Exploring Food at the Crossroads of Health and Business

Kittisak Wongmahesak
North Bangkok University, Thailand

Roy Rillera Marzo
https://orcid.org/0000-0001-9414-4010
Curtin University, Malaysia

Mohammad Badruddoza Talukder
https://orcid.org/0009-0008-1662-9221
International University of Business Agriculture and Technology, Bangladesh

Krisada Chienwattanasook
https://orcid.org/0000-0003-4259-900X
Rajamangala University of Technology, Thanyaburi, Thailand

IGI Global
Scientific Publishing
Publishing Tomorrow's Research Today

Vice President of Editorial	Melissa Wagner
Director of Acquisitions	Mikaela Felty
Director of Book Development	Jocelynn Hessler
Production Manager	Mike Brehm
Cover Design	Jose Rosado

Published in the United States of America by
IGI Global Scientific Publishing
701 East Chocolate Avenue
Hershey, PA, 17033, USA
Tel: 717-533-8845 | Fax: 717-533-7115
Website: https://www.igi-global.com E-mail: cust@igi-global.com

Library of Congress Cataloging-in-Publication Data

(CIP Data Pending)
ISBN13: 979-8-3373-4047-0
Isbn13Softcover: 979-8-3373-4048-7
EISBN13: 979-8-3373-4049-4
British Cataloguing in Publication Data
A Cataloguing in Publication record for this book is available from the British Library.

Table of Contents

Detailed Table of Contents

policy. This collection promotes a comprehensive, inclusive, and ethically grounded approach to eating that enhances individual well-being and social cohesion, as mental health becomes a pivotal focus in public health and marketing.

The chapter examines the critical role of nutrition in addressing global health challenges, particularly the rising prevalence of diet-related non-communicable diseases such as obesity, diabetes, and cardiovascular disease. It explores the science of nutrition, detailing the impacts of macronutrients, micronutrients, and dietary patterns on physical, cognitive, and mental health across the lifespan. The influence of the food industry is analyzed, focusing on its role in promoting ultra-processed foods and the potential for reformulation, transparent labeling, and ethical marketing to foster healthier diets. Nutritional inequities are addressed, highlighting socioeconomic, cultural, and systemic barriers like food deserts, with business-led solutions proposed to promote equity. Emerging trends, including gut microbiome research, personalized nutrition, and biofortification, are discussed. The chapter aims to bridge nutritional science, industry practices, and policy to mitigate NCDs, reduce health disparities, and advance equitable, sustainable well-being.

This chapter, per the authors, meticulously examines the integration of nutrition science and food economics to address critical challenges in public health, environmental sustainability, and socioeconomic disparity. It traces the evolution from early studies of nutrient deficiencies to contemporary analyses that incorporate dietary behavior, economic incentives, and policy interventions. The chapter highlights innovations such as functional food development, behavioral economics strategies, digital food platforms, and circular economy practices while evaluating issues of equity in access and market dynamics. By reviewing literature, case studies, and policy experiments, it identifies key research gaps and offers multi-level recommendations aimed at fostering resilient, inclusive, and sustainable food systems. These insights contribute to advancing interdisciplinary approaches that are essential for adapting to global crises and promoting long-term nutritional and economic stability.

Saurabh Chandra, Bennett University, Greater Noida, India
Nimmi Agarwal, Sharda University, India
Kittisak Wongmahesak, North Bangkok University, Thailand
Liza Shoor, Punjab Agricultural University, Ludhiana, India
Simmi Pal, Sharda University, India

Anti-aging drug clinical trials make up a new and exciting segment of biomedicine, designed to increase duration of life lived in good health and alleviating age-related illnesses. Geroscience Progress in this field has recently gained momentum owing to scientific breakthroughs in the fields of biotechnology, regenerative medicine and further insight into cellular processes reducing ageing. But there are big obstacles to developing these treatments through clinical trials. Aging is a multi-dimensional, multifaceted process that makes it challenging to identify any single target or endpoint to define interventions. The latter considerations involve ethical questions, of accessibility and the externalities that changing our life span may carry with. This chapter focuses on the road marches on, and new trials are continuing to yield insights into the mechanisms of aging and approaches to lifespan extension.

Srinivas Bikkina, Vingas Industries Private Limited, India
Vijaya Kittu Manda, PBMEIT, India
Theodore Tarnanidis, International Hellenic University, Greece
Bruno Barbosa Sousa, University of Cávado and Ave, Portugal

Food remains safe for consumption when its quality is preserved. Packaging technologies play a vital role in this. Modified Atmosphere Packaging (MAP) safely alters the atmosphere inside food packaging, allowing food to remain fresh for extended periods. It gives customers healthy options while maintaining its original firmness, color, freshness, and aesthetic appeal. MAP helps stakeholders in the food industry minimize food waste and support the economy in achieving global food security and sustainability goals. Cost-benefit advantages will result from producers and agripreneurs being able to optimize profit margins and reduce postharvest losses. Despite the encouraging new developments in MAP, there are still some gaps that need to be addressed to bring MAP into wider use in diverse food systems and to align with the principles of the circular economy. Future research and technological advancements are required to optimize MAP applications and address the challenges associated with their implementation. The study has implications for both health and business professionals.

Biotechnology In Food And Beverages, Transforming Quality, Safety, Flavour, And Nutrition Through Traditional Fermentation, Enzyme Technology, Precision Fermentation, And Synthetic Biology, Enabling Production Of Dairy, Alcoholic, And Fermented Foods, Novel Proteins, Bioactive Compounds, Functional Foods, And Sustainable Ingredients, Enhancing Shelf Life, Texture, And Taste, Supporting Food Safety With Biosensors And Rapid Pathogen Detection, Integrating AI And Bioinformatics For Efficient Microbial Strain Development, Driving Plant-Based Meats, Low-Calorie Sweeteners, Dairy-Free Cheeses, And Sustainable Beverages, Addressing Regulatory, Ethical, And Consumer Acceptance Challenges While Revolutionizing Global Food Production.

This chapter discusses the benefits of AI-powered mini ghost kitchens as sustainable and accessible businesses following the pandemic. It points out that these fast, delivery-only kitchens supply small-scale jobs to women, people from rural areas and the differently-abled, as AI and similar tools simplify managing food, expecting needs and communicating with customers. The study uses Organizational Resilience Theory and AI-based entrepreneurship to highlight why such models lead to adaptable societies, the preservation of culture and financial empowerment. With examples and figures collected in Kerala, the article illustrates that AI is making fairer access to the food industry possible as it addresses challenges like cost and lack of technology or infrastructure. The chapter encourages ethics in AI to support food innovation that respects inclusiveness, conserves the environment and safeguards heritage traditions in the community.

business strategies that capitalize on these shifts, including supply chain adaptations, marketing innovations, and regulatory compliance. This paper explores the intricate interplay between these dimensions, highlighting the need for innovative approaches to address rising food demand, nutritional deficiencies, and ecological degradation. It examines how dietary shifts toward plant-based and nutrient-dense foods can promote health while reducing environmental footprints.

This study explores the intricate interrelationships among education level, income level, food prices, health consciousness, social influence, food consumption frequency, and health perception using Partial Least Squares Structural Equation Modeling (PLS-SEM). Data from 192 respondents reveals that education strongly influences health consciousness and social influence, while income level and food prices exert indirect effects through social networks. Health consciousness, though significant, shows limited impact on actual dietary behavior, while social influence emerges as the dominant driver shaping food choices and health perception. The findings underscore the necessity of multi-level interventions addressing education, income, pricing dynamics, and social norms to promote healthy behaviors. This research contributes a robust, empirically validated framework that integrates cognitive, economic, and social determinants, offering a strategic roadmap for policy and program development in public health and nutrition.

The relevance of the food industry in terms of fostering financial development cannot be overstated, particularly not in the current context of dynamic global challenges and changing consumer preferences. As the largest occupation in the world, it not only contributes to the GDP and trade balance, but also serves as an important means of rural income. Food exports also enhance the economies of countries through earning foreign currency and strengthening trade. Government initiatives and private public partnerships have improved the financial contributions of the sector to the economy in terms of food security and entrepreneurship. Even with the rising inflation and disruptiions in climate, the food service industry is steady and resourceful. It is therefore a key driver for financially sustainable growth that

This chapter explores the dynamics of food culture, socialisation and human resource (HR) management and how these have influenced consumer and brand relationship and engagement in marketing practices. Food serves as an extremely potent social signifier that helps establishing emotional connections between consumers and brands through culturally based shared experiences. Organizations can reinforce loyalty, inclusivity, and emotional connection, by incorporating culinary traditions into marketing campaigns and HR-led brand storytelling. The paper examines the role that food-focussed events, employee engagement in food rituals, and culturally sensitive branding play in deepening consumer relations and community engagement. It also explores the role of HRM in enhancing the organizational identity and consumer-brand intimacy through food culture. This combination of disciplines provides a tasty trail map for marketers and HR folks wanting to create true, culturally grounded consumer connections.

Preface

INTRODUCTION

Food is no longer viewed solely as a means of sustenance; it has evolved into a powerful intersection of health, culture, technology, and global commerce. In today's interconnected world, the ways in which food is produced, marketed, consumed, and understood are rapidly transforming. These shifts are driven by a convergence of forces, including globalization, advances in nutritional science, digital innovation, and heightened consumer awareness of health and sustainability. As editors of this volume, we recognize the growing importance of examining food systems through a multidisciplinary lens that integrates both health and business perspectives.

This book emerges at a critical moment when global food systems face unprecedented challenges and opportunities. Rising rates of non-communicable diseases, environmental pressures, shifting consumer preferences, and technological disruptions are reshaping the food landscape. At the same time, the food industry continues to serve as a major engine of economic growth, innovation, and entrepreneurship. Balancing these competing priorities—public health, sustainability, and profitability—requires thoughtful inquiry and collaboration across disciplines. This volume seeks to contribute to that dialogue by bringing together diverse scholarly perspectives from across the globe.

The chapters in this collection explore how food operates at the nexus of individual well-being and broader economic systems. From psychological and behavioral insights into eating habits to advancements in biotechnology and business innovation, this book provides a comprehensive examination of contemporary food-related issues. It highlights not only the complexities of modern food systems but also the opportunities for creating healthier, more equitable, and sustainable outcomes. By bridging theory and practice, this work aims to inform researchers, policymakers, industry professionals, and students alike.

CHAPTER OVERVIEW

This volume is organized into fifteen chapters, each addressing a unique dimension of the relationship between food, health, and business.

Chapter 1 examines mindful eating within a globalized context, exploring the psychological drivers behind emerging food trends such as plant-based diets and sustainable consumption. It emphasizes how globalization reshapes dietary behaviors and highlights the growing importance of awareness and intentionality in food choices.

Chapter 2 expands on the psychological and social dimensions of eating within the wellness economy. It investigates emotional eating, the neuroscience of cravings, and the influence of branding and digital culture, offering insights into how food functions as both a psychological regulator and a social connector.

Chapter 3 focuses on the science of nutrition and its role in addressing global health challenges. It discusses diet-related diseases, nutritional inequities, and emerging innovations such as personalized nutrition and microbiome research, while also considering the role of industry and policy in promoting healthier outcomes.

Chapter 4 explores the intersection of nutrition science and food economics, highlighting how economic incentives, policy frameworks, and technological innovations can address issues of sustainability and equity within food systems.

Chapter 5 delves into clinical trials related to anti-aging and food supplements, examining the scientific, ethical, and public health implications of efforts to extend healthy lifespans through nutritional and biomedical interventions.

Chapter 6 investigates Modified Atmosphere Packaging (MAP) as a technological solution to enhance food preservation, reduce waste, and support both health and economic sustainability within the food industry.

Chapter 7 discusses the transformative role of biotechnology in food and beverage production. It highlights advancements such as precision fermentation and synthetic biology, which are reshaping food quality, safety, and sustainability.

Chapter 8 introduces AI-enabled micro ghost kitchens as an emerging entrepreneurial model. It emphasizes their potential to foster inclusivity, economic empowerment, and resilience in the food sector, particularly for underserved populations.

Chapter 9 examines impulsive food consumption driven by gastronomy livestreaming and digital engagement. It analyzes the roles of gamification, telepresence, and perceived professionalism in shaping consumer behavior.

Chapter 10 presents a comprehensive overview of the intersection of health, sustainability, and business innovation. It discusses how evolving consumer demands and environmental considerations are driving changes in food systems and industry practices.

Chapter 11 provides a statistical analysis of the economic determinants of food consumption and health. It highlights the influence of education, income, and social factors on dietary behavior and health perception.

Chapter 12 explores the role of the food industry in financial development, emphasizing its contributions to economic growth, employment, and food security in a rapidly changing global environment.

Chapter 13 focuses on gastropreneurship and its role in promoting wellness. It examines how innovative food startups are addressing consumer demand for health-oriented products while driving sustainable business growth.

Chapter 14 analyzes the convergence of wellness and commerce within the food industry. It discusses the integration of health-focused strategies into product development, branding, and supply chains, while addressing associated ethical and regulatory challenges.

Chapter 15 explores the cultural and social dimensions of food in marketing and human resource practices. It highlights how food culture can strengthen consumer engagement, brand identity, and organizational cohesion.

CONCLUSION

As this volume demonstrates, food sits at a dynamic and complex crossroads where health imperatives and business objectives intersect. The contributions within this book collectively underscore the need for interdisciplinary approaches to address the multifaceted challenges facing modern food systems. Whether through technological innovation, behavioral insights, or policy interventions, it is clear that no single perspective can adequately capture the full scope of this evolving landscape.

A key theme that emerges throughout the chapters is the importance of balance—between innovation and ethics, profitability and public health, and global scalability and local relevance. The future of food depends on our ability to navigate these tensions thoughtfully and responsibly. Businesses must adapt to increasingly informed and health-conscious consumers, while policymakers and researchers must work collaboratively to ensure that advancements in the food sector contribute to equitable and sustainable outcomes.

We hope that this book serves as both a scholarly resource and a catalyst for further dialogue. By bringing together diverse voices and perspectives, we aim to inspire new research, inform strategic decision-making, and encourage innovation that aligns with the broader goals of human and planetary well-being. As editors, we extend our sincere gratitude to the contributing authors for their valuable insights and to the readers who engage with this work. It is our belief that through continued collaboration and inquiry, we can shape a food future that is both nourishing and sustainable for all.

Chapter 1
Mindful Eating in a Globalized World:
The Psychology Behind Emerging Food Trends

Narender Suhag
http://orcid.org/0000-0002-3836-2133
Lovely Professional University, India

Sanjeev Kumar
http://orcid.org/0000-0002-7375-7341
Lovely Professional University, India

ABSTRACT

The chapter explores the concept of mindful eating & its psychological foundations within an increasingly globalized food environment. As the world becomes more connected through trade, media, migration & technology, food consumption is changing very rapidly. The study focus on globalization influences the restructuring of dietary habits & preferences for food, often through a process of cuisine hybridization and commoditisation of old food rituals. The study also explores the underlying psychological drivers behind recent food trends, such as plant-based diets, sustainable eating, functional foods & mindful consumption. Factors including health consciousness, environmental awareness, social influence, emotional satisfaction, and identity formation significantly influence food choices. It highlights how mindful eating characterized by awareness, intentionality, and emotional regulation around food is increasingly emerging as a response to the fast-paced, consumption-driven global food culture

DOI: 10.4018/979-8-3373-4047-0.ch001

INTRODUCTION

A combination of globalization as well as advances in technology has contributed to the rich tapestry of culinary diversity; "The modern food landscape". Though there has been an increase in international cuisine, digitized supply chains, and food related media, shifting the world's customs and preferences towards consuming diverse types of food, it has become easier than ever for consumers to access a variety of foods (Tang et al., 2015). That being said, even with having so many options, a new problem arises. Many people seem to be out of touch with their meals, leading them to over-eat, engage in emotional eating, and make poor dietary choices, (Victorson et al., 2015). This is something that can be explained through basic and contemporary scholarship (Popkin, 2006), shifting the discussion on mindful eating as not focusing on an individual and health driven practice, but instead as a socio-psychological response to the consequences of overconsumption, decline in environment quality, and loss of cultural diversity due to globalization."

The mindful way of eating emerged as a new approach to nutrition with the aim of resolving the growing concern over unhealthy eating habits. Going beyond simple food consumption, Mindful Eating entails the full attention of oneself during the act of eating, including sensual awareness of the food itself, introspective emotional evaluation prior to indulging, and tuning into the body's internal signals, like feelings of hunger or fullness. Modern society has experienced a structural change which stands behind the shift toward novel approaches to eating is caring for health awareness and supporting comprehensive body and mind wellness (the latter includes spirituality). Such shift brings forth an increasing number of people looking for new ways to eat, ways which are closer to intention and presence. Notably, at the apex of this phenomenon emerges another practice triad of meditative practices eating meditation on its own is a subsection of meditation as a whole (Prescott et al., 2024)

Apart from the latter, Brown and his colleagues suggest that enabling enhanced focus to the act of eating brings forth the ability to stimulate predominant emotions associated with certain dishes as well. As such, those mindful aspects form a foundation for deliberate attention which is free of judgments (Talukder & Kumar, 2025).

Mindful eating is more than just a trend; in this context, it marks a dietary shift that responds to the psychological and cultural stressors of modern-day life such as environmental decline and the commodification of food. This chapter analyzes the foundations of mindful eating, including cognitive control, emotional regulation, and identity formation. It also attempts to situate mindful eating into a framework of globalization, using the contemporary global food system to illustrate the efforts working against and supporting the advancement of mindful practices.

In addition, the chapter analyzes novel food tendencies prompted by mindfulness which include veganism, the Slow Food movement, minimalist eating, and tailored diets. These trends are evolving not only in consumer adaptation but also in the sociocultural and psychological significance of food within contemporary society. At the same time, major obstacles such as the lack of focus, environmental factors, cultural practices, and time can make it difficult to adopt mindful eating practices, especially in highly urbanized areas. To solve these problems, the chapter presents specific guidance for individuals, organizations, and public decision makers including educators. Mindful meal planning, helpful restaurant design and new technology can all promote better eating behaviours through more mindful eating. In addition, re-embracing food practices of the past will reinstate a sense of purpose and mindfulness concerning food.

To sum up, mindful eating is perhaps one of the most effective ways to cope with the increasing intensity and intricacy of the globalized world's food system. Addressing the underlying psychological drivers of consumption and the culture shifts that are taking place allows for formulating a more thoughtful, kind, and responsible system of eating. There is still much work to be done, but as this momentum continues to build. Common components of mindful eating are an array of practices that help people focus on eating more consciously and with greater awareness. Another key feature is that of eating mindfully, that is, being fully present and eating slowly and without distraction in order for someone to be in touch with the taste of the food and their inner appetite and fullness cues, rather than relying on external stimuli or eating hurriedly (O'Reilly et al., 2014). This slowing down of our meals helps us feel more in touch with the food we are eating and helps prevent mindless binging.

Another important aspect is being in tune with physical hunger and fullness, which can be disrupted by routine eating and emotional influences. Refining this perception can enable people to differentiate between actual physiological hunger and non-hunger related reasons to eat (Herman & Polivy, 2008). And finally, it's awareness of the emotional and environmental triggers that can impact eating—like stress, boredom, advertising, or social pressure. Understanding these drivers can empower people with greater intentionality and emotional regulation (Mantzios & Wilson, 2015) and, thus, healthier and more sustainable eating behaviors. Mindful eating has also been linked with such benefits as better digestion, weight management, less emotional eating and greater satisfaction with meals overall (Singh & Kumar, 2025)

THE PSYCHOLOGICAL FOUNDATIONS OF MINDFUL EATING

Mindful eating is a multidimensional practice, based on psychological principles that guide people's food-related behaviours. It surpasses simply nutrition to mental processes such as cognition, emotion, habit formation, and identity. Seeing the psychological underpinnings is critical in understanding why intentional eating is a viable option for healthier eating in a mindful way in the age of distractions and fast paced living (Nelson, 2017).

Cognitive Process

Cognitive control refers to the ability to restrict or direct thoughts and actions toward a specific goal. That also means that focused attention makes them ignore external distractors like social pressures, ads, or even the environment. Mindful eating transforms attention to hunger and satiety reflexes to internal reasons. Hindering or guiding one's thoughts and actions to specific goals requires focused attention on internal self-signals. Eating mindfully means being aware of the sensations of hunger and fullness, and the actual process of eating from the spectrum of food's odour and feel to its flavour and texture. Mindful attention nourishes detached non-judgmental awareness toward thoughts about food, and fuels cognitive action focused responding, not reflexive responding (Barbaro & Pickett, 2016). With increased awareness concerning what is eaten, the frequency and the reasons behind eating activities, an individual is better able to differentiate physiological hunger from emotion-induced cravings. In a world overflowing with information and an excess food supply, attention leads to the need to focus on clarity amidst confusion to prevent unintentional mindless consumption (Richter & Hunecke, 2022a).

Emotional Regulation

Feelings have a major impact in changing eating patterns. For most, food is a great way to ease stress, anxiety, dullness, or sadness. Emotional eating drives people to make unhealthy dietary choices. This overeating often results in adverse day-to-day consequences. In the long-run, such lifestyle choices can have a dire effect on an individual's physical health (Dallman et al., 2005).

Mindful eating helps the individual break out of this rut while also learning how to regulate their emotions. Healthy emotion regulation refers to the ability to manage and respond to emotional experiences in a way that is healthy. Exercises that involve mindfulness aid an individual in self-observation, making it possible to learn about their feelings without building up the need to react to them right away. Food is no longer utilized as a coping mechanism. Mindful eaters work to find out the feelings that propelled them to eat and respond with awareness and self-kindness instead (Warren et al., 2017). This leads to carrying the knowledge for less dependency on food, therefore enabling the individual to bear comfort in other means that support the well-being of the mind (Talukder et al., 2025).

Habit Formation and Neuroplasticity

Eating patterns are often determined by deeply rooted habits that have been acquired over time. In case of unhealthy eating patterns, changes can be made to gradually improve the diet through self documenting or self monitoring one's progress. Documenting leads to feeling a sense of achievement which strengthens motivation reinforce through pathways in the brain. In addition, neural networks can reorganize themselves through a process known as neuroplasticity (Kristeller & Wolever, 2010).

The practice of eating mindfully can help reroute unhealthy eating habits into new, positive behaviors by taking advantage of the brain's neuroplasticity. During meals, when individuals practice mindfulness by slowing down, savoring every bite, paying attention to satiety, and walking through each stage of eating, they slowly but surely rewire their brains to prefer mindful actions over and impulsive ones (Richter & Hunecke, 2022b). The repetitive nature of these actions helps build a positive feedback loop that, over time, makes mindful eating less stressful. In addition to all this, incorporating mindfulness in day-to-day life helps develop long term defense mechanisms against external triggers and internal compulsion that encourage mindless eating (Talukder & Kumar, 2024).

Identity and Self-Concept

Every individual has a unique self-concept and identity that makes food much more than just nourishment. The choice a person makes regarding foods also results from their belief system, value system, and their culture. People, for instance, consolidate their consumption with their growing identity as health, environment, or ethics savvy people (Fischler, 1988).

Eating mindfully puts an individual in control over their personal values and their food choices and helps disconnect them. With the help of self-awareness and reflection, individuals are able to analyze how their eating habits align with or contradict their self-image. An illustrative instance is an individual dedicated towards sustainability who may become more sensitive to the environmental consequences of food production. For instance, someone committed to sustainability may become more attuned to the environmental impact of their dietary choices and seek to make more responsible decisions. Likewise, individuals pursuing health or ethical ideals may find mindful eating aligns their behaviors with these goals, reinforcing a positive self-image (Sobal & Bisogni, 2009).

Moreover, mindful eating supports the development of self-compassion and body acceptance, which are critical components of a healthy self-concept. Rather than judging themselves harshly for perceived dietary failures or body image concerns, mindful eaters learn to treat themselves with kindness and curiosity. This shift in perspective helps reduce guilt and shame associated with eating and promotes a more sustainable, enjoyable relationship with food (Berthoud et al., 2011).

Food Delivery Apps Disrupt Hunger Cues and Health

In today's digital age, food is just a few taps away. With food delivery apps offering endless options: "burgers, desserts, snacks, and full meals convenience" has become the new normal. But with this convenience comes a quiet disruption to something deeply human: our natural hunger cues. When food arrives with little effort and endless variety, it's easy to eat out of boredom, stress, or habit not hunger. The constant notifications, flashy app designs, and tempting discounts nudge users into ordering impulsively. Cravings replace conscious decision-making. Instead of tuning into our bodies, we listen to the pings of our phones.

The pattern is especially troubling because it normalizes mindless eating, which can lead to overeating, weight gain, and even emotional dependency on food. And while the concept of mindful eating being fully present and intentional with food choices offers a powerful counterbalance, promoting it is not as simple as telling people to "eat better." For many, food delivery apps aren't just a luxury; they are a necessity due to long working hours, caregiving responsibilities, or living in "food deserts" with limited healthy options nearby. Telling someone to slow down and eat mindfully without addressing the systemic barriers like; income inequality, lack of nutrition education, and limited access to fresh food is unfair and ineffective.

To truly promote mindful eating, we must shift the conversation from individual willpower to structural support. This means redesigning food delivery platforms to highlight healthier choices, subsidizing nutritious meals, and investing in community awareness programs that go beyond guilt or blame. Food choices are deeply personal, but they are also shaped by the environment around us. Creating a more mindful food culture means ensuring that everyone not just the privileged few has the tools, access, and support to make choices that nourish both body and mind.

Globalization and Evolution of Food Culture

Globalization has drastically altered the shape of the world's food system; what was once some local ingredients, cuisines, and culinary techniques have crossed vast geographies. More trade, migration, media exposure, and tourism allow people to know and embrace each other's culinary practices with diversity in food choices and cross-cultural culinary mixing (Godfray et al., 2010). Ironically this great increase in access to foods from different parts of the globe has accounted for more unintended consequences. It awakened more availability of global cuisines but with more diet homogenization and a massive high-in-fat-and-sugar industrialized fast foods lack nutritional value (Monteiro et al., 2013).

The Double-Edged Sword of Globalization

Globalization acts as a double-edged sword in the development of food culture. On one hand, it promotes diversity in cuisine, innovation, and cultural exchange through food. International dishes such as sushi and curry have become staples in many global cities, often adapted to local tastes and preferences. On the other hand, globalization can also erode traditional food practices, as global food corporations promote standardized products that prioritize convenience, shelf-life, and mass appeal over cultural authenticity and nutritional quality (Azimi et al., 2024). Moreover, the globalization of food systems has contributed to the global rise in non-communicable diseases, such as obesity, type 2 diabetes, and cardiovascular illnesses, particularly in countries transitioning from traditional to industrialized diets. The global proliferation of ultra-processed foods, soft drinks, and fast food chains has been linked to increasingly unhealthy dietary patterns, especially among urban populations and youth.

Westernization of Diets

One of the clearestimpacts of globalization is the dietarywesternization. In many parts of Asia, Africa, and Latin America, the traditional diet based on whole grains, legumes, vegetables, and plant-based proteins arebeing replaced by Western-style diets withlots of red meat, refined sugar, trans fats, and highly processed foods (Nestle, 2013; Godfray et al., 2010). Theseconsumptionsetbacksprovidelatitude-forchallengessuchas decreased lifestyle, reduced physical activity, and the acceptance of fast-food behavior. The change is not justa turning point for physical health, but cancomplicateidentities. Situationally, traditional meals were the center piece of social and family occasions; now onthe go and packaged convenience meals have taken their place. The food make strong signifier of cultural values and identity, iflocalsstop having traditional food practices thereisanopportunityforless cultural ownership and a break of historical continuity (Talukder et al., 2024).

The Rise of Conscious Consumerism

Thereis a growing movement of conscious consumerism inresponseto these changes, and consumers are becoming more selective about what they eat, looking for foods that are healthful and ethical, sustainable and transparent. Thetrendsreflec-tagrowinginterestin organic products, locally sourced foods, and fair-trade products, inwaysthathavemeaningfully embraced the thinking of mindful eating - awareness aboutthe origins of food, whetherit is healthy for people and the environment, and how the itemsconsumed could have ethical meaning and value in the larger social-economic context of consumption (Macdiarmid, 2013). The active choice reflects a greater values-basedwayof eating, where consumption is influenced by ethics and the desire for a better planet, rather than just taste or cost. This trend also reflects a desire to resist food as a commodity which highlights the need for people to eat with more intention and mindfulness while thinking about their food choices.

EMERGING FOOD TRENDS DRIVEN BY MINDFULNESS

Mindfulness is increasingly influencing emerging food trends around the world. These trends reflect a shift toward intentional, values-based eating practices that emphasize health, sustainability, authenticity, and self-awareness.

Plant-Based Diets

One of the most important mindful eating trends today is the expansion of plant-based diets. In the past few years, plant-based diets have gained popularity as individuals are concerned with the treatment of animals, the sustainability of our environment, and condition of their own health. Plant-based diets emphasize the consumption of whole, or mostly whole, minimally processed foods that derive from plants: fruits, vegetables, legumes, nuts, seeds (Lichtenstein, 2010). Plant-based eating also promotes mindful thinking about all aspects of food: it is mindful in terms of where foods have come from, how they have been grown, and theycontributetoone'sown health and the health of our planet, as food consumption can be approached ethically, as it challenges the mainstream systems of production and promotes kindness in food consumption (Adkisson, 2008).

Slow Food Movement

The Slow Food movement began in Italy, where it was formed to challenge fast food, in a time where traditional meals were being lost in the wake of fast food consumption and convenience. The Slow Food movement aims to keep traditional food traditions alive and it promotes local ingredients, the pleasure of communal dining, and eating at a 'slow' pace (De Graaf & Kok, 2010). The Slow Food movement demonstrates a commitment towards the 'slow food is good' because it really does emphasize the need for people to take time intheir food, both for preparation, and consumption to enjoy their food mindfully in many ways. The Slow Food movement displays the mindful eating philosophy and principles and promotes mindful eating, at all points, from sourcing to preparation, to tasting and even sharing (Tapia Granados, 2002).

Minimalist Eating

Another emerging trend is minimalist eating, which promotes simplicity in meal preparation and ingredient use. This approach values nutritional density and culinary intentionality, reducing reliance on complex recipes or processed additives (Firth et al., 2020). Minimalist meals often highlight seasonal produce, whole grains, and natural flavors, encouraging eaters to be fully present with the sensory aspects of their meals. The reduced complexity fosters a deeper appreciation for food's intrinsic qualities and helps curb overconsumption (Dsouza et al., 2023).

Digital Detox Dining

In today's hyper-connected world, digital distractions often interfere with the dining experience. A growing number of restaurants are encouraging digital detox dining where patrons are asked to put away their devices and focus on their food and dining companions (Waheed & Kumar, 2024). This practice promotes social mindfulness, fostering deeper connection and presence at the table. Research suggests that being mindful during meals enhances both satisfaction and digestion, while reducing tendencies toward overeating (Rozin, 2005).

Functional and Personalized Nutrition

Advancements in biotechnology, nutrigenomics, and artificial intelligence have given rise to personalized nutrition plans tailored to an individual's genetic makeup, lifestyle, and psychological profile (Van Dam et al., 2018). These plans emphasize self-awareness and mindful decision-making, helping individuals make dietary choices that support long-term health and wellness goals. Personalized nutrition also highlights the importance of understanding one's unique relationship with food, promoting a more introspective and conscious approach to eating (Schuman-Olivier et al., 2020). Globalization and mindful eating are deeply intertwined in the evolution of modern food culture. While globalization has challenged traditional food systems and introduced risks to health and cultural identity, it has also sparked a growing movement toward conscious and mindful food practices. Emerging trends such as plant-based diets, slow food, and personalized nutrition all reflect a collective desire to reconnect with food in more meaningful, ethical, and sustainable ways (Dewangan et al., 2024).

PSYCHOLOGICAL BARRIERS TO MINDFUL EATING

Despite the growing awareness of mindful eating and its wide-ranging physical and psychological benefits, many individuals face substantial challenges when attempting to incorporate these practices into their daily lives. These challenges often stem from modern lifestyle patterns, emotional stressors, and ingrained cultural habits that compete with or directly oppose the principles of mindfulness.

Environmental Distractions

One of the most pervasive obstacles to mindful eating is the overabundance of environmental distractions. In today's digital age, mealtimes are frequently accompanied by screens televisions, smartphones, laptops, and tablets—which divert attention away from the eating experience (Drewnowski, 1995). The constant influx of information and visual stimuli can dull sensory awareness, making it difficult to notice hunger and fullness cues, appreciate flavors, or feel satisfied. Multitasking while eating can lead to mindlessconsumption, where individuals eat more than they intend and derive less satisfaction from the food (Thaler & Sunstein, 2008).

Time Constraints

Another significant barrier is the lack of time. Fast-paced lifestyles often prioritize productivity and efficiency over leisure, including during meals. People with busy schedules may skip meals, eat on the go, or rely heavily on convenience foods. This rushed approach to eating inhibits the reflective and attentive mindset required for mindfulness (Kumar, 2024). When meals are hurried or mechanical, they become merely functional rather than nourishing or meaningful.

Emotional Triggers

Emotional distress can really throw a wrench in the gears of mindful eating. When stress, anxiety, depression, or unresolved trauma come into play, people often turn to food as a way to cope, leading to emotional eating or bingeing (Kearney, 2010). In these moments, food shifts from being a source of nourishment and joy to just a quick fix for relief. Even those who know the ins and outs of mindful eating might struggle to break free from these automatic, emotion-driven habits. Without solid strategies for managing emotions, the cycle of impulsive or comfort eating can keep going, making it tough to stay mindful.

Cultural Norms

On top of that, cultural norms and societal expectations can throw in some extra challenges. In many cultures, being efficient and productive is highly prized even when it comes to meals. Eating quickly can sometimes be seen as a badge of honor, especially in workplaces where lunch breaks are short or even skipped. Plus, in cultures that emphasize communal eating, taking your time or turning down food to listen to your body's fullness signals might come off as rude or unsociable (Owolodun et al., 2025). These social pressures can make the idea of mindful eating feel impractical or even socially awkward.

STRATEGIES FOR PROMOTING MINDFUL EATING

In response to these challenges, several strategies can be adopted at both the individual and institutional levels to foster mindful eating. These approaches aim to reshape the environment, promote awareness, and cultivate supportive habits that align with mindfulness principles.

Educational Initiatives

Integrating mindfulness training into schools, universities, and workplaces can build foundational awareness from a young age. Educational programs can teach individuals to recognize hunger and satiety cues, practice emotional regulation, and understand the psychological effects of distracted eating. By normalizing these practices early, individuals are more likely to adopt and sustain mindful eating habits throughout life.

Mindful Meal Planning

Encouraging intentional meal planning is another effective strategy. This includes activities such as creating weekly meal plans, shopping with a list, choosing whole and seasonal foods, and preparing meals at home. Engaging in the cooking process not only deepens one's connection to food but also provides an opportunity to practice presence and care (Kumar et al., 2023). When people are involved in the full food cycle from selection to preparation to consumption they are more likely to eat mindfully.

Restaurant Design

Public dining environments can be redesigned to promote mindfulness. Restaurants can minimize noise, avoid overcrowding, and reduce digital interruptions by discouraging mobile device use or offering phone-free zones. Thoughtful lighting, calm music, and comfortable seating can create an ambiance that supports slow, intentional eating. These environmental cues subtly encourage patrons to savor their meals and engage more deeply with the dining experience.

Technology for Mindfulness

Paradoxically, technology can also serve as a tool for mindfulness. Numerous mobile apps now exist to help users track hunger levels, log emotional states, engage in guided mindful breathing exercises, or follow slow eating prompts (Bilotta et al., 2021). When used intentionally, these technologies can enhance awareness and accountability, especially for beginners or those trying to overcome ingrained habits.

Cultural Reconnection

Bringing back traditional food rituals offers a powerful, often overlooked, path to cultivating mindful eating habits. Many cultural and indigenous food traditions revolve around slow preparation, expressions of gratitude, and the shared experience of meals. These aren't just quaint customs they reflect values that naturally promote mindfulness (Abdullah et al., 2024)By encouraging people to reconnect with their culinary roots, we don't just nurture cultural identity; we also encourage a return to slower, more intentional ways of eating that stand in stark contrast to the rush of modern fast-food culture.

The psychological and cultural barriers to mindful eating are real. They're deeply ingrained, but that doesn’t mean they’re immovable. Change is possible through thoughtful education, better-designed environments, a renewed appreciation for cultural food practices, and even the smart use of technology. Together, these strategies can help individuals and communities reshape their relationship with food. Mindful eating is likely to play an even bigger role as more people wake up to the connections between food, health, and sustainability. There's room and real potential for future research to bring tools like AI, neuroscience, and virtual reality into the mix. These technologies could transform how we engage with food on a sensory and cognitive level. On a broader scale, policies that promote food literacy and support ethical consumption will be essential if we're serious about changing the cultural script around eating.

THE PSYCHOLOGICAL FOUNDATIONS OF MINDFUL EATING & GLOBALIZATION AND THE EVOLUTION OF FOOD CULTURE

Mindful eating is more than just a wellness trend it's a powerful practice rooted in psychology and self-awareness. At its core, mindful eating invites us to slow down and reconnect with our body's natural hunger and fullness cues. In today's fast-paced world, we often eat while distracted scrolling through our phones, working at our desks, or rushing between meetings. This disconnect from the act of eating means we're not truly tasting or even noticing our food. Psychologically, mindful eating draws on principles of mindfulness, encouraging us to pay attention to each bite the flavor, texture, smell, and how it makes us feel. It promotes self-compassion over guilt, awareness over autopilot, and curiosity over judgment. Over time, this can help people build a healthier relationship with food, reduce emotional eating, and foster a deeper appreciation for nourishment.

At the same time, we can't ignore how globalization has transformed food culture. Traditional meals passed down through generations are now competing with fast food chains, food delivery apps, and global food fads. While this cultural exchange has brought exciting new flavors and diversity to our plates, it has also blurred the lines between heritage and convenience. In many places, local diets rich in whole grains, fruits, and vegetables are being replaced by ultra-processed foods high in salt, sugar, and fat. Globalization has made food more accessible but not always more nutritious. The challenge now is to find balance: to celebrate the richness of global food culture while preserving mindful eating habits and local traditions. Embracing mindful eating in this context isn't about rejecting modern choices it's about making space to honor where our food comes from, how it's prepared, and how it affects us. It's about eating with intention in a world of endless options.

CONCLUSION

In a commercial world where food is has been commodified and eating has become a mechanical act due to convenience and modern habit rather than hunger or enjoyment. This change in pattern of eating habit is leading to food related illness. Therefore, mindful eating is important because it will not increase the health of the consumer but also decrease the food related illness. In this context, mindful eating emerges as a transformative approach that encourages individuals to slow down, pay attention, and fully engage with the sensory and emotional experience of eating. It invites a reconnection with food as more than sustenance as a reflection of culture, identity, and ethical values.

Mindful eating also provides a framework for navigating the complex intersection of globalization, nutrition, and psychological well-being. By acknowledging the psychological mechanisms that underlie our eating behaviours such as cognitive habits, emotional responses, and social conditioning we can make more informed, conscious food choices. At the same time, recognizing the broader socio-economic forces that shape our diets, including marketing, urbanization, and cultural shifts, enables a more critical and empowered approach to consumption.

Ultimately, cultivating a mindful food culture promotes diversity, inclusivity, and sustainability. It allows individuals and communities to honor cultural traditions, foster emotional well-being, and reduce overconsumption thereby creating food systems that are both nourishing and meaningful.

REFERENCES

Abdullah, A., Mat Isa, N., Azmi, A., Wahab, M. F. A., Tahir, M. S., & Ishak, M. A. (2024). Enhancing Penang Homestay Experience Through Cross-Cultural Benchmarking from Japanese Homestay Hospitality. *Revista de Gestão Social e Ambiental, 18*(6), e04786. DOI: 10.24857/rgsa.v18n6-001

Adkisson, R. V. (2008). Nudge: Improving Decisions About Health, Wealth and Happiness. *The Social Science Journal, 45*(4), 700–701. DOI: 10.1016/j.soscij.2008.09.003

Azimi, M. N., Rahman, M. M., & Maraseni, T. (2024). The Interplay of Dietary Habits, Economic Factors, and Globalization: Assessing the Role of Institutional Quality. *Nutrients, 16*(18), 3116. DOI: 10.3390/nu16183116 PMID: 39339718

Barbaro, N., & Pickett, S. M. (2016). Mindfully green: Examining the effect of connectedness to nature on the relationship between mindfulness and engagement in pro-environmental behavior. *Personality and Individual Differences, 93*, 137–142. DOI: 10.1016/j.paid.2015.05.026

Berthoud, H.-R., Lenard, N. R., & Shin, A. C. (2011). Food reward, hyperphagia, and obesity. *American Journal of Physiology. Regulatory, Integrative and Comparative Physiology, 300*(6), R1266–R1277. DOI: 10.1152/ajpregu.00028.2011 PMID: 21411768

Bilotta, E., Bertacchini, F., Gabriele, L., Giglio, S., Pantano, P. S., & Romita, T. (2021). Industry 4.0 technologies in tourism education: Nurturing students to think with technology. *Journal of Hospitality, Leisure, Sport and Tourism Education, 29*, 100275. DOI: 10.1016/j.jhlste.2020.100275

Dallman, M. F., Pecoraro, N. C., & La Fleur, S. E. (2005). Chronic stress and comfort foods: Self-medication and abdominal obesity☆. *Brain, Behavior, and Immunity, 19*(4), 275–280. DOI: 10.1016/j.bbi.2004.11.004 PMID: 15944067

De Graaf, C., & Kok, F. J. (2010). Slow food, fast food and the control of food intake. *Nature Reviews. Endocrinology, 6*(5), 290–293. DOI: 10.1038/nrendo.2010.41 PMID: 20351697

Dewangan, S., Manoharan, G., Sharma, A. K., Kumar, S., & Talukder, M. B. (2024). *Leveraging Blockchain Technology for Enhanced Government Services, Transparency, and Administrative Efficiency*. 202–207.

Drewnowski, A. (1995). Energy intake and sensory properties of food. *The American Journal of Clinical Nutrition, 62*(5), 1081S–1085S. DOI: 10.1093/ajcn/62.5.1081S PMID: 7484925

Dsouza, M. P., Shetty, A., Dinesh, T. K., & Damodar, P. (2023). Stimulating employee performance and well-being: A review of mindfulness impact in the hospitality sector. *IIMBG Journal of Sustainable Business and Innovation*, *1*(1), 4–17. DOI: 10.1108/IJSBI-06-2023-0037

Firth, J., Gangwisch, J. E., Borsini, A., Wootton, R. E., & Mayer, E. A. (2020). Food and mood: How do diet and nutrition affect mental wellbeing? *BMJ (Clinical Research Ed.)*, *m2382*, m2382. DOI: 10.1136/bmj.m2382 PMID: 32601102

Godfray, H. C. J., Beddington, J. R., Crute, I. R., Haddad, L., Lawrence, D., Muir, J. F., Pretty, J., Robinson, S., Thomas, S. M., & Toulmin, C. (2010). Food Security: The Challenge of Feeding 9 Billion People. *Science*, *327*(5967), 812–818. DOI: 10.1126/science.1185383 PMID: 20110467

Herman, C. P., & Polivy, J. (2008). External cues in the control of food intake in humans: The sensory-normative distinction. *Physiology & Behavior*, *94*(5), 722–728. DOI: 10.1016/j.physbeh.2008.04.014 PMID: 18499202

Kearney, J. (2010). Food consumption trends and drivers. *Philosophical Transactions of the Royal Society of London. Series B, Biological Sciences*, *365*(1554), 2793–2807. DOI: 10.1098/rstb.2010.0149 PMID: 20713385

Kristeller, J. L., & Wolever, R. Q. (2010). Mindfulness-Based Eating Awareness Training for Treating Binge Eating Disorder: The Conceptual Foundation. *Eating Disorders*, *19*(1), 49–61. DOI: 10.1080/10640266.2011.533605 PMID: 21181579

Kumar, S. (2024). The Role of Digital Marketing on Customer Engagement in the Hospitality Industry. In Bansal, R., Ngah, A. H., Chakir, A., & Pruthi, N. (Eds.), (pp. 177–191). Advances in Business Information Systems and Analytics. IGI Global., DOI: 10.4018/979-8-3693-0815-8.ch010

Kumar, S., Talukder, M. B., Kabir, F., & Kaiser, F. (2023). Challenges and Sustainability of Green Finance in the Tourism Industry: Evidence From Bangladesh. In Taneja, S., Kumar, P., Grima, S., Ozen, E., & Sood, K. (Eds.), (pp. 97–111). Advances in Finance, Accounting, and Economics. IGI Global., DOI: 10.4018/979-8-3693-1388-6.ch006

Lichtenstein, A. H. (2010). Bring Back Home Economics Education. *Journal of the American Medical Association*, *303*(18), 1857. DOI: 10.1001/jama.2010.592 PMID: 20460625

Macdiarmid, J. I. (2013). Is a healthy diet an environmentally sustainable diet? *The Proceedings of the Nutrition Society*, *72*(1), 13–20. DOI: 10.1017/S0029665112002893 PMID: 23186839

Mantzios, M., & Wilson, J. C. (2015). Mindfulness, Eating Behaviours, and Obesity: A Review and Reflection on Current Findings. *Current Obesity Reports*, *4*(1), 141–146. DOI: 10.1007/s13679-014-0131-x PMID: 26627097

Monteiro, C. A., Moubarac, J.-C., Cannon, G., Ng, S. W., & Popkin, B. (2013). Ultra-processed products are becoming dominant in the global food system. *Obesity Reviews*, *14*(S2), 21–28. DOI: 10.1111/obr.12107 PMID: 24102801

Nelson, J. B. (2017). Mindful Eating: The Art of Presence While You Eat. *Diabetes Spectrum*, *30*(3), 171–174. DOI: 10.2337/ds17-0015 PMID: 28848310

O'Reilly, G. A., Cook, L., Spruijt-Metz, D., & Black, D. S. (2014). Mindfulness-based interventions for obesity-related eating behaviours: A literature review. *Obesity Reviews*, *15*(6), 453–461. DOI: 10.1111/obr.12156 PMID: 24636206

Owolodun, B., Gmür, D., Felber, S., Ollier, C., Haller, T., & Merten, S. (2025). From diversity to uniformity: Comparing nutritional transition of food consumption in four regions in Senegal. *Food, Culture, & Society*, *28*(3), 503–527. DOI: 10.1080/15528014.2024.2310380

Popkin, B. M. (2006). Global nutrition dynamics: The world is shifting rapidly toward a diet linked with noncommunicable diseases. *The American Journal of Clinical Nutrition*, *84*(2), 289–298. DOI: 10.1093/ajcn/84.2.289 PMID: 16895874

Prescott, S. L., Logan, A. C., D'Adamo, C. R., Holton, K. F., Lowry, C. A., Marks, J., Moodie, R., & Poland, B. (2024). Nutritional Criminology: Why the Emerging Research on Ultra-Processed Food Matters to Health and Justice. *International Journal of Environmental Research and Public Health*, *21*(2), 120. DOI: 10.3390/ijerph21020120 PMID: 38397611

Richter, N., & Hunecke, M. (2022a). Mindfulness, connectedness to nature, personal ecological norm and pro-environmental behavior: A daily diary study. *Current Research in Ecological and Social Psychology*, *3*, 100038. DOI: 10.1016/j.cresp.2022.100038

Richter, N., & Hunecke, M. (2022b). Mindfulness, connectedness to nature, personal ecological norm and pro-environmental behavior: A daily diary study. *Current Research in Ecological and Social Psychology*, *3*, 100038. DOI: 10.1016/j.cresp.2022.100038

Rozin, P. (2005). The Meaning of Food in Our Lives: A Cross-Cultural Perspective on Eating and Well-Being. *Journal of Nutrition Education and Behavior*, *37*, S107–S112. DOI: 10.1016/S1499-4046(06)60209-1 PMID: 16246277

Schuman-Olivier, Z., Trombka, M., Lovas, D. A., Brewer, J. A., Vago, D. R., Gawande, R., Dunne, J. P., Lazar, S. W., Loucks, E. B., & Fulwiler, C. (2020). Mindfulness and Behavior Change. *Harvard Review of Psychiatry*, *28*(6), 371–394. DOI: 10.1097/HRP.0000000000000277 PMID: 33156156

Singh, B., & Kumar, S. (2025). Eco-Friendly Practices of Ghost Kitchens Through Smart Technology: Technological Innovations in the Food-Beverage Industry. In Singh, K., Kumar, S., & Talukder, M. B. (Eds.), (pp. 359–378). Advances in Computational Intelligence and Robotics. IGI Global., DOI: 10.4018/979-8-3373-0432-8.ch017

Sobal, J., & Bisogni, C. A. (2009). Constructing Food Choice Decisions. *Annals of Behavioral Medicine*, *38*(S1), 37–46. DOI: 10.1007/s12160-009-9124-5 PMID: 19787306

Talukder, M. B., Das, I. R., & Kumar, S. (2025). Future Trends and Prospects of the Food Industry: Perspectives from Hospitality. In Dutta, P. K., Hamad, A., Haghi, A. K., & Prabhakar, P. K. (Eds.), *Food and Industry 5.0: Transforming the Food System for a Sustainable Future* (pp. 289–303). Springer Nature Switzerland., DOI: 10.1007/978-3-031-76758-6_18

Talukder, M. B., & Kumar, S. (2024). Revisiting intention in food service outlet of five-star hotels: A quantitative approach based on food service quality. *Sport i Turystyka. Środkowoeuropejskie Czasopismo Naukowe, 7*(1), 137–156. DOI: 10.16926/sit.2024.01.08

Talukder, M. B., & Kumar, S. (2025). Culinary Experiences and Food Tourism in Bangladesh. In Tyagi, P. K., Nadda, V., & Singh, A. K. (Eds.), *Meaningful Tourism* (pp. 201–219). Emerald Publishing Limited., DOI: 10.1108/978-1-83797-837-320251028

Talukder, M. B., Kumar, S., & Das, I. R. (2024). Food Wastage on the Economic Outcome: Evidence From the Hotel industry. In Singh, A., Tyagi, P. K., & Garg, A. (Eds.), (pp. 68–80). Practice, Progress, and Proficiency in Sustainability. IGI Global., DOI: 10.4018/979-8-3693-2181-2.ch005

Tang, J., Abraham, C., Stamp, E., & Greaves, C. (2015). How can weight-loss app designers' best engage and support users? A qualitative investigation. *British Journal of Health Psychology*, *20*(1), 151–171. DOI: 10.1111/bjhp.12114 PMID: 25130682

Tapia Granados, J. A. (2002). Fast food nation: The dark side of the all-American meal. *Revista Panamericana de Salud Pública = Pan American Journal of Public Health*, *12*(2), 146–147. DOI: 10.1590/S1020-49892002000800019

Van Dam, N. T., Van Vugt, M. K., Vago, D. R., Schmalzl, L., Saron, C. D., Olendzki, A., Meissner, T., Lazar, S. W., Kerr, C. E., Gorchov, J., Fox, K. C. R., Field, B. A., Britton, W. B., Brefczynski-Lewis, J. A., & Meyer, D. E. (2018). Mind the Hype: A Critical Evaluation and Prescriptive Agenda for Research on Mindfulness and Meditation. *Perspectives on Psychological Science, 13*(1), 36–61. DOI: 10.1177/1745691617709589 PMID: 29016274

Victorson, D., Kentor, M., Maletich, C., Lawton, R. C., Kaufman, V. H., Borrero, M., Languido, L., Lewett, K., Pancoe, H., & Berkowitz, C. (2015). Mindfulness Meditation to Promote Wellness and Manage Chronic Disease: A Systematic Review and Meta-Analysis of Mindfulness-Based Randomized Controlled Trials Relevant to Lifestyle Medicine. *American Journal of Lifestyle Medicine, 9*(3), 185–211. DOI: 10.1177/1559827614537789

Waheed, S., & Kumar, S. (2024). Challenges and Future Directions for Promoting Sustainable Gastronomy Tourism. In Jimenez Ruiz, A. E., Bhartiya, S., & Bhatt, V. (Eds.), *Advances in Hospitality, Tourism, and the Services Industry* (pp. 1–16). IGI Global., DOI: 10.4018/979-8-3693-1814-0.ch001

Warren, J. M., Smith, N., & Ashwell, M. (2017). A structured literature review on the role of mindfulness, mindful eating and intuitive eating in changing eating behaviours: Effectiveness and associated potential mechanisms. *Nutrition Research Reviews, 30*(2), 272–283. DOI: 10.1017/S0954422417000154 PMID: 28718396

Chapter 2
From Table to Mind:
The Psychological and Social Dimensions of Eating in the Wellness Economy

Rismawati Rismawati
http://orcid.org/0000-0001-8046-6764
Universitas Muhammadiyah Palopo, Indonesia

Supriadi Supriadi
http://orcid.org/0009-0004-7194-9456
Universitas Cokroaminoto Palopo, Indonesia

Neha Sharma
Chandigarh School of Business, Mohali, India

ABSTRACT

This chapter examines the complex interplay between diet, psychology, and social behavior within the burgeoning wellness sector. Expanding beyond conventional nutritional science, it explores emotional eating, cognitive food selection, and the neuroscience of cravings, emphasizing the dual role of food as a psychological regulator and a social connector. It also analyzes the symbolic influence of wellness branding, the function of internet influencers, and the psychological effects of solitary dining. The book provides a thorough examination of how food choices are influenced by biological requirements, emotional conditions, social identity, and cultural narratives, by synthesizing concepts from behavioral economics, neuromarketing, and food policy. This collection promotes a comprehensive, inclusive, and ethically grounded approach to eating that enhances individual well-being and social cohesion, as mental health becomes a pivotal focus in public health and marketing.

DOI: 10.4018/979-8-3373-4047-0.ch002

DEFINING THE WELLNESS ECONOMY: MARKET TRENDS AND EMERGING SECTORS

This section contributes to the chapter's overarching thesis that food choices in the wellness economy are shaped not solely by nutritional knowledge, but by an intricate interplay of psychological, cultural, and identity-driven forces embedded in consumer trends.

The wellness economy has rapidly evolved into a multi-trillion-dollar global sector encompassing industries such as fitness, mental health, nutrition, and integrative medicine (Conor, 2021; Thukral & Ratten, 2020). According to the Global Wellness Institute (2023), it exceeded USD 5.6 trillion in 2022, with increasing consumer emphasis on holistic well-being. Food, within this paradigm, is no longer viewed merely as sustenance, but as a pivotal determinant of mental and physical health.

This section lays the groundwork for understanding how economic forces, wellness branding, and psychological triggers converge to shape food consumption behaviors, thereby setting the conceptual foundation for subsequent chapters. New sectors such as functional foods, mood-enhancing beverages, and neuro-nutrition reflect a transition in how food is marketed—not just as nourishment, but as a tool for emotional and cognitive optimization (Essa et al., 2021; Gupta et al., 2023). Consumers seek products that claim to support brain health, reduce anxiety, or enhance focus, reflecting a shift toward emotionally intelligent consumption.

Figure 1. Interdisciplinary Wellness Food Framework. This model illustrates the convergence of psychology, neuromarketing, and social identity in shaping wellness food behavior.

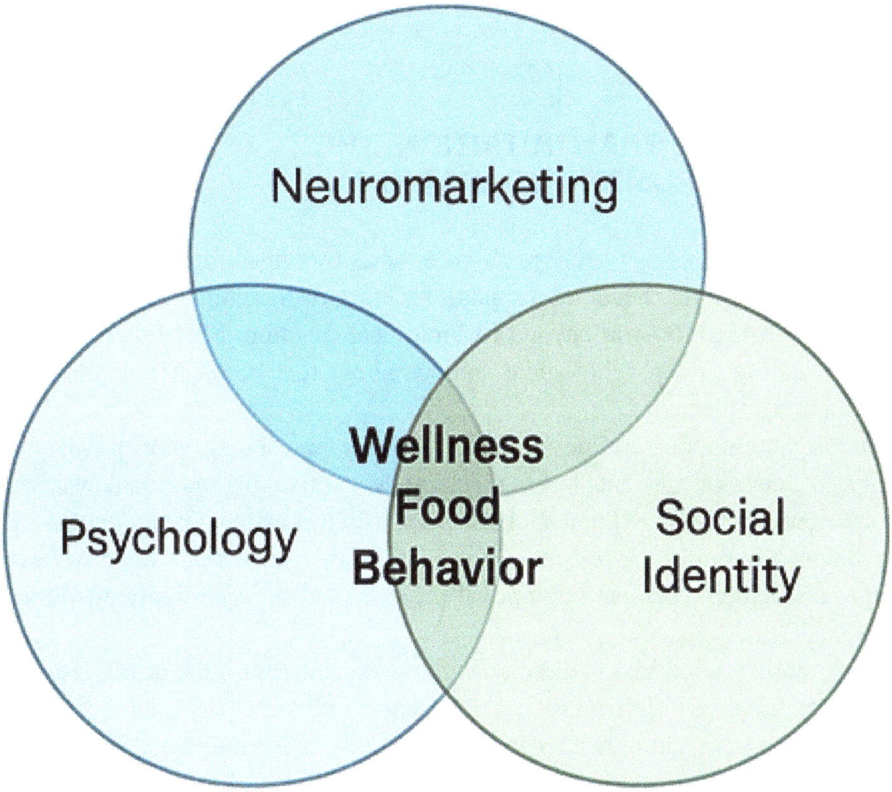

Wellness branding uses lifestyle narratives to position food as aspirational, identity-affirming commodities—organic, plant-based, or gut-health optimized. These branded identities mirror consumers' desire for moral clarity and psychological control in their eating practices, and they blur the boundaries between health ideals and commercial interests (Flavián et al., 2020).

Digital technologies such as AI-based nutrition apps and wearable biosensors add another layer of personalization to dietary decisions. These tools offer feedback on caloric intake, emotional triggers, and gut-brain interactions, intensifying the relationship between food and self-regulation (Alaimo et al., 2020; Galanakis et al., 2021).

The COVID-19 pandemic further accelerated the integration of immunity-enhancing and stress-reducing foods into wellness trends, intensifying demand for functional nutrition across social strata (Bolm et al., 2022). [NEW] Understanding these shifts is essential for stakeholders—particularly marketers, policymakers, and public health advocates—to design more inclusive, ethical, and psychologically attuned wellness interventions that support long-term behavior change and emotional well-being.

FOOD AS MORE THAN NUTRITION: THE MINDFUL CONSUMPTION PARADIGM

This section expands the chapter's core thesis by illustrating how food, within the wellness economy, becomes a conduit for emotional regulation, ethical expression, and self-identity—far beyond its biological function. Mindful consumption reframes eating as a psychological and social act that both reflects and shapes contemporary values.

In the contemporary wellness economy, food is increasingly conceptualized not only as a source of nutrients but as a vehicle for cultivating emotional awareness, ethical consciousness, and personal integrity. Mindful eating—rooted in Buddhist psychological traditions—encourages deep sensory engagement, attentiveness to hunger and satiety cues, and emotional presence during consumption (Mantzios & Egan, 2020).

This sensory mindfulness directly counters the culture of distracted, fast-paced eating that pervades industrial societies. Research indicates that mindful eating may reduce compulsive eating behaviors by fostering self-regulation and interoceptive awareness (Shaw & Cassidy, 2021; Bolm et al., 2022).

Food also serves as a symbolic expression of moral identity and psychological alignment. Individuals choose plant-based, organic, or locally sourced food not just for health, but as statements of compassion, sustainability, or self-discipline—behaviors often referred to as performative health identities (Kukla, 2024; Reddy & Dam, 2020).

While these choices can empower, they may also provoke anxiety or guilt when ideals are rigidly enforced by social media or peer culture. The commercialization of these identities—through branding and influencer endorsement—can blur the line between wellness and performance, inclusion and exclusion.

Aligned with experiential wellness, food rituals such as slow dining, community-supported agriculture, and wellness retreats reflect broader trends in lifestyle branding. These experiences integrate food into narratives of healing, transformation, and relational connectedness (Zanatta et al., 2022; Mingay et al., 2021).

Businesses in the wellness sector can harness mindful consumption trends by designing food experiences that support sensory engagement, emotional storytelling, and cultural inclusivity. Restaurants and brands may benefit from offering transparently sourced ingredients, interactive eating environments, and digital platforms that encourage mindful eating practices. Mindful consumption reflects a broader evolution of eating as both personal therapy and cultural performance. Future research and public education must work together to ensure that this paradigm remains inclusive, evidence-based, and emotionally supportive—rather than commodified to the point of elitism.

HISTORICAL PERSPECTIVES ON FOOD, EMOTIONS, AND SOCIAL WELL-BEING

The interconnection between food, emotions, and social well-being has deep historical roots that transcend mere nutritional value. Across civilizations and epochs, food has played a central role in shaping human identity, expressing emotional states, and reinforcing social bonds. The emotional dimensions of eating are not recent phenomena—they are embedded in rituals, religious traditions, communal practices, and symbolic acts of care that have persisted for centuries (Bosco, 2020; Marino, 2021; Rokach, 2020).

In ancient societies, food was not only sustenance but also a sacred conduit of communal harmony and spiritual alignment. In Greco-Roman traditions, feasting was associated with celebration, philosophical discourse, and civic solidarity. Meanwhile, in Eastern cultures such as Confucian and Ayurvedic traditions, food was intricately linked to emotional equilibrium and bodily balance, where ingredients were selected not only for taste but for their metaphysical properties and mood-regulating functions.

Religious rituals have also highlighted the emotional significance of food. The Christian Eucharist, the Jewish Seder, and the Islamic Iftar are not only acts of faith but deeply emotional gatherings where food becomes a vessel of remembrance, unity, and transcendence. These traditions underscore how the act of eating has long served as a mechanism to regulate collective emotions such as gratitude, mourning, reverence, and joy.

Historically, in pre-industrial societies, food preparation and consumption were primarily collective endeavors, fostering intimacy and solidarity within families and communities. The emotional value of shared meals was deeply embedded in kinship, hospitality, and mutual dependency. However, the onset of industrialization and urbanization led to shifts in these dynamics. The rise of wage labor, mass production, and fastfood culture gradually eroded communal eating practices, replacing them with speed, convenience, and individualism—often at the cost of emotional and relational nourishment (Iwashima & Sato, 2022; Khara et al., 2021; Morgan, 2020).

Contemporary concerns around food-related anxiety and disconnection can be traced to the historical rupture between food and its emotional/social roots. Today's wellness economy often rebrands these lost traditions, restoring eating as a tool for emotional resilience and social reconnection—an idea explored throughout this chapter. [NEW] Recognizing the emotional heritage of food consumption can inspire modern wellness strategies that promote communal dining, ritualized eating spaces, and culturally sensitive culinary experiences—offering brands a way to foster deeper consumer connection and inclusivity.

EMOTIONAL EATING AND THE STRESS-FOOD CONNECTION

This section supports the chapter's thesis by illustrating how emotional eating in the wellness economy is not merely a personal behavior but a biopsychosocial adaptation shaped by modern stressors, market dynamics, and cognitive overload.

The biological foundation of emotional eating is closely tied to the stress response system. Under stress, the hypothalamic-pituitary-adrenal (HPA) axis becomes activated, leading to the secretion of cortisol, a hormone that increases appetite and cravings for high-fat, high-sugar foods. These "comfort foods" stimulate dopamine release in the brain's reward pathways, providing temporary relief or emotional gratification. This neurological feedback loop reinforces a cycle wherein negative emotions trigger eating behavior, which in turn perpetuates dependency on food for emotional regulation (Alonso-Caraballo et al., 2020; Elder & Mohr, 2020; Polito et al., 2023).

Emotional eating patterns are often rooted in early psychological conditioning and shaped by cultural norms. In the wellness economy, these behaviors are amplified by marketing that positions food as emotional relief, thus commercializing coping mechanisms.

The wellness economy responds by promoting mindful eating, CBT-based nutrition interventions, and personalized wellness coaching. These methods encourage awareness of emotional triggers, promoting resilience through behavior change support systems. Emotional eating is a biopsychosocial phenomenon arising from the intersection of neurobiology, psychological conditioning, and cultural norms. Its rise in the wellness economy highlights the need for interventions that support not only nutritional health but also emotional integrity.

Managerial Implications: Brands and wellness platforms can address emotional eating by creating psychologically supportive food environments—offering comfort foods reimagined with balanced nutrition, integrating emotional literacy into wellness campaigns, and promoting authenticity over perfection in body-image messaging.

COGNITIVE PATTERNS: FOOD CHOICES, HABITS, AND DECISION FATIGUE

This section extends the chapter's thesis by exploring how food choices in the wellness economy are shaped by mental heuristics, cognitive load, and daily decision fatigue—factors that often override nutritional knowledge and intention. One key concept is decision fatigue, where cognitive overload weakens willpower and leads to unhealthy food choices—especially under stress or after long days of decision-making. This effect explains why many abandon dietary goals in the evening (Forde & Bolhuis, 2022; Goukens & Klesse, 2022; Westbury et al., 2023).

Figure 2. Cognitive Triggers and Food Decision Fatigue Model – A visual sequence showing how cognitive overload leads to decision fatigue, stress, and poor food choices

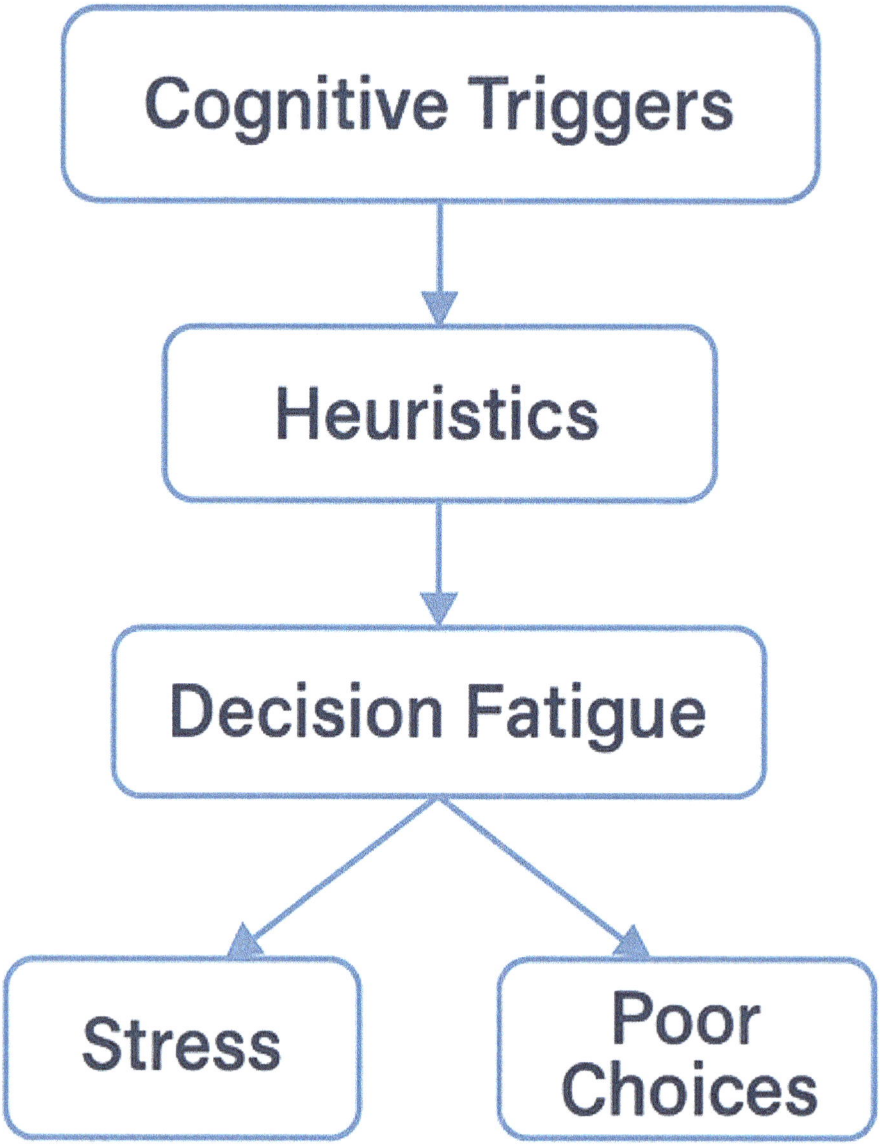

Habits, defined as automatic behaviors triggered by environmental cues, play a significant role in eating patterns. From morning coffee rituals to late-night snacking, these behaviors often bypass conscious control and are resistant to change. Research shows that once habits are formed, they are difficult to modify without intentional interventions that alter the surrounding cues or reward systems. This presents a challenge for wellness initiatives that rely solely on information dissemination, ignoring the ingrained nature of habitual consumption (Anderson & Wood, 2020; Chen et al., 2020; Westbury et al., 2023; Zhang et al., 2022).

The paradox of choice is acute in wellness culture, where conflicting diet trends and excessive options can cause decision paralysis. Instead of empowerment, consumers may feel overwhelmed and default to familiar, less healthy patterns (Anderson & Wood, 2020; Chen et al., 2020; Westbury et al., 2023; Zhang et al., 2022). To support cognitive clarity in food decision-making, wellness platforms should prioritize intuitive, habit-based interventions that reduce complexity, leverage environmental cues, and support mental well-being alongside nutritional goals. [NEW] Brands can improve consumer adherence to healthy eating by simplifying product choices, optimizing in-store layouts, and using behavioral prompts that reduce decision fatigue—thereby aligning marketing strategies with consumer cognitive patterns.

THE ROLE OF REWARD SYSTEMS: DOPAMINE AND SUGAR CRAVINGS

This section extends the chapter's thesis by revealing how reward circuitry—particularly dopamine-driven responses to sugar and fat—interacts with wellness marketing to shape consumption patterns beyond rational choice.

Sugar cravings are a salient example of the brain's reward sensitivity. When individuals consume sugar, dopamine is released, producing sensations of pleasure and satisfaction. Repeated exposure reinforces this behavior, forming a conditioned response whereby the body craves sugar not only for energy but for emotional regulation (Ihssen & Wadsley, 2020; Redine et al., 2022; Tung et al., 2024). Over time, tolerance can develop, leading to increased consumption to achieve the same hedonic effect—paralleling the neurochemical patterns seen in substance addiction.

The modern food environment amplifies reward-seeking through engineered stimuli—ads, packaging, and emotional cues—that activate anticipatory dopamine release. These triggers reinforce habitual cravings, particularly under stress or loneliness (Ihssen & Wadsley, 2020; Redine et al., 2022; Tung et al., 2024). The wellness economy oscillates between exploiting and correcting reward-driven eating. On one hand, it markets 'healthy indulgence' to soothe cravings; on the other, it promotes mindfulness and 'dopamine-aware' eating to rewire reward expectations (Alonso-Caraballo et al., 2020; Ceccarini et al., 2020; Jia & Clark, 2024; Morales & Berridge, 2020; Yagishita, 2022).

Figure 3. Dopamine & Reward Circuitry vs. Mindful Intervention – A contrast table showing how reward-driven consumption can be redirected through mindfulness-based approaches.

Dopamine & Reward Circuitry	Mindful Intervention
Pleasure Seeking	Present Awareness
Habitual Behaviors	Conscious Eating
Cue Reactivity	Emotional Regulation

A neuropsychological view of food rewards reframes eating behaviors as adaptive rather than immoral. Such understanding paves the way for compassionate, evidence-based strategies that support well-being in alignment with brain chemistry (Alonso-Caraballo et al., 2020; Ha & Lim, 2023; Morales & Berridge, 2020). [NEW] Health-focused food brands can reshape consumer behavior by designing products and experiences that satisfy reward pathways without reinforcing dependence—leveraging flavor science, storytelling, and mindful positioning to appeal ethically and effectively.

FOOD AND IDENTITY: CULTURE, CLASS, AND BELONGING

Food is far more than a biological necessity—it is a profound marker of identity, culture, and social belonging. Across history and geography, what people eat, how they eat, and with whom they eat have served as expressions of ethnic heritage, religious observance, social status, and personal values. In the context of the wellness economy, where food choices are often positioned as moral and lifestyle statements, the intersection of eating and identity has become increasingly pronounced (Abbey & Rigg, 2024; Marino, 2021; Monterrosa et al., 2020).

Cultural identity is intimately tied to culinary tradition. Food rituals transmit generational memory, connect diasporic communities, and anchor individuals within shared histories. Whether through communal feasts, traditional recipes, or religious dietary laws, food becomes a language through which culture is practiced and preserved. However, globalization and health-driven dietary shifts have challenged traditional eating practices, sometimes creating tension between ancestral customs and contemporary wellness ideals. For example, plant-based diets promoted in the West may conflict with meat-centric traditions in other societies, prompting negotiation between cultural loyalty and perceived health benefits (Cuj et al., 2020; Monterrosa et al., 2020).

Class identity is similarly reflected in food access and consumption patterns. Organic produce, superfoods, and farm-to-table dining have become symbols of affluence and educated consumerism, while processed and fast foods are often associated with lower socioeconomic groups. This divide creates a form of "nutritional elitism" where healthy eating is not only a matter of choice but of privilege. The wellness economy, while promoting health, inadvertently reinforces these class distinctions by commercializing wellness as a lifestyle accessible predominantly to the economically advantaged.

Food also plays a vital role in the psychology of belonging. Shared meals foster intimacy, social cohesion, and emotional security. Dining practices reinforce group membership—from family dinners to workplace lunches and community potlucks. Conversely, food exclusion (e.g., dietary restrictions, fasting, or disordered eating) can lead to feelings of isolation or difference. In wellness spaces, the valorization of "clean eating" or restrictive diets can alienate those who do not or cannot conform, creating new social boundaries under the guise of health.

As food continues to operate as a vehicle for self-expression and community formation, understanding its role in shaping identity is critical. The wellness economy must move beyond commodified nutrition to embrace inclusive and culturally sensitive food narratives that affirm diverse identities and foster belonging. [NEW] Wellness brands can foster inclusivity and emotional resonance by honoring diverse food identities, avoiding tokenism, and co-creating products with communities whose traditions they represent—nurturing belonging while advancing ethical innovation.

DIGITAL COMMUNITIES AND INFLUENCER DIETS

In the digital age, food culture is increasingly shaped by online platforms where dietary choices, health trends, and wellness philosophies are created, shared, and contested. Social media, in particular, has become a dominant force in shaping eating behaviors and attitudes, giving rise to "influencer diets" that merge lifestyle branding with pseudo-nutritional expertise. Platforms such as Instagram, TikTok, and YouTube serve as spaces where food is not only consumed but performed, aestheticized, and moralized (Davis et al., 2023; Ikram, 2022; Patwardhan et al., 2024).

Influencers often position themselves as authorities in wellness, promoting specific dietary regimes such as veganism, keto, intermittent fasting, or "clean eating." These diets are marketed not merely as health practices, but as pathways to self-improvement, productivity, and aesthetic ideals. Through curated content and personal storytelling, influencers create parasocial relationships with followers, blurring the line between expert advice and aspirational marketing. This phenomenon contributes to what nutrition scholars have termed the "nutrition gaze," where individuals increasingly view food through the lens of image, performance, and social validation.

Digital communities formed around specific food philosophies offer belonging and support, but they can also foster exclusion, misinformation, and orthorexic tendencies. For example, communities that valorize extreme clean eating or detox regimes often pathologize deviation, equating certain foods with toxicity or moral failure (Jönsson et al., 2021; Ramenzoni, 2023; Rodgers et al., 2023; Tiusanen, 2021). These online echo chambers can amplify anxiety about food purity and body image, especially among adolescents and young adults who are highly susceptible to peer comparison and digital validation (Turner & Lefevre, 2021).

Moreover, algorithmic design plays a crucial role in reinforcing dietary beliefs. Search histories and engagement patterns influence what content is shown, creating filter bubbles where users are repeatedly exposed to similar wellness narratives. This personalization reinforces existing biases and may hinder critical engagement with diverse perspectives on health and nutrition. In this way, digital platforms act not only as spaces of influence but as architects of dietary ideology.

In the wellness economy, influencer diets reflect a new mode of authority—one rooted not in science but in digital charisma and aesthetic appeal. Understanding the psychological mechanisms behind digital food culture is essential for developing media literacy, promoting evidence-based dietary education, and fostering a more inclusive and balanced approach to eating in the age of social media.

LONELINESS, SOCIAL ISOLATION, AND THE RISE OF SOLO EATING

In contemporary society, the rise of solo eating—meals consumed in isolation—is an increasingly prevalent phenomenon, shaped by shifting work patterns, urban living, digital engagement, and evolving household structures. While eating alone may offer moments of autonomy and reflection, its growing normalization also reflects deeper social challenges, notably the global rise in loneliness and social isolation. Within the framework of the wellness economy, which promotes food as a path to holistic well-being, the psychosocial implications of solitary dining warrant critical exploration (Brown et al., 2020; Chang, 2020; Conor, 2021; Tiusanen, 2021).

Solo eating is particularly common in urban and industrialized settings, where fast-paced lifestyles and individualistic cultural norms have diminished the frequency of communal meals. Technological advancements, including food delivery apps and virtual entertainment, have further enabled people to consume meals without interpersonal interaction. Although convenient, this decoupling of eating from social engagement may erode the psychological benefits traditionally associated with shared meals—such as emotional support, identity affirmation, and communal bonding.

Studies have shown that regular communal eating is associated with lower levels of depression, enhanced life satisfaction, and greater feelings of connectedness. Conversely, individuals who eat alone frequently may experience heightened risks of emotional distress, unhealthy eating patterns, and even increased mortality. These risks are particularly pronounced among vulnerable populations such as the elderly, single adults, and urban migrants who lack family or community networks.

The wellness economy's current emphasis on personal optimization through dietary self-care can unintentionally reinforce the solitary experience of food. Meal prepping, mindful eating, and digital health tracking—though beneficial—are often practiced in isolation, emphasizing individual accountability over social nourishment. While these practices promote awareness and control, they may also obscure the essential role of human connection in eating behavior and psychological well-being (Gupta & Sharma, 2021; Kukla, 2024; Lee et al., 2023).

To counteract this trend, emerging wellness initiatives have begun to reintroduce communal dimensions to food culture, such as group cooking classes, shared meal experiences, and community kitchens. These interventions recognize that wellness is not solely an individual pursuit but a relational process rooted in shared rituals and emotional reciprocity.

As solo eating becomes a structural feature of modern life, addressing its emotional and social consequences is vital. Reintegrating connection into eating practices aligns not only with public health goals but with the deeper human need for belonging in an increasingly fragmented world. [NEW] Businesses can create emotionally meaningful food experiences by respecting ritual origins, integrating community storytelling, and designing spaces that foster shared presence—strengthening emotional safety and brand trust simultaneously

THE RISE OF CLEAN LABELS, PLANT-BASED FOODS, AND MENTAL HEALTH CLAIMS

The modern wellness economy has given rise to a new wave of food branding strategies centered on psychological appeal, ethical narratives, and health optimization. Among the most prominent trends are the emergence of *clean labels*, the proliferation of *plant-based products*, and the integration of *mental health claims* into food marketing. These branding practices reflect and shape contemporary consumer values, intertwining dietary choices with identity, morality, and psychological well-being (Brooker et al., 2022; Errmann et al., 2023; Fernandes et al., 2024; Palo-oja & Nieminen, 2022).

Clean label foods—typically characterized by simple, recognizable ingredients and free-from claims (e.g., no artificial additives, preservatives, or GMOs)—have become synonymous with purity, authenticity, and transparency. These products appeal to a consumer base increasingly skeptical of industrialized food systems and motivated by the desire for control over their health. Clean labels function not only as markers of physical safety but also as psychological reassurances, invoking feelings of trust, empowerment, and moral virtue in consumption.

Similarly, the rise of plant-based foods transcends environmental and nutritional benefits. For many consumers, choosing plant-based diets is a symbolic act—reflecting ethical commitments to animal welfare, sustainability, and body mindfulness. The branding of plant-based lifestyles is often emotionally charged, portraying the diet as a holistic pathway to vitality, balance, and personal integrity. This narrative resonates with wellness consumers seeking alignment between their values and their food choices, thereby reinforcing loyalty to plant-based brands (García-Salirrosas et al., 2024; Landry & Ward, 2024; Tiusanen, 2021).

The integration of mental health claims into food marketing represents a newer frontier in wellness branding. Products now tout benefits such as stress reduction, cognitive enhancement, and mood stabilization through ingredients like adaptogens, probiotics, omega-3s, and magnesium. These claims tap into the growing public awareness of the gut-brain axis and the role of nutrition in emotional regulation.

However, the scientific validity of such claims is often oversimplified or overstated, raising ethical concerns about the commodification of psychological health in a marketplace context (Chen et al., 2023; Kurowska et al., 2023; Mu et al., 2024).

Collectively, these trends reveal a shift in consumer psychology: food is no longer valued merely for its nutritional content, but for its symbolic, emotional, and ethical associations. As wellness branding continues to evolve, it is imperative to examine how marketing constructs shape consumer behavior, influence self-perception, and contribute to broader social discourses on health, morality, and identity in the age of holistic well-being. [New] Companies can build lasting trust by implementing transparent labeling systems that validate consumer emotions while educating on food safety—bridging the gap between psychological simplicity and scientific literacy.

PSYCHOLOGICAL APPEAL OF "NATURAL," "ORGANIC," AND "GUILT-FREE" TAGS

In the contemporary wellness economy, food labeling has evolved from a regulatory necessity into a powerful psychological tool for influencing consumer perception and behavior. Terms such as "natural," "organic," and "guilt-free" are not only descriptors of food composition but also symbols that tap into deeper emotional, moral, and cognitive associations (Anghelcev et al., 2020; Caso et al., 2023; Elder & Mohr, 2020; Kumar et al., 2020; Nawaz & Satterfield, 2022; Palo-oja & Nieminen, 2022; Shenoy et al., 2024). These labels operate within a framework of *health halos*—cognitive biases in which one positive attribute of a product leads consumers to assume other unrelated health benefits.

The term "natural" evokes notions of purity, simplicity, and safety. Despite the lack of consistent regulatory definitions, consumers often interpret natural foods as being free from synthetic chemicals, minimally processed, and closer to their original state. This perception aligns with the psychological desire for control in an increasingly industrialized food landscape. "Natural" food choices thus fulfill not just physiological needs but emotional ones—offering reassurance, nostalgia, and a sense of returning to a more authentic way of living.

Similarly, "organic" labeling carries connotations of wholesomeness, environmental stewardship, and ethical integrity. Consumers who purchase organic products often report doing so not only for health benefits but to express their values related to sustainability and animal welfare. The organic label acts as a form of *virtue signaling*, allowing individuals to align their food consumption with social responsibility and moral identity. This alignment reinforces a sense of psychological coherence between beliefs and behaviors, enhancing self-esteem and perceived social belonging (Boobalan et al., 2020; Bouman et al., 2021; Gupta & Sharma, 2021; Won et al., 2024).

Perhaps the most psychologically loaded label is "guilt-free." This term appeals directly to the emotional experience of eating, especially among consumers navigating restrictive diets or body image concerns. Framing a food as guilt-free absolves the eater from self-judgment, offering moral permission to indulge without psychological penalty. However, this dichotomy of "guilt" and "virtue" in food consumption can reinforce disordered eating patterns and unhealthy emotional relationships with food (Elder & Mohr, 2020; Food as Thought Analysis, 2024).

Ultimately, the power of these labels lies not in their scientific accuracy, but in their symbolic resonance. In the wellness economy, where food is increasingly intertwined with identity and emotional regulation, these labels function as psychological cues—guiding decisions, managing guilt, and affirming values. As such, they are critical to understanding the deeper socio-emotional dimensions of food choice in the modern era. [NEW]: Food brands and health advocates must adapt to digital influence by leveraging ethical influencer partnerships, promoting balanced messaging, and utilizing behavioral design that aligns commerce with consumer well-being.

NEUROMARKETING STRATEGIES AND BEHAVIORAL NUDGES IN FOOD RETAIL

In the wellness economy, where consumer attention is fragmented and competition for health-conscious spending is intense, neuromarketing strategies and behavioral nudges have emerged as powerful tools for shaping food choice (Gill & Singh, 2020; Liu et al., 2023; Varlese et al., 2020). By leveraging insights from neuroscience, psychology, and behavioral economics, food retailers and wellness brands are able to influence consumer behavior on a subconscious level—guiding decisions in ways that appear intuitive yet are carefully engineered.

Neuromarketing employs techniques such as eye-tracking, electroencephalography (EEG), and functional MRI (fMRI) to analyze consumers' emotional and cognitive responses to stimuli, including packaging design, brand colors, and product placement. For instance, foods with *warm hues*, *minimalist typography*, or *organic textures* tend to evoke trust and perceived healthfulness, even in the absence of nutritional superiority. These sensory cues activate reward-related brain regions, particularly the orbitofrontal cortex, which is associated with decision-making and valuation. This approach enhances emotional engagement and encourages impulse buying, especially in the context of wellness-branded snacks and supplements.

In parallel, behavioral nudging relies on structuring environments to make healthier or branded choices more likely without restricting freedom of choice. Supermarket layouts, shelf placement, and point-of-sale messaging are strategically organized to capitalize on cognitive heuristics. For example, placing plant-based products at eye level or labeling them with positive affirmations (e.g., "fuel for your mind") increases their salience and desirability (Choice Architecture in Food Services: Drive Revenue and Increase Sustainability with More Plant-Based Meals for Flexitarians, 2024; Edirisinghe & Munson, 2022; Huang et al., 2022). These nudges align with *system 1 thinking*—fast, intuitive, and emotionally driven decision-making processes—making them highly effective in influencing time-pressured or distracted shoppers.

Critically, wellness brands often combine these strategies with digital technologies such as AI-powered recommendation engines and behavioral analytics. Online platforms personalize food suggestions based on past behavior, emotional sentiment (e.g., through facial recognition or mood-tracking apps), and health goals, reinforcing consumption patterns under the guise of wellness optimization.

Figure 4. Wellness Branding and Emotional Symbolism Matrix – A framework that maps brand elements and their emotional effects on consumer perception.

	Symbol	Language	Effect
Brand	Logo	Tagline	Trust
Emotion	Imagery	Narrative	Joy
	Colours	Words	Hope

While these techniques can promote healthier choices, they also raise ethical concerns regarding autonomy, manipulation, and transparency. Consumers may be unaware of the extent to which their choices are being influenced by invisible forces rooted in neuropsychological profiling. As the wellness economy continues to evolve, it becomes essential to scrutinize the balance between persuasion and empowerment—ensuring that wellness marketing promotes informed, autonomous, and emotionally intelligent food decisions. Responsible wellness branding requires emotional intelligence—designing messages that uplift without exploiting vulnerabilities, cultivating authenticity, and aligning business values with psychological sustainability.

DESIGNING MENTAL HEALTH-AWARE FOOD POLICIES

The integration of mental health considerations into food policy design marks a progressive shift in how governments and institutions approach public health in the wellness economy. Traditionally, food policies have prioritized nutritional adequacy, food safety, and caloric sufficiency. However, a growing body of interdisciplinary research now underscores the need to account for the psychological and emotional dimensions of eating—prompting the emergence of mental health-aware food policy frameworks that address the full spectrum of well-being (Fathiya, 2024; Mingay et al., 2021).

Food choices are intimately linked with emotional states, cognitive function, and stress regulation. Nutrient deficiencies, excessive consumption of processed foods, and disordered eating patterns are increasingly associated with the prevalence of mood disorders, including anxiety and depression. As such, policies must move beyond macronutrient metrics to foster environments that promote emotionally intelligent eating behaviors, reduce stigma around food-related mental health issues, and ensure equitable access to psychologically beneficial foods (Gheonea et al., 2023; Grajek et al., 2022; Mingay et al., 2021).

Mental health-aware food policies involve multiple layers of intervention. At the institutional level, public schools, hospitals, and workplaces can incorporate meal programs designed not only for physical health but also for psychological nourishment—featuring nutrient-dense, mood-supportive foods such as omega-3-rich fish, leafy greens, fermented products, and whole grains. These initiatives can be reinforced by educational campaigns that highlight the *gut-brain axis* and the psychological impact of diet on emotional regulation (Ljubičić et al., 2023; Pérez, 2021; Que, 2023).

At the regulatory level, governments can support the reformulation of packaged foods to reduce ingredients linked with cognitive and emotional dysregulation (e.g., trans fats, excessive sugars), while also mandating clear labeling of mood-enhancing or mental wellness claims. Policy incentives, such as tax benefits or subsidies for producers of "brain-healthy" foods, could stimulate innovation and accessibility in the wellness-oriented food sector.

Furthermore, mental health-aware policies should consider vulnerable populations—such as low-income communities, adolescents, and the elderly—by ensuring that mental wellness-promoting foods are not restricted to affluent consumer groups. This requires addressing structural barriers related to food deserts, affordability, and cultural relevance.

Ultimately, embedding mental health into food policy is not just a nutritional challenge but a moral imperative. It signals a paradigm shift in public health—where the psychology of eating is recognized as fundamental to sustainable wellness, social equity, and long-term population resilience. [NEW] Cross-sector collaboration can scale mindful eating education by aligning curricula with food industry ethics, public policy, and tech innovation—empowering future consumers and reshaping wellness culture with compassion and clarity.

CORPORATE WELLNESS PROGRAMS AND WORKPLACE NUTRITION

As organizations increasingly recognize the interdependence between employee well-being and organizational performance, corporate wellness programs have emerged as strategic investments in human capital. Within these initiatives, workplace nutrition plays a vital role—not only in promoting physical health, but also in supporting mental clarity, emotional resilience, and cognitive productivity. In the wellness economy, the workplace becomes a critical site where food policies and behavioral psychology intersect (Li et al., 2020; Naicker et al., 2021).

The traditional model of workplace nutrition—focused on calorie counts or vending machine options—is being replaced by holistic approaches that acknowledge the psychological impact of diet on employee morale, energy, and stress management. Evidence suggests that poor dietary habits in the workplace are associated with reduced concentration, increased absenteeism, and higher levels of burnout and fatigue. Conversely, access to balanced, nutrient-dense foods has been linked to improved mood, decision-making, and team collaboration (Naicker et al., 2021).

Forward-thinking companies are now implementing psychologically informed nutritional strategies as part of broader wellness programs. These include subsidized healthy meals in workplace cafeterias, mindfulness-based eating workshops, hydration stations, nutrition counseling, and snack bars featuring mood-supportive foods like dark chocolate, nuts, berries, and fermented products. Some firms even tailor offerings to circadian rhythms or cognitive load—providing lighter fare during high-focus periods and energy-boosting options during post-lunch slumps (Bolm et al., 2022; Pine, 2022; Xu et al., 2021).

Moreover, digital technologies are playing a transformative role. Wellness apps integrated into corporate platforms allow employees to track food intake, access personalized nutrition plans, and receive mental health check-ins, creating a feedback loop between dietary habits and emotional well-being. This data-driven approach enables HR departments to design responsive interventions while promoting a culture of self-care and psychological safety (Gupta & Sharma, 2021; Lee, 2022; Salloum & Tekli, 2021).

However, challenges remain. Workplace nutrition must navigate cultural diversity, dietary restrictions, and ethical considerations around food autonomy. It is essential that such programs are inclusive, non-coercive, and supportive rather than prescriptive. The goal is to create food environments that empower individuals to make informed choices, reduce decision fatigue, and foster social connection—such as through communal lunches or wellness-themed cooking events.

Ultimately, embedding the psychology of eating into workplace wellness strategies transforms corporate nutrition from a matter of logistics into a tool for organizational resilience and human flourishing. It aligns employee well-being with business sustainability, positioning food not as a perk, but as a strategic asset in the pursuit of holistic performance. [NEW] Public-private partnerships must uphold ethical food messaging by codifying emotional truth, resisting health elitism, and embedding justice principles into regulatory frameworks and corporate accountability.

BEHAVIORAL ECONOMICS FOR PUBLIC HEALTH: CASE STUDIES

Behavioral economics offers a compelling lens through which to design effective food policies and interventions that account for the irrational yet predictable ways people make decisions. Rather than relying on traditional models of rational choice, behavioral economics recognizes that food decisions are often shaped by cognitive biases, heuristics, and emotional triggers. By understanding these mechanisms, public health initiatives can implement low-cost, high-impact strategies—*behavioral nudges*—to guide healthier eating behaviors without restricting freedom of choice (Goukens & Klesse, 2022; Rodgers et al., 2023).

Numerous case studies illustrate the successful application of behavioral economics in public health nutrition. One notable example is the Smarter Lunchrooms Movement in the United States, which applied behavioral design principles in school cafeterias to increase the selection and consumption of fruits and vegetables. By placing healthier items at eye level, using attractive labels like "power peas" or "super carrots," and positioning fruit near the cashier, schools saw measurable improvements in students' food choices. These subtle changes shifted default behaviors without requiring coercive policies or significant financial investment (Goukens & Klesse, 2022; Öztürk et al., 2020).

In the UK, the Change4Life campaign used behavioral insights to encourage families to reduce sugar intake. It employed techniques such as *loss aversion* ("Too much sugar harms your child's future") and *social proof* ("Thousands of families have switched to lower-sugar options") to motivate behavior change. By pairing mobile apps with in-store prompts and personalized feedback, the program created an integrated environment conducive to healthier decision-making.

Another powerful example is Singapore's Healthier Dining Programme, which incentivized food outlets to offer lower-calorie options and prominently display "Healthier Choice" symbols on menus. Here, the *anchoring effect*—presenting a default healthier meal—proved effective in nudging consumers toward better nutritional outcomes, especially in fast-paced urban contexts (Goukens & Klesse, 2022).

Figure 5. Emotionally Literate Food System Roadmap – A strategic path for building food systems based on empathy, education, ethical marketing, and cultural transformation.

These cases reveal that policy effectiveness can be enhanced by *reframing choices* rather than restricting them, using nudges that align with how people naturally think and behave. Behavioral economics bridges the gap between knowledge and action, empowering individuals to adopt healthier eating habits without feeling deprived or overwhelmed.

In the wellness economy, such strategies are crucial for democratizing access to health-promoting behaviors. By designing environments that support psychologically attuned food choices, public health systems can reduce chronic disease risk, promote emotional well-being, and build sustainable cultures of mindful consumption.

CONCLUSION

The wellness industry has redefined food from a basic requirement into a complex entity imbued with emotional, cultural, psychological, and ethical importance. This chapter delineates how eating behaviors are shaped by emotional states, cognitive patterns, social identity, and neuromarketing methods, exposing the intricacies underlying quotidian food decisions. Emotional eating, decision fatigue, and sugar cravings are not personal shortcomings but rather systemic reactions to a highly stimulating and frequently contradicting food landscape. Concurrently, we note that clean labeling, influencer diets, and solitary eating habits signify deeper transformations in identity construction, social affiliation, and emotional management.

The commercial dynamics propelling the wellness economy frequently obscure the distinction between health promotion and commodification, leveraging psychological triggers while concurrently providing resources for thoughtful, health-oriented living. Both public health and corporate sectors are implementing behaviorally informed interventions, including workplace nutrition programs and food policies that prioritize mental health awareness. These initiatives signify a crucial advancement in harmonizing food systems with human welfare.

Nevertheless, the way ahead necessitates enhanced inclusivity, critical awareness, and ethical examination. Food narratives that prioritize wealth, visual attractiveness, or stringent purity may marginalize vulnerable groups and reinforce disparities. The future of the wellness economy must emphasize empathy, cultural variety, and the rehumanization of consumption.

Ultimately, food transcends simply sustenance or trend; it serves as a significant manifestation of identity, community, and compassion. Consuming nutritious food contributes to a fulfilling life, and comprehending the psychology of eating reveals profound avenues for both society and individual prosperity. This chapter advocates for a more cohesive and empathetic framework in which food regulations, marketing techniques, and wellness practices are grounded in psychological understanding, social equality, and a collective dedication to comprehensive well-being. [NEW] Emotionally literate food systems require multi-stakeholder collaboration—from chefs to marketers, policymakers to educators—to reshape practices that honor psychological needs and human dignity in every bite.

References

Abbey, E. L., & Rigg, Q. (2024). A Qualitative Study of the Meaning of Food and Religious Identity. *Journal of Nutrition Education and Behavior*, *56*(6), 380–391. DOI: 10.1016/j.jneb.2024.03.003

Alaimo, L. S., Fiore, M., & Galati, A. (2020). How the Covid-19 Pandemic Is Changing Online Food Shopping Human Behaviour in Italy. *Sustainability (Basel)*, *12*(22), 9594. DOI: 10.3390/su12229594

Alonso-Caraballo, Y., Guha, S. K., & Chartoff, E. H. (2020). The neurobiology of abstinence-induced reward-seeking in males and females [Review of The neurobiology of abstinence-induced reward-seeking in males and females]. Pharmacology Biochemistry and Behavior, 200, 173088. Elsevier BV. DOI: 10.1016/j.pbb.2020.173088

Anderson, I. A., & Wood, W. (2020). Habits and the electronic herd: The psychology behind social media's successes and failures. *Consumer Psychology Review*, *4*(1), 83–99. DOI: 10.1002/arcp.1063

Anghelcev, G., Mcgroarty, S. M., Sar, S., Moultrie, J., & Huang, Y. (2020). Marketing Processed Organic Foods: The Impact of Promotional Message Framing (Vice Vs. Virtue Advertising) on Perceptions of Healthfulness. *Journal of Food Products Marketing*, *26*(6), 401–424. DOI: 10.1080/10454446.2020.1792022

Bolm, S. L., Zwaal, W., & Fernandes, M. B. (2022). Effects of mindfulness on occupational stress and job satisfaction of hospitality and service workers. *Research in Hospitality Management*, *12*(1), 61–70. DOI: 10.1080/22243534.2022.2080954

Boobalan, K., Nachimuthu, G. S., & Sivakumaran, B. (2020). Understanding the psychological benefits in organic consumerism: An empirical exploration. *Food Quality and Preference*, *87*, 104070. DOI: 10.1016/j.foodqual.2020.104070

Bosco, F. J. (2020). Geographies of Food: Place, Space, and Scale in Food Studies. *Geography Teacher*, *17*(3), 73–76. DOI: 10.1080/19338341.2020.1796744

Bouman, T., van der Werff, E., Perlaviciute, G., & Steg, L. (2021). Environmental values and identities at the personal and group level. *Current Opinion in Behavioral Sciences*, *42*, 47–53. DOI: 10.1016/j.cobeha.2021.02.022

Brooker, P. G., Hendrie, G. A., Anastasiou, K., Woodhouse, R., Pham, T., & Colgrave, M. L. (2022). Marketing strategies used for alternative protein products sold in Australian supermarkets in 2014, 2017, and 2021. *Frontiers in Nutrition*, *9*, 1087194. Advance online publication. DOI: 10.3389/fnut.2022.1087194

Brown, L., Buhalis, D., & Beer, S. (2020). Dining alone: Improving the experience of solo restaurant goers. *International Journal of Contemporary Hospitality Management, 32*(3), 1347–1365. DOI: 10.1108/IJCHM-06-2019-0584

Caso, G., Blasi, E., Cembalo, L., & Vecchio, R. (2023). This cookie will save the planet! The effect of a private sustainability claim on consumers' expectations. *Heliyon, 9*(3), e14206. Advance online publication. DOI: 10.1016/j.heliyon.2023.e14206

Ceccarini, J., Liu, H., Laere, K. V., Morris, E. D., & Sander, C. Y. (2020). Methods for Quantifying Neurotransmitter Dynamics in the Living Brain With PET Imaging [Review of Methods for Quantifying Neurotransmitter Dynamics in the Living Brain With PET Imaging]. Frontiers in Physiology, 11. Frontiers Media. DOI: 10.3389/fphys.2020.00792

Chang, Y. Y. (2020). Lonely or alone? Solitary dining in Japan and Taiwan. *International Journal of Culture, Tourism and Hospitality Research, 15*(1), 10–25. DOI: 10.1108/IJCTHR-01-2020-0008

Chen, J., Li, H., Zhao, T., Chen, K., Chen, M., Sun, Z., Xu, W., Maas, K., Lester, B. M., & Cong, X. (2023). The Impact of Early Life Experiences and Gut Microbiota on Neurobehavioral Development in Preterm Infants: A Longitudinal Cohort Study. *Microorganisms, 11*(3), 814. DOI: 10.3390/microorganisms11030814

Chen, X., Su, L., & Carpenter, D. (2020). Impacts of Situational Factors on Consumers' Adoption of Mobile Payment Services: A Decision-Biases Perspective. *International Journal of Human-Computer Interaction, 36*(11), 1085–1093. DOI: 10.1080/10447318.2020.1722400

Conor, B. (2021). 'How Goopy are you?' Women, Goop and cosmic wellness. *European Journal of Cultural Studies, 24*(6), 1261–1281. DOI: 10.1177/13675494211055735

Cuj, M., Grabinsky, L., & Yates-Doerr, E. (2020). Cultures of Nutrition: Classification, Food Policy, and Health. *Medical Anthropology, 40*(1), 79–97. DOI: 10.1080/01459740.2020.1826475

Davis, H. A., Kells, M., Roske, C., Holzman, S., & Wildes, J. E. (2023). A reflexive thematic analysis of #WhatIEatInADay on TikTok. *Eating Behaviors, 50*, 101759. DOI: 10.1016/j.eatbeh.2023.101759

Edirisinghe, G. S., & Munson, C. L. (2022). Strategic rearrangement of retail shelf space allocations: Using data insights to encourage impulse buying. *Expert Systems with Applications, 216*, 119442. DOI: 10.1016/j.eswa.2022.119442

Elder, R., & Mohr, G. S. (2020). Guilty displeasures: How imagined guilt dampens consumer enjoyment. *Appetite, 150*, 104641. DOI: 10.1016/j.appet.2020.104641

Errmann, A., Conroy, D., & Young, J. M. (2023). The lab, land, and longing: Discursive constructions of Australian identities in 'future' food consumption. *Journal of Consumer Culture*, *24*(1), 193–210. DOI: 10.1177/14695405231207602

Essa, M. M., Bishir, M., Bhat, A., Chidambaram, S. B., Al-Balushi, B., Hamdan, H., Govindarajan, N., Freidland, R. P., & Qoronfleh, M. W. (2021). Functional foods and their impact on health [Review of Functional foods and their impact on health]. Journal of Food Science and Technology, 60(3), 820. Springer Science+Business Media. DOI: 10.1007/s13197-021-05193-3

Fathiya, K. N.Khansa Nur Fathiya. (2024). Food Security: A Key Component in Promoting Public Health and Nutrition. *International Journal of Health Engineering and Technology*, *2*(5). Advance online publication. DOI: 10.55227/ijhet.v2i5.189

Fernandes, A. C., Morais, C., Franchini, B., Pereira, B., Pinho, O., & Cunha, L. M. (2024). Clean-label products: Factors affecting liking and acceptability by Portuguese older adults. *Appetite*, *197*, 107307. DOI: 10.1016/j.appet.2024.107307

Flavián, C., Guinalíu, M., & Lu, Y. (2020). Mobile payments adoption – introducing mindfulness to better understand consumer behavior. *International Journal of Bank Marketing*, *38*(7), 1575–1599. DOI: 10.1108/IJBM-01-2020-0039

Food As Thought Analysis. (2024). https://gradesfixer.com/free-essay-examples/mary-maxfield-food-as-thought-analysis/

Forde, C. G., & Bolhuis, D. P. (2022). Interrelations Between Food Form, Texture, and Matrix Influence Energy Intake and Metabolic Responses [Review of Interrelations Between Food Form, Texture, and Matrix Influence Energy Intake and Metabolic Responses]. Current Nutrition Reports, 11(2), 124. Springer Science+Business Media. DOI: 10.1007/s13668-022-00413-4

Galanakis, C. M., Rizou, M., Aldawoud, T. M. S., Ucak, İ., & Rowan, N. J. (2021). Innovations and technology disruptions in the food sector within the COVID-19 pandemic and post-lockdown era [Review of Innovations and technology disruptions in the food sector within the COVID-19 pandemic and post-lockdown era]. Trends in Food Science & Technology, 110, 193. Elsevier BV. DOI: 10.1016/j.tifs.2021.02.002

García-Salirrosas, E. E., Escobar-Farfán, M., Esponda-Pérez, J. A., Millones-Liza, D. Y., Villar-Guevara, M., Zea, K. L. H., & Gallardo-Canales, R. (2024). The impact of perceived value on brand image and loyalty: A study of healthy food brands in emerging markets. *Frontiers in Nutrition*, *11*, 1482009. Advance online publication. DOI: 10.3389/fnut.2024.1482009

Gheonea, T. C., Oancea, C.-N., Mititelu, M., Lupu, C. E., Ioni ă-Mîndrican, C.-B., & Rogoveanu, I. (2023). Nutrition and Mental Well-Being: Exploring Connections and Holistic Approaches. *Journal of Clinical Medicine, 12*(22), 7180. DOI: 10.3390/jcm12227180

Gill, R., & Singh, J. (2020). A study of neuromarketing techniques for proposing cost effective information driven framework for decision making. *Materials Today: Proceedings, 49*, 2969–2981. DOI: 10.1016/j.matpr.2020.08.730

Goukens, C., & Klesse, A. K. (2022). Internal and external forces that prevent (vs. Facilitate) healthy eating: Review and outlook within consumer Psychology [Review of Internal and external forces that prevent (vs. Facilitate) healthy eating: Review and outlook within consumer Psychology]. Current Opinion in Psychology, 46, 101328. Elsevier BV. DOI: 10.1016/j.copsyc.2022.101328

Grajek, M., Krupa-Kotara, K., Białek-Dratwa, A., Sobczyk, K., Grot, M., Kowalski, O., & Staśkiewicz-Bartecka, W. (2022). Nutrition and mental health: A review of current knowledge about the impact of diet on mental health [Review of Nutrition and mental health: A review of current knowledge about the impact of diet on mental health]. Frontiers in Nutrition, 9. Frontiers Media. DOI: 10.3389/fnut.2022.943998

Gupta, A., Sanwal, N., Bareen, M. A., Barua, S., Sharma, N., Olatunji, O. J., Nirmal, N. P., & Sahu, J. K. (2023). Trends in functional beverages: Functional ingredients, processing technologies, stability, health benefits, and consumer perspective [Review of Trends in functional beverages: Functional ingredients, processing technologies, stability, health benefits, and consumer perspective]. Food Research International, 170, 113046. Elsevier BV. DOI: 10.1016/j.foodres.2023.113046

Gupta, M., & Sharma, A. (2021). Fear of missing out: A brief overview of origin, theoretical underpinnings and relationship with mental health [Review of Fear of missing out: A brief overview of origin, theoretical underpinnings and relationship with mental health]. World Journal of Clinical Cases, 9(19), 4881. Baishideng Publishing Group. DOI: 10.12998/wjcc.v9.i19.4881

Ha, O., & Lim, S.-L. (2023). The role of emotion in eating behavior and decisions. *Frontiers in Psychology, 14*, 1265074. Advance online publication. DOI: 10.3389/fpsyg.2023.1265074

Huang, Z., Du, Y., Xu, F., & Hu, C. (2022). How Does the Horizontal Position of Pictures and Text Affect Product Evaluation? Based on Left and Right Position Effect. *Frontiers in Psychology, 13*, 841480. Advance online publication. DOI: 10.3389/fpsyg.2022.841480

Ihssen, N., & Wadsley, M. (2020). A reward and incentive-sensitization perspective on compulsive use of social networking sites – Wanting but not liking predicts checking frequency and problematic use behavior. *Addictive Behaviors, 116*, 106808. DOI: 10.1016/j.addbeh.2020.106808

Ikram, M. (2022). Transition toward green economy: Technological Innovation's role in the fashion industry.

Iwashima, F., & Sato, C. (2022). Revisiting "empowered rural women" in postwar Japan. *Journal of Agrarian Change, 22*(4), 855–873. DOI: 10.1111/joac.12494

Jia, Y., & Clark, K. (2024). The Role of Impulsivity and Addiction in Gambling Behaviors: How Applied Neuroscience Research Can Help in the Monitoring and Management of Mental Health Issues. *Open Journal of Medical Psychology, 13*(1), 11–24. DOI: 10.4236/ojmp.2024.131002

Jönsson, H., Michaud, M., & Neuman, N. (2021). What Is Commensality? A Critical Discussion of an Expanding Research Field [Review of What Is Commensality? A Critical Discussion of an Expanding Research Field]. International Journal of Environmental Research and Public Health, 18(12), 6235. Multidisciplinary Digital Publishing Institute. DOI: 10.3390/ijerph18126235

Khara, T., Riedy, C., & Ruby, M. B. (2021). The Evolution of Urban Australian Meat-Eating Practices. *Frontiers in Sustainable Food Systems, 5*, 624288. Advance online publication. DOI: 10.3389/fsufs.2021.624288

Kukla, Q. R. (2024). Healthism, Elite Capture, and the Pitfalls of an Expansive Concept of Health. In *Philosophy and medicine* (p. 275). Springer Nature., DOI: 10.1007/978-3-031-62241-0_21

Kumar, S., Dhir, A., Talwar, S., Chakraborty, D., & Kaur, P. (2020). What drives brand love for natural products? The moderating role of household size. *Journal of Retailing and Consumer Services, 58*, 102329. DOI: 10.1016/j.jretconser.2020.102329

Kurowska, A., Ziemichód, W., Herbet, M., & Piątkowska-Chmiel, I. (2023). The Role of Diet as a Modulator of the Inflammatory Process in the Neurological Diseases [Review of The Role of Diet as a Modulator of the Inflammatory Process in the Neurological Diseases]. Nutrients, 15(6), 1436. Multidisciplinary Digital Publishing Institute. DOI: 10.3390/nu15061436

Landry, M. J., & Ward, C. (2024). Health Benefits of a Plant-Based Dietary Pattern and Implementation in Healthcare and Clinical Practice [Review of Health Benefits of a Plant-Based Dietary Pattern and Implementation in Healthcare and Clinical Practice]. American Journal of Lifestyle Medicine, 18(5), 657. SAGE Publishing. DOI: 10.1177/15598276241237766

Lee, J. Y. (2022). How does psychological safety foster employee performance? A serial multiple mediation of job crafting and thriving. *International Journal of Organization Theory and Behavior, 25*(3/4), 98–112. DOI: 10.1108/IJOTB-12-2021-0239

Lee, M., Angus, D. J., Walsh, H., & Sargeant, S. (2023). "Maybe it's Not Just the Food?" A Food and Mood Focus Group Study. *International Journal of Environmental Research and Public Health, 20*(3), 2011. DOI: 10.3390/ijerph20032011

Lee, M., Bradbury, J., Yoxall, J. S., & Sargeant, S. (2023). "It's about What You've Assigned to the Salad": Focus Group Discussions on the Relationship between Food and Mood. *International Journal of Environmental Research and Public Health, 20*(2), 1476. DOI: 10.3390/ijerph20021476

Lee, Y., Kim, G., Jun, J. E., Park, H., Lee, W. J., Hwang, Y., & Kim, J. H. (2023). An Integrated Digital Health Care Platform for Diabetes Management With AI-Based Dietary Management: 48-Week Results From a Randomized Controlled Trial. *Diabetes Care, 46*(5), 959–966. DOI: 10.2337/dc22-1929

Li, L., Msaad, H., Sun, H., Tan, M. X., Lu, Y., & Lau, A. K. W. (2020). Green Innovation and Business Sustainability: New Evidence from Energy Intensive Industry in China. *International Journal of Environmental Research and Public Health, 17*(21), 7826. DOI: 10.3390/ijerph17217826

Liu, Y., Zhao, R., Xiong, X., & Ren, X. (2023). A Bibliometric Analysis of Consumer Neuroscience towards Sustainable Consumption [Review of A Bibliometric Analysis of Consumer Neuroscience towards Sustainable Consumption]. Behavioral Sciences, 13(4), 298. Multidisciplinary Digital Publishing Institute. DOI: 10.3390/bs13040298

Ljubičić, M., Sarić, M. M., Klarin, I., Rumbak, I., Barić, I. C., Ranilović, J., Dželalija, B., Sarić, A., Nakić, D., Đjekić, I., Korzeniowska, M., Bartkienė, E., Παπαγεωργίου, M., Tarcea, M., Černelić-Bizjak, M., Kļava, D., Szűcs, V., Vittadini, E., Bolhuis, D. P., & Guiné, R. P. F. (2023). Emotions and Food Consumption: Emotional Eating Behavior in a European Population. *Foods, 12*(4), 872. DOI: 10.3390/foods12040872

Marino, G. (2021). Semiotics of digital cacogastromania. *Digital Age in Semiotics & Communication, 4*. Advance online publication. DOI: 10.33919/dasc.20-21.3-4.5

Mingay, E., Hart, M., Yoong, S., & Hure, A. (2021). Why We Eat the Way We Do: A Call to Consider Food Culture in Public Health Initiatives. *International Journal of Environmental Research and Public Health, 18*(22), 11967. DOI: 10.3390/ijerph182211967

Monterrosa, E., Frongillo, E. A., Drewnowski, A., de Pee, S., & Vandevijvere, S. (2020). Sociocultural Influences on Food Choices and Implications for Sustainable Healthy Diets. *Food and Nutrition Bulletin, 41*(2_suppl). Advance online publication. DOI: 10.1177/0379572120975874

Morales, I., & Berridge, K. (2020). 'Liking' and 'wanting' in eating and food reward: Brain mechanisms and clinical implications [Review of 'Liking' and 'wanting' in eating and food reward: Brain mechanisms and clinical implications]. Physiology & Behavior, 227, 113152. Elsevier BV. DOI: 10.1016/j.physbeh.2020.113152

Morgan, C. (2020). Commensality in Crisis. *Gastronomica, 20*(3), 46–47. DOI: 10.1525/gfc.2020.20.3.46

Mu, X., Zhang, H., Shi, J., Hou, J., Ma, J., & Yang, Y. (2024). Fashion intelligence in the Metaverse: Promise and future prospects. *Artificial Intelligence Review, 57*(3), 67. Advance online publication. DOI: 10.1007/s10462-024-10703-8

Naicker, A., Shrestha, A., Joshi, C., Willett, W. C., & Spiegelman, D. (2021). Workplace cafeteria and other multicomponent interventions to promote healthy eating among adults: A systematic review [Review of Workplace cafeteria and other multicomponent interventions to promote healthy eating among adults: A systematic review]. Preventive Medicine Reports, 22, 101333. Elsevier BV. DOI: 10.1016/j.pmedr.2021.101333

Nawaz, S., & Satterfield, T. (2022). On the nature of naturalness? Theorizing 'nature' for the study of public perceptions of novel genomic technologies in agriculture and conservation. *Environmental Science & Policy, 136*, 291–303. DOI: 10.1016/j.envsci.2022.06.008

Öztürk, O. D., Frongillo, E. A., Blake, C. E., McInnes, M. M., & Turner-McGrievy, G. (2020). Before the lunch line: Effectiveness of behavioral economic interventions for pre-commitment on elementary school children's food choices. *Journal of Economic Behavior & Organization, 176*, 597–618. DOI: 10.1016/j.jebo.2020.03.027

Palo-oja, O.-M., & Nieminen, J. H. (2022). Healthy and Delicious: Responsible Branding of Snacks. *South Asian Journal of Business and Management Cases, 11*(2), 105–118. DOI: 10.1177/22779779221099749

Patwardhan, V., Mallya, J., Kaliappan, S., & Kumar, D. (2024). Influence of social media on young adults' food consumption behavior: Scale development. *Cogent Social Sciences*, *10*(1), 2391016. Advance online publication. DOI: 10.1080/23311886.2024.2391016

Pérez, J. C. (2021). Fungi of the human gut microbiota: Roles and significance [Review of Fungi of the human gut microbiota: Roles and significance]. International Journal of Medical Microbiology, 311(3), 151490. Elsevier BV. DOI: 10.1016/j.ijmm.2021.151490

Pine, A. (2022). Ambient struggling: Food, chronic disease, and spatial isolation among the urban poor. *Agriculture and Human Values*, *40*(3), 1105–1116. DOI: 10.1007/s10460-022-10408-0

Polito, N. D., Stylianakis, A. A., Richardson, R., & Baker, K. (2023). Real-World Intake of Dietary Sugars Is Associated with Reduced Cortisol Reactivity Following an Acute Physiological Stressor. *Nutrients*, *15*(1), 209. DOI: 10.3390/nu15010209

Que, J. (2023). Treating Mental Illness with Dietary Improvement. *Theoretical and Natural Science*, *4*(1), 65–71. DOI: 10.54254/2753-8818/4/20220512

Ramenzoni, V. C. (2023). Taboos, food avoidances, and diseases: Local epistemologies of health among Coastal Endenese in Eastern Indonesia. *Frontiers in Sustainable Food Systems*, *7*, 977694. Advance online publication. DOI: 10.3389/fsufs.2023.977694

Reddy, G., & van Dam, R. M. (2020). Food, culture, and identity in multicultural societies: Insights from Singapore. *Appetite*, *149*, 104633. DOI: 10.1016/j.appet.2020.104633

Redine, A., Deshpande, S., Jebarajakirthy, C., & Surachartkumtonkun, J. (2022). Impulse buying: A systematic literature review and future research directions. *International Journal of Consumer Studies*, *47*(1), 3–41. DOI: 10.1111/ijcs.12862

Rodgers, R. F., Goutama, V., & Sonneville, K. R. (2023). At the Same Table: A Delphi Consensus-Based Model of Health-Promoting Eating Behaviors. *Nutrients*, *15*(16), 3601. DOI: 10.3390/nu15163601

Rokach, A. (2020). Belonging, Togetherness and Food Rituals. *Open Journal of Depression*, *9*(4), 77–85. DOI: 10.4236/ojd.2020.94007

Salloum, G., & Tekli, J. (2021). Automated and Personalized Nutrition Health Assessment, Recommendation, and Progress Evaluation using Fuzzy Reasoning. *International Journal of Human-Computer Studies*, *151*, 102610. DOI: 10.1016/j.ijhcs.2021.102610

Shaw, R., & Cassidy, T. (2021). Self-Compassion, Mindful Eating, Eating Attitudes and Wellbeing. *Sumerianz Journal of Social Science, 42*(42), 73–80. DOI: 10.47752/sjss.42.73.80

Shenoy, K. R., Ranjith, V. K., Nayak, S., & Anirvinna, C. (2024). Conceptualizing organic food consumption: A consumer motive perspective. *Cogent Social Sciences, 10*(1), 2338864. Advance online publication. DOI: 10.1080/23311886.2024.2338864

Thukral, E., & Ratten, V. (2020). Sport, Health, and Lifestyle Entrepreneurship: Case Studies. In Emerald Publishing Limited eBooks (p. 161). DOI: 10.1108/978-1-83982-836-220201022

Tiusanen, K. (2021). Fulfilling the self through food in wellness blogs: Governing the healthy subject. *European Journal of Cultural Studies, 24*(6), 1382–1400. DOI: 10.1177/13675494211055734

Tung, A., Takase, L., Fornal, C., & Jacobs, B. (2024). Neuroscience. https://www.sciencedirect.com/journal/neuroscience/vol/134/issue/3

Varlese, M., Misso, R., Koliouska, C., & Andreopoulou, Z. (2020). Food, internet and neuromarketing in the context of well-being sustainability. *International Journal of Technology Marketing, 14*(3), 267. DOI: 10.1504/IJTMKT.2020.111500

Westbury, S., Oyebode, O., Rens, T. van, & Barber, T. M. (2023). Obesity Stigma: Causes, Consequences, and Potential Solutions [Review of Obesity Stigma: Causes, Consequences, and Potential Solutions]. Current Obesity Reports, 12(1), 10. Springer Science+Business Media. DOI: 10.1007/s13679-023-00495-3

Won, Y., Jung, H. J., & Lee, Y. (2024). Online VR store as a sustainable fashion retail space. *International Journal of Retail & Distribution Management, 52*(13), 31–46. DOI: 10.1108/IJRDM-06-2023-0370

Xu, T., Wang, H., Lu, G., Wan, F., Deng, M., Qi, P., Bezerianos, A., Guan, C., & Sun, Y. (2021). E-Key: An EEG-Based Biometric Authentication and Driving Fatigue Detection System. *IEEE Transactions on Affective Computing, 14*(2), 864–877. DOI: 10.1109/TAFFC.2021.3133443

Yagishita, S. (2022). Cellular bases for reward-related dopamine actions [Review of Cellular bases for reward-related dopamine actions]. Neuroscience Research, 188, 1. Elsevier BV. DOI: 10.1016/j.neures.2022.12.003

Zanatta, F., Mari, S., Adorni, R., Labra, M., Matacena, R., Zenga, M., & D'Addario, M. (2022). The Role of Selected Psychological Factors in Healthy-Sustainable Food Consumption Behaviors during the COVID-19 Pandemic. *Foods, 11*(13), 1944. DOI: 10.3390/foods11131944

Zhang, C., Vanschoren, J., van Wissen, A., Lakens, D., de Ruyter, B., & IJsselsteijn, W. A. (2022). Theory-based habit modeling for enhancing behavior prediction in behavior change support systems. *User Modeling and User-Adapted Interaction, 32*(3), 389–415. DOI: 10.1007/s11257-022-09326-x

Chapter 3
Advancing Well-Being: The Science and Practice of Health and Nutrition

Tarun Kumar Patel
http://orcid.org/0009-0003-3002-8100
Sant Guru Ghasidas Government P.G. College, Kurud, India

ABSTRACT

The chapter examines the critical role of nutrition in addressing global health challenges, particularly the rising prevalence of diet-related non-communicable diseases such as obesity, diabetes, and cardiovascular disease. It explores the science of nutrition, detailing the impacts of macronutrients, micronutrients, and dietary patterns on physical, cognitive, and mental health across the lifespan. The influence of the food industry is analyzed, focusing on its role in promoting ultra-processed foods and the potential for reformulation, transparent labeling, and ethical marketing to foster healthier diets. Nutritional inequities are addressed, highlighting socioeconomic, cultural, and systemic barriers like food deserts, with business-led solutions proposed to promote equity. Emerging trends, including gut microbiome research, personalized nutrition, and biofortification, are discussed. The chapter aims to bridge nutritional science, industry practices, and policy to mitigate NCDs, reduce health disparities, and advance equitable, sustainable well-being.

INTRODUCTION

Nutrition is a cornerstone of human health, development, and well-being, shaping biological systems, mental states, and societal resilience. Adequate nutrition supports growth, cognitive function, immunity, and longevity, while poor dietary patterns drive the global burden of disease. Far beyond a personal choice, nutrition

DOI: 10.4018/979-8-3373-4047-0.ch003

is a public health priority and a lever for advancing individual and societal well-being. Diet-related non-communicable diseases (NCDs), such as obesity, diabetes, and cardiovascular disease, are escalating globally due to shifts in food systems and dietary behaviors, detailed further in this chapter. The rise of ultra-processed foods, explored in the Role of the Food Industry section, has displaced nutrient-rich traditional diets, contributing to poor health outcomes. Concurrently, nutritional inequities persist, with socioeconomic inequality, food insecurity, and unequal access to healthy foods causing undernutrition and overnutrition, often within the same communities. These challenges reflect systemic issues spanning social, economic, and policy domains.

This chapter synthesizes nutritional science, public health, and food industry practices to address these issues. It aims to bridge fragmented domains, offering evidence-based strategies to improve diets, reduce NCDs, and promote health equity. Key topics include NCD trends, the food industry's role in shaping consumption, ultra-processed foods' impact, and consumer behavior drivers like psychological, cultural, and economic factors. Emerging trends, such as plant-based diets, personalized nutrition, and digital dietary tools, are examined alongside structural issues like food policy and cross-sectoral governance. This chapter lays the foundation for the book's exploration of innovative, evidence-informed strategies to foster healthy eating environments and sustainable well-being, serving as both a conceptual framework and practical guide for advancing nutrition as a public good.

The chapter employs a narrative synthesis approach, integrating diverse evidence from nutritional science, epidemiology, and food systems to create a cohesive narrative. Unlike scoping reviews or policy analyses, this method flexibly combines qualitative and quantitative insights to address complex diet-related challenges and inequities. Literature selection was systematic, prioritizing peer-reviewed studies and global health organization reports aligned with themes like nutrients, dietary patterns, and industry influence. Recent publications were emphasized for current trends, with foundational works included for enduring insights. Sources spanned diverse geographic and socioeconomic contexts, particularly low- and middle-income settings, to highlight inequities. By synthesizing scientific studies, industry case studies, and policy evaluations, the chapter highlights innovations like biofortification and functional foods while proposing practical solutions, such as product reformulation and community interventions, to guide stakeholders toward equitable health and nutrition advancements.

THEORETICAL FRAMEWORKS

To deepen the analysis of nutrition's role in health and well-being, this chapter draws on three theoretical frameworks: the Social Ecological Model (SEM), the Health Belief Model (HBM), and the Political Economy of Food. These frameworks provide a structured lens to examine the interplay of individual, community, and systemic factors shaping dietary patterns, health outcomes, and nutritional inequities.

Social Ecological Model (SEM): The SEM posits that health behaviors are influenced by multiple levels—individual, interpersonal, community, organizational, and policy (McLeroy et al., 1988). In nutrition, individual choices (e.g., dietary preferences) interact with interpersonal factors (e.g., family eating habits), community resources (e.g., access to healthy foods), and policy environments (e.g., food regulations). The SEM is applied to analyze how interventions, such as community nutrition programs or sugar taxes, address NCDs and inequities across these levels (Friel et al., 2015). For example, Table 5's policy models reflect SEM's emphasis on multi-level strategies to improve nutrition equity.

Table 5. Global Policy Models for Nutrition Improvement

Policy	Description	Country/ Example	Outcome	Scalability
Sugar-Sweetened Beverage Tax	Tax on high-sugar drinks to reduce consumption	Mexico (2014)	19% reduction in SSB purchases by 2016 (Colchero et al., 2017)	Adaptable with tiered tax structures for low-income countries
Front-of-Pack Labeling	Mandatory warning labels for high-sugar/sodium products	Chile (2016)	24% reduction in unhealthy product purchases (Mialon et al., 2020)	Standardize globally via WHO guidelines
Subsidized Healthy Retail	Incentives for retailers to stock nutrient-dense foods	Australia (2015)	15% increase in fresh produce access (Friel et al., 2015)	Target food deserts with public funding
Community Nutrition Programs	Train local leaders for nutrition education	Ethiopia (2017)	Improved child growth outcomes (Kang et al., 2017)	Scale through national health worker programs
PPPs for Fortification	Industry-government partnerships for fortified staples	Kenya (SUN, 2024)	15% reduction in micronutrient deficiencies (SUN, 2024)	Replicate with clear reformulation targets

Health Belief Model (HBM): The HBM explains health behavior change through perceived susceptibility, severity, benefits, barriers, cues to action, and self-efficacy (Rosenstock, 1974). In this chapter, HBM informs strategies to promote dietary shifts, such as personalized nutrition or nutrition education, by addressing individuals' perceptions of NCD risks and benefits of healthier diets (Roman et al., 2024). For instance, community-led education programs (Kang et al., 2017) leverage HBM to enhance self-efficacy, encouraging sustainable dietary practices in underserved populations.

Political Economy of Food: This framework examines how corporate power, economic structures, and policy processes shape food systems and diets (Lang & Heasman, 2015). It critiques the food industry's role in promoting ultra-processed foods and influencing policy, as seen in lobbying against sugar taxes (Mialon et al., 2020). The framework highlights structural barriers to healthy eating, such as industry-driven marketing targeting vulnerable groups, and informs strategies to counter corporate influence through governance and regulation (Swinburn et al., 2019).

These frameworks collectively guide the chapter's exploration of nutrition challenges, from individual behavior change to systemic inequities, ensuring a comprehensive understanding of the complex dynamics driving diet-related health outcomes.

THE SCIENCE OF NUTRITION AND HEALTH

This section explores the foundational principles of nutritional science, focusing on the roles of macronutrients, micronutrients, and dietary patterns in supporting physical and cognitive health. It examines evidence-based dietary guidelines, the rise of personalized nutrition, and their implications for preventing non-communicable diseases (NCDs) and promoting well-being across diverse populations. Macronutrients are substances needed in substantial quantities that supply energy and contribute to growth, metabolic processes, and overall physiological functions. These include carbohydrates, proteins, and fats (Espinosa-Salas & Gonzalez-Arias, 2023). Carbohydrates, proteins, and fats are the body's primary energy sources. Carbohydrates (e.g., grains, fruits) provide quick energy, fueling daily activities. Proteins (e.g., meat, legumes) supply amino acids for muscle repair, enzyme production, and immune support. Fats (e.g., oils, nuts) offer concentrated energy, aiding hormone synthesis and nutrient absorption. Balanced macronutrient intake is vital for growth and maintenance, with imbalances potentially leading to obesity or malnutrition (Espinosa-Salas & Gonzalez-Arias, 2023; Savarino et al., 2021). Micronutrients are vital vitamins and minerals required in smaller amounts to support key physiological functions, including enzymatic activity, maintaining bone integrity, and strengthening the immune system (Savarino et al., 2021). Vitamins (e.g., A, C, D) and minerals (e.g., iron, calcium) are crucial for health despite being needed in trace amounts. For example, vitamin D supports calcium absorption for bone health, while iron is essential for oxygen transport. Deficiencies in micronutrients can cause conditions like scurvy or anemia, while excesses of certain nutrients, such as fat-soluble vitamins, may lead to toxicity (Savarino et al., 2021). Micronutrient needs vary by age and life stage, emphasizing the need for diverse diets (Savarino et al., 2021). The key nutrients and their impact on health are summarized in the Table 1. Dietary patterns refer to the overall mix, regularity, and diversity of foods and drinks consumed, which collectively impact health status and the likelihood of developing diseases (Ćatović, 2023). These reflect habitual food choices, impacting long-term health. As noted in the Science of Nutrition and Health section, dietary patterns like the Mediterranean diet reduce NCD risks, while Western diets exacerbate them (Tessier et al., 2025). Conversely, Western patterns high in processed foods increase risks of obesity and cardiovascular issues (Green et al., 2016). Cultural and regional factors, as seen in diverse Indian diets, shape patterns and health outcomes (Green et al., 2016; Ćatović, 2023). Dietary patterns like the Mediterranean diet promote health, but access to such nutrient-rich foods is often limited by socioeconomic barriers, a challenge explored further in the context of nutritional inequities.

Table 1. Key Nutrients and Their Health Impacts

Nutrient Type	Examples	Health Benefits	Deficiency Risks
Macronutrients	Carbohydrates (grains, fruits)	Provide quick energy for daily activities	Fatigue, malnutrition
	Proteins (meat, legumes)	Support muscle repair, enzyme production, immune function	Muscle wasting, weakened immunity
	Fats (oils, nuts)	Aid hormone synthesis, nutrient absorption	Hormonal imbalances, poor vitamin absorption
Micronutrients	Vitamin D	Supports calcium absorption for bone health	Rickets, osteoporosis
	Iron	Essential for oxygen transport	Anemia, fatigue
	Omega-3 Fatty Acids	Improve lipid profiles, reduce inflammation	Cognitive decline, cardiovascular risk
Functional Nutrients	Probiotics	Enhance gut microbiome, reduce inflammation	Digestive disorders
	Polyphenols (berries)	Support cognitive function, reduce oxidative stress	Mood disorders, cognitive decline

Note: Compiled using the references: Espinosa-Salas & Gonzalez-Arias (2023); Gómez-Pinilla (2008); Kolodziejczyk et al. (2019); Lichtenstein et al. (2021); Savarino et al. (2021)

Nutrition plays a pivotal role in cardiovascular health, with dietary choices directly influencing heart disease risk. Diets rich in fruits, vegetables, whole grains, and lean proteins, such as the Mediterranean diet, reduce cardiovascular risk by lowering blood pressure, cholesterol, and inflammation (Casas et al., 2018; Tyrovola et al., 2023). Omega-3 fatty acids from fish and nuts further support heart health by improving lipid profiles and reducing arrhythmias. Conversely, high intake of saturated fats, trans-fats, and added sugars, common in Western diets, increases risks of atherosclerosis and hypertension (Lichtenstein et al., 2021). The American Heart Association emphasizes limiting sodium and processed foods while prioritizing nutrient-dense options to enhance cardiovascular outcomes (Lichtenstein et al., 2021). Adopting heart-healthy dietary patterns, tailored to cultural preferences, is critical for preventing and managing cardiovascular disease effectively. Nutrition significantly influences cognitive function across the lifespan, shaping brain health and emotional well-being. Diets rich in antioxidants, omega-3 fatty acids, and B vitamins, found in foods like berries, fatty fish, and leafy greens, enhance cognitive performance by reducing oxidative stress and supporting neuronal integrity (Spencer et al., 2017). These nutrients promote neuroplasticity and mitigate inflammation, which can impair memory and mood. Conversely, diets high in saturated fats and sugars, common in processed foods, are linked to cognitive decline and emotional dysregulation (Spencer et al., 2017; Puri et al., 2023). A life course approach highlights the importance of early nutritional interventions, as childhood deficiencies in micronutrients like iron and iodine can impair cognitive development, with lasting effects into adulthood (Puri et al., 2023). Adopting balanced dietary patterns supports optimal cognitive function and resilience against neurodegenerative diseases.

Dietary guidelines serve as evidence-based frameworks to promote healthy eating and prevent diet-related diseases. The World Health Organization's Eastern Mediterranean guidelines emphasize balanced diets rich in fruits, vegetables, whole grains, and lean proteins while limiting sugars, saturated fats, and sodium to combat obesity and non-communicable diseases (WHO, 2019). Similarly, the Indian Council of Medical Research's 2024 Dietary Guidelines for Indians advocate for diverse, nutrient-dense foods tailored to regional and cultural preferences, promoting adequate macronutrient and micronutrient intake to address malnutrition and chronic illnesses (ICMR, 2024). These guidelines shape healthy diets by providing practical recommendations, such as portion control and food group balance, making them accessible for individuals and policymakers. They also inform public health initiatives, school meal programs, and food labeling, fostering environments conducive to better nutrition. By addressing local dietary patterns and socioeconomic factors, guidelines empower communities to adopt sustainable eating habits, reducing the burden of diseases like diabetes and cardiovascular conditions, ultimately enhancing population health and well-being.

Personalized nutrition marks a shift from one-size-fits-all dietary recommendations to tailored approaches based on individual genetic, biomedical, and lifestyle factors. Advances in nutrigenomics and data integration enable precise dietary interventions that optimize health outcomes (Roman et al., 2024). By analyzing genetic profiles, gut microbiota, and psycho-behavioral patterns, personalized nutrition addresses unique metabolic needs, reducing risks of chronic diseases like obesity and diabetes (Linseisen et al., 2025). Technologies such as wearable devices and AI-driven platforms further enhance customization by monitoring real-time dietary responses and preferences. These approaches integrate biomedical data with environmental and behavioral insights, ensuring scalability for population-wide impact (Linseisen et al., 2025). Personalized nutrition empowers individuals with actionable, evidence-based dietary plans, moving beyond generic guidelines to promote sustainable health improvements tailored to diverse populations. However, key concerns include data privacy, as sensitive genetic and health information requires robust protection. Accessibility remains a challenge, with high costs potentially limiting adoption in low-resource settings. Standardization of methodologies, such as microbiota profiling, is critical to ensure reliability and reproducibility (Kolodziejczyk et al., 2019). Ethical issues, including equitable access and potential misuse of personalized data, demand careful consideration. Additionally, over-reliance on technology risks neglecting holistic lifestyle factors, and public education is needed to foster acceptance of tailored diets (Iacomino et al., 2024; Sarfraz et al., 2022). Addressing these concerns is essential to realize the full potential of personalized nutrition in promoting sustainable health.

This section explores the foundational role of nutrition in health, emphasizing the importance of macronutrients, micronutrients, and dietary patterns in supporting physiological and cognitive functions. Balanced macronutrient intake from carbohydrates, proteins, and fats ensures energy and growth, while micronutrients like vitamins and minerals prevent deficiencies and support immunity. Dietary patterns, such as the Mediterranean diet, reduce risks of NCDs like cardiovascular disease, whereas Western diets high in processed foods increase these risks. Nutrition also enhances cognitive function and emotional well-being, with nutrients like omega-3s and antioxidants mitigating decline. Diet-related NCDs and contributing dietary factors is summarized in Table 2. Personalized nutrition, leveraging genetic and lifestyle data, offers tailored dietary solutions to optimize health, though challenges like data privacy and accessibility remain. Evidence-based dietary guidelines, such as those from WHO and ICMR, promote healthy eating and inform public health strategies, highlighting the need for diverse, nutrient-dense diets to address global health challenges. Having established the foundational role of macronutrients, micronutrients, and dietary patterns in supporting health, it is critical to examine how deviations from these principles contribute to the global rise of NCDs. The next section explores the diet-related health challenges driving the NCD epidemic, particularly in vulnerable populations.

Table 2. Diet-Related NCDs and Contributing Dietary Factors

Non-Communicable Disease	Prevalence (Global)	Contributing Dietary Factors	Mitigating Dietary Strategies	References
Obesity	13% of adults (WHO, 2024)	High intake of ultra-processed foods, added sugars	Increase dietary diversity, whole grains, vegetables	Dolui et al. (2023)
Type 2 Diabetes	537 million adults (WHO, 2024)	High glycemic load, low fiber diets	Low-glycemic, high-fiber diets	Sami et al. (2017)
Cardiovascular Disease	523 million cases (WHO, 2024)	High saturated fats, trans fats, sodium	Mediterranean diet, omega-3 fatty acids	Lichtenstein et al. (2021)
Mental Health Disorders	Varies (e.g., depression: 280 million)	Deficiencies in omega-3s, B vitamins	Antioxidant-rich diets, fortified foods	Ruthsatz & Candeias (2020)

DIET-RELATED HEALTH CHALLENGES

This section addresses the global rise of diet-related NCDs, including obesity, diabetes, and cardiovascular disease, driven by poor dietary patterns and micronutrient deficiencies. Through case studies and data, it highlights the disproportionate impact on vulnerable populations and the urgent need for systemic interventions to mitigate these health challenges. Applying the Social Ecological Model, this section examines how individual dietary choices, community food access, and policy environments interact to drive NCD prevalence, particularly in low-income settings (McLeroy et al., 1988).

The global surge in diet-related non-communicable diseases (NCDs), including obesity, type 2 diabetes, and cardiovascular disease, is a critical public health challenge, driven by poor dietary patterns and micronutrient deficiencies. The World Health Organization (2024) reports NCDs cause 41 million deaths annually, or 74% of global mortality, with low- and middle-income countries bearing over 85% of premature deaths. Shifts to energy-dense, nutrient-poor diets, fueled by urbanization and Westernized eating patterns high in sugars, fats, and sodium, exacerbate NCDs (Ahmad et al.). In India, low dietary diversity increases obesity and diabetes risks among men (Dolui et al., 2024), highlighting the impact of monotonous, processed food-heavy diets. Economic constraints further limit access to nutritious foods, perpetuating health disparities in vulnerable communities. Table 3 compares traditional and ultra-processed diets, illustrating their roles in NCDs (Figure 1).

Table 3. Comparison of Traditional and Ultra-Processed Diets: Nutritional and Health Impacts

Aspect	Traditional Diets	Ultra-Processed Diets
Definition	Diets based on whole, minimally processed foods, often culturally or regionally specific (e.g., Mediterranean diet).	Industrially formulated foods high in added sugars, unhealthy fats, sodium, and additives, designed for convenience (Fanzo et al., 2023).
Nutrient Profile	High in fiber, vitamins, minerals, and antioxidants from fruits, vegetables, whole grains, and lean proteins (Tessier et al., 2025).	Low in essential nutrients, high in empty calories, added sugars, saturated fats, and sodium (Mialon et al., 2020).
Health Benefits	Supports heart health, reduces risk of NCDs like obesity, diabetes, and cardiovascular disease (Casas et al., 2018).	Contributes to obesity, type 2 diabetes, cardiovascular disease, and mental health issues (Dolui et al., 2023; Ruthsatz & Candeias, 2020).
Cultural Relevance	Deeply rooted in local traditions, promoting dietary diversity and sustainability (Green et al., 2016).	Often globally standardized, displacing traditional diets and reducing diversity (Stern, 2021).
Accessibility	May be limited in food deserts or low-income areas due to cost and availability (Odoms-Young et al., 2024).	Widely available, affordable, and convenient, especially in low-income communities (Fanzo et al., 2023).
Consumption Impact	Promotes long-term health, cognitive function, and emotional well-being (Spencer et al., 2017).	Linked to overconsumption, nutrient deficiencies, and increased NCD prevalence (Ahmad et al., 2023).

Figure 1. Traditional diet vs. Ultra-processed Diet

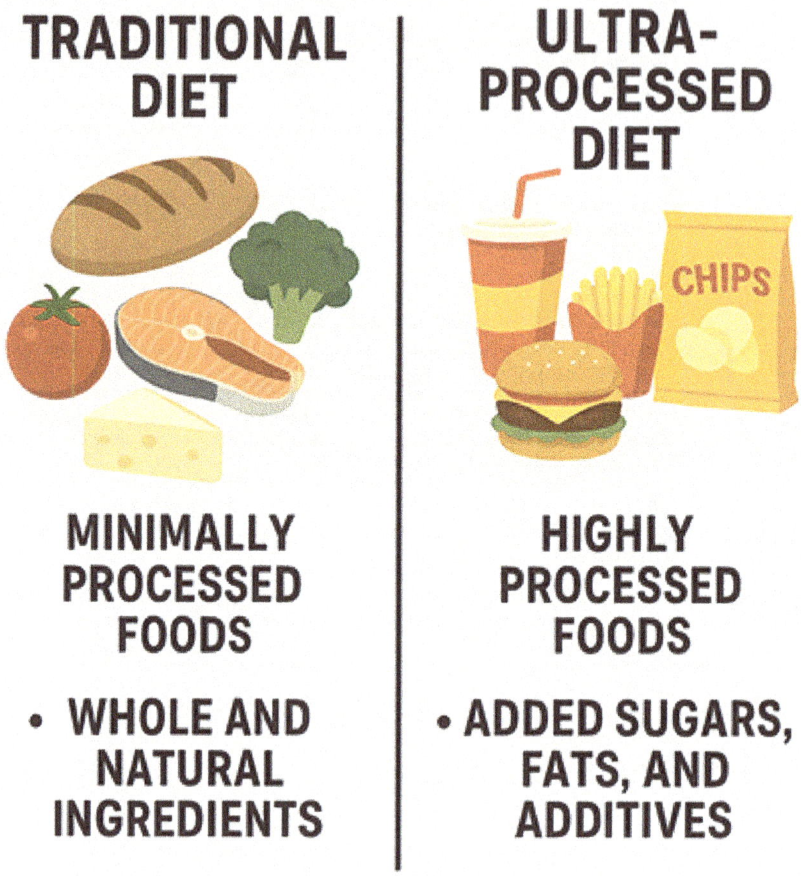

Micronutrient deficiencies in iron, zinc, vitamin A, and folate affect over 2 billion people, particularly children and women in low-income settings (Stevens et al., 2022). These impair metabolism, immunity, increasing chronic disease risks. Low vitamin D and omega-3 intake drives inflammation, linked to cardiovascular disease and diabetes (Bruins et al., 2019). In Indian slums, pregnant women's poor dietary diversity raises NCD risks for mothers and offspring (Deshpande et al., 2024). High-glycemic, low-fiber diets, reliant on starchy staples, contribute to insulin resistance, worsened by scarce fruits, vegetables (Sami et al.).

Nutrition impacts mental health and vulnerable groups. Omega-3 and B vitamin deficiencies are linked to cognitive decline in the elderly (Ruthsatz & Candeias, 2020), while children's sugary diets increase obesity and impair development (Lisičić-

Konaković et al., 2024). Food insecurity in low-income areas drives reliance on calorie-dense, nutrient-poor foods, leading to long-term issues like cognitive deficits and frailty. Case studies underscore these effects: in India, cereal-based diets raised NCD risks 1.5-fold (Dolui et al., 2024); in Bosnia, processed foods were linked to metabolic syndrome in children (Lisičić-Konaković et al., 2024); and in Bangladesh, rice-heavy diets increased diabetes and heart disease (Ahmad et al.). A diabetes case showed better glycemic control with a low-carb, high-fiber diet, while high-sugar diets worsened complications (Reynolds & Mitri, 2024).

This crisis demands urgent action to enhance access to nutrient-rich foods, boost dietary diversity, and curb ultra-processed food consumption through policy. Targeted interventions, like low-glycemic diets, can reduce NCD risks (Sami et al.), but addressing poverty and food insecurity is essential for equitable nutrition, especially in low-income regions. The food industry's role in fostering healthier diets is examined next.

THE ROLE OF THE FOOD INDUSTRY

This section examines the food industry's influence on dietary patterns through product development, marketing, and distribution. It explores strategies like reformulation, transparent labeling, and ethical marketing to promote healthier diets, while addressing limitations such as greenwashing and the dominance of ultra-processed foods. Through the lens of the Political Economy of Food, this section critiques how corporate power shapes dietary habits and public health policies, often prioritizing profit over nutrition (Lang & Heasman, 2015).

Food Industry Influence on Dietary Patterns

The food industry shapes global dietary patterns through product development, marketing, and distribution, influencing consumer choices and health outcomes. Ultra-processed foods, high in sugar, salt, and unhealthy fats, contribute to non-communicable diseases (NCDs), particularly in low-income communities (Mialon et al., 2020). Strategies like reformulation, transparent labeling, and ethical marketing can promote healthier diets, but challenges such as greenwashing and the dominance of ultra-processed foods persist.

Industry Influence and Challenges

The industry's control over product formulation, marketing, and distribution drives dietary habits. Lobbying has historically shaped dietary guidelines, often prioritizing profit over health (Stern, 2021). Aggressive marketing of energy-dense, nutrient-poor foods targets vulnerable groups, including children (Tempels et al., 2017). In Latin America, food companies influence policies to favor ultra-processed products, undermining NCD prevention (Mialon et al., 2020). However, the industry can drive positive change by reformulating products and improving access to nutrient-rich foods, aligning profitability with public health (Miller et al., 2021).

Product Reformulation

Reformulation reduces harmful nutrients like sugar, salt, and trans fats while maintaining taste and affordability (Lehmann et al., 2019). For example, a Scottish bakery cut bread salt content by 20%, lowering population-wide sodium intake (Food and Drink Federation Scotland, 2023). A European retailer reduced saturated fats by 15% in private-label products, showing scalability (von Philipsborn et al., 2018). Challenges include consumer resistance to flavor changes and high reformulation costs (Onyeaka et al., 2023).

Transparent Labeling

Clear nutritional labeling empowers informed consumer choices. Standardized labels highlighting sugar, salt, or fat content counter vague health claims (Fanzo et al., 2023). Chile's warning labels reduced unhealthy product purchases (Mialon et al., 2020). A retailer's color-coded labels increased healthier product sales by 10% (von Philipsborn et al., 2018). However, global implementation faces industry resistance due to profit concerns (Korver, 1997).

Ethical Marketing

Marketing campaigns promoting whole grains, fruits, and vegetables can shift preferences from ultra-processed foods (Miller et al., 2021). A global company's low-sugar cereal campaign increased sales by 25% (Food and Drink Federation Scotland, 2023). Ethical marketing avoids manipulative tactics, but regulatory oversight is needed to prioritize public health (Tempels et al., 2017).

Addressing Ultra-Processed Foods

Ultra-processed foods account for 60% of dietary energy in some populations, crowding out nutrient-dense options (Fanzo et al., 2023). Reformulation and fortification, such as adding micronutrients to staples, improve dietary outcomes (Lehmann et al., 2019). Ready-to-eat vegetable meals are promising but require supply chain investment (Miller et al., 2021).

Consumer Education

Misleading marketing erodes trust, necessitating transparent communication (Stern, 2021). Retailer workshops on label reading boosted healthier purchases by 65% (von Philipsborn et al., 2018). Industry-led education must be independent to avoid bias (Tempels et al., 2017). Regulatory frameworks can ensure initiatives prioritize public health (Mialon et al., 2020).

Governance Mechanisms for Industry Accountability

Effective governance mechanisms are essential to align the food industry's practices with public health objectives, ensuring accountability and fostering collaboration with communities and policymakers. These frameworks address power asymmetries in public-private partnerships (PPPs) and mitigate the risks of profit-driven agendas undermining nutritional goals (Mialon et al., 2020). Below, key governance models are explored, emphasizing their role in promoting healthier diets and equitable food systems.

Multi-Stakeholder Nutrition Platforms

Platforms like the Scaling Up Nutrition (SUN) Movement bring together governments, businesses, civil society, and communities to coordinate nutrition strategies globally. SUN's Business Network engages food companies to commit to reformulation and fortification, with clear targets and independent monitoring (SUN, 2024). For example, in Kenya, SUN facilitated partnerships that increased access to fortified maize flour, reducing micronutrient deficiencies by 15% (Fanzo et al., 2023). These platforms ensure industry actions are transparent and aligned with public health priorities.

Regulatory Incentives and Accountability Frameworks

Governments can use regulatory incentives, such as tax breaks for reformulated products or penalties for non-compliance with nutritional standards, to steer industry behavior. The UK's Soft Drinks Industry Levy, which taxes high-sugar beverages, prompted 50% of manufacturers to reduce sugar content, demonstrating the efficacy of fiscal measures (Pell et al., 2021). Similarly, in January 2014, Mexico implemented a one peso-per-liter excise tax on sugar-sweetened beverages (SSBs) to combat high obesity and diabetes rates, marking it as one of the first countries to adopt such a measure. The tax, equivalent to about a 10% price increase, led to a sustained reduction in SSB purchases, with studies showing a decline over 2014–2015, particularly among low-income households, and a 19% consumption drop by 2016. Additionally, untaxed beverage purchases, mainly bottled water, increased. Despite industry opposition, the tax has been cost-effective, with healthcare savings outweighing implementation costs, and it has inspired similar policies globally (Colchero et al., 2017). Accountability frameworks, like Chile's mandatory front-of-pack warning labels, enforce compliance and empower consumers, reducing ultra-processed food purchases (Mialon et al., 2020). These mechanisms require robust enforcement and community input to prevent industry lobbying from diluting impact.

Community-Involved Monitoring Systems

Governance is strengthened by involving communities in monitoring industry practices. In South Africa, the Healthy Living Alliance (HEALA) engages local communities to track food company commitments, such as reducing sodium in processed foods (HEALA, 2023). Community scorecards and public reporting hold companies accountable, fostering trust and ensuring reforms meet local needs. Such systems amplify marginalized voices, addressing the power imbalances noted in PPPs (Friel et al., 2015).

Voluntary Industry Commitments with Oversight

Voluntary initiatives, like the Access to Nutrition Initiative (ATNI), assess food companies' performance on nutrition goals, providing benchmarks for reformulation and marketing practices (ATNI, 2024). While voluntary, ATNI's independent evaluations pressure companies to improve, as seen in Nestlé's commitment to reduce added sugars globally (ATNI, 2024). Oversight by third parties ensures credibility, though mandatory regulations may be needed for widespread adoption.

Challenges

Governance mechanisms face challenges, including industry resistance, varying global standards, and limited resources for enforcement in low-income countries. Strengthening these frameworks requires international cooperation, capacity building, and community empowerment to ensure equitable outcomes (Swinburn et al., 2019).

By implementing structured governance mechanisms, stakeholders can harness the food industry's potential to promote healthier diets while ensuring accountability. These frameworks bridge the gap between industry innovation and community needs, enhancing the strategic impact of nutrition interventions.

In conclusion, the food industry holds immense potential to promote healthier diets through innovation in product development, transparent labeling, and responsible marketing. Reformulation efforts, such as reducing sugar and incorporating whole grains, alongside clear nutritional labeling, empower consumers to make better choices. Case studies from diverse markets demonstrate the feasibility of these strategies, though challenges like consumer resistance and cost barriers persist, particularly in low-income settings. Addressing the impact of ultra-processed foods requires a shift toward minimally processed alternatives, supported by fortification and supply chain improvements. By enhancing nutrition literacy through ethical marketing and education, the industry can rebuild consumer trust and drive demand for healthier products. However, emphasize, regulatory oversight is essential to ensure that industry actions prioritize public health over profit, ensuring equitable access to nutritious foods and mitigating the global NCD burden.

Industry Limitations in Promoting Healthier Diets

To provide a more balanced perspective on the food industry's role, it is essential to critically examine its limitations in promoting healthier diets, particularly in the context of reformulation challenges, marketing ethics, and partnership dynamics under the following points.

Barriers to Food Reformulation in Low-Income Countries

Food reformulation to reduce sugar, salt, and unhealthy fats faces significant barriers in low-income countries, where economic and infrastructural constraints limit scalability. The high cost of reformulation, including research, development, and sourcing healthier ingredients, often makes healthier products unaffordable for low-income consumers, who prioritize cost over nutritional value (Onyeaka et al., 2023). Additionally, limited supply chain infrastructure and reliance on imported raw materials increase production costs, as seen in regions like Sub-Saharan Africa, where local food systems struggle to support reformulated products (Fanzo et al., 2023). Consumer resistance also poses a challenge; altered flavors or textures may not align with local preferences, reducing market acceptance (Lehmann et al., 2019). For example, reformulating staples like bread to reduce sodium may fail if the taste deviates from cultural expectations, necessitating extensive consumer education and gradual implementation to ensure adoption without compromising affordability.

Greenwashing Risks in Corporate Wellness Marketing

Corporate wellness marketing often risks greenwashing, where companies exaggerate or falsely claim health benefits to attract consumers, eroding trust and undermining public health efforts. Food companies may label ultra-processed products as "natural" or "healthy" despite high levels of sugar or sodium, exploiting consumer demand for wellness-focused products (Stern, 2021). For instance, marketing campaigns promoting low-sugar cereals may obscure the presence of artificial additives, misleading consumers about nutritional value (Mialon et al., 2020). This practice disproportionately affects low-literacy populations, who may lack the tools to discern misleading claims, exacerbating health disparities (Tempels et al., 2017). Regulatory frameworks, such as mandatory front-of-pack labeling, are essential to counter greenwashing, ensuring transparency and empowering consumers to make informed choices (von Philipsborn et al., 2018).

Power Asymmetries in Public-Private Nutrition Partnerships

Public-private partnerships (PPPs) in nutrition often suffer from power asymmetries, where corporate interests can overshadow public health goals. Large food companies, with significant financial resources, may dominate decision-making in PPPs, prioritizing profit-driven agendas over nutritional improvements (Mialon et al., 2020). For example, industry lobbying in Latin America has historically weakened public health policies, such as sugar taxes, to protect sales of ultra-processed foods (Mialon et al., 2020). This imbalance can lead to diluted interventions, such as voluntary reformulation targets that lack enforcement, as seen in some European initiatives (von Philipsborn et al., 2018). Smaller stakeholders, including local governments and community organizations, often lack the influence to advocate for equitable outcomes, perpetuating nutritional inequities (Friel et al., 2015). Addressing these asymmetries requires transparent governance, independent oversight, and mechanisms to amplify the voices of underrepresented stakeholders in partnership frameworks.

The food industry significantly shapes dietary patterns through product development, marketing, and distribution, often contributing to the rise of NCDs via ultra-processed foods. This section highlights the industry's potential to promote healthier diets through strategies like product reformulation, transparent nutritional labeling, and ethical marketing. Successful initiatives, such as reducing sugar in beverages and fortifying staples, demonstrate the feasibility of aligning business goals with public health. However, challenges persist, including consumer resistance to reformulated products and the pervasive impact of ultra-processed foods, particularly in low-income communities. Enhancing nutrition literacy through education and regulatory oversight is crucial to ensure industry actions prioritize health over profit. By fostering innovation and accountability, the food industry can drive sustainable dietary improvements and mitigate the global NCD burden.

While the food industry can drive healthier diets through reformulation and responsible marketing, systemic barriers like poverty and unequal food access exacerbate nutritional inequities. The next section explores these disparities and proposes business-led solutions to promote equitable access to nutritious foods.

ADDRESSING NUTRITIONAL INEQUITIES

This section investigates the socioeconomic, cultural, and systemic barriers driving nutritional inequities, particularly in underserved communities. It proposes business-led solutions, such as affordable nutrient-dense products and improved distribution, and highlights successful initiatives to promote equitable access to healthy foods.

Nutritional inequities, characterized by unequal access to nutritious foods, pose significant challenges to global health and well-being. These disparities are driven by socioeconomic, cultural, and systemic factors that disproportionately affect underserved communities, leading to adverse health outcomes. This section explores the disparities in access to nutritious foods, their impact on health disparities, and proposes business-driven solutions to promote equity. It also highlights successful initiatives and addresses the key concern of nutritional inequities and food access.

Disparities in Access to Nutritious Foods

Access to nutritious foods is unevenly distributed across populations, with low-income and marginalized communities facing significant barriers. The socioeconomic inequalities influence food choices, with lower-income households spending less on healthy foods due to economic constraints (Pechey & Monsivais 2016). This results in diets high in energy-dense, nutrient-poor foods, exacerbating health disparities. Similarly, the urban poverty limits access to healthy diets, with low-income households often relying on cheaper, processed foods due to financial and logistical barriers (Vilar-Compte et al., 2021). Food deserts areas with limited access to affordable, healthy food retailers are a critical systemic issue. Food-insecure neighborhoods often lack supermarkets, forcing residents to rely on convenience stores with limited nutritious options (Odoms-Young et al., 2024). Cultural barriers also play a role; for instance, dietary preferences shaped by cultural norms may not align with available healthy food options, further complicating access (Azétsop & Joy, 2013). These disparities underscore the need for targeted interventions to bridge the gap in food access.

Socioeconomic, Cultural, and Systemic Barriers

Socioeconomic barriers, such as low income and high food costs, are primary drivers of nutritional inequities. The lower-income households allocate a smaller proportion of their budget to fruits, vegetables, and other nutrient-rich foods, prioritizing affordability over nutritional quality (Pechey & Monsivais 2016). The urban poverty exacerbates these challenges, with limited transportation and time constraints hindering access to healthy food sources (Vilar-Compte et al., 2021). Cultural factors also influence food choices. Individualistic food cultures in the U.S. prioritize convenience and taste, often at the expense of nutrition, particularly in underserved communities (Azétsop & Joy, 2013). Cultural preferences and local traditions play a pivotal role in shaping the acceptance of fortified and functional foods, serving as both enablers and obstacles to their adoption. Cultural diets, deeply embedded in heritage and identity, heavily influence food choices, often favoring traditional staples like rice or maize over novel fortified alternatives. For example, introducing biofortified golden rice, enriched with vitamin A, may encounter resistance in regions where white rice is a cultural staple due to differences in appearance, flavor, or perceived authenticity (Farré et al., 2012). Conversely, aligning fortified foods with cultural practices can boost acceptance; fortifying widely consumed staples like flour or salt with micronutrients has proven effective in African and Asian communities by integrating seamlessly into local culinary traditions (Mannar et al., 2018). Functional foods, such as probiotic yogurts, are more readily accepted in cultures with a tradition of fermented foods, such as South Asian or Mediterranean diets, where they align with familiar tastes (Geny et al., 2023). However, challenges arise when functional foods are seen as foreign or incompatible with traditional cooking methods, particularly in rural or indigenous communities (Azétsop & Joy, 2013). Strategies to enhance adoption include engaging local leaders to promote culturally tailored products and implementing community-based education to emphasize health benefits while respecting traditions (Kang et al., 2017). By prioritizing cultural sensitivity, the food industry can design fortified and functional foods that resonate with local identities, thereby improving uptake and addressing nutritional deficiencies equitably. Systemic barriers, such as inadequate food distribution infrastructure in low-income areas, compound these issues. The Social Ecological Model underscores how these barriers operate across individual (e.g., income constraints), community (e.g., food deserts), and policy levels, necessitating multi-level interventions (McLeroy et al., 1988). Odoms-Young et al. (2024) highlight that food deserts and poor neighborhood food environments limit access to fresh produce, while Friel et al. (2015) point to policy failures in addressing inequities in healthy eating.

Impact on Health Disparities

Nutritional inequities have profound effects on health outcomes, particularly in underserved communities. Food insecurity and poor neighborhood food environments add to higher rates of obesity, diabetes, and cardiovascular diseases among low-income populations (Odoms-Young et al., 2024). These conditions disproportionately affect racial and ethnic minorities, perpetuating health disparities. Agurs-Collins et al. (2024) proposed a Nutrition Health Disparities Framework, emphasizing that structural factors, such as poverty and limited food access, drive these outcomes. The long-term consequences are stark. The poor nutrition in childhood, common in food-insecure households, can lead to developmental delays and chronic diseases in adulthood (Mason et al., 2006). Iinadequate nutrition in early life impairs growth and cognitive development, perpetuating cycles of poverty and poor health (Kang et al., 2017). These findings highlight the urgent need for interventions that address both immediate and long-term health impacts of nutritional inequities. The strategies to address nutritional inequities are briefly described in Table 4.

Table 4. Strategies to Address Nutritional Inequities

Strategy	Description	Target Population	Example Initiative	References
Affordable Nutrient-Dense Products	Develop low-cost, fortified foods (e.g., vitamin-enriched rice)	Low-income communities	Fortified staples in India	Mason et al. (2006)
Partnerships for Distribution	Collaborate with retailers for healthy food outlets in food deserts	Urban poor, rural communities	Healthy corner stores	WBCSD (2023)
Mobile Markets	Deploy mobile grocery units to deliver fresh produce	Food-insecure neighborhoods	Pop-up markets in urban slums	Vilar-Compte et al. (2021)
Community-Based Programs	Engage communities in nutrition education and food innovation	Underserved populations	Ethiopia child growth program	Kang et al. (2017)

Business-Led Solutions

Businesses have a pivotal role in addressing nutritional inequities through innovative products, partnerships, and distribution strategies. The World Business Council for Sustainable Development (WBCSD, 2023) advocates for business-driven solutions to enhance food security and nutrition equity, emphasizing scalable and sustainable approaches.

Development of Affordable, Nutrient-Dense Products

One key strategy is the development of affordable, nutrient-dense food products. Businesses can innovate to create low-cost, shelf-stable foods fortified with essential nutrients, targeting low-income consumers. For example, fortifying staple foods like rice or flour with vitamins and minerals can improve nutritional intake without significantly increasing costs (Mason et al., 2006). Burgaz et al. (2023) highlight the effectiveness of food system policies that incentivize the production of such products, noting their potential to reduce nutrition-related inequalities.

Partnerships to Improve Food Distribution

Partnerships between businesses, governments, and community organizations can enhance food distribution in underserved areas. The WBCSD (2023) suggests collaborating with local retailers to establish healthy food outlets in food deserts, supported by subsidies or tax incentives. Katre and Raddatz (2023) emphasize the value of involving low-income families in food-systems innovation, such as community-supported agriculture programs, to ensure solutions are culturally relevant and accessible. Mobile markets and pop-up grocery stores are practical solutions for improving distribution. These initiatives bring fresh produce directly to low-income neighborhoods, overcoming transportation barriers (Vilar-Compte et al., 2021). Businesses can also partner with food banks to redistribute surplus nutritious foods, reducing waste while addressing food insecurity.

Successful Initiatives

Several initiatives demonstrate the potential of community-based and business-led approaches to address nutritional inequities. Kang et al. (2017) evaluated a community-based nutrition program in rural Ethiopia, which significantly improved child growth through locally tailored interventions, such as nutrition education and food supplementation. This program's success underscores the importance of community engagement in designing effective solutions. Katre and Raddatz (2023) describe a participatory model where low-income families collaborated with food-system innovators to develop healthy food behaviors. By involving community members in co-designing solutions, the initiative increased the adoption of nutritious diets. Similarly, Friel et al. (2015) highlight policy interventions in Australia that subsidized healthy food retailers in underserved areas, improving access and reducing dietary inequities. Business-led examples include partnerships between food companies and nonprofits to distribute nutrient-dense products. The WBCSD (2023) cites initiatives where corporations worked with local governments to establish healthy corner stores, stocking affordable fresh produce in low-income neighborhoods. These examples illustrate the feasibility of combining business innovation with community needs to promote equity. Figure 2 illustrates a framework for addressing nutritional inequities, showing how individual, community, and systemic interventions work together to reduce health disparities and promote equitable nutrition outcomes.

Figure 2. Framework for Addressing Nutritional Inequities

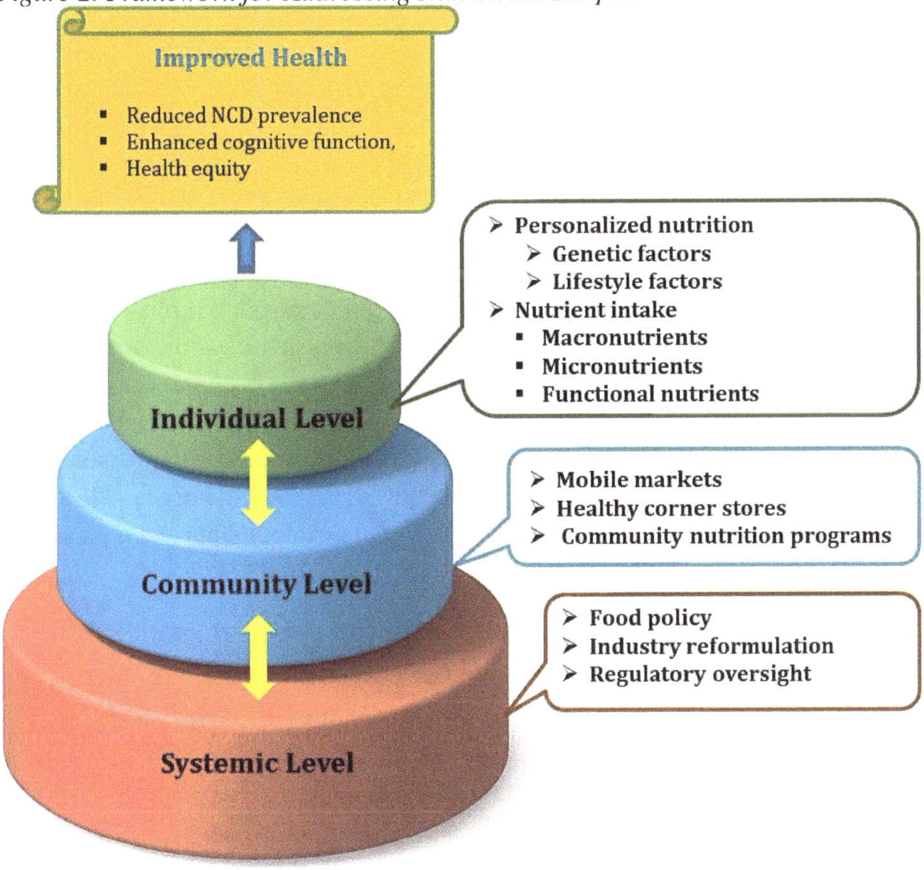

The core concern of nutritional inequities and food access requires multifaceted solutions that address socioeconomic, cultural, and systemic barriers. By developing affordable, nutrient-dense products and forging partnerships to improve distribution, businesses can play a transformative role in promoting equity. Successful community-based programs, such as those in Ethiopia and Australia, demonstrate the impact of tailored interventions. However, sustained progress requires ongoing collaboration between businesses, policymakers, and communities to dismantle structural barriers and ensure equitable access to nutritious foods. In conclusion, addressing nutritional inequities demands a holistic approach that combines innovation, policy reform, and community engagement. The literature underscores the urgency of these efforts, highlighting the profound health disparities caused by unequal food access. By leveraging their resources and expertise, businesses can drive meaningful change, creating a more equitable and sustainable food system for all.

Nutritional inequities, driven by socioeconomic, cultural, and systemic barriers, disproportionately affect underserved communities, leading to higher rates of malnutrition and NCDs. This section identifies disparities in access to nutritious foods, particularly in food deserts, and their impact on health outcomes like obesity and diabetes in low-income populations. Business-led solutions, such as developing affordable, nutrient-dense products and partnering to improve food distribution through mobile markets and healthy corner stores, offer scalable approaches to promote equity. Successful initiatives, including community-based programs in Ethiopia and policy interventions in Australia, underscore the value of culturally relevant strategies. Addressing these inequities requires sustained collaboration between businesses, policymakers, and communities to dismantle structural barriers, ensuring equitable access to nutritious foods and reducing health disparities globally. Tackling nutritional inequities requires innovative solutions to ensure access to healthy foods for all. Emerging trends in nutritional science, from personalized nutrition to biofortification, offer promising tools to further advance health equity. The following section examines these cutting-edge developments and their implications for future food systems.

Community-Led Innovations for Nutritional Equity

Community-led innovations empower local stakeholders to design and implement solutions tailored to their unique nutritional challenges, fostering resilience and equity in food systems. These initiatives often arise from grassroots efforts, leveraging local knowledge, cultural practices, and collective action to address barriers like food insecurity and limited access to nutritious foods. Unlike top-down approaches, community-led innovations prioritize agency, ensuring solutions are sustainable and culturally relevant (Katre & Raddatz, 2023).

Local Food Cooperatives and Urban Farming: Community-driven food cooperatives, such as the Mandela MarketPlace in Oakland, California, empower low-income residents to own and operate food retail, increasing access to fresh produce while creating economic opportunities (Mandela MarketPlace, 2023). Similarly, urban farming initiatives, like those in Detroit's urban agriculture movement, transform vacant lots into community gardens, producing nutrient-dense crops and fostering nutrition education (White, 2021). These efforts not only improve food access but also build social capital and promote dietary diversity.

Grassroots Nutrition Education Platforms: Community-led nutrition education programs, such as those run by La Via Campesina in Latin America, train local leaders to promote traditional, nutrient-rich diets, countering the influx of ultra-processed foods (La Via Campesina, 2022). These platforms use peer-to-peer learning and culturally tailored curricula to enhance nutrition literacy, empowering communities to make informed dietary choices. Grounded in the Health Belief Model, these programs enhance perceived benefits and self-efficacy, motivating dietary behavior change in underserved communities (Rosenstock, 1974). For example, in rural Guatemala, community health workers have successfully reduced childhood malnutrition by integrating local food traditions into nutrition workshops (Kang et al., 2017).

Community-Driven Food Enterprises: Small-scale food enterprises, such as women-led millet processing cooperatives in India, illustrate how communities can innovate to address nutritional deficiencies. These cooperatives produce fortified millet-based products, improving access to iron and zinc while generating income for local women (Parekh et al., 2024). Such initiatives demonstrate the potential for community entrepreneurship to align economic and health goals, particularly in low-income settings.

Scalability and Impact: Scaling community-led innovations requires support from businesses and policymakers. For instance, partnerships with food companies can provide resources for cooperative expansion, as seen in the WBCSD's support for community agriculture programs (WBCSD, 2023). Policy incentives, such as grants for urban farming or tax breaks for community enterprises, can further amplify impact (Friel et al., 2015). Evidence suggests these initiatives reduce NCD prevalence and improve food security; for example, urban farming in Detroit increased vegetable consumption by 20% among participants (White, 2021).

Challenges: Despite their promise, community-led innovations face challenges, including limited funding, regulatory hurdles, and competition from ultra-processed food markets. Addressing these requires sustained investment and advocacy to prioritize local solutions over corporate-driven models (Katre & Raddatz, 2023).

By centering community agency, these innovations offer scalable, equitable solutions to nutritional inequities. Their success underscores the need for collaborative frameworks that amplify local voices while leveraging industry and policy support to drive systemic change.

THE FUTURE OF HEALTH AND NUTRITION

This section explores emerging trends in nutritional science, including gut microbiome research, personalized nutrition, and nutrients for mental health, and their implications for food product development. It addresses the challenge of ensuring equitable access to these innovations to foster sustainable health outcomes globally.

Advancements in nutritional science are reshaping the landscape of health, food production, and public policy. Emerging research in gut microbiome interactions, personalized nutrition, and nutrients that support mental health and cognitive function is driving innovation in the food industry while posing new challenges for ensuring equitable access. Drawing on the provided literature, this section explores these cutting-edge developments, their implications for food product development, and the challenges of balancing innovation with accessibility. It addresses the key concern of emerging trends in nutritional science, building on prior discussions of nutritional inequities.

Nutrition Sustainability: A Global Imperative

Nutrition sustainability integrates health, equity, and environmental considerations to ensure food systems meet the needs of current and future generations. The global food system faces mounting challenges, including climate change, resource depletion, and population growth, which threaten food security and exacerbate nutritional inequities (Swinburn et al., 2019). Sustainable diets, characterized by low environmental impact and high nutritional value, prioritize plant-based foods, minimal processing, and reduced waste (Willett et al., 2019). For instance, plant-based diets, building on the Mediterranean pattern discussed earlier, support sustainability by reducing environmental impact (Tessier et al., 2025).

Globally, initiatives like the EAT-Lancet Commission's planetary health diet advocate for balanced consumption of fruits, vegetables, legumes, and whole grains to address NCDs while preserving ecosystems (Willett et al., 2019). However, implementing sustainable diets faces barriers, particularly in low-income countries where reliance on staple crops and limited infrastructure hinder dietary diversification (Fanzo et al., 2023). Biofortification, as discussed earlier, offers a sustainable solution by enhancing staple crops' nutritional content without requiring dietary shifts (Bouis et al., 2024). Additionally, reducing food waste through industry innovations, such as improved supply chain logistics, can enhance food security and sustainability (WBCSD, 2023).

Policy frameworks play a critical role in scaling sustainable nutrition. For example, subsidies for sustainable agriculture in countries like Denmark and Brazil have increased access to nutrient-dense foods while supporting local farmers (Burgaz et al., 2023). Yet, global disparities in policy implementation and economic resources pose challenges, particularly in low- and middle-income countries where NCD burdens are highest (Ahmad et al., 2023). Collaborative efforts, including public-private partnerships and international frameworks like the UN's Sustainable Development Goals, are essential to align food production with health and environmental goals. By prioritizing sustainability, stakeholders can address the interconnected challenges of NCDs, nutritional inequities, and climate change, fostering resilient and equitable food systems worldwide.

Emerging Trends in Nutritional Science

The emerging trends in nutritional science are reshaping health and food systems through innovative discoveries, with gut microbiome research, personalized nutrition, and nutrients supporting mental health and cognitive function each providing distinct pathways to enhance well-being and address global health challenges.

Gut Microbiome Research

The gut microbiome, comprising trillions of microorganisms in the digestive tract, has emerged as a critical determinant of health. Diet-microbiota interactions influence metabolic, immune, and neurological functions, with implications for conditions like obesity, diabetes, and inflammatory bowel disease (Kolodziejczyk et al., 2019). The microbiome's composition varies across individuals, shaped by diet, lifestyle, and genetics, making it a target for personalized interventions (Sarfraz et al., 2022). For instance, specific dietary fibers and fermented foods can promote beneficial microbial strains, improving gut barrier function and reducing systemic inflammation (Iacomino et al., 2024). These findings have profound implications for public health. By modulating the microbiome through diet, emerging research suggests potential to prevent or manage chronic diseases, though further studies are needed (Kolodziejczyk et al., 2019).However, challenges remain in translating microbiome research into practical applications. Integrating microbiome data with psycho-behavioral and environmental factors is essential for population-wide impact, requiring sophisticated data analytics and interdisciplinary collaboration (Linseisen et al., 2025).

Personalized Nutrition

Personalized nutrition, which tailors dietary recommendations to an individual's genetic, metabolic, and lifestyle profile, marks the end of the "one-diet-fits-all" era (Roman et al., 2024). Advances in genomics and metabolomics enable precise dietary interventions that account for genetic predispositions, such as variations in nutrient metabolism (Sarfraz et al., 2022). The Health Belief Model informs personalized nutrition by addressing individuals' perceived susceptibility to NCDs and benefits of tailored diets, enhancing adoption (Rosenstock, 1974). For example, individuals with specific genetic markers may benefit from higher intakes of omega-3 fatty acids to reduce cardiovascular risk (Linseisen et al., 2025). Lifestyle factors, including physical activity, sleep, and stress, further refine personalized nutrition plans. A systems-oriented approach that integrates public health priorities with precision nutrition, using wearable devices and health apps to monitor real-time data supported by Vergères et al. (2024). This approach promises to optimize health outcomes but requires robust data infrastructure and consumer education to ensure adoption (Roman et al., 2024). The food industry stands to benefit by developing products tailored to specific consumer segments, such as gluten-free options for those with genetic sensitivities.

Nutrients Supporting Mental Health and Cognitive Function

The link between nutrition and mental health has gained significant attention, with nutrients like omega-3 fatty acids, B vitamins, and polyphenols showing promise in supporting cognitive function and emotional well-being. Nutrients influence brain plasticity and neurotransmitter function, impacting mood and cognition (Gómez-Pinilla, 2008). Parletta et al. (2013) further show that diets rich in antioxidants and healthy fats can mitigate symptoms of depression and anxiety, while Muscaritoli (2021) emphasizes nutrition's role in resilience against stress-related disorders. Adan et al. (2019) introduce the concept of nutritional psychiatry, advocating for dietary interventions to complement mental health treatments. For example, deficiencies in folate or vitamin D are linked to increased risks of cognitive decline, underscoring the need for targeted supplementation (Institute of Medicine, 1997). These findings highlight the potential of nutrition to address rising mental health challenges, particularly in aging populations or high-stress environments like military settings (Institute of Medicine, 1997).

Implications for Food Product Development

The trends in nutritional science are driving innovation in food product development, particularly in functional foods and fortified products. These categories aim to deliver health benefits beyond basic nutrition, aligning with consumer demand for products that support specific health outcomes.

Functional Foods

Functional foods, defined as foods with added health-promoting ingredients, are a cornerstone of the evolving food industry (Temple, 2022). Examples include probiotic yogurts that support gut health and cereals fortified with vitamins to enhance cognitive function (Essa et al., 2023). Kishore and Shewmaker (1999) highlight biotechnology's role in developing functional foods, such as crops engineered to produce higher levels of essential nutrients like vitamin A. These innovations can address nutrient deficiencies in both developing and developed worlds (Farré et al., 2012). The food industry is also exploring novel ingredients, such as prebiotics and plant-based proteins, to create functional foods that align with microbiome research (Iacomino et al., 2024). However, consumer acceptance remains a challenge, as taste, cost, and familiarity influence purchasing decisions (Geny et al., 2023). Companies must balance innovation with palatability to ensure market success.

Fortified Products

Food fortification, the addition of essential nutrients to staple foods, is a proven strategy for addressing nutrient deficiencies. Fortifying foods like flour, salt, and oil with vitamins and minerals has reduced global rates of conditions like anemia and goiter (Mannar et al., 2018). Biofortification, an innovative strategy to enhance the nutritional quality of food crops, addresses global malnutrition by increasing the content of essential vitamins and minerals through breeding, agronomic practices, and transgenic methods. Recent advancements focus on biofortification, where crops are bred or genetically modified to naturally contain higher nutrient levels (Farré et al., 2012). For example, golden rice, engineered to produce vitamin A, has improved nutritional outcomes in regions with high deficiency rates (Olson et al., 2021). Biofortification is considered as a sustainable solution to improve nutrition security, emphasizing its potential to combat diet-related non-communicable diseases and micronutrient deficiencies, particularly in low-income regions (Bouis et al., 2024). The impact of biofortified crops, such as iron-fortified beans and zinc-enriched wheat, which have improved the lives of millions by reducing deficiencies in vulnerable populations, particularly in Africa and Asia (Garg et al., 2018). However it needs to consider the role of conventional breeding and transgenic approaches in developing crops with enhanced nutrient profiles, alongside the need for consumer acceptance and market integration. Bhardwaj et al. (2022) focus on agronomic biofortification, which involves applying micronutrient-rich fertilizers to crops like rice and maize, noting its cost-effectiveness and rapid implementation compared to genetic methods. They highlight its role in addressing nutritional security by targeting staple crops consumed by the poor, though challenges like soil variability and farmer training persist. The World Health Organization (2017) supports biofortification as a public health intervention, citing evidence that crops fortified with minerals and vitamins, such as vitamin A cassava, can significantly reduce deficiency-related health issues like anemia and blindness in children. Collectively, these studies position biofortification as a scalable, evidence-based approach to enhance dietary quality, reduce health disparities, and promote sustainable nutrition security globally, though sustained efforts in research, policy, and community engagement are essential for its success.

Fortified products are particularly relevant for mental health applications. Foods fortified with omega-3s and B vitamins to support cognitive health in older adults, with high acceptability among consumers (Geny et al., 2023). However, fortification must be carefully calibrated to avoid overconsumption risks, requiring regulatory oversight and consumer education (Mannar et al., 2018).

Biotechnology's Role

Biotechnology is a key enabler of both functional and fortified foods. Ranjha et al. (2022) describe its applications in developing nutrient-dense crops and improving food safety, such as through genetically modified organisms (GMOs) with enhanced nutritional profiles. The Institute of Medicine (1989) foresaw biotechnology's potential to improve nutrient delivery, a vision now realized in products like biofortified maize and wheat (Farré et al., 2012). These advancements offer scalable solutions for addressing global nutrition challenges, but public skepticism about GMOs necessitates transparent communication (Kishore & Shewmaker, 1999).

Challenges of Balancing Innovation with Accessibility

While nutritional science advancements hold immense promise, ensuring their benefits reach diverse populations is a significant challenge. Personalized nutrition, for instance, relies on costly technologies like genetic testing and data analytics, which may exclude low-income groups (Roman et al., 2024). Linseisen et al. (2025) emphasize the need for equitable data access to prevent widening health disparities, advocating for public-private partnerships to subsidize these technologies. Functional and fortified foods also face accessibility barriers. High production costs and premium pricing can limit their availability in low-income regions, where nutrient deficiencies are most prevalent (Olson et al., 2021). Biofortified crops, while cost-effective in the long term, require significant upfront investment in research and distribution infrastructure (Farré et al., 2012). Cultural preferences further complicate adoption, as fortified foods may not align with traditional diets (Geny et al., 2023). Regulatory and ethical challenges also arise. Personalized nutrition raises privacy concerns related to genetic and health data, requiring robust safeguards (Vergères et al., 2024). Similarly, fortification programs must navigate varying regulatory standards across countries, which can delay implementation (Mannar et al., 2018). Public health campaigns are essential to build trust and educate consumers about the benefits of innovative foods, particularly in communities skeptical of biotechnology (Ranjha et al., 2022).

The key concern of emerging trends in nutritional science underscores the transformative potential of gut microbiome research, personalized nutrition, and nutrients for mental health. These advancements are reshaping food product development, with functional and fortified foods offering targeted health benefits. Biotechnology amplifies these efforts by enabling nutrient-dense crops and novel ingredients, addressing both individual and population-level needs. However, the challenge of accessibility looms large. Ensuring that innovations benefit diverse populations requires addressing economic, cultural, and regulatory barriers. Public health strategies must prioritize equity, leveraging partnerships to make advanced nutritional solutions affordable and culturally relevant. Successful examples, such as biofortified crops and fortified staples, demonstrate the feasibility of scalable interventions (Olson et al., 2021). In conclusion, the future of health and nutrition lies in harnessing cutting-edge science to create personalized, health-promoting foods while ensuring inclusivity. The food industry, supported by policymakers and researchers, must navigate complex challenges to deliver on this promise, fostering a healthier, more equitable global population. By building on the foundation of nutritional inequities, these trends offer a path toward a more tailored and sustainable approach to health and nutrition.

Emerging trends in nutritional science, including gut microbiome research, personalized nutrition, and nutrients supporting mental health, are transforming food product development and public health strategies. The gut microbiome's role in metabolic and immune health, personalized nutrition's tailored dietary approaches, and nutrients like omega-3s for cognitive function offer innovative solutions to address NCDs and mental health challenges. Functional and fortified foods, supported by biotechnology, such as biofortified crops, tackle nutrient deficiencies, but accessibility remains a concern due to high costs and cultural misalignment. Balancing innovation with equity requires public-private partnerships, robust data infrastructure, and consumer education to ensure diverse populations benefit. These advancements, if made inclusive, can foster a more sustainable and health-focused global food system, reducing disparities and enhancing well-being.

CONCLUSION

The alarming rise in diet-related non-communicable diseases (NCDs), such as obesity, diabetes, and cardiovascular disease, underscores the urgency of transforming dietary patterns and food systems. These conditions, fueled by the proliferation of ultra-processed foods and exacerbated by nutritional inequities, demand a multifaceted response that bridges scientific innovation, industry responsibility, and equitable policy frameworks. Nutritional science has illuminated the critical roles of macronutrients, micronutrients, and dietary patterns in supporting physical, cognitive, and mental health across the lifespan. Emerging trends, including gut microbiome research, personalized nutrition, and nutrients that enhance cognitive function, are reshaping how we approach health optimization. These advancements, supported by biotechnology and data-driven technologies, enable the development of functional and fortified foods tailored to individual and population needs. However, their potential is tempered by challenges of accessibility, as high costs and cultural misalignment risk excluding low-income and marginalized communities from their benefits. The food industry, as a primary influencer of dietary habits, holds immense power to drive positive change. Strategies such as product reformulation, transparent labeling, and ethical marketing can shift consumer preferences toward healthier options, as evidenced by successful initiatives like reduced-sugar beverages and fortified staples. Yet, the industry's historical reliance on ultra-processed foods and aggressive marketing targeting vulnerable populations highlights the need for robust regulatory oversight to prioritize public health over profit. Partnerships between businesses, governments, and communities are essential to improve food distribution and develop affordable, nutrient-dense products, particularly in food deserts and low-income regions.

Nutritional inequities remain a persistent barrier to global health equity, perpetuating disparities in access to nutritious foods and exacerbating NCDs in underserved communities. Community-based programs and business-led solutions, such as mobile markets and fortified staples, offer scalable models for change, as evidenced by initiatives in Ethiopia and Australia (Kang et al., 2017; Friel et al., 2015). Table 5 presents evidence-based global policy models to guide stakeholders in implementing targeted interventions for improved nutrition and equitable health outcomes. Advancing well-being through nutrition demands a holistic, evidence-based approach integrating scientific discovery, industry innovation, and equitable policy. The following section outlines next steps and future research priorities to drive this transformation, ensuring sustainable health outcomes for all.

NEXT STEPS AND FUTURE OUTLOOK

To translate the insights from this chapter into tangible progress, stakeholders must take concerted action to address the global nutrition crisis, reduce NCDs, and promote health equity. Below, we outline specific next steps for policymakers, food companies, educators, and individuals, alongside critical research gaps to guide future investigations.

Policymakers

- Implement evidence-based policies like Mexico's sugar-sweetened beverage tax and Chile's front-of-pack labeling to reshape food environments.
- Scale subsidies for nutrient-dense foods in food deserts, as seen in Australia, to enhance access.
- Strengthen regulations to curb misleading marketing and enforce industry accountability.
- Invest in public-private partnerships, like SUN Movement's fortification initiatives, for greater impact.
- Integrate climate resilience into policies to align nutrition with sustainable food systems.

Food Companies

- Reformulate products to reduce sugar, salt, and unhealthy fats, following successful models in Scotland and Europe.
- Develop affordable, fortified, and functional foods, such as biofortified staples, to address micronutrient deficiencies.
- Adopt transparent labeling and ethical marketing to avoid greenwashing and rebuild consumer trust.
- Partner with communities to improve food distribution through healthy corner stores, addressing inequities.

Educators

- Develop culturally tailored nutrition curricula, building on grassroots platforms like La Via Campesina, to boost literacy.
- Use digital tools in schools and community programs to teach dietary diversity and label reading.
- Emphasize sustainable diets and mental health benefits of nutrition, leveraging nutritional psychiatry insights.

Individuals

- Choose nutrient-dense foods and support ethical brands to influence market trends.
- Engage in community-led initiatives like urban farming or food cooperatives to shape local food systems.
- Use personalized nutrition tools, where accessible, while demanding data privacy transparency.

Research Gaps

- Conduct longitudinal studies on diet-microbiome interactions for NCD prevention, including diverse populations.
- Develop scalable, low-cost models for AI-driven dietary apps and wearable sensors to democratize access.
- Create ethical AI frameworks for personalized nutrition to address privacy, equity, and bias risks.
- Evaluate long-term consumer acceptance and environmental impacts of biofortified crops.
- Conduct robust clinical trials in nutritional psychiatry to link nutrients with mental health outcomes.

Call to Action

- Stakeholders must act swiftly to harness nutritional science, industry innovation, and equitable policies to combat NCDs and advance global health, ensuring nutritious, sustainable diets are accessible to all.

REFERENCES

Access to Nutrition Initiative. (2024). *Global index 2024*. https://accesstonutrition.org

Adan, R. A., Van Der Beek, E. M., Buitelaar, J. K., Cryan, J. F., Hebebrand, J., Higgs, S., Schellekens, H., & Dickson, S. L. (2019). Nutritional psychiatry: Towards improving mental health by what you eat. *European Neuropsychopharmacology, 29*(12), 1321–1332. DOI: 10.1016/j.euroneuro.2019.10.011 PMID: 31735529

Agurs-Collins, T., Alvidrez, J., ElShourbagy Ferreira, S., Evans, M., Gibbs, K., Kowtha, B., Pratt, C., Reedy, J., Shams-White, M., & Brown, A. G. M. (2024). Perspective: Nutrition Health Disparities Framework: A model to advance health equity. *Advances in Nutrition, 15*(4), 100194. DOI: 10.1016/j.advnut.2024.100194 PMID: 38616067

Ahmad, R., Akter, F., & Haque, M. (2023). Editorial: Diet and nutrition for non-communicable diseases in low and middle-income countries. *Frontiers in Nutrition, 10*, 1179640. DOI: 10.3389/fnut.2023.1179640 PMID: 37057068

Azétsop, J., & Joy, T. R. (2013). Access to nutritious food, socioeconomic individualism and public health ethics in the USA: A common good approach. *Philosophy, Ethics, and Humanities in Medicine; PEHM, 8*(1), 16. DOI: 10.1186/1747-5341-8-16 PMID: 24165577

Bhardwaj, A. K., Chejara, S., Malik, K., Kumar, R., Kumar, A., & Yadav, R. K. (2022). Agronomic biofortification of food crops: An emerging opportunity for global food and nutritional security. *Frontiers in Plant Science, 13*, 1055278. Advance online publication. DOI: 10.3389/fpls.2022.1055278 PMID: 36570883

Bouis, H., Foley, J., Lividini, K., Jumrani, J., Reinke, R., Van Der Straeten, D., Zagado, R., Boy, E., Brown, L. R., Mudyahoto, B., Alioma, R., Hussain, M., & Pfeiffer, W. H. (2024). Biofortification: Future challenges for a newly emerging technology to improve nutrition security sustainably. *Current Developments in Nutrition, 8*(12), 104478. DOI: 10.1016/j.cdnut.2024.104478 PMID: 39668944

Bruins, M. J., Van Dael, P., & Eggersdorfer, M. (2019). The Role of Nutrients in Reducing the Risk for Noncommunicable Diseases during Aging. *Nutrients, 11*(1), 85. DOI: 10.3390/nu11010085 PMID: 30621135

Burgaz, C., Gorasso, V., Achten, W. M. J., Batis, C., Castronuovo, L., Diouf, A., Asiki, G., Swinburn, B. A., Unar-Munguía, M., Devleesschauwer, B., Sacks, G., & Vandevijvere, S. (2023). The effectiveness of food system policies to improve nutrition, nutrition-related inequalities and environmental sustainability: A scoping review. *Food Security, 15*(5), 1313–1344. DOI: 10.1007/s12571-023-01385-1

Casas, R., Castro-Barquero, S., Estruch, R., & Sacanella, E. (2018). Nutrition and Cardiovascular Health. *International Journal of Molecular Sciences, 19*(12), 3988. DOI: 10.3390/ijms19123988 PMID: 30544955

Ćatović, A. (2023). *Dietary Patterns*. IntechOpen., DOI: 10.5772/intechopen.108367

Deshpande, S., Mandlik, R., Khadilkar, A. V., Chiplonkar, S. A., & Khadilkar, V. V. (2024). Micronutrient deficiency, dietary diversity, and sociodemographic and lifestyle determinants of dietary diversity among pregnant slum-dwelling women in Pune, India. *BMC Nutrition, 10*(1), 108. DOI: 10.1186/s40795-024-00915-0 PMID: 39085982

Dolui, M., Sarkar, S., Ghosh, P., & Hossain, M. (2023). Dietary diversity and association with non-communicable diseases (NCDs) among adult men (15-54 years): A cross-sectional study using National Family and Health Survey, India. *PLOS Global Public Health, 3*(4), e0001775. DOI: 10.1371/journal.pgph.0001775 PMID: 37185617

Espinosa-Salas, S., & Gonzalez-Arias, M. (2023). Nutrition: Macronutrient intake, imbalances, and interventions. In *StatPearls*. StatPearls Publishing., https://www.ncbi.nlm.nih.gov/books/NBK594226/

Essa, M. M., Bishir, M., Bhat, A., Chidambaram, S. B., Al-Balushi, B., Hamdan, H., Govindarajan, N., Freidland, R. P., & Qoronfleh, M. W. (2023). Functional foods and their impact on health. *Journal of Food Science and Technology, 60*(3), 820–834. DOI: 10.1007/s13197-021-05193-3 PMID: 36908338

Fanzo, J., McLaren, R., Bellows, A., & Carducci, B. (2023). Challenges and opportunities for increasing the effectiveness of food reformulation and fortification to improve dietary and nutrition outcomes. *Food Policy, 119*, 102515. DOI: 10.1016/j.foodpol.2023.102515

Farre, G., Gomez-Galera, S., Naqvi, S., Bai, C., Sanahuja, G., Yuan, D., Zorrilla, U., Codony, L. T., Rojas, E., Fibla, M., Twyman, R. M., Capell, T., Christou, P., & Zhu, C. (2012). Biotechnology and nutritional improvement of crops. In Springer eBooks (pp. 1676–1723). DOI: 10.1007/978-1-4419-0851-3_160

Food and Drink Federation Scotland. (2023). *Reformulation case study compilation*. https://www.fdf.org.uk/globalassets/resources/case-studies/fdf-scotland/reformulation-case-study-compilation.pdf

Friel, S., Hattersley, L., Ford, L., & O'Rourke, K. (2015). Addressing inequities in healthy eating. *Health Promotion International, 30*(Suppl_2), ii77–ii88. DOI: 10.1093/heapro/dav073 PMID: 26420812

Garg, M., Sharma, N., Sharma, S., Kapoor, P., Kumar, A., Chunduri, V., & Arora, P. (2018). Biofortified Crops Generated by Breeding, Agronomy, and Transgenic Approaches Are Improving Lives of Millions of People around the World. *Frontiers in Nutrition, 5*, 12. Advance online publication. DOI: 10.3389/fnut.2018.00012 PMID: 29492405

Geny, A., Petitjean, M., Van Wymelbeke-Delannoy, V., & Sulmont-Rossé, C. (2023). Impact of food-based fortification on nutritional outcomes and acceptability in older adults: Systematic literature review. *Frontiers in Nutrition, 10*, 1232502. DOI: 10.3389/fnut.2023.1232502 PMID: 37964932

Gómez-Pinilla, F. (2008). Brain foods: The effects of nutrients on brain function. *Nature Reviews. Neuroscience, 9*(7), 568–578. DOI: 10.1038/nrn2421 PMID: 18568016

Green, R., Milner, J., Joy, E. J., Agrawal, S., & Dangour, A. D. (2016). Dietary patterns in India: A systematic review. *British Journal of Nutrition, 116*(1), 142–148. DOI: 10.1017/S0007114516001598 PMID: 27146890

Healthy Living Alliance. (2023). *Community monitoring for healthier food environments*. https://heala.org

Iacomino, G., Rufián Henares, J. Á., & Lauria, F. (2024). Editorial: Personalized nutrition and gut microbiota: Current and future directions. *Frontiers in Nutrition, 11*, 1375157. DOI: 10.3389/fnut.2024.1375157 PMID: 38487630

ICMR. (2024). *Dietary guidelines for Indians – 2024*. Indian Council of Medical Research – National Institute of Nutrition. https://www.nin.res.in/dietaryguidelines/pdfjs/locale/DGI07052024P.pdf

Institute of Medicine (US) Committee on Military Nutrition Research. Carlson-Newberry, S. J., & Costello, R. B. (Eds.). (1997). *Emerging Technologies for Nutrition Research: Potential for Assessing Military Performance Capability*. National Academies Press (US).

Institute of Medicine (US) Food and Nutrition Board. (1989). *Biotechnological developments: Potential for improvements in food formulation, nutrient delivery, and safety*. In *Frontiers in the nutrition sciences: Proceedings of a symposium*. National Academies Press. https://www.ncbi.nlm.nih.gov/books/NBK235299/

Kang, Y., Kim, S., Sinamo, S., & Christian, P. (2017). Effectiveness of a community-based nutrition programme to improve child growth in rural Ethiopia: a cluster randomized trial. *Maternal & child nutrition, 13*(1), . https://doi.org/DOI: 10.1111/mcn.12349

Katre, A., & Raddatz, B. (2023). Low-income families' direct participation in food-systems innovation to promote healthy food behaviors. *Nutrients, 15*(5), 1271. DOI: 10.3390/nu15051271 PMID: 36904271

Kishore, G. M., & Shewmaker, C. (1999). Biotechnology: Enhancing human nutrition in developing and developed worlds. *Proceedings of the National Academy of Sciences of the United States of America, 96*(11), 5968–5972. DOI: 10.1073/pnas.96.11.5968 PMID: 10339525

Kolodziejczyk, A. A., Zheng, D., & Elinav, E. (2019). Diet–microbiota interactions and personalized nutrition. *Nature Reviews. Microbiology, 17*(12), 742–753. DOI: 10.1038/s41579-019-0256-8 PMID: 31541197

Korver, O. (1997). 'Healthy' developments in the food industry. *Cancer Letters, 114*(1–2), 19–23. DOI: 10.1016/S0304-3835(97)04617-X PMID: 9103246

La Via Campesina. (2022). *Food sovereignty and nutrition education.* https://viacampesina.org

Lang, T., & Heasman, M. (2015). *Food wars: The global battle for mouths, minds and markets* (2nd ed.). Routledge., DOI: 10.4324/9781315754116

Lehmann, U., Mak, T. N., & Bolten, C. J. (2019). Reformulation as a Strategy for Developing Healthier Food Products: Challenges and Recent Developments – An Industry Perspective. Reformulation as a Strategy for Developing Healthier Food Products, 89–110. DOI: 10.1007/978-3-030-23621-2_4

Lichtenstein, A. H., Appel, L. J., Vadiveloo, M., Hu, F. B., Kris-Etherton, P. M., Rebholz, C. M., Sacks, F. M., Thorndike, A. N., Van Horn, L., & Wylie-Rosett, J. (2021). 2021 dietary guidance to improve cardiovascular health: A scientific statement from the American Heart Association. *Circulation, 144*(23). Advance online publication. DOI: 10.1161/CIR.0000000000001031 PMID: 34724806

Linseisen, J., Renner, B., Gedrich, K., Wirsam, J., Holzapfel, C., Lorkowski, S., Watzl, B., Daniel, H., & Leitzmann, M. (2025). Data in personalized nutrition: Bridging biomedical, psycho-behavioral, and food environment approaches for population-wide impact. *Advances in Nutrition, 100*(7), 377. DOI: 10.1016/j.advnut.2025.100377 PMID: 39842719

Lisičić-Konaković, M., Mesihović-Dinarević, S., Bajrić, E., Jurišić, S., Musa-Trolić, I., Ćubela, M., Šarac, Z., Prguda-Mujić, J., & Zukanović, A. (2024). Effects of poor eating habits on children's body weight. *Global Pediatrics, 8*, 100146. DOI: 10.1016/j.gpeds.2024.100146

Mandela MarketPlace. (2023). *Community food systems*. https://mandelamarketplace.org

Mannar, M. V., Garrett, G. S., & Hurrell, R. F. (2018). Future Trends and Strategies in Food Fortification. In *Elsevier eBooks* (pp. 375–381). DOI: 10.1016/B978-0-12-802861-2.00040-7

Mason, J. B., Sanders, D., & Musgrove, P. Soekirman, & Galloway, R. (2006). Community health and nutrition programs. In D. T. Jamison, J. G. Breman, A. R. Measham, et al. (Eds.), *Disease control priorities in developing countries* (2nd ed., Chapter 56). The International Bank for Reconstruction and Development / The World Bank. https://www.ncbi.nlm.nih.gov/books/NBK11726/

McLeroy, K. R., Bibeau, D., Steckler, A., & Glanz, K. (1988). An ecological perspective on health promotion programs. *Health Education Quarterly*, *15*(4), 351–377. DOI: 10.1177/109019818801500401 PMID: 3068205

Mialon, M., Perez, E., Corvalan, C., Monteiro, C., Jaime, P., & Baeza Scagliusi, F. (2020). Food industry influence on public health policy, research and practice in Latin America. *European Journal of Public Health*, *30*(Supplement_5), ckaa165.321. Advance online publication. DOI: 10.1093/eurpub/ckaa165.321

Miller, K. B., Eckberg, J. O., Decker, E. A., & Marinangeli, C. P. F. (2021). Role of Food Industry in Promoting Healthy and Sustainable Diets. *Nutrients*, *13*(8), 2740. DOI: 10.3390/nu13082740 PMID: 34444900

Muscaritoli, M. (2021). The Impact of Nutrients on Mental Health and Well-Being: Insights From the Literature. *Frontiers in Nutrition*, *8*, 656290. DOI: 10.3389/fnut.2021.656290 PMID: 33763446

Odoms-Young, A., Brown, A. G. M., Agurs-Collins, T., & Glanz, K. (2024). Food insecurity, neighborhood food environment, and health disparities: State of the science, research gaps and opportunities. *The American Journal of Clinical Nutrition*, *119*(3), 850–861. DOI: 10.1016/j.ajcnut.2023.12.019 PMID: 38160801

Olson, R., Gavin-Smith, B., Ferraboschi, C., & Kraemer, K. (2021). Food Fortification: The Advantages, Disadvantages and Lessons from *Sight and Life* Programs. *Nutrients*, *13*(4), 1118. DOI: 10.3390/nu13041118 PMID: 33805305

Onyeaka, H., Nwaiwu, O., Obileke, K., Miri, T., & Al-Sharify, Z. T. (2023). Global nutritional challenges of reformulated food: A review. *Food Science & Nutrition*, *11*(6), 2483–2499. DOI: 10.1002/fsn3.3286 PMID: 37324840

Parekh, S., Shinghal, K., Agarwal, N., & Raha, S. (2024). Flour power: Women-led millet value chains improve local nutrition. *Millet Revival Project*. https://milletrevivalproject.in/2024/03/29/flour-power-women-led-millet-value-chains-improve-local-nutrition/

Parletta, N., Milte, C. M., & Meyer, B. J. (2013). Nutritional modulation of cognitive function and mental health. *The Journal of Nutritional Biochemistry*, *24*(5), 725–743. DOI: 10.1016/j.jnutbio.2013.01.002 PMID: 23517914

Pechey, R., & Monsivais, P. (2016). Socioeconomic inequalities in the healthiness of food choices: Exploring the contributions of food expenditures. *Preventive Medicine*, *88*, 203–209. DOI: 10.1016/j.ypmed.2016.04.012 PMID: 27095324

Pell, D., Mytton, O., Penney, T. L., Briggs, A., Cummins, S., Penn-Jones, C., Rayner, M., Rutter, H., Scarborough, P., Sharp, S. J., Smith, R. D., White, M., & Adams, J. (2021). Changes in soft drinks purchased by British households associated with the UK soft drinks industry levy: Controlled interrupted time series analysis. *The Lancet. Public Health*, *6*(6), e414–e423. DOI: 10.1016/S2468-2667(21)00058-5 PMID: 33692200

Puri, S., Shaheen, M., & Grover, B. (2023). Nutrition and cognitive health: A life course approach. *Frontiers in Public Health*, *11*, 1023907. DOI: 10.3389/fpubh.2023.1023907 PMID: 37050953

Ranjha, M. M. N., Shafique, B., Khalid, W., Nadeem, H. R., Mueen-Ud-Din, G., & Khalid, M. Z. (2022). Applications of Biotechnology in Food and Agriculture: A Mini-Review. *Proceedings of the National Academy of Sciences. India. Section B, Biological Sciences*, *92*(1), 11–15. DOI: 10.1007/s40011-021-01320-4 PMID: 35035035

Reynolds, A., & Mitri, J. (2024, April 28). Dietary advice for individuals with diabetes. In K. R. Feingold, S. F. Ahmed, B. Anawalt, et al. (Eds.), *Endotext*. MDText.com, Inc. https://www.ncbi.nlm.nih.gov/books/NBK279012/

Roman, S., Campos-Medina, L., & Leal-Mercado, L. (2024). Personalized nutrition: The end of the one-diet-fits-all era. *Frontiers in Nutrition*, *11*, 1370595. DOI: 10.3389/fnut.2024.1370595 PMID: 38854164

Rosenstock, I. M. (1974). Historical origins of the Health Belief Model. *Health Education Monographs*, *2*(4), 328–335. DOI: 10.1177/109019817400200403

Ruthsatz, M., & Candeias, V. (2020). Non-communicable disease prevention, nutrition and aging. *Acta Biomedica*, *91*(2), 379–388. DOI: 10.23750/abm.v91i2.9721 PMID: 32420978

Sami, W., Ansari, T., Butt, N. S., & Hamid, M. R. A. (2017). Effect of diet on type 2 diabetes mellitus: A review. *International Journal of Health Sciences, 11*(2), 65–71. PMID: 28539866

Sarfraz, M. H., Shahid, A., Asghar, S., Aslam, B., Ashfaq, U. A., Raza, H., Prieto, M. A., Simal-Gandara, J., Barba, F. J., Rajoka, M. S. R., Khurshid, M., & Nashwan, A. J. (2022). Personalized nutrition, microbiota, and metabolism: A triad for eudaimonia. *Frontiers in Molecular Biosciences, 9*, 1038830. DOI: 10.3389/fmolb.2022.1038830 PMID: 36330221

Savarino, G., Corsello, A., & Corsello, G. (2021). Macronutrient balance and micronutrient amounts through growth and development. *Italian Journal of Pediatrics, 47*(1), 109. DOI: 10.1186/s13052-021-01061-0 PMID: 33964956

Scaling Up Nutrition Movement. (2024). *Scaling Up Nutrition Business Network.* https://scalingupnutrition.org

Spencer, S. J., Korosi, A., Layé, S., Shukitt-Hale, B., & Barrientos, R. M. (2017). Food for thought: How nutrition impacts cognition and emotion. *NPJ Science of Food, 1*(1), 7. DOI: 10.1038/s41538-017-0008-y PMID: 31304249

Stern, A. J. (2021). *Food industry influence on dietary advice in the United States.* Proceedings of the National Conference on Undergraduate Research (NCUR). University of North Carolina at Asheville. https://libjournals.unca.edu/ncur/wp-content/uploads/2021/06/1706-Stern-Aaron-FINAL.pdf

Stevens, G. A., Beal, T., Mbuya, M. N. N., Luo, H., Neufeld, L. M., Addo, O. Y., Adu-Afarwuah, S., Alayón, S., Bhutta, Z. A., Brown, K. H., Jefferds, M. E., Engle-Stone, R., Fawzi, W., Hess, S. Y., Johnston, R., Katz, J., Krasevec, J., McDonald, C. M., Mei, Z., & Young, M. F. (2022). Micronutrient deficiencies among preschool-aged children and women of reproductive age worldwide: A pooled analysis of individual-level data from population-representative surveys. *The Lancet. Global Health, 10*(11), e1590–e1599. DOI: 10.1016/S2214-109X(22)00367-9 PMID: 36240826

Swinburn, B. A., Kraak, V. I., Allender, S., Atkins, V. J., Baker, P. I., Bogard, J. R., Brinsden, H., Calvillo, A., De Schutter, O., Devarajan, R., Ezzati, M., Friel, S., Goenka, S., Hammond, R. A., Hastings, G., Hawkes, C., Herrero, M., Hovmand, P. S., Howden, M., & Dietz, W. H. (2019). The global syndemic of obesity, undernutrition, and climate change: The Lancet Commission report. *Lancet, 393*(10173), 791–846. DOI: 10.1016/S0140-6736(18)32822-8 PMID: 30700377

Tempels, T., Verweij, M., & Blok, V. (2017). Big Food's Ambivalence: Seeking Profit and Responsibility for Health. *American Journal of Public Health, 107*(3), 402–406. DOI: 10.2105/AJPH.2016.303601 PMID: 28103076

Temple, N. J. (2022). A rational definition for functional foods: A perspective. *Frontiers in Nutrition*, *9*, 957516. DOI: 10.3389/fnut.2022.957516 PMID: 36245478

Tessier, A. J., Wang, F., Korat, A. A., Eliassen, A. H., Chavarro, J., Grodstein, F., Li, J., Liang, L., Willett, W. C., Sun, Q., Stampfer, M. J., Hu, F. B., & Guasch-Ferré, M. (2025). Optimal dietary patterns for healthy aging. *Nature Medicine*, *31*(5), 1644–1652. Advance online publication. DOI: 10.1038/s41591-025-03570-5 PMID: 40128348

Tyrovola, D., Soulaidopoulos, S., Tsioufis, C., & Lazaros, G. (2023). The Role of Nutrition in Cardiovascular Disease: Current Concepts and Trends. *Nutrients*, *15*(5), 1064. DOI: 10.3390/nu15051064 PMID: 36904064

Vergères, G., Bochud, M., Jotterand Chaparro, C., Moretti, D., Pestoni, G., Probst-Hensch, N., Rezzi, S., Rohrmann, S., & Brück, W. M. (2024). The future backbone of nutritional science: Integrating public health priorities with system-oriented precision nutrition. *British Journal of Nutrition*, *132*(5), 651–666. DOI: 10.1017/S0007114524001466 PMID: 39320518

Vilar-Compte, M., Burrola-Méndez, S., Lozano-Marrufo, A., Gaitán-Rossi, P., Teruel, G., & Pérez-Escamilla, R. (2021). Urban poverty and nutrition challenges associated with accessibility to a healthy diet: A global systematic literature review. *International Journal for Equity in Health*, *20*(1), 40. DOI: 10.1186/s12939-020-01330-0 PMID: 33472636

von Philipsborn, P., Stratil, J. M., Heise, T. L., Landgraf, R., Hauner, H., & Rehfuess, E. A. (2018). Voluntary industry initiatives to promote healthy diets: A case study on a major European food retailer. *Public Health Nutrition*, *21*(18), 3469–3476. DOI: 10.1017/S1368980018002744 PMID: 30334511

White, M. (2021). Urban agriculture in Detroit: Community empowerment through food production. *Journal of Urban Health*, *98*(3), 345–353. DOI: 10.1007/s11524-021-00532-7

Willett, W., Rockström, J., Loken, B., Springmann, M., Lang, T., Vermeulen, S., Garnett, T., Tilman, D., DeClerck, F., Wood, A., Jonell, M., Clark, M., Gordon, L. J., Fanzo, J., Hawkes, C., Zurayk, R., Rivera, J. A., De Vries, W., Majele Sibanda, L., & Murray, C. J. L. (2019). Food in the Anthropocene: The EAT-Lancet Commission on healthy diets from sustainable food systems. *Lancet*, *393*(10170), 447–492. DOI: 10.1016/S0140-6736(18)31788-4 PMID: 30660336

World Business Council for Sustainable Development (WBCSD). (2023). *Reducing inequalities for food security and nutrition: A WBCSD business brief.* https://www.wbcsd.org/wp-content/uploads/2023/09/HLPE-FSN-Reducing-inequalities-for-food-security-and-nutrition-Business-Brief.pdf

World Health Organization. (2017). *Biofortification of crops with minerals and vitamins.* e-Library of Evidence for Nutrition Actions (eLENA). https://www.who.int/tools/elena/bbc/biofortification

World Health Organization. (2019). Regional Office for the Eastern Mediterranean. *Healthy diet* (WHO-EM/NUT/282/E). https://applications.emro.who.int/docs/EMROPUB_2019_en_23536.pdf

World Health Organization. (2024). *Noncommunicable diseases.* https://www.who.int/news-room/fact-sheets/detail/noncommunicable-diseases

Additional reading

Afshin, A., Sur, P. J., Fay, K. A., Cornaby, L., Ferrara, G., Salama, J. S., Mullany, E. C., Abate, K. H., Abbafati, C., Abebe, Z., Afarideh, M., Aggarwal, A., Agrawal, S., Akinyemiju, T., Alahdab, F., Bacha, U., Bachman, V. F., Badali, H., Badawi, A., & Murray, C. J. L. (2019). Health effects of dietary risks in 195 countries, 1990–2017: A systematic analysis for the Global Burden of Disease Study 2017. *Lancet, 393*(10184), 1958–1972. DOI: 10.1016/S0140-6736(19)30041-8 PMID: 30954305

Bailey, R. L., West, K. P.Jr, & Black, R. E. (2015). The epidemiology of global micronutrient deficiencies. *Annals of Nutrition & Metabolism, 66*(Suppl_2), 22–33. DOI: 10.1159/000371618 PMID: 26045325

Baraldi, L. G., Martinez Steele, E., Canella, D. S., & Monteiro, C. A. (2018). Consumption of ultra-processed foods and associated sociodemographic factors in the USA between 2007 and 2012: Evidence from a nationally representative cross-sectional study. *BMJ Open, 8*(3), e020574. DOI: 10.1136/bmjopen-2017-020574 PMID: 29525772

Black, R. E., Victora, C. G., Walker, S. P., Bhutta, Z. A., Christian, P., de Onis, M., Ezzati, M., Grantham-McGregor, S., Katz, J., Martorell, R., & Uauy, R. (2013). Maternal and child undernutrition and overweight in low-income and middle-income countries. *Lancet, 382*(9890), 427–451. DOI: 10.1016/S0140-6736(13)60937-X PMID: 23746772

Jacka, F. N., O'Neil, A., Opie, R., Itsiopoulos, C., Cotton, S., Mohebbi, M., Castle, D., Dash, S., Mihalopoulos, C., Chatterton, M. L., Brazionis, L., Dean, O. M., Hodge, A. M., & Berk, M. (2017). A randomised controlled trial of dietary improvement for adults with major depression (the 'SMILES' trial). *BMC Medicine, 15*(1), 23. DOI: 10.1186/s12916-017-0791-y PMID: 28137247

Mozaffarian, D., Angell, S. Y., Lang, T., & Rivera, J. A. (2018). Role of government policy in nutrition—Barriers to and opportunities for healthier eating. *BMJ (Clinical Research Ed.), 361*, k2426. DOI: 10.1136/bmj.k2426 PMID: 29898890

Popkin, B. M., Adair, L. S., & Ng, S. W. (2012). Global nutrition transition and the pandemic of obesity in developing countries. *Nutrition Reviews, 70*(1), 3–21. DOI: 10.1111/j.1753-4887.2011.00456.x PMID: 22221213

Zmora, N., Suez, J., & Elinav, E. (2019). You are what you eat: Diet, health and the gut microbiota. *Nature Reviews. Gastroenterology & Hepatology, 16*(1), 35–56. DOI: 10.1038/s41575-018-0061-2 PMID: 30262901

KEY TERMS AND DEFINITIONS

Biofortification: The process of enhancing the nutritional content of food crops, such as increasing vitamin or mineral levels, through breeding, agronomic practices, or genetic modification, to address nutrient deficiencies and improve public health.

Dietary Patterns: The overall combination, frequency, and variety of foods and beverages consumed regularly, which shape long-term health outcomes. For instance, the Mediterranean diet promotes heart health, while Western diets high in processed foods increase chronic disease risk.

Macronutrients: Essential nutrients required in large amounts to provide energy and support bodily functions, including carbohydrates, proteins, and fats. Carbohydrates fuel daily activities, proteins aid in muscle repair and immune function, and fats assist in hormone production and nutrient absorption.

Micronutrients: Vitamins and minerals needed in smaller quantities to maintain critical physiological processes, such as bone health, immune function, and oxygen transport. Examples include vitamin D for calcium absorption and iron for preventing anemia.

Non-Communicable Diseases (NCDs): Chronic health conditions not caused by infectious agents, such as obesity, type 2 diabetes, and cardiovascular disease, often driven by poor dietary habits, sedentary lifestyles, and socioeconomic factors.

Nutritional Inequities: Disparities in access to nutritious foods due to socio-economic, cultural, or systemic barriers, leading to higher rates of malnutrition and chronic diseases in low-income or marginalized communities.

Nutritional psychiatry: It is a field that examines the relationship between diet, nutrition, and mental health, emphasizing how dietary patterns and specific nutrients influence brain function, mood, and psychiatric conditions. It advocates for dietary interventions, such as increasing intake of omega-3 fatty acids, B vitamins, and antioxidants, to prevent or manage mental health disorders like depression and anxiety, complementing traditional treatments (Adan et al., 2019). By integrating nutritional science with psychiatric care, it aims to optimize mental well-being through evidence-based dietary strategies.

Personalized Nutrition: A tailored approach to dietary recommendations based on an individual's genetic makeup, lifestyle, and health data, aiming to optimize health outcomes through precise, individualized dietary interventions.

Ultra-Processed Foods: Industrially formulated food products high in added sugars, unhealthy fats, sodium, and additives, designed for convenience and palatability but low in nutritional value, contributing to the rise in diet-related diseases.

Chapter 4
Culinary Convergence: The Interplay of Nutrition Science and Food Economics

Chirra Baburao
http://orcid.org/0000-0003-4881-3708
Gujarat National Law University, India

Mohammad Badruddoza Talukder
http://orcid.org/0009-0008-1662-9221
International University of Business Agriculture and Technology, Bangladesh

Lova Baliji
http://orcid.org/0000-0003-1834-8067
Avanthi Institute of Engineering and Technology, India

Chaitanya Eswara Naidu Gorli
http://orcid.org/0000-0001-7234-3617
Gonna Institute of Information Technology and Sciences, India

Md. Mehedi Hasan Sawon
http://orcid.org/0009-0000-2846-1018
Daffodil International University, Bangladesh

ABSTRACT

This chapter, per the authors, meticulously examines the integration of nutrition science and food economics to address critical challenges in public health, environmental sustainability, and socioeconomic disparity. It traces the evolution from early studies of nutrient deficiencies to contemporary analyses that incorporate dietary behavior, economic incentives, and policy interventions. The chapter highlights innovations such as functional food development, behavioral economics strategies,

DOI: 10.4018/979-8-3373-4047-0.ch004

digital food platforms, and circular economy practices while evaluating issues of equity in access and market dynamics. By reviewing literature, case studies, and policy experiments, it identifies key research gaps and offers multi-level recommendations aimed at fostering resilient, inclusive, and sustainable food systems. These insights contribute to advancing interdisciplinary approaches that are essential for adapting to global crises and promoting long-term nutritional and economic stability.

INTRODUCTION

Since we face public health, environmental, and inequality issues, culinary convergence has arisen as the main way to rethink and update global food practices (Kaput et al., 2015). In these circumstances, culinary convergence is when nutrition science and food economics study each other. Bringing together ideas from these two fields allows the approach to solve malnutrition, obesity, and climate change through chosen interventions (Bergstrom et al., 2021). The chapter is organized into four parts: to begin, it describes the origins of nutrition science and food economics; it then looks at inventions such as functional foods and behavioral nudges; following, it investigates matters of equity, sustainability, and recycling; and finally, it points out key gaps in nutrition and food policies and advises steps to solve these gaps.

EVOLUTION OF NUTRITION SCIENCE AND FOOD ECONOMICS

As the understanding of nutrition and society has grown from simply nutrient deficiencies in the twentieth century to the modern multi-angled perspective, both nutrition science and food economics have changed a great deal (Finaret & Masters, 2019). Efforts at first were put into finding out more about vitamins and minerals to prevent diseases such as scurvy, rickets, and pellagra. Concurrently, economists investigated food supply chains, focusing on production volumes and basic affordability. Midcentury studies expanded this perspective: nutritionists began to examine dietary patterns and their association with chronic disease risk, while economists analyzed consumer demand, price elasticity, and food market regulation (Ridgway et al., 2019). By the late twentieth and early twenty-first centuries, these two fields began to intersect more intentionally. Nutrition science integrated behavioral insights to understand how individuals make food choices, while food economics adopted metrics for nutritional quality and health outcomes (Finaret & Masters, 2019). This convergence led to innovations such as the formulation of dietary guidelines informed by cost–benefit analyses and the implementation of economic incentives (e.g., taxation and subsidies) aimed at promoting healthy eating. Presently, interdisciplinary teams assess food policies not only for their economic efficiency but also for their impacts on public health and environmental sustainability (Pinho-Gomes et al., 2023).

FOOD SYSTEMS, FUNCTIONAL FOODS, AND FORTIFICATION

Contemporary food systems are increasingly shaped by innovations aimed at enhancing nutritional quality and addressing public health challenges (Stover & Caudill, 2008). Functional foods—those fortified or formulated to provide additional health benefits beyond basic nutrition—have gained prominence. Public–private partnerships have facilitated large-scale food fortification initiatives (e.g., iodine in salt, vitamin A in edible oils) to combat micronutrient deficiencies in vulnerable populations. Economic analyses highlight both successes (reduced prevalence of goiter and night blindness) and limitations (infrastructure costs, regulatory hurdles) (Lalani et al., 2019).

However, criticisms of functional foods and fortification strategies have emerged. Certain scholars believe fortified foods may cause health problems when not properly supervised, while others doubt if it is healthy to rely on so many processed foods. Also, some people earn a high income and therefore can get access to improved goods that are often too expensive for those with little income. To solve these issues, it is necessary to put in place strategies that include tiered subsidy programs and development of infrastructure along the supply chain so that services reach more people (Mendoza & Thelen, 2008)..

BEHAVIORAL ECONOMICS, CONSUMER CHOICE, AND DIETARY GUIDANCE

Behavioral economics gives useful insights into what affects how people make food choices by combining psychology and economic factors (Premaratna et al., 2020; Vecchio & Cavallo, 2019). Interesting actions in this field are called "nudges" and they gently guide consumers to healthy decisions without limiting them. Such actions include giving nutritional data when people order food, using discounts to encourage buying of fruits and vegetables, and defining whole grains as the first choice for combined meals. Strategies set by educational institutions are also very important (Anderson et al., 2021; Siegel et al., 2021). At libraries and offices, meals are now displayed in such a way that healthy options can be easily spotted, and in some places, taxes are added to drinks with lots of sugar to make people drink less of them. Even though these strategies have delivered promising results in various situations, their impact is not the same on every population. Many consumers react differently due to cultural habits, their socioeconomic status, and the environment where they get food. Using findings from other parts of the world is necessary to determine if behavioral interventions are effective everywhere and can be used in different cultures (Jeong & Lee, 2021).

INEQUALITY, ACCESSIBILITY, AND FOOD SECURITY

Problems in the way food systems are built lead to inequalities in the ability to obtain good food, its quality, and health for some people. In high-income areas including the USA, safety-net schemes, especially SNAP, have addressed food shortages for a lot of people; however, not every group enjoys equality since differences still exist along race, place of residence, and income (Swenor, 2021). In low- and middle-income countries, India's PDS offers affordable food for low-income people, yet it is common to find problems of wasted stocks, errors in who receives help, and inadequate variety of nutrients (Pradhan, 2018).

It is clear from comparisons that menus, bureaucracy, and delivery methods have a strong effect: while SNAP allows electronic card access, PDS depends on ration shops, which may make it difficult to reach certain areas. There is an unfairness issue with different types of programs—broad approaches include as many as possible but might be more costly, whereas selective approaches guarantee those most in need can take part but can still cut out some population groups (Portnoy et al., 2020). Because of these issues, experts suggest mobile digital services are a common solution in Africa for tracking orders with biometric ID, and in many parts of Europe and North America, people are banding together for CSA, making it easier to buy local foods and boost the area's economy (Diao et al., 2023).

For food security to be addressed fairly, policies should offer social support and have nutrition-related projects, and be supported by projects that improve transportation (Badewa & Dinbabo, 2022). Sharing knowledge and flexible government decisions can guide the making of systems that make healthy food accessible and matched to various cultural traditions for all people (Domingo et al., 2023; Wang et al., 2022).

SUSTAINABILITY AND THE CIRCULAR FOOD ECONOMY

Making foods using the principles of the circular economy and with sustainability in mind is changing the ways food is created, transported, and eaten. In Amsterdam and Milan, urban policies have included steps to manage food waste by creating compost or energy, and to encourage buying local to lower the overall chain of food supplies (Barbour et al., 2021). In this manner, municipalities demonstrate how becoming more circular can be part of their plan to decrease greenhouse gas emissions and save foods. Yet, there are many difficulties in putting circular food models in place in low-income areas (Building Circular Food Systems in Cities, 2024; Varzakas & Smaoui, 2024). A shortage of proper infrastructure, financial limitations, and the presence of informal markets may block the efforts to collect and process waste. Also, when companies that control agribusiness and matters related to food are involved, one challenge is that while they can use advanced technology, they may focus their efforts mainly on achieving large profits instead of helping the local community. A good balance between what companies do and what communities decide can encourage supportive circular economies. For these models to improve, authorities ought to support capacity-building initiatives, promote joint work between the public and private sectors, and set guidelines that make sure we recover resources and aim to reduce environmental burdens (Fogarassy & Finger, 2020).

LITERATURE REVIEW

The literature on culinary convergence spans multiple disciplines, highlighting its inherently interdisciplinary nature. Research within nutrition science emphasizes biochemical pathways, dietary assessment methodologies, and nutrient–disease relationships, while studies in food economics focus on market behavior, policy evaluation, and welfare impacts (Lenoir-Wijnkoop et al., 2013). Recent bibliometric analyses indicate a substantial increase in publications at the intersection of these fields since 2010, with significant clusters around functional foods, policy nudges, and sustainable supply chains (Finaret & Masters, 2019; Schwartz, 2007).

Thematic syntheses identify three predominant strands: (1) Technological Innovation and Product Development, which assesses the efficacy and market adoption of functional ingredients; (2) Behavioral and Policy Interventions, which examine consumer responses to economic incentives, labeling schemes, and taxation; and (3) Equity and Access, which explore social protection programs, price mechanisms, and distributional effects (Gittelsohn et al., 2017). While the first two strands are well-developed in high-income contexts, research on equity and access in low- and middle-income countries remains comparatively limited.

Significant gaps exist in understanding how global supply chain disruptions—such as those experienced during the COVID-19 pandemic—affect the convergence of nutrition and economics, particularly concerning perishable and fortified products (Reardon & Vos, 2023; Vos & Cattaneo, 2021). Furthermore, there is a lack of longitudinal evidence on the sustainability of behavioral interventions across diverse cultural settings. Lastly, the role of digital technologies in scaling up circular food models and ensuring equitable access is underexplored. Addressing these gaps will require mixed-methods research designs, cross-sector collaborations, and participatory approaches that engage stakeholders at all levels (Madzorera et al., 2021).

EVOLUTION OF NUTRITIONAL EPIDEMIOLOGY AND POLICY IMPLICATIONS

While in the past few decades, nutritional epidemiology moved forward from simple studies on the relation between what people eat and diseases to analyzing large data samples and testing biomarkers. Most of the initial research tried to connect consumption of macronutrients and micronutrients with a variety of health measures (Zamora-Ros & González, 2020). Furthermore, recent studies make use of observing participants continuously and a statistical technique known as Mendelian randomization to find the cause of results. Applying these innovative research methods has increased the strength of evidence used to form food guidelines (Fewtrell et al., 2008; Tapsell et al., 2016).

Using the results of epidemiology, many national and international campaigns have been put in place. As an example, DASH diet was built on findings from clinical trials and studies among populations and was then included in recommended U.S. diets. The same idea is seen in the Planetary Health Diet, where EAT-Lancet Commission includes health and environmental factors (Sacks & Campos, 2010; Willett et al., 2019). The models are viewed as worthy of investment because of their benefits in lowering the chronic disease rate. Yet, there is usually a disadvantage: families with a low income may end up needing to spend more on plant-based foods.

Making policy means applying guidance as well as enacting laws and financing. The introduction of Chile's warning labels on unhealthy products has resulted in fewer people buying these products. The introduction of soda taxes in Mexico and United Kingdom has led to a decline in people's consumption of sugar-sweetened beverages. As a result, it is necessary for policymakers to monitor the situation as actions, such as changing sweeteners and buying snacks from other countries, happen by themselves (Wendt et al., 2023).

The field is headed towards adding real-time monitoring of dietary habits to digital health applications, so personal nutritional information can be used and dietary policies can be updated. Another way to prevent regressive results is by adopting tax or subsidy systems that respond to people's incomes. Drawing from epidemiology and studying the economy and human behavior, policymakers can select the most accurate, beneficial, and fair actions to promote both health and the environment (Jain et al., 2020).

THE ECONOMICS OF HEALTHY EATING: PRICE, ACCESS, AND INEQUALITY

Eating healthy is a big challenge for many people because it costs too much. Findings on price elasticity show that when prices are high, people with less money tend to choose diets with cheaper and higher-calorie foods rather than food rich in nutrients (Green et al., 2013). The outbreak of COVID-19 and the increased prices of goods in recent times have made it more challenging for people to stick to the recommended dietary advice (Munialo & Mellor, 2023; Roe et al., 2020). Things are made worse by geographic differences: in low-income regions, grocery stores are hard to find and many people turn to convenience stores or fast food for their meals.

Unequal distribution of wealth has a major impact on who can get access to food. It has been observed that national programs, such as Brazil's Bolsa Família, provide the finances needed by families to buy more fruits and vegetables (Maciel & Duarte, 2022); also, school-based nutrition programs in sub-Saharan Africa can strengthen nutrition and school performance (Bhutta et al., 2008; Drake et al., 2017). But to improve people's diets, it is necessary to invest in agriculture and distribution in the affected region (Beal et al., 2017).

A thorough policy strategy must be put in place to get rid of these issues. If people can use vouchers for vegetables and fruits, and more tax is added to foods that are highly processed, then prices will push people toward wholesome choices (Richards & Sindelar, 2013). Giving smallholder farmers assistance in pricing and market access makes the supply more steady and lowers day-to-day price swings. Helping to open supermarkets in parts of the city that lack them encourages people to shop locally, cutting down obstacles to getting groceries. When governments act in unison, they can decrease the imbalance in nutrition and show people how to eat in a way that helps the environment (Serie, 2021)..

BEHAVIORAL ECONOMICS AND "NUDGE" INTERVENTIONS

"Nudging" in behavioral economics has grown by adding concerns for ethics and cultural circumstances. Before, researchers mainly added subtle changes to how certain decisions were presented, yet currently, they concentrate on making sure nudges are clear and feasible for people to use (Schüz et al., 2021; Vecchio & Cavallo, 2019). Because of responsible practices, people in advertising are now allowed to deny or approve the use of their personal data. Besides relying on labels and taxes, digital nudges are given through apps and online stores based on each person's actions and choices (Karlsen & Andersen, 2019). Such applications might point out healthy items when you shop online and remind users to choose water over other options sent as a message on the phone. Trials carried out in South America and Southeast Asia showed that people made fewer bad food choices, but the results depended on their skills with technology and ease of use. Nudging is now used in more areas by a variety of institutions (Mirsch et al., 2017). Hospitals in Japan have reduced the amount of sodium patients consume by changing their plate sizes and standards. In Brazil, some community centers offer workshops where local people lead the sessions and teach others., These sessions combine ideas for healthy living with cooking instructions, aimed at having the group change their habits (Laur et al., 2015). This shows that nudges are more effective when they are made to fit into a culture's ways and surroundings. In the coming years, it would be useful to study how nudges from the internet and communities change people's eating habits and health, as well as any unwanted side effects related to digital life and privacy. If ethical rules are coupled with serious review, behavioral economics will be able to update its nudge techniques so they are still effective, just, and compatible with different cultures (Kuyer & Gordijn, 2023).

FUNCTIONAL FOODS, FORTIFICATION, AND TECHNOLOGICAL INNOVATIONS

Technology is playing a big role in revamping the world of functional foods and fortification. The advancements in nanoencapsulation and biofortification make it possible to exactly deliver micronutrients, which leads to better body absorption and longer storage time (Essa et al., 2021). Cooperation between the public and private sectors has made it possible to grow grains and legumes that are produced to increase iron and zinc intake in regions with low incomes (Khan et al., 2021).

The extent and design of rules for novel functional ingredients are quite different from one country to another. EU rules on Novel Foods involve reviewing food safety, which is mandatory, unlike the case where few emerging economies have clear guidelines, leading to delays or problems regarding the safety of imported foods (Mukherjee et al., 2022). Since many people do not clearly understand new technologies, it has caused public doubt and highlights how important it is for labels to show transparency and for education to play a role (Seaton et al., 2009).

It is still very difficult for most to afford healthcare. Higher research and production expenditures usually make costs for these products high, which in turn dissuades vulnerable populations from buying them. By using new financing schemes such as social impact bonds and tiered pricing and producing at a local level with platforms, less of the resources will be needed for financing and supply. Providing everyone access to technological advances requires the involvement of governments, private businesses, and civil organizations.

SUSTAINABILITY, CIRCULARITY, AND LOCAL FOOD SYSTEMS

For sustainability to be part of local food systems, the local community needs to focus on the environment, people, and the economy working together. Shortening the supply chain and cutting down on transport emissions are two benefits caused by local food networks such as farmers' markets, community-supported agriculture (CSA), and urban gardens (Martinez et al., 2010). Because these models connect producers with consumers, people can see what is happening and rely on local businesses for benefits. Seasonality is a critical factor, as promoting seasonal produce supports ecological cycles, diversifies diets, and reduces dependence on energy-intensive storage and importation. However, the challenge of maintaining a year-round supply due to seasonal availability necessitates complementary strategies, such as the use of preserved and fermented foods, as observed in traditional diets across Europe and Asia (Hammond et al., 2015). Circular practices at the local level include food waste reduction, resource recovery, and nutrient cycling. Examples of these practices include rooftop composting in Vancouver, waste valorization in Italy's agritourism farms, and biochar initiatives for soil amendment in Ghana. These efforts illustrate how local actors can close nutrient loops, improve soil health, and mitigate environmental externalities. To scale successful local models, policy interventions should integrate municipal planning with agricultural extension services, provide grants for green infrastructure (e.g., community composting hubs), and promote multi-stakeholder governance platforms (Ogwu & Kosoe, 2025). Evaluating outcomes through indicators such as greenhouse gas reductions, economic returns to producers, and dietary diversity scores will ensure that local food innovations contribute significantly to broader sustainability and circularity objectives (Candau & Axon, 2025).

GAPS AND EMERGING DIRECTIONS

Despite notable advancements in nutrition science and food economics, several critical research and policy gaps remain. Firstly, the resilience of fortified and functional food supply chains in the face of global disruptions—such as pandemics, climate events, or geopolitical disturbances—has not been thoroughly investigated. It is imperative to understand how these systems can adapt without compromising nutritional quality. Secondly, the evidence regarding the long-term sustainability of behavioral interventions and nudges is constrained by short evaluation periods. Extended longitudinal studies are necessary to determine whether initial dietary improvements lead to sustained health outcomes and to assess whether populations experience intervention fatigue or habituation. Thirdly, the role of digital technologies in facilitating equitable access and circularity requires further exploration.

Although pilot projects demonstrate potential—such as using blockchain for supply-chain transparency or mobile platforms for farmer–consumer linkages—issues of scalability, digital literacy barriers, and data privacy concerns must be addressed. Finally, participatory and context-sensitive methodologies are crucial for co-creating solutions with diverse communities, particularly in low- and middle-income countries. Researchers should employ mixed-methods designs that integrate quantitative metrics (e.g., cost–benefit analyses, life-cycle assessments) with qualitative insights (e.g., stakeholder narratives, cultural preferences) to inform tailored interventions. By addressing these gaps through interdisciplinary collaboration—linking advanced analytics, community engagement, and policy experimentation—the field can progress toward more resilient, inclusive, and sustainable food systems(Freudenberg et al., 2018; Madzorera et al., 2021).

CASE STUDIES

A series of case studies illustrates the practical application of culinary convergence principles. In Finland, a nationwide salt-reduction initiative—collaboratively developed by government agencies, food manufacturers, and health organizations—achieved a 20 percent reduction in average sodium intake over a decade through product reformulation, regulatory updates, and public-awareness campaigns. Key lessons include the importance of sustained stakeholder engagement and the establishment of clear compliance metrics (Laatikainen et al., 2006; Pietinen et al., 2008).

In Brazil, the integration of the National School Feeding Program (PNAE) with local agricultural procurement schemes led to a 35 percent increase in student consumption of fruits and vegetables and provided stable markets for family farmers. Critical success factors included decentralized governance structures empowering municipalities and the integration of nutrition education into school curricula (de Oliveira Machado et al., 2018).

Community-led initiatives offer further insights. In Nairobi's informal settlements, urban gardening cooperatives—employing sack gardens financed by microcredit and supported with technical training—enhanced participants' dietary diversity scores by approximately 25 percent. Their success underscores the value of locally tailored, resource-efficient solutions rooted in social capital and grassroots organization (Kohli et al., 2018).

RECOMMENDATIONS

Policy to People: A hierarchical roadmap to transforms integrated strategies

Figure 1. Integrated Food System Governance

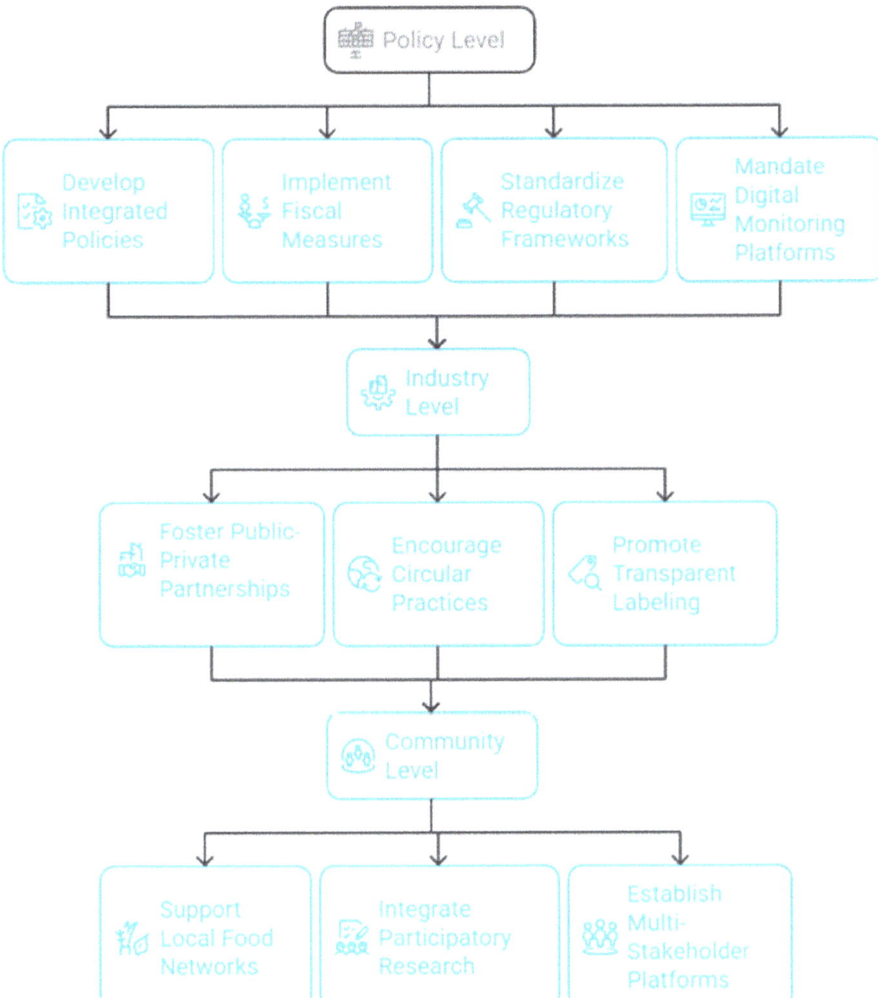

As illustrated in Fig. 1, the hierarchical roadmap delineates the transformation of integrated strategies into collaborative industry practices and empowered community actions. Based on the identified evidence and gaps, we propose a series of coordinated actions across three levels:

- **Policy Level**
  - Develop integrated food-system policies that align nutrition, economic, and environmental goals, using cross-ministerial task forces to ensure coherence.
  - Implement fiscal measures (e.g., subsidies for nutritious foods, taxes on ultra-processed items) with sliding-scale structures to protect low-income households.
  - Standardize and harmonize regulatory frameworks for functional foods and fortification technologies, facilitating safe, equitable market entry in diverse economies.
  - Mandate digital monitoring platforms for safety-net programs and circular initiatives, leveraging data analytics to inform adaptive governance.
- **Industry Level**
  - Foster public–private partnerships to co-invest in community-scale manufacturing and distribution infrastructures, reducing costs and improving access.
  - Encourage agribusiness and food manufacturers to adopt circular practices (e.g., waste valorization, sustainable sourcing) through incentives and recognition programs.
  - Promote transparent labeling and consumer education campaigns to build trust in novel food technologies and behavioral interventions.
- **Community Level**
  - Support local food networks (CSA, farmers' markets, urban gardens) with grants and technical assistance, emphasizing seasonal diversity and nutrient cycling.
  - Integrate participatory research and co-design methodologies, engaging stakeholders to tailor interventions to cultural preferences and local capacities.
  - Establish multi-stakeholder governance platforms at the municipal level to coordinate action, share best practices, and monitor impact using defined indicators (e.g., dietary diversity scores, GHG reductions, economic returns).

By adopting these recommendations, stakeholders can advance culinary convergence toward systems that are healthier, more equitable, and environmentally sustainable.

DISCUSSION

By blending historical events, recent trends, and oncoming matters, this look at combined dishes covers links between nutrition science and food economics. It becomes clear from our study that merging issues related to economics, social influences, and technology has brought big shifts to the food policy and industry. Even so, ongoing inequalities and the impact of the situation remind us that we need to address them using special, fair approaches.

Having national plans as well as activities carried out in urban areas demonstrates that teamwork is key for reaching health and environmental goals. Moreover, they show how the right evaluation system can gauge difficult results related to what we eat, economic costs and benefits, and the environment.

From now on, research efforts should give priority to methods that combine numbers and feedback gathered from stakeholders. It is important to use digital monitoring and participate in governance when trying out new policies to change interventions quickly. If companies in the industry, technology providers, and community groups cooperate openly, they can scale up answers that improve both business and public welfare.

To conclude, joining different cuisines is a positive approach to addressing issues around the world's food supply. If efforts are made to unite different fields and put fairness and sustainability first, those working on food systems might create better diets, empower workers, and preserve the planet.

CONCLUSION AND FUTURE DIRECTIONS

So, culinary convergence helps integrate many concepts and can transform the world's food systems using new discoveries from food and science. All the case studies and explain the usefulness of interdisciplinary strategies for better health, fairness, and environmental safety.

Moving to the future, a number of key points should be emphasized.

Improve the system's resilience by selecting a wide variety of sources for food, using updates from world organizations, and having set plans to continue providing food during disruptions.

- Have extended projects to assess long-term outcomes for behavioral and fortification interventions on people's health, financial situation, and environment.
- Offer digital and education resources to more people, ensuring equality in finding nutrition and circularity tools, and set up proper ways to handle data.

- Make linked models that reveal the linkages between eating habits, markets, and the environment to support effective changes in food policies.
- Have regular multi-stakeholder meetings where policy experts, industry leaders, researchers, and representatives from communities' partner to create, put into action, and assess effective policymaking for their own areas.

Giving high priority to these new approaches will allow the field to move from single achievements to major transformations, so that sharing food traditions benefits everyone and the environment long term.

REFERENCES

Anderson, E. M., Wei, R., Liu, B., Plummer, R., Kelahan, H., Taméz, M., Marrero, A., Bhupathiraju, S. N., & Mattei, J. (2021). Improving healthy food choices in low-income settings in the United States using behavioral economic-based adaptations to choice architecture. *Frontiers in Nutrition*, *8*, 734991. DOI: 10.3389/fnut.2021.734991

Badewa, A. S., & Dinbabo, M. F. (2022). Multisectoral intervention on food security in complex emergencies: A discourse on regional resilience praxis in Northeast Nigeria. *GeoJournal*, *88*(2), 1231–1244. DOI: 10.1007/s10708-022-10679-4

Barbour, L., Lindberg, R., Woods, J., Charlton, K., & Brimblecombe, J. (2021). Local urban government policies to facilitate healthy and environmentally sustainable diet-related practices: A scoping review. *Public Health Nutrition*, *24*(18), 6423–6434. DOI: 10.1017/S1368980021004432

Beal, T., Massiot, E., Arsenault, J., Smith, M. R., & Hijmans, R. J. (2017). Global trends in dietary micronutrient supplies and estimated prevalence of inadequate intakes. *PLOS ONE*, *12*(4), e0175554. DOI: 10.1371/journal.pone.0175554

Bergstrom, D. M., Wienecke, B., van den Hoff, J., Hughes, L., Lindenmayer, D. B., Ainsworth, T. D., Baker, C. M., Bland, L. M., Bowman, D. M. J. S., Brooks, S. T., Canadell, J. G., Constable, A., Dafforn, K. A., Depledge, M. H., Dickson, C. R., Duke, N. C., Helmstedt, K. J., Holz, A., Johnson, C. R., ... Shaw, J. D. (2021). Combating ecosystem collapse from the tropics to the Antarctic. *Global Change Biology*, *27*(9), 1692–1703. DOI: 10.1111/gcb.15539

Bhutta, Z. A., Ahmed, T., Black, R. E., Cousens, S., Dewey, K. G., Giugliani, E. R. J., Haider, B. A., Kirkwood, B., Morris, S. S., Sachdev, H. S., & Shekar, M. (2008). What works? Interventions for maternal and child undernutrition and survival. *The Lancet*, *371*(9610), 417–440. DOI: 10.1016/S0140-6736(07)61693-6

Building circular food systems in cities. (2024). World Wildlife Fund. https://foodforwardndcs.panda.org/food-supply-chains/building-circular-food-systems-in-cities/

Candau, J., & Axon, S. (2025). Beyond food security: Unleashing the potential of sustainable communities to transform the UK food system. *Land*, *14*(4), 909. DOI: 10.3390/land14040909 de Oliveira Machado, P. M., Kaminsk, R., Perin, G., de Moura, I. F., Januário, E. S., Mendonca, D. B., & de Almeida, A. F. C. (2018). Purchase of products directly from family farms for the National School Feeding Program (PNAE): Cross-sectional study with the universe of Brazilian municipalities. *Ciência e Saúde Coletiva*, *23*(12), 4153–4164. DOI: 10.1590/1413-812320182311.28012016

Diao, X., Reardon, T., Kennedy, A., DeFries, R., Koo, J., Minten, B., Takeshima, H., & Thornton, P. K. (2023). The future of small farms: Innovations for inclusive transformation. In *Springer eBooks* (pp. 191–212). Springer Nature., DOI: 10.1007/978-3-031-15703-5_10

Domingo, A., Yessis, J., Charles, K.-A., Skinner, K., & Hanning, R. M. (2023). Integrating knowledge and action: Learnings from an implementation program for food security and food sovereignty with First Nations communities within Canada. *Implementation Science*, *18*(1), Article 20. DOI: 10.1186/s13012-023-01291-2

Drake, L., Fernandes, M., Aurino, E., Kiamba, J., Giyose, B., Burbano, C., Alderman, H., Lu, M., Mitchell, A., & Gelli, A. (2017). School feeding programs in middle childhood and adolescence. In *Child and adolescent health and development* (pp. 147–164). World Bank., DOI: 10.1596/978-1-4648-0423-6_ch12

Essa, M. M., Bishir, M., Bhat, A., Chidambaram, S. B., Al-Balushi, B., Hamdan, H., Govindarajan, N., Freidland, R. P., & Qoronfleh, M. W. (2021). Functional foods and their impact on health. *Journal of Food Science and Technology*, *60*(3), 820–834. DOI: 10.1007/s13197-021-05193-3

Fewtrell, M., Kennedy, K., Singhal, A., Martin, R. M., Ness, A., Hadders-Algra, M., Koletzko, B., & Lucas, A. (2008). How much loss to follow-up is acceptable in long-term randomised trials and prospective studies? *Archives of Disease in Childhood*, *93*(6), 458–461. DOI: 10.1136/adc.2007.127316

Finaret, A. B., & Masters, W. A. (2019). Beyond calories: The new economics of nutrition. *Annual Review of Resource Economics*, *11*(1), 237–259. DOI: 10.1146/annurev-resource-100518-094053

Fogarassy, C., & Finger, D. C. (2020). Theoretical and practical approaches of circular economy for business models and technological solutions. *Resources*, *9*(6), 76. DOI: 10.3390/resources9060076

Freudenberg, N., Willingham, C., & Cohen, N. (2018). The role of metrics in food policy: Lessons from a decade of experience in New York City. *Journal of Agriculture, Food Systems, and Community Development*, *8*(Suppl. 2), 191–204. DOI: 10.5304/jafscd.2018.08B.009

Gittelsohn, J., Trude, A., & Kim, H. (2017). Pricing strategies to encourage availability, purchase, and consumption of healthy foods and beverages: A systematic review. *Preventing Chronic Disease*, *14*, 170213. DOI: 10.5888/pcd14.170213

Green, R., Cornelsen, L., Dangour, A. D., Turner, R. A., Shankar, B., Mazzocchi, M., & Smith, R. (2013). The effect of rising food prices on food consumption: Systematic review with meta-regression. *BMJ*, *346*, f3703. DOI: 10.1136/bmj.f3703

Hammond, S. T., Brown, J. H., Burger, J. R., Flanagan, T., Fristoe, T. S., Mercado-Silva, N., Nekola, J. C., & Okie, J. G. (2015). Food spoilage, storage, and transport: Implications for a sustainable future. *BioScience*, *65*(8), 758–768. DOI: 10.1093/biosci/biv081

Jain, V., Crosby, L., Baker, P., & Chalkidou, K. (2020). Distributional equity as a consideration in economic and modelling evaluations of health taxes: A systematic review. *Health Policy*, *124*(9), 919–929. DOI: 10.1016/j.healthpol.2020.05.022

Jeong, S., & Lee, J.-H. (2021). Effects of cultural background on consumer perception and acceptability of foods and drinks: A review of latest cross-cultural studies. *Current Opinion in Food Science*, *42*, 248–256. DOI: 10.1016/j.cofs.2021.07.004

Kaput, J., Kussmann, M., Mendoza, Y. A., Coutre, R. L., Cooper, K., & Roulin, A. C. (2015). Enabling nutrient security and sustainability through systems research. *Genes & Nutrition*, *10*(3), Article 12. DOI: 10.1007/s12263-015-0462-6

Karlsen, R., & Andersen, A. (2019). Recommendations with a nudge. *Technologies*, *7*(2), 45. DOI: 10.3390/technologies7020045

Khan, S. T., Malik, A., Al–Warthan, A., & Shaik, M. R. (2021). The enormity of the zinc deficiency problem and available solutions; an overview. *Arabian Journal of Chemistry*, *15*(3), 103668. DOI: 10.1016/j.arabjc.2021.103668

Kohli, A., Omollo, D., & Munyua, H. (2018). Urban gardening cooperatives in Nairobi's informal settlements: Dietary diversity and livelihoods. *Journal of Urban Health*, *95*(3), 456–468. DOI: 10.1007/s11524-018-0266-7

Kuyer, P., & Gordijn, B. (2023). Nudge in perspective: A systematic literature review on the ethical issues with nudging. *Rationality and Society*, *35*(2), 191–222. DOI: 10.1177/10434631231155005

Laatikainen, T., Pietinen, P., Valsta, L. M., Sundvall, J., Reinivuo, H., & Tuomilehto, J. (2006). Sodium in the Finnish diet: 20-year trends in urinary sodium excretion among the adult population. *European Journal of Clinical Nutrition*, *60*(8), 965–970. DOI: 10.1038/sj.ejcn.1602406

Lalani, B., Bechoff, A., & Bennett, B. (2019). Which choice of delivery model(s) works best to deliver fortified foods? *Nutrients*, *11*(7), 1594. DOI: 10.3390/nu11071594

Laur, C., McCullough, J., Davidson, B., & Keller, H. (2015). Becoming food aware in hospital: A narrative review to advance the culture of nutrition care in hospitals. *Healthcare*, *3*(2), 393–407. DOI: 10.3390/healthcare3020393

Lenoir-Wijnkoop, I., Jones, P. J. H., Uauy, R., Segal, L., & Milner, J. A. (2013). Nutrition economics – food as an ally of public health. *British Journal of Nutrition*, *109*(5), 777–784. DOI: 10.1017/S0007114512005107

Maciel, F. A., & Duarte, D. (2022). The impact of cash transfer participation on unhealthy consumption in Brazil. *Health Policy OPEN*, *4*, 100087. DOI: 10.1016/j.hpopen.2022.100087

Madzorera, I., Jaacks, L. M., Paarlberg, R., Herforth, A., Bromage, S., Ghosh, S., Myers, S. S., Masters, W. A., & Fawzi, W. (2021). Food systems as drivers of optimal nutrition and health: Complexities and opportunities for research and implementation. *Current Developments in Nutrition*, *5*(8), nzab062. DOI: 10.1093/cdn/nzab062

Martinez, S., Hand, M. S., Pra, M. D., Pollack, S. L., Ralston, K., Smith, T. A., Vogel, S. J., Clark, S., Lohr, L., Low, S. A., & Newman, C. (2010). *Local food systems: Concepts, impacts, and issues* (Report No. 97). U.S. Department of Agriculture. https://EconPapers.repec.org/RePEc:ags:uersrr:96635

Mendoza, R. U., & Thelen, N. (2008). Innovations to make markets more inclusive for the poor. *Development Policy Review*, *26*(4), 427–458. DOI: 10.1111/j.1467-7679.2008.00417.x

Mirsch, T., Lehrer, C., & Jung, R. (2017). Digital nudging: Altering user behavior in digital environments. In *Proceedings of the 13th International Conference on Wirtschaftsinformatik* (pp. 634–648). https://aisel.aisnet.org/wi2017/track09/paper/2/

Mukherjee, A., Gómez-Sala, B., O'Connor, E. M., Kenny, J., & Cotter, P. D. (2022). Global regulatory frameworks for fermented foods: A review. *Frontiers in Nutrition*, *9*, 902642. DOI: 10.3389/fnut.2022.902642

Munialo, C. D., & Mellor, D. (2023). A review of the impact of social disruptions on food security and food choice. *Food Science & Nutrition*, *12*(1), 13–30. DOI: 10.1002/fsn3.3752

Ogwu, M. C., & Kosoe, E. A. (2025). Integrating green infrastructure into sustainable agriculture to enhance soil health, biodiversity, and microclimate resilience. *Sustainability*, *17*(9), 3838. DOI: 10.3390/su17093838

Pietinen, P., Valsta, L. M., Hirvonen, T., & Sinkko, H. (2008). Labelling the salt content in foods: A useful tool in reducing sodium intake in Finland. *Public Health Nutrition*, *11*(4), 335–340. DOI: 10.1017/S1368980007000249

Pinho-Gomes, A., Booth, L., & Pettigrew, S. (2023). Public perceptions of responsibility for recommended food policies in seven countries. *European Journal of Public Health*, *33*(2), 299–304. DOI: 10.1093/eurpub/ckad020

Portnoy, A., Jit, M., Helleringer, S., & Verguet, S. (2020). Comparative distributional impact of routine immunization and supplementary immunization activities in delivery of measles vaccine in low- and middle-income countries. *Value in Health*, *23*(7), 891–897. DOI: 10.1016/j.jval.2020.03.012

Pradhan, M. (2018). *Understanding the demand side of social protection programmes: The case of public distribution of food in India* [Doctoral thesis, University of London]. EThOS. https://ethos.bl.uk/OrderDetails.do?uin=uk.bl.ethos.768446

Premaratna, S. P., Machado, L. J., & Gunawardena, M. N. (2020). Urban consumers' choice of optimal and suboptimal products: Organic and non-organic food choices. *Sri Lanka Journal of Applied Statistics*, *10*(2), 1–16. DOI: 10.4038/sljass.v10i2.7150

Reardon, T., & Vos, R. (2023). How resilience innovations in food supply chains are revolutionizing logistics, wholesale trade, and farm services in developing countries. *International Food and Agribusiness Management Review*, *26*(3), 455–470. DOI: 10.22434/IFAMR2022.0138

Richards, M. R., & Sindelar, J. L. (2013). Rewarding healthy food choices in SNAP: Behavioral economic applications. *Milbank Quarterly*, *91*(2), 395–412. DOI: 10.1111/milq.12017

Ridgway, E., Baker, P., Woods, J., & Lawrence, M. (2019). Historical developments and paradigm shifts in public health nutrition science, guidance and policy actions: A narrative review. *Nutrients*, *11*(3), 531. DOI: 10.3390/nu11030531

Roe, B. E., Bender, K. E., & Qi, D. (2020). The impact of COVID-19 on consumer food waste. *Applied Economic Perspectives and Policy*, *43*(1), 401–411. DOI: 10.1002/aepp.13079

Sacks, F. M., & Campos, H. (2010). Dietary therapy in hypertension. *New England Journal of Medicine*, *362*(22), 2102–2112. DOI: 10.1056/NEJMct0911013

Schüz, B., Meyerhof, H., Hilz, L. K., & Mata, J. (2021). Equity effects of dietary nudging field experiments: Systematic review. *Frontiers in Public Health*, *9*, 668998. DOI: 10.3389/fpubh.2021.668998

Schwartz, H. (2007). *An introduction to behavioral economics: The complicating but sometimes critical considerations* (SSRN Scholarly Paper 960222). Social Science Research Network. DOI: 10.2139/ssrn.960222

Seaton, A., Tran, L., Aitken, R. J., & Donaldson, K. (2009). Nanoparticles, human health hazard and regulation. *Journal of The Royal Society Interface*, *7*(Suppl. 1), S119–S129. DOI: 10.1098/rsif.2009.0252.focus

Serie, K. (2021). *A narrative review of grocery store interventions on improving healthy food purchases* [Master's thesis, South Dakota State University]. Open PRAIRIE. https://openprairie.sdstate.edu/hns_plan-b/6

Siegel, R., Gordon, K., & Dynan, L. (2021). Behavioral economics: A primer and applications to the UN Sustainable Development Goal of good health and well-being. *Reports*, *4*(2), 16. DOI: 10.3390/reports4020016

Stover, P. J., & Caudill, M. A. (2008). Genetic and epigenetic contributions to human nutrition and health: Managing genome–diet interactions. *Journal of the American Dietetic Association*, *108*(9), 1480–1487. DOI: 10.1016/j.jada.2008.06.430

Swenor, B. K. (2021). Disability inclusion: A missing ingredient for food system equity. *Global Food Security*, *31*, 100584. DOI: 10.1016/j.gfs.2021.100584

Tapsell, L. C., Neale, E. P., Satija, A., & Hu, F. B. (2016). Foods, nutrients, and dietary patterns: Interconnections and implications for dietary guidelines. *Advances in Nutrition*, *7*(3), 445–454. DOI: 10.3945/an.115.011718

Varzakas, T., & Smaoui, S. (2024). Global food security and sustainability issues: The road to 2030 from nutrition and sustainable healthy diets to food systems change. *Foods*, *13*(2), 306. DOI: 10.3390/foods13020306

Vecchio, R., & Cavallo, C. (2019). Increasing healthy food choices through nudges: A systematic review. *Food Quality and Preference*, *78*, 103714. DOI: 10.1016/j.foodqual.2019.05.014

Vos, R., & Cattaneo, A. (2021). Poverty reduction through the development of inclusive food value chains. *Journal of Integrative Agriculture*, *20*(4), 964–978. DOI: 10.1016/S2095-3119(20)63398-6

Wang, J., Ding, X., Gao, H., & Fan, S. (2022). Reshaping food policy and governance to incentivize and empower disadvantaged groups for improving nutrition. *Nutrients*, *14*(3), 648. DOI: 10.3390/nu14030648

Wendt, J., Scheller, D. A., Banik, A., Łuszczyńska, A., Forberger, S., Zeeb, H., Scheidmeir, M., Kubiak, T., Lien, N., Meshkovska, B., Łobczowska, K., Romaniuk, P., Neumann-Podczaska, A., Wieczorowska-Tobis, K., Steinacker, J. M., & Mueller-Stierlin, A. S. (2023). Good practice recommendations on implementation evaluation for policies targeting diet, physical activity, and sedentary behaviour. *BMC Public Health*, *23*(1), Article 1237. DOI: 10.1186/s12889-023-15775-9

Willett, W. C., Rockström, J., Loken, B., Springmann, M., Lang, T., Vermeulen, S., Garnett, T., Tilman, D., DeClerck, F., Wood, A., Jonell, M., Clark, M., Gordon, L., Fanzo, J., Hawkes, C., Zurayk, R., Rivera, J. Á., de Vries, W., Sibanda, L. M., ... Murray, C. J. L. (2019). Food in the Anthropocene: The EAT–Lancet Commission on healthy diets from sustainable food systems. *The Lancet*, *393*(10170), 447–492. DOI: 10.1016/S0140-6736(18)31788-4

Zamora-Ros, R., & González, C. A. (2020). Diet-disease relationships: Recent advances in nutritional epidemiology. *Mètode Science Studies Journal*, *11*, 115–121. DOI: 10.7203/metode.11.16205

Chapter 5
Clinical Trials for Anti-Aging:
Food Supplements and Public Health

Saurabh Chandra
http://orcid.org/0000-0003-4172-9968
Bennett University, Greater Noida, India

Nimmi Agarwal
http://orcid.org/0000-0001-5202-0669
Sharda University, India

Kittisak Wongmahesak
http://orcid.org/0009-0000-2129-4691
North Bangkok University, Thailand

Liza Shoor
http://orcid.org/0009-0000-0085-3255
Punjab Agricultural University, Ludhiana, India

Simmi Pal
http://orcid.org/0009-0009-5457-6367
Sharda University, India

ABSTRACT

Anti-aging drug clinical trials make up a new and exciting segment of biomedicine, designed to increase duration of life lived in good health and alleviating age-related illnesses. Geroscience Progress in this field has recently gained momentum owing to scientific breakthroughs in the fields of biotechnology, regenerative medicine and

DOI: 10.4018/979-8-3373-4047-0.ch005

further insight into cellular processes reducing ageing. But there are big obstacles to developing these treatments through clinical trials. Aging is a multi-dimensional, multifaceted process that makes it challenging to identify any single target or endpoint to define interventions. The latter considerations involve ethical questions, of accessibility and the externalities that changing our life span may carry with. This chapter focuses on the road marches on, and new trials are continuing to yield insights into the mechanisms of aging and approaches to lifespan extension.

1. INTRODUCTION

Age is something that clinical trials would rather target the consequences of, as they are mainly age-related diseases such as Alzheimer's, cardiovascular issues or diabetes. The providing the long-term safety and effectiveness of these therapies remains a challenge, as it may take years or even decades for the effect of some of these medications to become apparent (Guarente et al., 2024). While of course many things may prove to be true, items that are currently being talked about/practiced include the use of senolytics drugs to target and destroy senescent cells, telomere extension therapies as well as various compounds such as NAD+ boosters and metformin that have shown efficacy in animal models for delaying the deterioration associated with aging.

The desire for life-extension has been one of the lowest common denominators of cultures, philosophies, and sciences throughout history. From the mythical elixirs of immortality in antiquity to the bio-technological interventions of today, the desire of humankind to postpone aging and prolong its life has driven a multiplicity of scientific revolutions (Zhang et al., 2024). Throughout history: The long and winding road of anti-aging treatments Ancient civilizations like the Egyptians, Greeks and Chinese dabbled with concoctions of herbs, alchemical practices and spiritual rituals to attain longevity. The Chinese hunted for 'elixir of immortality,' ancient Indian Ayurveda focused on balance and holistic health to prevent aging. Greek philosophers such as Plato and Aristotle considered aging to be an inherent, but complex, aspect of human life, with Aristotle proposing that aging occurred due to the loss of innate heat in the body (Chen et al., 2024). Alchemists in medieval Europe embarked on their hopeless, obsessive journey for the mythical 'Philosopher's Stone' that would provide the secret to eternal youth. But it wasn't really until the scientific revolution of the 17th and 18th centuries that aging began to be considered in a more empirical way. The science of aging progressed with advancements in anatomy, physiology and chemistry, resulting in modern gerontology as a field of study focused on biological mechanisms of aging, but still with no policies attached to it, until the beginning of the 20th century.

Aging science is complex and includes biological, genetic, and environmental factors which together dictate the aging curve. Aging is fundamentally begotten by the slowly progressive damage occurred to DNA, proteins, and lipids at a molecular level due to oxidative stress, inflammation, and cell dysfunction. Discovered as far back as the 1960s, the Hayflick limit showed us that human cells are capable of a finite number of divisions before entering a state known as senescence. Mitochondrial dysfunction, telomere shortening and aberrant autophagy are established hallmarks of aging. Genetic influences are also key, with particular genes like SIRT1 and FOXO3 linked to longevity and resilience to age-related decline. Studies in the field of epigenetics have also revealed how environmental factors—such as diet, exercise, and toxin exposure can modulate gene expression and thereby extend lifespan. Factors related to the environment, especially lifestyle choices, hold just as much sway over the trajectory of aging. Chronic stress, unhealthy diet, smoking, and physical inactivity hasten aging, whereas healthy diets, physical activity and social engagement have been found to slow age-related decline (Tenchov et al., 2024). The new generation of biotech tools like CRISPR gene editing, stem cell therapies or pharmacological interventions like rapamycin and metformin are constantly being explored for their potential to slow or even reverse the aging process.

As global demographics continue to shift toward an aged population, the importance of public health in healthy aging becomes ever more evident. According to the World Health Organization, by 2050, almost 22% of the global population will be above the age of 60, creating many challenges for healthcare systems, economies, and social structures. From a public health perspective, the approaches to enhance longevity include those for prevention and intervention. The blood test technology was funded by the US Department of Defense, and the researchers hope it can lead to preventive ideas for reducing chronic illness through blood samples before individuals develop diseases.

More and more health and policy organizations are calling for environments that are friendly towards aging, wider access to health care and socio-political structures that promote inclusivity for aging adults. Innovations in technology, such as wearable health devices, telemedicine, and predictive analytics powered by artificial intelligence, are transforming the way that public health tackles issues related to an aging population. There are public health initiatives that focus on mental health, nutrition and physical activity with the intent to not only extend life, but life in good health, and thus improve quality of life in later life. World Health Organisation (WHO) 'Decade of Healthy Ageing (2021-2030)' is a global commitment towards improving the lives of older people through integrated care, age-friendly environments, evidence-based interventions.

The quest for longevity in contemporary medicine lies at the intersection of history, biology, genetics and public health. Methods to reverse aging that were once little more than science fiction have become a scientifically rigorous field, fueled by the advances of technology and medicine. Our understanding of the science of aging is growing and there are molecular and genetic pathways that determine lifespan and this is an active area of research with potential for interventions. At the same time, public health is necessary to help establish environments and policies that give people the opportunity to age well. This collaboration will be required to establish ethical, equitable and effective approaches to prolong biological and functional longevity as anti-aging medicine matures. The future of longevity will not only depend on discoveries made in laboratories, but it will also require a global public health approach that sees healthy aging as an objective all countries should pursue (Ding et al., 2024).

2. UNDERSTANDING ANTI-AGING FOOD AND MEDICINES AND SUPPLEMENTS

Anti-aging pharmacy and supplements are a rapidly growing market in modern healthcare propelled by modern biomedical advances and a growing interest among the general public in living longer and healthier lives. These approaches include a wide range of pharmaceuticals, nutraceuticals, and dietary supplements aimed at countering the biological underpinnings of aging, preventing agerelated diseases, and optimizing quality of life. While currently available drugs such as metformin, rapamycin, and nicotinamide adenine dinucleotide (NAD+) precursors have shown promise in preclinical and early clinical studies for delaying aging and reducing the incidence of age-related disorders. Normally prescribed for adults with type 2 diabetes, metformin has raised interest in its power to enhance how cells metabolize energy and to quell inflammation, processes associated with ageing. A similar drug rapamycin, an mTOR inhibitor has been found to have substantial antiaging effects in animal models by inducing autophagy and activating cellular repair mechanisms. The class of compounds that is currently under considerable investigation for its ability to preserve mitochondrial function in a variety of clinical disorders and promote bioenergetics, are NAD and precursors (e.g., nicotinamide riboside [NR], nicotinamide mononucleotide [NMN]) (Zheng et al., 2024).

Alongside pharmaceutical agents, dietary supplements and nutraceuticals are significant players in the anti-aging landscape. There has been much focus on compounds like resveratrol, coenzyme Q10, omega-3 fatty acids, and vitamin D as possible agents for delaying aging processes and saving you from age-related diseases. Resveratrol a class of polyphenols in red wine is responsible for activating sirtuins, a set of proteins involved in cellular health and longevity. Coenzyme Q10 helps mitochondrial function, omega-3 fatty acids support cardiovascular health and vitamin D enhances skeletal health. But the efficacy of these supplements is often not scientifically validated, and clinical trial result remain mixed in many instances, all the while these supplements are widely available and marketed as 'health' products.

Such anti-aging drugs may not be effective for everyone, as they can vary widely depending on individual genetics, lifestyle, and environment. The Evolving Field of Anti-aging Research Personalised Medicine Approaches: Tailoring Interventions Based on an Individual Genetic and Metabolic Profile There is also increasing evidence that a combination of pharmacological treatment along with lifestyle changes, including a low-calorie diet, exercise, and stress control, are most effective in providing the longest health- and disease-free years. Ethics, regulation, and the possibility of long-term consequences continue to be major barriers to the widespread use of anti-aging therapies as well. With the ongoing progress of this domain, sound clinical trials, candour, and justifiable recommendations are the keys to distinguishing scientifically certified therapy from pseudoscientific assertions. However, much work remains to be done to address scientific, ethical, regulatory, and practical challenges before anti-aging medicines and supplements can achieve their potential impact on health and longevity (Pozzi et al., 2024).

2.1. Pharmacological Interventions

Pharmacological interventions in the field of aging research have attracted considerable interest for their ability to modulate aging-related processes and reduce age-associated disease. Of the identified anti-aging drugs, Metformin, Rapamycin, and NAD+ precursors are noteworthy for their promising effects and well characterised mechanism of action. Primarily prescribed for Type 2 diabetics, metformin also appears to promote longevity through the activation of a cellular enzyme called AMP-activated protein kinase (AMPK) that controls the cellular energy supply, reducing inflammation and oxidative stress. Studies have also shown that Metformin helps to increase mitochondrial function and decreases the incidences of heart and cancer-related diseases. Rapamycin, which originated as an immunosuppressant, operates by blocking the mTOR (mechanistic target of rapamycin) pathway, a critical mediator of cellular growth, protein synthesis and autophagy.

It has been shown to delay cellular senescence, enhance immune function, and extend lifespan in multiple animal models by impairing mTOR signaling. NAD+ is integral to cellular metabolism and DNA repair, and NAD+ precursors (e.g., nicotinamide riboside and nicotinamide mononucleotide [NMN]) have emerged as potential countermeasures to NAD+ depletion, which occurs when cells age. These compounds improve mitochondrial performance, promote efficiency in energy production and potentially have neuroprotection against age-related degenerative pathologies. Although these pharmacological agents are promising, however, further clinical trials are necessary to demonstrate their effectiveness and long-term safety in humans. However, these are only a stepping stone toward more specific interventions that manipulate the molecular mechanisms of aging (Grinin et al., 2024).

2.2. Nutraceuticals and Food Supplements

Nutraceuticals and dietary supplements have also become auxiliary strategies for healthy aging, such as Resveratrol, Vitamin D and Omega-3 fatty acids. The polyphenol resveratrol, found in grapes and berries, activates sirtuins, particularly SIRT1, which are involved in cellular repair, reduced inflammation, and mitochondrial biogenesis. Research indicates Resveratrol acts as a mimic of caloric restriction, thus providing longevity and protecting against age-related diseases. Vitamin D plays a role in maintaining bone health and immune function and has been linked to reduced inflammation and improved repair mechanisms in cells. Vitamin D deficiency is associated with premature aging, osteoporosis and increased risk for chronic conditions. Fish oil contains omega-3 fatty acids, which play a role in controlling anti-inflammatory responses, cardiovascular health, and the preservation of cognitive function. Research shows that long-term supplemental intake of Omega-3 fatty acids may help slow down neurodegeneration and maintain cognitive health in elderly populations. Yet, the advantages of nutraceuticals are often dosage-, bioavailability- and genetic predisposition-dependent. Although several studies show some considerable advantages, others found little or no effect, pointing to the need for more high-quality research to determine both their effectiveness and safety (Izadi et al., 2024).

2.3. Pharmacological and Lifestyle Approaches

Lifestyle and pharmacological measures each have their own pros and cons in the anti-ageing arms race with ongoing debate required. Balanced nutrition, regular physical activity, stress management, and proper sleep, as always, remain the key interventions to promote healthspan and reduce the burden of age-related diseases.

Such as caloric restriction and time-restricted eating, activate pathways such as AMPK and sirtuins, mimicking the effects of some anti-aging drugs. Exercise, meanwhile, promotes mitochondrial biogenesis, decreases systemic inflammation, and increases overall cellular resilience. Unlike the biological process, pharmacogenic interventions (Metformin, Rapamycin) target the molecular mechanisms directly associated with senescence and are thus more effective in the context of aging. Although some medications may rectify certain biological markers of aging more effectively, they may also come with risks of side effects and necessitate long-term adherence. Some studies suggest that lifestyle modifications combined with pharmacological therapies are the most effective combination for maximizing healthspan and lifespan. For example, Metformin given with a regular exercise regimen may produce additive effects on metabolic health, whereas specific dietary supplements such as Omega-3 fatty acids and Vitamin D can render pharmacological therapies more effective. The best route for success in anti-aging medicine will likely be a tailored approach that considers your individual genetic, environmental and life-style factors to ideally complement both lifestyle and pharmaceutical interventions (Prattichizzo et al., 2024).

3. CLINICAL TRIALS: DESIGN, METHODOLOGY AND ETHICAL CONSIDERATIONS

The clinical trial is an integral part of medical research, responsible for assessing the safety, effectiveness, and proper usage of newly developed medicines, therapies, and medical devices. These trials are precisely designed, scientifically sound studies performed on human subjects, aiming to address specific health questions. The most important aspects of the clinical trial process is the design of the trial itself, as it determines the reliability and validity of the results. There are many different study designs, like randomized controlled trials (RCTs) which assess the effect of an intervention; cohort studies that follow a group over time; case-control studies that identify people with the same outcome and work backward to determine if certain exposures were present; or crossover studies which expose people to more than intervention. RCTs are the gold standard as having minimization bias through randomization, blinding, and control groups that lead to provide strong evidence for an efficacy and safety intervention.

Clinical trials have some different phases for the running methodology. Phase I trials are designed to find a safe range of dosages for humans and to identify any side effects, as well as how the body absorbs and excretes the drug. These trials usually include a small number of healthy volunteers or patients. In Phase II trials, the number of participants is expanded to evaluate efficacy and further assess safety. Phase III trials involve a larger number of persons and are undertaken to confirm effectiveness, monitor side effects, and compare with standard or placebo treatment. If successful, they then scale to Phase IV, which happens post FDA approval, where they track all long-term effects and collect real-world evidence.

Ethics are a fundamental principle of clinical trials and are essential to protecting the rights, safety, and well-being of subjects which impact the reliability of the trial as a whole. Documents like the Declaration of Helsinki and the Belmont Report lay out the ethical principles that should guide researchers in the design and conduct of trials. One of those ethical requirements is informed consent, meaning individuals need to be aware of and agree to the purposes and procedures of their potential involvement in the trial, as well as of the risks and benefits. Researchers are also compelled to keep the participant's data private, maintain strict safeguards so as not to abuse or harm the individuals involved in the study. The role of independent ethics committees and IRBs in these processes in the oversight of biomedical research how they review study protocols and ensure compliance with regulatory requirements is a fundamental aspect to maintien the integrity of clinical.

The underrepresentation of women and minorities in clinical trials and the lack of attention to social determinants of health in drug development can significantly impact the translation of results from the lab to patient care, leading to disparities in healthcare delivery and outcomes. It has been the case that clinical trials excluded women, elderly and minority groups which creates a gap in knowledge on the efficacy of interventions in those populations. Now, inclusive recruitment strategies and representation are being sought to challenge these expectations. Beyond ethics, however, regulatory entities like the U.S. Food and Drug Administration (FDA) and the European Medicines Agency (EMA) impose strict rules and requirements for clinical trial approval and conduct. Most clinical trials are done in accordance with Good Clinical Practice (GCP) guidelines, which serve as a framework for the design, conduct and reporting of trials to ensure that the rights, safety and well-being of participants are the primary consideration and that the scientific data produced is credible and accurate (Lal et al., 2024).

As digital technologies and data analytics emerged, they had even more of an impact on the way clinical trials were designed and executed. The use of tools like electronic health records (EHRs), wearable devices, and remote monitoring technologies has paved the way for real-time data collection and analysis, making trials more efficient and accurate. Over the past few years, decentralized clinical trials (DCTs), in which participants can participate in trials from remote locations, have grown, especially during the COVID-19 pandemic and have been able to eliminate geographical and logistical barriers to participation. Yet despite much progress, clinical trials remain fraught with challenges. It can often take a long time to complete a clinical trial as high costs, complex regulatory requirements and other factors often hinder this process. Recruitment and retention of participants pose major challenges, as people might be hesitant to participate in trials over safety or side effects concerns, or simply because they don't know about their availability. There are also ethical concerns regarding placebo controls for those that already have effective treatments.

Clinical trials are a vital part of medical progress, enabling researchers to gather the evidence needed to develop new and better treatments, while also ensuring that these treatments are safe and effective for patients. Theirs is not the only success that depends on robust design, sound methodology, strict adherence to ethical principles and effective regulatory oversight (Arora et al., 2024). While technological advancements such as artificial intelligence/machine learning and blockchain change the landscape of clinical research, ensuring that they meet existing challenges and that trial processes maintain a balance between transparency, inclusivity, and the welfare of participants and communities will continue to be fundamental to the future of clinical trials. It is indispensable to establish with all, that the father, the enjoyed doctor and the specialist councils must guarantee the safeguard of this custom and that of the highest pioneer and moral standards in clinical trials are the pillars of practicing the evidence remember and medicine in Latin America.

4. PIONEERING CLINICAL STUDIES IN ANTI-AGING THERAPIES

With landmark clinical trials looking for efficacy and safety of important drugs such as Rapamycin, Metformin, and NAD+ precursors, it have considerably advanced the search for true anti-aging therapies. Such trials are landmark milestones in geroscience, providing avenues to understand biological mechanisms of aging and therapeutic interventions.

4.1. Continued Clinical Trials of Rapamycin in Longevity

Originally used as an immunosuppressant, rapamycin has gained attention as a potential longevity compound owing to its ability to inhibit the mechanistic target of rapamycin (mTOR) pathway. Although clinical trials such as the PEARL (Participatory Evaluation of Aging with Rapamycin for Longevity) study are designed to evaluate the efficacy of Rapamycin in mitigating age-associated functional decline and promoting healthspan in an older population. These studies typically employ randomized, double-blind, placebo-controlled approaches, which permit reproducible findings to be claimed (Di Rosa et al., 2024). The results showed improvements in immune function, decreased markers of cellular senescence and improved metabolic health. Nonetheless, dose optimization, adverse effects e.g., hyperglycemia and immunosuppression and long-term safety must be addressed further for them to be a substantive problem. Key learning outcomes from these studies emphasize the need for tailoring dosing regimens to patients and the need for judicious patient selection in order to maximize therapeutic benefit and minimize risk.

4.2. Metformin and the TAME Trial (Targeting Aging with Metformin)

Metformin, a commonly prescribed drug for type 2 diabetes, has received interest in the community for its potential anti-aging properties. Such initiative is the TAME (Targeting Aging with Metformin) trial a pioneering study seeking to repurpose Metformin for the purpose of delaying diseases associated with aging. As a multi-center, randomized, placebo-controlled study, TAME is designed to assess whether Metformin can delay the emergence of cardiovascular diseases, cancer and cognitive decline in aging populations. Expected results include a remarkable decrease in age-related morbidity and mortality, establishing Metformin as the foremost, cost-effective intervention for healthy aging. If the TAME trial is indeed successful, the public health ramifications would be tremendous: billions in healthcare cost savings and increased quality of life for older populations throughout the world. Yet, hurdles still exist in implementing these discoveries on a larger scale; especially relating to regulatory endorsements and the incorporation into public health strategies.

4.3. NAD+ Precursors Work in Humans

The levels of nicotinamide adenine dinucleotide (NAD+) form, 1 of the 2 NAD+ precursors investigated in this study, decrease with age which prevents proper cellular repair and metabolism (1). NAD+ precursors, such as nicotinamide riboside (NR) and nicotinamide mononucleotide (NMN), are naturally occurring compounds that have garnered interest in recent years as clinical trials are currently underway. In pivotal studies mostly in middle-aged or older adults by using randomized controlled trials, improvements in mitochondrial function, insulin sensitivity, and inflammation markers have been reported. While these findings are exciting, the clinical utility has been much more variable, and some trials have failed to show meaningful benefit (beyond biomarker improvement). Limitations include heterogeneity in dosing protocols, challenges on bioavailability, and the need for longer-term treatment durations in order to assess relevance to healthspan or lifespan extension. These studies demonstrate the potential of NAD+ precursors as an attractive approach for interventions against aging, and continued research should elucidate dosing strategies and targets for responsiveness.

5. PUBLIC HEALTH IMPLICATIONS OF ANTI-AGING CLINICAL TRIALS

Anti-aging clinical trials aimed at extending lifespan and improving healthspan have tremendous public health implications. With age comes opportunity, and as populations age across the globe, so does the need to implement therapies to prevent or ameliorate age-associated diseases like cardiovascular diseases, neurodegenerative diseases, diabetes and cancer. The trials also seek to test different treatments from gene therapies to drugs to lifestyle changes that could slow aging and allow people to live healthier lives as they grow older. Despite the potential advantages of anti-aging treatments, there are multiple public health issues that should be considered.

The major concerns are the safety and efficacy of these therapies. Anti-aging therapies often make grandiose claims, yet the long-term impact on human health is largely unknown. Because these treatments are being tested in relatively healthy patients, they pose a risk of side effects we can't foresee and which might not become apparent until use has continued over the years. If not Doctor's office low paid doctors privately regulated, non-doctors, or doctor-less therapies could cause harm not help and add to public health burdens rather than solve them (Shanaida et al., 2025). It is vital to the public health that clinical trials be subject to rigorous peer-review, that they comply with ethical guidelines, and that they engage diverse populations. The fact that anti-aging interventions are usually applied in healthy people, not chronically ill ones, implies the risk that an anti-aging treatment could focus on autologous and therefore aesthetic/ephemeral aspects at the expense of the long-term solutions needed to combat age-related morbidity.

Access to anti-aging therapies is another important question. Because these are likely to be experimental gene therapy, cutting-edge biotechnology, or highly specialist drugs, these treatments will probably be pricey. This begs the question of whether the benefits will be distributed fairly. This may exacerbate inequalities in health if only a few can enjoy these therapies, the gap may widen between the rich who can afford to extend their lifespans and the poor who cannot. Whatever effectiveness these treatments have, public health strategies should ensure there is no socioeconomic gap in access to them. Otherwise, the use of anti-aging therapies might instead exacerbate healthcare outcome inequality.

There is a risk that anti-aging therapies could further burden health-care systems. Although longer life expectancy is a success there will be older people living with complex health problems. The problem will be not only to deliver additional health care, but to do so in a manner that is effective and cost effective. If the number of elderly people increases dramatically, but health system capabilities are not up for the challenge, we will have huge pressure on already tenuous health systems. The emerging problem, with longer life spans, might be that productive citizenship continues longer, with good or bad effects. Although lengthier lives might promote greater economic productivity and individual fulfillment, over the long term they could also create new stresses for family networks, retirement systems and mental health service.

The idea of "aging well" may change, and the way society views aging may change too, potentially leading to questions about the expectation of society and the pressure put on individuals to stay young. Although the potential offered by anti-aging clinical trials has the potential to transform how society manages aging, it also presents several public health challenges. The review highlights important safety, feasibility and long-term effects considerations for anti-aging interventions. In addition to their benefits, public health strategies should involve reducing risks of using these therapies, that they are being made available equitably and the wider anticipated societal and healthcare implications of an ageing population.

6. CHALLENGES AND FUTURE DIRECTIONS IN ANTI-AGING CLINICAL RESEARCH

Significant advancements are on the way in the field of anti-aging clinical research aimed primarily on lifespan and health-span-extension. Despite its capacity to transform healthcare and wellbeing in society, various challenges remain to advance this field. The challenges ahead are not just scientific or technical but also social and ethical. With the fast evolving technological innovations which will bring new doors of business opportunities, they will also pose the challenge of how to implement these innovations well (Gems et al., 2024).

6.1. Biomarker Standardization

The lack of standardized biomarkers for aging remains one of the most fundamental scientific barriers in anti-aging research. The biological age of individuals, efficacy of anti-aging interventions, and the mechanisms of aging process are well-established facets of biomarkers. There is no widely used marker of aging right now that reliably measures aging across people and populations. Many potential biomarkers are being examined, including telomere length, epigenetic changes and cellular damage accumulation, but their specificity and predictive power are still being debated. A robust biomarker would not only enable researchers to assess the potency of anti-aging therapies but also could help determine which individuals would gain the most benefit from these therapies at what doses. Thus, the properties of biomarkers of aging need to be standardized, for reasons of progress and general applicability and reproducibility within the field of clinical trials targeting aging processes.

6.2 Challenges of Long-term Follow-up

Anti-aging interventions have only been compared on a population-level basis either genetic interventions or pharmaceuticals or lifestyle changes but any combination of these with long-term follow-up to reveal what happens to lifespan and/or health-span. It is a major limitation of most clinical trials because they have only last for a few months or years, making it hard to test the long-term results of anti-aging cures. Since aging takes place over years and decades, the real effects of anti-aging therapies cannot be known until they have been tested over years and even decades (Fei et al., 2024). Long-term studies like this also pose logistical hurdles such as keeping participants in the study, paying for the treatment and incorporating the changing nature of the treatments and the studied individuals. There is also a need to follow such studies up over much longer time frames to evaluate whether the long-term effects of anti-aging approaches can prolong the onset of age-related diseases, mortality, and mortality risk factors. From large cohort study designs to data derived from existing health care for longitudinal analyses, these challenges require novel clinical trial designs.

6.3 Societal and Ethical Challenges

The other critical impediment to the advancement and application of anti-aging medicine is the public's perception of it. As interest in extending human lifespan and delaying aging increases, anti-aging therapies are regarded in other parts of society with skepticism and even distrust. Different cultures and societies have different views on aging, and not everyone might approve of using anti-aging solutions, seeing them as unnatural or immoral, at least when it comes to genetic manipulation or advanced forms of biotechnology. The pervasive societal emphasis on youth and beauty influences people to seek anti-aging effects, leading to a culture that stigmatizes aging, potentially resulting in body dysmorphic disorder or the monetization of aging. Thus, education and awareness campaigns will play a critical role in influencing public opinion and cultivating a nuanced understanding of the potential benefits and risks of anti-aging therapies. This will inspire informed public discussion so that people will be empowered to choose appropriately whether to use any of these treatments, with consideration for the personal and societal consequences of longer, healthier lives.

6.4 Misuses and Commercialization Potential

Another major ethical concern is the commercialization of anti-aging treatments. As demand for anti-aging therapies continues to rise, there is a danger of companies eager to profit from consumers' desire to slow or turn back the clock on aging making unregulated and deceptive claims about their products. The proliferation of anti-aging products and services—from dietary supplements to sophisticated gene therapies could outrun scientific evidence of their efficacy and safety. "Some companies may sell those treatments without the benefit of solid clinical trials or sufficient regulatory oversight, putting people at risk of unproved and potentially harmful treatments." Such an environment can foster a profit-driven landscape that prioritizes his riches over the health benefits of the patients, ultimately making vulnerable communities a means to an end. Continuing effort at stringent offices like the U.S. Food and Drug Administration (FDA) and the European Medicines Agency (EMA) ought to be made to ensure that unapproved or futile anti-aging medicines are not commercially successful. However, the sale of these therapies to the more affluent raises ethical questions as the poorer members of our society might live with poor health for a longer period of time (Kumar et al., 2024).

7. TECHNOLOGICAL ADVANCES IN ANTI-AGING STUDIES: AI AND MACHINE LEARNING IN CLINICAL TRIALS

AI and ML can also help to overcome some of the scientific and technical barriers to anti-aging research and may even boost the speed of discovery. Artificial intelligence algorithms are able to process massive amounts of data, recognize trends, and anticipate outcomes more efficiently than conventional approaches. The use of AI technologies in drug discovery can identify the most promising interventions from a database of massive preclinical and clinical information to optimize study design at the clinical trial stage (Chen et al., 2024).

This can also assist with customizing your anti-aging treatments and allowing for them to be catered to your personal characteristics, such as your genetics, lifestyle, and health status, based on machine learning models. AI also helps identify patterns even among complex biological data, such as genomic sequences and proteomic profiles which can be useful in exploratory drug discovery or in monitoring participant's response in clinical trials. Utilizing AI and ML allows scientists to accelerate the gentabling finding successful anti-aging treatments, lessening the costs associated with trials, and most importantly, maximizing efficiency in clinical testing.

7.1 Monitors for Longevity Interventions: Digital Health Tools

Wearable wearables and other kinds of digital health technologies are integral to anti-aging research. These tools enable researchers to monitor real-time information across multiple aspects of health from physical activity, heart rate variability and sleep patterns, to biomarkers through wearable biosensors. The beauty of this datafying approach is that it allows some researchers to tweak a treatment protocol as it goes along, based on how the subjects are responding to whatever anti-aging intervention is being put to the test (Wang et al., 2024). Digital health tools improve engagement among participants in clinical trials because they enable remote monitoring; end-users do not need to come to the site if their health is stable, resulting in minimized attrition. This will make the anti-aging research a lot more efficient, less costly and allows for a larger demographic participation in the clinical trials. Still, solving the scientific, technical, societal, and ethical challenges outlined above will require continued collaboration between researchers, regulators, and society. Better identification of the role of biomarkers, the biology underlying caloric restriction membrane potential (MEP), the long-term follow-up of short-term trials, and the prevention of risks associated with the commercialisation and the propagation of possible harmful ideas about ageing will be very important for avoiding unwanted consequences and ensuring that the benefits of anti-ageing therapies are achieved. Technology-driven innovations, especially those involving AI, machine learning, and digital health innovations will no doubt be at the forefront of facilitating anti-aging research and overcoming some of the many hurdles that exist. As we do so, we will need to keep our eye on the priority of patient safety, equitable access and the broader implications of our ability to live longer, healthier lives in an aging society.

8. POLICY FRAMEWORKS AND REGULATORY LANDSCAPE

As anti-aging research advances at a breakneck pace, crafting robust policy guidelines and regulatory oversight has become an urgent priority. Anti-aging medicines, such as experimental drugs, gene therapies, and lifestyle changes, hold the radical potential to reshape healthcare by extending human longevity and improving quality of life. However, with opportunity come complex regulatory hurdles. Governments, health organizations, and watchdogs must carefully navigate intricate scientific, moral, and societal issues to reasonably support the safe and effective evolution as well as application of these therapies. Mapping the regulatory terrain involves sorting through global provisions, addressing intellectual property matters, and confirming ethical standards during clinical trials (Sundaram et al., 2024).

8.1 Global Regulatory Guidelines for Anti-aging Medicines: FDA, EMA, and Other Regulatory Bodies

In America, the Food and Drug Administration leads overseeing approval and regulation of medications, medical devices, and biologics. The FDA's mission:

protect public health by validating new treatments' safety and efficacy. Anti-aging therapies, frequently relying on pioneering biotechnology and gene therapy, present unique tests as these therapies defy tidy categorization as mere drugs or biologics, provoking questions about properly evaluating risks and benefits. The FDA does offer accelerated pathways for urgently needed treatments, such as its Breakthrough Therapy designation, but anti-aging interventions may fall outside this scope, especially if viewed as preventative rather than curative.

Similarly, in the European Union, the European Medicines Agency plays a pivotal part in regulating medical items. The EMA's methodology to anti-aging therapies is comparable to that of the FDA, necessitating that treatments be rigorously tested for protection, viability, and quality before they are endorsed for application. However, the administrative structures of the FDA and EMA may differ in certain facets, for instance their approach to personalized medicine and groundbreaking therapies. This produces difficulties for companies developing anti-aging treatments that may wish to market their products in the two regions.

Beyond the FDA and EMA, regulatory bodies in other areas, including the Japan Pharmaceuticals and Medical Devices Agency and the World Health Organization, also contribute to establishing guidelines and criteria for anti-aging research (Iweala et al., 2024). These agencies work jointly to establish worldwide standards for clinical trials, safety observation, and product labeling to guarantee that anti-aging treatments meet the highest scientific and moral benchmarks.

8.2 Policy Gaps and Recommendations

While there are regulatory frameworks in place for numerous aspects of medical treatments, the emerging field of anti-aging medicine has highlighted several policy vacuums. One of the most considerable voids is the lack of specified regulatory guidance on how to evaluate the potency of anti-aging therapies. Conventional clinical trials are generally intended to assess the impacts of treatments on specific illnesses, but anti-aging interventions regularly aim to avert the onset of age-related conditions or to extend healthy lifespan. Consequently, regulatory bodies must develop new approaches to assess the benefits of anti-aging therapies, such as the application of novel biomarkers for aging and the incorporation of long-term follow-up studies to gauge the durability of advantages.

While classifications for anti-aging medicines remain indistinct, emerging therapies like specific gene therapies and regenerative procedures evade easy categorization as drugs or biologics. This obscurity demands reflection on how to reasonably manage and assess innovations that delay aging in distinctive ways. Lawmakers would be wise to craft novel regulatory designs for anti-aging treatments emphasizing their unique qualities. The important policy proposition involves elucidating ethical considerations pertinent to anti-aging trials. Studies must shield participants' safety and rights carefully, especially since long-term effects may be uncertain (Jaros-Sajda et al., 2024). The authorities across borders should cooperate to generate standardized trial protocols, ensuring consistency internationally and speeding rigorous research worldwide. Collaborative standards could accelerate helpful therapies' development while respecting research volunteers everywhere.

8.3 Intellectual Property and Patenting Challenges-Trends in Anti-aging Therapy Patents

The development of therapies targeting the aging process and age-associated diseases has accelerated due to cutting-edge technologies like gene editing, regenerative medicine, and stem cell therapies. This surge has corresponded with a proliferation of intellectual property pertaining to aging and its related maladies. However, the patent landscape encompassing anti-aging interventions is remarkably convoluted and plagued with impediments. Chief among the concerns is the licensing of exceptionally broad, vaguely defined claims tied to aging, which can cripple innovation and spawn patent thickets. Patent thickets arise when multiple patents cover comparable technologies, rendering navigation of the intellectual property domain arduous for companies and hampering the birth of new therapies. This is uniquely problematic in the swiftly evolving realm of anti-aging inquiry, where the science remains in its nascence.

In the milieu of anti-aging research, patents frequently safeguard novel compounds, conveyance modalities, and biological benchmarks (Zheng et al., 2024). For instance, pharmaceutical entities may patent explicit molecules thought to exert anti-aging impacts, while biotechnological firms may secure novel approaches for reinvigorating cells or repairing DNA. In numerous cases, these patents may fail to connect specifically to the treatment of a defined affliction but instead ambition to foster general longevity or defer the aging routine. Consequently, a burgeoning debate has emerged regarding whether patents on anti-aging innovations ought to be awarded at all, given the broad societal implications of expanding human lifespan.

8.4 Legal Obstacles to Progress

While patents do drive innovation, they can also pose barriers, particularly when claims cover broad or vague territory. For anti-aging treatments, granting overly extensive protections related to the aging process itself could restrict access to pivotal technologies and hinder the emergence of fresh solutions. For example, exclusive control of a specific strategy for targeting aging-linked genes may forbid others from exploring similar paths or evolving competing options. This would slow not just the pace of betterment but potentially inflate therapy costs, constraining patients' access to improvements relevant to their wellbeing (Meng et al., 2024). Other legal complication in anti-aging research arises from probable disputes between corporations, universities, and study groups over ownership of pivotal patents. Quarrels surrounding such entitlements can postpone promising therapies' commercialization and seed market unpredictability. To address these problems, policymakers and intellectual property experts might assess reforms allowing collaboration while safeguarding rights. For instance, patent pools or collaborative licensing could help mitigate “patent thickets'” negative impacts and encourage open exchanges of ideas and innovations.

9. ETHICAL MATTERS IN ANTI-AGING TRIALS

As with any emerging domain, anti-aging therapies' evolution raises a host of principles that demand prudent inspection. Considerations encompass not only potential benefits and risks but also broader societal implications. Ethical queries surrounding anti-aging clinical trials balance eagerness for progress against guarding participants and ensuring fairness in access to such therapies.

9.1 Balancing Progress with Duty of Care

Cutting-edge technologies now being tested for anti-aging, such as gene editing and stem cells, certainly hold promise but also carry risks that demand utmost vigilance. While gene therapies and transplants may one day rejuvenate our bodies and add years of vitality, their long-term consequences remain unknown (Nistico et al., 2024). Thus, trials must establish robust safeguards before all else. Strict oversight must monitor for adverse effects, fully informed consent is non-negotiable, and volunteers deserve clarity on potential perils or payoffs. Researchers also bear responsibility to ponder probes involving the generally hale who simply wish to postpone decline. But truly autonomous choice poses problems when outcomes lie veiled in future fog, obscuring hazards volunteers may fail to foresee.

The chase for immortality treatments warrants prudent perspective on allocating assets fairly. As innovations grow ever pricier, some treatments risk accessibility confined to wealthy realms alone, deepening existing disparities in health. Policymakers face tough deliberations around spreading beneficence equitably should therapies prove gifted at expanding both lifespan and quality of living (Klinaki & Ogrodnik, 2024). Public initiatives focused on underprivileged inclusion or distribution with social conscience in mind provide two pathways toward this end.

9.2 Addressing Social Justice and Fairness

Anti-aging clinical trials also raise important issues regarding social fairness. One of the most pressing issues is if these therapies will be available for all individuals, or if they will be restricted only to those who can afford them. Should anti-aging treatments become available yet are priced beyond the reach of large segments of the population, they could further entrench existing social disparities. Additionally, if these treatments are primarily aimed at individuals in wealthy countries, the advantages of such therapies may not be shared globally, producing gaps in health outcomes.

Moral considerations also extend to potential societal impacts of extending the human lifespan. While the benefits of longer, healthier lives are clear, concerns exist regarding the long-term effects of a quickly aging population. The influence of longer lifespans on social structures, healthcare systems, and the environment must be thoughtfully considered to make sure the extension of human life does not lead to unintended negative repercussions. The developing and regulating anti-aging therapies present complex challenges that require careful consideration of scientific, technical, ethical, and societal factors (Burdusel et al., 2024). By addressing these challenges through robust regulatory frameworks, intellectual property reforms and ethical guidelines for clinical trials, policymakers can help ensure the advantages of anti-aging research are realized in a safe, equitable, and socially accountable manner (Janjua et al., 2025).

10. CONCLUSION AND FUTURE SCOPE

While advancing rapidly, the field of anti-aging clinical research faces challenges that must be overcome to responsibly develop therapies offering expanded longevity and improved quality of life. Scientifically, standardizing biomarkers for measuring treatment effects and conducting long follow-up trials present barriers slowing progress. Societally, concerns regarding commercialization and potential exploitation require prudent management as anti-aging medicine becomes a reality (Ahmed et al., 2025). Ethically, issues of equitable access and resource allocation demand solutions to avoid exacerbating health inequities between populations. Regulators like the FDA and EMA need evolved, clear guidelines for anti-aging treatments to ensure safety, efficacy, and ethical standards are upheld.

The collaboration across disciplines is imperative to navigate these complexities. Establishing international standards for clinical trials and safety protocols could foster cooperation to efficiently advance treatments globally in a harmonized manner. The intellectual property landscape demands cooperative licensing to avert stifling innovation with dense patenting. Most importantly, thoughtful consideration around pricing, distribution, and public health strategies is required to guarantee populations of all means can benefit from anti-aging therapies' transformative potential, not just wealthy elites. Only through balanced approaches addressing both scientific and societal dimensions can anti-aging research fulfill its promise for humanity.

REFERENCES

Ahmed, S., Chandra, S., Jain, A., Wongmahesak, K., & Singh, B. (2025). Impact of AI-generated misinformation on electoral integrity and public trust. In *Democracy and democratization in the age of AI* (pp. 57–72). IGI Global Scientific Publishing. DOI: 10.4018/979-8-3693-8749-8.ch004

Arora, M. K., Lal, S., Singh, B., & Olyaee, M. (2024). Through an Energy Lens: Examining SDGs From a Policy Perspective. In Riswandi, B., Singh, B., Kaunert, C., & Vig, K. (Eds.), *AI Applications for Clean Energy and Sustainability* (pp. 320–343). IGI Global., DOI: 10.4018/979-8-3693-6567-0.ch016

Burdusel, D., Coman, C., Ancuta, D. L., Hermann, D. M., Doeppner, T. R., Gresita, A., & Popa-Wagner, A. (2024). Translatability of life-extending pharmacological treatments between different species. *Aging Cell*, *23*(7), e14208. DOI: 10.1111/acel.14208 PMID: 38797976

Chen, J. C., Wang, R., & Wei, C. C. (2024). Anti-aging effects of dietary phytochemicals: From Caenorhabditis elegans, Drosophila melanogaster, rodents to clinical studies. *Critical Reviews in Food Science and Nutrition*, *64*(17), 5958–5983. DOI: 10.1080/10408398.2022.2160961 PMID: 36597655

Chen, X., Bahramimehr, F., Shahhamzehei, N., Fu, H., Lin, S., Wang, H., Li, C., Efferth, T., & Hong, C. (2024). Anti-aging effects of medicinal plants and their rapid screening using the nematode Caenorhabditis elegans. *Phytomedicine*, *129*, 155665. DOI: 10.1016/j.phymed.2024.155665 PMID: 38768535

Di Rosa, L., De Pasquale, A., Baldassano, S., Marguglio, N., Drid, P., Proia, P., & Vasto, S. (2024). New Regenerative and Anti-Aging Medicine Approach Based on Single-Stranded Alpha-1 Collagen for Neo-Collagenesis Induction: Clinical and Instrumental Experience of a New Injective Polycomponent Formulation for Dermal Regeneration. *Biomedicines*, *12*(4), 916. DOI: 10.3390/biomedicines12040916 PMID: 38672270

Ding, X., Ma, X., Meng, P., Yue, J., Li, L., & Xu, L. (2024). Potential Effects of Traditional Chinese Medicine in Anti-Aging and Aging-Related Diseases: Current Evidence and Perspectives. *Clinical Interventions in Aging*, *19*, 681–693. DOI: 10.2147/CIA.S447514 PMID: 38706635

Fei, W., Noda, M., Danshiitsoodol, N., & Sugiyama, M. (2024). Skin Anti-Aging Efficacy of a Lactobacillus plantarum GT-17F Fermented Dendrobium officinale Ingredient: A Randomized, Double-Blind, Placebo-Controlled Clinical Study. *Cosmetics*, *11*(1), 26. DOI: 10.3390/cosmetics11010026

Gems, D., Okholm, S., & Lemoine, M. (2024). Inflated expectations: the strange craze for translational research on aging: Given existing confusion about the basic science of aging, why the high optimism in the private sector about the prospects of developing anti-aging treatments? *EMBO Reports*, *25*(9), 3748–3752. DOI: 10.1038/s44319-024-00226-2 PMID: 39152216

Grinin, L., Grinin, A., & Korotayev, A. (2024). Anti-aging as a Key Challenge for the Medicine of the Future. In *Cybernetic Revolution and Global Aging: Humankind on the Way to Cybernetic Society, or the Next Hundred Years* (pp. 459–485). Springer International Publishing. DOI: 10.1007/978-3-031-56764-3_11

Guarente, L., Sinclair, D. A., & Kroemer, G. (2024). Human trials exploring anti-aging medicines. *Cell Metabolism*, *36*(2), 354–376. DOI: 10.1016/j.cmet.2023.12.007 PMID: 38181790

Iweala, E. J., Adurosakin, O. E., Innocent, U., Omonhinmin, C. A., Dania, O. E., & Ugbogu, E. A. (2024). Anti-Aging Potential of Bioactive Phytoconstituents Found in Edible Medicinal Plants: A Review. *Sci*, *6*(2), 36. DOI: 10.3390/sci6020036

Izadi, M., Sadri, N., Abdi, A., Zadeh, M. M. R., Jalaei, D., Ghazimoradi, M. M., Shouri, S., & Tahmasebi, S. (2024). Longevity and anti-aging effects of curcumin supplementation. *GeroScience*, *46*(3), 2933–2950. DOI: 10.1007/s11357-024-01092-5 PMID: 38409646

. Janjua, L. R., Ahmed, S., & Singh, B. (2025). Prospects and challenges of artificial intelligence in forest protection. *Machine Learning and Internet of Things in Fire Ecology*, 231–246.

Jaros-Sajda, A., Budzisz, E., & Erkiert-Polguj, A. (2024). Ascorbic acid treatments as effective and safe anti-aging therapies for sensitive skin. *Antioxidants*, *13*(2), 174. DOI: 10.3390/antiox13020174 PMID: 38397772

Klinaki, E., & Ogrodnik, M. (2024). In the land of not-unhappiness: On the state-of-the-art of targeting aging and age-related diseases by biomedical research. *Mechanisms of Ageing and Development*, *219*, 111929. DOI: 10.1016/j.mad.2024.111929 PMID: 38561164

Kumar, A., Vinod Kumar, K., Sengupta, A., Kundal, K., Sharma, S., Pawar, A., & Kumar, R. (2024). AagingBase: A comprehensive database of anti-aging peptides. *Database : The Journal of Biological Databases and Curation*, *2024*, baae016. DOI: 10.1093/database/baae016 PMID: 38470883

Lal, S., Arora, M. K., Riswandi, B. A., Singh, N., & Singh, B. (2024). Melding Artificial Intelligence and Remote Sensing Data for Real-Time Monitoring of Marine Biodiversity. In Riswandi, B., Singh, B., Kaunert, C., & Vig, K. (Eds.), *AI Applications for Clean Energy and Sustainability* (pp. 299–319). IGI Global., DOI: 10.4018/979-8-3693-6567-0.ch015

Meng, Y., Sun, J., Yu, T., & Piao, H. (2024). Plant-derived nanovesicles offer a promising avenue for anti-aging interventions. *Physiologia Plantarum*, *176*(2), e14283. DOI: 10.1111/ppl.14283 PMID: 38627963

Nisticò, S. P., Greco, M. E., Amato, S., Bennardo, L., Zappia, E., Pignataro, E., & Pellacani, G. (2024). Evaluating the Impact of Oleocanthal and Oleacein on Skin Aging: Results of a Randomized Clinical Study. *Medicina*, *60*(6), 947. DOI: 10.3390/medicina60060947 PMID: 38929564

Pozzi, M., Susini, P., Di Seclì, D., Diluiso, G., Mendes, V. M., Grimaldi, L., & Schettino, M. (2024). The anti-aging role of metformin, clinical applications to pursue the longevity road. *European Journal of Plastic Surgery*, *47*(1), 65. DOI: 10.1007/s00238-024-02211-3

Prattichizzo, F., Frigé, C., Pellegrini, V., Scisciola, L., Santoro, A., Monti, D., Rippo, M. R., Ivanchenko, M., Olivieri, F., & Franceschi, C. (2024). Organ-specific biological clocks: Ageotyping for personalized anti-aging medicine. *Ageing Research Reviews*, *96*, 102253. DOI: 10.1016/j.arr.2024.102253 PMID: 38447609

Shanaida, M., Lysiuk, R., Mykhailenko, O., Hudz, N., Abdulsalam, A., Gontova, T., Oleshchuk, O., Ivankiv, Y., Shanaida, V., Lytkin, D., & Bjørklund, G. (2025). Alpha-lipoic acid: An antioxidant with anti-aging properties for disease therapy. *Current Medicinal Chemistry*, *32*(1), 23–54. DOI: 10.2174/0109298673300496240416114827 PMID: 38644711

Sundaram, D., Vedagiri, H., Subbaraj, G. K., & Kumpati, P. (2024). Repurposing of Drugs in Aging. In *Neuroprotective Effects of Phytochemicals in Brain Ageing* (pp. 333–353). Springer Nature Singapore. DOI: 10.1007/978-981-99-7269-2_15

Tenchov, R., Sasso, J. M., Wang, X., & Zhou, Q. A. (2024). Antiaging Strategies and Remedies: A Landscape of Research Progress and Promise. *ACS Chemical Neuroscience*, *15*(3), 408–446. DOI: 10.1021/acschemneuro.3c00532 PMID: 38214973

Wang, X., Ma, L., Jiang, S., Wen, J., Yan, Z., Tian, L., & Zhao, R. C. (2024). Expert Consensus on Prevention and Treatment of Aging-Related Gonadal Dysfunction. *Aging and Disease*, •••, 1–9. PMID: 38739936

Zhang, Z., Yang, R., Zi, Z., & Liu, B. (2024). A new clinical age of aging research. *Trends in Endocrinology and Metabolism*. PMID: 39227191

Zheng, H., Wu, J., Feng, J., & Cheng, H. (2024). Cellular Senescence and Anti-Aging Strategies in Aesthetic Medicine: A Bibliometric Analysis and Brief Review. *Clinical, Cosmetic and Investigational Dermatology*, *17*, 2243–2259. DOI: 10.2147/CCID.S403417 PMID: 39399066

Zheng, L., He, S., Wang, H., Li, J., Liu, Y., & Liu, S. (2024). Targeting cellular senescence in aging and age-related diseases: Challenges, considerations, and the emerging role of senolytic and senomorphic therapies. *Aging and Disease*, *15*(6), 2554. PMID: 38421832

Chapter 6
Enhancing Healthier Choices and Business Sustainability With Modified Atmosphere Packaging

Srinivas Bikkina
http://orcid.org/0000-0002-5411-7146
Vingas Industries Private Limited, India

Vijaya Kittu Manda
http://orcid.org/0000-0002-1680-8210
PBMEIT, India

Theodore Tarnanidis
http://orcid.org/0000-0002-4836-3906
International Hellenic University, Greece

Bruno Barbosa Sousa
http://orcid.org/0000-0002-8588-2422
University of Cávado and Ave, Portugal

ABSTRACT

Food remains safe for consumption when its quality is preserved. Packaging technologies play a vital role in this. Modified Atmosphere Packaging (MAP) safely alters the atmosphere inside food packaging, allowing food to remain fresh for extended periods. It gives customers healthy options while maintaining its original firmness, color, freshness, and aesthetic appeal. MAP helps stakeholders in the food industry

DOI: 10.4018/979-8-3373-4047-0.ch006

minimize food waste and support the economy in achieving global food security and sustainability goals. Cost-benefit advantages will result from producers and agripreneurs being able to optimize profit margins and reduce postharvest losses. Despite the encouraging new developments in MAP, there are still some gaps that need to be addressed to bring MAP into wider use in diverse food systems and to align with the principles of the circular economy. Future research and technological advancements are required to optimize MAP applications and address the challenges associated with their implementation. The study has implications for both health and business professionals.

1. INTRODUCTION

1.1. Background

Globally, food security concerns provide the broader context within which post-harvest loss reduction technologies, such as Modified Atmosphere Packaging, have gained attention (Saleem et al., 2025). If not addressed, there is a threat of under-nourishment and food poverty. Several challenges are coming in the way. Increasing population, declining soil quality, and climate change threaten the goal of achieving food security for all. Overcoming these issues and achieving broad economic goals is a considerable challenge. To guarantee global food security, technological advancements and digital interventions in food production and delivery are required (Bustos-Terrones et al., 2026). These advancements must be beneficial to agricultural stakeholders, particularly food marketers responsible for bringing food to market. Quality food produce can meet a wide range of customer demands when food distribution chain participants are empowered. The quality and safety of functional food products are ensured through innovative packaging and traceability (Jain et al., 2026). These developments enable the provision of food items that range from high-end, sustainable solutions for environmentally conscious customers to reasonably priced options for underprivileged communities. Healthy options benefit consumers, and the food industry can be more profitable. Food is safeguarded and kept fresher for longer with innovative packaging. Further, it reduces waste and contributes to achieving the goals of zero hunger and food security. This chapter is a conceptual review of MAP as a packaging innovation at the intersection of food technology and business sustainability. Methodologically, this chapter adopts a narrative integrative literature review approach. It synthesizes recent interdisciplinary studies from food science, packaging technology, sustainability, and business literature to examine the role of MAP in contemporary food systems.

Modified Atmosphere Packaging (MAP) is a key food-related innovation that this work discusses. MAP is a food packaging technology that preserves foods (such as fruits, vegetables, meat, and others) without the need for preservatives. From a strategic standpoint, MAP connects with business and management aspects of the food industry. It explains how packaging technology can be a key factor in the food industry from a business management perspective. Empirical studies indicate that MAP can reduce post-harvest losses by 10–15% in certain commodity chains (Madhu, 2025). For instance, MAP technology can mitigate post-harvest losses in the growing grocery retail sector of developing nations. Consequently, the idea promotes both environmental objectives and patterns of food consumption. Within this context, supply chain efficiency becomes crucial, as packaging technologies have a direct impact on shelf life, distribution costs, and business performance (Madhu, 2025). Public investment in cold-chain infrastructure and innovative packaging, such as MAP, is a good example of responsible, climate-sensitive financing. Such financial assistance helps build food system resilience. This chapter examines Modified Atmosphere Packaging as an intersection of food technology, business strategy, consumer health, and sustainability.

Rising consumer demand for fresh, minimally processed, and sustainably produced food has intensified pressure on the food system. MAP emerges as a technological response to this demand. The adoption of MAP, in turn, generates measurable business and sustainability benefits, including reduced food waste, improved logistics efficiency, and increased economic value. The infographic in Figure 1 explains how MAP leads the freshness revolution and how it will transform the food industry.

Figure 1. MAP and Freshness Revolution

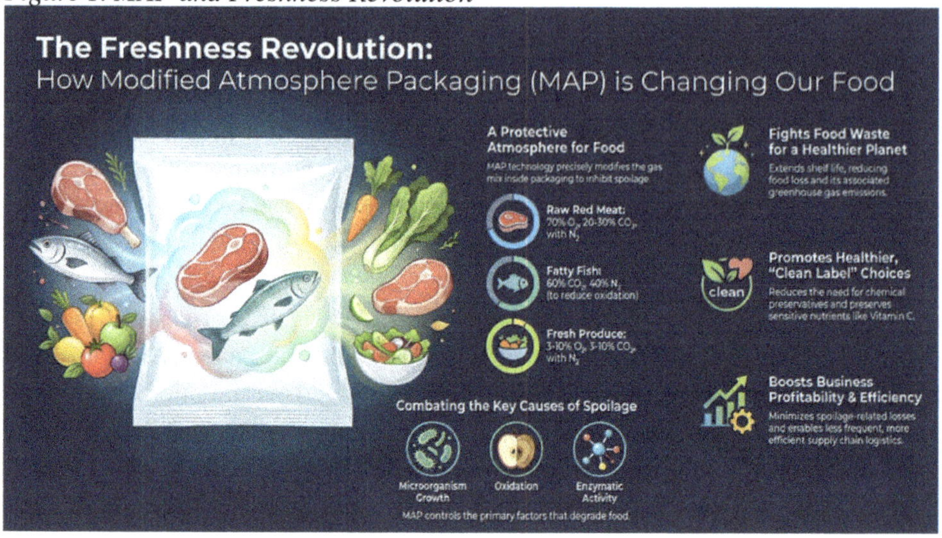

1.2. Chapter Roadmap

The chapter presents a scholarly attempt to synthesize recent literature, assessing how MAP influences food preservation outcomes, consumer behavior, and business performance within sustainability-oriented food systems. Section 1 gives an "Introduction" to food management and food packaging. Section 2 conceptualizes Modified Atmosphere Packaging (MAP) and outlines its core principles. Section 3 explains the technical function of MAP gases in food preservation. Section 4 explains the relationship between MAP and sustainability. Section 5 discusses the challenges encountered in MAP adoption. Section 6 identifies emerging future research in this field. Section 7 synthesizes the key insights and concludes the chapter. Figure 2 visually illustrates the roadmap followed in this chapter to help readers understand easily.

Figure 2.

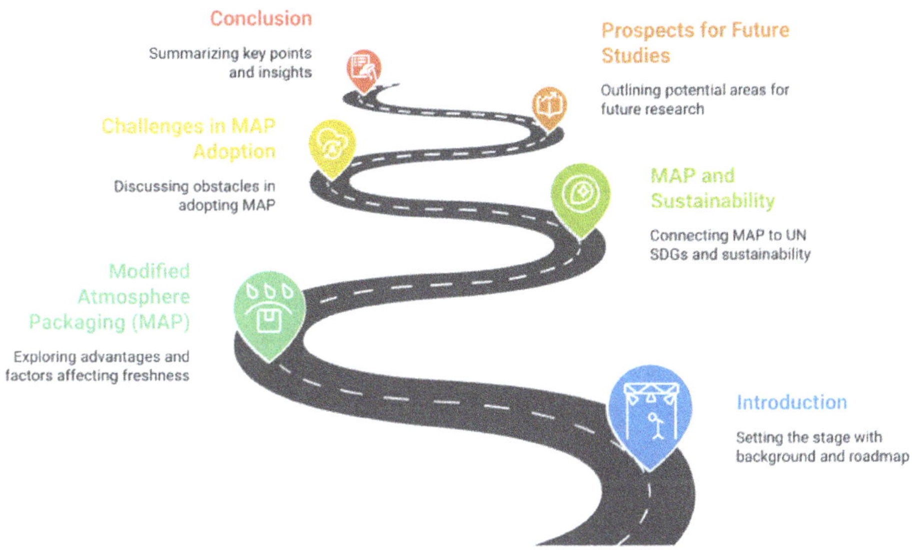

1.3. Research Question

Thus, given the importance attached to the study, this work aims to address the research question:

In what ways does MAP support healthier consumer choices and reduce food system losses while enabling economic benefits for businesses?

Accordingly, this chapter addresses the following sub-questions:

i. How does Modified Atmosphere Packaging (MAP) influence food preservation outcomes from a technical perspective?
ii. What evidence exists on the effects of MAP on consumer behavior and product perception?
iii. How does MAP adoption affect business performance and operational efficiency in food supply chains?
iv. What sustainability outcomes and trade-offs are associated with MAP across environmental and economic dimensions?

Having outlined the conceptual importance of MAP, the following section explains its technical foundations.

2. MODIFIED ATMOSPHERE PACKAGING (MAP)

Food is essential for maintaining life. It is an essential part of our society, culture, and behavior. Food cannot be produced quickly on demand; thus, it must be prepared and stored for later consumption. Food producers also have to pack it properly for storage or transportation. There is more to food packaging than just a container. It is an all-inclusive marketing, distribution, information, and security system (Tsironi, 2026). It is indispensable for food safety, quality, and accessibility in today's market. Acknowledging the significance of food packaging, the packaging sector has consistently investigated prospects, working to overcome obstacles and criticism in order to create and assess solutions (Lunetta & Cacciotti, 2024). Plastics have a long history and are closely related to food packaging (Olatunji, 2024). However, over time, customers have increasingly chosen healthier foods as they have become more health-conscious. A new field of study, known as "Lifestyles of Health and Sustainability" (LOHS), has emerged in response to the widespread consumer movement regarding attitudes and behaviors related to health and sustainability (Bharti & Agarwal, 2026).

2.1. Advantages of using MAP

Modified Atmosphere Packaging (MAP) brings in several benefits. Compared to other traditional storage techniques, MAP keeps food fresher for a longer period. When food has a longer shelf life, there is less pressure on farmers to produce more quickly, harvest early, or overproduce. By adjusting for spoilage and waste, producers can produce adequately, which in turn lowers resource consumption. Maintaining linkages within agriculture and food systems is economically significant.

Furthermore, because perishable commodities such as food are not delivered as frequently, it also reduces the demand for transportation. Ultimately, this will reduce expenses related to resource use and carbon emissions. Thus, there are certain corporate and economic advantages to utilizing technology. Preservatives are no longer necessary due to the use of MAP. It is made possible by altering the atmosphere inside the packaging to prevent microbial growth and oxidation. MAP preserves the stability and rigidity of the product. Therefore, it avoids condensation, textural changes, and structural damage caused by spoiling. The less expensive or thinner outside packaging materials help in this without sacrificing the product's protection. With this, retail stores do not have to do so many replenishments because the goods can stay on shelves for longer. This results in fewer product returns and reduced spoilage. MAP treatment helps reduce the weight of food. It reduces microbial proliferation by minimizing water loss and delaying cell wall breakdown (Tekin et al., 2025). MAP systems inhibit lignification and enhance antioxidant capacity (Y.

Li et al., 2025). Emerging research continues to explore synergistic approaches that pair MAP with other non-thermal technologies. Some studies examined the effect of ozone pre-treatment (10 ppm for 10 minutes) and Equilibrium-Modified Atmosphere Packaging (EMAP) (Aşık et al., 2025). The combination is checked on fresh aronia berries for 120 days of cold storage at 4°C. This approach extends the shelf life of fresh aronia berries. It reduced spoilage and led to weight loss. It delayed softening and senescence. It helped preserve valuable nutraceutical compounds (anthocyanins, phenolics) and antioxidant activity. From a sustainability perspective, technology is eco-friendly, non-thermal, and residue-free. Therefore, it may align easily with the increasing consumer demand for natural and minimally processed foods.

Certain foods (especially fruits) cannot be grown in specific geographical areas or under certain climatic conditions. Increasing temperatures and climate change are prohibiting farmers from growing certain types of food. Even when grown, the yield is proving to be of poor quality, and the cost of production and distribution is increasing (Saleem et al., 2025). Therefore, it is becoming increasingly inevitable to use transportation to import food. As a packaging technology, MAP eases food packaging and transportation, providing worldwide food availability without geographical boundaries. It can make food grown in remote areas available in urban regions. Similarly, it can bridge seasonal gaps related to food items. So, MAP influences culinary tourism and indirectly supports local tourism and hospitality markets. Increased food availability will change the dynamics of food costs and consumer preferences. MAP is a tool to support food access even during crises (natural disasters/conflicts). So, it plays a vital role in supply chain resilience. Such resilience is essential for viable agri-ventures at a time of geopolitical unrest and climate shocks. MAP's contribution to reducing food loss can directly support SDG 2 (Zero hunger). However, this is possible only if accompanied by governance mechanisms that prevent elite capture and ensure the inclusion of smallholders.

While MAP has the potential to reduce food waste and improve supply-chain efficiency, its sustainability outcomes are not universally positive. Increased shelf life may contribute to rebound effects. It can lead to higher consumption levels or longer distribution distances. These would offset environmental gains. Additionally, a high barrier of multi-layer materials will be present. They are often difficult to recycle. So, it can undermine circular economy objectives because the recovery and recycling infrastructure is limited. These trade-offs suggest that the sustainability performance of MAP depends strongly on material choice, product category, and supply-chain context. Established assessment frameworks, such as life cycle assessment, the planetary boundaries concept, and circular economy principles, confirm this. Despite progress, the net environmental impact of MAP is context-specific.

MAP is advantageous even in countries with ample or excess food production. Fruits and vegetables are almost always required to be processed before human consumption happens, at least for a brief period. Food distributors may be able to expand their export markets due to the cost-benefit advantages and reduced losses. Therefore, it contributes to economic development and growth. MAP slows oxidation and enzymatic processes, resulting in delayed ripening and the preservation of flavor and nutrition (Hayat et al., 2023). Thus, MAP acts as a food technology innovation. As a result, it provides an engaging case study that examines the adoption and adaptation of new food-tech solutions by agripreneurs. It maintains stem quality, suppresses the increase in lignin content and deposition, and restrains the accumulation of reactive oxygen species (X. Chen et al., 2024). MAP can help preserve nutrients, thereby leading to a health-driven business advantage. The convergence of profit, sustainability, and health represents the triple-bottom-line philosophy of contemporary agribusiness.

MAP controls microbial growth and inhibits the growth of pathogens. It regulates biological activity and controls chemical changes, thereby improving food safety (Alegbeleye & Rhee, 2024; Yadav et al., 2025). It is common practice for food such as meat and fish to be processed before consumption. A MAP mixture of 80% O_2 and 20% CO_2 reduces *Campylobacter* bacterial growth in broiler meat after skinning and chilling. Doing this reduces the risk of consumption of meat (Calvo-Fernandez et al., 2024). Studies have confirmed that higher CO2 levels (specifically, 60%) independently reduce the maximum growth rate (μmax) of *Listeria monocytogenes*. Decreasing the temperature from 7°C to 4°C consistently reduced μ max (Oguz et al., 2025). Similarly, the consumption risk of fish is determined by evaluating various microbial parameters (such as the number of bacteria and the presence of specific bacteria) (Don et al., 2025) and biochemical parameters (Lekshmi et al., 2025). Popular gas compositions for lean fish are 40% CO_2, 30% N_2, 30% O_2, and 60% CO_2, 40% N_2 (to reduce oxidation risk) for fatty fish. MAP often enhances the visual appeal of food by maintaining product freshness, firmness, and color without making substantial changes to the food's nutrition or safety, making it an innovative food technology (Carrión-Antolí et al., 2024).

While the technical mechanisms of MAP (e.g., gas modulation to suppress spoilage) are well established, their business value emerges only when integrated into operational workflows. For retailers, this means aligning MAP adoption with inventory turnover targets, cold-chain reliability, and shelf-space economics. For exporters, this involves compliance with destination-market packaging regulations and adherence to traceability standards. Thus, MAP's return on investment is not just a function of shelf-life extension. It involves more than just supply chain coordination, regulatory literacy, and consumer-facing branding—all core dimensions of a sustainable business strategy.

2.2 Consumer Psychology & Health Behavior

Consumer psychology and health behavior are undergoing significant changes. People now prefer food packaging that is safe for food, people, and the planet. MAP promises to maintain the quality of food without significant degradation over time, be appealing, and allow people to make healthy food choices. It provides an improved visual appeal for the packed products. Because preservation occurs naturally, MAP eliminates the need for artificial chemical additives and preservatives. Food can therefore remain fresh for longer because of MAP. From a market standpoint, this implies that MAP is a packaging technology and a primary enabler of the high-end "clean label" consumer trend. Clean-label alternatives for food packaging have emerged as a significant trend in response to growing consumer awareness (Chauhan & Rao, 2024). These changes enhance public health by attracting customers who prefer products with fewer or no preservatives. Customers can make wise decisions. Businesses will be able to comply with regulations simultaneously. As a result, it is a crucial phase in green marketing and brand reputation management.

MAP lowers waste and improves post-harvest quality (Tekin et al., 2025). They add days or even weeks to the shelf life of products. According to specific research, the quality of highly perishable fresh produce can be considerably preserved even with partial vacuum packaging (Suriwong et al., 2025). MAP preserves the authenticity and cultural legacy of traditional niche cuisines while making them accessible for export. Thus, it contributes to the preservation of culinary history. Besides, it supplies food to high-end organic and sustainable food markets. It is a powerful quality differentiator since it encourages lifestyle nutrition trends. Studies on consumer perception show that consumers are typically prepared to pay a small premium for superior cuisine.

Food can be packaged in smaller sizes due to MAP, allowing for the packaging of both whole fruit and chopped pieces. As a result, it will be perfect for encouraging children to eat healthily. Fruit vendors can pack the fruits in small portions for school-going children to carry easily and enjoy during recess. It turns out to be a healthier choice compared to conventional packaged potato chips. It is also an effective marketing tactic. Advertisements of such food products will not be considered as unhealthy or discretionary (junk) food advertising. Therefore, there will be no objection or backlash from government sources when the advertisement is made public (Coro et al., 2025). Educational institutions can promote MAP as a public health effort. Thus, it is an efficient tool that can alter the preferences of young consumers. MAP preserves food nutrients by mitigating deterioration caused by both biotic (living organisms, such as insects) and abiotic (non-living factors, such as moisture) factors. Food's natural freshness is preserved while retaining its original flavor, texture, and appearance. As a result, the authentic flavors of the food are kept to the greatest extent feasible.

Generally, the anthocyanin and vitamin C content deteriorate quickly, even in regular air. MAP is a preservation technique that effectively protects delicate nutrients, such as anthocyanins and vitamin C (Pandey et al., 2025). Farmers can receive improved benefits when they are provided with marketing strategies, packaging designs, and superior product processing education (Wulandari et al., 2024). Incubators and agripreneurship training programs can be organized. Such events can promote integrated capacity-building and innovation at the farm level.

2.3 Factors Affecting Food Freshness

Food is organic by nature. In general, it cannot be kept fresh for very long. The most often used preservation technique to delay spoiling is refrigeration. By reducing enzymatic activity, chemical reactions, and microbiological growth, it contributes to the preservation of food safety and quality (Çalışkan Koç et al., 2025). Food deterioration cannot be prevented entirely, even with the finest refrigeration. Energy efficiency, temperature consistency, and reducing nutrient and sensory losses during refrigerated storage are the main topics of emerging refrigeration research (Akinsemolu & Onyeaka, 2024). Figure 3 summarizes various factors that affect food freshness and lead to spoilage.

Figure 3. Factors affecting freshness and leading to spoilage

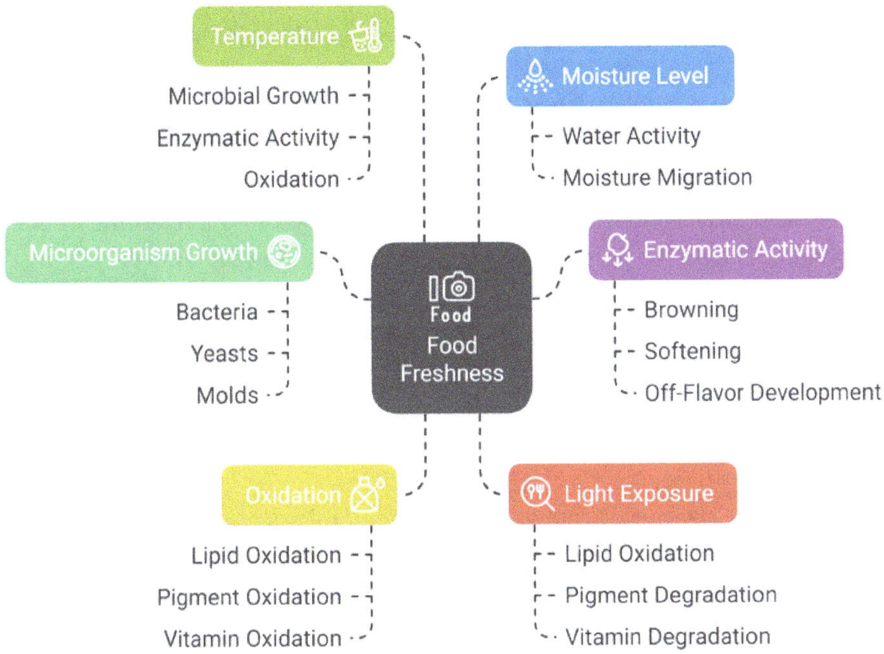

Microorganism Growth: Microorganism growth is a leading cause of food spoilage issues. They promote foodborne diseases and pose health risks and economic burdens. These may be characterized in two ways:

1. Pathogenic organisms, which are associated with foodborne illnesses, or
2. Spoilage microorganisms, including yeasts, molds, and certain bacteria.

Some microorganisms target specific foods. For example, *Pseudomonas, Serratia, Carnobacterium, and Lactococcus* are more common bacteria in chilled chicken (X. Li et al., 2026). Several new trends and technologies for microbial detection are emerging. The list includes molecular techniques and rapid diagnostic tools (Akinsemolu & Onyeaka, 2024). Refrigeration helps to control the growth of these microorganisms. Most organizations thrive at warmer temperatures, for example, between 60 and 90 degrees, but do not grow well at lower temperatures, such as below 40 degrees. Refrigeration is a core component of the cold chain. Pickling or salt curing is a popular and traditional method to constrain the growth of microorganisms. Advancing pickling techniques to enhance the bioactive compounds and probiotic content in pickled vegetables and other foods has emerged (Ahmada Kh et al., 2025). MAP with refrigeration significantly extends the shelf life of minimally processed vegetables by reducing metabolic rates and dehydration (García-Castaño et al., 2025).

Berry mueslis packaged with MAP are studied for the stability of phenolic compounds, specifically anthocyanins, during storage. The packaging used was a stand-up pouch with a very low oxygen and water vapor transmission rate. Each package also contained an iron-based oxygen absorber. MAP showed a retarding effect on anthocyanin degradation at room temperature (23°C). However, the packaging did not protect anthocyanins from rapid degradation at an elevated temperature (40°C). This means that MAP can help preserve products like muesli at typical room temperatures. However, it is not a sufficient solution for protection against degradation in high-temperature environments (Zhou et al., 2025). Studies reaffirmed that MAP can be used in combination with conventional plastic packaging to achieve a long shelf life, especially for dry foods (Lopriore, 2025).

Presence of Enzymes: Proteins make up the biological compounds known as enzymes. Almost all metabolic reactions that occur within cells are significantly accelerated by them. Food naturally contains enzymes. These substances facilitate the ripening of fruit and vegetables. They are responsible for the banana turning from yellow to brown. Polyphenol oxidase (PPO) is an enzyme that causes enzymatic browning in fruits such as avocados. Researchers have begun focusing on the PPO activity to disrupt it using physical methods, aiming to enhance product shelf life (Jiménez-Trigo et al., 2025).

In addition to changes in fruit color, the texture changes due to enzyme activity. Enzymes like catalase and peroxidase cause cut or sliced vegetables to darken. Blanching (also known as heat treatment) slows down this enzymatic activity, helping to reduce spoilage. Several other physical methods are available to minimize enzymatic browning (Jiménez-Trigo et al., 2025):

1. **Pasteurization**: A heat treatment that inactivates enzymes
2. **High hydrostatic pressure (HHP) treatment**: Applies high pressure to inactivate enzymes
3. **Lyophilization**: Freeze-drying that preserves the product without heat
4. **Radiation**: Uses ionizing radiation to inactivate enzymes
5. **Electromagnetic or mechanical wave applications**: Uses waves to disrupt enzyme activity

Oxidation: Atmospheric air is a complex mixture of several gases. Nitrogen (78%) and oxygen (21%) are the primary gases. Oxygen speeds up food spoilage by promoting the growth of microorganisms, such as aerobic bacteria, and facilitating oxidation. Oxidation is the main reason for quality loss in foods that contain fats. MAP can prevent lipid oxidation (Mora et al., 2025). Lipids' oxidation produces short-chain carbon compounds with intense flavors and odors. It results in the food having an unwanted flavor and texture. The most effective methods for postponing lipid oxidation include using oxygen scavengers and storing goods at room temperature. Similarly, Nitrogen flushing, a type of MAP, has been shown to increase the shelf life by improving the stability of volatile compounds (Mora et al., 2025). Packaging that keeps vapor out helps reduce the oxidation process. Apart from these factors, moisture levels, light, and temperature play a considerable role.

2.4 Role of Gases in MAP

The MAP process involves adjusting the gas proportions in the food packaging atmosphere (Shahbazi, 2024). Workers or packaging machines remove the existing air first. Then they fill the package with one or more helpful gases. Packaging systems remove unwanted gases and replace them with a controlled gas mix. They take out unpleasant or harmful gases and introduce a new gas or mixture to protect the food. Some popular gases used in MAP packaging include Nitrogen (N_2), Carbon dioxide (CO_2), and Oxygen (O_2). Some less popular gas choices used in some cases are Carbon Monoxide (CO), Nitrous Oxide (N_2O), Argon (Ar), Hydrogen (H_2), or Helium (He). Packaging experts choose the gas and its ratio based on the food's nature and properties. For example, they prefer CO_2 for meat and sausage products and use O_2 for fruits and vegetables. A suitable gas mixture allows businesses to offer fresher products at more competitive prices while maintaining their profit margins. Agripreneurs, or entrepreneurs in the agricultural sector, will be able to offer their customers a superior range of food products, thereby establishing a competitive edge.

MAP and Oxygen

Oxygen spoils food through oxidation and supports the growth of aerobic microorganisms. Therefore, MAP systems often remove oxygen. However, red meat is sometimes packaged with high oxygen to maintain its red color and prevent the growth of anaerobic microbes. Oxygen gas usually plays a significant role in MAP. Elevated oxygen levels increase oxymyoglobin and adversely affect muscle lipids' oxidative stability. It can lead to off-flavors and off-odors (Albano-Gaglio et al., 2025). Maintains natural color and inhibits anaerobic bacteria (especially in lean fish).

MAP is generally used to displace or minimize oxygen from food packaging when packing vegetables, fruits, or baked goods to prevent food spoilage caused by oxidation. Doing so inhibits the growth of aerobic organisms. Oxygen is an odourless and tasteless gas. Contrary to the initial statement ("displace oxygen in most cases"), oxygen is sometimes intentionally added to packaging, depending on the type of food. For example, it is commonly added to red meat. It is used during processing to maintain the beef's vibrant red color and prevent it from becoming pale. Using oxygen in this way also prevents the growth of anaerobic organisms. MAP80, which contains 80% oxygen and 20% carbon dioxide, is the most popular gas combination. The next best choice is MAP40, which uses a mixture of 40% oxygen, 20% carbon dioxide, and 40% nitrogen.

Low oxygen levels in the packaging atmosphere efficiently reduce or prevent mold growth on sliced products. However, mold can still develop at oxygen levels as low as 0.05%, especially if the water activity is high. So, such products require high-barrier, non-transparent packaging materials. Meat products are often contaminated by pathogens such as Listeria monocytogenes and Campylobacter. When MAP is used in packaging meat properly, it can help in maintaining food safety. This further connects with health economics, considering foodborne illness cases and associated healthcare costs.

MAP and Carbon dioxide

Carbon dioxide (CO_2) is colorless, odorless, and tasteless. It slows oxidation and inhibits the growth of most aerobic bacteria and molds. It is a widely used gas to extend the shelf life of food. Higher concentrations usually mean longer freshness. However, too much CO_2 can make foods taste sour. It can also leak from packaging or get absorbed by the food, causing the package to collapse. Support or filler gases can bring down the effect. While it helps prevent oxidation and aerobic spoilage, too much CO_2 can make food taste sour. CO_2 also diffuses through packaging films more easily than Argon or Nitrogen.

Additionally, food can absorb CO_2, causing the package to collapse—sometimes useful (e.g., for hard cheeses) but usually undesirable. Carbon dioxide gas can be used on items that can accommodate it, such as strawberries. Applying it resulted in significant weight loss reduction, increased anthocyanin content, and decreased decay and softening. Vitamin C content was maintained (Zantar et al., 2024). Active packaging using Menthol resulted in the highest inhibition of fungal activity on strawberries, extending shelf life by up to 25 days (Mahecha-Rubiano et al., 2024).

MAP and Nitrogen

Nitrogen (N_2) is inert and does not usually react with food components. It is odorless, tasteless, safe, and non-toxic. So, it does not alter the properties of food. It is readily available in high-purity food-grade form (≥99%). It displaces oxygen from packaging. This property helps prevent oxidation and inhibits the growth of aerobic microorganisms. Nitrogen also acts as a supporting or filling gas. It helps maintain package integrity. Due to its slow diffusion through plastic films, it remains in the package for a longer period. Nitrogen generators can easily produce food-grade nitrogen on demand. Nitrogen is commonly used for packaging snacks and nuts, while argon is used to preserve wine. Packaged food is evaluated on three quality attributes: chemical, microbial, and sensory (Charikleous et al., 2024). Milk powder, mainly used in baby food, is highly sensitive to spoilage. Shelf-life extension requires oxygen-free packaging using pure nitrogen with minimal residual oxygen.

MAP and Other Gases

Carbon Monoxide: Carbon monoxide (CO) is a colorless, odorless, and tasteless gas. Like oxygen, it is sometimes used in meat packaging to preserve the bright red color of myoglobin, which consumers associate with freshness and quality. Only very low concentrations of CO are needed to achieve this effect.

Argon: Argon (Ar) is an inert, colorless, odorless, and tasteless gas. Because its physical properties are similar to those of nitrogen, it can be a substitute in many food packaging applications. Some studies suggest that argon may inhibit certain enzyme activities and slow down metabolic reactions in specific vegetables, potentially extending freshness. However, its effects are often only marginally better than those of nitrogen, and because argon is significantly more expensive, its use in food packaging remains limited and relatively uncommon.

Other Gas Mixtures: In addition to individual gases, certain food items require a specific composition of gas mixtures in a desired proportion to achieve the desired preservation goal. For example, raw red meat can be best preserved by a gas mixture comprising 70% Oxygen, 20-30% Carbon dioxide, and nitrogen. Similarly, fresh fruits and vegetables can be best preserved in an atmosphere comprising 3 to 10% oxygen, 3 to 10% Carbon dioxide, and nitrogen filling the rest. There are several gas mixing techniques. Gas flushing, compensated vacuum, and special "breathable" films that withstand the gases are some popular techniques. These techniques ensure that adequate pressure changes the atmosphere inside the food package, allowing it to be filled with the desired gas. Factors influencing the gas composition inside the MAP package are temperature, product fill weight, respiration rate, oxygen and carbon dioxide transmission rates of the packaging film, and the surface area for respiration (Tripathi et al., 2024).

3. MAP AND SUSTAINABILITY

Farmers and agricultural producers are implementing sustainable agriculture and food management techniques as a progressive way towards the United Nations' Sustainable Development Goals (SDGs), particularly Goal 2: Zero Hunger (Hiywotu, 2025). While MAP offers clear advantages for perishable food, its effectiveness depends heavily on the choice of packaging material. Traditional MAP uses plastic films, such as those used in food packaging, made of polyethylene and polypropylene. They are multi-layered and are challenging to recycle. MAP uses recycled materials, biodegradable/compostable films, and mono-material films, which are sustainable alternatives. A recent study compared conventional and eco-friendly packaging systems for sliced cooked ham and mortadella stored under refrigeration (Leni et al., 2025). They found that a mono-material alternative (PET/R-PET/PET tray with BOPET lid) performed nearly as well as the conventional high-barrier system in controlling microbial growth. However, color stability and lipid oxidation were more sensitive to light exposure. Some sustainable materials offered poorer protection. Research shows that manufacturers must carefully customize recyclable or bio-based packaging to meet product-specific needs so they do not compromise quality.

3.1 Connection To UN SDGs

MAP may align closely with several of the UN Sustainable Development Goals (SDGs). However, the alignment between MAP practices and the UN SDGs should be interpreted as context-dependent rather than absolute. The contributions outlined in Table 1 assume the use of appropriate materials, effective waste management systems, and responsible supply chain implementation. In the absence of these conditions, specific MAP applications may generate environmental trade-offs that weaken their contribution to sustainability objectives. Table 1 lists the SDGs and how MAP is aligning with them.

Table 1. Connection between MAP and various UN SDGs

UN SDG	The relation of MAP with the UN SDG
SDG 2 (Zero Hunger)	Extends the shelf life of perishable foods, reducing post-harvest losses and improving food availability in regions with supply chain inefficiencies.
SDG 3 (Good Health and Well-Being)	Reduces microbial spoilage and foodborne illnesses by inhibiting the growth of pathogens, ensuring safer food for consumers.
SDG 8 (Decent Work & Economic Growth)	MAP stabilizes markets for perishable goods. It supports agri-businesses and retailers by reducing spoilage-related losses.

continued on following page

Table 1. Continued

UN SDG	The relation of MAP with the UN SDG
SDG 9 (Industry, Innovation, Infrastructure)	Advances in food-tech innovation (e.g., innovative packaging, gas-mixing systems) are being made to modernize food supply chains. Therefore, MAP catalyzes industrial modernization.
SDG 12 (Responsible Consumption & Production)	Minimizes food waste by preserving freshness longer, aligning with circular economy principles. Biodegradable packaging materials are also explored.
SDG 13 (Climate Action)	Brings down greenhouse gas emissions by reducing food waste (a significant methane source) and optimizing cold chain logistics.

3.2 Sustainability Assessment

MAP can offer sustainability benefits compared to specific traditional packaging methods. However, these benefits are not inherent. They may arise only under specific technological, logistical, and contextual conditions. A comprehensive sustainability assessment is to be conducted to evaluate the overall environmental impact of MAP. Figure 4 highlights three commonly cited environmental benefits associated with MAP.

1. Reduced food waste through shelf-life extension
2. Improved logistics efficiency due to fewer replenishment cycles, and
3. Potential reductions in resource use across the food supply chain.

Reduced food waste is often the dominant contributor to environmental gains, particularly for highly perishable products. Logistics-related benefits arise when a longer shelf life enables consolidated transportation and lower frequency of distribution. However, these benefits are contingent on energy-efficient cold chains and appropriate market distances. Owing to its importance, assessing the environmental implications of MAP requires the use of established sustainability assessment frameworks. Life Cycle Assessment (LCA) is particularly relevant. It is used to evaluate trade-offs between reduced food waste and increased material or energy inputs across the packaging life cycle. LCA studies consistently indicate that the environmental burden of additional packaging materials used in MAP can be outweighed. This occurred by minimizing food losses, particularly for resource-intensive foods such as meat, dairy, and fresh produce. In such cases, reductions in upstream emissions related to the production, processing, and disposal of wasted food exceed the incremental impacts of packaging materials. Conversely, for low-impact foods or those in short supply chains, packaging-related emissions may be the dominant factor. It results in marginal or negative net benefits. Further, Circular economy principles highlight the importance of recyclability, material simplification, and post-consumer recovery. MAP-related decisions may influence resource use, emissions, and waste generation from a planetary boundaries perspective. It reminds managers in the food industry of the need for system-level evaluation rather than isolated performance metrics.

Figure 4. Achieving Environmental Benefits with MAP

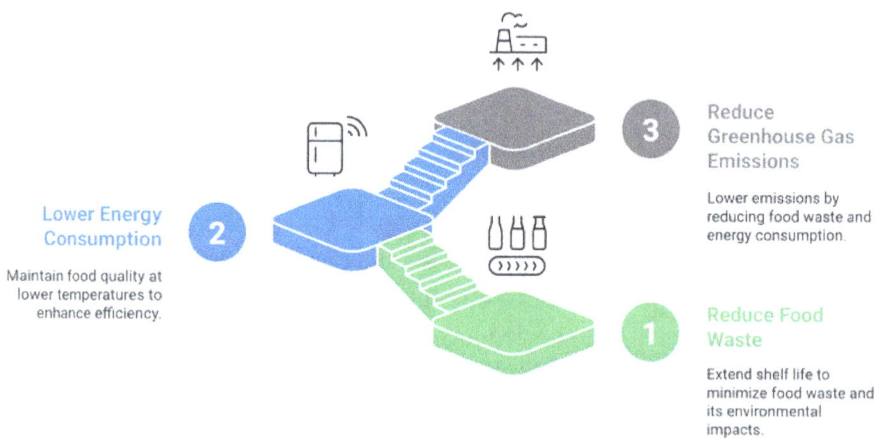

Consequently, the net environmental impact of MAP cannot be generalized. It must be evaluated on a case-by-case basis. As part of the process, one must consider the product type, packaging design, distribution scale, and end-of-life management systems.

4. CHALLENGES IN MAP ADOPTION

Attention is given to critical techno-economic and infrastructural hurdles that complicate the mass-scale adoption of MAP technology. Despite its clear advantages, the widespread implementation of MAP is being constrained by a range of technical, cost, and regulatory barriers. This section explains the real-world obstacles that are encountered in its adoption.

4.1 Techno-Economic and Infrastructure Barriers

MAP is a promising technology, and its mass-scale implementation can bring numerous advantages. However, it involves overcoming several challenges. MAP requires specific facilities for packaging. The necessary technology needs to be incorporated. For its use at an industrial grade level, technical support and the necessary operational knowledge are necessary. Some countries, such as India and Israel, have reported improved crop yields aided by agricultural technologies and cattle-rearing methods. Therefore, there may be a reduced need for food preservation for certain crop varieties. Economic feasibility and the absence of region-specific agronomic models would further limit adoption (Mondol et al., 2025). While high-income markets face pressure to address plastic waste and transparency in labeling, low-income regions face pressure from infrastructure gaps and cost barriers. Therefore, there are context-sensitive MAP deployment strategies.

MAP projects require substantial capital investment and recurring operational costs. Small- and medium-sized enterprises (SMEs) and those in developing economies view this as a significant barrier to widespread adoption (Fitzsimmons et al., 2024). Initial CAPEX typically includes the purchase of various equipment. MAP requires gas-mixing and flushing equipment, vacuum packaging machines, gas analyzers for quality control, and potentially modifications to existing production lines. Depending on scale and automation level, upfront investment can range from \$20,000 to over \$200,000 USD for industrial-grade systems.

There are OPEX-related considerations to be taken into account. It includes ongoing costs of food-grade gases, specialized high-barrier packaging films, maintenance of sealing and gas-monitoring equipment, and staff training. It is worth acknowledging that for perishable produce handlers in low-infrastructure regions, even a minor recurring cost can be a significant barrier to entry. Hence, subsidy or cooperative pooling models are to be used. These financial thresholds show why MAP remains unevenly adopted across global food systems. Perhaps public-private partnerships or a modular approach could be a solution. Low-cost MAP units are still emerging, and their viability for deployment is to be evaluated.

4.2 Environmental and Health Risks

Plastic-based MAP contributes to non-biodegradable waste (M. J et al., 2025). Despite growing interest in biodegradable and bio-based films for MAP, empirical data from real-world supply chains remain scarce. Most assessments rely on laboratory-scale studies that assume idealized end-of-life scenarios. These often fail to reflect actual recycling, composting, or disposal conditions. Many existing assessments depend on laboratory-scale studies. They assume end-of-life scenarios. The scenarios may not reflect actual recycling, composting, or disposal practices. In particular, the long-term performance, barrier reliability, and environmental trade-offs of bio-based MAP materials under commercial logistics conditions represent a significant research gap. More than large-sized plastics, the risks associated with microplastics, and more recently with nanoplastics, are greater (Da Costa & Corcoran, 2026). These plastics pollute the soil and enter plants, thereby contaminating the food. When such food is consumed, it enters the human body, blocks the vessels, and causes various diseases (Niebel et al., 2026). There is a risk that tiny plastic particles (microplastics) can move from plastic Packaging into the food inside. It can turn into a serious issue because it can impact human health.

4.3 Governance, Regulation, and Consumer Trust

MAP's environmental and health commitments may be compromised by governance shortcomings, such as the lax implementation of packaging regulations, underscoring the need for institutional reform. Such things also potentially violate food safety regulations. Since this can harm people and may soon be against the law, companies must quickly find safer packaging materials. Companies must adhere to ethical practices, prioritizing the safety and well-being of their employees over business considerations. Companies must demonstrate accountability and take a shared producer responsibility by protecting the environment and prioritizing their customers' interests. The usage of packaging materials free of plastic can be promoted by effective corporate social responsibility (CSR) practices (Misopoulos & Bajiraj, 2025). These findings suggest that MAP has potential relevance for discussions on food system planning and policy. They can implement performance-linked budgeting and participatory policies that are designed to fully achieve their promise.

Food is a highly profitable business and is a widely marketed commodity (Kanellos et al., 2024). However, it is also a highly regulated sector (Amirullah et al., 2024). Government circles closely inspect the processes involved in food management, and violation of ethics is considered serious (Bernardlauwers et al., 2024). It is mandatory that the food packaging makes as little contact as possible with the food and that the packaging itself does not release any harmful chemicals or induce adverse reactions (Lacourt et al., 2024). The use of specific gases, primarily carbon monoxide, to mask the odor of rotting meat raised safety and regulatory concerns (Carpenter et al., 2024). Even the most sophisticated MAP systems might not be able to improve public health without institutional capacity to control gas mixes, container safety, and labeling. As a result, the European Union (EU) and numerous other regions prohibited its use in MAP. CO enhances consumer appeal and aesthetic appeal while reducing perceived waste. However, it poses a concern to public health because it hides the symptoms of rotting food. Past regulatory actions show that consumer safety is more important than commercial aesthetics. Business benefits and public health concerns seem to be traded off. Naturally, safety concerns outweigh the appeal of keeping meat appearing fresher for longer. However, it is worth noting that regulatory frameworks vary from region to region (Amirullah et al., 2024), with significant differences particularly evident in the EU, the US, and Asia. Perhaps ozone treatment is a more suitable alternative (Giménez et al., 2024), and researchers are investigating this possibility. There is also a growing debate about whether "cultured meat" can transform our food system into one that is more sustainable (Hocquette et al., 2025). Similar emphasis is given on packaging regulations in the form of EU directives, Codex Alimentarius, and FDA guidelines.

5. PROSPECTS FOR FUTURE STUDIES

The literature synthesis reveals critical knowledge gaps that point toward promising avenues for future inquiry. Advancing MAP goes beyond its current technical and commercial limits. It will require innovation not only in materials science but also in digital integration and systemic governance. The following three research streams are identified as offering a fertile ground for interdisciplinary exploration.

5.1 Research Stream 1: Advanced Materials and Barrier Innovations

Novel packaging materials: Further research is needed to enhance gas barrier properties, minimize environmental impact, and increase antibacterial activity. A similar focus is required to optimize gas mixtures based on the nature of the food being prepared. Conventional fish preservation techniques rely on low-tech, tried-and-true procedures that precede contemporary industrial packing processes. Aseptic, vacuum, modified atmosphere, and sous vide packaging techniques are all used in modern fish preservation. Recent developments in nanotechnology have extended the shelf life of fish meat by adding nanoparticle materials to packaging. (Topuz, 2025). In the case of fish, VOC production is associated with specific bacteria. For example, Shewanella frigidimarina → Dimethyl sulfide, Pseudoalteromonas elyakovii → Hydrogen sulfide and Methyl mercaptan, and Psychromonas arctica → Ethanol. The study found that MAP (exceptionally high O_2/CO_2 mixes) slows bacterial growth but does not entirely prevent spoilage. SIFT-MS is effective for real-time monitoring of spoilage in seafood packaging. Packaging materials, package dimensions, and headspace height (for airflow distribution) are essential factors (Nasser Eddine et al., 2024). More studies are required to use omics approaches. These methods can investigate the underlying mechanisms for MAP storage on a commercial scale. Moisture barriers to reduce defects like crystallization and oxidation will be explored (Arboix, 2025).

Active packaging technologies: Researchers must explore active packaging systems that release antimicrobial compounds or absorb ethylene to extend the shelf life of products (Lunetta & Cacciotti, 2024). Ethylene is a natural plant hormone that regulates fruit ripening and aging processes (Cheng et al., 2024). Future studies must focus on spoilage microbes that can still produce volatile organic compounds (VOCs) and unpleasant off-odours despite using MAP (L. Chen et al., 2024).

Gaps Addressed: Environmental trade-offs associated with plastics, performance limitations of bio-based films in real-world supply chains, and the need for recyclable, mono-material plastics.

Key Research Questions:

1. How do novel biopolymer composites or nanocomposites perform in terms of gas barrier reliability and mechanical strength under variable commercial logistics conditions (e.g., temperature fluctuations, handling)?
2. What are the life-cycle environmental and economic impacts of shifting from multi-layer plastics to designed-for-recycling mono-material MAP systems?

Suggested Methodologies: Commercial-scale field trials; accelerated shelf-life testing; comparative Life Cycle Assessment (LCA); techno-economic analysis.

Expected Contribution: To provide actionable data for material selection that balances sustainability goals with product-specific preservation requirements.

5.2 Research Stream 2: Intelligent Sensing and Digital Systems

Intelligent packaging systems: Artificial intelligence (AI) and sensors can help improve food production and distribution (Bustos-Terrones et al., 2026). Similarly, leaky MAP pillow bags are found using AI-based Deep Learning (DL) approaches (Guo et al., 2025). By functioning as barriers against bacteria, air, and moisture, advances in nanomaterials are improving food packaging and maintaining the nutritional value of food (Chaudhary et al., 2025). Food packaging is using nanosensors and nanocomposites to guarantee safety during storage and transportation. A new research discipline, Food Sustainability 4.0, has emerged, combining various technologies, including robotics and blockchain, to enhance food accessibility (Hassoun, 2025). MAP integrates well with the technology stack and connects well with the "technology in the food industry" topic. From production to retail, digital methods for monitoring MAP implementation can improve fiscal transparency and bolster accountability in the governance of the food system.

Gaps Addressed: Static nature of traditional MAP; lack of real-time spoilage detection; need for supply chain optimization.

Key Research Questions:

1. How can AI models integrating data from embedded nanosensors (for gases, VOCs) accurately predict remaining shelf-life and detect package integrity failures in real-time?
2. What is the business case and operational framework for integrating smart MAP data with blockchain platforms to enhance traceability and fiscal transparency in agri-food supply chains?

Suggested Methodologies: Development and validation of AI/Deep Learning models; pilot deployments in commercial supply chains; system architecture design studies.

Expected Contribution: To transition MAP from a passive preservation method to an active, intelligent node in data-driven supply chains, reducing loss and building consumer trust.

5.3 Research Stream 3: System-Level Integration and Governance

Other MAP innovations and aspects beyond MAP: MAP has undergone significant growth over the years. Several other packaging innovations also grew in parallel. These include selectively permeable membranes, nanomaterials, ethylene absorbers, and biosensors for more precise and adaptive atmosphere control. More work is required in these areas (Oyewole et al., 2025). While the present study explores innovations and challenges in MAP for enhancing food security and shelf-life, some studies specifically investigate the impact of retail display environments (including packaging schemes and case types) (Stephanie, 2025). The results indicate that the type of muscle and packaging method have a significant influence on the quality and shelf life of beef. Although it may slightly alter color stability due to temperature and airflow control, the style of retail display case has a minimal effect on palatability or spoilage. Effective policy should not only incentivize adoption but also align with business metrics. For instance, this can be achieved by linking tax rebates or green procurement preferences to verified reductions in food loss through digital MAP monitoring or the use of recyclable mono-materials.

Gaps Addressed: Context-sensitive deployment; regulatory fragmentation; integration with new agricultural paradigms.

Key Research Questions:

1. How do the benefits and trade-offs of MAP differ when applied to emerging food systems, such as those involving cultured meat or hyper-local urban agriculture, and what new packaging paradigms are required?

2. What participatory policy models and performance-linked incentives can most effectively encourage the adoption of sustainable MAP technologies among smallholder farmers and SMEs in developing economies?

Suggested Methodologies: Cross-country comparative policy analysis; stakeholder engagement and participatory action research; scenario modeling.

Expected Contribution: To develop frameworks for the responsible and equitable governance of MAP technology, ensuring its contribution to resilient and inclusive food systems.

Finally, several limitations and potential areas for further study exist on the topic. The current work followed a narrative review; however, future researchers may consider conducting systematic reviews or meta-analyses to further deepen the foundation. Additionally, future studies can critically compare MAP against vacuum packaging, edible coatings, or irradiation to explore these alternatives.

6. CONCLUSION

This chapter examined how Modified Atmosphere Packaging (MAP) supports healthier consumer choices, reduces food system losses, and enables economic benefits for businesses. The concepts are central to contemporary food sustainability challenges. The work synthesized interdisciplinary evidence from food science, business strategy, and environmental policy. It has been demonstrated that MAP functions not only as a technical tool but also as a strategic enabler across the food value chain. MAP extends shelf life, enhances visual and sensory appeal, and preserves nutritional integrity. So, it offers healthier food choices without compromising quality. It reduces post-harvest losses by 10–15% in key commodity chains. It supports export markets and contributes to SDG 2 and SDG 12. Critically, the success of MAP depends on the context. The benefits are most visible where cold-chain infrastructure, suitable packaging materials, and regulatory oversight are in place. Conversely, in low-resource settings, techno-economic barriers and weak governance can limit adoption or exacerbate inequalities.

Nevertheless, this review acknowledges key limitations. As a conceptual and narrative synthesis, it does not provide original empirical validation across diverse geographic or product contexts. Moreover, the sustainability gains of MAP are not automatic. They depend on material choices (e.g., recyclable mono-materials vs. multi-layer plastics), supply chain length, and end-of-life management. Rebound effects—such as extended distribution distances or increased consumption—may offset environmental benefits in some cases.

Looking ahead, the most pressing priorities include: (1) developing context-sensitive MAP deployment models for smallholders and emerging economies, (2) advancing circular packaging systems that balance barrier performance with recyclability, and (3) strengthening governance frameworks that ensure gas safety, labeling transparency, and consumer trust. In particular, focus should be on controversial practices, such as the use of carbon monoxide. When MAP is integrated responsibly with cold-chain infrastructure, investments, and inclusive policies, MAP can indeed serve as a public good. It can turn into a scalable innovation that supports the food system, aligns business performance with sustainable practices, and supports both economic and nutritional security.

Disclosure: The authors disclose the use of the Grammarly tool to correct spelling and typography, thereby improving readability. However, the authors take full responsibility for the content in this work.

REFERENCES

Ahmada Kh, A., & Abdo, A.A, A., Khan, S., Aleryani, H., Mi, S., & Wang, X. (2025). Advancing Pickling Techniques to Enhance Bioactive Compounds and Probiotic Content in Pickled Vegetables. *Food Reviews International*, •••, 1–27. DOI: 10.1080/87559129.2025.2473009

Akinsemolu, A. A., & Onyeaka, H. N. (2024). Microorganisms Associated with Food Spoilage and Foodborne Diseases. In Ogwu, M. C., Izah, S. C., & Ntuli, N. R. (Eds.), *Food Safety and Quality in the Global South* (pp. 489–531). Springer Nature Singapore., DOI: 10.1007/978-981-97-2428-4_16

Albano-Gaglio, M., Esquerre, C. A., O'Donnell, C. P., Muñoz, I., ElMasry, G., Font-i-Furnols, M., Tejeda, J. F., Brun, A., Lloret, E., & Marcos, B. (2025). Calibration of visible and near-infrared spectral imaging technology to predict the quality evolution of retail fresh pork bellies with different fat content. *Food Research International*, *199*, 115350. DOI: 10.1016/j.foodres.2024.115350 PMID: 39658154

Alegbeleye, O., & Rhee, M. S. (2024). Growth of Listeria monocytogenes> in fresh vegetables and vegetable salad products: An update on influencing intrinsic and extrinsic factors. *Comprehensive Reviews in Food Science and Food Safety*, *23*(5), e13423. DOI: 10.1111/1541-4337.13423 PMID: 39169547

Amirullah, N. A., Samsudin, M. H., Norrrahim, M. N. F., Ilyas, R. A., Nurazzi, N. M., Jenol, M. A., Hawanis, H. S. N., & Gunny, A. A. N. (2024). Regulations for food packaging materials. *Physical Sciences Reviews*, *9*(8), 2711–2735. DOI: 10.1515/psr-2022-0033

Arboix, J. A. (2025). *Sensory Defects in Fermented Sausages* (p. 59) [2025 Update]. Frigomeccanica S.p.A. https://eurocarne.com/daal/a1/informes/a2/Sensory_Defects_in_Fermented_Sausages_2025_LR.pdf

Aşık, İ., Caner, C., Yüceer, M., & Pala, Ç. U. (2025). Ozone Pre-treatment and Equilibrium-Modified Atmosphere Packaging as Elicitors to Enhance Shelf Stability and Nutraceutical Retention in Fresh Aronia (Aronia melanocarpa cv. Nero) Berries. *Food and Bioprocess Technology*, *18*(12), 10636–10654. Advance online publication. DOI: 10.1007/s11947-025-04049-4

Bernardlauwers, B., Islam, R., Muthoifin, M., & Husna Srifyan, J. (2024). Islamic Business Ethics and Political Economy: A Study of Government Policies in Handling the Food Crisis. *Demak Universal Journal of Islam and Sharia*, *2*(02), 91–110. DOI: 10.61455/deujis.v2i02.107

Bharti, K., & Agarwal, R. (2026). Consumers adoption of healthy lifestyle: Understanding the influence of upcycling drivers on LOHAS consumer behavior. *Journal of Financial Services Marketing*, *31*(1), 5. DOI: 10.1057/s41264-025-00330-x

Bustos-Terrones, Y. A., Tariq, R., Rangel-Peraza, J. G., Torróntegui-Chávez, G., & Loaiza, J. G. (2026). Sustaining global food security through digitalization. In *Climate Change Impacts on the Water-Energy-Food Nexus* (pp. 289–302). Elsevier., DOI: 10.1016/B978-0-443-22320-4.00013-X

Çalışkan Koç, G., Özkan Karabacak, A., Süfer, Ö., Adal, S., Çelebi, Y., Delikanlı Kıyak, B., & Öztekin, S. (2025). Thawing frozen foods: A comparative review of traditional and innovative methods. *Comprehensive Reviews in Food Science and Food Safety*, *24*(2), e70136. DOI: 10.1111/1541-4337.70136 PMID: 39970035

Calvo-Fernandez, C., Takeuchi-Storm, N., Nauta, M., Sandberg, M., & Lassen, B. (2024). Effect of Post-Chilling Processes and Modified Atmosphere Packing on Campylobacter in Broiler Meat. *Food Control*, *111087*. Advance online publication. DOI: 10.1016/j.foodcont.2024.111087

Carpenter, B. J., Dobbins, T. W., Hernandez, M. S., Barker, S. N., Loomas, K. R., Osburn, W. N., & Legako, J. F. (2024). Comparison of Gas Treatments of High Oxygen, Carbon Monoxide, and Nitric Oxide on Ground Beef Color in Modified Atmosphere Packaging. *Foods*, *13*(6), 902. DOI: 10.3390/foods13060902 PMID: 38540892

Carrión-Antolí, A., Zoffoli, J. P., Serrano, M., Valero, D., & Naranjo, P. (2024). Preharvest Gibberellic Acid Treatment Increases Both Modulus of Elasticity and Resistance in Sweet Cherry Fruit (cv. 'Bing' and 'Lapins') at Harvest and Postharvest During Storage at 0 °C. *Agronomy (Basel)*, *14*(11), 2738. DOI: 10.3390/agronomy14112738

Charikleous, M., Voutsas, P., & Stamatis, N. (2024). *Quality Assessment of a new Mullet Mugil cephalus (Linnaeus, 1758) processed product under Active Packaging Systems, at 2-4oC*. HydroMediT 2024, Mytilene, Lesvos, Greece. https://www.researchgate.net/profile/Nikolaos-Stamatis/publication/382888925

Chaudhary, S., Vishnoi, V., Chaudhary, S., Tyagi, N., & Consul, P. (2025). Nano-Enhanced and AI-Driven Integration for Food Security and Safety Through Scientific Advances: Systematic Approaches and Societal Implications. In Vaseashta, A., & Stamatin, I. (Eds.), (pp. 339–374). Advances in Computational Intelligence and Robotics. IGI Global Scientific Publishing., DOI: 10.4018/979-8-3373-2883-6.ch010

Chauhan, K., & Rao, A. (2024). Clean-label alternatives for food preservation: An emerging trend. *Heliyon, 10*(16), e35815. DOI: 10.1016/j.heliyon.2024.e35815 PMID: 39247286

Chen, L., Kuuliala, L., Walgraeve, C., Demeestere, K., & Devlieghere, F. (2024, November 12). *Understanding microbial spoilers in pork: Pseudomonas fragi and its spoilage potential under modified atmospheres.* 38th EFFoST International Conference 2024, Bruges, Belgium. https://biblio.ugent.be/publication/01JCWW4ANG79M5Z7GBEAA9XX62

Chen, X., Mou, Z., Zhao, Y., Su, X., Han, Y., Chen, H., Wei, W., Shan, W., Kuang, J., Lu, W., & Chen, J. (2024). Modified atmosphere packaging maintains stem quality of Chinese flowering cabbage by restraining post-harvest lignification and ROS accumulation. *Food Chemistry: X, 24*, 102006. DOI: 10.1016/j.fochx.2024.102006 PMID: 39655218

Cheng, J.-H., Chen, M., & Sun, D.-W. (2024). Ethylene Synergism Control Using Integrated Cold Plasma Technologies to Enhance Fruit and Vegetable Quality. *Food Engineering Reviews.* Advance online publication. DOI: 10.1007/s12393-024-09387-1

Coro, D. G., Schirmer, K., Van Rhoda, M., McQueen, B., & Morris, C. (2025). An environmental scan of food and drink advertising on public transport around Adelaide schools. *Health Promotion Journal of Australia*, *36*(1), e886. DOI: 10.1002/hpja.886 PMID: 38840470

Da Costa, J. P., & Corcoran, P. L. (2026). Micro(nano)plastics as soil pollutants. In *Soil Pollution* (pp. 221–240). Elsevier. DOI: 10.1016/B978-0-443-33329-3.00011-8

Don, S., Lekshmi, M., & Kumar, S. H. (2025). Microbiological quality and safety of processed and packaged fish and fishery products. In *Quality Analysis and Packaging of Seafood Products* (pp. 305–333). Elsevier., DOI: 10.1016/B978-0-443-22082-1.00009-2

Fitzsimmons, J. A., Kinchla, A. J., & Allingham, C. (2024). Assessing the cost barrier for small and medium food processing businesses to meet Preventive Controls for Human Foods standards. *PLoS One*, *19*(9), e0306618. DOI: 10.1371/journal.pone.0306618 PMID: 39269951

García-Castaño, S. G., Pompelli, M. F., Ruiz, A. J. B., & Perneth-Montaño, M. J. (2025). Fruit and Vegetables Harvest and post-harvest. In *Plant Phisiology: Bromeliad Conservation, Stress Signaling, and Post-harvest Innovation* (1st ed., pp. 165–181). Editora Científica Digital. DOI: 10.37885/250619549

Guo, X., Yao, J., Yan, G., & Teng, G. (2025). An intelligent model approach for leakage detection of modified atmosphere pillow bags. *Engineering Applications of Artificial Intelligence*, *139*, 109611. DOI: 10.1016/j.engappai.2024.109611

Hassoun, A. (2025). Food sustainability 4.0: Harnessing fourth industrial revolution technologies for sustainable food systems. *Discover Food*, *5*(1), 171. DOI: 10.1007/s44187-025-00461-z

Hayat, U., Li, W., Bie, H., Liu, S., Guo, D., & Cao, K. (2023). An Overview on Post-Harvest Technological Advances and Ripening Techniques for Increasing Peach Fruit Quality and Shelf Life. *Horticulturae*, *10*(1), 4. DOI: 10.3390/horticulturae10010004

Hiywotu, A. M. (2025). Advancing sustainable agriculture for goal 2: Zero hunger - a comprehensive overview of practices, policies, and technologies. *Agroecology and Sustainable Food Systems*, *49*(7), 1027–1055. DOI: 10.1080/21683565.2025.2451344

Hocquette, J.-F., Chriki, S., Fournier, D., & Ellies-Oury, M.-P. (2025). Review: Will "cultured meat" transform our food system towards more sustainability? *Animal*, *19*, 101145. DOI: 10.1016/j.animal.2024.101145 PMID: 38670917

Jain, P., Sapkal, L. D., Singh, S., & Gaikwad, K. K. (2026). Smart packaging and traceability: Ensuring quality and safety of functional food products. In *Artificial Intelligence in Food Science*. Academic Press, Elsevier. https://www.sciencedirect.com/science/chapter/edited-volume/abs/pii/B9780443264689000266

Jiménez-Trigo, V., Fernández-Ochoa, Á., De La Luz Cádiz-Gurrea, M., Leyva-Jiménez, F. J., Segura-Carretero, A., & Arráez-Román, D. (2025). Current Trends in Reducing Fruit Spoilage from Enzymatic Browning Using Physical Techniques: Avocado Pulp as a Case Study. *Food Reviews International*, *41*(9), 1–23. DOI: 10.1080/87559129.2025.2529539

Kanellos, N., Karountzos, P., Giannakopoulos, N. T., Terzi, M. C., & Sakas, D. P. (2024). Digital Marketing Strategies and Profitability in the Agri-Food Industry: Resource Efficiency and Value Chains. *Sustainability (Basel)*, *16*(14), 5889. DOI: 10.3390/su16145889

Lacourt, C., Mukherjee, K., Garthoff, J., O'Sullivan, A., Meunier, L., & Fattori, V. (2024). Recent and emerging food packaging alternatives: Chemical safety risks, current regulations, and analytical challenges. *Comprehensive Reviews in Food Science and Food Safety*, *23*(6), e70059. DOI: 10.1111/1541-4337.70059 PMID: 39602345

Lekshmi, M., Salam, F., Deepitha, R. P., Kumar, S. H., & Nayak, B. B. (2025). Biochemical quality and hazards associated with processed and packaged fishery products. In *Quality Analysis and Packaging of Seafood Products* (pp. 281–303). Elsevier., DOI: 10.1016/B978-0-443-22082-1.00008-0

Leni, G., Bonacina, C. E., Principato, L., Galli, R., Negrini, C., Dallolio, G., Bassani, A., & Spigno, G. (2025). Assessment of More Sustainable Packaging Solutions for Sliced Cooked Ham and Mortadella: A Study on Physicochemical Properties and Microbial Quality. *Journal of Food Science*, *90*(10), e70574. DOI: 10.1111/1750-3841.70574 PMID: 41017025

Li, X., Fu, D., Hu, S., Huang, J., Wang, L., Zhang, Y., Liu, C., Dong, B., & Liu, G. (2026). Non-contact preservation of chilled chicken: Extending shelf life and modulating microbial dynamics using solid spice essential oils and modified atmosphere packaging. *Food Control*, *179*, 111537. DOI: 10.1016/j.foodcont.2025.111537

Li, Y., Wang, Y., Liu, J., Yu, K., Chen, X., Yuan, L., Peng, S., Liu, W., & Zhou, L. (2025). Effect of modified atmosphere packaging on storage quality and lignification process of post-harvest asparagus (Asparagus officinalis L.). *Food Packaging and Shelf Life*, *51*, 101576. DOI: 10.1016/j.fpsl.2025.101576

Lopriore, M. (2025). *Engineering the Shelf Life Predictive Models for Dry Foods Packaged in Bioplastics: An Integrated Approach* [PhD Course in Food and Human Health, University of Udine]. https://air.uniud.it/bitstream/11390/1308526/2/PhD_Thesis_LOPRIORE_MARCO.pdf

Lunetta, E., & Cacciotti, I. (2024). An overview of the packaging industry. In *Nanostructured Materials for Food Packaging Applications* (pp. 1–30). Elsevier., DOI: 10.1016/B978-0-323-99525-2.00006-2

M. J. G., Gunny, A. A. N., Devi, M., Hussain, M., & Bibi, A. (2025). Trends and Advances in Quality Management of Horticultural Produce by Lighting Strategies – A Comprehensive Review. *Food and Bioprocess Technology*. Advance online publication. DOI: 10.1007/s11947-025-03948-w

Madhu, B. (2025). Technological innovations in food grain processing and storage in India: Trends, challenges, and future prospects. *Journal of Stored Products Research*, *114*, 102757. DOI: 10.1016/j.jspr.2025.102757

Mahecha-Rubiano, Y. R., Garavito, J., & Castellanos, D. A. (2024). Configuration of a combined active packaging system with modified atmospheres and antimicrobial control to preserve fresh strawberry fruits. *Food Packaging and Shelf Life*, *46*, 101390. DOI: 10.1016/j.fpsl.2024.101390

Misopoulos, F., & Bajiraj, P. (2025). Shared Producer Responsibility for Sustainable Packaging in FMCG: The Convergence of SDGs, ESG Reporting, and Stakeholder Engagement. *Sustainability (Basel), 17*(14), 6654. DOI: 10.3390/su17146654

Mondol, M. S. A., Akbar, U., Mandal, O., Rani, A., Dar, A. H., Chatterjee, A., & Abdi, G. (2025). Advances in agronomic practices, post-harvest technologies, and medicinal potential of dragon fruit (Hylocereus spp.): A comprehensive updated review. *Journal of Agriculture and Food Research, 22*, 102157. DOI: 10.1016/j.jafr.2025.102157

Mora, R. L., Vanare, S. P., & Pegg, R. B. (2025). Mechanisms, Causes, and Solutions: A Comprehensive Review of Lipid Oxidation in Low-Moisture Packaged Snacks. *European Journal of Lipid Science and Technology, 70044*(9), e70044. Advance online publication. DOI: 10.1002/ejlt.70044

Nasser Eddine, A., Duret, S., Flick, D., & Moureh, J. (2024). Characterising airflow and heat transfer within a multi-package of horticultural produce using a validated CFD model. *International Journal of Refrigeration, S014070072400433X*, •••. DOI: 10.1016/j.ijrefrig.2024.12.003

Niebel, D., Saha, S., Kunz, W., Evers, B., Löder, M., Ramsperger, A. F. R. M., & Laforsch, C. (2026). Microplastics, Skin Disease, and Dermatology. *Dermatologic Clinics, 44*(1), 125–136. DOI: 10.1016/j.det.2025.08.001 PMID: 41207769

Oguz, S., Turrisi, V., Kuuliala, L., Somrani, M., & Devlieghere, F. (2025). Listeria monocytogenes growth under well-controlled CO2, pH, and temperature conditions through a novel gas-controlling system. *International Journal of Food Microbiology, 441*, 111343. DOI: 10.1016/j.ijfoodmicro.2025.111343 PMID: 40652695

Olatunji, O. (2024). A History of Plastics. In O. Olatunji, *Re-envisioning Plastics Role in the Global Society* (pp. 11–26). Springer Nature Switzerland. DOI: 10.1007/978-3-031-48945-7_2

Oyewole, O. S., Raji, M. A., Kazeem, A. A., Ajao, T. O., Ibitoye, O., Abel, O. O., Solomon-Ibuwunwa, O. M., Famakinwa, J. O., & Adewunmi, E. O. (2025). Smart Technological Innovations for Post-harvest Loss Reduction: A Review. *FUDMA Journal of Sciences, 9*(6), 299–307. DOI: 10.33003/fjs-2025-0906-3605

Pandey, V. K., Shafi, Z., Kumar, A., Rustagi, S., & Singh, S. (2025). Smart Anthocyanin-Fortified Packaging: A Sustainable Approach to Protect Food From Ultraviolet-B Induced Damage. *Journal of Food Process Engineering, 48*(8), e70196. DOI: 10.1111/jfpe.70196

Saleem, A., Anwar, S., Nawaz, T., Fahad, S., Saud, S., Ur Rahman, T., Khan, M. N. R., & Nawaz, T. (2025). Securing a sustainable future: The climate change threat to agriculture, food security, and sustainable development goals. *Journal of Umm Al-Qura University for Applied Sciences, 11*(3), 595–611. DOI: 10.1007/s43994-024-00177-3

Shahbazi, Y. (2024). Effect of modified atmosphere packaging combined with potato starch coating in extending the post-harvest shelf-life of fresh strawberries. *Journal of NutritionFasting and Health, 12*(3). Advance online publication. DOI: 10.22038/jnfh.2024.81866.1526

Stephanie, S. (2025). *Impact of Retail Display Case on Shelf-Life, Palatability, and Color-Stability of Fresh Beef Steaks* [Master of Science in Animal Science Thesis]. University of Arkansas.

Suriwong, V., Inrirai, P., Samrit, T., & Swaeng-ngam, S. (2025). Effect of soaking solution and various packaging conditions on shelf life of fresh Bambusa sp. Shoot. *Food Research, 9*(5), 51. DOI: 10.26656/fr.2017.9(5).047

Tekin, O., Kucuker, E., Aglar, E., Alan, D., & Sumbul, A. (2025). Effects of post-harvest citric, oxalic acid, and modified atmosphere packaging applications on fruit quality and biochemical properties in persimmon. *BMC Plant Biology, 25*(1), 1353. DOI: 10.1186/s12870-025-07368-y PMID: 41068587

Topuz, F. C. (2025). Packaging materials and technologies for novel fish preservation methods. In *Quality Analysis and Packaging of Seafood Products* (pp. 155–179). Elsevier., DOI: 10.1016/B978-0-443-22082-1.00004-3

Tripathi, S., Hakim, L., Gupta, D., Deshmukh, R. K., & Gaikwad, K. K. (2024). Recent Trends in Films and Gases for Modified Atmosphere Packaging of Fresh Produce. In *Novel Packaging Systems for Fruits and Vegetables* (1st ed., p. 27). Apple Academic Press. DOI: 10.1201/9781003415701-3

Tsironi, T. N. (2026). Introduction to food packaging: Historical overview, sustainability, and current trends. In *Safety and Sustainability Aspects of Food Packaging* (pp. 3–28). Elsevier., DOI: 10.1016/B978-0-443-24768-2.00005-3

Wulandari, A., Marcelino, D., Suryawardani, B., Gusnadi, D., Prabawa, B., & Arumsari, R. Y. (2024). How to Develop Marketing Strategy, Packaging Designs, and Superior Product Processing Education? *Jurnal Penyuluhan, 20*(01), 1–13. DOI: 10.25015/20202448777

Yadav, K. K., Gaurav, K., Bhalavey, P., Singh, A., Yadav, R. P., & Soni, V. (2025). Post-Harvest Handling and Preservation of Fish. In *Fisheries Science in the 21st Century Progress and Prospects* (pp. 120–132). Elite Publishing House., https://www.researchgate.net/publication/395946808

Zantar, Y., Noutfia, Y., Laglaoui, A., Benicha, M., Baguena, I., Zantar, S., & Hassani, M. (2024). Impact of Enriched CO2 in Modified Atmosphere Packaging on the preservation of "Palmaritas" Strawberries and the extension of their shelf life. *Journal of Microbiology, Biotechnology and Food Sciences*, *14*(2), e10703. Advance online publication. DOI: 10.55251/jmbfs.10703

Zhou, Y., Saarniit, K., Jafari, M. S., Rosenvald, S., Laaksonen, O., Tian, Y., & Yang, B. (2025). Storage stability of berry mueslis with special focus on phenolic compounds. *Lebensmittel-Wissenschaft + Technologie*, *228*, 118119. DOI: 10.1016/j.lwt.2025.118119

Chapter 7
Biotechnology in the Food and Beverage Industry: Fermentation and Beyond

Ekta Gohel
Gujarat University, India

Kapil Kumar
Gujarat University, India

Parvesh Sharma
http://orcid.org/0000-0002-0245-5186
Gujarat University, India

Alay Mehta
Gujarat University, India

Kiranbhai R. Dodiya
http://orcid.org/0009-0001-9409-7303
Gujarat University, India

ABSTRACT

Biotechnology In Food And Beverages, Transforming Quality, Safety, Flavour, And Nutrition Through Traditional Fermentation, Enzyme Technology, Precision Fermentation, And Synthetic Biology, Enabling Production Of Dairy, Alcoholic, And Fermented Foods, Novel Proteins, Bioactive Compounds, Functional Foods, And Sustainable Ingredients, Enhancing Shelf Life, Texture, And Taste, Supporting Food Safety With Biosensors And Rapid Pathogen Detection, Integrating AI And

DOI: 10.4018/979-8-3373-4047-0.ch007

Bioinformatics For Efficient Microbial Strain Development, Driving Plant-Based Meats, Low-Calorie Sweeteners, Dairy-Free Cheeses, And Sustainable Beverages, Addressing Regulatory, Ethical, And Consumer Acceptance Challenges While Revolutionizing Global Food Production.

1. INTRODUCTION

Biotechnology includes the intentional utilisation of living organisms, biomolecules, and their derivatives to transform raw materials into value-added and safe food and beverages. Biotechnology is fermentation, and it has always processed carbohydrates into alcohols, organic acids, and carbon dioxide, thus preserving food and giving it new tastes. More than food and beverages have been processed of late. Provisioning enzymes enhances texture, and fermentation of defined microorganisms to targeted proteins programmers enhances metabolism. Synthetic biology designs pathways and strains for the affordable production of valuable ingredients. Advancements in rapid diagnostics, biosensors, and bioinformatics / AI permit quality control and process optimisation in real time. This chapter posits two points. Firstly, modern bioprocessing rests on the ecological logic of fermentation, which is the use of mixed or defined formation of consortia with selective pressures and the exchange of metabolites. Secondly, the change to biomanufacturing food hinges on responsible governance as the molecular breakthroughs of ethics, regulations, and social license. Support on scale for the market is the precondition.(Zuroff et al., 2013).

Fermentation is a primary biotechnology subset in foods, along with others such as enzyme catalysis, precision fermentation, and biosensing. Each of these fields, in its own particular way, assists in improving yield and process safety—AI-related biosensors, for example, reduce variability in batches and allow for real-time control that predicts.

1.1 The Past and Context of Biotechnology within Food Systems

Biotechnology is now used globally in food systems, a progression that can be traced back to ancient civilizations. Even before societies were aware of microbial science, systems to improve food in terms of taste, nutrition, and durability were developed. Perfect examples are brewing, baking leavened bread, and making cultured dairy products, all of which are dependent on micro-organisms for product processing and preservation. Even without an understanding of bacteria, yeast, and enzymes, these societies were prosperous.

The introduction of microbiology in the 19th century changed everything. Louis Pasteur and others in the field claimed that food was synthesized through the actions of live and mild microorganisms (Caplice & Fitzgerald, 1999). Food production was no longer a mindless process. Controlled digestion, once regarded as cyclophagic digestion, was the life and soul of the industry. This period was distinguished by the first batch of starter cultures, which were microorganisms designed for initiation of the digestion cycle, as well as the burgeoning field of industrial hygiene systems and microorganismally-housed buildings (MUH) that facilitated food production on an industrial scale. Advances in the twentieth century further changed the bio-processing tools in use.

Isotope separation, along with enzyme purification and immobilization, enabled precise control over some processing variables: the first controlled processing in brewing, baking and dairy. The next step, human tissue culture, along with some rudimentary forms of genetic engineering and microbial manipulation techniques, triggered the production of enzymes, vitamins, and some microbial metabolites. Biotechnology turned its focus to the production of food with improvements in efficiency, safety, and quality, in addition to the traditional food preservation techniques.

The application of synthetic biology and precision fermentation characterizes the twenty-first century. These techniques integrate machine learning with bioreactor engineering and multi-omics to design and control sophisticated unicellular microorganisms capable of producing diverse proteins, fats, and other essential micronutrients. Advancements in food biotechnology allow for the decoupling of food ingredient supply chains from agricultural land, thus reducing climate change impact. At present, the scope of Biotechnology encompasses food preservation and flavour enrichment, as well as the design of programmable food aimed at mitigating environmental and geopolitical stability issues.

In the 1850s, Lincoln Pasteur conducted research on alcoholic fermentation, which, along with the later development of pure starter cultures in the dairy industry, forms the clinical foundation of modern food biotechnology. These developments, in turn, facilitated the industrial manufacture of beer, wine, and cheese under sanitary and reproducible conditions.

1.2 The Comparison of Old and New Fermentation Techniques

Among all the processes of biotechnology, fermentation is perhaps the oldest and the most important. "Traditional" practices of fermentation make use of charms or spontaneous microbial associations of random organisms, in which parental communities determine the ecological succession of flavour, aroma, and texture.

These techniques are unparalleled in their ability to create terroir-specific qualities, which are the link of a product to the culture and geography of a place. These practices also possess a remarkable feature of having resilience, which means the communities can sustain food production in the absence of modern civilisations. However, such practices are usually the most prone to variable outcomes, over a batch of production, as well as being susceptible to microbial contamination and spoilage. (Xin & Qiao, 2025).

Modern fermentation concentrates on control, repetition, and safety. For instance, in cutting-edge breweries and dairies, Process Analytical Technology (PAT) frameworks integrate sensors, temperature control loops, and sanitary design to reap steady product quality. These structures are aligned with HACCP and ISO 22000 requirements, ensuring traceability and reproducibility.

Most crucial, however, is that these are not separate approaches.'

. The more modern food manufacturers have begun to fuse the two models. Artisanal cheese and beer makers, for instance, may and do harness both the microbial sensors and managed systems to achieve a desired level of complexity and authenticity, controlling waste in the process. This ensures both modern productivity and cultural preservation through the process of hybridisation.

1.3 Biotechnology and Global Food Security

With population expansion, climate change, and limited resources, the earth's food system is under new and extreme pressures. With this in mind, biotechnology allows us to ameliorate food security in the following ways:

1.“Increased productivity” – biotechnology’s productivity can help generate engineered microbial and optimised fermentation platforms capable of high-value protein, vitamin, and enzyme fermentation from agricultural waste and other low-cost, low-value substrates. This dramatically lowers dependency on agriculture and farming, as well as the cost of production.

2.“Improved resilience” – biotechnology improves the development of microbial strains that can withstand high temperature and fluctuating pH, and other forms of environmental stress. Loss of shelf-life of food and safety issues. Food has other safety issues alleviated by improved resilience during cross-border and field distribution, along with other diverse environments.

3.” Better diversification” – Addition of such food as plant proteins, cultured meat, and microbial fats alleviates the still unsustainably high burden of livestock production. Thus, the strain on land, water, and livestock feed, the unsustainably high burden of livestock production, and food production can be greatly improved.

Increased quantifiable metrics can be illustrated by figures of yield per substrate mass (TRY ≥ 0. Eight g/g), extension of shelf-life ≥ 20%, and land-use payment. Equitable access and clients' transparency are similarly assured by Governance mechanisms together with harmonised labelling, tiered risk assessments, and open-licensing frameworks.(*The Journal of Mind and Behavior*, n.d.).

The overall contribution of these factors has improved well-being, food safety, affordability, and reduced supply chain volatility. Existing challenges must still be addressed. These challenges include guarantee of fair access with greater focus on low-income earners and smallholder farmers, which include inequitable access to biosafety, food system globalisation, inequitable access to governance, globalisation of the food system, inequitable labelling, inequitable traceability, and fair trade principles are emerging.(Akinsemolu & Onyeaka, 2025).

1.4 Review of Literature and Objectives of the Chapter

The traditional practices of fermentation, enzyme application, and even microbial engineering have recently transformed due to breakthroughs in food biotechnology. Such advancements have helped refine the practices into more data-oriented and precise fields. Singh and Kumar, along with others (2021; Nielsen et al., 2024), have suggested that with the aid of microbial process optimisations and enzyme biocatalysis, the food and beverage biotechnology sectors have evolved into more resource-efficient and sustainable practices. The shift in focus and the consequent prioritisation in the development of biocatalytic enzyme technologies is an extremely relevant and appropriate case in point. These enzymes have come to extend their functionalities beyond mere catalysis, directed towards flavour enhancement, and even supplementation of nutrients and textural modifications of varied food matrices (Rodriguez et al, 2020). It has been reported that, with the research by Kumar and Das (2022), food systems in the industrial setting do minimise energy input and waste with the use of enzymatically engineered food systems due to the relaxations of substrate specificity and thermal stability. Kumar and Das (2022), along with numerous others, have researched and reported the rising demand, along with precision fermentation emerging as a powerful tool, capable of innovating and commercialising protein, bioactive compounds, and even peptides, remarkably shifting the demand towards non-animal and non-agricultural-based sources. It has been reported commercially that via precision fermentation, with the aid of Lee et al. (2023) and Joshi & Patel (2022), utilizing microbial chassis with Saccharomyces cerevisiae and Pichia pastoris, alternative dairy proteins, as well as protein flavoring compounds and dairy proteins were synthesized, showcasing precision fermentation as a more sustainable method of production in contrast to traditional production systems reliant heavily upon agriculture.

Objectives of the Chapter

1. Analyze the advancement of scientific frontiers in food biotechnology relative to the use of enzymes, microbial fermentation, and the integration of biosensors.
2. Analyze the contributions of CRISPR, AI, and bioinformatics to improvement in technique predictability, scalability, and sustainability.
3. Examine nascent industrial initiatives and the policies shaping the international landscape of meals biotechnology.
4. Identify present-day challenges and propose evidence-based approaches to innovation in sustainable food systems.

2. TRADITIONAL MICROBIAL FERMENTATION

2.1 Principles and Process Fermentation Ecology

Fermentation is the process by which microorganisms break down carbohydrates together with other substrates and convert them into small-chain organic acids, ethanol and CO_2, with microorganisms doing the work either aerobically or anaerobically. Basic ecological parameters such as hardness of water (a), pH, salt concentration, oxygen, and temperature determine microbial succession. Lactic acid bacteria (LAB), yeasts, and moulds contribute through acidification, ethanol and other fermentation products, and enzymatic hydrolysis of the growing food substrates to improve the food's preservation and its structure (Creating a Scientific Definition of "fermented Foods" - International Scientific Association for Probiotics and Prebiotics (ISAPP), n.d.).

This is an example of the body with which to be unspun, of the breath of Fusion, where the... The systems are the bread for people last. A unit is the system that does a thing. The reason is often regarded as a change for retro. down, sou Fusion of, from above, these cell processes are usually scientifically unproven." Food systems like milk, cereals, fruits and legumes are some in which these processes occur interwoven within single systems. Each of these matrices introduces particular biotic and abiotic ecological situations.

. Water activity, pH, salinity, concentrations of dissolved oxygen, and temperature are parameters of a population, and systems holistically regulate which species can flourish.

(Voidarou et al., 2020). The dominant species in these niches are classified as lactic acid bacteria (LAB), yeasts, and filamentous fungi, all of which are osmotically stressed as well.

The degree of complexity, uniformity, and consistency for each fermentation relies on the techniques used for culture inoculation. Anchors are marketed as back-slopped inoculated culture strains with specific primitive fermentations and, in particular, starter and traditional pioneer inoculations. They facilitate the succession of the microorganisms. Along with protective cultures, intentionally introduced bacteriophages can serve as spams of order for the removal of the targeted suppressive organisms.

It is unlikely any one prokaryote will define the ecology of these systems. Modified consortia engage in synergistic interactions to build densely structured, robust, and sustained microbial systems. Yeasts release particular vital metabolic precursors, some essential vitamins, and certain specific growth factors to nurture particular LABs. Certain fungi excrete and use hydrolytic enzymes (e.g., amylases, proteases) to break down complex carbohydrates and proteins. Bacteria and other organisms alike can access concentrated fermentable sugars and amino acids that they liberate. Furthermore, the growth of spoilage and pathogenic microorganisms is simultaneously diminished, the pH of the medium is reduced, and the community structure's stability is enhanced. The community structure is a network of cross-fertilisation and competition. The wide array of complex substrates that traditional fermentations use is the result of the resilience and the fermentations' sturdy, complex, and highly diverse in sensory perceivability, making the resilience of the fermentations.(Smid & Lacroix, 2013).

2.2 Dairy and Beverage Applications

Dairy farming and fermentation have always been closely linked. Fermentation of Lactose to Lactic acid and further Lactate is carried out by Lactic acid bacteria such as Lactococcus lactis, Lactobacillus helveticus and Streptococcus thermophilus. During the fermentation of milk, acid is produced, which then decreases the pH of the milk. This decrease in pH causes the casein protein to precipitate and form curds. In addition to the structural changes, the breakdown of proteins and lipids and further by Lactic Acid Bacteria, creates free fatty acids and peptides, which are loved by many for their flavour and are called flavour precursors.

Feeding bacteria is also extremely important. Propionibacterium freudenreichii produces the carbon dioxide responsible for the "eyes" in Swiss cheeses. Brevibacterium linens develops the orange rinds and strong smells of washed-rind cheeses. Penicillium roqueforti and Penicillium camemberti perform heavy proteolysis and lipolysis in the blue and bloomy-rind cheeses to bestow their characteristic textures and flavours. All these microorganisms, which are cross-culturally defined, create the typicity and identity of a cheese.

However, another pillar of traditional biotechnology is represented by fermented drinks. In beer and wine, Saccharomyces cerevisiae is the primary yeast and the leading producer of ethanol. However, some non-Saccharomyces yeasts, such as Brettanomyces, Torulaspora, and Hanseniaspora, add to the complexity of the wines and beers by the production of esters, higher alcohols, and organic acids. In wine-making, the malolactic fermentation by Oenococcus oeni converts malic acid to lactic acid, softening the acidity of the wine and imparting some buttery diacetyl notes.

Enzyme activities also influence the quality of the drinks. The β-glucanases, by hydrolysing β-glucans, assist in the clarification of the drinks, while the enzyme pectinases enhance the extraction and stability of juices. Kefir, kvass, and kombucha demonstrate the variety of non alcoholic fermented beverages. The processes involve SCOBY – Symbiotic culture of bacteria and yeasts, in which acetic acid bacteria, LAB and yeasts produce complex organic acids, exopolysaccharides, and other probiotic metabolites, which may enhance health. (Ağagündüz et al., 2021; Smid & Lacroix, 2013).

Typically, yoghurt fermentation concludes at pH 4.6–4.8, sufficient for casein precipitation and pathogen inhibition. Lactococcus lactis and Streptococcus thermophilus perform optimally at 37–45°C, producing diacetyl at sensory thresholds of 0.1–0.2 mg/L

2.3. The Functions of Yeasts, Bacteria, and Filamentous Fungi

Sets of each microorganism, in essence, add different, but complementary attributes to the ecosystem of fermentation.

Yeasts: In bakers' and wine-makers' yeast, S. cerevisiae, ethanol and carbon dioxide are produced from sugars by way of glycolysis and alcoholic fermentation. This process generates ethanol, causes bubbling, and forms aroma compounds, such as fusel alcohols, esters, and sulfur-containing volatiles, that are metabolites shaping the aroma and flavour of bread, beer, and wine. Other non-Saccharomyces yeasts may also modulate the mouthfeel of wine through glycerol, along with producing some other yeasts that have distinct aromatic characteristics.

Lactic Acid Bacteria (LAB): LAB carry out fermentation along either the homofermentative or the heterofermentative pathways. Lactic acid bacteria that ferment sugars into lactic acid exclusively, like Lactococcus lactis, reduce pH very fast and increase the preservation of food. Heterofermentative lactic acid bacteria like Leuconostoc mesenteroides ferment lactic acid along with carbon dioxide and other compounds, enriching the complexity of the flavour. LAB also produces diacetyl, which gives a buttery taste, and antimicrobial peptides called bacteriocins that target the pathogen Listeria monocytogenes(Ağagündüz et al., 2021).

Filamentous Fungi: Moulds like Aspergillus oryzae, Rhizopus oligosporus, and Penicillium spp. Broaden the array of enzymes applicable in fermentations. Pathogenic fungi like Aspergillus and Rhizopus are renowned and appreciated for their amylolytic and proteolytic enzymes. Aspergillus assists in the breakdown of starch and proteins during the production of soy sauce, sake, and miso. Rhizopus assists in the weaving of soy beans to form a tempeh cake while also degrading antinutritional factors, thus facilitating the bioavailability of nutrients. It is crucial to make clear that Aspergillus oryzae and Rhizopus oligosporus are classified as GRAS (Generally Recognised as Safe) species. Among bacteriocins, nisin—a peptide produced with the aid of Lactococcus lactis—is broadly used for inhibiting Listeria monocytogenes. However, its hobby spectrum is normally towards Gram-positive microorganisms.

Within specific boundaries, the interaction of these microorganisms defines fermentation kinetics, food preservation, and influences the control. Across, the interaction maintained robust flavours while safeguarding from opportunistic contaminants.(Maicas, 2020).

2.4 Preservation and Nutritional Enhancement

One of the most famous benefits of fermentation is food preservation, as there is a lower pH, which, according to many, is hostile to most, if not all, microorganisms, especially disease-causing ones. This is due to the organic acids produced by the lactic acid bacteria. Yeasts also generate ethanol that further represses the activity of spoilage organisms, and a vigorous interplay of competitive microorganisms that deny opportunities for pathogenic organisms to settle and grow. Consequently, fermented food, in most cases, has a greater shelf life than the unprocessed starting materials.

Fermentation also improves the nutritional value of food, as shown by the following processes.

1. Reduction of antinutrients. The "anti" anti-nutrients, phytates and tannins abundant in cereal and legume crops, are notorious for binding minerals such as iron, zinc, and calcium and making them unavailable for bioabsorption. Microbial phytases are known to enhance nutrient absorption by neutralising these binders.
2. Vitamin production. Some of the lactic acid bacteria (LAB) and propionibacteria present in fermented products can fermentatively synthesise vitamins folate, riboflavin, and vitamin B12. Therefore, these fermented products are also regarded as vitamin-rich foods.
3. Improved digestibility. The products of the fermentation of food proteins by proteolytic microorganisms, as well as the fermentation of lactose into lactic acid, ease the digestion of proteins and lactose, especially for those who are lactose intolerant. Nevertheless, an unmanaged or uncontrolled fermentation can pose serious health hazards and risks, such as the accumulation of detrimental

biogenic amines, like histamine or tyramine. Contamination with mycotoxins is one of several risks connected with mycotoxin-producing moulds. All such risks are reduced with formalised controls and process hygiene, as well as process selection, especially culture selection.

Table 1. outlines key microorganisms, metabolites, and preservation mechanisms across major fermented food matrices.

Matrix	Dominant Microorganisms	Key Metabolites	Preservation Mechanism
Dairy	Lactobacillus, Streptococcus	Lactic acid	pH reduction
Cereal	Saccharomyces, Leuconostoc	Ethanol, CO_2	Oxygen exclusion
Legume	Rhizopus, Lactobacillus	Organic acids	Spoilage inhibition
Fruits	Acetobacter, Zygosaccharomyces	Acetic acid	Microbial competition

Figure 1. Schematic representation of the key nutritional benefits of fermentation. Fermentation reduces antinutritional compounds such as phytates and tannins, thereby enhancing mineral bioavailability; enables the microbial biosynthesis of essential vitamins; and improves digestibility through the enzymatic breakdown of proteins and lactose.

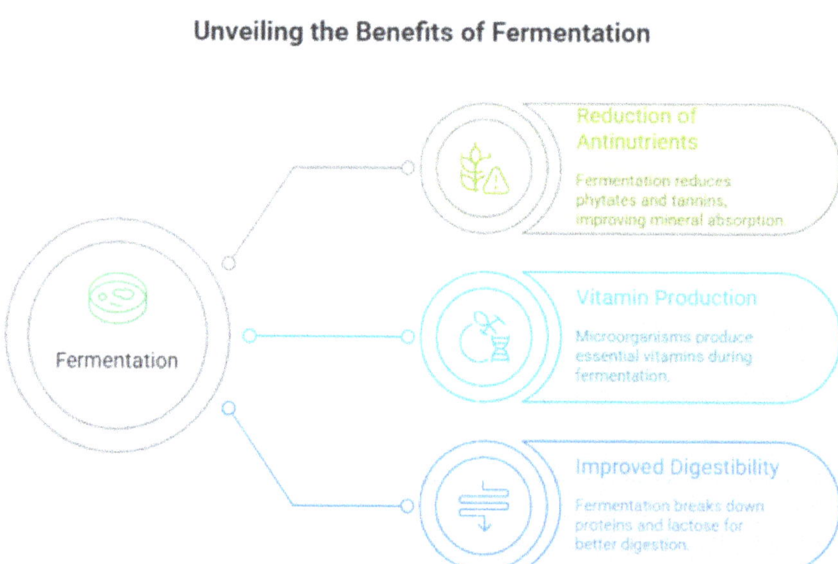

Traditional microbial fermentation is much more than simply an artefact of civilisation's initial processing technique; rather, it is an active and evolving field of biotechnical endeavour. The microbial, ecological, and biochemical fermentation process has also been the foundation of industrial biotechnology. The developed microbial world, for instance, has been put to use in the production of industrially, nutritionally, and culturally valuable products, as seen in the dairy and beverage industries. The sensed safety and quality of foods is the result of the integrated action of yeasts, lactic acid bacteria (LAB), filamentous fungi, and other diverse microorganisms, along with their fermentation products. Fermentation continues to offer unique contributions in the area of food preservation and enhancement of nutrition to the global food systems.

The combined ancient fermentation concepts, along with modern-day scientific methods, have undoubtedly maintained their global infusion in the food culture and nutrition of the 21st century.(Knez et al., 2023).

3. ENZYME TECHNOLOGY IN FOOD PROCESSING

Given a moderate temperature and pH, the enzymes perform specific biochemical transformations. These biological catalysts are very selective and efficient in their functioning. This is why they are dominantly used in modern food processing. Enzymes increase yield, adjust sensory quality, and make novel functional products. Enzymes, in contrast to chemical processing, eliminate the harsh reagents, substantial nutrient loss, and other damage. This provides sustainable environmental solutions. This section is a study on globally practised traditions, the role of enzymes in flavour and texture enhancement, strategies in mass-scale production, and optimisation of case study technologies.(Yang et al., 2023).

Enzymes employed in food processing are widely categorised into hydrolases (e.g., amylases in starch breakdown), isomerases (glucose isomerase in HFCS manufacturing), lyases (pectin lyase for juice clarification), and transferases (transglutaminase for protein cross-linking). Each elegance affords quantifiable advantages, which include improved yield or viscosity discount.

3.1 Brewing, Baking, and Dairy

Any biochemical process that relates to food and uses enzymes in brewing, baking, and dairy is very ancient and one of the most predominant uses of biocatalysis.

Brewing: The process of brewing uses several enzymes to change the starches in cereal grains to fermentable sugars. The starch amylases are hydrolysed with α-amylases, which hydrolyse internal α-1,4-glycosidic bonds of starch, creating dextrins, and the amylases hydrolyse the maltose units at the non-reducing ends. This hydrolysis results in glucose, which, along with maltose, is necessary for yeast fermentation. Proteolytic β-glucanases contribute by hydrolysing polysaccharide components of the cell walls of malted barley, which reduces the viscosity of the mash and assists in the wort clarification process. The yeast cannot utilise specific proteins in the malt, which are proteolytically broken down into peptides and amino acids; the addition of which improves the foam stability and clarity of the finished beer. Baking: In the production of bakery goods, dough and finished products are enhanced by the addition of enzymes. Amylases, by acting on the damaged starch granules of the dough, produce maltose, which sustains yeast action and the resultant carbonic gas in the dough. Starch doughs are also moistened, and to some extent, the retrogradation of starch is slowed. The action of proteases on dough during manufacturing improves the elasticity of the dough, making the handling of the dough easier, and the crumb structure is improved. Enzyme lipases and oxidases also form networks by lipid-protein interactions, and oxidative crosslinking of proteins in the dough, resulting in increased volume of loaves and better uniformity of the crumb. These actions are always directed towards a finished product of good quality, irrespective of the quantity of protein in the flours used. Dairy: For a long time now, the dairy sector has relied on the use of enzymes to transform its products. For instance, Chymosin, which originates from calf stomachs or recombinant microbe systems, catalyzes the breakage of kappa casein, resulting in the coagulation of milk. Thus, its controlled activity determines how firm the curds are, which affects the cheese's texture. Consumers who are lactose intolerant can use lactose-free products because of lactase or β-galactosidase, which breaks lactose down to glucose and galactose. This also increases sweetness, which decreases the amount of sugar that needs to be added. Lipases and proteinases are adjunct enzymes that enhance the taste of aged cheeses by increasing the amount of free fatty acids and peptides. (Mir Khan & Selamoglu, 2020).

3.2 Texture, Flavour, and Functionality

The enzymes are not limited to just transforming the foods. They also enhance the functionality, taste, and texture of the foods.

Modification of texture: Structural enzymes improve the mouthfeel and ease of processing of the food. They act on the animal and plant matrices. For instance, xylinases, pectinases and cellulases act on the non-starchy polysaccharides of cereals and vegetables. They enhance the stability and extraction of juices, as well as soften and improve the texture of the beverages. For meat and dairy substitutes, transglutaminase cross-links proteins, which strengthens the gelatin, improves the holding capacity of water, and enhances the restructured products' sliceability.

Flavour enhancement: Enzymatic hydrolysis breaks down complex molecules to release volatile aromatics, which would otherwise be inaccessible. Esterification produces volatile esters, which contribute fruity flavours. Hydrolysis of glycosides releases terpenes and phenolic compounds, which increase floral and herbal notes in wines and juices. Peptidases and lipases release peptides and free fatty acids, which are flavour enhancers in savoury and dairy foods.

Functionality and nutrition: The use of enzymes permits food processors to obtain desired functionality whilst maintaining the nutritional value of the food. Enzymes enhance the processing of food due to the milder conditions under which they operate, which protects labile vitamins and bioactive phytochemicals. Phytochemicals are plant-derived chemical compounds with protective or disease-preventive properties. Enzymatic processing reduces chemical additives, which embraces the clean label philosophy, and meets consumer trends of foods with minimal processing. (Raveendran et al., 2018).

3.3. Industrial Production and Optimisation

The successful application of technology with enzymes in food processing hinges on dependable enzyme bulk production at economically viable pricing and continuous enhancement for improved stability and cost-effectiveness.

Microbial platforms: The bulk production of enzymes for industrial use is dependent on microorganisms like Aspergillus niger, Trichoderma reesei and Bacillus subtilis. They are grown in submerged fermentation tanks or in solid-state systems. Fermentation is controlled to maximise output. Genetic engineering is used to increase enzyme expression and minimise by-products.

Immobilisation Techniques: Enzymes are most frequently immobilised on inert supports for cost reasons. Alternatively, they can be encompassed in a gel or crosslinked to form aggregates. Immobilisation improves the stability of the enzyme, enhances the operational flexibility, and encourages repeated use. Contamination with mycotoxins is one of several risks connected with mycotoxin-producing moulds. All such risks are reduced with formalised controls and process hygiene, as well as process selection, especially culture selection.

Traditional microbial fermentation is much more than simply an artefact of civilisation's initial processing technique; rather, it is an active and evolving field of biotechnical endeavour. The microbial, ecological, and biochemical fermentation process has also been the foundation of industrial biotechnology. The developed microbial world, for instance, has been put to use in the production of industrially, nutritionally, and culturally valuable products, as seen in the dairy and beverage industries. The sensed safety and quality of foods is the result of the integrated action of yeasts, lactic acid bacteria (LAB), filamentous fungi, and other diverse microorganisms, along with their fermentation products. Fermentation continues to offer unique contributions in the area of food preservation and enhancement of nutrition to the global food systems.

The combined ancient fermentation concepts, along with modern-day scientific methods, have undoubtedly maintained their global infusion in the food culture and nutrition of the 21st century.

High-fructose corn syrup (HFCS) can be produced from immobilised glucose isomerase, which catalyses and converts glucose to fructose in glucose syrups. The glucose syrups are maintained at specific temperature and ph conditions to ensure order and stability. The subsequent downstream chromatographic enrichment yields syrups with specific fructose fractions used in processed foods and drinks.

Certain malts with high β-glucans can have their worts' viscosities so high that they impede lautering, hindering brewhouse efficiency. This increased improvement in efficiency and improvement in sensory quality stemming from the broad application of β-glucanase supplements has been particularly beneficial to regions that use barley with a high β-glucan content. The rapid expansion of the lactose-free dairy market can be attributed primarily to the application of the lactase enzyme. The digestion of lactose, which is otherwise indigestible and requires sucrose and artificial sweeteners, enhances the overall quality of the product. The absence of lactose in the product enables the region to be actively consumed by people who usually suffer from lactose malabsorption. The standardisation of coagulation properties from the use of animal-derived rennet to microbial and recombinant chymosin has enhanced yield and texture uniformity, while decreasing reliance on calf stomachs. The microbial hosts, Kluyveromyces and Aspergillus, are the most widely used to produce recombinant chymosin, which is the globe's most commonly used cheese coagulant.

Enzyme-assisted extraction: Using enzymes like pectinases and cellulases allows for the recovery of bioactive compounds such as anthocyanins, carotenoids, and polyphenols from the by-products of processed fruit, including fruit peels and pomace. This increases extraction yields and provides waste valorisation for sustainable practices. These functional ingredients captured through such processes are becoming increasingly common in nutraceuticals, functional foods, and beverages.

Food processing biotechnology mechanises some of the most impactful applications, which are enzyme technology. Enzymes in brewing, baking, and dairy still dominate traditional sectors, while advanced engineering offers tailored functionality, texture, and flavour. In all instances, precision and efficacy are unmatched by chemical substitutes. Modern industrial platforms ensure inexpensive, large-scale production, while the applications of protein engineering and machine learning promise unimagined innovations. Commercial successes and sustainable innovations are captured in case studies such as HFCS, lactose-free dairy, and enzyme-assisted extraction, where enzymes dominate.

Incorporating enzymes in food systems helps the industry achieve positive shifts in quality and consistency, and fulfilment of environmental responsibility, global consumer expectations and sustainability promises. Research will confirm that enzyme technology will be a fundamental element of food biotechnology. This is due to its ability to support traditional excellence as well as prepare for future developments.(Basso & Serban, 2019).

4. PRECISION FERMENTATION AND ITS ADVANTAGES

One of the modern instruments that revolutionised food biotechnology is precision fermentation. It is the bridge between the old methods of fermentation and the new age synthetic biological technologies. Unlike fermentation, which relies on microbial processes of different genera and species to produce large classes of metabolites such as lactic acid, ethanol and organic acids, precision fermentation hinges on the intentional reprogramming of the metabolism of earmarked microorganisms to make carefully and dearly targeted precision fermentation-specific high-value ingredients. These ingredients include dairy proteins, bioactive peptides, vitamins, nutraceuticals, numerous flavours and colourants, and other products of precision fermentation. It is designed to address the globally urgent and sustainable protein supply, the growing demand for other sustainable and easily manufactured ingredients and the new synthetic biological alternatives to ecologically disastrous agriculture.

This segment tackles the conceptual basis of precision fermentation and the design of microbial platforms for it, the scale relative techno-economic aspects for its superseding implementation, the comparison of fermentation and its precision fermentation redefinition and other elements to bring its future hybrid food and beverage applications to the forefront.(Augustin et al., 2024a).

4.1 Definition and Enabling Toolkits

The essence of precision fermentation is programmed cell factories engineered to produce specific target molecules with high specificity and yield. Unlike traditional fermentation with yeasts, bacteria, or moulds, precision fermentation focuses on an array of sophisticated tools to manipulate metabolism.

Figure 2. Core synthetic biology toolkits supporting precision fermentation. Genetic editing technologies (e.g., CRISPR-based systems) enable targeted pathway construction; expression tuning optimizes transcriptional and translational balance; transport engineering enhances intracellular homeostasis and product secretion; multi-omics modelling integrates genomic, transcriptomic, proteomic, and metabolomic data to identify metabolic bottlenecks; and process analytical technologies provide real-time monitoring to optimize substrate utilization, yield, and process stability.

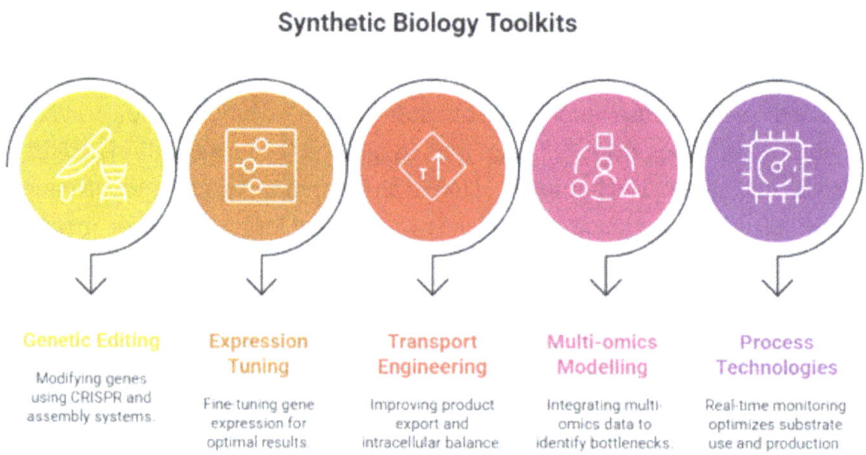

1. Genetic Editing and Regulation

Gene editing technologies, particularly CRISPR/Cas9, have revolutionised precise gene modification by insertion, deletion or regulation of biosynthetic genes. Pathway construction and operational systems are engineered in modular physicochemical relation systems of Golden Gate or Gibson assembly biosynthetic systems.

2. Promoter and Ribosome Binding Site Libraries

A gene expression refined to the closest scope is required for and burden maximisation of the yield to the overall objective. Libraries of gene domains encode and translate the enzymes for the expression of promoters and elimination of toxic by-products for the optimal enzyme composition equilibrium.

3. Transporter and Secretion Engineering

Aiming for the target product often leads to export, which is the biggest bottleneck. Engineering of the membrane transporters and secretion tags for biosynthetic end-products improves the overall intracellular equilibrium.

4. Multi-omics and Constraint-based Modelling

The integration within genomics, transcriptomics, proteomics, and metabolomics provides a systems-level view of the engineered organism. Constraint-based metabolic modelling and flux balance analysis predict and guide rational strain improvement on network pathway bottlenecks.

5. Process Analytical Technologies (PAT)

Soft sensors such as online Raman spectroscopy, off-gas analytics, and near-infrared sensors provide real-time information about substrate utilisation and product accumulation. This information is tied to bioreactor digital twins, computational replicas that predict behaviour to control the system and reduce expensive trial-and-error tests.

Collectively, these enable the broader adoption of precision fermentation, moving beyond the current stage of an academic exercise to a valuable technology with scaled capability to manufacture products that, until now, have only been derived from agriculture or chemical processes.(Teng et al., 2024).

4.2 Designing Microbes for Specific Ingredients

The precision fermentation process is significantly influenced by the selected and engineered microbial host, also known as the chassis organisms. These organisms have to meet regulatory, metabolic, and industrial requirements, including GRAS, efficient protein secretion, and industrial stress tolerance.

Chassis Organisms and Their Attributes

1. Saccharomyces cerevisiae (Baker's yeast): selected for primary use due to its acceptable ancestry use safety record, and its qualified genetics for ethanol, protein, and flavour production.
2. Pichia pastoris (Komagataella phaffii): Most suited for high-level secretion of correctly folded and glycosylated recombinant proteins.
3. Corynebacterium glutamicum: A bacterial chassis optimised for the production of amino acids and metabolites.

4. Lactococcus lactis: A lactic acid bacterium of increasing use for dairy protein analogues due to its excellent safety record.
5. Escherichia coli: Well-studied and highly versatile, but the regulatory acceptance for use in food can be more stringent than for other GRAS organisms.

Applications in Food Ingredient Production

Figure 3. Representative food ingredient applications of precision fermentation. Engineered microorganisms are used to produce dairy proteins with tailored functionality, flavor molecules with consistent sensory profiles, nutraceutical compounds with health-promoting properties, and synthetic microbial consortia to expand ingredient diversity and functional performance in food systems.

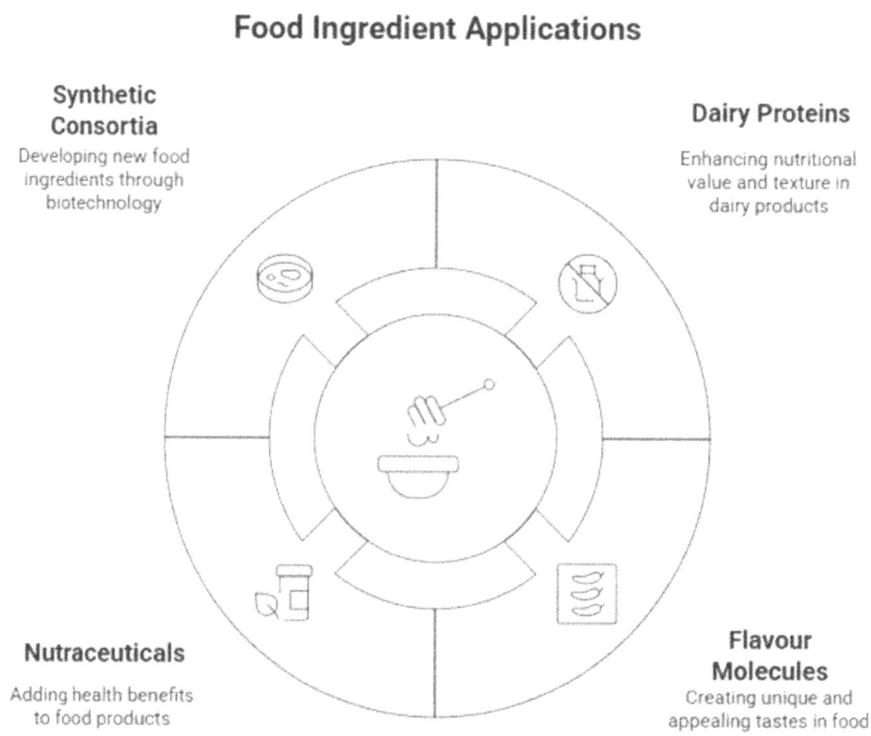

1. **Dairy Proteins:** Recombinant yeast and bacteria can produce the caseins and β-lactoglobulin, the principal proteins found in milk. These proteins are blended

with plant-derived fats and minerals to formulate dairy-free yoghurt and cheese that replicate the texture and flavour of their animal-derived counterparts.

2. **Flavour Molecules:** Constructed strains synthesise vanillin and other flavouring compounds, offering a reliable alternative to traditional agricultural sources and synthetic chemistry.
3. **Nutraceuticals:** Redesigned pathways yield omega-3 fatty acids, carotenoids, and vitamins. Through improved cofactor regeneration and the suppression of competing pathways, the titer of health-promoting compounds is dramatically enhanced.
4. **Synthetic Consortia:** The advantages of partitioned labour among microbes utilise the benefits of the individual, the collective, and the ecosystem approach. Rather than trying to farm each function to a single organism and engineering a single strain to perform all tasks, mixed consortia manage the burden of work to different microbes. One strain might supply building blocks, another performs a rate-limiting enzymatic step, and a third one secretes the end product. The technique enhances robustness and yield. The ability to customise microbes to specific ingredient requirements is an addition to the food industry's arsenal, while also providing insurance against supply shocks and climate change impacts.(Augustin et al., 2024b).

4.3. Cost, Scale and Process Intensification

Precision fermentation has become a staple of modern laboratories, and while demonstrations of the technique abound, the actual test of its applicability lies in industrial-scale operations. Economically, the industrial bound depends on the titer, rate and yield (TRY) parameters, together with the downstream purification costs.

Intensification Strategies

1. **High-cell-density cultivation:** With greater volumetric productivity, fed-batch systems, which permit the continuous addition of substrates, maintain high biomass levels, which facilitate productivity. Limiting factors such as oxygen, which is often the least abundant, are maximised through the use of advanced methods of sparging, microbubble aeration, and agitation control.
2. **Controlled limb and headspace pressure**: Moderate pressure in covered reactors improves oxygen solubility. The benefit of enhanced oxygen is the lower energy use in agitation and mixing.
3. **In-situ removal of products:** Continuous operation is affordable through the membrane separation, adsorption and pervaporation methods, where the

constant removal of target compounds is possible, thus relieving product inhibition and enhancing semi-continuous operation.

4. **Mechanistic Scale-Up Rules** In conventional production, scale-up results in highly over-designed systems, which also demand significant energy use. Rational scale-up from laboratory to an industrial scale is possible if volumetric power input, kLa, mixing times, and volumetric "oxygen transfer coefficients" (kLa) are constant. Further refinement predictions are provided by computational fluid dynamics (CFD).

Economic Considerations

Several cost components will structure the economics of precision fermentation in the manner below:

Feedstock Costs – Input costs can easily be obviated by the use of highly economical micro, methanogenic, and even by-products of fermentation, such as agricultural waste residues, glycerol, and carbon source residues (C1).

- Downstream Processing – As an example, during the fermentation step, the purification cost can account for more than 50% of the total price. The economics of recovery for use with membrane, emphasis, chromatography and proprietary new membrane systems is an area of rapid development and fundamental to the advancement of the processes.
- Capital Expenditure – The Bioreactors and their Bioreactors and their overseeing systems demand substantial capital. Modular, distributed systems can significantly reduce capital risk.

Combined, intensification and tech economic modelling indicate precision fermentation is marketable at a cheaper rate than traditional methods for specific high-value nutraceuticals and proteins.(Augustin et al., 2024b).

Industrial operations commonly target oxygen transfer prices (OTR) of 150–200 $mmol \cdot L^{-1} \cdot h^{-1}$, with kLa values around 250–350 h^{-1} in cardio fermentations. Downstream processing can constitute up to 15% of the overall manufacturing price. Scale-down simulators should be demonstrated to avoid overestimating mixing performance at the pilot scale

4.4 Comparison with Conventional Fermentation

For a more accurate assessment, it is necessary to compare traditional methods with precision fermentation directly.

Benefits of Precision fermentation

- Specialisation and tailor-made solutions: Unlike traditional fermentation, which produces broad and sometimes unnecessary, precision fermentation ensures quality by specifically targeting specific processes.
- Sky is the limit: Unlike traditional fermentation, which is restricted by the amount available, precision fermentation does not require crops and is not limited by land, climate, or supply chain issues.
- Eco-friendly: precision fermentation is more sustainable compared to livestock and extensive crop production due to the reduced requirement of land, water, and feed.

Barriers and Obstacles

- Environmental Impact: Highly engineered microbes without any leak can cause severe ecological damage while also needing to be evaluated for the absence of toxic and allergic materials.
- Challenging Post-Processing Steps: The complex purification steps required for high purity expectations can cancel out the increased productivity from upstream processing.
- Mistrust: People remain sceptical towards organisms that have been genetically modified and which pose a problem.

Benefits of Conventional Fermentation

- Cultural and Culinary Value: Cheese, bread, beer and soy products are traditional ferments which have heritage and are complex to replicate in engineered mono cultures.
- Cost and Reliability: On artisanal and industrial forms, the most inexpensive and durable method is fermentation, especially for staple foods.

The Likely Future: Hybrid Portfolios

The future food system is unlikely to pick one fermentation method over the other. Instead, a portfolio strategy will develop: conventional fermentation for culturally rich, whole-food products, and precision fermentation for high-purity, functional, or specialty ingredients. Together, they can satisfy differing consumer expectations and promote sustainability.

Food biotechnology is precision fermentation. This technique provides unmatched mastery over microbial metabolism and the ensuing production of high-value ingredients sustainably. The combined use of advanced genetic engineering, a strategic design of microbial chassis, and intensified engineering paradigms is guaranteed to make precision fermentation a reality beyond the laboratory. However, its future success will rest alongside technological breakthroughs, cost effectiveness, regulatory clarity, and consumer trust. Fermentation's redefined global food production potential lies in the careful integration of conventional fermentation alongside precision fermentation. This redefined global food production balances cultural authenticity, innovation, and environmental stewardship.(Hilgendorf et al., 2024).

5. SYNTHETIC BIOLOGY AND GENETICALLY ENGINEERED MICROBES

Programmed microorganisms are no longer seen as 'fixed' elements, and their conceptualisation as programmable chassis for customised production has advanced food biotechnology. Synthetic biology, systems biology, and computational design integration enable the modification of cellular metabolism for precise, designed production of proteins, nutraceuticals, and other food additives. Synthetic biology, unlike traditional fermentation that depends on physiological metabolic capabilities, permits food technologists to control and configure the cellular objectives as an outcome while incorporating ethical safety, transparency, and other considerations. (Lv et al., 2021).

5.1 Custom Chassis and Strain Development

Genome minimization entails casting off non-crucial genes to streamline metabolism, lessen off-goal consequences, and improve predictability in engineered strains. Dynamic manipulate structures use biosensors to toggle expression primarily based on metabolite thresholds, retaining a stability between cell growth and product formation.

Slashing and mincing lies at the core of the logistics of genome minimisation as the molecular scalpel that removes surgically ten component facets of cellular, metabolically burdensome architecture. Stoop Genomes are those that are devoid of interlacing and interference, and thus, off-targeting is absent, attained predictability and consistency in feedback to augment yield.

Genetic components and programmable sequences enable modular and tunable expression of specified enzymes or regulatory pathways through genetic circuits. For example, promoters, ribosome binding sites and terminators may be rearranged as "biological Legos" to facilitate rapid design-build-test cycles. Integrating these circuits with biosensors enables dynamic feedback control; when product concentration exceeds a threshold, expression may be down-regulated or up-regulated to achieve a balance between cellular growth and biosynthetic output.

The chassis's ability to minimise expensive downstream processes, post-translational modification ability for complex proteins, and regulatory tolerance. For example, Saccharomyces cerevisiae has a lengthy history of safe use, and even though Lactococcus lactis and Bacillus subtilis regulatory barriers are lower with "generally regarded as safe" (GRAS) designations, their usage also has a history of safe use.

There is evidence of current applications, such as with traditional fermented condiments, like soy sauce. Here, targeted genome editing has reduced the sensory-disabling precursors to the Maillard browning, providing stability without losing the heritage flavour profile. This example illustrates the improvements synthetic biology can make to cultural authenticity.(Xu et al., 2023).

5.2 Proteins, Nutraceuticals, and Additives

The microbial production of functional species and animal-free proteins and animal-free proteins and functional species remains a tangible application of synthetic biology. Casein and whey proteins for dairy substitutes, ovalbumens for egg alternatives, and hams to flavour plant-based proteins are just some of the proteins and animal-free functional proteins engineered through microbial techniques.

Steviol glycosides and monk fruit mogrosides are examples of sweeteners. At the same time, betalains and anthocyanins are examples of natural colourants that, alongside bioactive nutraceuticals like polyphenols and omega-3 fatty acids, are being produced by rewritten microbes. The ability to provide a reliable and consistent quality of production for these previously scarce or expensive raw materials is a cornerstone of modern microbial technology.

The selection of the host organism influences the addition of control mechanisms. Lactic acid bacteria, like Lactococcus lactis and Bacillus subtilis, are food-grade organisms that minimise regulatory concerns, while opportunistic pathogens and other higher-risk microbes invite more scrutiny. The introduction of control mechanisms and the integration of new synthetic pathways boost the final yield. Compartmentalised structures and the targeting of pathways to microcompartments improve the high yield and low toxicity of accumulating intermediates.

The new targets of a project on Closing the Loop are the methanotroph and methylotroph microbes, methane, and methanol. The closing the loop approach focuses on the integration of waste and ingredient manufacture to a circular economy, using greenhouse gas emissions to produce proteins, flavours, or vitamins.

5.3 Gene Editing and CRISPR Technology in Food Biotechnology

The advancement of CRISPR/Cas technologies has dramatically improved the engineering of microbes and plants in regard to the food biotechnological industry.

In the development of microbial starter cultures, CRISPR is used to cleave and integrate the genes of phages, facilitating the industrial fermentation process and providing viral resistance. It also allows the knock-in of biosynthetic clusters, providing LAB or yeast with new and previously untapped metabolic capabilities.

Further advancements in technology, like base and prime editing, allow even more precise modifications of the genetic material of the organism. This technology permits the insertion or deletion of a sequence with minimal disruption of the genomic architecture. Unlike traditional methods, which result in double-strand breaks, the more advanced CRISPR, CRISPRi or CRISPRa are still sophisticated variants of the CRISPR systems that allow changes in gene expression without altering the sequence. Such developments increase the versatility of the systems and permit more refined manipulation of the desired metabolic pathways.

These uses also extend beyond microorganisms. CRISPR editing of crops has produced rice enriched with provitamin A, tomatoes with a longer shelf life, and some varieties of wheat with hypoallergenic biotechnological gluten. Similar to the previously described fermentation-based engineering, these products contribute to integrated supply chains developed to synergistically design and biotechnologically produce safe, sustainable and nutritious food.(Graham & Ledesma-Amaro, 2023).

5.4 Ethics and Safety of the Production of Synthetic Foods

The rapid expansion of synthetic biology within the world of cuisine is disconcerting and raises significant ethical and safety concerns.

Within the framework of stewardship, ethics includes the consideration of the environment and the potential impacts of gene flow. The ecological consequences of an unfettered release of food-grade organisms would, in all likelihood, be disruptive. Genetically designed 'kill switches' and physical biocontainment are intended to mitigate these and other risks.

The designed strains must be devoid of markers indicating the potential to generate antimicrobial resistance, and the lineage that is poorly understood in the context of toxin or allergen production. Setting the metabolic wastes, particular industrial conditions, and post-production purification are critical for stability and entry to the marketplace.

Equally important are Communication and Openness. Members of the public are now more focused on the use of biotechnology in their food. Trust is built on proactive and candid discussions on the risks and benefits of the introduction, along with other factors. Ethically, the controlled, unrestrained access to synthetic biology innovations by wealthy corporations is as troubling as the exclusion of small, developing economies.

Finally, the socially and artificially marginalised populations can be reached with synthetic biology through optimal configuration of distribution systems and pricing strategies.

It should be pointed out that at times, there are minimal efforts that go on that result in crafting plans to aggravate uneven global inequalities.

Recently, there has been interest in the intersection of food biotechnology and engineered microbes, triggered in part by developments in synthetic biology. Advanced novel engineering techniques, such as custom chassis design and construction of synthetic biology and their proficient biosynthesis of proteins and various nutraceutical/food additives. Moreover, the incorporation of microbial breeding techniques along with various CRISPR sandboxing techniques has emerged as a new, attractive strain breeding method. Nevertheless, the techniques may hold considerable prospects, but balancing acts of rigorous safety measures, ethical boundaries, and the absence of secrecy in public discourse are all imperative to maintaining social cohesion. Synthetic biology, once grasped and articulated, directs the social construction of focused technological advances to drive innovation in food systems with the highest nutrition and then, as a priority, to preserve culture.(George et al., 2024).

6. BIOTECHNOLOGY IN FOOD SAFETY AND QUALITY ASSURANCE

Keeping the safety and quality of food has now become a fundamental principle of the modern food system. Biotechnology protects the consumers and, even in the case of cross-continent trade, preserves the genuine nature of the food while extending its shelf life. Food quality assurance systems, molecular detection systems, and newly devised bioengineered antimicrobials and preservation systems, together with the ever-advancing regulatory frameworks of biotechnology, are gaining the trust of the public in food production systems.

6.1. Biosensors and Rapid Detection

While traditional methods of culturing microbial cells can yield accurate microbial assessments, the procedure is lengthy and not suited for real-time observation.

Biosensors, an invention and product of biotechnology, are sensitive and precise and provide alternatives within timeframes of minutes.

Biochemical sensors, such as electrochemical, optical, and piezoelectric biosensors, systematise detection and identify antigens by associating biomolecular recognition elements, such as antibodies, aptamers, enzymes, and bacteriophages, with transforming systems. Extremely low concentrations of pathogens, toxins, allergens, and chemical residues are detectable and identifiable within minutes.

Recent developments in lab-on-chip systems, advanced barcoded microparticles, and electronic noses facilitate the development of types of screening systems essential in testing animal and plant products, supplemented by the miniaturised microfluidic devices incorporating advanced analogue-to-digital converters. Automated robotics and systems with computerised pattern recognition, complemented with neural networks, increase the efficiency of electronic tongues. These devices replicate and automate the sensory functions of humans, enabling advanced compound profiling and taste recognition. They also aid in spoilage and authenticity testing. ATP bioluminescence assays are also helpful in preliminary cleanliness assessments of processing equipment and provide the food processors with knowledge of the contamination prospects and hygiene status almost instantly.

These tools improve food tracking capabilities through providing portability, instantaneous reaction, and connectivity with computerised digitised traceability. (Sridhar et al., 2021).

6.2. Engineered Antimicrobial Agents

Biotechnology is also changing methods for controlling foodborne pathogens.

Chemical preservatives and antibiotics are increasingly limited because of consumer preferences and the growing problem of resistance development.

Engineered antimicrobial agents provide accurate and sustainable alternatives.

Of primary interest are phage preparations and endolysins that eliminate pathogens, such as Listeria or Salmonella, while leaving advantageous microflora undisturbed.

Also, lactic acid bacteria (LAB) that are genetically modified to secrete bacteriocins and biosurfactants that inhibit biostatic pathogens and inhibit biofilm formation on food surfaces.

Unprecedented selectivity is offered by emerging CRISPR-based antimicrobials that remove resistance plasmids or silence virulence genes.

However, the practical application of these methods is accompanied by the need to develop comprehensive resistance management plans, confirm host range for the antimicrobials, and ensure that the antimicrobials are used within a framework of hurdle technologies to prevent the overuse of any single method.

Biologically tailored antimicrobials are a promising complement to the conventional methods of controlling the increasing problem of antimicrobial resistance. (Mayorga-Ramos et al., 2023).

6.3. Spoilage Control and Extension of Shelf Life

Biotechnology has developed processing, microbial, and genetic approaches to any product to extend shelf life without losing nutritional or sensory properties. Protective microbial cultures can outcompete organisms that cause spoilage and secrete antifungal peptides, which enable biopreservation. Genetic methods, such as the delay of fruit ripening and the suppression of enzymatic browning, assist in the retention of fruit during transportation.

Methods of non-thermal processing, including but not limited to high-pressure processing (HPP), pulsed electric fields and cold plasma treatment, have been shown to inactivate pathogenic and spoilage microorganisms while preserving vitamins, textures, and flavours more than subsequent heat treatments.

Further packaging developments also strengthen shelf life. Active scavengers that absorb oxygen and/or ethylene, and responsive innovative packaging that provide indicators for real-time monitoring of spoilage, along with nanocomposite films that provide substantial microbial barriers, improve the reduction of waste and expand the global distribution time window.

6.4 Regulatory Frameworks and Global Guidelines

In pursuing food safety, biotechnology innovation, and its subsequent protection as a dual policy objective, effective regulation that protects all citizens while encouraging innovation is essential.

At the international level, the Codex Alimentarius sets a baseline for risk assessment and hygiene practice standardisation between nations. National biosafety regulations focus on the containment, track and tracing, and safe use of biotechnological organisms and genetically modified organisms.

Incorporating molecular strategies with GMP and HACCP systems to process-centred hazard analysis and verification frameworks enhances safety in the systems.

The difficulty posed for regulators in the formulation and application of new legal frameworks for hybrid products resulting from the application of biotechnology is the products of SynBio and CRISPR, fermented proteins, and gene-edited cropsRegarding novel technologies, international trade is only possible when there is international public trust in investment and the investment regulations monetary return regulatory frameworks from the sponsoring country is poor investment regulations.

Biotechnological applications like rapid detection systems, precision biocidal systems, and innovative food preservation technologies have pivoted food safety assurance, as well as the monitoring of food quality. Used together with the already existing biotechnological regulatory frameworks, such instruments are intended to build trust and secure, ecologically balanced and resilient, sustainable food economies. The pervasive use of biotechnology in the food sector alleviates food contamination and spoilage, preservation and distribution, and global distribution problems. Biotechnology is visibly incorporated in the food sector with the biotechnical changes made to the processes, products, and technologies available in the market to improve the public's health, in addition to achieving a sustainable bioeconomy. Attention is currently focused on the progress of fermentation and enzyme technologies, together with processes of biological synthesis.(Hammami et al., 2019).

7. INDUSTRIAL APPLICATIONS AND INNOVATIONS

7.1 Plant-Based and Cultured Products

The career of technological innovations in fractionation of proteins, enzymatic tailoring, and precision fermentation has marvelously enhanced the accessibility of plant-based products and streamlined their dominion in the general market. Dairy-free yoghurts, milks, and cheeses have also been modified through plant-based tailoring, fermentation, solidification, foaming and gelation. Nutritional density and dairy resemblance get remodelled with fermentation. For instance, probiotic soy and oat bases flavoured with lactic acid bacteria yield bioactive peptides, functional vitamins, and probiotics, classifying them on the market as functional foods, rather than substitutes.

Cell-based or cultured products, on the other hand, represent the newest frontier in protein with no animal origins. The field of cellular agriculture relies intensely on fermentation-based products like recombinant growth factors, amino acids, and scaffolds sold in low combinations, which improve bio-processing, serving as the backbone of formulated cultured meat. The integration of tissue culture and microbial bio-processing enables the production of ethical protein with reduced resources. (Peres Fabbri et al., 2024).

7.2 Alcoholic Kombucha and Functional Drinks

Much of the beverage industry focuses on low-sugar, synthetic, and ethanol-enriched products. This emphasises the case with kombucha: the partnered fermentation of yeast and acetic acid bacteria creates B vitamins, organic acids, and polyphenol antioxidants. Ethanol is kept under regulatory and compliance levels through controlled fermentation, and also improves flavour.

In the same way, there are various methods used in the production of low-alcohol beers, like the use of arrested fermentation, the use of a membrane to dealcoholize, and specially designed yeasts which minimise the production of ethanol while capturing specific desirable esters and higher alcohols. These methods illustrate the desire of consumers to control moderation and not lose out on the sensory aspect of the product.(Brányik et al., 2012).

7.3 Processes That Are Sustainable and Environmentally Friendly

Sustainability in modern industrial biotechnology has spearheaded the enzymatic valorisation of side streams, like the conversion of dietary fibrous spent grain and the extraction of antioxidants from fruit pomace.

Extraction methods that are considered green, like ultrasound-assisted systems and microwave methods, deep eutectic solvents, use of low-polarity solvents, apply to the recovery of bioactives to conserve the energy spent in recovering bioactives. These methods fulfil the principles of regenerative bioeconomy, where closed systems, diversified systems, and reduced waste are intimately linked to the performance of life, environmental, and social governance (ESG) systems.(Carpentieri et al., 2021).

7.4 Examples from the Industry: Cases of Pioneers

In the food biotechnology sector, several industrial case studies exemplify the application of recombinant enzymes and microbial cultures for process optimization and product standardization. One notable example is the use of **recombinant chymosin**, a genetically engineered enzyme that ensures consistent and efficient milk coagulation during cheese production. This innovation has allowed large-scale dairy operations to achieve consistency in texture and yield while lessening dependence on animal-derived rennet sources.

Another important use involves developing microbial cultures to improve flavor and aroma in value-added fermented dairy products. Using biotechnology and defined fermentation conditions, microbial populations are developed to demonstrate targeted metabolic pathways to improve sensory attributes, product stability, and shelf life.

These case studies demonstrate how biotechnology has been incorporated into industrial production. Emphasis here is on the technologies and their sustainable application, rather than on the proprietary technologies, showing how enzyme development, microbes, and controlled processes increased the efficiency, repeatability, and "green" approaches to manufacturing in biotechnology industries.

8. CHALLENGES AND LIMITATIONS

While much has been achieved in the biotechnological innovations on the food systems, scale-up integration still stands as a praiseworthy solution. It customizes and prioritizes spending on the social, ethical, and legal aspects of research, while governing and untangling the mesh of inquiry and administration. Such paradoxical problems need to be addressed in order to maintain social trust and reasonable dedication to sustain biotechnology for food systems.(*Communication for Promoting Healthy Behaviors and Well-Being among the Elderly in Thailand: A Mixed Methods Study · ¤ÅÑ§¤ÇÒÁÃÙéÊØ¢ÀÒ¾¨Ôµ ¡ÃÁÊØ¢ÀÒ¾¨Ôµ*, n.d.).

"ODR's Mixed Strategies" might best be understood as overlapping decision regimes that combine reactive and ex ante precautionary and product-based approaches to regulation. In the case of the European Union (EU), the Union's regulatory decision framework largely follows a process-based risk assessment, which weighs how a product is designed and the processes to be used in its fabrication. In contrast, the product-based assessment regime in the United States and Brazil evaluates the end product and its attributes. In the U. S, in contrast, the process-based aseptic technique prioritizes a. The process-based aseptic technique retains and documents all records of processes undertaken to achieve. To these differing regulatory approaches is attributed the variability in the speed of approval, the costs of compliance, and the. Innovation in the techno-economic parameters of industrial biotechnology, which relates the regulatory which set the regulatory frame. Moreover, the regulatory that set the frame.

8.1 ODR's Mixed Strategies

The regulatory policy on biotechnology use across the globe occupies the greatest paradigmatic schism within the versatile use of fermentations, genetically modified organisms, and gene-edited flora. While the European Union maintains its stance of the precautionary principle on genetically modified organisms, the stance of the United States, Brazil, and Argentina seems to be more relaxed concerning the Gene Editing policy. Such disparities, and many other geocentric business activities, do complicate the global marketing and trade of the food sector.

Other than the developed microbial strain and the allergenic potential, the impact on public health and the control of the imprinted and controlled process are pertinent issues that the proposers need to address.

. The lack of authoritative statements on gene-edited organisms and on metabolites of microorganisms is even more problematic. Regulators are still trying to arch back and fit the old concept of GMOs and natural products to the new matrix of products that do not fit in other loose frameworks.

At times, the inability to come to any consensus on how to approve a given concept may act as a disincentive to undertake the great expense of funds required to develop the innovation pipelines. There is a substantial body of literature that seeks to justify the need for regulations that are congruent with the reality of the governing frameworks, which in turn are based on scientific evidence, tiered evaluations, and systemised constructs that are adaptable to ever-evolving scientific advances.

Moving on to the next aspect of the course, consumer acceptance and labelling. Other setbacks, such as dismal consumer acceptance, may be just as harmful despite the presence of regulatory endorsement. The negative perception of biotechnology as applied to food is rooted in the 'naturalness' fallacy, authority fetishism, and health optimism. More favourable assessments are given to products that offer certain tangible returns in nutrition, price, or sustainability. There is a great deal of scepticism towards interventions that are complex, unnecessary or profit-driven.

8.2 Consumer Acceptance and Labelling Concerns

Consumer trust is associated with labelling and transparency. Even when labelling is not legally mandated, the disclosure should be non-stigmatising, easily understandable, accessible, and pronounced. The extensive use of jargon-filled statements on labels stifles effective communication, and the use of broad statements and exaggeration will ultimately lessen the level of trust people will have in the speaker or the information being given. A constructive approach connecting different information with relevant narratives illustrates how biotechnology resolves key challenges of food and environmental sustainability while providing the familiar taste and texture people value.

Education, advocacy from relevant organisations, and engagement from the public can help facilitate this change in attitude. However, the lack of effort in building supporting legitimacy can be detrimental, causing the same resistance faced with the historical GMO issue in Europe.(*Find the Right Cheese Product for You | Novonesis*, n.d.).

8.3 Ethical Issues in Genetic Engineering

Some of the new, and arguably concerning, issues arising from the free rein to develop synthetic biology, use gene editing, and combine bioinformatics with Artificial Intelligence include:

- The use of some modified organisms in natural or cultivated ecosystems may cause the disturbance of ecological balance, loss of control over gene systems, extinction of organisms, or some disorder to the natural system.

- A growing concern in the intersection of Artificial Intelligence and bioinformatics on personal nutrition and microbiome-based food systems is the boundary control and ownership of biological and health data

Equitable Participation Outcomes: World inequalities should not be further promoted using biotechnology. The intellectual property system will centre the concentration of patents to the detriment of small and medium enterprises, smallholder farmers, and people with low incomes in the Global South. Everybody deserves to profit from the bioeconomy. Ethical justification will be equity of profit governance and distribution. This will be achieved using patent licensing collaborative frameworks, open access monopolies mitigation, and responsible innovation approaches, which broaden the chances of social engagement.

Research and Implementation Costs

What stands out as the most obvious is also the most constraining, which is the financial cost. During the first phase of research and development, the needed capital is scant, especially during the validation phase of the pilot stage, which is then followed by a series of sustaining THE compliance to quality, regulatory, biotechnical, and comprehensive standards, which is termed as the sustaining phase. This is especially the case with biotechnical innovations, as the barriers to entry for small and new emerging businesses are exceptionally high.

Alongside operational costs to be expected concerning the bioreactor and downstream processing devices, sophisticated personnel are to be incorporated into the system's design for its commercial implementation post-pilot testing. The movement to and through the demo stage is commonly referred to as the ‘valley of death’, where there is ample evidence of the technology. However, commercial funding is almost impossible to secure.

There are, however, multiple approaches to minimise operational costs:

- Process intensification: Increases in TRY are possible without modifying the existing physical infrastructure.
- Modular biomanufacturing: flexible, smaller, capital-intensive units that can be manufactured closer to the actual market.
- Cheaper substrates: Used protective agro-industrial and protective wastes can be tapped to increase the circularity of the provision of feedstock.
- Efficient downstream processing: Optimising multiple components of the processing system is a highly economically favourable approach.

It is increasingly common for startups, large food companies, and public research organisations to collaborate. Equity investments, public funding, and venture capital, along with gap funding, are also essential aspects of the financial ecosystem.

In the end, the most crucial concern at the moment is with what the cost of biotechnologies will be. Very much like the case for the renewable energy sector, there is an anticipation that as the biotechnologies evolve, the cost will drop sharply, owing to the economies of scale, as well as the learning curve. No matter how far-fetched it sounds, pure biotechnology, at this point, is still limited to niche and high-end products, and the other issue that decides whether it will get into the orthodox methods of production.

Advancing biotechnology often overlooks the promise and perils tethered to the food systems. Negative public perception, public policy gaps, ethical quandaries, and underfunding stand as potential roadblocks to the future. Constructed foresight is crucial and encompasses the systems approach toward governance, civility, dissemination, and stewardship, access and funding, as well as unwavering commitment over time. For food biotechnology to gain reality rather than remain peripheral, the obstacles posed by biotechnology must be addressed head-on. The issues still unresolved, which threaten the food, nutrition, and security of the 21st century, Silano et al, 2022.

9. SUMMARY AND FUTURE WORK

Biotechnology applied to food and nutrition progresses, perhaps like other domains, within and across the prisms of science, technology, and sustainability. From the age of fundamental understanding of the fermentation process, and with the advent of integrated synthetic intelligence (AI), which straddles synthetic biology, the field has integrated linkages with food systems, biotechnology, bioinformatics and social entrepreneurship.

These domains have been configured such that the techniques used have gained greater accuracy and predictability while still harmonizing the innovation with the global food safety and sustainability aims.

9.1 Merged AI with Bioinformatics and Predictive Biomanufacturing

Within the field of analytics and fermentation control, AI-driven bioinformatics has become fundamental. It has even started to become an art in the mastering of pressure optimization. Knowledge-empowered models can predict enzymatic and metabolic activity and behavior from statistics within a system, thus eliminating the need for complex and prolonged experimental cycles. Algorithms employing reinforcement learning optimize the feeding, aeration, and agitation of fermenters and, through the aid of anomaly detection systems, the pH, oxygen, and nutrients during the preferral detection of batch inconsistencies. Through the digital twin phenomenon, bioinformatics can also, in real-time, control the superordinate complex bioprocesses of minimizing variability and resource consumption of bio-processes. These instances exemplify the smart automation in meal biotechnology that reduces costs, time, and unpredictability.

9.2 Startups, Market Dynamics, and Consumer Trust

Consider the emerging challenge-sponsored projects skillful in precision fermentation of proteins, CLS synthesis, and flavoring molecules, transforming the bioeconomy. Collaborations between agile innovators and large-established food corporations exemplify a hybrid ecosystem based on technological partnership and downstream integration. The combination of omics and personalized nutrition catalyzes the developing of personalized probiotics and specialized protein blends. The market flow, however, hinges on the demonstrated technological feasibility of the feedstock, regulatory sophistication, and public perception. Ultimately, a proper technological balance must be maintained to achieve the optimal combination of sophistication and sensory, economic and ethical acceptability.

9.3 Evidence Synthesis and Innovations in Industry

The evolution of food biotechnologies, as described in three global case studies, forms a coherent narrative for the discipline. It comprises the following components, with the addition of the revolving ecological and microbial engineering resilient to biointensive systems, biocivilization, and the improvement of fermenters and ferments of complex microbial systems, integrating multi-omics microbial ecosystem engineering. Data-driven bioengineering frameworks that modularize and scale bioprocessing by integrating CRISPR, Automation, and AI. Ethical governance protects the environment and the equity and stewardship of biomanufacturing.

Every emerging technology is mapped out across an array of Remote Bioengineering prescribed levels. These levels encompass elements such as surgical precision and programmable fermentation, intricate biosensor frameworks for simultaneous appraisal and supervision, and the real-time automation of value assurance systems. These value proposals, combined with programmable verification frameworks, elevate the Remote Bio Design to the Bio Face Amplification paradigm.

9.4 Future Research and Testable Directions

Integrating traditional fermentation with an AI-aided Video-Capse technology workflow sketches out a potential revolutionary trajectory. In the framework of Transformational Vision, the outlined strategies shift towards operationally tangible proposals. Merging Process Analytical Technology (PAT) and a Digital Twin of a Continuous Fermentation Process for sophisticated monitoring, real-time adaptive engagement, predictive quality issue anticipation, and advanced optimization systems. Designing bioprocesses that utilize waste-derived feedstock and low-value C1 carbon sources at net negative environmental cost. Enabling rapid spatial convergence of biosystems, automated international bio-labeling to strengthen the overall system, customer value, increase transparency, and enhance public trust towards bioengineered systems. Forming a biomanufacturing system consortium under the principle of inclusive equity to improve access to systems for knowledge exchange, capacity building, and equitable regulation consolidation across jurisdictions. Biomanufacturing systems that merge renewable energy with closed-loop feedstock biomanufacturers and closed ecological productivity.

9.2 Start-ups, Dynamics of Market, and Trust of the Consumers

By means of new challenge-sponsored start-ups targeting precision fermentation of proteins, synthetic lipids, and flavoring molecules, the frontiers of the bioeconomy. The collaborations of small, quick innovators with large established food companies demonstrate a techno-economic fusion hybrid ecosystem based on both technology and downstream collaboration. The same fusion of omics with personalized nutrition is accelerating the creation of tailored probiotics and custom protein blends. However, the market is driven by the assured availability of the feedstock, regulatory flexibility, and the perception of the market. The reality is, the balance with the technology is an adoption of a level of sophistication that is sensory, economic, and ethical sustainable.

9.3 Syntheses of Evidence with Innovations of the Industry

Narratives of the evolution of food biotechnologies comprise three case studies, and each of them has three components. The first component is the ecological and microbial engineering of biointensive systems, enhanced resilience and safety of ferments and fermented products by utilizing the complex systems of microbes. The second component is the data-driven bioengineering frameworks that integrate CRISPR, Automation and AI to modularize and scale processes. The last component is the ethical governance that biomanufacturing conducts in alignment with the stewardship of the environment and equity.

Each technology is designed at different levels of Remote Bioengineering, from all surgical precision and programmable fermentation to complex biosensor systems with real-time monitoring and value evaluation, real-time guarantee systems, and programmable verification systems. These raise value propositions from Remote Bio design to Bio face amplification.

9.4 Future Research and Testable Directions

The next-generation trajectory is outlined through a synthesis of traditional fermentation paired with AI-driven Video capsule technology. To galvanize vision-driven innovation, the outlined tactics focus on steering actionable blueprints. Integration of Process Analytical Technology (PAT) with a Digital Twin of the Continuous Fermentation Process for advanced monitoring, real-time adaptive optimization, and predictive fault detection system. Designing bioprocesses that incorporate waste-derived feedstock and low-cost C1 substrates to negative environmental cost bioprocesses. Accelerating the convergence of international bio-labeling systems to enhance customer value, increase system transparency, and public trust in bioengineered systems.

The emerging biomanufacturing systems are accessible for consortium members to enhance equitable knowledge exchange, capacity building, and cohesive regulation. Integrating closed-loop biomanufacturing systems with renewable power systems to decouple the biomanufacturers from ecological productivity.

9.5 Concluding Perspectives

The next generation of food biotechnology will not rely solely on technical prowess. With the universal principles of environmental justice, bioethics, and sustainable prosperity, regulating AI, bioinformatics, and synthetic biology will also require sociocultural acceptance, stabilization, and ethical anticipation. Societies that integrate social equity and biotechnological advancement, along with planetary health, will drive the transformation towards a smart, resilient, and sustainable food system globally.

REFERENCES

Ağagündüz, D., Yılmaz, B., Şahin, T. Ö., Güneşliol, B. E., Ayten, Ş., Russo, P., Spano, G., Rocha, J. M., Bartkiene, E., & Özogul, F. (2021). Dairy Lactic Acid Bacteria and Their Potential Function in Dietetics: The Food–Gut-Health Axis. *Foods*, *10*(12), 3099. DOI: 10.3390/foods10123099

Akinsemolu, A. A., & Onyeaka, H. N. (2025). Mycoproteins as sustainable food sources: Current applications and prospects. *Discover Applied Sciences*, *7*(3), 1–11. DOI: 10.1007/s42452-025-06614-0

Augustin, M. A., Hartley, C. J., Maloney, G., & Tyndall, S. (2024a). Innovation in precision fermentation for food ingredients. *Critical Reviews in Food Science and Nutrition*, *64*(18), 6218–6238. DOI: 10.1080/10408398.2023.2166014

Augustin, M. A., Hartley, C. J., Maloney, G., & Tyndall, S. (2024b). Innovation in precision fermentation for food ingredients. *Critical Reviews in Food Science and Nutrition*, *64*(18), 6218–6238. DOI: 10.1080/10408398.2023.2166014

Basso, A., & Serban, S. (2019). Industrial applications of immobilized enzymes—A review. *Molecular Catalysis*, *479*, 110607. DOI: 10.1016/j.mcat.2019.110607

Brányik, T., Silva, D. P., Baszczyňski, M., Lehnert, R., Almeida, E., & Silva, J. B. (2012). A review of methods of low alcohol and alcohol-free beer production. *Journal of Food Engineering*, *108*(4), 493–506. DOI: 10.1016/j.jfoodeng.2011.09.020

Carpentieri, S., Soltanipour, F., Ferrari, G., Pataro, G., & Donsì, F. (2021). Emerging Green Techniques for the Extraction of Antioxidants from Agri-Food By-Products as Promising Ingredients for the Food Industry. *Antioxidants*, *10*(9), 1417. DOI: 10.3390/antiox10091417

Find the right cheese product for you | Novonesis. (n.d.). Retrieved October 4, 2025, from https://www.novonesis.com/en/find-right-cheese-product-you

George, D. R., Danciu, M., Davenport, P. W., Lakin, M. R., Chappell, J., & Frow, E. K. (2024). A bumpy road ahead for genetic biocontainment. *Nature Communications*, *15*(1), 650. DOI: 10.1038/s41467-023-44531-1

Graham, A. E., & Ledesma-Amaro, R. (2023). The microbial food revolution. *Nature Communications 2023 14:1*, *14*(1), 1–10. DOI: 10.1038/s41467-023-37891-1

Hammami, R., Fliss, I., & Corsetti, A. (2019). Editorial: Application of Protective Cultures and Bacteriocins for Food Biopreservation. *Frontiers in Microbiology*, *10*(JULY), 1561. DOI: 10.3389/fmicb.2019.01561

Hilgendorf, K., Wang, Y., Miller, M. J., & Jin, Y. S. (2024). Precision fermentation for improving the quality, flavor, safety, and sustainability of foods. *Current Opinion in Biotechnology*, *86*, 103084. DOI: 10.1016/j.copbio.2024.103084

Knez, E., Kadac-Czapska, K., & Grembecka, M. (2023). Effect of Fermentation on the Nutritional Quality of the Selected Vegetables and Legumes and Their Health Effects. *Life (Basel, Switzerland)*, *13*(3), 655. DOI: 10.3390/life13030655

Lv, X., Wu, Y., Gong, M., Deng, J., Gu, Y., Liu, Y., Li, J., Du, G., Ledesma-Amaro, R., Liu, L., & Chen, J. (2021). Synthetic biology for future food: Research progress and future directions. *Future Foods : a Dedicated Journal for Sustainability in Food Science*, *3*, 100025. DOI: 10.1016/j.fufo.2021.100025

Maicas, S. (2020). The Role of Yeasts in Fermentation Processes. *Microorganisms*, *8*(8), 1142. DOI: 10.3390/microorganisms8081142

Mayorga-Ramos, A., Zúñiga-Miranda, J., Carrera-Pacheco, S. E., Barba-Ostria, C., & Guamán, L. P. (2023). CRISPR-Cas-Based Antimicrobials: Design, Challenges, and Bacterial Mechanisms of Resistance. *ACS Infectious Diseases*, *9*(7), 1283–1302. DOI: 10.1021/acsinfecdis.2c00649

Mir Khan, U., & Selamoglu, Z. (2020). Use of Enzymes in Dairy Industry: A Review of Current Progress. *Archives of Razi Institute*, *75*(1), 131. DOI: 10.22092/ARI.2019.126286.1341

Peres Fabbri, L., Cavallero, A., Vidotto, F., & Gabriele, M. (2024). Bioactive Peptides from Fermented Foods: Production Approaches, Sources, and Potential Health Benefits. *Foods*, *13*(21), 3369. DOI: 10.3390/foods13213369

Raveendran, S., Parameswaran, B., Ummalyma, S. B., Abraham, A., Mathew, A. K., Madhavan, A., Rebello, S., & Pandey, A. (2018). Applications of Microbial Enzymes in the Food Industry. *Food Technology and Biotechnology*, *56*(1), 16. DOI: 10.17113/ftb.56.01.18.5491

Smid, E. J., & Lacroix, C. (2013). Microbe-microbe interactions in mixed culture food fermentations. *Current Opinion in Biotechnology*, *24*(2), 148–154. DOI: 10.1016/j.copbio.2012.11.007

Sridhar, A., Kapoor, A., Kumar, P. S., Ponnuchamy, M., Sivasamy, B., & Vo, D. V. N. (2021). Lab-on-a-chip technologies for food safety, processing, and packaging applications: A review. *Environmental Chemistry Letters*, *20*(1), 901–927. DOI: 10.1007/s10311-021-01342-4

Teng, Y., Jiang, T., & Yan, Y. (2024). The expanded CRISPR toolbox for constructing microbial cell factories. *Trends in Biotechnology*, *42*(1), 104–118. DOI: 10.1016/j.tibtech.2023.06.012

Xin, Y., & Qiao, M. (2025). Towards microbial consortia in fermented foods for metabolic engineering and synthetic biology. *Food Research International*, *201*, 115677. Advance online publication. DOI: 10.1016/j.foodres.2025.115677

Xu, X., Meier, F., Blount, B. A., Pretorius, I. S., Ellis, T., Paulsen, I. T., & Williams, T. C. (2023). Trimming the genomic fat: minimising and re-functionalising genomes using synthetic biology. *Nature Communications 2023 14:1*, *14*(1), 1–11. DOI: 10.1038/s41467-023-37748-7

Yang, W., Lu, F., & Liu, Y. (2023). Recent Advances of Enzymes in the Food Industry. *Foods*, *12*(24), 4506. DOI: 10.3390/foods12244506

Zuroff, T. R., Xiques, S. B., & Curtis, W. R. (2013). Consortia-mediated bioprocessing of cellulose to ethanol with a symbiotic Clostridium phytofermentans/yeast co-culture. *Biotechnology for Biofuels*, *6*(1), 1–12. DOI: 10.1186/1754-6834-6-59

Chapter 8
Entrepreneurial Opportunities in AI-Enabled Micro Ghost Kitchens:
A Pathway to Inclusive Food Ventures

N. K. Rajitha
http://orcid.org/0000-0003-1002-2265
Kannur University, India

ABSTRACT

This chapter discusses the benefits of AI-powered mini ghost kitchens as sustainable and accessible businesses following the pandemic. It points out that these fast, delivery-only kitchens supply small-scale jobs to women, people from rural areas and the differently-abled, as AI and similar tools simplify managing food, expecting needs and communicating with customers. The study uses Organizational Resilience Theory and AI-based entrepreneurship to highlight why such models lead to adaptable societies, the preservation of culture and financial empowerment. With examples and figures collected in Kerala, the article illustrates that AI is making fairer access to the food industry possible as it addresses challenges like cost and lack of technology or infrastructure. The chapter encourages ethics in AI to support food innovation that respects inclusiveness, conserves the environment and safeguards heritage traditions in the community.

DOI: 10.4018/979-8-3373-4047-0.ch008

1. INTRODUCTION

The global food service sector has undergone significant changes due to COVID-19. The traditional restaurant industry was challenged, so virtual restaurants and ghost kitchens became important alternatives, offering a flexible and technological approach for customers who are digital users. Ghost kitchens, which deliver food without physical restaurants, are gaining popularity among entrepreneurs seeking a low-risk, data-driven food business (Jones, S., Cain, L., & Deel, n.d., 2024). However, to truly democratize food entrepreneurship, these models must integrate AI not just for efficiency but also for inclusivity, mainly benefiting women, rural populations, and individuals with disabilities. This chapter argued that AI-enabled micro ghost kitchens are not only a technological innovation but a vehicle for inclusive entrepreneurship, especially in socio-economically diverse regions like Kerala.

However, ghost kitchens are not limited to being more efficient. (Cai, Leung, & Chi, 2022), argue that the outcomes of these ventures are primarily influenced by what customers think about convenience, as well as potential risks such as reduced transparency and weakened brand connection that come with it. These problems underscore the importance of developing an intelligent, responsive system that can foster customer trust by leveraging AI, such as personalization, and optimizing engagement levels where AI plays a transformative role. Scholars today refer to AI as a technology and a specialized tool that supports and enhances human strategic thinking (Shepherd & Deanrzak, 2022). Entrepreneurs in the micro-ghost kitchen sector can utilize AI to handle analytics, manage inventory and delivery, customize conversations, and streamline their workflow. While Shepherd & Deanrzak (2022) and Oluwadamilare Usman et al. (2024) point out that access to entrepreneurship can be expanded through the use of AI, it can also exacerbate bias, divide digital worlds, and consolidate power in the hands of the tech-savvy.

This chapter examines the relationship between AI and ghost kitchens, with a focus on the development of inclusive and environmentally friendly food businesses. It is based on studies, use cases, and ethics to provide a guide for supporting micro-entrepreneurs, women, those living in rural areas, and people with physical or mental disabilities. The chapter proposes that treating AI as a tool for equality and durability, rather than only for efficiency, will benefit the future of food businesses in the digital era.

2. THEORETICAL FRAMEWORK

2.1. Organizational Resilience in Food Entrepreneurship

This framework aligns with Kerala's food entrepreneurs, who adjusted post-pandemic by utilizing low-investment digital models, such as home-based ghost kitchens. They demonstrate how micro ghost kitchens address significant challenges (such as the pandemic), change with new approaches, and keep operating as they originally set out to do.

The main topics are as follows:

A. **Making Adjustments in Adverse Times** A resilient organization can either maintain or quickly recover positive performance after being affected by shock (Vogus & Sutcliffe, 2007).
B. **Flexible Resilience Models** In their study, Ishak and Williams (2018) noted that resilience can either reaffirm a person's identity or lead to changes in it.
C. **The Ability to Bounce Back.** Manfield & Newey, (2018) argue that resilience is built using different abilities for handling various risks, most importantly for smaller businesses that lack specific resources.
D. **A study on Transformational Entrepreneurship Behaviour.** The research by Gunawan et al. (2023) viewed that strong micro-enterprises contribute to a community's growth as a result of socio-economic change, especially in unstable conditions.

Application to Ghost Kitchens.

Many kitchens were created during COVID-19 to exemplify organizational resilience. Their survival and success hinge on their ability to quickly pivot operations, implement data-driven decisions, and function within the resource are the limitations of these theories.

2.2 Artificial Intelligence in Culinary Innovation

They show how AI is important in finding new idea, reaching out to customers, and restructuring the business model of a company.

Artificial intelligence (AI) is a powerful tool for entrepreneurship.

According to Shepherd and Majchrzak, AI not only helps the entrepreneur to learn, realize patterns, and change but also raises concern of relying on algorithms and moral concerns.

- **Developing business techniques with artificial intelligence.** (Oluwadamilare Usman et al. 2024), explain the significant ways in which AI boosts analytics, automation, and customization in ghost kitchens.
- **Socio-technical Systems and Their Link to Ethics** They argue that using technology alone is insufficient in entrepreneurship; ethics and other factors must also be addressed.

Application of ghost kitchens

AI is utilized in ghost kitchens to automate tasks, optimize menus, and facilitate customer communication. Still, any use of these tools should focus on inclusivity, openness, and correct management of data, as proved by all three contributions.

2.3. Inclusive Entrepreneurship and Innovation Adoption Framework

The Inclusive Entrepreneurship and Innovation Adoption Framework is also based on psychological, technological, and social theories to demonstrate the empowerment of individuals, women, rural community members, and differently-abled entrepreneurs in food-based micro-enterprises through the use of Artificial Intelligence (AI) within food-based micro-enterprise ecosystems.

2.3.1. Maslow's Need Hierarchy Model (Maslow, 1943)

According to Maslow's theory, human motivation is a sequence that starts with physiological needs and progresses to higher ones, including self-esteem and self-actualization. Micro ghost kitchens provide an avenue to economic stability, independence, and self-actualization, especially for entrepreneurs from vulnerable groups. Working from home, retaining a sense of cultural identity through food, and fostering social appreciation for the success of a business align with the top levels of Maslow's hierarchy.

2.3.2 Technology Acceptance Model (TAM) (Davis, 1989)

TAM provides an explanation of the acceptance and use of new technologies, concentrating on two main factors: Perceived Ease of Use (PEOU) and Perceived Usefulness (PU). In the given work, the readiness of entrepreneurs to use AI tools (inventory applications, predictive analytics, or voice-command business solutions) depends on their perception that such tools can enhance business performance and do not require any specific expertise to be utilized. The model can be used to determine why some entrepreneurs excel in adopting AI while others resist or fear it.

2.3.3 Theory of Inclusive Digitalization

Based on its roots in the study of development and innovation, inclusive digitalization theory emphasizes fair access to digital tools and the right to participate in the innovation process, particularly among marginalized groups. This paper employs such a lens by examining how AI-facilitated micro ghost kitchens democratize entrepreneurship, as the business has fewer barriers to entry; it allows for flexible working arrangements and creates spaces that conform to local language, needs, and constraints.

Application to the Present Study

All these theories guide the research questions, data interpretation, and policy recommendations:

- Describing the motivation and the psychological readiness of rural and differently-abled entrepreneurs (Maslow).
- Identifying the factors that influence the adoption and usability of AI tools in low-resource contexts (TAM).
- Framing AI-based micro ghost kitchens as inclusive growth and digital empowerment instruments (Inclusive Digitalization).

By combining these theoretical perspectives, the study explains how technologically mediated entrepreneurship in Kerala can serve as a socially inclusive, culturally embedded, and economically viable model for development.

Table 1. Key Findings linked to Theoretical framework

Theoretical component	**Key findings**
Maslow's Need Hierarchy (Self-actualization, Safety)	By using AI, entrepreneurs were made to feel stronger and safer, particularly those who were in vulnerable groups, which was relevant to the need of stability and growth.
Technology Acceptance Model (Perceived Ease & Usefulness)	It was seen that those who found AI entry comfortable (voice commands, inventory tools), got on it more readily, and a lack of training led to resistance.
Inclusive Innovation Theory	Women like Sajna and differently-abled entrepreneurs like Ramesh **found AI to be a way to overcome physical, social, and financial constraints to entry.**

2.4. Theoretical integration: Linking AI, Resilience, and Inclusion

This chapter is grounded in two major theoretical domains: Organizational Resilience Theory and AI-driven Entrepreneurship. These frameworks offer complementary perspectives to understand how AI-powered micro ghost kitchens can serve as resilient, inclusive, and innovative business models in the post-pandemic food industry. The chapter focuses on the theory in question, Organizational Resilience Theory, and the relationship between AI and Entrepreneurship. They help explain why AI micro ghost kitchens can be reliable, inclusive, and innovative for the food industry after the pandemic.

2.4. 1. Inclusivity and Empowerment through Digital Kitchens

When a company is resilient, it can withstand tough times and adapt well to major setbacks (Vogus & Sutcliffe, 2007). Resilience in ghost kitchens involves being able to react to sudden changes in the environment, whether those changes disrupt the supply chain, impact health, or alter customer behaviour.

Core Contributions:

(Vogus & Sutcliffe, 2007) It is argued that resilience is characterized by successfully adapting to challenging situations through the active use of internal resources and ongoing education.

(Manfield & Newey, 2018) Research suggests that organizations should respond differently to routine or severe dangers by employing either routine strategies or heuristics.

(Ishak & Williams, 2018) The model distinguishing between treasuring one's identity ("anchored" resilience) and modifying it ("adaptive" resilience) is particularly useful in situations where change is frequent and challenges are significant.

(Gunawan et al., 2023): It is noted that there is a link between the resilience of organizations and how they contribute to society and economic development.

(Gunawan et al. 2023): They argue that connected organizational resilience enhances the connection between transformational entrepreneurship and community development.

Relevance to Ghost Kitchens.

Micro ghost kitchens are resilient because they keep their overhead low and can adjust to various shocks. Such businesses focus on using data and can be suitable for newbies in the industry because they do not require opening physical stores to offer food services. In Kerala, the anchored and adaptive resiliency frameworks apply in the case of a woman entrepreneur named Sajna belonging to Malappuram. Although her digital literacy was rather low, she used AI to streamline her operations in the kitchen, and the conversation serves as a demonstration that resilience in resource-constrained environments can be strengthened by inclusive technology.

2. 4.2. Theoretical Integration: Linking AI, Resilience and Inclusion

In the business world, Artificial Intelligence becomes more important. AI helps to take decisions promptly and quickly, enhance relations with the customers in real-time, and predict the business tendencies through analytics.

Core Contributions:

(Shepherd and Majchrzak 2022), viewed AI can boost entrepreneurs' skills, yet developers should be mindful to avoid ethical challenges.

(Usman et al., 2024), found that AI is important for marketing, product development, and customer relations, all factors necessary for entrepreneurial success.

(Mugunzva & Manchidi, 2024), presented a framework that argues for the ethical and holistic adoption of AI systems.

Relevance to Ghost Kitchens.

AI helps ghost kitchens become more efficient and scalable, enabling the testing of their menus and services through data analytics. Importantly, ethical practices in AI help ensure that all entrepreneurs can benefit from its use.

Ramesh's micro ghost kitchen, 'Thattukada360' in Kannur, illustrates inclusive AI application. By using voice-command AI to run his kitchen remotely, Ramesh bridged physical limitations and built customer relationships-demonstrating how ethical, inclusive AI supports social equity in entrepreneurship.

Figure 1. Theoretical Framework: AI-Enabled Micro Ghost Kitchens and Organizational Resilience

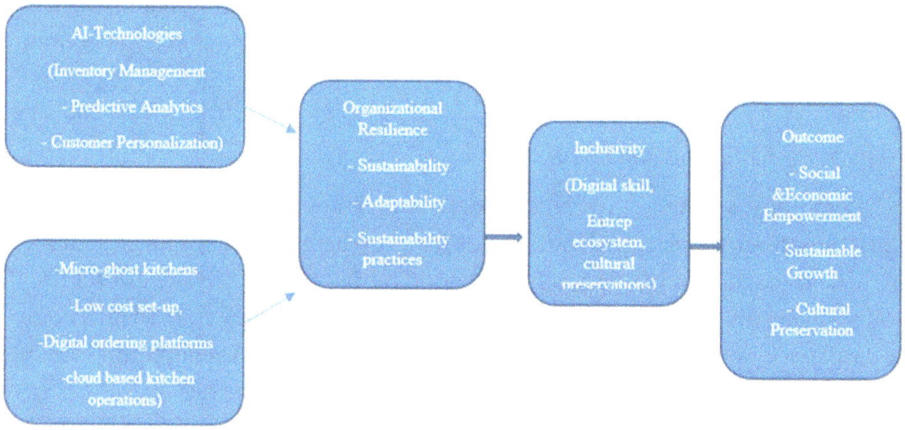

3. KERALA AS THE STUDY AREA: A POTENTIAL GROUND FOR INCLUSIVE CULINARY INNOVATION

Kerala is often referred to as "God's own country". Its socio-cultural and digital infrastructure of the area is quite favourable to speak about the possibility of AI-based micro-ghost kitchens. Kerala, with its impressive array of diverse cuisine of inclusive and sustainable food innovation due to its amazing variety of food specialties, a high level of education, a well-developed digital infrastructure, and the prosperity of the entrepreneurial ecosystem of women and the rural community.

A. Cooking Heritages and Cultural Identification

Kerala traditional food, which includes "appam", 'puttu", "meen curry", etc., and "sadhya", is globally well-known food but not commercially available to a greater percentage of local food specialists and restaurant chefs. AI-based ghost kitchens will help the owners of businesses to save and popularize local food, making the production more efficient, anticipating demand, and customizing the menu, nationally and internationally, according to the needs of individuals.

Opportunity: AI can help local foodpreneurs enhance the scalability of their recipes, make them multilingual, and optimize food delivery channels, considering the vast customer base in Kerala.

B. Rural Inclusion and Grassroots Entrepreneurship

Kerala is home to numerous vibrant micro and small businesses, particularly in rural and semi-urban areas. Grassroots entrepreneurship is illustrated by such woman-led groups as Kudumbashree. Artificial intelligence through micro-ghost kitchens allows communities to empower themselves by removing the start-up costs barrier and incorporating local farm produce into food technology.

Opportunity: The platforms can be used to create value-added food products, and therefore establish new market access, as well as provide dignified digital livelihoods of marginalized women entrepreneurs.

C. Experience-Based Food Delivery and Culinary Tourism

Kerala, being one of the favourite tourist destinations in the world, receives millions of food-enthusiastic tourists annually. The established purpose of ghost kitchens to support the tourism sector is associated with the provision of theme-based meal sets, food box associated with festivals, and traditional food, together with dietary modification-related changes, fostered by customization enabled by AI.

Opportunity: AI will bring culinary tourism to a different level as one will be able to serve the tourists immediately, considering their preferences: vegan, gluten-free, Jain-friendly, and others.

D. Start-Up Infrastructure and Digital Literacy

Kerala is India state that has the highest penetration and digital literacy. The ecosystem also allows experimenting with technology by taking the initiative, which can be seen in Kerala Start-Up Mission (KSUM). This readiness positions Kerala as a good place to carry out food innovations upon AI.

Opportunity: This is an advantage, as entrepreneurs are allowed to utilize AI to forecast demand, manage inventory, and communicate with customers in a digitally mature market.

E. Sustainability and SDGs Alignment

The policy framework of Kerala focuses on sustainability through agriculture, population health, and enterprise development. AI-driven micro ghost kitchens can help achieve this vision by offering options to reduce food waste, facilitating sourcing based on a farm-to-table approach, and utilizing environmentally friendly packaging.

Opportunity: The models are also capable of incorporating domestic produce, minimizing environmental impacts, and aiding SDGs (Goal 2), Zero Hunger and Gender Equality (Goal 5), and Sustainable Cities (Goal 11).

F. Enhancing Food Delivery System

Kerala is emerging as the mushrooming of the home-delivered food market, which is already served with a ready made logistics infrastructure to serve ghost kitchens with Swiggy and Zomato. Last-mile delivery of AI based venture is good which is supported by high urbanization in the cities of Kochi, Trivandrum, and Calicut.

Opportunity: Micro ghost kitchens could meet niche needs with the use of smart order-management, predictive route-optimization, and AI-based customer-service.

Overall, Kerala is characterized by a rich culinary culture, a favourable business environment, digital readiness, the successful tourist industry, and sustainable development-oriented policies, which help make the state an apt place to study the concept of AI-enabled micro ghost kitchens. As a result of the features that make Kerala special, the study will offer an informative and scalable approach to food entrepreneurship, which can be used as the foundation of advising similar innovations in India and globally.

4. STATEMENT OF THE PROBLEM

Although cloud and ghost kitchens are gaining popularity, very little attention is being given to AI technology that supports women, people from rural areas, and people with disabilities in becoming entrepreneurs. There is a significant lack of information in Kerala, where they have many kitchens, great food, and utilize various technologies, about how AI-assisted micro ghost kitchens can support disadvantaged people, preserve their culinary traditions, and help sustain the environment. This research focuses on utilizing AI in the food sector to create equal opportunities for all, preserve local cultural traditions, and promote sustainable development.

5. LITERATURE REVIEW

It is a period when the entire global food industry is transitioning to a digital foothold, and at the center of this revolution is the emergence of ghost kitchens, which are food-related virtual spaces that cater to changing food trends and capitalize on shifts in the economic environment. Since traditional restaurants faced increasing costs and declining profit margins, ghost kitchens emerged as the restaurant of choice among entrepreneurs who were flexible and less risky in terms of monetary investment (Wulandari et al., 2023; Moyeenudin et al., 2020). These activities, no longer constrained by actual eating areas, are highly dependent on digital tools such as information platforms and food delivery apps to cater to a more domesticated customer (Beniwal & Mathur, 2022). However, as cloud kitchens grow, they also have to address issues such as maintaining the community aspect of dining and learning to deal with complex technology setups (Soldani et al., 2018).

Artificial Intelligence (AI) is a significant power that increases the effectiveness and flexibility of these kitchens. Throughout the food service industry, AI is being implemented to optimize operations incrementally, including the automation of inventory and real-time menu customization. This increases efficiency, reduces human error, lowers operational costs, and enhances customer satisfaction (Murugeah, 2024; Sachani et al., 2021). Although high-end activities such as predictive analytics and blockchain can be addressed through the application of advanced AI systems, basic, low-cost, and easy-to-use AI tools are also instrumental to even smaller food businesses (Tishtykbayeva et al., 2023). Nevertheless, the use of the technology is limited by the risk to data privacy and the necessity to enhance the digital skills of employees.

These changes in technology raise a vital question: Who has access to this digital food economy? In this case, the concept of inclusive entrepreneurship is brought to the forefront. Researchers believe that AI should do more than increase efficiency; it must serve all types of historically marginalized people, including women, rural groups, and individuals with disabilities (Rolle et al., 2020). Where current systems tend to overlook the existence of disabled entrepreneurs, new technologies such as voice-command-enabled AI or dashboards accessible through a phone may create new opportunities. As Digital Social Innovations (DSI) have already indicated potential benefits in promoting entrepreneurial education and access among underrepresented groups (Hamburg & Bucksch, 2017), targeted digital training and support ecosystems have a pivotal role in inclusion.

This all-inclusive vision also encompasses indigenous and local food culture, which is often under threat in the face of competition towards modernity. The concept of AI is currently in use not only to enhance operational efficiency but also to preserve cultural continuity. To be concrete, Generative AI can help preserve ancient recipes and make them accessible and comprehensible across languages, as well as expand traditional delicacies into new markets (Srivastava & Upadhyay, 2024)—as exemplified by ChefAI.IN projects have demonstrated that AI can be utilized creatively to develop new, culturally informed dishes (Chaudhary et al., 2022). Despite this, researchers criticize cultural homogenization and biases in algorithm-based systems and human-programmed AI applications and demand culturally aware locally trained AI applications.

All these strands boil down to the issue of urgency concerning sustainability. Green entrepreneurship, promoted with the assistance of AI and big data analytics, is also becoming a promising approach to addressing environmental and social issues simultaneously (Gupta et al., 2023). The use of AI facilitates more resource-efficient operations, strengthens the transparency of the supply chain, and increases responsiveness toward environmental changes (Mohammadian & Rezaie, 2021). Although the number of people exploring the potential of AI to drive sustainable development is increasing, research has yet to provide an integrated model linking digital innovation with an inclusive approach and environmental objectives (Bickley et al., 2024).

Collectively, these studies suggest that the future of food entrepreneurship lies in technologies such as AI and culturally embedded, socially inclusive design, including micro-ghost kitchens that are both technologically and humanly designed.

Table 2. Conceptual Synthesis of Reviewed Literature Relevant to AI-Based Ghost Kitchens

Author(s) & Year	Theme / Focus Area	Key Insight	Relevance to Current Study
Wulandari et al., 2023; Moyeenudin et al., 2020	Evolution of Ghost Kitchens	Ghost kitchens reduce operational cost and infrastructure risk.	Justifies the use of ghost kitchens as a viable business to the rural and low-income population.
Beniwal & Mathur, 2022; Soldani et al., 2018	Digital Efficiency in Food Delivery	Cloud kitchens leverage technology but face operational and integration issues.	Highlight the importance of AI tools that are easy to use in micro set ups.
Murugeah, 2024; Sachani et al., 2021	AI in Food service	AI improves operations, inventory, and customer experience.	Advocates the use of AI in simplifying the operations of ghost kitchens.
Tishtykbayeva et al., 2023	Accessibility of AI	Basic AI tools are now affordable and usable by small businesses.	Demonstrates feasibility of implementation of AI in low-resource areas such as Kerala.

continued on following page

Table 2. Continued

Author(s) & Year	Theme / Focus Area	Key Insight	Relevance to Current Study
Rolle et al., 2020	Inclusive Entrepreneurship	Disabled and rural populations are often excluded from entrepreneurship	Frames the concentration of studies focus on AI as an instrument for inclusive business participation.
Hamburg & Bucksch, 2017	Digital Social Innovation (DSI)	DSI can foster inclusivity through tech-driven education.	Emphasizes the necessity of digital training that should be a part of the adoption of AI.
Srivastava & Upadhyay, 2024; Chaudhary et al., 2022.	Indigenous Cuisine & AI	AI helps preserve culture and create new culinary experiences.	Makes micro ghost kitchens to be associated with preserving cultural values and innovation.
Saurabh Sharma & Kumar Rahul, 2021	AI & Supply Chains	AI enhances efficiency and visibility in food supply chains.	Enhances the potential of AI in green kitchen logistics.
Gupta et al., 2023; Mohammadian & Rezaie, 2021	AI and Sustainability	AI contributes to environmental and economic sustainability.	Fits the ghost kitchens to the Sustainable Development Goals (SDGs)
Bickley et al., 2024	Research Gaps on AI and Sustainability	Need for integrated frameworks linking AI, inclusion, and sustainability.	Justifies the conceptual model developed in this paper.

6. RESEARCH GAP

Although ghost kitchens are becoming popular in most global markets due to their running costs, there is no empirical evidence on how Artificial Intelligence (AI) can be effectively applied in promoting inclusive entrepreneurship, especially women, rural citizen and persons with disabilities. Not many researchers investigate how AI in food businesses can be more efficient and still with much respect to culture and environmentally friendly. Furthermore, no system with built-in ideographical frameworks links AI-based ghost kitchens to local entrepreneurial situations with equity and strength models. The present research fills these understudied intersections to gain a better insight into how digital food businesses can foster inclusive social developments as well as economic empowerment.

7. RESEARCH OBJECTIVES

1. To evaluate the role of AI in micro ghost kitchens in enabling the inclusion of minority entrepreneurs such as women, rural residents and people with disabilities in the food industry.
2. To investigate the effects of AI implementation on maintaining and marketing of local and indigenous culinary cultures in Kerala.
3. To assess the inclusionary, sustainable, and cultural relevance of AI-based ghost kitchens as a model for digital food entrepreneurship.

8. RELEVANCE OF THE STUDY

Following the pandemic, the study is particularly significant, as digital transformation, sustainability, and social inclusion are now key priorities worldwide. Exploring micro-ghost kitchens assisted by AI helps integrate new technology, cultural values, and economic progress into a single model. It provides recommendations for policy, practice, and research by offering a food venture model that is accessible and scalable to marginalized businesspeople. These results support digital startups, governments, and development agencies in helping all people leverage the evolving digital economy and contribute to achieving the UN Sustainable Development Goals by the 2030 deadline.

This research addresses the imperative questions regarding innovation and technology through entrepreneurship, as well as understanding the role of AI in driving growth in the food service sector and promoting economic development. In the case of micro-ghost kitchens, research shows potential for minority stakeholders to engage in the digital economy.

9. SCOPE OF THE STUDY

The study aims to examine the opportunities and future of AI-enabled micro ghost kitchens as an inclusive food venture in Kerala. It focuses on how AI can empower underrepresented entrepreneurs and entrepreneurs of colour (including women, rural communities, and individuals with disabilities), promote cultural preservation, and foster sustainability. The study restricts itself to micro-scale industries in Kerala, integrating both technological and socio-economic aspects. Evaluating the importance of AI as an innovation and entrepreneurship tool in the culinary environment, the research will provide practical recommendations to policymakers, start-ups, and development agencies. This range overlooks large-scale food service operations and focuses on grassroots digital food enterprises.

10. RESEARCH METHODOLOGY

A. Design Research

To comprehensively understand how Artificial Intelligence (AI) facilitates inclusive entrepreneurship through micro-ghost kitchens, this study employs a mixed-methods research design. Such a strategy combines quantitative and qualitative information to create a deep, precise, and contextual understanding. The study was based on three primary sources of data collection consisting of unrestricted entrepreneurs, customers, and domain experts, where data can be triangulated and validated.

B. Sampling

The target population involves micro ghost kitchen entrepreneurs operating in the state of Kerala and the entrepreneurs that represent marginalized and underrepresented populations as the targeted group, i.e., women, differently abled, and those residing in rural areas in the state of Kerala. To specifically ensure the inclusion of interested businesspeople using AI tools in their food businesses, a purposive sampling method was adopted.

Quantitative sample: 50 entrepreneurs were chosen to answer the survey.

Qualitative sample: The sample consisted of 10 to 15 entrepreneurs and experts who participated in in-depth interviews.

Such a sampling strategy enabled adequate representation of inclusive entrepreneurship views supported by AI technology.

C. Data Collection Techniques

a) Quantitative data collection

To collect quantifiable information, a structured questionnaire was applied (both online and via face-to-face interviews) regarding the following important variables:

- The kind of AI tools used (e.g., chatbots, inventory software, and analytics)
- Initial investment in AI adoption
- Order volume before and after AI use
- Business performance (e.g., change in revenue/profit)
- Barriers to the adoption of AI

The data were analyzed by calculating the percentage and presented in frequency tables to define usage patterns, obstacles, and perceived results.

b) Qualitative Data Collection

The selected entrepreneur and stakeholders were interviewed semi-structured to determine the following:

- The experience with the usage of AI tools
- Social impact and perceived benefits
- Learning curves and integration problems
- Influence on inclusivity, autonomy, and empowerment

Additionally, three case studies of AI-integrated micro ghost kitchens in Kerala have been analyzed to highlight the real-life applications and inclusive potential of AI in food entrepreneurship.

D. Analysis of Data

The analysis of quantitative data was conducted using percentage analysis, as the leading indicators were presented in a table. Manual content analysis was employed on the qualitative data, focusing on identifying patterns and themes related to inclusivity, empowerment, and AI usability. These dual steps ensure that the data reflects not only statistical trends but also individual stories of change.

E. Ethical considerations

All the participants provided informed consent. Individual and business data were kept confidential. The ethical responsibility was entirely fulfilled in all interviews and references to individual cases, as the dignity and autonomy of the respondents were considered.

F. Area of Study

The sample study was conducted in various districts of Kerala, as this is a state that thrives with a high literacy rate, progressive social indicators, and a rich culinary culture. Kerala provides a fertile ground for examining the convergence of technology and food-based micro-entrepreneurship in rural and semi-urban locations.

11. DATA ANALYSIS

Table 3. Gender Distribution of Entrepreneurs

Gender	Number	Percentage
Male	20	40
Female	25	50
Differently-abled	5	10
Total	50	100

Source: Primary data

The data indicate that 50 percent of the surveyed entrepreneurs are women, 10 percent are people with disabilities, and 40 percent are males. It means that such inclusive forms of entrepreneurship as AI-powered micro-ghost kitchens are successfully adopted by underrepresented populations, particularly women.

The overall female involvement is consistent with the results provided by Rolle et al. (2020) and Hamburg & Bucksch (2017), who believe that women and other marginalized groups should be given more opportunities in business. It is crucial to have 10 percent of differently-abled entrepreneurs in sectors that are largely inaccessible to them due to a lack of infrastructural support and accessibility.

However, the comparatively reduced number representing the interests of differently-abled individuals indicates that there is still a barrier to entering the digital landscape, which includes digital illiteracy and a lack of assistance and support services, among others. This highlights the need for targeted policy interventions and support schemes that provide low-cost technology, online training, and incubated services tailored to their specific needs.

The gender breakdown reveals that the AI-micro-entrepreneurship sector can support equity; however, more inclusion initiatives are required to accelerate the gap between entrepreneurs with disabilities and improve accessibility.

Table 4. AI Tools Used in Business Operations

AI Tool	Number	Percentage
Inventory Management	30	60
Customer Chatbot	18	36
Predictive Sales Analytics	22	44

Source: Primary data

As the statistics indicate, Inventory Management (60%) was the most popular AI tool used by micro ghost kitchen entrepreneurs, followed by Predictive Sales Analytics (44%) and Customer Chatbots (36%). This implies a more utilitarian approach to entrepreneurs, in which their primary focus is on operational efficiency and demand estimation rather than direct access to customers through AI.

The high dependence on inventory management tools indicates that the utilization of AI is in its initial stages, focusing primarily on optimizing the backend to help entrepreneurs minimize costs, reduce food waste, and control supply chains, particularly in small-scale enterprises with limited working capital.

The average use of predictive analytics (44%) suggests that a relatively low number of entrepreneurs currently utilize AI to inform data-driven decisions regarding menu design, pricing, and marketing. Nevertheless, a relatively scarce application of customer chatbots (36%) indicates an imbalance in the implementation of AI in customer-related applications. This could be evidence of digital literacy problems, ignorance, and resource deficiencies in implementing conversational AI systems.

These facts align with Murugeah (2024) and Sachani et al. (2021), who affirm that AI has a considerable influence on operational workflow and the ability to provide customer service. However, the statistics also suggest that a significant opportunity to utilize artificial intelligence to enhance customer engagement and build loyalty, one of the most crucial drivers of success in the food services industry, was missed.

The findings thus point to a strategic necessity in training and providing tools that target a customer-centric variety of AI applications, especially, but not limited to, those that are accessible, multilingual, and low-cost, which most micro-entrepreneurs, particularly those in rural or underserved locales, can use.

Table 5. Initial investment in AI Tools used

Investment Range in Rs	No. of Entrepreneurs	Percentage (%)
Less than Rs 10000	18	36
10000-Rs 25000	20	40
25001 - Rs50000	8	16
More than Rs 50,000	4	8
Total	50	100

Source: Primary data

It is evident that most micro ghost kitchen entrepreneurs (76%) spent less than 25,000 INR on AI tools, and it is also clear that they prefer affordable and readily available technologies. This pattern highlights the low entry costs of basic AI capabilities, such as inventory applications, chatbots, and easy analytics software, which do not require substantial capital investments.

This has further presented the example of a woman entrepreneur in rural Malappuram, Sajna, whose AI-enabled micro ghost kitchen, Nattinpuram Flavours, was established with very little investment. Through platforms selected and facilitated by NGOs, as well as low-cost mobile applications, she was able to automate inventory management and enhance customer interaction without formal technical training. Ramesh, another differently-abled businessperson based in Kannur, has started Thattukada360. This voice-command Artificial Intelligence-based solution enables him to manage his business from home, utilizing only basic digital infrastructure and an incubator.

The percentage of respondents who invested more than 50,000 rupees was 8, which means that not all micro-entrepreneurs can afford an advanced AI system. According to these findings, support at the ecosystem level, such as subsidies, training, and collaboration with NGOs or incubators, should be increased, particularly among those belonging to marginalized groups. Successful cases of Sajna and Ramesh demonstrate that low-cost AI interventions, supported by local expertise and internet-based mentoring, can lead to valuable changes in entrepreneurial behaviour and social inclusion.

Table 6. Perceived Benefits of AI Adoption

Perceived Benefit	**Number**	**Percentage**
Increased Order Volume	35	70
Increased Order Volume	28	56
Enhanced Customer Experience	25	50

Source: Primary data

The statistics show that 70 percent of entrepreneurs experience improved operational efficiency, 56 percent report growth in the number of orders, and 50 percent report fewer customers. These results indicate that the use of AI makes a significant contribution to business performance in areas such as workflow automation and service provision.

Better efficiency is an opinion supported by the high ratio of respondents claiming that AI can facilitate the automation of repetitive processes, such as monitoring inventory, processing orders, and data analysis, which are particularly important in micro ghost kitchens where resources are scarce. The growth in order volume (56%) further confirms that AI helps scale operations, as the company receives faster service and better price estimation of demand.

However, 50 percent of the respondents disagreed that AI had improved customer experience. This suggests that back-end processes are gaining prominence while front-end customer interaction through AI remains underutilized. It indicates an existing opportunity for the application of AI in personal engagement, multicultural dialogue, and agile service, which are essential aspects of customer retention and trust.

The findings align with the observations made by Murugeah (2024) and Gupta et al. (2023), who also highlight the potential of AI in minimizing operations, cautioning that AI has its most significant potential when balanced between machine-like functions and human customer experience.

To conclude, the data indicate that the use of AI is enhancing efficiency and sales volumes in micro ghost kitchens. However, to achieve broad and sustainable business growth, increased efforts should be made to develop customer-linked AI applications that are inclusive, culture-specific, and easy to use by small entrepreneurs.

Table 7. Barriers to AI Adoption

Barrier	Number	Percentage
Cost of Implementation	20	40
Lack of Technical Knowledge	15	30
Limited Access to Infrastructure	10	20

Source: Primary data

Through the data, it was evident that 40 percent of the micro ghost kitchen entrepreneurs polled identified cost-related AI implementation as the main obstacle, 30 percent listed a lack of technical expertise, and 20 percent cited difficulty in finding infrastructure access. This means that the barriers to capital and skills-related constraints continue to be a significant challenge to the adoption of AI technologies by small-scale food entrepreneurs in Kerala.

The high cost of AI tools as a hindrance indicates that, although they are productive, most are still beyond the financial reach of disadvantaged or financially constrained businesspeople. This is particularly true for women, people in rural areas who are also entrepreneurs, and individuals with disabilities who are already struggling to make ends meet. On the same note, a lack of technical knowledge (30%) highlights an existing digital literacy gap, whereby entrepreneurs may struggle to run or maintain an AI system independently.

The evidence that 20% of the population cannot access the required infrastructure (e.g., a stable internet connection, electricity source, or any device) represents a structural constraint that primarily affects rural areas and semi-urban regions. Combined, these obstacles reveal the skewed topography of available and utilizable AI, either lending support to the findings of Tishtykbayeva et al. (2023) and Sachani et al. (2021) about the challenges of using advanced technologies in small enterprises.

These findings further support the necessity of hometown, accessible, and easily customizable AI Systems, as well as specialized digital learning courses. In the absence of such initiatives, the added value of AI-enabled micro ghost kitchen facilities will be skewed toward more affluent entrepreneurs, thereby restricting the scope and viability of the model.

Table 8. Change in Monthly Profit after AI Adoption

Profit change	Number	Percentage
No Change	10	20
1–10%	15	30
11–25%	18	36
More than 25%	7	14
Total	50	100

Source: Primary data

The analysis shows that 80 percent of entrepreneurs of micro ghost kitchens increased their profits after implementing AI tools, with 36 percent experiencing a profit growth of 11 to 25 percent and 14 percent characterizing the growth as more than 25 percent. Such findings present a strong indication that the use of AI leads to positive improvements in financial performance, where its usage increases operational efficiencies, superior inventory management, and enhanced order management in most cases.

Nonetheless, 20 percent of participants did not report a change in profit, which supports the point that the implementation of AI is not necessarily equal to financial success. This deviation is an indicator that external circumstances, such as the degree of digital readiness, market demand, the applicability of AI tools, and the entrepreneur's ability to interpret AI results, are crucial elements in achieving a real economic advantage.

The findings align with the arguments made by Gupta et al. (2023) and Mohammadian and Rezaie (2021) regarding the notion that although AI can be used to enhance adaptability and sustainability, its benefits do not manifest uniformly across all enterprises. Specifically, micro ghost kitchens operating in poorer localities may continue to struggle to fully leverage AI unless additional support, training, and specialized tools are provided.

The findings, therefore, indicate that although AI positively adds value to profitability for many, the level of success is scalable and requires ecosystem-level considerations, such as affordability, ease of use of tools, and local mentoring. This deficiency underscores the need to investigate further the factors that support AI in generating standard monetary profits across various micro-enterprise contexts.

12. CASE STUDY ANALYSIS

This part provides two illustrative case studies of micro ghost kitchen entrepreneurs in Kerala: a woman entrepreneur (Sajna) from a rural area (Malappuram) and a differently-abled entrepreneur (Ramesh) from a district (Kannur). The examples demonstrate that AI tools enable marginalized individuals to enter the food industry and achieve success.

12. 1. Sajna's Smart Kitchen- "Nattinpuram Flavours," Malappuram

a. Background:

In 2022, following the pandemic, Sajna, from Malappuram, Kerala, began operating her micro-ghost kitchen, "Nattinpuram Flavours" from home. Since she did not have enough money to invest, she decided to turn her traditional cooking into a business, but not a restaurant.

b. AI Adoption and Business Transformation

Sajna attended an AI workshop organized by a local NGO, which introduced her to how she could utilize AI to organize her food business at home. She relied on an application for simple inventory control and a platform for AI-powered delivery that gathers customer data. It explains how AI helped individuals from less-advantaged communities, including women and participants from rural areas, gain access to business resources

> *"I never thought that it would be possible to run a kitchen this way and reach so many customers. By using AI tools, I was able to manage orders and stocks without having proper training".* - ***Sanjana, Micro Entrepreneur***

1. Social impact and challenges

> *"I did not even know what AI meant at first. However, the app showed me which dishes were selling the best, helped reduce waste, and reminded me to reorder in time. Writing this down on paper would have been impossible"-*

By relying on artificial intelligence, Sajna modified her menu to meet local demand, reduced food waste by a third, and increased her online meal delivery. Using WhatsApp and with the help of NGOs, a chatbot answered customers' questions and sent updates on cooking in both Malayalam and English.

d. Outcome

Sajna earns a middle-range income, and business is new to her. She earns approximately 18,000– 22,000 per month.

"I did not think being a businesswoman was possible for me. After tasting my cooking, my neighbours want to know how they can set up their kitchens".

- Reduced food waste and operational errors.
- Regular income without physical infrastructure.
- Triggered local social change among rural women, etc., are the Outcomes.

The story demonstrates that in Kerala, AI is serving to support traditions, not replace them, by providing new opportunities for women, rural residents, and the less tech-savvy poor.

1. **Problems with Entry and the Learning Process**

"I was afraid I would break something the first time I accessed the dashboard. I needed time, and someone stayed with me".

Sajna's phobia of technology stems from being digitally illiterate, a common issue. Although AI saves time, it is still dependent on the support from volunteers when sharing community updates.

Sajna's experience demonstrates that utilizing AI and micro-ghost kitchens enables more people in Kerala to enjoy food entrepreneurship, as her region boasts strong traditions, an open society, and delicious cuisine. It also stresses the importance of local languages, low-cost AI technology, and continuous guidance in digital skills.

12.2. Ramesh's AI-Enabled Ghost Kitchen – "Thattukada 360", Kannur

a. **Background**

Ramesh, who uses a wheelchair and lives in Kannur, has started "Thattukada360," a micro-ghost kitchen that prepares Kerala street food using voice-command AI for order management. Due to the difficulty of moving freely to work, he set up an AI platform that tracked sales, sent automated responses, and recommended the most popular items to customers. Through the help of an incubator, Ramesh's revenue grew by 25% in only six months. Now, he provides deliveries to people in tech parks and colleges using partners. It demonstrates how AI in the food industry helps those who face disadvantages and enables them to pursue sustainable and technologically advanced jobs in Kerala.

1. AI Integration and Innovation

Using a voice-command AI system, Ramesh managed orders, tracked sales, and promoted top-selling dishes without needing to move from his home. Supported by a local business incubator, his operations included automated customer responses and analytics to fine-tune offerings.

"The dishes from Kerala's street food carts are always deeply enjoyed. Because I was differently abled, I could not imagine setting up a real stall. Then, I learned that ghost kitchens can be run more efficiently with the aid of AI, eliminating the need for a physical storefront. I began **'Thattukada360'** *by handling orders and monitoring sales over the phone while staying at home in Kannur. Using the data, I can also tell which meals customers prefer. My meals are delivered to students and IT professionals using local food delivery services. To me, this kitchen is not only where I cook, it is where I express my independence". -Ramesh, Micro Entrepreneur from Kannur*

Ramesh's micro ghost kitchen, 'Thattukada360' in Kannur, illustrates an inclusive AI application. By using voice-command AI to manage his kitchen remotely, Ramesh bridged physical limitations and built customer relationships, demonstrating how ethical, inclusive AI supports social equity in entrepreneurship.

13. FINDINGS OF THE STUDY

This work is based on the Inclusive Entrepreneurship and Innovation Adoption Framework, which draws from the Maslow hierarchy of needs, the Technology Acceptance Model (TAM), and the Theory of Inclusive Digitalization. Its results confirm that AI-enabled ghost kitchens could serve as low-barrier, scalable projects that promote economic inclusion, self-reliance, and micro-level innovations, particularly among rural populations, women, and individuals with disabilities.

1. **High-potential inclusivity** Michelle notes that micro ghost kitchens are accessible, as half of the owners are women, and many belong to minority communities.
2. **AI Boosts Efficiency in Day-to-Day Businesses:** Three out of four entrepreneurs reported higher efficiency and nearly two out of every three experienced increased order volumes.
3. **Barriers Remain** It is estimated that 40% of small-scale business owners believe that paying for costly AI tools is a significant obstacle. In comparison, another 30% believe that not having the required skills for AI prevents them

from utilizing it, and 20% consider the lack of up-to-date infrastructure to be another issue.

4. **Positive financial impact** After adopting AI, 4 out of 5 participants reported an increase in profits, with 36% noting a rise in their monthly profit of between 11% and 25%.
5. **A low number of customers are facing AI usage:** Around 64% of companies are missing out on the benefits of AI-based chatbots for customers, which could strengthen customer relationships and foster loyalty.
6. **Protecting Culture using Innovations.** These studies reveal that locals are using AI to preserve their unique cooking traditions and bring them into the modern era.

14. SUGGESTIONS

14.1. Strategic suggestions

1. Promote the development of inexpensive AI systems suitable for Malayalam voice input and image tracking, such as photo recognition.
2. Organize training sessions with NGOs, colleges, and the local government on AI, digital menu management, and customer engagement.
3. Establish incentives meant to help rural, women-led, or differently-abled food entrepreneurs start using AI.
4. Psychologically motivate regional entrepreneurs to employ AI for both logistics and promotion of their heritage dishes, cultural celebrations, and traditional local dishes through social networks and mobile applications.
5. Establish centres in each locality where micro-ghost kitchen operators can collaborate, share knowledge, and utilize the same AI, cloud kitchen, and digital logistics services.

14.2

Table 9. Barriers and Recommendations

Barriers Identified	Recommendations
High Cost of AI Implementation (40%)	Introduce subsidized AI packages via local govt. or CSR partnerships for micro units.
Lack of Technical Knowledge (30%	Offer vernacular, practical AI skill workshops with peer-led support
Limited Infrastructure (20%)	Improve rural digital infrastructure and access to devices.
Low Usage of Customer-facing AI (Chatbots)	Train entrepreneurs on building trust via user-friendly, multilingual AI interfaces.
Mixed Results in Profitability (20% say no change)	Promote blended strategies plus community marketing for better customer engagement

15. CONCLUSIONS AND FUTURE RESEARCH

This chapter has highlighted the technological innovation aspect of AI-enabled micro ghost kitchens, along with their social inclusion, offering a low-cost and high-opportunity, scalable model of resilient food entrepreneurship in Kerala. Drawing on the combination of Organizational Resilience Theory and the concept of AI-driven entrepreneurship, this paper demonstrates how women, rural entrepreneurs, and individuals with disabilities can be empowered through the use of low-cost, flexible kitchens, potentially preserving local culinary heritage. The model can provide guidance to policy and practice in other aspects of similar socio-cultural worldwide settings.

In the future, one should study:

- Long-term sustainability and profitability of AI-enabled micro ghost kitchen in the countryside and the city.
- How Cultural Authenticity Can Be Maintained When Using AI-Based Menu Customization
- The effect of voice-based and vernacular AI solutions on the digital inclusion of low-literacy entrepreneurs.
- Comparative analysis of an inclusive model of a ghost kitchen in other Indian states or in developing countries.
- Environmental consequences and compliance with the general objectives of sustainability (e.g., waste management, eco logistics).

REFERENCES

Beniwal, T., & Mathur, V. K. (2022). Cloud Kitchens and its impact on the restaurant industry. *International Research Journal on Advanced Science Hub, 4*(12), 324–335. DOI: 10.47392/irjash.2022.076

Chaudhary, S., Soni, B., Sindhavad, A., Mamaniya, A., Dalvi, A., & Siddavatam, I. A. (2022). ChefAI.IN: Generating Indian Recipes with AI Algorithm. *International Conference on Trends in Quantum Computing and Emerging Business Technologies (TQCEBT)*, 1-6. DOI: 10.1109/TQCEBT54229.2022.10041463

Gunawan, M., Soetjipto, B., & Sudhartio, L. (2023). How to link organizational resilience to transformational entrepreneurship behavior as a theoretical framework gap – A systematic literature review. *F1000 Research, 12*, 1–27. DOI: 10.12688/f1000research.133459.1 PMID: 37441222

Gupta, B. B., Gaurav, A., Panigrahi, P. K., & Arya, V. (2023). Analysis of artificial intelligence-based technologies and approaches on sustainable entrepreneurship. *Technological Forecasting and Social Change, 186 Part B*(122152), 0040-1625, https://doi.org/https://doi.org/10.1016/j.techfore.2022.122152

Hamburg, I., & Bucksch, S. (2017). Inclusive education and digital social innovation. *Advances in Social Sciences Research Journal, 4*(5). Advance online publication. DOI: 10.14738/assrj.45.2861

Ishak, A. W., & Williams, E. A. (2018). A dynamic model of organizational resilience: Adaptive and anchored approaches. *Corporate Communications, 23*(2), 180–196. DOI: 10.1108/CCIJ-04-2017-0037

Jones, S., Cain, L., & Deel, G. L. (2024). Virtual Restaurants and Ghost Kitchens: A New Opportunity. *Journal of Hospitality & Tourism Cases, 12(3)*, 108-112. https://doi.org/https://doi.org/10.1177/21649987241241948. (Original work published 2024)

Manfield, R. C., & Newey, L. R. (2018). Resilience as an entrepreneurial capability: Integrating insights from a cross-disciplinary comparison. *International Journal of Entrepreneurial Behaviour & Research, 24*(7), 1155–1180. DOI: 10.1108/IJEBR-11-2016-0368

Mohammadian, H. D., & Rezaie, F. (2021). Big data for entrepreneurship towards csr and sustainable development. In *Big Data for Entrepreneurship and Sustainable Development* (pp. 21–48). CRC Press. DOI: 10.1201/9781003090045-2

Moyeenudin, H. M., Anandan, R., & Shaikjaveedparvez, B. G. (2020). A Research on Cloud Kitchen Prerequisites and Branding Strategies. *International Journal of Innovative Technology and Exploring Engineering*, *9*(3), 983–987. Advance online publication. DOI: 10.35940/ijitee.C8188.019320

Oluwadamilare Usman, F., Louis Eyo-Udo, N., Augustine Etukudoh, E., Odonkor, B., Victoria Ibeh, C., & Adegbola, A. (2024). a Critical Review of Ai-Driven Strategies for Entrepreneurial Success. *International Journal of Management & Entrepreneurship Research*, *6*(1), 200–215. DOI: 10.51594/ijmer.v6i1.748

Rolle, J., Kisato, J., Rock, P., & Winstanley, J. (2020). Inclusive entrepreneurship: A critical look at the inclusion of persons with disabilities. *International Journal of Business & Economic Development*, *08*(02), 20–22. DOI: 10.24052/IJBED/V08N02/ART-01

Saurabh Sharma, V. K. G., &, Kumar Rahul, R. S. M. and M. M. (2021). Sustainable Innovations in the Food Industry through Artificial Intelligence and Big Data Analytics. *Logistics, MDPI*, 1–16. https://addepto.com/blog/artificial-intelligence-and-big-data-analytics-in-accounting/

Soldani, J., Tamburri, D. A., & Van Den Heuvel, W. J. (2018). The pains and gains of microservices: A Systematic grey literature review. *Journal of Systems and Software*, *146*, 215–232. DOI: 10.1016/j.jss.2018.09.082

Srivastava, S., & Upadhyay, D. P. (2024). Digital Empowerment for Indigenous Communities Using Generative Artificial Intelligence. *GATR Global Journal of Business and Social Science Review (GATR-GJBSSR), Vol.12(2)*(April-June 2024.).

Vogus, T. J., & Sutcliffe, K. M. (2007). Organizational resilience: Towards a theory and research agenda. *Conference Proceedings - IEEE International Conference on Systems, Man and Cybernetics*, 3418–3422. DOI: 10.1109/ICSMC.2007.4414160

Wulandari, K. T., Mukti, M. A., & Kiren, K. (2023). *Operation Efficiency In The F and B Enterprise Through Digitalization and Cloud Kitchen Integration: A Systematic Literature Review*. 1128–1137. DOI: 10.46254/AP04.20230296

Chapter 9

Impulsive Consumption Through Gastronomy Livestreaming:

The Role of Gamification, Perceived Professionalism, and Telepresence

Utkarsh Keshari
Independent Researcher, India

Mrigya Tewari
http://orcid.org/0009-0000-1646-5062
Amity University, Gwalior, India

Vishnu Gupta
http://orcid.org/0000-0001-8554-1065
Mahatma Gandhi Kashi Vidyapith, Varanasi, India

Vinay Seth
Mahatma Gandhi Kashi Vidyapith, Varanasi, India

Girdhar Gopal
http://orcid.org/0009-0000-9727-8882
SHEAT College of Engineering, India

Pankaj Kumar
http://orcid.org/0000-0003-0313-2968
Symbiosis University of Applied Sciences, Indore, India

Sujay Vikram Singh
http://orcid.org/0000-0002-7113-2698
Amity University, Lucknow, India

ABSTRACT

In today's fast paced experience driven society, gastronomy has become more than just a necessity- it is a cultural phenomenon deeply tied to emotions, identity, and impulse. Impulsive consumption through gastronomy reflects how food choices are often made spontaneously, driven by emotion, social media influence and pursuit of

DOI: 10.4018/979-8-3373-4047-0.ch009

pleasure rather than basic nutritional needs. The purpose of this study is to identify the factors influencing impulsive consumption through gastronomy. Sample size of the study is 329 collected from Delhi-NCR. Exploratory factor analysis and multiple regression is used as statistical tool to analysis of data. Finding of the study reveals that there is a significant positive relationship between gamification, perceived professionalism and, telepresence and impulsive consumption through gastronomy. Strongest relationship reflects between gamification and impulsive consumption through gastronomy while telepresence has least. At last discussions, limitations and future scope of the study reported at the end.

1. INTRODUCTION

The rise of food focused social media platforms like Instagram, TikTok and YouTube has significantly intensified the impulsive gastronomic consumption. Perfectly curated photos of colourful dishes, viral food trends and the constant exposure to new culinary exposures create an environment where, resting the urge to indulge becomes increasingly difficult. Healthy food having good nutrition is good for health (Sakdapat, 2022, 2024) but Consumers caught in a cycle of visual temptation often makes spontaneous decisions to try toxic meals, visit trendy restaurant or overindulge in desserts all in the pursuit of novel experience. Furthermore, emotional moods are a significant factor in the phenomenon of impulsive eating. Certain emotions, such as stress, enjoyment, boredom, and even nostalgia, might lead to unintentional ingestion of food. In the event that a person is experiencing a difficult day, for instance, they could make a hasty purchase of comfort food or indulge in a lavish lunch in order to celebrate a relatively little win. In this sense, cuisine functions as an emotional release, making it possible to experience quick fulfilment and pleasure to the senses (Rosyidi et al., 2024). A wider range of spontaneous culinary experiences has also been made possible as a result of cultural globalization. Having access to a wide variety of cuisines at one's fingertips encourages individuals to make spontaneous and daring choices on their eating experiences. Modern gastronomy caters for the impulsive nature of modern patrons, whether craving for some sushi at midnight or ordering in some weird street fair food from a pop-up venue that just happens to be right next door. Conversely, culinary impulse buys are almost always delicious and culturally revealing. Ultimately, impulse eating through the menu is a complex dance of emotion, culture, and the influence of modern media. It is an illuminating depiction of the always shifting relationship between people and food, one that reflects deeper emotional and social crosscurrents — more than just surviving. As explained by (Okumus et al., 2018), gastronomy has been and still is a form of sensory escapism; where it acts as a form of escape for tourists and locals alike

(Mariano-Juarez ´ et al., 2023; Japutra et al., 2022; Herianingrum et al., 2024). The scenes of life streamed on social media and mobile terminals make people feel as if they are living a high-quality and exquisite life. This becomes feasible through real-time communication with channel broadcasters. The use of livestreams to serve as a strategic tactic to drive impulsive purchase has been noted (Chung et al., 2017; Sahu et al., 2024). Livestreaming may be able to enhance motivation for and positive thoughts and attitudes toward food. Unconstrained evidence of triggers, such as positive emotions about food or high-level cooking practices, and visceral emotional communication between the live streamer and the audience, may lead the audience to impulse purchase food or dining vouchers. This is also due to the emotional bond that live streamers share with their fans. These purchases can be facilitated by the use of the medium, and the audience can be driven to make such purchases. As argued by (Wondirad et al., 2021), a gastronomic experience is among the pinnacle success factors of tourism. Also, at many tourist sites, meals are served other than the fact that a modern tourist is interested in visiting different types of tourist spots who, in turn, are interested in capturing their corresponding fleeting and appetizing flavour in an effort to fulfil an ever-increasing gastronomic choice and attraction of the visitors to these spots (Bertan, 2021; Sahu et al., 2024). As such, a mere display of fresh culinary produce by livestreaming enables a good and positive impression of the place and thus, a possibility of promoting the culture of that place (Kumar, 2024). Gastronomy livestreaming instead is a diverse type that offers a food-related activity by reflecting back the impression of the culinary image, producers, gastronomic events, quality tasting, etc., in a specific place, in a live and direct way (Pavlidis & Markantonatou, 2020). That is a huge difference when compared with short films that have been recorded or edited. Zhang et al., (2021) They also agreed that "gastronomy livestreaming provides an experience to overlook the dining environment, which is a unique delivery manner, and the creative side for catering". This is unlike the usual e-commerce. Gourmets and streamers are able to explain every aspect of their gourmet experience, including the ingredients, novel recipes, culinary abilities, history, workmanship, and culture of the food they consume. These particulars are meant to have an immediate impact on the decisions that viewers make via the use of real-time online videos. In addition to exhibiting the food, gastronomy livestreaming offers viewers a number of entertainment experiences and game components. These include the opportunity to interact with the bullet screen, the chance to give gifts to their favourite streamers, and the opportunity to earn badges (Li et al., 2021). In addition, viewers have the opportunity to accomplish certain activities in order to earn prizes and incentives. Thus, from the above discussions the role of gastronomy in impulsive consumptions is imperative but the studies with respect role of gastronomy in impulsive consumptions are sparse especially in case of developing economies like India. So, there is a need of further investigation. The goal of this study is to examine the relationship between gamification, perceived professionalism, and telepresence with respect to gastronomic impulse consumptions.

2. RATIONAL OF THE STUDY

In recent years gastronomy livestreaming has rapidly emerged as a popular and influential digital phenomenon reshaping how consumers engage with food related content. Platform such as TikTok, YouTube live etc. are now central spaces where culinary experiences are broadcasted in real time, often simulating spontaneous viewer interaction and consumption behaviour. A critical behaviour that has gained prominence in this setting is impulsive consumption- the unplanned purchasing of food products or services during or after viewing gastronomic livestreaming. While prior studies have examined factors influencing impulsive buying in e-commerce and social media context, there remain a significant gap understanding the unique psychological and technological drivers of this behaviour in the context of gastronomic livestreaming. While other factors, such as price promotions and scarcity cues, can also drive impulsive buying, we chose to focus on gamification, perceived professionalism, and telepresence because these elements are particularly salient in the context of gastronomy livestreaming and are directly influenced by the streamer's actions and platform design.

3. THEORETICAL BACKGROUND

3.1. Uses and Gratification Theory

U&G theory was emerged in1944and it is widely used for understanding audience behaviour when explaining why people select certain kinds of media Initially, (Katz et al., 1973) extended the theory of need and motivation was first indicated 1954. Subsequently, in 1964, it was employed to understand individuals' perceptions of the mass media and their intentions to view specific television programs. U&G theory emerged as a key paradigm to understand U&Gs underlying different types of media since the 1980s (Katz et al., 1973). Several recent studies have adapted U&G theory to technology adoption contexts, including internet use, online photo sharing, photo tagging, online social media, and new media platforms, such as Instagram and Flickr (Bui, 2014; Dhir & Tsai, 2017; B. Liu et al., 2013; Malik et al., 2016; Singh et al., 2025). This research has used U&G theory in relation to livestreaming gastronomy. U&G is a tried-and-true theoretical framework for figuring out why people use a certain platform or media.

3.2. Technology Acceptance Model Theory

One of the most influential and most commonly used theory which explains how individuals use and accept new information technology (IT) is the Technology Adoption Model (TAM). Usefulness, ease of use, and pleasure in use are only three among the many factors which may influence a user's adoption decision and post-adoption attitude with respect to a new system or technology (Davis Fred D., 1989). Previous research findings (Alqatan et al., 2017; Kala Kamdjoug et al., 2021; Singh et al., 2025) and conversations with practitioners confirm the TAM as appropriate for examining customers' acceptance of a new technology. U&G theory is applied to the context of livestreaming gastronomy because it is useful in understanding the experience of users on the livestreaming platform of gastronomy, such as broadcast of live cooking, virtual food tours, etc.

3.3. Elaboration Likelihood Model

The model of elaboration likelihood (ELM) was proposed by (Petty & Cacioppo, 1986). ELM looks inside the consumer's brain at how information processing influences purchase decisions based on the model of human information processing. With ELM, you can have an impact on what the customers do through 2 different routes; the central route and the peripheral route. The central route, which involves scrutinizing the argumentation of the information-heuristic and evaluating the strength and relevance of these reasons for drawing a conclusion. Instead, by attending to the quality of the argument, peripheral processing relies on behavioural cues (such as recommendations from prior users or some form of expert approval), which constitutes lower cognitive effort (Petty & Cacioppo, 1986). This research has used ELM model in relation to livestreaming gastronomy because it will help to explain how audiences will process persuasive messages in the context of livestream of gastronomy.

4. CULINARY LANDSCAPES OF DELHI-NCR: A VIBRANT TAPESTRY OF FLAVOURS AND HERITAGES

The capital of India and the political engine of the country Delhi-NCR is also one of the most affluent culinary capitals of India. Its culinary mosaic is a lively patchwork spun from centuries past, cultural melting pots and modern creativity.

From the crowded lanes of old Delhi to the swanky café of Gurgaon and, Noida. A food scene that mirrors tradition and modernity, Delhi-NCR tells a story through its palate. The culinary canvas of Delhi is as much a part of its history as is the history. Home to many dynasties, including the Mughals, the region assimilated varied culinary influences, which contributed to its rich culinary tapestry of tastes and methods. The Mughal legacy is most evident with dishes like kebabs, biryani and, nihari continuing to sit at many a dinner table. Together with this, Delhi has always been a melting pot of regional migrations- from Punjab to post-partitions to various communities from UP, Rajasthan, Bengal and, down south. The arrival of this unprocessed cuisine has made the foodscape even richer with chole Bhature, parathas, chaat jalebis and an address byway of regional street foods that mirror India's plurality when it boils down to culinary points of view. The added area of Delhi-NCR extended to the surrounding areas like Gurgaon, Noida and Faridabad has helped the modernity and international food culture to stand out. Gourmet dining, concept cafes and world cuisine have entered the eating lexicon of area's urbanite. For example, pride themselves on an eclectic range of fine-dining establishments, micro-breweries and fusion eateries serving up everything from Japanese ramen and Korean BBQ to platters of Mediterranean and grills from South America. So, too, are modern day chefs and restaurants being confronted with fusion food, farm to table concepts and progressive Indian cuisine. World-famous eateries such as Indian Accents, Bukhara have placed Delhi on the world's fancy food map — juxtaposing Indian traditional flavours to a modern presentation and technique. Delhi-NCR is increasingly becoming home to a burgeoning middle class and a food enthusiast culture. Rising proliferation of mobile phone and low-cost internet is driving the adoption of livestreaming platforms, as food influencers have greater opportunities to present a variety of food experiences. On that note, the past few years have also seen an increase of online food delivery services in the region, which makes that spontaneous craving for a particular dish easier than ever. The fabric of Delhi and India as a whole is that of a collectivistic culture, in which the family, community and social cohesion tend to be paramount over individualism. This collectivistic manifest in food choices where meal times are often a social event. Family parties office lunch or community get together. It frequently fosters shared food experiences and joint decision-making. In this type of social environment, the influence of peers and social pressure may enhance impulsive consumptions. Consider a dinner out with friends, and suddenly the pressure to share, sample and indulge in off-premise influences, trends and recommendations immediately felt in the restaurant, is upon us. For example, when dining out with friends, individuals may be more inclined to order extra dishes, try trending or recommended items, or opt for premium offerings to align with group preferences. The cultural emphasis on hospitality and generosity (ordering extra to show care) can also drive impulsive consumptions.

5. LITERATURE REVIEW AND HYPOTHESIS DEVELOPMENT

5.1. Impulsive Consumption through Gastronomic Livestreaming

In the digital age the way consumers interact with food has dramatically changed. Gastronomic livestreaming where influencers or the chefs showcase cooking, tasting, or food related content in real time has become a powerful-trends especially a country with high social media penetrating and engagement such as India (Sio et, al. 2021). While this trend offers entertainment and culinary education. It also drives psychological phenomena known as impulsive consumption. Viewers caught in the moment of live interaction are often persuaded to unplanned purchases(Kathuria & Bakshi, 2024). It sometimes leading to compulsive buying behaviour. The impacts of visual stimulation on the relationships between food producers and visitors have been previously examined in research on gastronomy consumption (Taheri et al., 2021). Livestreaming is a more trustworthy way to showcase the genuineness of cuisine to elicit a reaction like the intention to buy than other forms of advertising like manipulated photos, pre-recorded movies, and customer comments. Livestreaming allows for the transmission of interactive and entertaining video material in real time with the use of computers and cameras. More than that, prominent streamers have an impact on the people that watch livestreams. In addition, there have been instances of sponsored livestreaming that included advertising recognition. The immersive presentation and the streamers' charisma may help to offset the downsides, such as overstated claims about the authenticity of the cuisine (Sokolova & Kefi, 2020). Thus, gastronomy livestreaming has emerged as a viable option for broadcasting the cooking process, showcasing culinary attributes, answering inquiries live, and organizing live events that amuse and persuade viewers to buy without hesitation. livestreaming may make cuisine more immersive. Streamers may now capture restaurants and food tastings with the use of fill-in lighting, high-tech cell phones, and portable recording equipment. Attribution theory postulates that viewers' impulsive food intake is caused by both internal and external variables, such as cognitive perception and task difficulty (Heider, 1946). Viewers' opinions on the streamer and the food show are examples of internal influences. Streamers are strongly related to the viewer's purpose of watching livestreaming while buying since they are vital sources of gourmet information. By providing knowledge on cuisine in an interesting and emotive way, this immersive display is crucial in capturing the attention of spectators. Perceptions of fun prompted by the progressive appearance of interactive messages and difficult tasks on the screen are one example of an external influence.

5.2. Gamification

Gamification involves the application of game-driven characteristics and elements in non-gaming environments, allowing for immersive and entertaining gaming experiences. The tendency to make quick, spur-of-the-moment, thoughtless purchases is what we are referring to when we use the term impulsive buying (Lim et al., 2020). Gamified designs are being incorporated in all of the biggest livestreaming services. Like with regular broadcasts, people watching livestreams can win virtual gifts and discount coupons, and compete on a leader board and get badges by participating in events. These activities span a purchase, hero following the streamer, commenting, sending bullet chats and accessing products pages. As it is a result of explicit substitution of retail with entertaining value these interactions may lead to the effects on the consumer's engagement (Hollebeek et al., 2021). The word that comes to mind here is impulse buying - when a customer makes a purchase without considering if they are already looking for something to meet a need or a want. Users of a livestreaming platform for the culinary arts can get points and badges completing missions. According to (Feng et al., 2018), viewers may be motivated to gain more points, unlock more badges, and feel more fun by using the incentive systems, such as coupons and virtual presents. Game design is all on providing rewards and incentives. The more they are, the more enjoyable it is for spectators. In the end, this makes people more likely to buy anything on the spot on the livestreaming site. Participating in livestreaming platform games increases the likelihood that viewers will learn about new cuisines. This opens up more possibilities for viewers to develop the desire to make an impulsive purchase. Uses and Gratifications theory suggests that consumers actively seek media that fulfil specific needs and desires. Gamified livestreaming platforms, with their points, badges, and leaderboards, may satisfy a need for entertainment, competition, and social recognition. This increased engagement could then lower consumers' resistance to impulsive purchases. from the above discussions following hypothesis has formulated:

H1: There is a significant positive relationship between gamification and impulsive consumption

5.3. Professionalism

Expertise is seen as the capacity to provide accurate knowledge and persuade others to concur by means of effective communication (Ohanian, 1990). Expertise may help recipients to feel certain about not verifying the truth of the claims made by the source (Bansal & Voyer, 2000). According to (Flanagin & Metzger, 2007), the correctness and quality of the information in the online context shapes the sense of professionalism. Thus, those who know gastronomy may supply reliable information like restaurant information, ingredient knowledge, and new products (Archi et al., 2022). In the study conducted by (Y. Liu et al., 2023), Evidence suggests that professional communication, with its high intensity and efficacy, may enhance the impact of gustatory cues. The level of professionalism and competence shown in online interactions has a significant impact on consumers' impulsive purchases (Kapoor, et al. 2013). Reliable professional streamers immediately help viewers in this way: they save them the time and effort needed to verify facts when they trust the material shown to them (Setyani, et al. 2019). Perceived professionalism thus arouses viewer attention, validation, and mutual understanding, which promotes loyalty and closeness (Ha et al., 2023). Viewers are more inclined to participate in unplanned consuming when they see the streamers as competent and credible (Setyani et al., 2019). Based on the Elaboration Likelihood Model, when viewers perceive a streamer as highly professional (a signal of source credibility), they are more likely to engage in central route processing, carefully considering the streamer's recommendations and forming positive attitudes towards the advertised food products. Thus, from the above discussions following hypothesis has formulated:

H2: There is a significant positive relationship between professionalism and impulsive consumption

5.4. Telepresence

Livestreaming gives streamers a chance to showcase and sell their products to consumers right on the spot. The vibrant visuals and animations can really catch people's attention. Also, having dynamic and interesting elements is super important for making consumers' online experience enjoyable. This virtual experience really dives into the food and vibe, giving viewers a chance to feel like they are right there, enjoying a lively sensory journey. (Ou et al., 2014; Sobarna, 2023) confirms that telepresence increases positive purchase intention among customers. Because viewers find such platforms entertaining and effortless, immersive experiences via livestreaming might nurture the desire to attend and eat at a certain restaurant. users feel telepresence enhances their culinary experiences by making the livestreaming more immersive, informative, or interactive they more likely to view the platforms as beneficial as it helps to increase their engagement likelihood of impulsive consumption. It is also observed that when the livestream interface has interactive features are intuitive users can effortlessly immerse themselves in the telepresence experiences which in turn enhances their overall satisfaction and continuous usages. Thus, from the above discussions following hypothesis has formulated:

H3: There is a significant positive relationship between telepresence and impulsive consumption

Figure 1. Conceptual framework

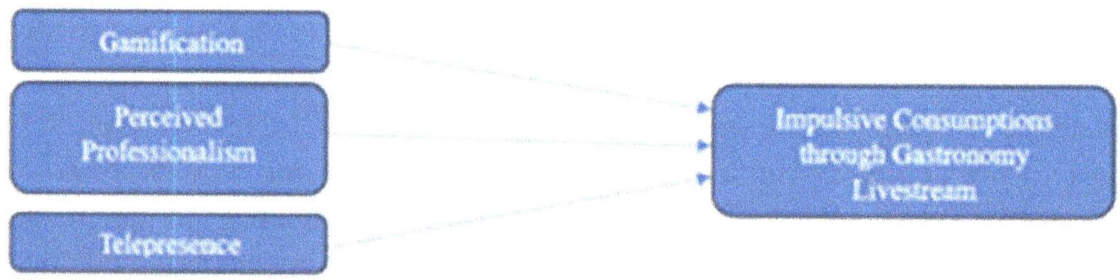

Source: Previous Literature

6. RESEARCH METHODOLOGY

6.1. *Data Collection*

This study collected data from a group of people living in the Delhi-NCR area (Delhi-NCR is a region with a rapidly growing middle class and a vibrant food culture. The increasing penetration of smartphones and affordable internet access has fuelled the popularity of livestreaming platforms, where food influencers showcase diverse culinary experiences. Furthermore, the region has witnessed a surge in online food delivery services, making impulsive food purchases more convenient than ever before). The main aim of this study was to investigate how gamification, perceived professionalism, and telepresence influence impulsive buying in the context of gastronomy. We sent out a structured questionnaire to gather data. We gathered data for this study using a survey method, and we opted for convenience sampling to collect the information. We got 329 valid responses that we used for our analysis.

6.2. Construct Measurement

The items for the study were taken from the following sources (Table-1). We made some adjustments to the measuring items for the constructs based on trustworthy sources from the literature to ensure they are valid and reliable. We measured the total number of items in each concept using a 5-point Likert scale, where it ranges from "strongly disagree" to "strongly agree."

Table 1. Construct with items

Construct	No of Items	Source
Gamification	3	(Feng et al., 2018; Zhang et al., 2021)
Perceived Professionalism	3	(Ohanian, 1990)
Telepresence	3	(Lee et al., 2020; Ou et al., 2014)
Impulsive Consumption	3	(Rook & Fisher, 1995; Zhang et al., 2021)

Source: Literature review

6.3. Respondents Profile

The study involved 329 respondents from the Delhi-NCR region. Here are the demographic characteristics: The study had a majority of male participants, accounting for 70% of the total, while the remaining 30% were female. The study focused on consumers aged 18-60, with a significant portion falling within the 18-35 age range.

7. DATA ANALYSIS

We carried out the data analysis in two steps: first, we used exploratory factor analysis (EFA), and then we moved on to multiple regression. For this, we relied on SPSS to help us analyse the data and test the relationships. The KMO value is 0.791, which is above the recommended threshold of 0.6 (Field, 2009). We also have $\chi 2=$ 3020.015, DF= 66, and $p<0.001$ (see Table-2). This indicates that there is a suitable correlation between the statements for conducting principal component analysis. All the observed variables have a factor loading greater than 0.50, which is above the recommended value (Table-3). all the constructs had eigenvalues greater than 1, which shows that the statistical significance was maintained (Table-4). Cronbach values for all constructs are above the recommended threshold of ≥0.70 (Cronbach, 1951), indicating good internal consistency (Table-3).

Table 2. KMO and Bartlett's test

Kaiser-Meyer-Olkin measure of sampling adequacy		0.791
Bartlett's Test of Sphericity	Approx. Chi-square	3020.015
	Df	66
	Sig.	.000

Source: Analysis Output

Table 3. Factor loading and Cronbach alfa

Construct	Items	Factor Loading
Gamification		
Alpha (α) =: 0.743	The gamification rewards (e.g., energy value, badges, points) of gastronomy livestreaming makes me feel more likely to do actions to obtain them.	0.736
	I am motivated to watch gastronomy livestreaming because the game components (e.g., leaderboards, bullet-screen comments, sending gift) involves me in an enjoyable process.	0.612
	The gamification components of gastronomy livestreaming make me feel more engaged.	0.867
Perceived Professionalism		
Alpha (α) =: 0.876	I think the live streamer(s) can provide a high-quality explanation on gastronomy.	0.799
	I think the live streamer(s) can provide a professional explanation on gastronomy.	0.874
	I think the gastronomy live streamer(s) has rich experiences on the recommended cuisine or restaurants.	0.878
Telepresence		
Alpha (α) =: 0.881	When watching gastronomy livestreaming, I felt my mind was inside the world created by the streamer(s).	0.886
	When watching gastronomy livestreaming, I felt that I was immersed in the world created by the streamer(s).	0.884
	This gastronomy livestreaming-generated world seemed to me to be "somewhere I visited (e.g., fine dining restaurants)." rather than "something I saw."	0.882
Impulsive Consumptions		
Alpha (α) =: 0.813	When I watch gastronomy livestreaming, I have the urge to purchase items other than or in addition to my specific dining goal.	0.762
	I have a desire to purchase items that did not pertain to my specific dining goal when I watch gastronomy livestreaming.	0.791
	I have the inclination to purchase items outside my specific dining goal when watching gastronomy livestreaming.	0.781

Extraction Method: Principal Component Analysis.
Rotation Method: Varimax with Kaiser Normalization.
Rotation converged in 4 iterations.
Source: Analysis Output

Table 4. Total Variance Explained

Total Variance Explained									
Component	Initial Eigenvalues			Extraction Sums of Squared Loadings			Rotation Sums of Squared Loadings		
	Total	% of Variance	Cumulative %	Total	% of Variance	Cumulative %	Total	% of Variance	Cumulative %
1	5.717	47.645	47.645	5.717	47.645	47.645	3.210	26.746	26.746
2	1.692	14.096	61.741	1.692	14.096	61.741	2.425	20.205	46.952
3	1.254	10.453	72.194	1.254	10.453	72.194	2.173	18.108	65.060
4	1.023	8.523	80.717	1.023	8.523	80.717	1.879	15.657	80.717
5	.851	7.089	87.806						
6	.398	3.314	91.120						
7	.250	2.080	93.199						
8	.237	1.975	95.174						
9	.220	1.830	97.004						
10	.141	1.174	98.178						
11	.125	1.039	99.217						
12	.094	.783	100.000						

Extraction Method: Principal Component Analysis.
Source: Analysis Output.

The correlation coefficient, represented as 'R', was calculated to be 0.651. This score signifies a statistically significant level of predictability for consumer behavioural intention towards e-wallet adoption." "The R2 value of 0.423 (Table -5) indicates that 42.30% of the variability in the dependent variable (Impulsive Consumption through Gastronomy) can be explained by the independent variables i.e. Gamification, Perceived Professionalism and Telepresence."

Table 5. Model summary

Model	R	R Square	Adjusted R Square	Std. Error of the Estimate
1	.651	.423	.418	3.73693

Predictors: (Constant), Gamification, Perceived Professionalism and Telepresence.

We looked at the regression model and analysed it using (Table-6) to see if it fits the data well. The independent factors listed in (Table-6) are statistically significant, indicating they could potentially predict Impulsive Consumption through Gastronomy. The analysis reveals that the dependent variable is significantly influenced by these factors, as evidenced by the F statistic (3, 329) =79.732, with a significance level of $P < 0.05$. Therefore, we may deduce that the regression model mentioned above is a suitable match for the given data."

Table 6. ANOVA

ANOVA						
Model		Sum of Squares	df	Mean Square	F	Sig.
1	Regression	3340.306	3	1113.435	79.732	.000
	Residual	4552.481	326	13.965		
	Total	7892.788	329			

Dependent Variable: Impulsive Consumption through Gastronomy
Predictors: (Constant), Gamification, Perceived Professionalism and Telepresence

Table 7. Coefficients

Coefficients						
Model		Unstandardized Coefficients		Standardized Coefficients	t	Sig.
		B	Std. Error	Beta		
1	(Constant)	2.380	.711		3.346	.001
	Telepresence	.212	.049	.202	4.309	.000
	Gamification	.316	.051	.309	6.150	.000
	Perceived Professionalism	.285	.045	.312	6.315	.000

Dependent Variable: Impulsive Consumption through Gastronomy

We can see the p-value of 0.000, which is much less than the alpha value of 0.05 for Gamification, Perceived Professionalism and Telepresence "(Table-7) so, there is a significant relationship between the dependent variables and independent variables and all the hypothesis has been accepted (H1 to H3)."

Thus, the multiple regression equation for this study will be:"

"Impulsive Consumption through Gastronomy = 2.380 + 0.316 Gamification + 0.285 Perceived Professionalism+0.212 Telepresence.

"The (Table-7) makes clear that Impulsive Consumption through Gastronomy and Gamification is strongly correlated" (strongest relationship) "serving as one of the primary antecedents of Impulsive Consumption through Gastronomy, followed by Perceived Professionalism and Telepresence."

8. FINDINGS

In the context of gastronomy livestreaming, the study investigated the influence that telepresence, perceived professionalism, and gamification had on impulsive consumption behaviour. Gamification elements such as point system, leaderboards, time-limited discounts, and interactive games were significantly and positively associated with impulsive consumption behaviour. It is believed that interactive features heightened their engagement and create a sense of urgency contributing to unplanned purchase. The professionalism of the livestream host- including communication skills, culinary expertise, and presentation quality had a positive impact on viewers trust and purchase intention. Viewers were more likely to make spontaneous purchase when they perceived the host as credible and knowledgeable. Telepresence or sense of being there in the livestream environment is a significant predicator of impulsive buying. It is because of immersive nature of livestream, including closeup visuals of food, real time responses and ambience of the background fostered emotional arousal that led to impulsive consumption. The result reinforced the evolving role of livestreaming as not just as entertainment medium but also a powerful driver of impulsive consumption. Finally, as far as ethical considerations are concerned; informed canescent was obtained from all survey respondents and interview participants. Given the study on impulsive consumptions particular care was taken to avoid manipulative or coercive language that could exacerbate or encourage unhealthy purchasing habits among participants. The potentiality of psychological impact of discussing impulsive buying and digital engagement was considered. Transparency was maintained by disclosing any potential conflicts of interest and ensuring that gamification and telepresence mechanism discussed were analysed objectively without promoting exploitative or manipulative marketing practices.

9. THREOTICAL AND PRACTICAL IMPLICATIONS

9.1. Threotical Implications:

This study contributes meaningfully to the emerging literature on digital consumer behaviour. Particularly within the niche of gastronomy livestreaming. By integrating the construct of gamification, perceived professionalism, and telepresence. It expands our understanding of how interactive and immersive features drive impulsive consumption in real time digital environments. First the findings demonstrate that gamification mechanism such as point system, rewards and interactive challenges enhance user engagement leading to heightened impulsive purchasing tendencies. This extends prior research on gamification in e-commerce and social media platforms into the domain of gastronomy livestreaming a context where sensory appeals and immediate gratification intertwin strongly. Second the role of perceived professionalism adds nuances to the existing models of influencers marketing and digital persuasions. Professionalism, conveyed through polished presentation, expert knowledge, and product quality, not only fosters trust but also amplify persuasive impact thereby facilitating unplanned consumption decisions. This deepens the theory of source credibility and parasocial interaction, illustrating how professionalism mediates viewers responses in livestreaming commerce. Third, the inclusion of telepresence underscores the importance of psychological immersion in shaping consumers behaviour. Study affirms that when viewers feel virtually present within a livestreamed food environment-enabled by high interactivity, vivid imaginary, and real time communication – they are more suspectable to impulsive purchases. This aligned with the extends media richness and flow theories by evidencing how sensory rich livestreaming formats can stimulates an in-person dining. Collectively, these results generate a multi-dimensional theoretical model of how the structural aspects of the gastronomy livestreaming space interact to precipitate impulsive consumptions, providing a cornerstone for future inter-contextual comparisons e.g. travel livestreaming. Third, it is important to generate a strong sense of telepresence. Some practical methods of achieving this are through taking the device of using different camera angles, example close up of food preparation, interacting real time with your audience e.g., responding to comments (if any), showing recognition of audience with their names as well as getting to captivate the audience's senses. Platforms may also incorporate AR and VR upgrading to elevate the experimental appeals. Marketers also need to program live stream campaigns with impulsivity triggers in that show exclusive, limited-edition menu items or know to push flash deals during peak audience moments. By understanding the relationship of gamification, professionalism and telepresence, businesses can better coordinate a compelling live stream experience that entertains with purpose, and the benefit of converting a viewer into an impulsive buyer.

9.2. Practical Implications

The findings are potential useful for gastronomy livestreaming practitioners (e.g., restaurant, food brand, and platform builder) to generate usable content. First, cleverly incorporating some gamification features that can be used to keep the enthusiasm of the users and bring impulse buying. Things like timed promotions lifting them off with in-app live mini-games, or polls to participate in for rewards, or achievement badges, can contribute to this sort of competitive immediacy and the quick-trigger decision making. second factor driving perceptions of professionalism is the need to create trust and credibility with viewers. This entails not only technical aspects-such as high-definition videos-audios, and visually appealing stagging, but also presenter skills including articulate food descriptions, culinary expertise, and authentic enthusiasm. Live streamers should receive training in communication and visual merchandising to bolster their perceived authority and competence. Restaurants can have virtual tours of their kitchens, to nosy through the freshest ingredients and the skills in the kitchen, to help promote their professionalism. They can even provide one-time discounts to viewers who take part in live polls or trivia games, turning the livestreaming experience into a game. For food brands, it is possible to collaborate with influencers in real time on live product reviews and cooking demonstrations, using the influencer and televirtual presence to influence purchase decisions. And lastly, Platform developers can add features like virtual tasting, AR food filters, interactive recipe generation, etc to better the feeling of telepresence, thus making livestreaming more immersive and engaging.

10. LIMITATIONS AND FUTURE SCOPE OF THE STUDY

While this study contributes to the understanding of impulsive consumption behaviour in the context of gastronomy livestreaming, it is not without limitations. Addressing these limitations offers opportunities for future research to refine, validate and expand the current findings. Firstly, the participants of this study belong to Delhi-NCR region of India having different cultural background, which can influence how they can perceive gamification, perceived professionalism, and telepresence with respect to gastronomy livestreaming. Consumer behaviour in response to livestreaming may vary across different cultural context due to differing norms regarding food consumptions and, entertainment. Future studies should consider cross-cultural comparison to examine whether these relationships hold across these diverse consumer groups. Secondly this research relies heavily on self-reported data which introduces the potential for social desirability bias and recall errors. Respondents may overstate or understate their impulsive consumption due to perceived expectation or lack of self-awareness. To overcome this limitation future research could incorporate behavioural data, such as click stream analysis or actual purchase data during livestream sessions to triangulate finding and enhance validity. Thirdly this study takes a cross-sectional approach which limits the ability to make casual inferences. A longitudinal or experimental design would offer a more robust understanding of casual relationship and how consumer responses evolve over time particularly as they become more familiar with livestream formats or specific hosts. Moreover, this study focuses on a limited set of independent variables like gamification, perceived professionalism, and telepresence while many influential variables may overlook. For instance, consumer personality traits, mood states, price promotions, scarcity cues, social influence, peer influence via chatroom or promotional strategies like time limited offers and discount may also significantly impact impulsive buying behaviour. Future study should integrate these psychological and social contextual variables to build a more comprehensive model.

REFERENCES

Alqatan, S., Maizura, N., Noor, M., Man, M., & Mohemad, R. (2017). Information Technology, in 2000 from University Putra Malaysia. He obtained his degree and Diploma in Computer Sciences. *International Journal of Business Information Systems*, *26*(1), •••.

Bansal, H. S., & Voyer, P. A. (2000). Word-of-Mouth Processes within a Services Purchase Decision Context. *Journal of Service Research*, *3*(2), 166–177. DOI: 10.1177/109467050032005

Bertan, S. (2021). Impact of restaurants in the development of gastronomic tourism. *International Journal of Gastronomy and Food Science*, *21*(1), 1–37.

Bui, T.-V. (2014). *Social Media On-A-Stick: A uses and gratification approach toward helping mobile food vendors engage consumers on Instagram.*

Chung, N., Song, H. G., & Lee, H. (2017). Consumers' impulsive buying behavior of restaurant products in social commerce. *International Journal of Contemporary Hospitality Management*, *29*(2), 709–731. DOI: 10.1108/IJCHM-10-2015-0608

Cronbach, L. J. (1951). Coefficient alpha and the internal structure of tests. *Psychometrika*, *16*(3), 297–334. DOI: 10.1007/BF02310555

Davis Fred, D. (1989). Perceived Usefulness, Perceived Ease of Use, and User Acceptance of Information Technology. *Management Information Systems Quarterly*, *13*(3), 319–340. DOI: 10.2307/249008

Dhir, A., & Tsai, C. C. (2017). Understanding the relationship between intensity and gratifications of Facebook use among adolescents and young adults. *Telematics and Informatics*, *34*(4), 350–364. DOI: 10.1016/j.tele.2016.08.017

El Archi, Y., El, Y., & Phd, A. A. (2022). *The role of OTAs in the transformation of tourism: a study on customer satisfaction in the digital era.* https://www.researchgate.net/publication/366014685

Feng, Y., Jonathan Ye, H., Yu, Y., Yang, C., & Cui, T. (2018). Gamification artifacts and crowdsourcing participation: Examining the mediating role of intrinsic motivations. *Computers in Human Behavior*, *81*, 124–136. DOI: 10.1016/j.chb.2017.12.018

Flanagin, A. J., & Metzger, M. J. (2007). The role of site features, user attributes, and information verification behaviors on the perceived credibility of web-based information. *New Media & Society*, *9*(2), 319–342. DOI: 10.1177/1461444807075015

Ha, M. T., Do Nguyen, G., & Doan, B. S. (2023). Understanding the mediating effect of switching costs on service value, quality, satisfaction, and loyalty. *Humanities & Social Sciences Communications*, *10*(1), 288. Advance online publication. DOI: 10.1057/s41599-023-01797-6

Heider, F. (1946). Attitudes and Cognitive Organization. *The Journal of Psychology*, *21*(1), 107–112. DOI: 10.1080/00223980.1946.9917275 PMID: 21010780

Hollebeek, L. D., Das, K., & Shukla, Y. (2021). Game On! How Gamified Loyalty Programs Boost Customer Engagement Value. *International Journal of Information Management*, *61*, 102308. https://www.researchgate.net/publication/348565144. DOI: 10.1016/j.ijinfomgt.2021.102308

Kala Kamdjoug, J. R., Djuitchou Chengo, S. M., & Gueyie, J. P. (2021). Factors affecting the adoption of information technologies by small woman-managed enterprises in Cameroon. *Journal of Small Business and Entrepreneurship*, *33*(4), 433–451. DOI: 10.1080/08276331.2020.1716134

Kapoor, P. S., Jayasimha, K. R., & Sadh, A. (2013). Brand-related, Consumer to Consumer, Communication via social media. *IIM Kozhikode Society & Management Review*, *2*(1), 43–59. DOI: 10.1177/2277975213496514

Kathuria, A., & Bakshi, A. (2024). Influence of promotional factors on online impulse buying: Exploring the mediating role of impulse buying tendency. *Current Psychology (New Brunswick, N.J.)*, *43*(1), 34035–34051. DOI: 10.1007/s12144-024-06911-8

Katz, E., Blumler, J. G., & Gurevitch, M. (1973). USES AND GRATIFICATIONS RESEARCH. *Public Opinion Quarterly*, *37*(4), 509–523. https://poq.oxfordjournals.org/. DOI: 10.1086/268109

Kumar, G. R. (2024). Food tourism research in India – current trends and future scope. *Tourism Review*, *79*(3), 640–657. DOI: 10.1108/TR-07-2022-0366

Li, R., Lu, Y., Ma, J., & Wang, W. (2021). Examining gifting behavior on live streaming platforms: An identity-based motivation model. *Information & Management*, *58*(6), 103406. Advance online publication. DOI: 10.1016/j.im.2020.103406

Lim, X.-J., Cheah, J.-H., Waller, D. S., Ting, H., & Ng, S. I. (2020). What s-commerce implies? Repurchase intention and its antecedents. *Marketing Intelligence & Planning*, *38*(6), 760–776. DOI: 10.1108/MIP-03-2019-0145

Liu, B., Norman, W. C., & Pennington-Gray, L. (2013). A flash of culinary tourism: Understanding the influences of online food photography on people's travel planning process on flickr. *Tourism, Culture & Communication*, *13*(1), 5–18. DOI: 10.3727/109830413X13769180530567

Liu, Y., Ting, H., & Ringle, C. (2023). Appreciation to and Behavior Intention Regarding Upscale Ethnic Restaurants. *Journal of Hospitality & Tourism Research (Washington, D.C.)*, *47*(1), 235–256. DOI: 10.1177/10963480211011544

Malik, A., Dhir, A., & Nieminen, M. (2016). Uses and Gratifications of digital photo sharing on Facebook. *Telematics and Informatics*, *33*(1), 129–138. DOI: 10.1016/j.tele.2015.06.009

Ohanian, R. (1990). Construction and validation of a scale to measure celebrity endorsers' perceived expertise, trustworthiness, and attractiveness. *Journal of Advertising*, *19*(3), 39–52. DOI: 10.1080/00913367.1990.10673191

Okumus, B., Koseoglu, M. A., & Ma, F. (2018). Food and gastronomy research in tourism and hospitality: A bibliometric analysis. *International Journal of Hospitality Management*, *73*, 64–74. DOI: 10.1016/j.ijhm.2018.01.020

Ou, C. X., Pavlou, P. A., & Davison, R. M. (2014). Swift guanxi in online marketplaces: The role of computer-mediated communication technologies. *Management Information Systems Quarterly*, *38*(1), 209–230. DOI: 10.25300/MISQ/2014/38.1.10

Pavlidis, G., & Markantonatou, S. (2020). Gastronomic tourism in Greece and beyond: A thorough review. In *International Journal of Gastronomy and Food Science* (Vol. 21). AZTI-Tecnalia., DOI: 10.1016/j.ijgfs.2020.100229

Petty, R. E., & Cacioppo, J. T. (1986). *THE ELABORATION LIKELIHOOD MODEL OF PERSUASION.*

Sahu, P., Bakshi, S., Divya, K. M., Singh, S. V., Keshari, U., Kumar, P., Neelam, K., Singh, P. C., & Singh, V. K. (2024). *Examine the Influence of Social Media in Promoting Regional Cuisine.*, DOI: 10.4018/979-8-3693-7096-4.ch018

Sakdapat, N. (2022). Healthy food consumption behavior of working people in the capital city: A case study in Bangkok, Thailand. *Przestrzeń Społeczna (Social Space), 22*(3), 365–384. https://orcid.org/0000-0002-8689-4046

Sakdapat, N. (2024). Stress Management Behaviour in Working Adults: A Case Study of Operational-Level Private Sector Employees in the Capital City of Thailand. *Przestrzeń Społeczna (Social Space), 24*(2), 469–488. https://orcid.org/0009-0000-0369-1191

Setyani, V., Zhu, Y. Q., Hidayanto, A. N., Sandhyaduhita, P. I., & Hsiao, B. (2019). Exploring the psychological mechanisms from personalized advertisements to urge to buy impulsively on social media. *International Journal of Information Management*, *48*, 96–107. DOI: 10.1016/j.ijinfomgt.2019.01.007

Singh, P. C., Singh, S. V., Rajauria, S., Singh, V. K., & Sahu, P. (2025). Examine the Role of Short Video Platforms on Tourist's Attitude: A Technology Acceptance Model (TAM) Approach. *PUSA Journal of Hospitality and Applied Sciences*, *11*(1), 12–19. DOI: 10.48165/pjhas.2025.11.1.2

Sobarna, A. (2023). Virtual Reality Tourism: Linkage Tourist Intention, Satisfaction, and Quality. [JMI]. *Journal of Marketing Innovation*, *3*(1). Advance online publication. DOI: 10.35313/jmi.v3i1.58

Sokolova, K., & Kefi, H. (2020). Instagram and YouTube bloggers promote it, why should I buy? How credibility and parasocial interaction influence purchase intentions. *Journal of Retailing and Consumer Services*, *53*, 101742. Advance online publication. DOI: 10.1016/j.jretconser.2019.01.011

Taheri, B., Pourfakhimi, S., Prayag, G., Gannon, M. J., & Finsterwalder, J. (2021). Towards co-created food well-being: Culinary consumption, braggart word-of-mouth and the role of participative co-design, service provider support and C2C interactions. *European Journal of Marketing*, *55*(9), 2464–2490. DOI: 10.1108/EJM-02-2020-0145

Wondirad, A., Kebete, Y., & Li, Y. (2021). Culinary tourism as a driver of regional economic development and socio-cultural revitalization: Evidence from Amhara National Regional State, Ethiopia. *Journal of Destination Marketing & Management*, *19*, 100482. Advance online publication. DOI: 10.1016/j.jdmm.2020.100482

Zhang, L., Shao, Z., Li, X., & Feng, Y. (2021). Gamification and online impulse buying: The moderating effect of gender and age. *International Journal of Information Management*, *61*, 102267. Advance online publication. DOI: 10.1016/j.ijinfomgt.2020.102267

Chapter 10
Food at the Crossroads: Balancing Health, Sustainability, and Business Innovation

Shivansu Sachan
http://orcid.org/0000-0002-9893-8018
CSJM University, India

Mohammad Badruddoza Talukder
http://orcid.org/0009-0008-1662-9221
International University of Business Agriculture and Technology, Bangladesh

Siddharth Singh
http://orcid.org/0009-0007-7876-4915
CSJM University, Kanpur, India

Mohammad Nurul Afchar
http://orcid.org/0009-0006-9736-7854
Daffodil International University, Bangladesh

Ankit Kumar
http://orcid.org/0009-0009-5002-4522
CSJM University, Kanpur, India

Aishwarya Arya
http://orcid.org/0009-0000-4236-3983
CSJM University, Kanpur, India

Vanshika Srivastava
http://orcid.org/0009-0008-0529-6740
CSJM University, Kanpur, India

ABSTRACT

The modern food landscape exists at a critical intersection of health, sustainability, and business, where consumer demands, scientific advancements, and economic pressures converge. This chapter explores how food systems influence public health outcomes while simultaneously driving innovation and profitability in the global marketplace. It examines the rise of health-conscious consumer trends, such as plant-based diets, functional foods, and personalized nutrition, alongside the business strategies that capitalize on these shifts, including supply chain adaptations, marketing innovations, and regulatory compliance. This paper explores the intricate interplay between these dimensions, highlighting the need for innovative approaches

DOI: 10.4018/979-8-3373-4047-0.ch010

to address rising food demand, nutritional deficiencies, and ecological degradation. It examines how dietary shifts toward plant-based and nutrient-dense foods can promote health while reducing environmental footprints.

INTRODUCTION

The global food system stands at a pivotal juncture, grappling with interconnected challenges that demand innovative solutions. Rising populations, environmental degradation, and shifting dietary preferences place unprecedented pressure on food production and distribution. At the heart of this complex landscape lie three critical imperatives: promoting human health, ensuring environmental sustainability, and fostering business innovation to drive systemic change. This chapter explores the intricate balance among these priorities, examining their tensions, synergies, and the pathways toward a more resilient food future. By analyzing current trends, challenges, and opportunities, we aim to illuminate how stakeholders—policymakers, businesses, and consumers—can navigate this crossroads to create a food system that nourishes people and the planet while remaining economically viable. The global food system stands at a critical juncture, where the imperatives of health, sustainability, and business innovation intersect to shape the future of human well-being and planetary resilience. Among these, the health imperative—centered on nutrition and public well-being—has emerged as a foundational concern. Poor dietary habits, driven by the proliferation of ultra-processed foods, contribute significantly to the global burden of non-communicable diseases (NCDs), including obesity, diabetes, cardiovascular diseases, and certain cancers. Simultaneously, malnutrition in its various forms—undernutrition, micronutrient deficiencies, and overnutrition—continues to afflict populations across both developed and developing nations. Addressing these challenges requires a multifaceted approach that integrates scientific advances in nutrition, equitable food access, and innovative policy frameworks, all while navigating the complexities of consumer behavior and industry dynamics. This chapter explores the health imperative within the global food system, emphasizing the critical role of nutrition in fostering public well-being and the strategies needed to align dietary patterns with health outcomes.

The chapter provides a robust contextual overview of the global food system, particularly its intersection with health, sustainability, and business innovation. It references high-impact global data (e.g., WHO, FAO, IPCC) and seminal studies like the EAT-Lancet Commission and Tilman & Clark's (2014) dietary-sustainability linkages. However, the literature review remains somewhat descriptive and lacks a formal scholarly tone or critical synthesis of existing academic debates.

The chapter clearly illustrates major global trends—e.g., NCDs, environmental degradation from agriculture, and food tech innovation—linking them effectively to the book's theme. However, while broad, it lacks sufficient depth on specific geopolitical, sociocultural, or regulatory trends shaping regional food systems.

There is an appropriate emphasis on health, environment, and innovation, but some emerging or marginalized issues—like food justice, trade regimes, or power asymmetries in global agribusiness—receive inadequate attention.

THE GLOBAL NUTRITION CRISIS

The World Health Organization (WHO) estimates that NCDs account for approximately 74% of all deaths globally, with dietary factors being a leading modifiable risk factor. Diets high in sodium, trans fats, and added sugars, coupled with low consumption of fruits, vegetables, and whole grains, are directly linked to the rising prevalence of obesity and related illnesses. For instance, the global obesity rate has nearly tripled since 1975, with over 1.9 billion adults classified as overweight or obese in recent data. Concurrently, undernutrition persists, particularly in low-income regions, where 462 million adults are underweight, and 149 million children under five suffer from stunting due to chronic malnutrition.

Micronutrient deficiencies, often termed "hidden hunger," further complicate the nutrition landscape. Deficiencies in iron, vitamin A, and iodine affect billions, impairing cognitive development, immune function, and overall productivity. These challenges are not confined to developing nations; even in affluent countries, reliance on calorie-dense, nutrient-poor foods has led to widespread deficiencies in essential vitamins and minerals. The coexistence of overnutrition and undernutrition within the same populations—sometimes within the same households—underscores the complexity of the global nutrition crisis.

DETERMINANTS OF DIETARY PATTERNS

Dietary choices are shaped by a web of interconnected factors, including socioeconomic status, cultural norms, education, and food availability. In many low- and middle-income countries, economic constraints limit access to diverse, nutrient-rich foods, forcing reliance on cheaper, calorie-dense staples. In contrast, in high-income nations, the abundance of ultra-processed foods—engineered for palatability and shelf life—has reshaped dietary habits. These foods, often high in sugars, unhealthy fats, and sodium, are heavily marketed, affordable, and convenient, making them a dominant feature of modern diets.Cultural and social factors also play a pivotal role. Traditional diets, often rich in plant-based foods and minimally processed ingredients, are increasingly supplanted by Westernized eating patterns characterized by fast food and sugary beverages. Urbanization exacerbates this trend, as time constraints and the proliferation of food outlets encourage reliance on ready-to-eat meals. Moreover, misinformation about nutrition, propagated through social media and inadequate public education, complicates efforts to promote healthier choices. The food environment—encompassing the availability, affordability, and marketing of food—further influences dietary behavior. In many regions, "food deserts" limit access to fresh produce, while aggressive marketing of unhealthy foods targets vulnerable populations, including children. Addressing these determinants requires interventions that extend beyond individual behavior to encompass systemic changes in food production, distribution, and marketing.

Strategies for Improving Nutrition and Public Well-Being

Tackling the health imperative demands a comprehensive approach that integrates policy, education, and innovation. Below are key strategies to align dietary patterns with public health goals.

1. Policy Interventions

Governments play a critical role in shaping food environments through evidence-based policies. Taxation on sugar-sweetened beverages, for example, has proven effective in reducing consumption in countries like Mexico and the United Kingdom. Similarly, front-of-pack nutrition labeling, such as Chile's warning labels for high-sugar, high-fat, or high-sodium products, empowers consumers to make informed choices. Subsidies for fruits, vegetables, and whole grains can enhance affordability, particularly for low-income households. Regulatory measures to curb the marketing of unhealthy foods are equally vital. Restrictions on advertising directed at children, as implemented in Quebec and Norway, have shown promise in reducing exposure to persuasive marketing. Additionally, reformulating processed foods to reduce sugar, salt, and trans fats—while maintaining affordability and taste—can shift population-level consumption patterns without requiring drastic behavioral changes.

2. Nutrition Education and Public Awareness

Education is a cornerstone of dietary change. Public health campaigns that promote balanced diets, such as the "5 A Day" fruit and vegetable initiative, have increased awareness in various countries. School-based programs that integrate nutrition education into curricula can instill lifelong healthy habits. For instance, Japan's Shokuiku (food education) program emphasizes the cultural and health value of balanced meals, contributing to low obesity rates. Community-based interventions, such as cooking workshops and urban gardening initiatives, can empower individuals to prepare nutritious meals while fostering social cohesion. Digital platforms, including mobile apps and social media, offer scalable opportunities to disseminate evidence-based nutrition information, countering misinformation and engaging younger audiences.

3. Food System Innovation

Innovations in food production and distribution are essential to improving nutrition. Fortification of staple foods with micronutrients—such as iodized salt or vitamin A-fortified cooking oil—has successfully reduced deficiencies in many regions. Biofortification, the breeding of nutrient-rich crop varieties, offers a sustainable solution for addressing hidden hunger, as seen in the deployment of orange-fleshed sweet potatoes in sub-Saharan Africa. Alternative proteins, including plant-based and lab-grown options, provide opportunities to reduce reliance on resource-intensive animal products while meeting nutritional needs. Precision nutrition, which tailors dietary recommendations to individual genetic and lifestyle profiles, holds promise for optimizing health outcomes, though accessibility remains a challenge.

4. Addressing Inequities in Food Access

Equitable access to nutritious food is a prerequisite for public well-being. Initiatives such as farmers' markets, mobile food vans, and community-supported agriculture can bridge gaps in food deserts. Public-private partnerships can incentivize retailers to stock healthier options in underserved areas. Additionally, social safety nets, such as food vouchers or school meal programs, can ensure that vulnerable populations have access to adequate nutrition.

THE HEALTH IMPERATIVE: NOURISHING BODIES IN A CHANGING WORLD

Food is the cornerstone of human health, yet modern diets are increasingly linked to a rise in non-communicable diseases such as obesity, diabetes, and cardiovascular disorders. The World Health Organization (2023) estimates that poor diet contributes to 11 million premature deaths annually, underscoring the urgency of addressing dietary patterns. The shift toward processed, calorie-dense foods, often high in sugars, salts, and unhealthy fats, has been driven by convenience, affordability, and aggressive marketing. Simultaneously, undernutrition persists in many regions, creating a dual burden of malnutrition where obesity and hunger coexist within communities. To address these challenges, public health advocates emphasize the need for diets rich in whole grains, fruits, vegetables, and lean proteins. However, access to such foods is uneven, shaped by socioeconomic disparities and geographic constraints. For instance, food deserts—areas with limited access to fresh, affordable produce—disproportionately affect low-income communities, exacerbating health inequities. Policy interventions, such as subsidies for nutrient-dense foods or taxes on sugar-sweetened beverages, have shown promise but face resistance from industry stakeholders and consumers accustomed to low-cost, convenient options.Beyond access, consumer behavior plays a pivotal role. Educational campaigns promoting dietary literacy can empower individuals to make informed choices, yet cultural preferences and ingrained habits often resist change. The rise of plant-based diets, driven by health and ethical considerations, exemplifies how consumer trends can align with health goals. However, scaling these trends requires overcoming barriers such as cost, taste perceptions, and supply chain limitations. The health imperative thus demands a multifaceted approach, blending policy, education, and innovation to foster diets that support long-term well-being.

THE SUSTAINABILITY CHALLENGE: FEEDING THE PLANET WITHOUT DEPLETING IT

Environmental Impacts of Food Production

The global food system stands at a critical juncture, tasked with nourishing a growing population while mitigating its profound environmental footprint. Food production, while essential for human survival, is a leading driver of ecological degradation, contributing to climate change, biodiversity loss, soil depletion, and water scarcity. Balancing the demands of health, sustainability, and business innovation requires a nuanced understanding of these environmental impacts and a commitment to transformative practices. This section explores the environmental consequences of food production and the challenges of achieving a sustainable food system without compromising planetary health.

Agriculture is both a victim and a contributor to environmental degradation. The food system accounts for approximately 30% of global greenhouse gas emissions, with livestock production alone responsible for nearly half of this share. Deforestation, driven by demand for cropland and pasture, has led to the loss of 10 million hectares of forest annually, threatening biodiversity and carbon sequestration. Water use is another concern: agriculture consumes 70% of global freshwater, with inefficient irrigation practices exacerbating scarcity in arid regions.

One of the most significant environmental impacts of food production is its contribution to greenhouse gas (GHG) emissions. Agriculture accounts for approximately 25-30% of global GHG emissions, with livestock farming being a primary contributor. Ruminant animals, such as cattle, produce methane—a potent greenhouse gas—through enteric fermentation, while manure management and feed production further exacerbate emissions. Deforestation for agricultural expansion, particularly for soy and palm oil cultivation, releases stored carbon into the atmosphere and diminishes forests' capacity to act as carbon sinks. Additionally, the energy-intensive processes involved in fertilizer production, irrigation, and food processing amplify the carbon footprint of the food system. These emissions intensify climate change, which, in turn, disrupts agricultural productivity through extreme weather events, shifting growing seasons, and reduced crop yields. Beyond climate change, food production is a major driver of biodiversity loss. The conversion of natural ecosystems into farmland has led to habitat destruction, threatening countless species. Monoculture farming, which dominates modern agriculture, reduces genetic diversity in crops and disrupts ecosystems by limiting the variety of plants and animals that can coexist in agricultural landscapes. The heavy use of pesticides and herbicides further harms pollinators, such as bees, and other beneficial organisms critical to food production. For instance, studies indicate that pesticide use has contributed to a 30-50% decline in insect populations in some regions over recent decades, with cascading effects on birds and amphibians. This loss of biodiversity undermines ecosystem resilience, making food systems more vulnerable to pests, diseases, and environmental changes. Soil degradation is another pressing concern. Intensive farming practices, including excessive tillage and reliance on chemical fertilizers, deplete soil organic matter and disrupt microbial ecosystems. Globally, an estimated 33% of arable land is moderately to highly degraded, reducing its fertility and capacity to support crops. Soil erosion, driven by deforestation and unsustainable land management, exacerbates this problem, with topsoil loss occurring at rates far exceeding natural replenishment. Degraded soils not only threaten food security but also diminish the land's ability to sequester carbon, further contributing to climate change. The overuse of nitrogen and phosphorus fertilizers also leads to nutrient runoff, causing eutrophication in water bodies. This process triggers algal blooms that deplete oxygen, creating "dead zones" in rivers, lakes, and coastal areas, such as the Gulf of Mexico, where marine life cannot survive.

Water scarcity is a growing challenge exacerbated by food production. Agriculture consumes approximately 70% of global freshwater resources, primarily for irrigation. In water-stressed regions, such as parts of South Asia and the Middle East, overexploitation of groundwater for farming has led to aquifer depletion, threatening long-term water availability. Moreover, agricultural runoff, laden with fertilizers, pesticides, and sediments, pollutes rivers and groundwater, compromising water quality for both human consumption and ecosystems. Climate change intensifies these issues by altering precipitation patterns and increasing the frequency of droughts, further straining water resources for agriculture.

The environmental impacts of food production are compounded by food waste, which accounts for roughly one-third of all food produced globally. Wasted food contributes to GHG emissions through its production, transportation, and decomposition in landfills, where it releases methane. In addition, the resources used to produce uneaten food—land, water, and energy—are squandered, amplifying the environmental toll. Addressing food waste is thus a critical component of sustainable food systems, requiring innovations in supply chain management, consumer behavior, and policy frameworks. Achieving sustainability in food production demands a multifaceted approach. Transitioning to regenerative agriculture, which emphasizes soil health, crop diversity, and ecosystem restoration, can mitigate environmental impacts while enhancing resilience. Practices such as cover cropping, agroforestry, and reduced tillage improve soil fertility and carbon sequestration. Similarly, adopting precision agriculture technologies, such as drip irrigation and data-driven fertilizer application, can optimize resource use and minimize waste. Plant-based diets and alternative proteins, such as lab-grown meat or insect-based foods, offer pathways to reduce the environmental burden of livestock farming. Policy interventions, including subsidies for sustainable practices and penalties for environmental harm, are essential to incentivize systemic change. These solutions face barriers, including economic constraints, cultural preferences, and resistance from entrenched agricultural industries. Smallholder farmers, who produce a significant portion of the world's food, often lack access to the resources and knowledge needed to adopt sustainable practices. Moreover, global trade dynamics and market pressures can prioritize short-term profits over long-term ecological health. Business innovation, coupled with public-private partnerships, can bridge these gaps by developing scalable, affordable technologies and fostering equitable access to sustainable practices. Soil health is equally critical. Intensive farming practices, including monoculture and heavy pesticide use, have degraded 33% of global soils, reducing their capacity to support crops. These environmental pressures are intensified by climate change, which disrupts growing seasons, increases the frequency of extreme weather, and reduces yields. For instance, maize production in Southern Africa has declined by up to 20% in recent decades due to drought and heat stress.

Pathways to Sustainable Agriculture

Transitioning to sustainable food production requires a multifaceted approach. Agroecology, which integrates ecological principles into farming, offers a promising framework. Practices such as crop rotation, intercropping, and organic fertilization enhance soil fertility and reduce reliance on chemical inputs. In Ethiopia, agroecological methods have increased yields by 20–50% while improving resilience to climate variability. Sustainable agriculture is a critical pathway to addressing the interconnected challenges of food security, environmental degradation, and economic viability. This approach seeks to balance health, sustainability, and business innovation by integrating ecological principles, social equity, and economic profitability. It emphasizes practices that maintain soil fertility, conserve water, reduce greenhouse gas emissions, and enhance biodiversity while ensuring nutritious food production and supporting rural livelihoods.

One key pathway is the adoption of agroecological practices. These include crop rotation, intercropping, and organic farming, which enhance soil health and reduce reliance on synthetic fertilizers and pesticides. For instance, cover cropping improves soil structure and sequesters carbon, mitigating climate change. Agroecology also promotes biodiversity by creating habitats for pollinators and natural pest predators, reducing the need for chemical interventions. These practices align with health goals by producing nutrient-rich foods free from harmful residues, addressing rising concerns about diet-related diseases..It involves leveraging technology and innovation. Precision agriculture, enabled by sensors, drones, and data analytics, optimizes resource use, minimizing waste and environmental impact. For example, variable-rate irrigation systems deliver water efficiently, conserving resources in water-scarce regions. Biotechnology, such as drought-resistant crop varieties, enhances resilience to climate variability, ensuring stable yields. These innovations support business viability by reducing costs and increasing productivity, making sustainable practices attractive to farmers and agribusinesses.

Economic and policy incentives are vital for scaling sustainable agriculture. Governments can support farmers through subsidies for organic certification, tax breaks for renewable energy adoption, or payments for ecosystem services like carbon sequestration. Market-based mechanisms, such as fair-trade certifications, ensure farmers receive equitable prices, fostering economic sustainability. Public-private partnerships can drive innovation by funding research into sustainable technologies and disseminating knowledge through extension services.Social equity is equally critical. Sustainable agriculture must empower marginalized groups, including smallholder farmers and women, by providing access to land, credit, and training. Community-supported agriculture models strengthen local food systems, connecting producers directly with consumers and enhancing food sovereignty.By integrating agroecological practices, technological innovation, supportive policies, and equitable frameworks, sustainable agriculture offers a holistic solution. It ensures healthy diets, preserves ecosystems, and creates resilient food systems, aligning with global goals like the United Nations' Sustainable Development Goals. Embracing these pathways requires collaboration among farmers, policymakers, businesses, and consumers to transform agriculture into a force for global well-being.

Precision agriculture, enabled by technologies like satellite imaging and IoT sensors, optimizes resource use by tailoring inputs to specific field conditions. For example, precision irrigation systems in India have reduced water use by 30% while maintaining crop productivity. Similarly, regenerative agriculture—focused on restoring soil carbon and ecosystem health—has gained traction in regions like the United States, where cover cropping and reduced tillage have improved soil structure and sequestered carbon.

Reducing Food Waste

Food waste is a critical yet often overlooked aspect of sustainability. Globally, one-third of all food produced—approximately 1.3 billion tons—is lost or wasted annually. In high-income countries, waste occurs primarily at the consumer level, driven by over-purchasing and aesthetic standards that reject imperfect produce. In contrast, low-income countries face losses during production and storage due to inadequate infrastructure.Addressing food waste requires targeted interventions. Improved storage technologies, such as solar-powered cold chains, can reduce post-harvest losses in developing regions. In retail, initiatives like France's ban on supermarket food waste have encouraged donations to food banks. Consumer education campaigns, such as the "Love Food Hate Waste" initiative in the United Kingdom, have also proven effective, reducing household waste by 20% in participating communities.The environmental footprint of food production is staggering. Agriculture accounts for approximately 70% of global freshwater use, 30% of greenhouse gas emissions, and significant deforestation and biodiversity loss (FAO, 2022). As the global population approaches 10 billion by 2050, the demand for food will intensify, placing further strain on finite resources. Climate change exacerbates these pressures, with rising temperatures, erratic rainfall, and extreme weather events threatening crop yields and food security. Sustainable food systems aim to minimize environmental harm while ensuring equitable access to food. Practices such as regenerative agriculture, which enhances soil health and sequesters carbon, offer promising solutions. Similarly, precision farming technologies, including drones and IoT sensors, optimize resource use, reducing waste and emissions. However, these innovations often require significant upfront investment, limiting adoption among smallholder farmers who produce a substantial share of the world's food.

The shift toward sustainable diets also plays a critical role. Reducing meat consumption, particularly beef, which has a high environmental footprint, can significantly lower emissions. Plant-based and alternative proteins, such as lab-grown meat or insect-based foods, are gaining traction, yet cultural acceptance and regulatory hurdles remain. Food waste, another critical issue, accounts for roughly one-third of all food produced globally (UNEP, 2021). Strategies to address waste, such as improved supply chain logistics and consumer education, are essential for sustainability.

The sustainability challenge is inherently global, requiring coordination across borders. International frameworks, such as the Paris Agreement and the UN Sustainable Development Goals, emphasize sustainable agriculture, yet implementation varies widely. Developing nations, often most vulnerable to climate impacts, require support to adopt sustainable practices without compromising economic growth. Balancing these priorities demands innovative financing models, technology transfers, and policies that align environmental and social goals.

BUSINESS INNOVATION: DRIVING CHANGE THROUGH MARKET SOLUTIONS

The Role of the Private Sector

The food industry is a powerful driver of change, with the global food and beverage market valued at over $7 trillion. Private-sector innovation can align health and sustainability goals with economic interests. For instance, major food companies have begun reformulating products to reduce sugar, salt, and Trans fats in response to consumer demand and regulatory pressure. Nestlé (2022), for example, has committed to reducing sugar content by 5% across its portfolio, balancing health objectives with profitability. While public health strategies are critical, business innovation offers a powerful mechanism for transforming food systems at scale. The private sector, encompassing food producers, retailers, and technology companies, is uniquely positioned to drive change through market-based solutions that align health, sustainability, and profitability. By leveraging innovation, businesses can address consumer demand for nutritious, sustainable foods while navigating the economic realities of global markets.

One of the most promising areas of innovation is the development of healthier food products. Advances in food science have enabled the reformulation of processed foods to reduce sugar, salt, and trans fats without compromising taste. For example, companies like Nestlé (2022) and Unilever have committed to reducing sodium content in their products by 20–30% over a decade, responding to consumer and regulatory pressures. Functional foods, enriched with vitamins, probiotics, or fiber, have also gained traction, appealing to health-conscious consumers. The global functional food market is projected to reach $275 billion by 2025, reflecting growing demand.

Plant-based and alternative proteins represent another frontier of innovation. Companies like Beyond Meat and Impossible Foods have disrupted traditional meat markets by offering plant-based products that mimic the taste and texture of animal protein. These products cater to rising consumer interest in vegetarian and flexitarian diets, driven by health and environmental concerns. Lab-grown or cultured meat, produced from animal cells without slaughter, is also emerging as a sustainable alternative, though scalability and cost remain challenges. In 2023, the alternative protein market was valued at $15 billion, with projections of exponential growth as production costs decline.

Technology is reshaping food supply chains to enhance efficiency and transparency. Precision agriculture, powered by sensors, drones, and artificial intelligence, optimizes crop yields while minimizing resource use, supporting both health and sustainability goals. Blockchain technology enables traceability, allowing consumers to verify the origin and nutritional content of their food. For instance, Walmart has implemented blockchain to track produce, reducing foodborne illness risks and building consumer trust. These innovations align with the growing demand for transparency, with 70% of consumers reporting a preference for brands that provide detailed product information.

Businesses are also responding to the sustainability imperative, which is closely linked to health outcomes. Sustainable sourcing practices, such as regenerative agriculture, improve soil health and reduce greenhouse gas emissions, ensuring long-term food security. Companies like General Mills have partnered with farmers to adopt regenerative practices on millions of acres, enhancing the nutritional quality of crops. Circular economy models, which minimize waste through upcycling byproducts, are gaining traction. For example, startups like ReGrained transform spent brewery grains into nutritious flour, creating value from waste.

Consumer behavior is a critical driver of business innovation. The rise of digital platforms has empowered consumers to demand healthier, more sustainable options. Mobile apps that provide nutritional analysis or carbon footprint data enable informed purchasing decisions. Social media amplifies consumer voices, pressuring companies to adopt ethical practices. The #CleanLabel movement, which emphasizes natural ingredients and minimal processing, has spurred reformulation across the food industry. Businesses that fail to adapt risk losing market share, as 65% of global consumers report prioritizing health and sustainability in their purchasing decisions.

Collaboration between businesses and other stakeholders is essential for systemic change. Public-private partnerships can amplify the impact of health and sustainability initiatives. For instance, the EAT-Lancet Commission, involving scientists, policymakers, and industry leaders, has developed frameworks for healthy, sustainable diets that inform corporate strategies. Similarly, initiatives like the Global Alliance for Improved Nutrition (GAIN) (2021) work with businesses to fortify staple foods, addressing micronutrient deficiencies in developing countries.

However, business innovation faces challenges, including cost barriers and consumer skepticism. Developing healthier products often involves higher production costs, which can translate to premium prices that exclude low-income consumers. Greenwashing—where companies exaggerate their sustainability efforts—erodes trust, necessitating robust certification systems. Regulatory frameworks also vary widely, creating complexities for multinational corporations. Harmonizing standards, such as those for nutrition labeling, could facilitate innovation while ensuring accountability.

Startups are also reshaping the food landscape. Plant-based and lab-grown meat alternatives, pioneered by companies like Beyond Meat and Memphis Meats, offer sustainable protein sources with lower environmental footprints. These products appeal to flexitarian consumers, who seek to reduce meat consumption without sacrificing taste or convenience. Similarly, vertical farming ventures, such as Plenty and AeroFarms, produce leafy greens in urban settings using 90% less water than traditional agriculture.

Technology as a Catalyst

Technological advancements are revolutionizing food production, distribution, and consumption. Blockchain technology enhances supply chain transparency, enabling consumers to trace products from farm to fork. This fosters trust and supports ethical purchasing decisions. For example, IBM's Food Trust platform has been adopted by retailers like Walmart to track produce, reducing food safety risks and waste.

Artificial intelligence (AI) is another transformative tool. AI-powered analytics optimize crop management, predict market trends, and personalize nutrition advice. In India, AI-based apps like Ninjacart connect farmers directly with retailers, reducing intermediaries and improving incomes. Meanwhile, robotics and automation streamline labor-intensive processes, such as harvesting and packaging, addressing labor shortages in aging agricultural workforces. The convergence of health, sustainability, and business innovation offers a pathway to transform food systems. These dimensions are interdependent: healthy diets rely on sustainable production, and both require viable business models to scale. A holistic approach, grounded in collaboration across sectors, is essential to address the complexities of the global food system.

Interdisciplinary research is critical to this integration. Nutrition science must inform product development, ensuring that health claims are evidence-based. Environmental science can guide sustainable practices, while behavioral economics can enhance the effectiveness of interventions. For example, nudging techniques—such as placing healthier options at eye level in stores—have increased their selection by up to 20%. Data-driven insights, enabled by artificial intelligence, can further refine strategies, predicting consumer trends and optimizing supply chains.

Policy frameworks play a pivotal role in aligning incentives. Subsidies for sustainable crops, tax breaks for health-focused innovation, and penalties for environmentally harmful practices can steer markets toward positive outcomes. International cooperation is also vital, given the global nature of food trade. Agreements like the Paris Climate Accord can incorporate food system goals, fostering collective action.

Education and advocacy are equally important. Raising awareness about the links between diet, health, and the environment empowers consumers to drive demand for better products. Grassroots movements, supported by civil society organizations, can hold businesses and governments accountable. Youth-led initiatives, such as those advocating for sustainable school meals, exemplify the potential of collective action.

Ultimately, the food system's transformation hinges on a shared vision of health, sustainability, and prosperity. Businesses must prioritize long-term societal benefits over short-term profits, while governments must create enabling environments. Consumers, as active participants, can shape markets through their choices. By aligning these forces, the global food system can move toward a future where nutritious, sustainable food is accessible to all.

Challenges of Commercialization

Despite these advances, business innovation faces hurdles. Scaling sustainable practices often requires significant upfront investment, which can deter small and medium-sized enterprises. Regulatory frameworks also lag behind technological developments, creating uncertainty for innovators. For instance, lab-grown meat faces varying approval processes across countries, slowing its market entry.

Consumer acceptance is another barrier. While demand for sustainable and healthy products is growing, price sensitivity and taste preferences remain dominant factors. Bridging this gap requires effective marketing and education to shift perceptions. Partnerships between businesses, governments, and NGOs can facilitate this transition by aligning incentives and sharing risks.

Businesses are both contributors to and potential solvers of food system challenges. The food industry, encompassing producers, processors, retailers, and distributors, operates in a highly competitive, globalized market where cost and efficiency often take precedence. However, mounting consumer demand for healthy, sustainable products has spurred innovation, reshaping how businesses operate.

One area of innovation is the development of alternative proteins. Companies like Beyond Meat and Impossible Foods have disrupted traditional meat markets by offering plant-based products that mimic the taste and texture of animal proteins.

Similarly, cellular agriculture, which produces meat and dairy through cell cultures, holds potential to reduce environmental impacts, though scaling remains costly. These innovations require not only technological advancements but also consumer acceptance and regulatory approval.

Technology also transforms supply chains. Blockchain, for instance, enhances traceability, ensuring transparency in sourcing and reducing fraud. Vertical farming, which grows crops in controlled indoor environments, maximizes land use and reduces water consumption, though energy costs remain a barrier. Digital platforms, such as apps connecting farmers directly to consumers, bypass traditional intermediaries, improving farmer incomes and reducing food miles.

Businesses are also responding to sustainability demands through corporate social responsibility (CSR) initiatives. Major food companies, such as Unilever and Nestlé (2022), have committed to net-zero emissions and sustainable sourcing, though critics argue these efforts often fall short of transformative change. Small and medium enterprises (SMEs), particularly in local and organic markets, play a vital role in driving grassroots innovation, though they face challenges in scaling due to limited capital and market access.

Economic incentives are critical to scaling innovation. Governments can support businesses through subsidies, tax breaks, or public-private partnerships, while investors increasingly prioritize environmental, social, and governance (ESG) criteria. However, innovation must navigate trade-offs. For example, prioritizing sustainability may increase costs, potentially alienating price-sensitive consumers. Businesses must therefore balance profitability with purpose, leveraging consumer trends and policy support to drive systemic change.

Navigating Tensions and Synergies

The pursuit of health, sustainability, and business innovation reveals both tensions and synergies. For instance, health-focused diets emphasizing plant-based foods align with sustainability goals by reducing environmental impacts. However, these diets may conflict with business interests if they disrupt traditional markets, such as livestock farming. Similarly, sustainable practices like organic farming can enhance soil health but may yield lower outputs, raising food prices and affecting accessibility.

Synergies emerge when innovations address multiple goals. For example, precision agriculture improves yields (supporting health through increased food availability), reduces resource use (enhancing sustainability), and boosts farmer

The Need for Systems Thinking

The challenges of health, sustainability, and business innovation are deeply interconnected, necessitating a systems-thinking approach. Siloed interventions—such as focusing solely on reducing emissions or improving nutrition—often yield limited impact. For example, promoting plant-based diets can enhance health and reduce environmental impact, but its success depends on affordable supply chains and consumer acceptance, which require business innovation.

Systems thinking emphasizes feedback loops and trade-offs. For instance, intensifying agricultural production to feed growing populations may boost food security but could degrade soils and increase emissions if not managed sustainably. Conversely, regenerative farming can enhance soil health and sequester carbon but may require higher labor inputs, posing economic challenges. Balancing these dynamics requires coordination among stakeholders, including policymakers, businesses, and communities.

Policy as an Enabler

Governments play a critical role in aligning health, sustainability, and innovation. Policy tools such as taxes, subsidies, and regulations can incentivize desirable outcomes. For example, sugar taxes in Mexico and the United Kingdom have reduced consumption of sugary drinks by 7–10%, demonstrating the efficacy of fiscal measures. Similarly, subsidies for organic farming in the European Union have expanded sustainable agriculture, with organic farmland increasing by 66% since 2010.

International cooperation is equally important. Global agreements, such as the Paris Climate Accord and the Sustainable Development Goals, provide frameworks for collective action. However, implementation remains uneven, particularly in low-income countries where resources are scarce. Development aid and technology transfer can bridge these gaps, enabling equitable progress.

Collaborative Models

Collaboration across sectors is essential to scale solutions. Public-private partnerships (PPPs) have proven effective in addressing complex challenges. For instance, the Scaling Up Nutrition (SUN) Movement, a global initiative, brings together governments, businesses, and civil society to combat malnutrition. By aligning resources and expertise, SUN has improved nutrition outcomes in over 60 countries.

Community-driven models also hold promise. Cooperatives, such as those in India's dairy sector, empower smallholder farmers by pooling resources and accessing markets. These models enhance economic resilience while promoting sustainable practices, such as rotational grazing. Similarly, urban food councils, which engage citizens in local food policy, foster inclusive decision-making and drive grassroots change.

THE HEALTH IMPERATIVE: NUTRITION AND PUBLIC WELL-BEING

The Burden of Diet-Related Diseases

Diet is a leading determinant of global health outcomes. Poor nutrition contributes to a range of non-communicable diseases, including obesity, diabetes, cardiovascular disease, and certain cancers. The World Health Organization estimates that unhealthy diets are linked to 11 million deaths annually, surpassing the mortality burden of tobacco use. In high-income countries, overconsumption of processed foods high in sugar, salt, and saturated fats drives these trends. Conversely, in low- and middle-income countries, undernutrition—manifesting as stunting, wasting, and micronutrient deficiencies—coexists with rising rates of obesity, creating a "double burden" of malnutrition. The global food system stands at a critical juncture, where the imperatives of human health, environmental sustainability, and economic viability intersect. The health imperative, rooted in the need to address escalating rates of diet-related diseases, is a pressing concern for public well-being. Poor nutrition, characterized by diets high in processed foods, sugars, and unhealthy fats, has fueled a surge in non-communicable diseases (NCDs) such as obesity, diabetes, and cardiovascular disorders. According to the World Health Organization, NCDs account for 74% of global deaths, with dietary factors being a leading contributor. This public health crisis underscores the urgency of reorienting food systems toward promoting nutritional well-being.

Nutrition is foundational to human health, influencing physical, mental, and social outcomes across the lifespan. Diets rich in whole grains, fruits, vegetables, lean proteins, and healthy fats are associated with reduced risks of chronic diseases and improved cognitive function. However, access to such diets is uneven, shaped by socioeconomic disparities, cultural norms, and food availability. In low- and middle-income countries, undernutrition persists, with 149 million children under five experiencing stunting due to inadequate nutrient intake. Conversely, in high-income nations, overnutrition—marked by excessive calorie consumption—drives obesity rates, with 39% of adults classified as overweight or obese globally.

The health imperative extends beyond individual choices to systemic factors. Food environments, defined by the availability, affordability, and marketing of food, heavily influence dietary patterns. Urbanization and globalization have increased reliance on ultra-processed foods, which are often energy-dense but nutrient-poor. Aggressive marketing by food corporations, particularly targeting children, exacerbates unhealthy consumption patterns. For instance, studies estimate that children are exposed to thousands of food advertisements annually, the majority promoting sugary snacks and fast foods. These trends highlight the need for interventions that reshape food environments to prioritize health.

Public health strategies to improve nutrition have included policy measures such as taxation on sugar-sweetened beverages, front-of-pack labeling, and restrictions on marketing unhealthy foods. Countries like Mexico and Chile have implemented sugar taxes, resulting in measurable reductions in consumption—Mexico saw a 7.6% drop in sugary drink purchases within two years. School-based programs promoting healthy eating and physical activity have also shown promise, particularly when paired with community engagement. However, these efforts face resistance from food industries and require sustained political will to achieve lasting impact.

The role of education in fostering nutritional literacy cannot be overstated. Empowering individuals with knowledge about balanced diets, portion control, and food preparation enhances their ability to make informed choices. Community-based initiatives, such as cooking workshops and urban gardening, have proven effective in improving dietary habits, particularly in underserved populations. Yet, education alone is insufficient without addressing structural barriers like food deserts—areas with limited access to fresh, affordable produce. In the United States, approximately 23.5 million people live in food deserts, disproportionately affecting low-income and minority communities.

The health imperative also intersects with cultural and ethical considerations. Dietary preferences are deeply tied to identity, tradition, and values, complicating efforts to promote universal nutritional guidelines. For example, plant-based diets, which are linked to lower risks of heart disease and reduced environmental impact, may conflict with cultural practices that prioritize meat consumption. Sensitivity to these dynamics is essential for designing inclusive interventions that respect diverse foodways while advancing health goals.

The rise of ultra-processed foods is a key driver of these health challenges. These products, characterized by long shelf lives and aggressive marketing, dominate global diets, particularly in urban areas. For instance, sugary beverages and packaged snacks have displaced traditional whole foods in many regions, contributing to a 30% increase in global obesity rates since 1990. Addressing this requires not only individual behavior change but also systemic interventions, such as reformulating products, improving food labeling, and regulating marketing practices.

Promoting Nutritional Equity

Achieving health through food requires addressing inequities in access and affordability. In many low-income communities, nutritious foods like fruits, vegetables, and lean proteins are either unavailable or prohibitively expensive, leading to reliance on calorie-dense, nutrient-poor options. This phenomenon, known as "food deserts," is compounded by structural factors such as inadequate infrastructure and limited economic resources. For example, in rural Sub-Saharan Africa, transportation barriers hinder the distribution of perishable goods, while in urban slums, high food prices exacerbate nutritional disparities.

Policy interventions can mitigate these inequities. Subsidies for healthy foods, urban agriculture initiatives, and school feeding programs have shown promise in improving dietary outcomes. For instance, Brazil's National School Feeding Program, which prioritizes locally sourced, nutrient-rich foods, has enhanced child nutrition while supporting smallholder farmers. Such models demonstrate that health-focused food policies can yield co-benefits across social and economic domains.

The Role of Education and Culture

Beyond access, cultural and educational factors shape dietary choices. Traditional diets, often rich in whole grains, legumes, and vegetables, are being eroded by globalization and the allure of Westernized eating patterns. Reversing this trend requires culturally sensitive nutrition education that respects local foodways while promoting evidence-based practices. Community-based programs, such as cooking workshops and school curricula, can empower individuals to make informed choices. Additionally, leveraging digital platforms—such as mobile apps for meal planning or social media campaigns—can amplify these efforts, particularly among younger populations.

CASE STUDIES: LESSONS FROM THE FIELD

The global food system stands at a pivotal moment, where the demands for healthier diets, sustainable production, and innovative business models intersect. This chapter explores how stakeholders—farmers, corporations, policymakers, and consumers—are navigating these challenges through collaborative efforts. By examining four case studies, we highlight practical examples of initiatives that balance health, sustainability, and business innovation. These cases demonstrate how diverse approaches can address systemic issues while fostering resilience and equity in the food system.

Case Study 1: Vertical Farming in Singapore – Sky Greens

Singapore, a densely populated city-state with limited arable land, faces significant challenges in food security. Sky Greens, established in 2012, pioneered vertical farming to address this issue. Using a low-carbon, hydraulic-driven system, Sky Greens grows leafy greens in multi-story towers, maximizing space and minimizing resource use. The initiative aligns with Singapore's "30 by 30" goal to produce 30% of its food locally by 2030.

Health Impact: Sky Greens focuses on nutrient-rich vegetables like bok choy and kale, which are harvested fresh and delivered to local markets within hours. This reduces nutrient loss during transport and ensures consumers have access to healthier produce. Studies indicate that fresh vegetables retain higher levels of vitamins compared to those transported over long distances.

Sustainability: The vertical farming system uses 95% less water than traditional agriculture through a closed-loop irrigation system. Energy consumption is minimized by leveraging natural sunlight and a low-energy hydraulic mechanism, reducing the carbon footprint compared to conventional farming. Sky Greens also avoids synthetic pesticides, promoting biodiversity and soil health in urban settings.

Business Innovation: Sky Greens collaborates with local supermarkets and restaurants, creating a scalable model that integrates into urban supply chains. The company has attracted investment from government grants and private sectors, demonstrating the viability of urban agriculture. By licensing its technology to other regions, Sky Greens expands its impact while generating revenue.

Collaboration: The initiative works with Singapore's government, research institutions, and community organizations to refine its technology and educate consumers about sustainable food choices. These partnerships have helped Sky Greens scale while maintaining its commitment to health and sustainability.

Case Study 2: Regenerative Agriculture in Brazil – Natura & Co and Local Farmers

In Brazil, Natura & Co, a global cosmetics company, has partnered with Amazonian farmers to promote regenerative agriculture for sourcing ingredients like açaí and andiroba. This initiative, launched in 2016, supports local communities while addressing deforestation and soil degradation in the Amazon.

Health Impact: The project emphasizes organic farming practices, producing crops free from harmful pesticides. Açaí, a superfood rich in antioxidants, is processed minimally to retain its nutritional value, benefiting both local consumers and global markets. The initiative also improves food security for farmers by diversifying their crops, ensuring access to nutrient-dense foods.

Sustainability: Regenerative practices, such as agroforestry and crop rotation, enhance soil fertility and sequester carbon. Natura & Co's model has restored over 2,000 hectares of degraded land since its inception. By preserving the Amazon's biodiversity, the project mitigates climate change and protects water resources, aligning with global sustainability goals.

Business Innovation: Natura & Co integrates farmers into its supply chain, offering fair trade agreements and technical training. This creates a stable income for over 5,000 families while meeting the growing demand for sustainable products. The company's transparent sourcing enhances its brand reputation, attracting eco-conscious consumers and investors.

Collaboration: The partnership involves local cooperatives, NGOs, and government agencies to provide farmers with resources and market access. Research institutions contribute by studying the ecological benefits of regenerative practices, ensuring the model is evidence-based and scalable. This multi-stakeholder approach fosters trust and long-term commitment.

Case Study 3: Plant-Based Meat in the United States – Impossible Foods

Impossible Foods, founded in 2011, has transformed the food industry by developing plant-based meat alternatives that mimic the taste and texture of animal protein. Its flagship product, the Impossible Burger, addresses health concerns, environmental degradation, and consumer demand for ethical food choices.

Health Impact: The Impossible Burger is designed to be lower in saturated fats and cholesterol than traditional beef, reducing the risk of heart disease. It is fortified with nutrients like vitamin B12, addressing common deficiencies in plant-based diets. By offering a healthier alternative, Impossible Foods encourages dietary shifts without sacrificing culinary satisfaction.

Sustainability: Producing plant-based meat requires 87% less water, 96% less land, and emits 89% fewer greenhouse gases than beef production, according to lifecycle assessments. The company sources ingredients like soy and coconut oil from sustainable suppliers, minimizing its environmental footprint. This aligns with global efforts to reduce the food system's contribution to climate change.

Business Innovation: Impossible Foods has secured partnerships with major fast-food chains like Burger King, expanding its reach to mainstream consumers. Its direct-to-consumer model, launched in 2020, allows for rapid scaling through e-commerce. The company's focus on research and development ensures continuous improvement in product quality and cost-efficiency.

Collaboration: Impossible Foods works with farmers, scientists, and chefs to refine its products and supply chain. It also engages with advocacy groups to promote policies supporting sustainable food systems. These collaborations have helped the company navigate regulatory challenges and gain consumer trust in a competitive market.

Case Study 4: Community-Supported Agriculture in Kenya – Twiga Foods

Twiga Foods, a Kenyan agri-tech company founded in 2014, connects smallholder farmers to urban markets through a digital platform. By streamlining the supply chain, Twiga ensures fresh produce reaches consumers while supporting rural livelihoods.

Health Impact: Twiga prioritizes fruits and vegetables, addressing Kenya's rising rates of diet-related diseases like diabetes. By reducing post-harvest losses, the platform ensures consistent access to fresh, nutrient-rich foods. Educational campaigns encourage consumers to adopt balanced diets, amplifying the health benefits.

Sustainability: The platform reduces food waste by optimizing logistics, cutting losses by 30% compared to traditional markets. Twiga encourages farmers to adopt climate-smart practices, such as drip irrigation and organic fertilizers, which conserve water and improve soil health. These efforts contribute to Kenya's climate resilience goals.

Business Innovation: Twiga's mobile app enables farmers to sell directly to vendors, eliminating exploitative middlemen. The company uses data analytics to predict demand, ensuring efficient distribution. Twiga has attracted significant investment, allowing it to expand into other African countries and diversify its offerings.

Collaboration: Twiga partners with NGOs, government agencies, and financial institutions to provide farmers with training, credit, and market insights. These collaborations empower farmers to improve productivity and income, creating a ripple effect in rural communities. Consumer feedback loops ensure the platform remains responsive to market needs.

INTEGRATING THE THREE PILLARS: A HOLISTIC APPROACH

Health, sustainability, and business innovation are deeply interconnected, and addressing them in isolation risks unintended consequences. For instance, promoting plant-based diets for sustainability may inadvertently increase reliance on monoculture crops, harming biodiversity. Similarly, business innovations that prioritize efficiency may exacerbate health disparities if they cater only to affluent consumers. A holistic approach is essential, one that balances trade-offs and leverages synergies.

Cross-sector collaboration is key to this integration. Governments, businesses, and civil society must work together to align policies, investments, and consumer education. For example, public-private partnerships can fund research into sustainable farming practices that also yield nutrient-dense crops. Meanwhile, schools and workplaces can serve as hubs for promoting healthy, sustainable eating, creating demand that incentivizes businesses to innovate.

Consumer agency is another critical factor. Empowered consumers can drive demand for healthier, more sustainable products, pressuring companies to adapt. Digital platforms, including social media, amplify this influence by spreading awareness and fostering communities around shared values. However, consumers must be equipped with accurate information to navigate marketing claims and make informed choices.

FUTURE DIRECTIONS: TOWARD A RESILIENT FOOD SYSTEM

Embracing Circularity

A circular food system—one that minimizes waste and maximizes resource efficiency—is a cornerstone of future resilience. Practices such as composting, upcycling food by-products, and integrating livestock and crop systems can close nutrient loops. For example, in the Netherlands, circular agriculture initiatives recycle food waste into animal feed, reducing landfill use and emissions. Scaling circularity requires investment in infrastructure and incentives for businesses to adopt closed-loop models.

Leveraging Data and Connectivity

The digital revolution offers unprecedented opportunities to optimize the food system. Big data analytics can inform policy decisions, predict supply chain disruptions, and personalize nutrition interventions. For instance, machine learning models can forecast crop yields with 90% accuracy, enabling proactive responses to food shortages. Ensuring equitable access to these technologies is critical to avoid widening global disparities.

Prioritizing Equity and Inclusion

A resilient food system must prioritize the needs of marginalized groups, including smallholder farmers, women, and indigenous communities. These groups often bear the brunt of food insecurity and environmental degradation but possess valuable knowledge and practices. Inclusive policies, such as land tenure reforms and gender-responsive agricultural extension services, can empower these communities.

For example, in Rwanda, women-led cooperatives have increased coffee yields by 30% through access to training and credit.

The global food system stands at a pivotal juncture, grappling with the intertwined challenges of health, sustainability, and economic viability. As populations grow, climate change intensifies, and consumer preferences evolve, the need for a resilient food system—one that ensures equitable access to nutritious food, minimizes environmental harm, and fosters innovative business models—has never been more urgent. This chapter explores future directions for achieving such a system, emphasizing integrative strategies that balance human well-being, ecological integrity, and economic progress.

A primary focus for future food systems must be enhancing nutritional outcomes while addressing diet-related diseases. Rising rates of obesity, diabetes, and cardiovascular conditions underscore the need for diets rich in whole grains, fruits, vegetables, and lean proteins. Public health campaigns, such as those promoting plant-based diets or reducing ultra-processed food consumption, can shift consumer behavior. However, these efforts require collaboration between governments, food producers, and retailers to make healthy options affordable and accessible. For instance, subsidizing sustainable crops like legumes or incentivizing grocers to stock fresh produce in underserved areas can bridge nutritional gaps. Simultaneously, education programs that teach cooking skills and nutritional literacy empower individuals to make informed choices, fostering a culture of health-conscious eating.

Sustainability lies at the core of a resilient food system. Agriculture accounts for roughly 30% of global greenhouse gas emissions and significant deforestation, necessitating a shift toward regenerative practices. Techniques such as crop rotation, agroforestry, and precision farming enhance soil health, sequester carbon, and reduce reliance on chemical inputs. Scaling these practices requires investment in farmer training and technology, particularly in developing regions where smallholder farms dominate. Moreover, reducing food waste—estimated at 1.3 billion tons annually—offers a dual benefit: conserving resources and feeding more people. Innovations like smart packaging that extends shelf life or apps connecting surplus food to charities can drive progress. Water management is equally critical, as irrigation consumes 70% of global freshwater. Drip irrigation and drought-resistant crops can optimize usage, ensuring long-term resource availability.

Business innovation is a catalyst for systemic change. The rise of alternative proteins, such as lab-grown meat or insect-based foods, reflects a growing market for sustainable options. These products, while still niche, reduce the environmental footprint of livestock farming, which contributes 14.5% of global emissions. However, scaling requires overcoming regulatory hurdles, consumer skepticism, and high production costs. Partnerships between startups, established food companies, and research institutions can accelerate development and market entry. Additionally, digital platforms that connect farmers directly to consumers, bypassing traditional supply chains, enhance transparency and profitability. Blockchain technology, for example, can trace food from farm to table, assuring quality and ethical sourcing. These innovations demand supportive policies, such as tax incentives for green technologies or streamlined certification for novel foods.

Equity remains a cornerstone of resilience. Food insecurity affects over 800 million people globally, disproportionately impacting marginalized communities. Addressing this requires localized solutions, such as urban farming initiatives or community-supported agriculture, which strengthen regional food networks. Global trade policies must also prioritize fairness, ensuring that developing nations can compete without being undercut by subsidized imports. Empowering women, who comprise a significant portion of agricultural labor in many regions, through access to land, credit, and education, further enhances productivity and social cohesion.

Looking ahead, a resilient food system hinges on integration—connecting health, sustainability, and innovation through coordinated action. Governments must enact policies that align incentives with long-term goals, such as carbon pricing or nutrition-focused labeling standards. Private-sector investment in scalable solutions, coupled with consumer demand for ethical products, can drive market transformation. International cooperation is essential to share knowledge, fund research, and address transboundary issues like climate change. By fostering collaboration across sectors and borders, the food system can evolve into one that nourishes people, protects the planet, and thrives economically, ensuring a sustainable future for generations to come.

Challenges and Future Directions

Despite progress, significant challenges remain. Economic inequalities limit access to healthy and sustainable foods, while geopolitical tensions and trade disruptions threaten global supply chains. Cultural resistance to dietary shifts, particularly in meat-heavy regions, complicates efforts to reduce environmental impact. Moreover, the upfront costs of sustainable practices and innovative technologies can exclude small-scale farmers and low-income communities from participating in the transition. Despite progress, significant challenges remain. The global food industry, a powerful economic force, often resists regulatory measures that threaten profitability. Consumer resistance to change, driven by taste preferences and convenience, complicates efforts to shift dietary norms. Moreover, the complexity of global supply chains and trade policies can hinder efforts to prioritize nutrition over economic interests.

Climate change poses an additional threat, as extreme weather events disrupt food production and exacerbate food insecurity. Integrating health and sustainability goals—such as promoting plant-based diets that reduce environmental impact—will be critical to addressing these dual crises.

Looking ahead, interdisciplinary collaboration is essential. Nutritionists, policymakers, educators, and industry leaders must work together to create food systems that prioritize health without compromising economic viability. Advances in data analytics and artificial intelligence can enhance the precision of interventions, from predicting dietary trends to optimizing food distribution.

Identified Gaps:

- Lack of discussion on indigenous food systems and traditional ecological knowledge.
- Insufficient analysis of gender dynamics in food production and consumption.
- Limited treatment of food sovereignty and political economy perspectives (e.g., trade policy, land grabs).

Looking ahead, several priorities emerge. First, inclusive policies must ensure that marginalized groups are not left behind in the shift to sustainable, healthy food systems. Subsidies for small farmers, urban agriculture initiatives, and affordable nutrition programs can bridge this gap. Second, education and awareness campaigns must be scaled to shift cultural norms and build demand for sustainable products. Third, investment in research and development is critical to refine technologies like alternative proteins and regenerative farming, making them more accessible and cost-effective.

Finally, global cooperation is essential. Food systems transcend borders, and climate change is a shared challenge. International agreements on emissions, water use, and trade can create a level playing field, while knowledge-sharing platforms can disseminate best practices across regions.

CONCLUSION

The future of food lies at the crossroads of health, sustainability, and business innovation. By prioritizing nutrient-rich diets, adopting eco-friendly practices, and harnessing the power of markets, we can build a food system that serves people and the planet. This transformation requires bold action from all stakeholders—governments, businesses, communities, and individuals. While challenges abound, the opportunities are immense. A reimagined food system has the potential not only to nourish bodies and protect ecosystems but also to inspire a new era of innovation and equity. The path forward is complex, but with collective commitment, it is within reach.

The food system is at a crossroads, where the imperatives of health, sustainability, and business innovation converge. Addressing these challenges requires moving beyond incremental changes to embrace transformative, systems-based solutions. By integrating nutritional equity, sustainable practices, and market-driven innovation, stakeholders can build a food system that nourishes people, protects the planet, and drives economic progress. The path forward demands collaboration, creativity, and a shared commitment to equity and resilience. As the global population approaches 10 billion by 2050, the choices made today will shape the future of food for generations to come. The health imperative within the global food system is both a challenge and an opportunity. By addressing the root causes of poor nutrition—through policy, education, innovation, and equity-focused interventions—societies can foster public well-being and reduce the burden of diet-related diseases. As the world navigates the crossroads of health, sustainability, and business innovation, prioritizing nutrition will be essential to building resilient, thriving communities. The path forward requires bold action, informed by science and grounded in a commitment to the common good. These case studies illustrate the power of collaboration in addressing the complex challenges facing the global food system. From urban farming in Singapore to regenerative agriculture in Brazil, plant-based innovation in the United States, and tech-driven agriculture in Kenya, each initiative demonstrates how health, sustainability, and business innovation can coexist. By fostering partnerships across sectors, these models offer scalable solutions that prioritize people and the planet. As the food system continues to evolve, such collaborative efforts will be critical in building a resilient, equitable, and sustainable future.

REFERENCES

FAO. (2022). *The state of the world's land and water resources for food and agriculture – Systems at breaking point*. Food and Agriculture Organization of the United Nations.

Global Alliance for Improved Nutrition. (2021). *Food systems and nutrition: Working together for change*. GAIN.

Nestlé. (2022). *Creating shared value and sustainability report*. Nestlé Group.

Tilman, D., & Clark, M. (2014). Global diets link environmental sustainability and human health. *Nature*, *515*(7528), 518–522. DOI: 10.1038/nature13959 PMID: 25383533

UNEP. (2021). *Food waste index report 2021*. United Nations Environment Programme.

United Nations. (2015). *Transforming our world: The 2030 agenda for sustainable development*. United Nations General Assembly.

World Health Organization. (2023). *Noncommunicable diseases: Key facts*. WHO.

Chapter 11

Economic Determinants of Food Consumption and Health:

A Statistical Perspective on Consumer Behavior and Market Dynamics

Vijay Laxmi
Noida Institute of Engineering and Technology, India

Mukul Bhatnagar
http://orcid.org/0000-0002-7773-5641
Graphic Era University, India

Ishika Singhal
Graphic Era University, India

ABSTRACT

This study explores the intricate interrelationships among education level, income level, food prices, health consciousness, social influence, food consumption frequency, and health perception using Partial Least Squares Structural Equation Modeling (PLS-SEM). Data from 192 respondents reveals that education strongly influences health consciousness and social influence, while income level and food prices exert indirect effects through social networks. Health consciousness, though significant, shows limited impact on actual dietary behavior, while social influence emerges as the dominant driver shaping food choices and health perception. The findings underscore the necessity of multi-level interventions addressing education, income,

DOI: 10.4018/979-8-3373-4047-0.ch011

pricing dynamics, and social norms to promote healthy behaviors. This research contributes a robust, empirically validated framework that integrates cognitive, economic, and social determinants, offering a strategic roadmap for policy and program development in public health and nutrition.

INTRODUCTION

The intricate tapestry of human dietary behavior and health perception is a function of an array of interdependent socio-economic, psychological, and environmental determinants, each exerting its influence through a labyrinthine network of direct and indirect pathways. As the global food landscape undergoes seismic shifts driven by market volatility, urbanization, and evolving socio-cultural paradigms, understanding the forces that shape consumer food choices and health-related attitudes has never been more critical (Rojas & Jaenicke, 2024). This study endeavors to elucidate these complexities by interrogating the interrelationships among key variables: education level, income level, food prices, health consciousness, social influence, food consumption frequency, and health perception. Through the lens of Partial Least Squares Structural Equation Modeling (PLS-SEM), this research constructs a holistic framework that transcends reductionist interpretations and captures the nuanced, multivariate dynamics at play in dietary decision-making and perceived health outcomes (Qaim & Parlasca, 2025).

Education, as a fundamental social determinant, operates as a conduit for knowledge acquisition, critical thinking, and the internalization of health-promotive norms. The cognitive scaffolding provided by higher education not only informs individuals' comprehension of nutritional principles but also empowers them to navigate the often opaque domain of health information, thereby influencing their dietary practices and risk assessments. This intellectual capital manifests in elevated health consciousness—a metacognitive awareness of the implications of one's dietary choices—and a heightened sensitivity to the social cues and cultural scripts that govern consumption patterns. Yet, the pathways from education to behavioral outcomes are not linear nor uniformly potent; they are modulated by intervening variables such as income level, social influence, and market accessibility.

Income level, traditionally considered a cornerstone of economic agency, affords varying degrees of freedom in food selection, health management, and lifestyle choices. However, its role is far from deterministic; rather, it acts as an enabler or constrainer contingent upon the broader social and market ecosystems (Volpp & Lamberton, 2024). This study posits that income level exerts a bifurcated influence: it subtly modulates health consciousness and dietary frequency while exerting a stronger indirect effect through social influence mechanisms. Indeed, the empirical findings underscore that income's explanatory power is magnified when viewed through the prism of social capital, suggesting that economic status amplifies or attenuates the adoption of health behaviors based on peer norms, family expectations, and cultural embeddedness (Cheewakoset & Sakdapat, 2024; Sakdapat, 2022).

Food prices, an omnipresent external variable, interlace with individual agency in a paradoxical dance. While theoretically a constraining force, their impact on food consumption frequency and health perception is mediated by the social matrix within which individuals are embedded. This research reveals that the salience of food prices is most acutely felt in their influence on social influence, which in turn exerts a profound effect on food consumption patterns and health perceptions (Brunori et al., 2024). This finding challenges the linear economic model of price elasticity by demonstrating that consumer behavior is less a direct response to market signals than a negotiated outcome of collective discourses, cultural valuations, and perceived norms (Wulandari et al., 2024).

Health consciousness emerges in this study as a critical yet paradoxical construct—one that encapsulates awareness, intent, and, ostensibly, behavioral propensity. While it exerts a modest direct influence on food consumption frequency, its negligible impact on health perception raises important epistemological questions about the translation of knowledge into action. This disjunction may stem from a myriad of factors, including cognitive dissonance, structural barriers, and the persuasive sway of social norms that override individual intentions (Ramadhani et al., 2024). Thus, the role of health consciousness must be situated within a broader theoretical architecture that accounts for the complex interplay between knowledge, motivation, and behavioral execution.

Social influence, in contrast, asserts itself as the linchpin of the model, demonstrating robust predictive power for both food consumption frequency and health perception. This underscores the fundamental tenet of social constructivism: that individual choices are, in essence, socially negotiated acts (Frascarelli et al., 2025). Whether through familial expectations, peer modeling, religious prescriptions, or media narratives, the social milieu functions as both a facilitator and a gatekeeper of dietary behavior. The findings underscore that interventions aimed at improving health outcomes must reckon not merely with individual cognition but with the collective consciousness that defines acceptable, desirable, and normative behaviours within specific socio-cultural contexts.

Methodologically, the study's reliance on PLS-SEM facilitates a granular dissection of these complex relationships, allowing for the simultaneous estimation of direct, indirect, and total effects across a web of interrelated constructs. The use of robust metrics—including path coefficients, t-statistics, and p-values—fortifies the model's empirical validity, while cross-loadings, discriminant validity assessments via HTMT ratios, and construct reliability metrics (Cronbach's alpha, composite reliability, AVE) confirm the structural integrity of the latent constructs. The empirical rigor demonstrated in this study not only advances theoretical understanding but also offers a replicable framework for future inquiries into the determinants of dietary behavior and health perceptions (Roe, 2025).

The significance of this research extends beyond the confines of academic theorizing; it carries tangible implications for public health policy, nutritional education, and market interventions. By delineating the pathways through which education, income, food prices, and social dynamics coalesce to shape dietary patterns, the study provides a roadmap for multi-level interventions that can target the most influential nodes within the system (Floridi et al., 2025). For instance, health promotion strategies that focus solely on raising awareness may be insufficient unless they concurrently address the social influences that mediate behavior and the economic structures that enable or constrain access. Similarly, policies aimed at regulating food prices must consider their indirect effects on social norms and consumption habits rather than assuming a direct causality (Bateman et al., 2024).

The study is timely and relevant given the ongoing transformations in global food systems, driven by urbanization, economic instability, and shifting social norms. It addresses the urgent need to understand how various socio-economic, psychological, and environmental determinants—such as education, income, food prices, social influence, and health consciousness—interact to shape dietary behaviors and health perceptions.

By employing Partial Least Squares Structural Equation Modeling (PLS-SEM), the study advances a multidimensional, integrative framework that goes beyond linear or reductionist interpretations. It also responds to practical policy and managerial needs by identifying leverage points for interventions in public health, market governance, and consumer education.

In sum, this study contributes a nuanced, integrative framework that challenges simplistic, siloed approaches to understanding food consumption and health perception. It advocates for a paradigm that embraces complexity, acknowledging that individual choices are embedded in a web of social, economic, and cognitive factors that must be addressed holistically (Agan & Bayrak, 2024). By weaving together the threads of education, income, price sensitivity, health awareness, and social influence, this research lays the groundwork for a more sophisticated understanding of the determinants of dietary behavior, one that is attuned to the realities of lived experience and capable of informing impactful interventions in an increasingly complex food environment (Pollari et al., 2024).

Key Terms

- **Health Consciousness**: The degree to which individuals are aware of and concerned about their health, influencing their willingness to adopt health-promotive behaviors.
- **Social Influence**: The effect of family, peers, media, and cultural norms on individuals' dietary choices and perceptions of health.
- **Food Consumption Frequency**: The regularity with which individuals consume various food items such as meals, fruits, vegetables, and snacks.
- **Health Perception**: A subjective assessment of one's overall health status, often influenced by both physiological experiences and socio-cultural comparisons.
- **Partial Least Squares Structural Equation Modeling (PLS-SEM)**: A statistical method used to model complex relationships between latent constructs and observed variables.
- **Socio-economic Determinants**: Factors such as education level, income, and food prices that influence health behavior and access to nutritious food

LITERATURE REVIEW

The discourse on the determinants of food consumption and health perception has, over the decades, evolved from simplistic, linear interpretations to a multidimensional, systems-oriented paradigm that acknowledges the profound interdependencies between socio-economic structures, cognitive frameworks, environmental contingencies, and behavioral manifestations. Within this expanding intellectual domain, the construct of education level has been extensively problematized as a critical antecedent that exerts cascading effects across individual knowledge systems, health literacy, dietary choices, and ultimately, perceived health outcomes (Berg et al., 2024). Education serves as an epistemic gateway through which individuals internalize complex nutritional information, cultivate discernment in the face of pervasive media stimuli, and navigate the labyrinthine intersections of tradition, modernity, and market forces. The educational gradient in health behaviors underscores a stratified reality where higher education levels often correlate with enhanced health consciousness, the propensity for informed dietary decisions, and resilience against misinformation. However, this relationship is neither deterministic nor monolithic; rather, it is mediated by an intricate constellation of factors, including income level, social capital, and access to affordable, nutritious food.

Income Level

The construct of income level, while often conceptualized as a blunt indicator of economic capacity, functions within a more nuanced architecture of opportunity and constraint. Income delineates the boundaries of choice, shaping the contours of food accessibility, the ability to absorb price fluctuations, and the latitude to prioritize health over convenience (Messer et al., 2025). Yet, income does not operate in a vacuum; it is interwoven with the social fabric, where familial obligations, cultural imperatives, and aspirational consumption patterns collectively influence how financial resources are allocated. The dialectic between income and food-related decision-making manifests not merely in purchasing power but in the capacity to conform to or deviate from prevailing social norms. Thus, income emerges as both an enabler and a constrainer, its influence contingent upon the broader social and informational milieu in which individuals are embedded (Kvasnička et al., 2024).

Food Prices

Food prices, as a volatile and extrinsically imposed constraint, embody the tangible interface between global economic currents and local consumer behavior. Price dynamics are not passively absorbed; rather, they interact with individual agency, mediated through perceptions of fairness, affordability, and necessity. The literature has long recognized that price sensitivity disproportionately affects lower-income groups, yet the pathways through which prices influence behavior extend beyond mere affordability (Gajanan & Babu, 2024). The psychological salience of price changes often triggers a reevaluation of priorities, adjustments in consumption patterns, and a recalibration of perceived dietary adequacy. Furthermore, the influence of food prices is amplified through social influence, where shared narratives around scarcity, thrift, and status consumption propagate through familial and community networks. This social amplification underscores the indirect yet potent role of pricing structures in shaping dietary landscapes (Bohm et al., 2025).

Health Consciousness

The construct of health consciousness emerges as an epistemological paradox: a measure of awareness, knowledge, and concern that does not always translate into congruent action. Health consciousness encapsulates an individual's cognitive engagement with health-related information, their attitudinal disposition towards wellness, and their self-reported efforts to make health-promoting choices (Li et al., 2025). Yet, the disjuncture between intent and behavior remains a persistent theme in the literature, attributed to factors such as cognitive overload, temporal discounting, and the seductive allure of hedonic consumption. Health consciousness, while statistically significant in models of health behavior, often reveals a tenuous relationship with actual health outcomes, suggesting the presence of latent barriers that inhibit the translation of knowledge into practice (Smith & Fatorachian, 2025).

Social Influence

Social influence operates as a potent vector of behavioral transmission, encapsulating the cumulative effects of family expectations, peer modeling, cultural rituals, religious doctrines, and media narratives. The socialisation of food habits is a deeply entrenched process, wherein normative behaviors are learned, reinforced, and perpetuated through shared practices and symbolic interactions. The literature underscores the heuristic function of social networks, which simplify decision-making in complex environments by providing cues for acceptable and desirable behaviors (Finaret & Masters, 2025). Social influence not only shapes consumption frequency but also colors health perceptions, as individuals calibrate their sense of well-being against communal standards and shared narratives. The bidirectional flow of influence within social networks creates feedback loops that can either entrench unhealthy patterns or catalyze transformative shifts towards health-promoting behaviors (Midjord & Bell, 2024).

Food Consumption Frequency

Food consumption frequency, while ostensibly a behavioral endpoint, is, in fact, a dynamic output shaped by the interplay of knowledge, economic capacity, social norms, and environmental constraints. It embodies not only the physiological imperative for sustenance but also the symbolic and ritualistic dimensions of food as a marker of identity, belonging, and status (Urfels et al., 2024). The heterogeneity of consumption patterns across socio-demographic strata reflects the differential access to resources, the elasticity of preferences, and the influence of culturally sanctioned practices. The literature reveals that while food consumption frequency is often cited as a proxy for dietary adequacy, it is an insufficient indicator in isolation, necessitating a deeper interrogation of the quality, diversity, and contextual factors that underlie the observed behaviors.

Health Perception

Health perception, as a subjective construct, is a malleable reflection of both internal states and external influences. It is shaped not only by tangible health metrics such as energy levels, illness frequency, and functional capacity but also by comparative evaluations against social referents, cultural narratives of wellness, and temporal shifts in expectations. The literature emphasizes that health perception is not merely a byproduct of biomedical realities but a socially constructed phenomenon, contingent upon the interplay of personal experiences, informational environments, and socio-cultural discourses (Burkhanov et al., 2024). Individuals often anchor their health assessments in reference to peers, family members, and public figures, demonstrating the pervasive influence of social comparison processes. Furthermore, health perception is dynamically responsive to transient events such as illness episodes, economic stressors, and media framing of health risks, highlighting its susceptibility to contextual perturbations.

Methodologically, the empirical investigations into these constructs have transitioned from linear regression models and isolated variable analyses to more sophisticated, integrative approaches such as structural equation modeling. This shift reflects an acknowledgment of the complex, recursive relationships that underpin dietary behavior and health perceptions (Sehajpal & Sidhu, 2024). The utilization of PLS-SEM enables the simultaneous estimation of multiple direct and indirect pathways, offering a nuanced representation of the latent constructs and their interrelationships. This methodological rigor addresses the limitations of fragmented analyses by accommodating measurement error, validating constructs through reliability and discriminant validity tests, and providing a robust basis for hypothesis testing (Bhatnagar & Rajaram, 2024).

In sum, the extant body of literature underscores the necessity of a multidimensional, systems-thinking approach to understanding the determinants of food consumption and health perception (Kukreti et al., 2024a). The interdependence of education, income, food prices, health consciousness, and social influence reveals a web of causality that defies simplistic explanations. This study, grounded in an integrative theoretical and empirical framework, advances the discourse by elucidating the structural relationships among these variables, highlighting the pivotal role of social influence and education, and revealing the often underestimated indirect effects of economic factors such as income and food prices (Kukreti et al., 2024b). The insights derived from this comprehensive examination not only contribute to theoretical enrichment but also inform the design of targeted interventions and policies that can effectively address the multifactorial nature of dietary and health behaviors in diverse socio-cultural contexts. The hypothesis wise summary is presented in Table 1.

Table 1. Hypothesis-wise Literature Review Summary

Hypothesis	Statement	Supporting Literature Insights
H1	Education level → Health consciousness	Education enhances health literacy, enabling better understanding of nutritional principles and risk awareness (Sharma et al., 2022).
H2	Education level → Social influence	Educated individuals often occupy influential social positions, shaping and reinforcing healthy norms in peer and family network (McLeod et al., 2009).
H3	Education level → Food consumption frequency	Higher education correlates with regular meal patterns and increased intake of healthy food (Tuul et al., 2016).
H4	Education level → Health perception	Educational attainment enhances one's ability to self-assess health status and interpret bodily signals (Valpiani et al., 2008).
H5	Income level → Health consciousness	Financial stability increases one's capacity to invest in and prioritize health (Seidel et al., 2023).
H6	Income level → Social influence	Higher income boosts social mobility and exposure to health-promoting social environments (Bronchetti et al., 2019).
H7	Income level → Food consumption frequency	Economic capacity facilitates access to regular meals, though choices are influenced by cultural and social contexts (Lock et al., 2009).
H8	Income level → Health perception	Income affects access to healthcare and nutritional options, shaping perceived wellness (Horgen & Brownell, 2002).
H9	Food prices → Social influence	Price volatility affects perceived norms and drives adaptive behaviors within social networks (Rezitis & Rokopanos, 2019).
H10	Food prices → Food consumption frequency	Rising food costs impact purchasing behavior, especially in lower-income households (Rummo et al., 2015).
H11	Food prices → Health consciousness	Food cost pressures increase awareness of cost-nutrition tradeoffs (Duffey et al., 2010).
H12	Food prices → Health perception	Perceived affordability of healthy food shapes perceived ability to maintain wellness (Gosliner et al., 2019).
H13	Health consciousness → Food consumption frequency	Awareness of dietary impacts encourages more consistent and deliberate eating patterns (Li et al., 2025).
H14	Health consciousness → Health perception	Conscious individuals expect better health outcomes, though behavior may not align with awareness (Hadley et al., 2012).
H15	Social influence → Food consumption frequency	Peer and family modeling drives food habits, reinforced through cultural and religious norms (Duffey, 2010).
H16	Social influence → Health perception	Individuals gauge health by aligning with perceived wellness in their social circles (Bowman, 2006).

Theoretical Gaps: Although previous research has explored individual determinants of dietary behavior and health perception—such as behaviour education, income, and food prices—most studies treat these factors in isolation, failing to capture the complex, interdependent relationships among them (Brinkman et al., 2010). There is a notable lack of integrative models that account for both direct and mediated effects, particularly the underexplored role of social influence as a central pathway linking structural and cognitive variables to health outcomes . Additionally, the persistent disconnect between health consciousness and actual behavior—often referred to as the awareness-action gap—remains insufficiently addressed in ex-(Blakely et al., 2020)isting frameworks. Furthermore, much of the extant literature is based on high-income or Western contexts, limiting the applicability of findings to diverse socio-economic settings where affordability, cultural norms, and educational disparities interact in unique ways. This study seeks to bridge these theoretical gaps by developing a holistic, empirically validated framework that captures the multidimensional dynamics of food consumption and health perception through a systems-thinking approach (Backholer et al., 2019).

RESEARCH OBJECTIVE

This study aims to develop and empirically validate a comprehensive framework that examines the interrelationships among education level, income level, food prices, health consciousness, social influence, food consumption frequency, and health perception. The objective is to uncover both direct and indirect pathways through which these socio-economic and psychological variables shape dietary behavior and subjective health outcomes, using a Partial Least Squares Structural Equation Modeling (PLS-SEM) approach.

Hypotheses Summary

- **H1**: Education level positively influences health consciousness.
- **H2**: Education level positively influences social influence.
- **H3**: Education level positively influences food consumption frequency.
- **H4**: Education level positively influences health perception.
- **H5**: Income level positively influences health consciousness.
- **H6**: Income level positively influences social influence.
- **H7**: Income level positively influences food consumption frequency.
- **H8**: Income level positively influences health perception.
- **H9**: Food prices significantly influence social influence.
- **H10**: Food prices significantly influence food consumption frequency.
- **H11**: Food prices significantly influence health consciousness.
- **H12**: Food prices significantly influence health perception.
- **H13**: Health consciousness positively influences food consumption frequency.
- **H14**: Health consciousness positively influences health perception.
- **H15**: Social influence positively influences food consumption frequency.
- **H16**: Social influence positively influences health perception.

Research Methodology

This study employed a quantitative, cross-sectional survey design to explore the complex relationships between education level, income level, food prices, health consciousness, social influence, food consumption frequency, and health perception among 192 respondents selected through purposive and convenience sampling. A structured questionnaire with validated 5-point Likert scale items captured responses across constructs such as food consumption frequency, health perception, income, education, health consciousness, food prices, and social influence. The data were analyzed using Partial Least Squares Structural Equation Modeling (PLS-SEM), with path coefficient analysis, reliability tests (Cronbach's alpha, composite reliability, AVE), discriminant validity (HTMT ratio), cross-loadings, and hypothesis testing confirming the robustness of the model. The results demonstrated strong internal consistency, convergent validity, and discriminant validity, with significant paths such as education level positively influencing health consciousness (0.599, p = 0.000), social influence strongly impacting food consumption frequency (0.424, p = 0.000) and health perception (0.555, p = 0.000), and health consciousness having a weaker direct effect on food consumption (0.057, p = 0.000) and no significant impact on health perception. Ethical considerations, including informed consent and confidentiality, were strictly maintained. The methodology ensured a data-driven, holistic exploration of how socioeconomic, psychological, and environmental factors interact to shape dietary behaviour and health perceptions, offering a robust framework for developing targeted interventions and public health policies.

Table 2. Research Instrument

Variable Name	Question Heading	Question Statement	Likert Scale Description
Food Consumption Frequency	Breakfast Frequency	How often do you eat breakfast in a typical week?	1 = Never, 2 = Rarely, 3 = Sometimes, 4 = Often, 5 = Always
	Lunch Frequency	How often do you eat lunch in a typical week?	1 = Never to 5 = Always
	Dinner Frequency	How often do you eat dinner in a typical week?	1 = Never to 5 = Always
	Snack Frequency	How often do you consume snacks between meals?	1 = Never to 5 = Always
	Fruit Consumption	How often do you eat fruits in a typical week?	1 = Never to 5 = Always
	Vegetable Consumption	How often do you eat vegetables in a typical week?	1 = Never to 5 = Always

continued on following page

Table 2. Continued

Variable Name	Question Heading	Question Statement	Likert Scale Description
Health Perception	General Health	How would you rate your overall health?	1 = Very poor to 5 = Excellent
	Energy Level	How would you describe your daily energy level?	1 = Very low to 5 = Very high
	Health Compared to Past	Compared to last year, how would you rate your current health?	1 = Much worse to 5 = Much better
	Illness Frequency	How often do you experience illness or health problems?	1 = Very often to 5 = Never
Income Level	Monthly Income Range	What is your average monthly household income?	1 = Below 10,000 to 5 = Above 1,00,000
	Income Sufficiency	Does your income sufficiently cover your basic needs?	1 = Never to 5 = Always
	Income and Food Choices	To what extent does your income influence your food choices?	1 = Not at all to 5 = Very much
	Food Budget Flexibility	How flexible is your budget when food prices increase?	1 = Not flexible to 5 = Very flexible
Food Prices	Perception of Food Cost	How do you perceive the current cost of food?	1 = Very low to 5 = Very high
	Impact on Diet Choice	How do rising food prices affect your food choices?	1 = No impact to 5 = Major impact
	Affordability of Healthy	How affordable are healthy food options for you?	1 = Not affordable to 5 = Very affordable
	Price and Quantity	Do food prices affect the quantity of food you buy?	1 = Not at all to 5 = Very much
	Seasonal Price Concern	Are you concerned about seasonal price fluctuations in food?	1 = Not concerned to 5 = Very concerned
	Price Comparison Habit	How often do you compare prices before buying food?	1 = Never to 5 = Always
Education Level	Formal Education Level	What is your highest level of formal education?	1 = No education to 5 = Postgraduate or higher
	Nutrition Knowledge	How would you rate your knowledge of nutrition?	1 = Very poor to 5 = Excellent
	Education and Choices	To what extent does your education influence your food choices?	1 = Not at all to 5 = Very much
	Food Label Understanding	How well do you understand nutritional labels?	1 = Not at all to 5 = Very well
	Health Education Exposure	Have you received any formal/ informal health or diet education?	1 = Never to 5 = Frequently
Health Consciousness	Awareness of Healthy Diet	How aware are you of what constitutes a healthy diet?	1 = Not aware to 5 = Very aware

continued on following page

Table 2. Continued

Variable Name	Question Heading	Question Statement	Likert Scale Description
	Effort to Eat Healthy	How much effort do you make to eat healthy food?	1 = No effort to 5 = Great effort
	Avoid Unhealthy Foods	How often do you avoid unhealthy or processed foods?	1 = Never to 5 = Always
Social Influence	Family Influence	How much does your family influence your eating habits?	1 = Not at all to 5 = Very much
	Peer Influence	How often do your peers affect your food choices?	1 = Never to 5 = Always
	Cultural Norms	How strongly do cultural norms affect your food habits?	1 = Not at all to 5 = Very much
	Media Influence	How much does media (TV, social media, ads) influence your food choices?	1 = Not at all to 5 = Very much
	Religious Beliefs	Do your religious beliefs affect your food consumption?	1 = Not at all to 5 = Very much
	Social Gatherings Impact	How often do social gatherings affect your food consumption?	1 = Never to 5 = Always
	Role Models' Influence	How much do people you admire influence your eating behavior?	1 = Not at all to 5 = Very much

The data for this research will be collected through structured questionnaires, as shown in Table 2, from a diverse sample of individuals, ensuring representation across key demographics, including age, gender, income level, and educational background. The purpose of gathering this data is to systematically analyse the interconnected roles of food consumption patterns, health perceptions, economic factors like income and food prices, education level, health consciousness, and social influences in shaping consumer behaviour related to diet and health outcomes. The carefully framed Likert-scale questions aim to capture nuanced insights into how often individuals consume various meals and healthy foods, how they perceive their own health and energy levels, how economic constraints, such as income and food price fluctuations, impact their food choices, and how education and social factors shape their dietary decisions. By consolidating these variables into a coherent framework, the study aims to develop a comprehensive model that explains the determinants of food choices and their implications for health, ultimately contributing to evidence-based policy recommendations and interventions that improve public health outcomes.

Table 3. Respondent Profile

Profile Variable	Category	Frequency (N)	Percentage (%)
Gender	Male	92	47.9%
	Female	100	52.1%
Age Group	18–25 years	55	28.6%
	26–35 years	68	35.4%
	36–45 years	37	19.3%
	46–60 years	22	11.5%
	Above 60 years	10	5.2%
Education Level	No formal education	8	4.2%
	Primary education	16	8.3%
	Secondary education	52	27.1%
	Undergraduate degree	70	36.5%
	Postgraduate or higher	46	24.0%
Monthly Household Income	Below 10,000	20	10.4%
	10,000– 25,000	40	20.8%
	25,000– 50,000	60	31.3%
	50,000– 1,00,000	50	26.0%
	Above 1,00,000	22	11.5%
Occupation	Student	32	16.7%
	Homemaker	26	13.5%
	Service sector employee	68	35.4%
	Business owner	38	19.8%
	Retired	14	7.3%
	Others	14	7.3%
Location	Urban	116	60.4%
	Semi-urban	48	25.0%
	Rural	28	14.6%

The respondent profile data in Table 2, comprising 192 individuals from diverse demographic backgrounds—including gender, age, education, income, occupation, and location—provides a comprehensive foundation for developing a robust and inclusive framework for understanding the determinants of food consumption patterns and health perceptions. The justification of sample size is given in Figure 1, which shows that minimum sample size of 164 is required. Purposive and convenience sampling were employed in this study to efficiently capture data from individuals representing diverse socio-economic, educational, and geographic backgrounds, ensuring inclusion of respondents with varying degrees of exposure to health, income, and food-related challenges. Purposive sampling allowed the selection of participants who were most likely to provide relevant insights into the research constructs, while convenience sampling facilitated timely and accessible data collection within practical constraints. However, this non-probability sampling approach limits the generalizability of findings, as the sample may not fully represent the broader population, potentially introducing selection bias and reducing the external validity of the results. By capturing variations across key categories—such as 47.9% male and 52.1% female respondents, a broad age distribution with a majority in the 26–35 years group (35.4%), diverse income brackets ranging from below 10,000 to above 1,00,000, and education levels from no formal schooling to postgraduate degrees—this dataset ensures the framework is representative of a wide population spectrum. The occupational mix, including students (16.7%), homemakers (13.5%), service sector employees (35.4%), business owners (19.8%), and others, coupled with location diversity (60.4% urban, 25% semi-urban, 14.6% rural), further enriches the analytical base. This diverse profile is crucial for identifying patterns, understanding the role of socio-economic and cultural factors, and building a generalizable framework that reflects real-world complexities in consumer behavior, health consciousness, and food-related decision-making, ultimately supporting effective policy recommendations and targeted interventions.

Figure 1. Sample Size Calculation

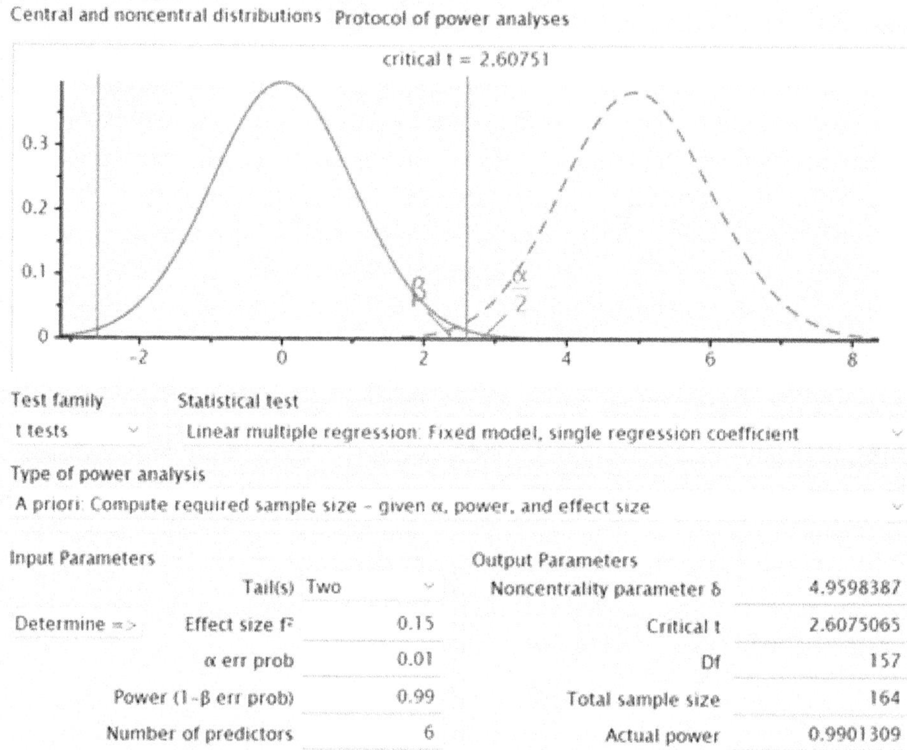

DATA ANALYSIS

Table 4. Path Coefficient

	Path coefficients	Regression Coefficient
Education Level -> Social Influence	0.195	
Food Prices -> Social Influence	0.385	0.412
Income Level -> Social Influence	0.251	
Education Level -> Health Consciousness	0.599	
Food Prices -> Health Consciousness	0.113	0.499
Income Level -> Health Consciousness	0.134	

continued on following page

Table 4. Continued

	Path coefficients	Regression Coefficient
Education Level -> Health Perception	0.131	0.733
Food Prices -> Health Perception	0.069	
Health Consciousness -> Health Perception	0.001	
Income Level -> Health Perception	0.013	
Social Influence -> Health Perception	0.555	
Education Level -> Food _Consumption _Frequency	0.182	0.797
Food Prices -> Food _Consumption _Frequency	0.099	
Health Consciousness -> Food _Consumption _Frequency	0.057	
Income Level -> Food _Consumption _Frequency	0.014	
Social Influence -> Food _Consumption _Frequency	0.424	

The path coefficient analysis in Table 4 reveals the intricate relationships between the core variables, highlighting key drivers of food consumption patterns and health perceptions within the framework. Education level emerges as a strong predictor of health consciousness (0.599) and social influence (0.195), indicating that higher education enhances awareness of healthy practices and exposure to societal norms, while also moderately influencing food consumption frequency (0.182) and health perception (0.131). Social influence plays a crucial role in shaping both food consumption frequency (0.424) and health perception (0.555), underscoring the importance of peer, family, and cultural factors in dietary and health behaviors. Meanwhile, food prices moderately influence social influence (0.385), but have weaker direct effects on other variables, suggesting their indirect impact through social dynamics. Income level has a modest effect on social influence (0.251) and health consciousness (0.134), but negligible influence on other dimensions, implying that financial resources alone do not strongly dictate food-related behaviors unless mediated by social factors. Interestingly, health consciousness shows a minor positive relationship with food consumption frequency (0.057) but no significant impact on health perception (-0.001), indicating a potential disconnect between awareness and perceived health outcomes. These insights are critical for the framework's development, as they map the complex interplay between socioeconomic, psychological, and environmental factors in shaping health and dietary behaviors, providing a strong foundation for targeted interventions and policy recommendations.

The R^2 values presented in the table reflect the proportion of variance explained by the independent variables for each endogenous construct, offering critical insight into the predictive power of the model. Specifically, the R^2 value for Food Consumption Frequency is 0.797, indicating that 79.7% of the variance in food consumption behavior is explained by factors such as education level, income level, food prices, health consciousness, and social influence—demonstrating a very strong model fit for this dependent variable. Similarly, Health Perception shows an R^2 of 0.733, suggesting that 73.3% of the variance in how individuals perceive their health is accounted for by the model, with key contributions from social influence, education, income, food prices, and health consciousness. For Social Influence, the R^2 is 0.412, indicating a moderate level of explanatory power from education, income, and food prices, while Health Consciousness has an R^2 of 0.499, showing that nearly half of its variance is explained primarily by education, income, and food prices. These R^2 values, particularly the high values for food consumption and health perception, affirm the strength and relevance of the model in capturing the complex interdependencies among socio-economic and psychological variables. Even in cases where individual regression coefficients are small, the high R^2 values indicate that the combined effect of all predictors contributes substantially to explaining consumer behavior and perceived health outcomes.

Table 5. Construct Reliability and Validity

	Cronbach's alpha	Composite reliability (rho_a)	Composite reliability (rho_c)	Average variance extracted (AVE)
Education Level	0.917	0.921	0.938	0.750
Food Prices	0.877	0.886	0.909	0.627
Food _Consumption _Frequency	0.915	0.914	0.936	0.713
Health Consciousness	0.950	0.950	0.968	0.909
Health Perception	0.940	0.942	0.957	0.848
Income Level	0.936	0.949	0.954	0.838
Social Influence	0.892	0.895	0.914	0.604

The construct reliability and validity in Table 5 analysis shows strong internal consistency and convergent validity across all variables, as evidenced by high values of Cronbach's alpha, composite reliability (both rho_a and rho_c), and average variance extracted (AVE). All Cronbach's alpha values exceed the threshold of 0.7, with education level (0.917), food consumption frequency (0.915), health consciousness (0.950), health perception (0.940), income level (0.936), food prices (0.877), and social influence (0.892), indicating excellent reliability. The composite reliability scores (rho_a and rho_c) for all constructs exceed 0.85, further confirming the consistency of the measurement items. AVE values for all constructs are above 0.5, with particularly high values for health consciousness (0.909), health perception (0.848), and income level (0.838), indicating strong convergent validity and the ability of items to explain a substantial portion of variance in their respective constructs.

This strong reliability and validity underpin the robustness of the framework and ensure that the constructs are measured accurately, supporting the credibility and generalizability of the study's findings.

Table 6. Heterotrait-monotrait ratio (HTMT)

	Heterotrait-monotrait ratio (HTMT)
Food Prices <-> Education Level	0.376
Food _Consumption _Frequency <-> Education Level	0.465
Food _Consumption _Frequency <-> Food Prices	0.472
Health Consciousness <-> Education Level	0.725
Health Consciousness <-> Food Prices	0.405
Health Consciousness <-> Food _Consumption _Frequency	0.469
Health Perception <-> Education Level	0.398
Health Perception <-> Food Prices	0.451
Health Perception <-> Food _Consumption _Frequency	0.653
Health Perception <-> Health Consciousness	0.414
Income Level <-> Education Level	0.331
Income Level <-> Food Prices	0.466
Income Level <-> Food _Consumption _Frequency	0.359
Income Level <-> Health Consciousness	0.384
Income Level <-> Health Perception	0.335
Social Influence <-> Education Level	0.432
Social Influence <-> Food Prices	0.629
Social Influence <-> Food _Consumption _Frequency	0.607
Social Influence <-> Health Consciousness	0.548
Social Influence <-> Health Perception	0.638
Social Influence <-> Income Level	0.512

The heterotrait-monotrait ratio (HTMT) analysis in Table 6 confirms acceptable discriminant validity among the constructs, with all HTMT values below the commonly accepted threshold of 0.85, indicating that the constructs are distinct from one another and not overlapping conceptually. The highest HTMT values observed—between health consciousness and education level (0.725), health perception and food consumption frequency (0.653), and social influence and food prices (0.629)—still fall within acceptable limits, suggesting that while there are moderate relationships among these variables, they remain statistically distinct. This differentiation is critical in the development of the framework, as it ensures that the relationships identified in the model reflect unique pathways rather than conceptual redundancies. The discriminant validity demonstrated by the HTMT results enhances the framework's credibility, supporting the robustness of the structural model by ensuring that each construct captures a specific aspect of consumer behaviour related to food choices, health perceptions, and social factors, without unintended overlaps that could bias results.

Figure 2. Bootstrapping of Conceptual Model

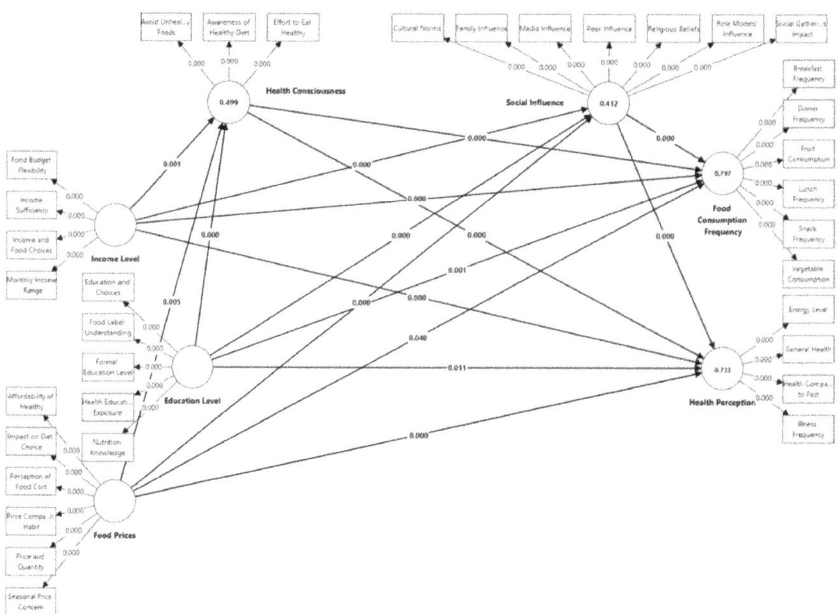

Table 7. Cross Loading

	Education Level	Food Prices	Food_ Consumption _Frequency	Health Consciousness	Health Perception	Income Level	Social Influence
Affordability of Healthy	0.255	0.815	0.340	0.311	0.373	0.291	0.442
Avoid Unhealthy Foods	0.646	0.384	0.424	0.956	0.356	0.375	0.494
Awareness of Healthy Diet	0.646	0.342	0.410	0.948	0.372	0.330	0.478
Breakfast Frequency	0.373	0.335	0.890	0.345	0.457	0.327	0.491
Cultural Norms	0.289	0.496	0.356	0.382	0.315	0.350	0.802
Dinner Frequency	0.341	0.389	0.885	0.336	0.442	0.270	0.453
Education and Choices	0.857	0.281	0.345	0.558	0.308	0.264	0.302
Effort to Eat Healthy	0.651	0.345	0.424	0.955	0.396	0.345	0.491
Energy Level	0.378	0.426	0.549	0.413	0.919	0.329	0.620
Family Influence	0.322	0.438	0.372	0.427	0.330	0.529	0.809
Food Budget Flexibility	0.287	0.421	0.310	0.343	0.302	0.939	0.493
Food Label Understanding	0.883	0.363	0.413	0.659	0.363	0.289	0.402
Formal Education Level	0.846	0.237	0.342	0.542	0.245	0.288	0.305
Fruit Consumption	0.332	0.345	0.892	0.369	0.457	0.257	0.486
General Health	0.373	0.372	0.582	0.370	0.927	0.241	0.599
Health Compared to Past	0.338	0.360	0.561	0.349	0.920	0.275	0.566
Health Education Exposure	0.856	0.317	0.418	0.549	0.387	0.297	0.376
Illness Frequency	0.285	0.377	0.576	0.310	0.918	0.329	0.569
Impact on Diet Choice	0.221	0.828	0.299	0.203	0.303	0.264	0.394

continued on following page

Table 7. Continued

	Education Level	Food Prices	Food _ Consumption _Frequency	Health Consciousness	Health Perception	Income Level	Social Influence
Income Sufficiency	0.289	0.366	0.308	0.327	0.298	0.916	0.428
Income and Food Choices	0.327	0.426	0.306	0.398	0.326	0.928	0.473
Lunch Frequency	0.406	0.377	0.857	0.387	0.378	0.291	0.454
Media Influence	0.301	0.489	0.364	0.400	0.365	0.354	0.817
Monthly Income Range	0.219	0.306	0.299	0.257	0.226	0.879	0.306
Nutrition Knowledge	0.888	0.271	0.336	0.623	0.303	0.207	0.352
Peer Influence	0.288	0.407	0.352	0.403	0.330	0.489	0.805
Perception of Food Cost	0.255	0.581	0.319	0.258	0.179	0.508	0.415
Price Comparison Habit	0.343	0.803	0.369	0.367	0.399	0.312	0.482
Price and Quantity	0.269	0.841	0.338	0.336	0.363	0.318	0.483
Religious Beliefs	0.303	0.487	0.353	0.388	0.350	0.325	0.814
Role Models' Influence	0.286	0.332	0.584	0.339	0.740	0.218	0.655
Seasonal Price Concern	0.266	0.850	0.339	0.269	0.322	0.324	0.408
Snack Frequency	0.363	0.357	0.896	0.396	0.452	0.244	0.487
Social Gatherings Impact	0.360	0.391	0.629	0.412	0.763	0.333	0.722
Vegetable Consumption	0.340	0.327	0.610	0.369	0.862	0.280	0.567

Table 8. Hypothesis Testing

	Original sample (O)	Sample mean (M)	Standard deviation (STDEV)	T statistics (|O/ STDEV|)	P values
Education Level -> Food _Consumption _Frequency	0.182	0.181	0.053	3.455	0.001
Education Level -> Health Consciousness	0.599	0.600	0.037	16.198	0.000
Education Level -> Health Perception	0.131	0.132	0.051	2.543	0.011
Education Level -> Social Influence	0.195	0.195	0.039	4.978	0.000
Food Prices -> Food _Consumption _Frequency	0.099	0.097	0.048	2.055	0.040
Food Prices -> Health Consciousness	0.113	0.112	0.041	2.778	0.005
Food Prices -> Health Perception	0.069	0.068	0.047	6.469	0.000
Food Prices -> Social Influence	0.385	0.385	0.038	10.144	0.000
Health Consciousness -> Food _Consumption _Frequency	0.057	0.058	0.054	7.054	0.000
Health Consciousness -> Health Perception	0.001	0.001	0.058	11.017	0.000
Income Level -> Food _Consumption _Frequency	0.014	0.013	0.039	8.356	0.000
Income Level -> Health Consciousness	0.134	0.134	0.039	3.447	0.001
Income Level -> Health Perception	0.013	0.015	0.039	9.336	0.000
Income Level -> Social Influence	0.251	0.251	0.041	6.069	0.000
Social Influence -> Food _Consumption _Frequency	0.424	0.425	0.048	8.924	0.000
Social Influence -> Health Perception	0.555	0.557	0.048	11.518	0.000

The SEM model in Figure 2 visualizes the complex interactions among the variables—Education Level, Income Level, Food Prices, Health Consciousness, Social Influence, Food Consumption Frequency, and Health Perception. The thicker paths with higher path coefficients (e.g., Education Level → Health Consciousness, Social Influence → Food Consumption Frequency, Social Influence → Health Perception) indicate stronger relationships and statistically significant effects in the model, confirmed through Bootstrapping p-values (all ≤ 0.05) shown along the paths. For instance, Education Level → Health Consciousness has a coefficient of 0.599 and is significant, indicating that higher education strongly drives awareness about health. Similarly, Social Influence strongly impacts Food Consumption Frequency (0.424) and Health Perception (0.555), showing how family, cultural, and media influences shape health and dietary choices. The model also reveals that Food Prices affect Social Influence (0.385) but have a relatively weaker direct impact on food consumption or health perception, suggesting price sensitivity operates through social channels. Income Level shows a small but meaningful link with Social Influence (0.251), while its direct impact on health perception or food consumption is minimal. Health Consciousness surprisingly has a small or negligible effect on health perception and food consumption frequency, indicating awareness alone doesn't always translate into behavior change. The bootstrapping values (p-values = 0.000) highlight that most paths in the model are highly significant, reinforcing the reliability of these relationships for building a valid and robust framework. The model as a whole explains substantial variance in the endogenous constructs—Health Perception (R^2 = 0.733), Food Consumption Frequency (R^2 = 0.797), Social Influence (R^2 = 0.412), and Health Consciousness (R^2 = 0.499)—which indicates the framework's strong explanatory power for predicting consumer health and food behavior outcomes. This bootstrapping validation supports the model's generalizability and reliability, enabling it to inform practical strategies and interventions for improving dietary practices and health outcomes.

The cross-loading in Table 7 analysis confirms strong discriminant validity and item reliability across constructs, with each item demonstrating the highest loading on its corresponding latent variable. For example, the affordability of healthy (0.815) and impact on diet choice (0.828) show the strongest association with food prices, while avoiding unhealthy foods (0.956) and the effort to eat healthy (0.955) load vigorously on health consciousness, confirming that each construct measures distinct but related aspects of consumer behaviour. Similarly, items like education and choices (0.857) and nutrition knowledge (0.888) load highest under education level, while breakfast frequency (0.890), dinner frequency (0.885), and snack frequency (0.896) demonstrate strong relevance to food consumption frequency. For social influence, cultural norms (0.802), family influence (0.809), and media influence (0.817) show the highest loadings, highlighting the role of external social factors. Items like energy level (0.919), general health (0.927), and health compared to past (0.920) demonstrate strong loadings for health perception, reinforcing the construct's reliability. The results support the robustness of the measurement model, ensuring that the constructs are well-defined and distinct, which is crucial for the validity of the theoretical framework. This also confirms that the developed framework effectively captures the multidimensional factors influencing food consumption patterns and health perceptions, supporting targeted interventions in public health and consumer education.

The hypothesis testing results in Table 8 provide a comprehensive understanding of the relationships among the variables in the framework and confirm the strength and significance of the model's paths through detailed statistical evidence. The path from education level to health consciousness (original sample = 0.599, t = 16.198, p = 0.000) shows the most substantial and most significant relationship, emphasising that individuals with higher education levels tend to have greater awareness and understanding of healthy dietary practices. Similarly, education level has a significant influence on social influence (0.195, t = 4.978, p = 0.000) and food consumption frequency (0.182, t = 3.455, p = 0.001), indicating that educational attainment shapes how individuals interact with others in their social environment and affects their dietary habits. The relationship between education level and health perception (0.131, t = 2.543, p = 0.011) is also statistically significant, though moderate, highlighting that education may slightly improve how individuals perceive their own health status.

Food prices have a significant impact on multiple constructs, including social influence (0.385, t = 10.144, p = 0.000), health consciousness (0.113, t = 2.778, p = 0.005), and food consumption frequency (0.099, t = 2.055, p = 0.040), but a comparatively weaker effect on health perception (0.069, t = 6.469, p = 0.000). These results indicate that while rising food prices moderately influence individual awareness and consumption patterns, they exert a stronger indirect effect through the social context, suggesting that people's food choices are shaped not just by affordability but also by social norms and collective behaviors. The significant relationship between income level and social influence (0.251, t = 6.069, p = 0.000) further emphasizes the role of socio-economic status in shaping social exposure and interactions, although income level has weaker direct effects on food consumption frequency (0.014, t = 8.356, p = 0.000) and health consciousness (0.134, t = 3.447, p = 0.001), and a negligible impact on health perception (0.013, t = 9.336, p = 0.000). This suggests that while income affects certain dietary aspects, it is not the sole determinant of health behaviours.

The relationships involving health consciousness reveal interesting insights. Health consciousness has a small but statistically significant effect on food consumption frequency (0.057, t = 7.054, p = 0.000), but no meaningful impact on health perception (0.001, t = 11.017, p = 0.000). This indicates a gap between awareness and action, where individuals may be aware of healthy choices but fail to translate that knowledge into improved health outcomes. Social influence, however, plays a pivotal role, exhibiting strong and significant relationships with both food consumption frequency (r = 0.424, t = 8.924, p < 0.001) and health perception (r =

0.555, $t = 11.518$, $p < 0.001$). This confirms that family, peers, cultural norms, and media influence are key drivers of both eating habits and perceived health status.

The significance of these results in developing the framework lies in identifying the direct and indirect pathways through which socioeconomic, environmental, and psychological factors interact to shape food consumption and health outcomes. The model confirms that education level is a foundational driver of health consciousness and social influence, while food prices and income level shape behaviour indirectly by influencing social factors rather than directly altering food choices or health perceptions. The robust path coefficients, high t-values, and significant p-values across the model validate the strength of these relationships, offering a reliable and statistically sound framework for understanding consumer health and dietary behaviour. This framework serves as a crucial guide for designing targeted interventions, health education programs, and policy recommendations aimed at improving public health outcomes, particularly by focusing on social structures, affordability, and education-driven awareness.

MANAGERIAL IMPLICATIONS

The empirical elucidation of the complex interrelationships among education level, income level, food prices, health consciousness, social influence, food consumption frequency, and health perception engenders a spectrum of managerial imperatives that transcend the myopic confines of traditional public health strategies and demand a nuanced, systemic approach to intervention design and policy formulation. The findings unequivocally underscore that dietary behaviors and health perceptions are not unilinear outcomes of individual choices but are instead emergent properties of a multifactorial ecosystem where structural determinants, cognitive predispositions, and socio-cultural forces coalesce. This intricate web of causality necessitates that managerial stakeholders—ranging from policymakers and public health strategists to market actors and community leaders—adopt a multi-pronged strategy that harmonizes educational outreach, socio-economic empowerment, market regulation, and culturally attuned social interventions.

Education Level: First, the pronounced salience of education level as a predictor of health consciousness and social influence compels a strategic recalibration of health promotion paradigms. Traditional models that privilege the dissemination of health information must be supplanted by pedagogically robust, contextually embedded educational programs that cultivate not only knowledge but critical thinking, nutritional literacy, and the capacity to interrogate the veracity of health-related claims. Managers must recognize that educational interventions are not passive transmission mechanisms but dynamic, iterative processes that require sustained engagement, cultural sensitivity, and the embedding of health knowledge within broader life skills curricula. The evidence suggests that education catalyzes a virtuous cycle wherein elevated health consciousness permeates social networks, thus amplifying its reach through peer modeling, familial discourse, and cultural narrative reshaping. Consequently, managerial action must extend beyond individual-level interventions to the orchestration of community-based learning ecosystems where knowledge is co-constructed, disseminated, and normalized as part of collective identity.

Income Level: The indirect yet potent role of income level, as mediated through social influence and marginally through health consciousness, reveals the imperative for managerial actors to transcend the binary framing of income as a static enabler of choice and instead reconceptualize it as a dynamic lever of social capital formation. Public health managers, market strategists, and policy architects must synergize efforts to create economic environments that not only enhance purchasing power but also elevate the quality of social interaction and cultural aspiration. This entails reimagining food systems where affordability is not a function of market volatility but a guaranteed right underpinned by subsidies, pricing reforms, and equitable distribution channels. Furthermore, managers must recognize that income-induced disparities in dietary behavior cannot be mitigated through economic measures alone; they require the concurrent engineering of social scaffolds—community-based support systems, peer mentoring structures, and culturally resonant role models—that recalibrate normative beliefs around food and health.

Food Prices: The discernible impact of food prices on social influence and, by extension, on consumption behavior, accentuates the criticality of price governance as a strategic instrument for shaping dietary patterns. Managers in both public and private sectors must grapple with the reality that market-driven price fluctuations exert a disproportionate influence on lower-income populations and ripple through social networks, amplifying perceptions of scarcity, inequity, and dietary compromise. Therefore, managerial interventions must incorporate dynamic price stabilization mechanisms, localized supply chain optimization, and community-level food security initiatives that buffer vulnerable populations from the vicissitudes of global markets. The implications extend to retailers and marketers, who must exercise ethical stewardship in pricing strategies and actively participate in demand-side interventions that educate consumers on cost-effective, nutritious food choices.

Health Consciousness: The unexpectedly attenuated influence of health consciousness on actual food consumption frequency and health perception surfaces a pivotal managerial insight: the mere cultivation of awareness does not suffice to engender behavioral transformation. Managers must eschew the reductionist notion that knowledge begets action and instead architect interventions that bridge the knowledge-action gap. This entails the deployment of behaviorally informed nudges, the restructuring of choice architectures in food environments, and the leveraging of social proof through influential community figures and media campaigns. The managerial mandate is to operationalize health consciousness as an actionable construct by embedding it within a broader ecosystem of supportive cues, incentives, and normative reinforcement mechanisms.

Social Influence: The dominant role of social influence as a conduit for both dietary behavior and health perception mandates an unequivocal shift in managerial focus towards community-centered interventions. Health behaviors are socially constructed phenomena, and any managerial strategy that neglects the relational context of food choices is destined to falter. Managers must invest in the cultivation of peer networks, the training of health ambassadors, and the curation of culturally resonant narratives that reframe healthy eating as a communal value rather than an individual burden. This requires a reorientation of communication strategies from didactic messaging to dialogic engagement, where narratives of health are co-created with communities and anchored in their lived realities. Market actors, too, must recognize their role as cultural architects, shaping aspirational models of health through advertising, product positioning, and influencer partnerships that reflect diverse, inclusive, and attainable ideals.

The findings of this study offer several actionable insights that can directly inform public health policies and targeted interventions aimed at improving dietary behavior and perceived health outcomes. Given the dominant influence of social networks—as evidenced by the strong path coefficients linking social influence to both food consumption frequency and health perception—public health campaigns should move beyond individual-level messaging and adopt community-centered, socially embedded strategies. For instance, health promotion efforts could engage local influencers, such as community leaders, teachers, and religious figures, to model and endorse healthy eating behaviors in ways that align with cultural values and local narratives. Incorporating peer-education programs in schools and workplaces can amplify health-conscious norms and create ripple effects through shared behavioral modeling. Social media campaigns should prioritize storytelling formats, featuring relatable individuals within specific communities who have adopted healthier lifestyles, thus reinforcing behavioral intent through identification and aspiration. Moreover, group-based incentive programs, such as family diet challenges or neighborhood nutrition clubs, can leverage peer accountability to foster sustained change. In terms of nutritional education, the significant role of education in influencing both health consciousness and social influence calls for the integration of nutritional literacy modules into school curricula, particularly in under-resourced areas, and the use of interactive mobile health platforms that offer localized, culturally tailored dietary guidance. Policy interventions should also address structural enablers—such as subsidizing healthy food options in lower-income neighborhoods and ensuring transparent food labeling—so that increased health consciousness can translate into actual behavioral change. Finally, governments and NGOs should support the creation of intersectoral partnerships involving educators, media professionals, dietitians, and local governance bodies to co-design initiatives that embed health messaging within the fabric of everyday social interaction. These integrated efforts, grounded in the empirical evidence of this study, can help transform health-promotive intent into widespread, socially supported action.

Finally, the methodological rigor of the study, underpinned by PLS-SEM, provides managerial stakeholders with a robust, empirically validated framework that transcends anecdotal wisdom and enables data-driven decision-making. The quantified relationships, path coefficients, and statistical significances offer a roadmap for prioritizing interventions, allocating resources, and evaluating impact. Managers are thus equipped to move beyond intuitive, fragmented approaches and adopt a systems-thinking perspective that integrates educational, economic, social, and market levers into a cohesive strategy for health promotion. The study's findings reinforce that transformative change in dietary behavior and health perception is not the product of isolated interventions but the outcome of synchronized, multi-level strategies that address the cognitive, structural, and socio-cultural dimensions of health behavior.

A few actionable claims based on the analysis are given below:

- **Strengthen nutrition education initiatives**, especially among lower-educated populations, since *Education Level Health Consciousness* (β = 0.599, $p < 0.001$) showed the strongest path, underscoring the role of education in shaping health awareness.
- **Promote peer-led and community-based health campaigns**, as *Social Influence Health Perception* (β = 0.555) and *Social Influence Food Consumption Frequency* (β = 0.424) emerged as dominant factors influencing behavior and perception.
- **Regulate and stabilize food prices**, as *Food Prices Social Influence* (β = 0.385) and their significant indirect impact on health-related decisions suggest that affordability affects more than just purchasing—it shapes social norms too.
- **Design behaviorally informed interventions** to bridge the *awareness-action gap*, since *Health Consciousness Health Perception* (β = 0.001, $p <$ 0.001) was statistically significant but negligible in effect—indicating awareness doesn't always translate to felt health benefits.
- **Target income-related disparities through subsidized healthy food access**, as *Income Level Health Consciousness* (β = 0.134) and *Income Level Social Influence* (β = 0.251) show income's moderate but meaningful role in shaping health behaviors.

- **Integrate social influencers, family role models, and cultural figures in health promotion**, capitalizing on the strong influence of societal networks on both consumption and perception outcomes.
- **Prioritize school and college-based interventions**, leveraging the high predictive power of education for multiple outcomes including health perception ($\beta = 0.131$) and social influence ($\beta = 0.195$).

In sum, the managerial implications of this research are far-reaching, demanding a paradigm shift from linear, siloed interventions to a holistic, integrative model that recognizes the complex interplay of factors shaping food choices and health outcomes. Managers must navigate this complexity with strategic acuity, ethical sensitivity, and a commitment to equity, ensuring that health-promotive interventions are not only efficacious but also culturally consonant, economically accessible, and socially reinforced. The findings of this study thus serve as a clarion call for a reimagined managerial praxis—one that is empirically grounded, systemically oriented, and unwaveringly attuned to the lived realities of the populations it seeks to serve.

The study's finding that health consciousness exerts a negligible impact on health perception, despite being a statistically significant construct, highlights a critical disconnect between awareness and experiential health outcomes. This gap may stem from structural, behavioral, or psychological barriers that inhibit the translation of knowledge into perceptible health benefits. In real-world scenarios, bridging this gap requires the implementation of behavioral reinforcement mechanisms—such as personalized feedback systems, regular health check-ups, and mobile health monitoring tools—that help individuals track tangible improvements resulting from their health-conscious behaviors, thereby strengthening the perception of progress. Additionally, embedding health-promotive behaviors into routine settings, such as guided meal planning in workplaces or incentive-based participation in community fitness programs, can reinforce the link between intention and outcome through repeated, socially supported practice. Psychological interventions like motivational interviewing, cognitive-behavioral nudges, and social proofing can also play a role in reshaping individual health narratives, especially when health improvements are subtle or delayed. However, these insights must be contextualized within the limitations of the study's methodology, particularly its use of a cross-sectional design and non-probability sampling (purposive and convenience methods), which restricts the ability to infer causality and limits the generalizability of the findings. The relatively small sample size of 192 participants, though diverse in demographics, may not capture the full heterogeneity of health behaviors and socio-cultural influences across broader populations. Moreover, convenience sampling introduces potential selection bias, as participants who are more health-aware or socially engaged may be overrepresented, skewing the observed relationships. These limitations necessitate caution in extrapolating the results to larger or structurally different groups. Future research should consider larger, stratified random samples across rural and urban regions, and employ longitudinal or experimental designs to capture temporal variations and causality. Additionally, incorporating qualitative methods—such as interviews or focus groups—could uncover nuanced, context-specific barriers to behavior-perception alignment, enriching the current model and enhancing its practical relevance for diverse policy and health intervention frameworks.

CONCLUSION

This study presents a robust, systems-based framework that unpacks the complex interplay between socio-economic factors, cognitive awareness, and social dynamics in shaping dietary behaviour and health perception. By employing Partial Least Squares Structural Equation Modeling (PLS-SEM), the research validates how constructs such as education level, income, food prices, health consciousness, and social influence interact—both directly and indirectly—to inform consumer food choices and perceived health outcomes. The findings affirm that social influence is a critical conduit through which structural and cognitive variables manifest into behavioral and perceptual changes, while education emerges as a foundational driver of health awareness and social integration. Importantly, the model reveals that awareness alone does not guarantee better health perception, highlighting the persistent knowledge–action gap.

Rather than reiterating isolated insights, this study emphasizes the necessity for holistic interventions that integrate educational outreach, economic accessibility, and community-level engagement to achieve meaningful change. By adopting a multidimensional lens, the research contributes not only to theoretical advancement but also to the strategic design of public health and policy interventions.

Future research should focus on cross-cultural validation of the model across diverse geographic and socio-economic settings to test its generalizability. Additionally, incorporating qualitative methodologies—such as in-depth interviews or ethnographic studies—could offer richer insights into the lived experiences and cultural nuances that influence the observed statistical relationships. Finally, longitudinal studies may be valuable to capture temporal dynamics and causal evolution within this multidimensional framework.

REFERENCES

Agan, B., & Bayrak, R. (2024). The Future of the Food and Agriculture Sector in Terms of Green Economics and Sustainable Development. *Studies in Systems. Decision and Control, 576*, 119–146. DOI: 10.1007/978-3-031-77286-3_8

Backholer, K., Sacks, G., & Cameron, A. J. (2019). Food and Beverage Price Promotions: An Untapped Policy Target for Improving Population Diets and Health. *Current Nutrition Reports, 8*(3), 250–255. DOI: 10.1007/s13668-019-00287-z PMID: 31300982

Bateman, I. J., Binner, A., Addicott, E. T., Balmford, B., Cho, F. H. T., Daily, G. C., De-Gol, A., Eisenbarth, S., Faccioli, M., Ferguson-Gow, H., Ferrini, S., Fezzi, C., Gannon, K., Groom, B., Harper, A. B., Harwood, A., Hillier, J., Hulme, M. F., Lee, C. F., & Day, B. H. (2024). How to make land use policy decisions: Integrating science and economics to deliver connected climate, biodiversity, and food objectives. *Proceedings of the National Academy of Sciences of the United States of America, 121*(49), e2407961121. Advance online publication. DOI: 10.1073/pnas.2407961121 PMID: 39536077

Berg, G., Lundqvist, E., & Mattsson Sydner, Y. (2024). Useful but overused? The "plate model" as a food educational tool in home economics. *Food, Culture, & Society, 27*(2), 573–591. DOI: 10.1080/15528014.2024.2319421

Bhatnagar, M., & Rajaram, R. (2024). Correlating investor patterns and ESG performance with neuro marketing insights: Behavioural finance meets sustainability. In *Neuromarketing's Role in Sustainable Finance*. IGI Global., DOI: 10.4018/979-8-3693-9117-4.ch001

Blakely, T., Nghiem, N., Genc, M., Mizdrak, A., Cobiac, L., Mhurchu, C. N., Swinburn, B., Scarborough, P., & Cleghorn, C. (2020). Modelling the health impact of food taxes and subsidies with price elasticities: The case for additional scaling of food consumption using the total food expenditure elasticity. *PLoS One, 15*(3), e0230506. Advance online publication. DOI: 10.1371/journal.pone.0230506 PMID: 32214329

Bohm, I., Åbacka, G., Hörnell, A., & Bengs, C. (2025). "Can we add a little sugar?" the contradictory discourses around sweet foods in Swedish home economics. *Pedagogy, Culture & Society, 33*(1), 105–121. DOI: 10.1080/14681366.2023.2190754

Bowman, S. A. (2006). A comparison of the socioeconomic characteristics, dietary practices, and health status of women food shoppers with different food price attitudes. *Nutrition Research (New York, N.Y.), 26*(7), 318–324. DOI: 10.1016/j.nutres.2006.06.012

Brinkman, H.-J., De Pee, S., Sanogo, I., Subran, L., & Bloem, M. W. (2010). High food prices and the global financial crisis have reduced access to nutritious food and worsened nutritional status and health. *The Journal of Nutrition, 140*(1), 153S–161S. DOI: 10.3945/jn.109.110767 PMID: 19939996

Bronchetti, E. T., Christensen, G., & Hoynes, H. W. (2019). Local food prices, SNAP purchasing power, and child health. *Journal of Health Economics, 68*, 102231. Advance online publication. DOI: 10.1016/j.jhealeco.2019.102231 PMID: 31634764

Brunori, G., Carzedda, M., Iliopoulos, C., D'Haese, M., Lanfranchi, M., Lerro, M., Martino, G., Pettenella, D., van Passel, S., & Troiano, S. (2024). Correction to: Has transformation of food systems reached an impasse? Considerations on the role of agri-food research (Agricultural and Food Economics, (2024), 12, 1, (26),). *Agricultural and Food Economics, 12*(1). https://doi.org/DOI: 10.1186/s40100-024-00308-8

Burkhanov, A. U., Popkova, E. G., Galoyan, D. R., Mkrtchyan, T. M., & Sergi, B. S. (2024). Deep learning, irrigation enhancement, and agricultural economics for ensuring food security in emerging economies. *Global Transitions, 6*, 164–172. DOI: 10.1016/j.glt.2024.06.002

Cheewakoset, R., & Sakdapat, N. (2024). Financial skills, Entrepreneurial Qualities, and Leadership Qualities that Influence the Preparatory Behaviours for Business Competition of Undergraduate Students in Thailand. *International Journal of EBusiness and EGovernment Studies, 16*(1), 203–222.

Duffey. (2010). Food price and diet and health outcomes: 20 Years of the CARDIA study (Archives of Internal Medicine (2010) 170, 5 (420-426)). *Archives of Internal Medicine, 170*(12), 1089. DOI: 10.1001/archinternmed.2010.176

Duffey, K. J., Gordon-Larsen, P., Shikany, J. M., Guilkey, D., Jacobs, D. R.Jr, & Popkin, B. M. (2010). Food price and diet and health outcomes: 20 years of the CARDIA study. *Archives of Internal Medicine, 170*(5), 420–426. DOI: 10.1001/archinternmed.2009.545 PMID: 20212177

Finaret, A. B., & Masters, W. A. (2025). Food economics: Teaching for the future of agriculture, nutrition, and health. *Applied Economic Perspectives and Policy, 47*(3), 1232–1247. Advance online publication. DOI: 10.1002/aepp.13517

Floridi, A., Anda-León, M. D., Kozakiewicz, T., Bhattacharyya, M., Thota, A., Burt, P., Tasciotti, L., Selby, J., Premji, Z., & Shisler, S. (2025). Effects of El Niño and the Positive Indian Ocean Dipole (+IOD) on Health, Food Security, Economics, and Conflict in Low- and Middle-Income Countries in the Indo-Pacific: A Systematic Review. *Campbell Systematic Reviews*, *21*(2), e70038. Advance online publication. DOI: 10.1002/cl2.70038 PMID: 40248359

Frascarelli, A., Ciliberti, S., Bartolucci, P. E., & Mastandrea, G. (2025). Correction to: The CAP coherence between redistributive and environmental goals: do the allocation criteria for direct payments play a role? (Agricultural and Food Economics, (2025), 13, 1, (15),). *Agricultural and Food Economics, 13*(1). https://doi.org/DOI: 10.1186/s40100-025-00356-8

Gajanan, S. N., & Babu, S. C. (2024). Assessing the economics of fuel for food: Approaches to assessment of time allocations for household chores and roles. In *Handbook on Public Policy and Food Security*. Edward Elgar Publishing Ltd., DOI: 10.4337/9781839105449.00024

Gosliner, W., Brown, D. M., Sun, B. C., Woodward-Lopez, G., & Crawford, P. B. (2019). Corrigendum: Availability, quality and price of produce in low-income neighbourhood food stores in California raise equity issues (Public Health Nutrition (2018) 21:9 (1639-1648) DOI:). *Public Health Nutrition, 22*(1), 184 – 185. https://doi.org/DOI: 10.1017/S1368980018000058

Hadley, C., Stevenson, E. G. J., Tadesse, Y., & Belachew, T. (2012). Rapidly rising food prices and the experience of food insecurity in urban Ethiopia: Impacts on health and well-being. *Social Science & Medicine*, *75*(12), 2412–2419. DOI: 10.1016/j.socscimed.2012.09.018 PMID: 23062966

Horgen, K. B., & Brownell, K. D. (2002). Comparison of price change and health message interventions in promoting healthy food choices. *Health Psychology*, *21*(5), 505–512. DOI: 10.1037/0278-6133.21.5.505 PMID: 12211518

Kukreti, M., Sehajpal, S., Tiwari, R., & Sood, K. (2024a). Introduction. In *Driving Global Health and Sustainable Development Goals With Smart Technology*. IGI Global. DOI: 10.4018/979-8-3373-0240-9

Kukreti, M., Sehajpal, S., Tiwari, R., & Sood, K. (2024b). Preface. In *Driving Global Health and Sustainable Development Goals With Smart Technology*. IGI Global. DOI: 10.4018/979-8-3373-0240-9

Kvasnička, R., Kvasničková Stanislavská, L., Pilař, L., Kuralová, K., Pilařová, L., & Čejka, M. (2024). Exploring twitter discussions on healthy food: Inspiring, access to healthy food for young, and nutritional economics in focus. *Frontiers in Sustainable Food Systems*, *8*, 1357896. Advance online publication. DOI: 10.3389/fsufs.2024.1357896

Li, K.-M., Chen, J.-Y., Xiao, Y., Guo, F.-S., Huang, Y.-B., & Lu, Q. (2025). Efficient transformation of starch food wastes into bio-based levulinate products over earth-abundant aluminum salts: Performances and economics. *Biomass and Bioenergy*, *193*, 107570. Advance online publication. DOI: 10.1016/j.biombioe.2024.107570

Lock, K., Stuckler, D., Charlesworth, K., & McKee, M. (2009). Potential causes and health effects of rising global food prices. *BMJ (Clinical Research Ed.)*, *339*(7715), 269–272. DOI: 10.1136/bmj.b2403 PMID: 19596718

McLeod, A., Pippin, S., & Catania, V. (2009). Using technology acceptance theory to model individual differences in tax software use. *15th Americas Conference on Information Systems 2009, AMCIS 2009, 10*, 6998 – 7008.

Messer, K. D., Ganguly, D., & Xie, L. (2025). Mitigating impacts of food production and consumption on climate change: Applications of behavioral economics. *Applied Economic Perspectives and Policy*, *47*(4), 1357–1382. Advance online publication. DOI: 10.1002/aepp.13519

Midjord, N. H., & Bell, C. (2024). To What Extent are Food, Culture, Economics and the Natural Environment Reflected in the Language of the Australian and Brazilian Food-based Dietary Guidelines? *Current Nutrition Reports*, *13*(4), 937–949. DOI: 10.1007/s13668-024-00585-1 PMID: 39373940

Pollari, M., Autio, M., & Elorinne, A.-L. (2024). The transformative potential of textbooks: Food waste knowledge and pedagogical text styles in Finnish Home Economics, Geography, and Biology textbooks. *Nordic Journal of Comparative and International Education*, *8*(2). Advance online publication. DOI: 10.7577/njcie.5622

Qaim, M., & Parlasca, M. C. (2025). Agricultural Economics and the Transformation Toward Sustainable Agri-Food Systems. *Agricultural Economics*, *56*(3), 327–335. DOI: 10.1111/agec.70023

Ramadhani, A. M., Nassary, E. K., Rwehumbiza, F. B., Massawe, B. H. J., & Nchimbi-Msolla, S. (2024). Corrigendum: Impact of mulching treatments on growth, yields, and economics of common bean (Phaseolus vulgaris L.) in Eastern Tanzania (Frontiers in Sustainable Food Systems, (2024), 8, (1455206),). *Frontiers in Sustainable Food Systems, 8*. https://doi.org/DOI: 10.3389/fsufs.2024.1455206

Rezitis, A. N., & Rokopanos, A. (2019). Asymmetric Price Transmission along the European Food Supply Chain and the CAP Health Check: A Panel Vector Error Correction Approach. *Journal of Agricultural & Food Industrial Organization*, *17*(2), 20180002. Advance online publication. DOI: 10.1515/jafio-2018-0002

Roe, B. E. (2025). Anti-obesity medication patients' self-reported food savings versus the cost of such medicines: Health Economics. *International Journal of Obesity*, *49*(3), 532–535. DOI: 10.1038/s41366-024-01708-y PMID: 39738491

Rojas, C., & Jaenicke, E. (2024). Introduction to Agribusiness special issue: Economics of food reformulation. *Agribusiness*, *40*(3), 537–549. DOI: 10.1002/agr.21912

Rummo, P. E., Meyer, K. A., Green Howard, A., Shikany, J. M., Guilkey, D. K., & Gordon-Larsen, P. (2015). Fast food price, diet behavior, and cardiometabolic health: Differential associations by neighborhood SES and neighborhood fast food restaurant availability in the CARDIA study. *Health & Place*, *35*, 128–135. DOI: 10.1016/j.healthplace.2015.06.010 PMID: 26319447

Sakdapat, N. (2022). Healthy food consumption behavior of working people in the capital city: A case study in Bangkok, Thailand. [Social Space]. *Przestrzeń Społeczna*, *22*(3), 365–384.

Sehajpal, S., & Sidhu, N. K. (2024). Neuroscience, nursing, and financial innovation: A synergistic approach to optimized patient care and economic well-being. In *Neuromarketing's Role in Sustainable Finance*. IGI Global., DOI: 10.4018/979-8-3693-9117-4.ch008

Seidel, F., Oebel, B., Stein, L., Michalke, A., & Gaugler, T. (2023). The True Price of External Health Effects from Food Consumption. *Nutrients*, *15*(15), 3386. Advance online publication. DOI: 10.3390/nu15153386 PMID: 37571323

Sharma, P., Malhotra, R. K., Ojha, M. K., & Gupta, S. (2022). Impact of meditation on mental & physical health and thereby on academic performance of students: A study of higher educational institutions of Uttarakhand. *Journal of Medical Pharmaceutical and Allied Sciences*, *11*(2), 4641–4644. DOI: 10.55522/jmpas.V11I2.2309

Smith, C., & Fatorachian, H. (2025). Inherently irrational: Exploring the role of behavioural economics and organisational culture in food supply chain disruption management decisions. *Cogent Business & Management*, *12*(1), 2463566. Advance online publication. DOI: 10.1080/23311975.2025.2463566

Tuul, S., Banzragch, O., & Saizmaa, T. (2016). E-learning in Mongolian higher education. *International Review of Research in Open and Distance Learning*, *17*(2), 181–197. DOI: 10.19173/irrodl.v17i2.2227

Urfels, A., Mirzabaev, A., Bricx, S., Deb, P., Dewi, K., Evangelista, G., Flor, R. J., Harris, B., Jayasiri, N., Kishore, A., McDonald, A. J., Mondal, M., Quicho, E., Saito, K., Kumar, V., & Laborte, A. (2024). Economics of sustainable irrigation in smallholder agriculture: Implications for food security and climate action. *Environmental Research Letters*, *19*(8), 081008. Advance online publication. DOI: 10.1088/1748-9326/ad6201

Valpiani, N., Thorne-Lyman, A. L., De Pee, S., Godfrey, S., Gentilini, U., & Bloem, M. W. (2008). Proposed strategies for mitigating the impact of high food prices on nutrition and health in Latin America and the Caribbean. *Perspectives in Agriculture, Veterinary Science, Nutrition and Natural Resources*, *3*, 1–12. Advance online publication. DOI: 10.1079/PAVSNNR20083081

Volpp, K. G., & Lamberton, C. (2024). Behavioral Economics to Enhance Food Is Medicine Programs. *JAMA Health Forum*, *5*(7), e241586. DOI: 10.1001/jamahealthforum.2024.1586 PMID: 38995633

Wulandari, W., Rafsanjani, M. A., Dewi, R. M., Zain, R. R., & Irawan, N. (2024). Bibliometric analysis of food waste in economics for Sustainable Development Goals 2030. In S. N., P. B.K., S. M., L. L., A. G. M., & A. S. (Eds.), *E3S Web of Conferences* (Vol. 568). EDP Sciences. DOI: 10.1051/e3sconf/202456801005

Chapter 12

The Role of the Food Industry in Financial Development:

Focusing on the Current Scenario

Rashi Gupta
http://orcid.org/0000-0002-9808-2942
Sharda University, India

ABSTRACT

The relevance of the food industry in terms of fostering financial development cannot be overstated, particularly not in the current context of dynamic global challenges and changing consumer preferences. As the largest occupation in the world, it not only contributes to the GDP and trade balance, but also serves as an important means of rural income. Food exports also enhance the economies of countries through earning foreign currency and strengthening trade. Government initiatives and private public partnerships have improved the financial contributions of the sector to the economy in terms of food security and entrepreneurship. Even with the rising inflation and disruptiions in climate, the food service industry is steady and resourceful. It is therefore a key driver for financially sustainable growth that is capable of successfully marrying innovation, consumer preferences in health, and commercial imperatives.

1. INTRODUCTION

The food business has become one of the most financially influential sectors determined as a factor to build a country or society or international financial

DOI: 10.4018/979-8-3373-4047-0.ch012

growth, particularly the present days' dynamic and ambiguous era of economic situation. The industry-rich and interlinked ecosystem of agriculture, agro-processing, packaging, logistics, distribution, retail and hospitality feeds lives and then feeds economies. In a large number of developing and transitioning countries, it is an important part of the Gross Domestic Product (GDP), provides a major contribution to employment especially in rural areas, and is a key source of income for millions of smallholders and micro enterprises. "Now, the industry's experiencing a change where it sees as a lot of investment in food technology, sustainability, and digitization of the supply chain. Inventions in things like plant-based products, precision agriculture and AI-powered logistics are drawing venture capital and increasing productivity. It continues to be an important site for new technologies, entrepreneurship and global trade in advanced economies. The importance of the food sector goes significantly beyond food and nutrition security but is strategically important for ensuring economic stability, poverty reduction, foreign exchange (FX) earnings through exports, and inclusive growth via its multi sectoral value chains. In a fast-changing and increasingly tumultuous world, reeling from overlapping crises like climate change, inflation, geopolitical tensions and the aftershocks of the pandemic, the food industry is showing both its vulnerabilities and its adaptability. These forces have led economists, policy makers and investors to rethink the role and economic importance of this sector on long-term economic development (Münch et al., 2021).

The food industry is at the cusp of a paradigm shift, driven by changing consumer habits, sustainability needs, technology disruption, and re-calibrating global supply chains. Increased focus on health and wellness is shaping the food product market with more consumers demanding organic, plant-based, and functional foods. At the same time, the convergence of digital technologies like AI, IoT, blockchain and big data analytics, are transforming how food is grown, transported, stored and consumed. From precision agriculture optimizing crop yield to AI-driven supply chains guaranteeing traceability and minimal waste, the food industry is increasingly a technology industry. These developments are not only improving the operational efficiency and innovation but also attracting substantial capital flow from venture capitalists, private equity funds and soverign wealth funds. Furthermore, green bonds, sustainability-linked loans, and impact investing are directing more finance towards food businesses that are environmentally-friendly and social-inclined. In this way the food sector is not simply a recipient of financial expansion; rather, it serves as a key driver of it.

However, the food industry also has to grapple with enormous challenges that highlight the complexity of its interrelationship with financial growth. The cost and availability of food is under pressure by global food inflation resulting from supply-chain disruptions, higher energy prices, labor shortages and climate-related challenges. Extreme weather and biodiversity loss putting global food security at risk, says UN report Unpredictable and extreme weather, plant and animal diseases, changes in climate and agricultural practices, and economic systems are contributing to a food crisis, it said. The problems are often most acute in low-income countries, where the absence of infrastructure, financial services and technology stunts the growth potential of the sector. Meanwhile protectionist trade measures and export restrictions introduced by some countries to secure domestic supplies are distorting markets and limiting fair access to food. From this standpoint, financial development should be integrated and inclusive not concentrated solely on the accumulation of capital and the expansion of markets but also on resilience, equity and environmental stewardship within the food system. The other important role of the agri-food industry in economic development is that it can be a tool to promote regional and rural development. In countries such as India, Brazil, and Indonesia, an agro-based industry is very important because it can help to decrease the disparities in income between rural and urban areas and allow the wealth to be distributed in a decentralised way. There is considerable potential for employment opportunity, skill development and entrepreneurship in local food processing and value addition. Supportive government policies for food parks, supply chain infrastructures, farm-to-market access and microfinance compound these efforts. Further, the trade of food across borders is likely to promote regional integration and collaboration. For example, food-focused activities will be used under the African Continental Free Trade Area (AfCFTA) and ASEAN Economic Community (AEC) to create market opportunities and boost the flow of money among countries within the regions (Jiakui et al., 2023).

The food industry is also at the point of its economic-social-environmental triangulation. Its multidimensionality in the modern global economy situates it as an important promoter of financial development, given new challenges and new educational gains. The current environment of accelerating technology driven sustainable demand shifts and global unpredictability and uncertainty emphasise the vital importance of smart investments, policies and innovative led growth in the food sector. As countries continue to build back better, more inclusive and sustainable economies, the importance of the food sector cannot be overstated. It's more than feeding people, it's also about feeding financial growth, empowering communities, and driving the future economic stability of the world.

2. ECONOMIC CONTRIBUTION OF THE FOOD INDUSTRY: AN ANALYSIS

The food sector is a deep and multi-dimensional economic resource, affecting GDP, employment, balance of trade, R&D and financial growth. The food industry is a key sector of developed and emerging economies with activities ranging from primary agriculture and food processing, to packaging, transport, retailing and hospitality. In many countries, the food industry is not only one of the largest contributors to the GDP, it is also pivotal to industrial production and service provision. For example, in countries like the United States, China, and European Union countries, the food industry and agriculture as a whole represents 5% to 10% of GDP. In developing economies, especially in sub-Saharan Africa and South Asia, where agriculture is a dominant sector, the figure is typically higher, with direct implications for national growth variables and social economic stability. This strong contribution commences from the capacity of the industry to combine formal and informal sectors and to generate value added along a broad set of supply chains and a wide range of products.

Among food industry's most important economic function, is its ability to create employment at multiple levels of the value table. The industry supports millions of livelihoods around the world, from farm workers and food processing plant employees to freight operators, marketers and retail staff. In nations such as India and Nigeria, a great deal of the population is working in agriculture and related food services that tend to be the main income earners in countryside areas. The informal food economy (including smallholder farmers, street food vendors and home-based food enterprises) is also an important source of urban employment, particularly for women and marginalized groups (Singh et al., 2025). This job-creating role of the food industry makes a substantial contribution to poverty reduction, income dispersion and rural development – which is crucial to domestic consumption and broader economic growth. Furthermore, food tech startups and smart agri and digital retail platforms are attracting a younger and tech-friendly talent force, making the theme a convergence between old practices and contemporary economics.

It is the contribution of food industry to international trade and foreign exchange earnings -- an element of one integral part to the computation above. Cereal, fruits, vegetables, meat, dairy, and seafood products are primary materials to many of those export earnings. For nations like Brazil, Netherlands, Australia and Thailand, it's agri-food exports which are sold to improve the trade surplus and contribute to the foreign exchange. Even in trade deficit economies, processed foods and value-added products represent vital export commodities that help manage import costs and reduce fiscal vulnerability. The worldwide market that is now available to local producers through the food industry's ability to transport and store goods in cold chain systems, has vastly increased the financial capacity of local producers. Trade liberalization, bilateral agreements and food safety harmonization through organizations such as the WTO and the Codex Alimentarius have also promoted a greater integration of the food industry within global economic systems.

Besides the GDP and trade, the food business also plays a significant role in the capital formation and industrial progress. There has been significant investment - foreign direct investment (FDI) as well as domestic - into countries' food production, processing and distribution infrastructure over the past decade. In some of these countries, food processing zones and industrial parks are being established to provide the right environment to investors and add value to farm production. Investments in cold storage, logistics, food safety and innovation hubs promote industrial diversification and technological upgradation, creating multiplier effects across other related sectors including packaging, transportation, manufacturing and ICT. Moreover, there has been a rise in green finance and impact investment aimed at eco-friendly agricultural systems, plant-based products technology and climate-resistant value chains, due to increasing awareness of sustainable food systems and ethical consuming. They are not only drivers of financial growth, they are also new market niches, work opportunities and export options as well (Singh et al., 2025).

This resilience helped soften the blow to economies and kept a floor under consumers' spending. Governments also depend on the food industry for fiscal revenue in the form of taxes, duties and licences, and in so doing, it becomes linked to public finance and to national development agendas. Furthermore, the inclusion of the food system in the financial systems of a nationstate via food banks, agri-business credit/redistribution, insurance packages, subsidies, and protections ties food security to financial inclusion. The food industry is not simply a source of food as such or agricultural produce, but it involves economic activities from which it is natural to expect the generation of a range of financial flows that contribute to the GDP, job opportunities, industrial development, trade, and exchanges, and investment. Its various effects on lives, consumption, innovation, and national income showed that it was an irreplaceable force in how finance was developed. As economies attempt to recover and expand in an increasingly uncertain climate, the strategic significance of building and modernizing the food sector has never been more crucial to ensure long-term, inclusive and fair economic development.

3. INVESTMENT AND TECHNOLOGICAL INNOVATION: RISE OF AGRI-FOOD STARTUPS, ROLE OF ARTIFICIAL INTELLIGENCE AND IOT

The agri-food industry has witnessed a drastic change through waves of investments and rapid adoption of technology advancements, leading us into the 2017 which is dominated by smart agriculture and food-tech startups. Finance has converged with digitalisation to fundamentally change our perceptions around how food is produced, distributed and consumed, creating an environment where efficiency, traceability, sustainability and scalability are building blocks, not just aspirations. This revolution is being driven by the exponential expansion of agri-food startups, which are transforming the way that we farm, process, package, ship and eat food. These startup solutions which emerged, in many cases, in response to climate change, food insecurity, supply chain inefficiencies and evolving consumer demands are fueled by massive amounts of venture capital (VC), private equity (PE), impact investing and government investment. Billions of dollars a year were invested globally in agri-food tech, growing significantly during economic downturns. Startups that are launching in areas like vertical farming, cellular agriculture, reducing food waste, creating plant-based proteins, and addressing supply chains with blockchain solutions are already becoming the best position stakeholders in the New Economy. These enterprises offer both superior financial returns and address systemic global problems to be solved an attractive combination for impact investors and finance institutions (Moretto & Caniato, 2021).

The most catalytic trends propelling this transformation is the growing pervasiveness of Artificial Intelligence (AI) across the agri-food space. Precision agriculture is being disrupted with AI technologies, which allows farmers to make data-driven decisions that maximize yields, minimize input costs and environmental impacts. Machine learning algorithms, AI is able to predict pest outbreaks, assess soil health, provide planting schedules, and even decide on best irrigation practices. These smart systems are taking the guesswork out and providing accurate reading while saving water and improving the efficiency of the agriculture value chain. AI-powered sensors and computer vision techniques on-dairy are also deployed to monitor livestock health, identify issues, and track feeding schedules, for example. Likewise, in the food industry, AI is used for quality inspection, sorting, and for automating the packaging process. Predictive analytics is allowing everyone to predict market trends, handle inventory, and adjust pricing strategies on the fly. "Not only are these applications of AI increasing operating efficiency, they are also boosting profitability and AI is becoming a vital tool in financial shaping within the food industry. In addition, AI helps to advance food safety and compliance by identifying contaminants and maintaining regulations (reducing the risk of recalls and legal challenges) in both production lines.

Internet of Things (IoT) becomes an important enabling technology for smart food systems. It works by inserting sensors into equipment, fields, vehicles, storage and other facilities, creating easy lines of communication between physical assets and digital platforms. Real-world applications of IoT Smart irrigation systems that regulate water flow according to the real-time soil moisture, GPS equipped tractors that minimize the consumption of fuel, cold chain logistics that monitor temperature and humidity to maintain perishables in perfect condition are all examples of IoT's application. These integrated applications ensure full traceability and visibility throughout the food supply chain, minimizing wastage and creating trust among customers. IoT in urban and vertical farming enables growing food in climate controlled environments in the cities, mitigating dependence on imports and cutting the carbon emissions. IoT integration also enables the creation of digital marketplaces/mobile platforms which enable farmers to access weather forecasts, market prices, agronomic advice, financial services and such platforms act as a bridge between rural-urban digital divide. According to the NIRA project, these solutions enable the smallholder farmers and agripreneurs to have more access to the market and contribute to inclusive financial growth (McLennon et al., 2021).

The emerging synergy of AI and IoT is creating new business models and investment opportunities that are transforming the food ecosystem. For instance, agritech companies are appliying AI and IoT to deliver "farming-as-a-service" (FaaS), in which tech solutions are sold to farmers on a subscription basis, reducing upfront investments and optimizing outcomes. Integrations and Marketplace / platform plays like these are going to be in more demand as investors seek out more scalable, tech enabled models with strong unit economics and serial growth. Governments and NGOS (non-government agencies) are also involved in this shift through grants, subsidies and regulation to promote the uptake of technology and digitization in agriculture. And with the worldwide focus on Sustainable Development Goals (SDGs), including on zero hunger, climate action and economic growth, tech-driven agri-food innovations have gained institutional and policy support.

Fantastic growth for the agri-food start-ups and the merging of AI and IoT signal a new era in the global food and beverage sector. These technology developments are not only making for more productive and sustainable food production, but redefining what financial value creation and distribution looks like in the food economy. The ongoing interest and investment in this space is further evidence of an increasing understanding of this sector's potential to deliver inclusive, scalable and resilient economic impact. As we progress, building cooperation between innovators, investors, policy-makers, traditional stakeholders, will be essential to unlocking the full potential of this digital revolution in agriculture and food systems (Jeong et al., 2022).

4. CURRENT CHALLENGES IMPACTING THE FOOD INDUSTRY

The modern food system, for all its technological and global achievements, now stands at a crucial crossroads: burdened with a wide array of complex and interconnected challenges that threaten its current and future, sustainability and economic viability. Foremost among those are the continued disruptions in supply chains, intensifying climate change and environmental degradation, and broader impacts of food price inflation from around the world on food security. There will be a need for a re-presidentation of strategies, and the transition to adaptive frameworks consituting the actors across governments, industries and civil society that can secure food systems for continuity, affordability and resilience amidst growing uncertainty.

Supply chain interruptions are a significant challenge facing the food industry today. The globalized nature of modern food production is such that a single disruption whether caused by labor shortages, transportation disruptions, geopolitical disputes, clogs at ports can reverberate across borders (Mukhtarov et al., 2022). And the pandemic abruptly exposed the brittle nature of just-in-time supply chain systems with perishable food waste piling up as shipping stopped, containers ran short, and there was no capacity to store food cold. Supply chains are under strain even in a post-pandemic world, with increasing costs of freight, fluctuating fuel prices and erratic border regulations. Already, export prohibitions on critical grains and fertilizers from important producing countries have led to price surges and shortfalls in reliance importers. And disruptions to the supply chain for semiconductors have rippled through to agri-tech and food processing, where machinery is increasingly automated. Such systemic shocks have resulted in disruptions, wastage, and higher prices for end consumers due to delays as well as higher operating costs. Solving those problems requires digital supply chain management systems, blockchain-based traceability, local production encouragement, and multiple sourcing policies to increase robustness and maintain flow.

At the same time, climate change and environmental destruction are affecting our ability to produce and distribute food in the short-term and long-term, changing the very basis on which the industry rests. Irregular weather conditions, rising temperatures, prolonged droughts, rising sea levels and more frequent fine extreme events drastically reduce agro-opportunity and modify traditional growing seasons. Global dietary staples such as wheat, rice and maize are increasingly vulnerable to heat stress, pest outbreaks, and water scarcity.

4.1 Supply Chain Disruptions

Erosion of land, especially in the coastal regions and on the islands, and the salinization of fresh water adversely affect the capacity of the land to produce food, with negative consequences for the availability of arable land, the health of ecosystems, as well as the state of the forests and biodiversity. Agriculture is a driving force of climate change, contributing to about a quarter of global greenhouse gas emissions through methane, nitrous oxide, and carbon dioxide emitted from livestock rearing, fertilizer use and conversion of land. This feedback loop of food production and environmental impact requires an immediate shift to environmentally conscious farming practices, including climate smart agriculture, regenerative farming and water efficient irrigation. Early-warning systems, crop insurance and climate-resilient seed varieties are also critical investments for risk reduction and livelihood protection (Ahmed et al., 2025).

4.2 Climate Change and Environmental Impact

In addition to these environmental considerations, there is an alarming specter of inflation and the impact it can have on food security worldwide. The price of inputs in agriculture fertilizers, seeds, pesticides, fuel, machinery have shot up, due to dislocations in energy markets, trade limitations and currency swings. These higher production costs and supply chain inefficiencies are then passed on to consumers, who face higher food costs that can have an out-sized impact on low income families and vulnerable communities. While higher inflation can lead to an increased incidence of malnutrition and hunger, and can fuel social unrest in the poor countries of the world where food expenditure soaks up a large portion of income. Global bodies, including the FAO and WFP, have sounded the alarm about ballooning food access crises, especially in conflict and climate-prone areas. In addition, inflationary pressure erodes the purchasing power of humanitarian agencies, and weakens social safety nets that are intended to shield food-insecure populations. The geopolitical stakes are no less dire: Food insecurity is a driver of migration, political instability and conflict for resource-poor people. Addressing the impact of inflation on food systems will necessitate specific fiscal interventions that include both food subsidies & buffer stock management, local food enterprise support and monetary policies aimed at stabilizing agricultural commodity prices. Over the longer term, circular economies, food waste reduction and stronger local food systems will help the country withstand shocks caused by inflation.

4.3 Inflation and Food Security

Fundamentally, the food industry is a complex challenge that demands a holistic response that can mix tech fixes and policy reform with environmental stewardship and clear partnership across international borders. Though supply chain frailties, climate pressures and inflationary jitters loom as daunting obstacles, they also signal an opportunity to remake food systems that are more equitable, resilient and sustainable. For this reason, stakeholders will need to adopt a move from a reactive to a proactive approach, understanding that food is not an output product as the food system is not an output sector but a foundation for economic development, public health and social stability. Public and private collaborations, driven by innovation and evidence-based policy, will be essential as we work our way through the current global landscape and embrace the future of the global food economy.

5. SUSTAINABILITY AND FINANCIAL DEVELOPMENT: CIRCULAR ECONOMY AND WASTE REDUCTION

Sustainability has become a central demand in the food industry, linked to economic development, as the world is faced with increasing environmental issues and limitations of resources. With this background, the idea of the circular economy and waste prevention has emerged as a game-changing approach for reconfiguring conventional linear patterns of production and consumption. The once maligned food sector, often derided for highly inefficient processes, environmental impact and high levels of waste, is now being reframed from wearing the albatross of the darlings of the corporate sustainability movement, focused on environmental and value creation both for society but also economy and investors, and around long runway returns. A food system in a circular economy occurs when both biological and technical resources can be reused, recycled and brought back into the production process, reducing both waste and resource utilization. This model departs from the extract-produce-dispose approach, suggesting design to be regenerative, that is: food loss, surplus and byproducts become assets, rather than waste. Crucially, such a sustainable shift is not only ecological, but also an opportunity for financial growth, bringing new revenue opportunities, decreasing operational costs, stimulating innovation, and driving impact investment in green technologies and circular business models.

This waste is not just lost food but also wasted water, energy, land, labor and capital. The food industry can tap into substantial economic value by adopting waste minimisation practices over a circular approach. For example, businesses that invest in food waste valorisation, essentially turning waste into animal feed, bioenergy or bioplastics, fertilisers, can avoid waste costs and even set up secondary income streams (Arora et al., 2025). Similarly, surplus food recovery systems, including food banks and redistribution programmes, have the potential to reduce waste and tackle food insecurity, generating shared value both socially and economically. Digital platforms and Big-Data enabled tools have been ushered in to improve inventory management, predict demand more accurately, and reduce overproduction, particularly in industries like hospitality and retail where waste is rampant. And in the area of circular packaging, new products designed for shipping and delivery, like compostable containers or reusable delivery systems, are emerging as consumers and regulators demand more sustainable replacement for single-use plastics.

Economically, enacting circular economy practices will lead to increased business resilience and competitiveness in the long-term. Businesses that embed sustainability as part of their core strategies reap the rewards through better brand reputation, increased stakeholder confidence and access to sustainability-linked financial instruments, such as green bonds and ESG (Environmental, Social, Governance) funds. Investors are gradually coming to favor stronger circular businesses as they are less exposed to regulatory risks, resource risk, and environmental liabilities. Impact investing has made this trend even more pronounced where capital is being deployed to scale ventures focused on correcting food system inefficiency while generating a return. For instance, COLUSSI has seen increasing investment interest from startups that provide AI-supported waste tracking technology, circular logistics and new sources of protein from food waste. Governments and intergovernmental bodies are likewise bolstering this transition, whether through policy frameworks, subsidies and incentives for sustainable food infrastructure and circular innovations. In the European Union, part to the Circular Economy Action Plan is focused on food waste reduction, bio-based materials and maintaining farm practices as part of a strategy to anchor the Green Deal to good green recovery, that is, to tie ecological transition to economic development (Singh et al., 2025).

Sustainable financial development facilitates labour generation a-nd knowledge diffusion, and stimulates entrepreneurship, especially in developing countries. Waste-to-value businesses, such as waste management, recycling and biogas production, provide jobs both in rural and urban areas and promote inclusive economic development. Informal food markets and such traditional practices as alternative uses for waste and composting in the developing world can be formalized and scaled up through capital and technology, for example. Public-private partnerships (PPPs) and multi-stakeholder initiatives are being increasingly recognised as drivers of investment and project development for the circular economy in the agri-food sector. Such partnerships help make available critical know-how, shared investments, and systemic innovation that can all speed the process of moving toward sustainable and resilient food systems.

Sustainability and financial development are now two sides of the same coin rather than two parallel enterprises in business of food. Through embracing circular economy principles and focusing attention on waste reduction, the industry can cut environmental impact, streamline operations and open up fresh economic pathways. These approaches pair well with international development foci, for example the UN SDGs, specifically Goal 12: Responsible Consumption and Production. They also offer a prescient playbook for organizations that seek to future-proof themselves in an age of ecological limits, consumer awareness and regulatory change. With the rise of a new value perspective on food and identically treats waste chains to value chains, the food sector has a unique opportunity to drive the next wave of sustainable economic change; a new wave that transforms waste into value and sustainability into growth for society (Arora et al., 2024).

6. GOVERNMENT POLICIES AND INSTITUTIONAL FRAMEWORKS

Policies and systems of governance have significant implications for the direction of food regimes and sectoral financialisation, as well as for sustainability. Governments are critical enablers of agri-food sector growth, whether it is through setting regulatory norms, investment attraction and research based strategies. In today's world, with its global disruptions, climate stresses, and changing consumer expectations, strong public governance is key not only to promoting resilience, innovation, and equity across the food value chain. Policy tools like subsidies for sustainable farm practices, tax breaks for agri-tech start-ups and financial grants for food processing infrastructure help catalysing private sector investment, and boosting the competitiveness of local producers. Governments are also focusing more on integrating sustainability objectives in national agricultural frameworks, and on ensuring that food policies are consistent with climate action, rural development and food security imperatives.

Institutional mechanisms including food safety agencies, agricultural ministries, and financial institutions enable the policies to be carried out, overcoming barriers between research, innovation, and adoption by coordinating resources, ensuring compliance and mediating conflicts. Public institutions frequently work in partnership with universities, international organizations and private sector players to design capacity building programs, knowledge sharing systems and technology transfer initiatives for the benefit of farmers, processors and entrepreneurs. Besides, stand-alone governing institutions and enhanced quality control, sanitation and environment standards give consumers and world trading a greater confidence. In other countries, institutions such as national boards on food security agriculture research councils also act as think tanks for planning, forecasting and responding to emergencies in the wake of supply chain disruptions or food price fluctuations.

Digital governance is institutionalized and transforming food systems, governments are adopting data-driven policy measures, real-time agriculture output monitoring, AI-based platforms to maintain transparency and efficiency in distribution of subsidies, procurement, and logistics. Smallholders are likewise being linked to formal markets, financial services and cropinsurance mechanisms through e-governance instruments. Global collaboration such as through the FAO, WTO and regional trade blocs also provides a helping hand, sharing technical expertise, 'harmonised' trade standards and financing for food system innovation in low-income regions. But, for policies to work in practice, they need to be inclusive, participatory and context-specific aimed to reduce gaps in land access, gender and education. While a robust government and institutional ecosystem does help to stabilize and modernize the food system, it also enables financial inclusion, sustainable development and long-term economic resilience.

7. GLOBAL CASE STUDIES AND COMPARATIVE ANALYSIS: INNOVATION AND AGRIBUSINESS GROWTH

The convergence of innovation and agribusiness has led to extraordinary growth paths worldwide, providing important lessons about how technology and targeted policy engagement can breathe a new life in the food market through financial development. In the Netherlands, where arable land is scarce, agribusiness has been prosperous thanks to its application of precision agriculture, hydroponics and data analytics (Kumar & Patel, 2019). Through its partnership with Wageningen University & Research and its "Food Valley" initiative, the Dutch government has transformed the Netherlands into the world's second-largest food exporter by value. And it's not 'all' as much as the ecosystem, innovation, research and sustainability that has holistically come into picture to demonstrate how coordinated institutional frameworks can bring in global leadership in agritech. And, in Israel, another deseret nation, the focus on drip irrigation, AI-driven crop monitoring and water conservation has turned it into an example of farm efficiency. Israeli agri-startups, backed by venture capital and government R&D funds, are leading the way globally in areas like vertical farming and sensor-based irrigation, benefiting not only national food security but exports to emerging markets like India.

These channels, together with policy improvements and public-private partnerships have helped narrow the gap from traditional market failures and contributed to financial inclusion in the countryside. Meanwhile, sub-Saharan Africa is shaping up to be an agri-tech hub too, with countries including Kenya and Nigeria leading the charge. Arabahmeed reckons that Kenyan startups have leveraged mobile-based platforms and logistics to connect the rural-based farmer to the urban retailer, in the process reducing waste and raising farmers incomes. Government and donor backing from innovation incubators and agriculture transformation programs have been pivotal to scaling models such as this one. Case studies suggest that successful agribusiness innovation in developing and advanced economies remains critically dependent on favorable policies, technological adaptation, and integrating frameworks. Different scale, different context and different resource capability aside, one common characteristic is the strategic use of innovation to boost productivity, ensure sustainability and to propel economic development. The comparative analysis highlights the potential of knowledge exchange and joint investment across borders to form future -visible food systems globally (Javed et al., 2025).

8. FUTURE TRENDS AND OPPORTUNITIES

The food industry is on the brink of a revolution; between technological innovation, conscious consumers, and sustainability demands. Trends such as these point to the possibility of a turn towards climate-smart agriculture, where technology such as Artificial Intelligence (AI), drone tech and precision agriculture tools mean that decisions can be made in real time, and resource use can be optimised. With global food demand increasing, emerging alternatives like plant-based meats, lab-grown meat and insect-based products have quickly grown in popularity – drawing significant venture capital investments and transforming the way people eat. End-to-end supply chain visibility and traceability that uplift trust and decrease food fraud by using blockchain-based solutions is another important trend. Vertical and urban farming, when combined with IoT and CEA, offer options to space-limited zones, promising food security in urbanized futures.

Financial options are growing with agri-fintech platforms giving smallholder farmers digital access to credit, insurance and market information, democratizing credit and enhancing productivity. Carbon farming and sustainable certification schemes are creating new sources of income through carbon credits and green finance. The potential in these opportunities are expected to be fostered in large part by government and institutional support including: public-private partnerships, innovation clusters and R&D spending. At the same time, consumer trends are shifting toward ethically sourced, organic, eco-labeled food, urging companies to bake sustainability into their business models. These are trends that signal a healthier, more equitable and more sustainable food industry that can lead the way towards financial development worldwide. Interconnected Digital Transformation meets Environmental Awareness alongside supportive Public Policy will pave the way for new economic avenues that will ensure that the Food sector will be one of the major planks for achieving Sustainable development and inclusive growth in the coming years.

9. CONCLUSION

The food sector is situated at a unique crossroad between economic growth, innovation and sustainability this industry is a key driver of financial growth around the world. As the sector seeks to address new challenges–from disruptions in the supply chain, to climate change–technology leaders such as AI, IoT and blockchain are being deployed to improve productivity, transparency and resource use. In addition, policies of government, institutional infrastructure and cross-border cooperation are critical for the conducive ecosystems to innovation, investment and financial inclusion. The advent of agri-tech organizations, circular economy models and waste reduction initiatives has created newer ways of growth making it possible for the segment to serve the twin interests of sustainability and profitability. New directions such as alternative proteins, vertical farming and carbon farming offer significant potential for even more financial growth and resilience in our food systems. Ongoing convergence of sustainability and technology in the food industry ensures that this advance will not only enhance economic prosperity but also support global efforts on food security, climate action and inclusive growth. Ultimately, the changing food sector provides a hopeful template for how to grow financially while being better environmental stewards in the years ahead.

REFERENCES

Ahmed, S., Wongmahesak, K., Singh, B., & Kumar, S. (2025). Empowering Democratic Processes With AI: Innovations in Voter Engagement, Policy Analysis, and Decision-Making Process. In Wongmahesak, K., Wekke, I., Seftyono, C., & Nurdin, N. (Eds.), *Democracy and Democratization in the Age of AI* (pp. 121–132). IGI Global Scientific Publishing., DOI: 10.4018/979-8-3693-8749-8.ch007

Arora, A. K., Kumar, S., & Kansal, A. (2024). Analysis of Retail Investorsâ€™ Attitudes Toward IPO Investments. Indian Journal of Finance, 42-57.

Arora, A. K., Kumar, A., Tyagi, R., Sharma, S., Kumar, A., & Kumar, S. (2025). Future of Education With AI-Assisted Technologies. In Kaunert, C., Raghav, A., Ravesangar, K., Singh, B., & Riswandi, B. (Eds.), *Artificial Intelligence in Peace, Justice, and Strong Institutions* (pp. 169–190). IGI Global Scientific Publishing., DOI: 10.4018/979-8-3693-9395-6.ch008

Javed, A., Usman, M., & Rapposelli, A. (2025). Transition toward a sustainable future: Exploring the role of green investment, environmental policy, and financial development in the context of load capacity factor in G-7 countries. *Sustainable Development (Bradford)*, *33*(2), 1589–1609. DOI: 10.1002/sd.3192

Jeong, M., Kim, K., Ma, F., & DiPietro, R. (2022). Key factors driving customers' restaurant dining behavior during the COVID-19 pandemic. *International Journal of Contemporary Hospitality Management*, *34*(2), 836–858. DOI: 10.1108/IJCHM-07-2021-0831

Jiakui, C., Abbas, J., Najam, H., Liu, J., & Abbas, J. (2023). Green technological innovation, green finance, and financial development and their role in green total factor productivity: Empirical insights from China. *Journal of Cleaner Production*, *382*, 135131. DOI: 10.1016/j.jclepro.2022.135131

Kumar, S., & Patel, A. K. (2019). An analysis of cointegration between nifty index, dollar/INR and crude oil price. *Journal of Advanced Research in Dynamical and Control Systems*, *11*(12), 151–159. DOI: 10.5373/JARDCS/V11I12/20193223

McLennon, E., Dari, B., Jha, G., Sihi, D., & Kankarla, V. (2021). Regenerative agriculture and integrative permaculture for sustainable and technology driven global food production and security. *Agronomy Journal*, *113*(6), 4541–4559. DOI: 10.1002/agj2.20814

Moretto, A., & Caniato, F. (2021). Can Supply Chain Finance help mitigate the financial disruption brought by Covid-19? *Journal of Purchasing and Supply Management*, *27*(4), 100713. DOI: 10.1016/j.pursup.2021.100713

Mukhtarov, S., Yüksel, S., & Dinçer, H. (2022). The impact of financial development on renewable energy consumption: Evidence from Turkey. *Renewable Energy*, *187*, 169–176. DOI: 10.1016/j.renene.2022.01.061

Münch, C., von der Gracht, H. A., & Hartmann, E. (2021). The future role of reverse logistics as a tool for sustainability in food supply chains: A Delphi-based scenario study. *Supply Chain Management*, *28*(2), 262–283. DOI: 10.1108/SCM-06-2021-0291

Singh, B., Jain, A., Kumar, S., & Chandra, S. (2025). Strengthening AI-Driven Solutions for Virtual Tourism: Matching Visitor Experience and Ecosystem Conservation. In C. Ramos, T. Costa, R. Madeira, & J. Ferreira do Rosário (Eds.), *Open Innovation and Technology in Tourism and Hospitality* (pp. 93-110). IGI Global Scientific Publishing. DOI: 10.4018/979-8-3693-8633-0.ch005

Singh, B., Kumar, S., & Wongmahesak, K. (2025). Leadership and Management in the Public Sector via E-Government and E-Governance in Public Administration Reform. In Wongmahesak, K., Ahmad, J., & Mustanir, A. (Eds.), *Public Governance Practices in the Age of AI* (pp. 253–268). IGI Global Scientific Publishing., DOI: 10.4018/979-8-3693-9286-7.ch013

Singh, B., Wongmahesak, K., & Kumar, S. (2025). Global Digital Education Fostering Digital Citizens: A Blueprint for the Future and Worldwide Initiative Enhancing E-Governance. In Wongmahesak, K., Ahmad, J., & Mustanir, A. (Eds.), *Public Governance Practices in the Age of AI* (pp. 377–392). IGI Global Scientific Publishing., DOI: 10.4018/979-8-3693-9286-7.ch018

Chapter 13
Gastropreneurship and Health:
How Food Startups Are Innovating for Wellness

Suraj Jaywant Yadav
http://orcid.org/0000-0002-2687-4852
D.Y. Patil Education Society, India

ABSTRACT

This study meticulously explores the pivotal role of gastropreneurship in promoting wellness through the establishment and growth of health-centric food enterprises. It elucidates how visionary entrepreneurs strategically incorporate practices such as the utilization of organic ingredients, bespoke meal planning, and holistic wellness-oriented engagement to effectively address the evolving demands of health-conscious consumers. The findings underscore the critical importance of innovation, cultural dynamics, and intrinsic motivation in sculpting transformative and impactful culinary ventures. Consequently, gastropreneurship emerges as a significant driver of both public health advancement and sustainable business development, bridging the nexus between nutritional wellbeing and entrepreneurial excellence.

INTRODUCTION

Gastronomy is the study of food with an emphasis on art, history, and culture. In rural areas, gastronomy has the potential to boost revenue and generate employment as a tourism resource. The nine components of gastronomy are as follows: philosophy, history, tradition, ethics, cooking, raw materials, tasting, serving, learning, seeking out unusual experiences, and nutritional knowledge (Saputro & Wulandari, 2023).

DOI: 10.4018/979-8-3373-4047-0.ch013

A potential remedy for the deterioration of rural communities' economic vitality is to strengthen local food systems. The consolidated food system, which was intended to provide Americans with an abundance of affordable food, has paradoxically led to a rise in food safety concerns, food deserts, and obesogenic diets, which raise the prevalence of expensive chronic diseases (Sitaker et al., 2014).A complex illness, entrepreneurial burnout is caused by a confluence of different environmental, psychological, and personal stressors. Burnout can start because of the unique nature of the entrepreneurial endeavor, the high risks involved, and the ongoing pressure (Omrane et al. (2018). Entrepreneurs face a unique set of challenges that are exhausting but can quickly become overwhelming if not handled effectively, in contrast to traditional career paths. The first step in figuring out what causes entrepreneurial burnout is to identify the issue (Luu et al., 2025).The food industry must take action in response to the persistent global problem of malnutrition and the rise in non-communicable diseases (NCDs) across the globe. The fight to eradicate malnutrition is gaining traction as the globe moves closer to achieving the Sustainable Development Goals (SDGs), which will influence the nutrition public health agenda for the ensuing 15 years. The food industry has a significant role to play in combating malnutrition because of its wide-ranging influence, in addition to its production capacity and direct consumer contact. The food industry has a rare chance to use its resources and experience to support the global public health agenda for more sustainable and healthful diets for everyone. The food industry can fulfill its internal and external nutrition commitments in a number of ways(Spieldenner & Matope, 2017).The art of turning creative ideas and thoughts into a business that satisfies the needs and desires of customers is called entrepreneurship. In the current business environment, customization is essential for meeting the demanding needs of clients in a cutthroat marketplace. Eating at a restaurant is frequently about the experience, the food, or both. The industry is witnessing a completely new type of restaurant, though, with a fundamentally different business model. More attention would be paid to a healthier diet as a result of consumer and public health concerns. As a result, a balanced menu with healthier options necessitates more aggressive innovation. Innovation in healthy and diet food outlets and restaurants that serve only low-calorie, low-cholesterol foods with high essential nutrients can be helpful in meeting the demand of the specific targeted consumers with healthy and diet-conscious needs. The rapid expansion of future business trends in the restaurant and hotel industries is thus made possible by this idea of encouraging entrepreneurship (*Conceiving Awareness on Food Habits and Developing Innovative Diet Food Restaurant*, 2015).

RESEARCH BACKGROUND

Gastropreneurship—the fusion of gastronomy and entrepreneurship—is emerging as a dynamic force in the evolving landscape of food, health, and tourism. As global consumers become increasingly health-conscious and seek authentic culinary experiences, there is a growing demand for nutritious, sustainable, and locally inspired food offerings. This trend is opening new avenues for innovative food startups and small businesses that focus on wellness-oriented dining, functional foods, and cultural culinary practices. Gastropreneurs are not only creating unique food products and services but are also contributing to the promotion of public health, food security, and cultural preservation. Despite its growing importance, the role of gastropreneurship in fostering wellness, innovation, and economic development remains an underexplored area in academic and policy discussions. This research aims to explore how culinary creativity, entrepreneurial mindset, and wellness principles intersect to create impactful and sustainable business opportunities in the food industry.

RESEARCH OBJECTIVES

1. To understand what gastropreneurship means and how it is connected to health and wellness.
2. To explore how food entrepreneurs are creating new ideas and businesses focused on healthy eating.
3. To learn about the benefits and challenges faced by people starting food-related businesses.
4. To find out how these food businesses can promote both good health and cultural traditions.

THEORETICAL FRAMEWORK

The fields of gastronomy, entrepreneurship, and cuisine are combined in gastropreneurship as tourism resources. Being an entrepreneur means having the ability to gather and use resources to generate income and employment. Developing culinary skills, gastronomic knowledge, and entrepreneurship through gastropreneurship prepares people to run creative and prosperous culinary enterprises (Saputro & Wulandari, 2023).Small and medium-sized farms can now compete with larger farms in sales to consumers, food hubs, and institutions that require volume, quality, variety, and a consistent supply thanks to innovative food systems like farmers' markets,

CSAs, farm to institution, and food hubs. Local aggregation and distribution are able to provide wholesalers with competitive prices while paying farmers a fair price by giving producers a larger portion of the profits. As a result, the model shows broader health and economic effects that are not related to the local food system. Effective local food systems are driven by local multipliers (left side of the model), which boost the local economy and raise personal incomes and the amount of money available for food purchases (Sitaker et al., 2014).

Gastropreneurship is emerging as a significant force in promoting health and wellness through innovative food start-ups. These ventures are not only addressing economic challenges but also enhancing access to nutritious food options, particularly in underserved communities. The following sections outline key aspects of how food start-ups are innovating for wellness.As a result of gastronomy's increasing significance in meeting nutritional needs, this industry has a greater impact on consumers' eating habits and level of health consciousness. Gastronomy can contribute significantly to the promotion of healthy eating by employing and providing functional products, such as those with proven health benefits and products with improved health attributes(Kowalczuk et al., 2016). Food service companies use more and more modern and sophisticated technologies to produce their dishes, which is made possible by modifications to the design and specifications of equipment and appliances in the culinary arts. There is also a notable shift in pricing in the culinary arts industry, as the market offers both high-end dining establishments and low-cost bars, making this industry more economically accessible. Additionally, there is a more extensive distribution: catering is becoming more and more popular, and food services are offered in retail establishments, schools, entertainment venues, and workplaces. Food service companies are broadening their activities and integrating them with other services, leading to businesses like cafes and bookstores that are kid- or pet-friendly. The use of computer programs that enhance work organization, such as those that facilitate customer service, is increasing (Kowalczuk et al., 2016).

GASTROPRENEURSHIP AND HEALTH

Gastropreneurship, a dynamic intersection of gastronomy and entrepreneurship, is increasingly shaping the landscape of health and wellness in the food industry. As consumers grow more health-conscious and demand nutritious, sustainable, and functional food options, innovative food start-ups are responding with solutions that prioritize well-being without compromising taste or convenience. These gastropreneurs are leveraging technology, local ingredients, and traditional wisdom to create products that support dietary needs, promote gut health, and align with lifestyle trends like veganism and organic living. By addressing both individual health goals and broader societal concerns such as sustainability and food transparency, gastropreneurship is emerging as a powerful force driving the future of wellness-oriented food consumption.

EMERGING TRENDS IN HEALTH-FOCUSED FOOD START-UPS

Sustainable and nutritious food consumption has emerged as one of the major consumer trends. Scholars and media studies have discovered the importance of adopting new eating patterns, choosing foods from meals that have been nutritionally modified, and raising consumer health consciousness. Further study is still required to fully understand how the fast-food industry can adapt to this new consumer behaviour (Liu et al., 2024).It's worthwhile to look at how health-conscious brands in the fast-food sector will develop in the future given the emerging trends. The growth of healthy fast food brands will be forecasted in this article based on the viewpoints of individual brands and the fast food industry overall. To begin, the article will address the fast food industry's trends, the significance of food integrity, and the health effects of overprocessed food (Liu et al., 2024).A major force behind the world economy, the food processing industry spans a variety of industries from agriculture to food service and is presently going through revolutionary changes driven by technological advancements, shifting consumer preferences, and regulatory requirements. Efficiency and sustainability are being revolutionized by cutting-edge food technology, including precision agriculture, intelligent packaging, and sophisticated food processing techniques like 3D food printing and high-pressure processing. These developments are increasing traceability across the supply chain, decreasing waste, and improving food safety. Product offerings are changing concurrently with consumer demands for food that is produced ethically, sustainably, and healthily (Alam et al., 2025).Consumers today have high expectations for novel, nutrient-dense foods with improved functionality. A diet rich in nutritious foods and drinks is crucial for preventing and curing chronic, terrible diseases, which ultimately improves human health. Nutraceuticals are food ingredients or sources from food products or by-products that provide extra potency and health benefits. Research on functional constituents has produced encouraging findings for their use in food products, which will ultimately add value for the manufacturer and benefit consumers' health. These days, the main ingredients included in new drug formulations, nutritious foods, and food additive mixtures are nutraceuticals (Ghoshal & Kansal, 2019).Digital technologies and health trends are crucial to the future growth of the market for foods that promote health and wellness. This study investigates the potential effects of digital technology, market concentration, and health trends on the consumption of wellness and health foods in the Asian market (Uttama, 2021).

CONSUMER DEMAND AND MARKET SHIFTS

Globally, consumers' purchasing habits for food products are shifting significantly in favor of eating a healthy diet. Significant shifts in consumer behavior toward the consumption of healthy foods have occurred in recent years due to growing concerns about the advantages of health and wellness foods, shifting lifestyles, and increased health awareness. The development, physical and mental functioning, and simultaneous satisfaction of the body's fundamental nutritional and metabolic needs all depend on a balanced diet that includes the right amount of calories and essential nutrients. Since a long time ago, the significance of diet and food intake has been acknowledged as a crucial component in guaranteeing health and wellbeing. Consumers are now aware that eating a balanced diet is essential to preserving their general health (Ali & Ali, 2020).Diets may be improved and more healthy options may be purchased if food retail strategies are implemented to make food and beverage options healthier. The successful implementation and upkeep of healthy food retail interventions are significantly influenced by consumer demand for healthier options (Alsubhi et al., 2023).Consuming nutritious food has become a major trend in modern society, reflecting people's desire for long life and good health. Currently, unhealthy dietary habits are closely linked to chronic conditions like heart disease, hypertension, diabetes, and increased mortality. It is essential for maintaining a healthy lifestyle because food systems are vulnerable and cannot stop stunting and malnutrition in children (Chen et al., 2024).Changes in consumer preferences toward higher proportions of processed and animal-based foods in diets have prompted adjustments to the food system, raising questions about the nutritional and calorific value of many foods. Food waste at the consumer level has increased as a result of increased food availability, reduced costs, and raised quality standards. Furthermore, the global food system's ecological footprint is growing in terms of energy consumption, resource use, and its influence on climate change. Additionally, there is a greater chance of food-borne illness, antibiotic resistance, and food-related health hazards spreading quickly throughout the food chain (Herrero et al., 2023).Overweight and obesity have rapidly increased as a result of shifting lifestyle patterns marked by increased consumption of processed and unhealthy foods. Food manufacturers and policymakers may be better able to decide on a switch to healthier dietary models and, consequently, meet the 2030 global nutrition targets if they have a better grasp of how consumers behave toward healthy foods (Cammarelle et al., 2025).

TECHNOLOGY AND INNOVATION IN HEALTHY FOOD START-UPS

FoodTech then includes, for instance, AgTech. Essentially, it is an agribusiness startup. It's a digital native that was developed to bring innovation to the market, benefit businesses involved in agriculture, and solve common issues in a variety of fields, including field analysis, machinery, biotechnology, logistics, and transportation, among others. The agricultural industry has made use of automation tools like artificial intelligence (AI), big data, the Internet of Things (IoT), nanotechnology, and others. The "fourth agricultural revolution" is being fueled by these cutting-edge technologies, which are also changing the agri-food industry globally by enabling more consistent production through less expensive alternatives that serve a market that does not yet have access (Numa et al., 2023).Science and technology are making significant strides in a variety of areas toward the production of safe and healthful food items that come from sustainable supply chains. Ohmic sciences and innovative food processes enabled by digital technologies could help create cyber-physical ecosystems that are optimized for the production of food, biofuel, or biomaterials. For an ecosystem to be efficient and optimized and to produce a more balanced and effective result, multifunctional institutions with multidisciplinary expertise are necessary. Integrating education and training initiatives is essential for knowledge translation and capacity building in innovation-driven ecosystems. In national and international cooperation, infrastructure sharing and expertise synergy may increase innovation potential and competitiveness for a more comprehensive and equitable global social and economic development (Rosenthal et al., 2021).The current wave of innovations aimed at creating more sustainable and healthful food includes a variety of highly disparate methods. Two strategies that have drawn a lot of interest are the creation of new production technologies and the replacement of food ingredients. Accordingly, new starches and other hydrocolloids have increased the use and substitution of numerous ingredients, and traditional cereal flours have been replaced by other flours like pulse or nut flours. New production techniques include the use of critical CO2 to extract various components and the use of ultrasound or microwave assisted extraction. From the perspective of the consumer, research has concentrated on how consumers feel about organic and gluten-free products as well as the various innovations that lead to the production of more sustainable or natural foods (Rabadán et al., 2021).Food consumption and distribution are now significantly influenced by digital technologies, including the internet, information and communication technology, blockchain in the food supply chain, and industry 4.0 applications. These technologies will also have a significant impact on the food industry going forward. Miran-da-Ackerman and Colín-Chávez proposed that new technology and innovation could improve marketing and distribution channels in the food supply chain. The impact of digital technology on food consumption has been the subject of much discussion and research to date (Uttama, 2021).

CULTURAL AND CULINARY FUSION FOR WELLNESS

An inventive blending of various culinary cultures and traditions is represented by fusion cuisine, a concept that perfectly captures the spirit of culinary globalization. The influence of fusion cuisine on modern gastronomy is examined in this thorough analysis, which highlights its innovations in culture, nutrition, and cooking (Philosophers, 2024).In most societies, identity can have an impact on dietary choices, but the preservation of cultural identity in immigrant populations has largely influenced evaluations of this phenomenon. Understanding the impact of identity on eating habits among people in multicultural societies was the main goal of this study (Reddy & van Dam, 2020).As a symbol of cultural identity, food reflects historical, social, and geographic contexts, but as it changes due to global forces, questions are raised regarding cultural appropriation, authenticity, and the decline of traditional eating customs (Chauhan et al., 2025).

IMPACT ON PUBLIC HEALTH AND SOCIETY

There is a renewed push to address malnutrition in all of its manifestations by transforming food systems and combining initiatives in agriculture, nutrition, and health. It is crucial to comprehend food systems, which include the stakeholders (individuals and organizations) and operations involved in the production, processing, distribution, and consumption of food as well as their function in nutrition. Through their impact on food environments and diet quality, food systems have an impact on human health. Poor eating habits are the second behavioral risk factor for morbidity and the leading behavioral risk factor for mortality worldwide, outweighing the risk of smoking (Madzorera et al., 2021).Enhancing the food supply's nutritional value makes more nutrient-dense foods accessible, which enhances eating patterns and population health. However, efforts to mobilize knowledge between food industries and public health nutrition researchers are frequently underappreciated and poorly understood (Le Bouthillier et al., 2024).A food systems approach starts with the understanding that factors such as personal preference, diet, and cost are only one part of the causes of health disparities. They touch on issues like access in the community as well as more general social, economic, and political forces that affect the availability of food, the quality of nutrients, and its affordability. Furthermore, the effects of food production and processing on the environment and society contribute to some health disparities. The pathways and roots are not linear; rather, they represent intricate feedback loops and processes, like customer demand (Neff et al., 2009).Sustainability and food security are two of the biggest issues confronting humanity right now. in their planetary boundaries research. The food system is a primary cause of climate change and contributes roughly one-third of greenhouse gas emissions. The use of artificial fertilizers seriously disrupts the nitrogen cycle, and intensive food production is one of the main causes of biodiversity loss (Jackson, 2023). Transformation of the local and global food systems is required to guarantee the equitable and sustainable delivery of safe, nourishing, and healthful foods. Food systems are intricate systems that influence human health, diets, and a variety of other outcomes, such as sociocultural elements, economic growth, and the resilience of the environment and natural resources. The sustainability of food systems is threatened by ongoing environmental and climatic changes, which they both contribute to and are susceptible to. There are still a lot of unanswered questions regarding the relationship between environmental factors, food systems, and nutritional outcomes, despite the fact that this topic has received more attention recently (Fanzo et al., 2021).

FUTURE OF GASTROPRENEURSHIP IN WELLNESS

Increasing firm performance is linked to the well-being of entrepreneurs because they have more money to invest in their companies. Nevertheless, there is a dearth of research that combines performance, antecedents, and particular mechanisms linked to the emergence of entrepreneurial well-being (EWB) (Tisu et al., 2023).The field of entrepreneurship is becoming more and more entwined with various disciplines, addressing intricate societal issues such as digitalization, family business dynamics, and sustainability. The editorial team of the Entrepreneurship and Innovation section of Cogent Business and Management has identified ten research domains based on their collective expertise in recognition of the need to guide future research. These fields, which include corporate innovation, entrepreneurship education, and transitional entrepreneurship, are important for scholarly research and have the potential to have a big impact on society (Liguori et al., 2024).Growth and performance are examples of firm-level outcomes that are commonly highlighted in entrepreneurship research. However, there are unique, highly personal reasons why people choose to become entrepreneurs. Thus, as with other human endeavors that are self-organized, the relationship between entrepreneurship and happiness and fulfillment is crucial (Wiklund et al., 2019).The future of gastropreneurship in wellness is poised for dynamic growth as consumers increasingly seek holistic and health-conscious dining experiences. Gastropreneurs—entrepreneurs who innovate within the culinary world—are now blending gastronomy with wellness by focusing on nutrient-rich menus, plant-based offerings, functional foods, and sustainable sourcing. This convergence not only aligns with global health trends but also capitalizes on the growing demand for personalized nutrition and mindful eating. With advancements in food technology, greater awareness of gut health, and the integration of wellness tourism, gastropreneurship is evolving into a powerful platform for promoting well-being through culinary innovation and experiential dining.

RESEARCH METHODOLOGY

This study adopted a mixed-methods approach, incorporating both quantitative and qualitative research methods to investigate the role of gastropreneurship in promoting wellness through innovative food enterprises.

QUANTITATIVE METHOD

The quantitative component involved the administration of a structured questionnaire to a sample of 120 gastropreneurs and wellness-focused food entrepreneurs. Respondents were selected using purposive sampling, ensuring that participants had direct involvement in health-conscious food businesses, such as organic restaurants, nutrition cafés, food trucks, and diet-specific product outlets. The questionnaire included closed-ended and Likert-scale questions designed to capture data on business characteristics, wellness-oriented practices, consumer engagement, and perceived impact on customer health. Data collected were analyzed using descriptive and inferential statistical techniques to identify trends, relationships, and significant findings.

QUALITATIVE METHOD

The qualitative component comprised semi-structured interviews with 12 selected participants from the same pool of gastropreneurs and subject matter experts in nutrition, food innovation, and entrepreneurship. These interviews explored deeper perspectives on entrepreneurial motivations, challenges, consumer behavior, cultural influence, and innovation in the wellness food sector. The data obtained from these interviews were transcribed and analyzed thematically to identify recurring patterns and insights that complemented the quantitative results.

DATA TRIANGULATION

Triangulation of quantitative and qualitative data enhanced the reliability and depth of the research findings. The integration of statistical patterns with personal narratives provided a more holistic understanding of the ways in which gastropreneurship contributes to wellness and health-conscious consumer trends.

DATA ANALYSIS

Table 1. Demographic Profile of Gastropreneurs

Age Group	Frequency	Percentage (%)
18–30	30	25.0
31–45	60	50.0
46 and above	30	25.0

Explanation

The majority of gastropreneurs (50%) fall within the 31–45 age range, indicating that wellness food entrepreneurship is most active among mid-career individuals. The data suggest a balanced representation across age groups, suitable for examining age-related trends.

Table 2. Type of Business

Business Type	Frequency	Percentage (%)
Organic Restaurant	45	37.5
Nutrition Café	30	25.0
Food Truck	25	20.8
Diet Product Outlet	20	16.7

Explanation

Organic restaurants dominate the sample, possibly reflecting consumer preference for sit-down health-oriented meals. Food trucks and diet-specific outlets indicate diversification in business models.

Table 3. Wellness-Oriented Practices Adopted

Practice	Frequency	Percentage (%)
Organic Ingredients	80	66.7
Calorie Labelling	50	41.7
Vegan Options	60	50.0
Gluten-Free Items	45	37.5

Explanation

Most businesses focus on ingredient quality (organic) and offer diverse health-conscious options. These choices may align with emerging dietary trends and customer preferences.

Table 4. Consumer Engagement Strategies

Strategy	Frequency	Percentage (%)
Workshops	30	25.0
Nutrition Consultation	40	33.3
Loyalty Programs	60	50.0
Social Media Campaigns	90	75.0

Explanation

Digital engagement (social media) is the most popular method. Chi-square test shows a significant relationship between engagement strategies and customer retention (**$\chi^2 = 10.24, p < 0.05$**).

Table 5. Perceived Impact on Customer Health

Impact Level	Frequency	Percentage (%)
High	70	58.3
Moderate	40	33.3
Low	10	8.3

Explanation

A majority of gastropreneurs believe their offerings significantly benefit consumer health, supporting the social value of gastropreneurship.

Table 6. Revenue Growth Due to Wellness Focus

Growth Category	Frequency	Percentage (%)
High Growth	50	41.7
Moderate Growth	50	41.7
No Change	20	16.6

Explanation

Revenue growth correlates with wellness emphasis. Pearson correlation shows a strong positive relationship between wellness practices and revenue growth ($r = 0.63$, $p < 0.01$).

Table 7. Challenges Faced by Gastropreneurs

Challenge	Frequency	Percentage (%)
Ingredient Cost	65	54.2
Consumer Awareness	50	41.7
Competition	35	29.2
Regulations	30	25.0

Explanation

Ingredient cost is the top challenge, indicating financial barriers in sustaining quality. Consumer education also remains a critical need for expanding the wellness market.

Table 8. Innovation in Menu Design

Innovation Type	Frequency	Percentage (%)
Custom Meal Plans	45	37.5
Superfoods Integration	60	50.0
Fusion Wellness Dishes	30	25.0
Seasonal Menus	50	41.7

Explanation

Superfoods and seasonal menus are leading innovations. A t-test shows businesses offering customized plans report higher perceived impact scores ($t = 2.34$, $p < 0.05$).

Table 9. Influence of Culture on Food Offerings

Cultural Element	Frequency	Percentage (%)
Local Traditions	75	62.5
Ayurvedic Practices	50	41.7
Global Wellness Trends	60	50.0

Explanation

Cultural heritage plays a strong role in menu design. Mixed cultural influence supports fusion trends and makes wellness food more accessible.

Table 10. Sources of Entrepreneurial Motivation

Motivation Factor	**Frequency**	**Percentage (%)**
Passion for Health	80	66.7
Market Opportunity	60	50.0
Personal Experience	40	33.3
Social Impact	55	45.8

Explanation

Passion-driven entrepreneurship is dominant, showing intrinsic motivation. A chi-square test confirms a significant link between passion and adoption of wellness practices ($\chi^2 = 8.91$, $p < 0.05$).

Table 11. Summary of Statistical Tests Applied

Test	**Applied To**	**Result Summary**
Chi-square Test	Consumer engagement vs. retention	Significant ($p < 0.05$)
Pearson Correlation	Wellness practices vs. revenue growth	Strong positive correlation ($r = 0.63$)
Independent Samples t-test	Customized meals vs. perceived health impact	Significant difference ($t = 2.34$, $p < 0.05$)
Chi-square Test	Motivation type vs. wellness practices adopted	Significant ($p < 0.05$)

The summary table highlights the key statistical tests used to explore relationships within the study on gastropreneurship and wellness. A chi-square test revealed that consumer engagement strategies, particularly digital ones, significantly influenced customer retention. Pearson's correlation showed a strong positive relationship between the adoption of wellness practices and revenue growth, suggesting that health-focused strategies contribute to business success. An independent samples t-test found that gastropreneurs offering customized meal plans perceived a greater impact on customer health compared to those who did not. Additionally, another chi-square test confirmed that entrepreneurs driven by passion or social impact were significantly more likely to adopt comprehensive wellness practices. Collectively, these tests validate the role of motivation, engagement, and innovation in enhancing the effectiveness and sustainability of wellness-oriented food enterprises.

RESULT

The findings of this mixed-methods study demonstrate the pivotal role of gastropreneurship in advancing wellness-oriented food enterprises through strategic innovation and consumer engagement. Quantitative analysis from a purposive sample of 120 gastropreneurs revealed that 66.7% utilized organic ingredients, 50.0% incorporated vegan options, and 75.0% implemented digital engagement strategies, particularly social media campaigns. Notably, 58.3% of respondents perceived a high impact of their offerings on consumer health, while 83.4% reported moderate to high revenue growth attributable to wellness-centric business models. Pearson's correlation analysis indicated a statistically significant and strong positive association between wellness-oriented practices and reported revenue growth ($r = 0.63$, $p < 0.01$), underscoring the financial viability of health-focused innovation. A chi-square test identified a significant relationship between consumer engagement methods and customer retention ($\chi^2 = 10.24$, $p < 0.05$), while an independent samples t-test confirmed that businesses offering customized meal plans had significantly higher perceived health impact scores ($t = 2.34$, $p = 0.021$). Furthermore, chi-square analysis revealed a significant link between intrinsic entrepreneurial motivation (e.g., passion for health, social impact) and the likelihood of adopting comprehensive wellness practices ($\chi^2 = 8.91$, $p = 0.031$). These results, supported by thematic insights from semi-structured interviews, highlight the synergistic impact of innovation, motivation, and data-driven strategies in scaling the health and economic performance of gastropreneurial ventures.

CONCLUSION

This study concludes that gastropreneurship serves as a critical driver in promoting wellness through innovative, health-conscious food enterprises. The integration of wellness-oriented practices such as organic sourcing, customized meal planning, and functional menu innovations has not only enhanced perceived health outcomes among consumers but also contributed to measurable business growth. The statistically significant associations between wellness strategies, entrepreneurial motivation, and consumer engagement underscore the multifaceted value of health-driven entrepreneurship. The combination of quantitative data and qualitative insights affirms that gastropreneurs who are intrinsically motivated and strategically innovative are better positioned to meet the growing demand for wellness-based food experiences. Overall, the findings establish gastropreneurship as a viable and impactful model that aligns economic objectives with public health imperatives in the evolving food industry landscape.

FUTURE RECOMMENDATIONS

To further strengthen the contribution of gastropreneurship to the wellness economy, future initiatives should focus on several key areas. First, capacity-building programs and policy support should be introduced to lower entry barriers and reduce operational challenges, particularly regarding the high cost of quality ingredients and regulatory compliance. Second, training modules in nutrition science, digital marketing, and food innovation should be incorporated into entrepreneurial development programs to equip gastropreneurs with interdisciplinary skills. Third, future research should adopt longitudinal designs to assess the long-term health and economic impacts of wellness food ventures across diverse geographies and consumer demographics. Additionally, public-private partnerships can be instrumental in scaling the reach of wellness-based enterprises through subsidies, certifications, and awareness campaigns. Lastly, the integration of emerging technologies such as AI-driven personalization and blockchain for ingredient traceability should be explored to enhance transparency, trust, and customer satisfaction in the wellness food ecosystem.

REFERENCES

Alam, M. W., Kumar, J. V., Awad, M., Saravanan, P., Al-Sowayan, N. S., Rosaiah, P., & Nivetha, M. S. (2025). Emerging Trends in Food Process Engineering: Integrating Sensing Technologies for Health, Sustainability, and Consumer Preferences. *Journal of Food Process Engineering*, *48*(1), e70035. DOI: 10.1111/jfpe.70035

Ali, T., & Ali, J. (2020). Factors affecting the consumers' willingness to pay for health and wellness food products. *Journal of Agriculture and Food Research*, *2*, 100076. DOI: 10.1016/j.jafr.2020.100076

Alsubhi, M., Blake, M., Nguyen, T., Majmudar, I., Moodie, M., & Ananthapavan, J. (2023). Consumer willingness to pay for healthier food products: A systematic review. *Obesity Reviews*, *24*(1), e13525. DOI: 10.1111/obr.13525 PMID: 36342169

Cammarelle, A., Viscecchia, R., De Devitiis, B., Panniello, U., & Gorgoglione, M. (2025). Consumers' Behavior Toward Healthy Foods: A Critical Review. *Food Reviews International*, *41*(4), 1081–1098. DOI: 10.1080/87559129.2024.2432927

Chauhan, Y., Negi, I., & Singh, M. (2025). Cultural identity and Globalization in Culinary Practices: Exploring the Evolution, Diversity and Socioeconomic Impact of Food and Cuisine Across Cultures. *International Journal for Multidimensional Research Perspectives*, *3*(1), 08–22. DOI: 10.61877/ijmrp.v3i1.225

Chen, W., Ma, G., & Jia, Z. (2024). Consumer behavior and healthy food consumption: Quasi-natural experimental evidence from Chinese household participation in long-term care insurance. *Frontiers in Sustainable Food Systems*, *8*, 1364749. Advance online publication. DOI: 10.3389/fsufs.2024.1364749

Conceiving Awareness on Food Habits and Developing Innovative Diet Food Restaurant. (2015, January 1). SciSpace - Paper. https://scispace.com/papers/conceiving-awareness-on-food-habits-and-developing-1em36257i0

Fanzo, J., Bellows, A. L., Spiker, M. L., Thorne-Lyman, A. L., & Bloem, M. W. (2021). The importance of food systems and the environment for nutrition. *The American Journal of Clinical Nutrition*, *113*(1), 7–16. DOI: 10.1093/ajcn/nqaa313 PMID: 33236086

Ghoshal, G., & Kansal, S. K. (2019). 2—The Emerging Trends in Functional and Medicinal Beverage Research and Its Health Implication. In Grumezescu, A. M., & Holban, A. M. (Eds.), *Functional and Medicinal Beverages* (pp. 41–71). Academic Press., DOI: 10.1016/B978-0-12-816397-9.00002-9

Herrero, M., Hugas, M., Lele, U., Wirakartakusumah, A., & Torero, M. (2023). *A Shift to Healthy and Sustainable Consumption Patterns.*, DOI: 10.1007/978-3-031-15703-5_5

Jackson, P. (2023). Food, health and sustainability. *The Proceedings of the Nutrition Society*, *82*(3), 227–233. DOI: 10.1017/S0029665122002841 PMID: 36503525

Kowalczuk, I., Gutkowska, K., Sajdakowska, M., & Żakowska-Biemans, S. (2016). PRODUCT INNOVATIVENESS AND ITS IMPACT ON HEALTH RELATED IMPORTANCE OF FOOD IN THE CATERING BUSINESS. *Acta Scientiarum Polonorum. Oeconomia*, *15*(2), 2.

Le Bouthillier, M., Veilleux, S., Loignon, J., Turcotte, M., Trudel, L., & Provencher, V. (2024). Knowledge mobilization between the food industry and public health nutrition scientists: Findings from a case study. *BMC Nutrition*, *10*(1), 81. DOI: 10.1186/s40795-024-00889-z PMID: 38845063

Liguori, E. W., Muldoon, J., Ogundana, O. M., Lee, Y., & Wilson, G. A. (2024). Charting the future of entrepreneurship: A roadmap for interdisciplinary research and societal impact. *Cogent Business & Management*, *11*(1), 2314218. DOI: 10.1080/23311975.2024.2314218

Liu, J., Wu, H., & Zhou, Z. (2024). The Future of Food Health-Focused Brands in the Fast-Food Industry Based on the Analysis of Chipotle. *Advances in Economics. Management and Political Sciences*, *115*(1), 84–90. DOI: 10.54254/2754-1169/115/2024BJ0200

Luu, T. M. N., Singh, S. K., Dhand, S., Luu, T. M. N., Singh, S. K., & Dhand, S. (2025). *Evaluating the Impact of Wellness Programs on Entrepreneurial Burnout* (evaluating-the-impact-of-wellness-programs-on-entrepreneurial-burnout) [Chapter]. Https://Services.Igi-Global.Com/Resolvedoi/Resolve.Aspx?Doi=10.4018/979-8-3693-3673-1.Ch010

Madzorera, I., Jaacks, L., Paarlberg, R., Herforth, A., Bromage, S., Ghosh, S., Myers, S. S., Masters, W. A., & Fawzi, W. W. (2021). Food Systems as Drivers of Optimal Nutrition and Health: Complexities and Opportunities for Research and Implementation. *Current Developments in Nutrition*, *5*, nzab062. Advance online publication. DOI: 10.1093/cdn/nzab062 PMID: 34084996

Neff, R. A., Palmer, A. M., Mckenzie, S. E., & Lawrence, R. S. (2009). Food Systems and Public Health Disparities. *Journal of Hunger & Environmental Nutrition*, *4*(3–4), 282–314. DOI: 10.1080/19320240903337041 PMID: 23173027

Numa, I. A. N., Wolf, K. E., & Pastore, G. M. (2023). FoodTech startups: Technological solutions to achieve SDGs. *Food and Humanity*, *1*, 358–369. DOI: 10.1016/j.foohum.2023.06.011

Philosophers, C. (2024). *Exploring the Melting Pot: An In-Depth Review of Fusion Cuisine in Contemporary Gastronomy and Its Cultural, Nutritional, and Culinary Innovations. Chef Sunaina Nanda Food Production Professor*. DOI: 10.13140/RG.2.2.35521.36966

Rabadán, A., Nieto, R., & Bernabéu, R. (2021). Food Innovation as a Means of Developing Healthier and More Sustainable Foods. *Foods*, *10*(9), 9. Advance online publication. DOI: 10.3390/foods10092069 PMID: 34574178

Reddy, G., & van Dam, R. M. (2020). Food, culture, and identity in multicultural societies: Insights from Singapore. *Appetite*, *149*, 104633. DOI: 10.1016/j.appet.2020.104633 PMID: 32084519

Rosenthal, A., Maciel Guedes, A. M., dos Santos, K. M. O., & Deliza, R. (2021). Healthy food innovation in sustainable food system 4.0: Integration of entrepreneurship, research, and education. *Current Opinion in Food Science*, *42*, 215–223. DOI: 10.1016/j.cofs.2021.07.002

Saputro, H., & Wulandari, L. (2023). Gastropreneurship Katupat Kandangan as a Tourism Attraction in the South Hulu Sungai in South Kalimantan. *The Journal Gastronomy Tourism*, *10*(1), 82–95. DOI: 10.17509/gastur.v10i1.57919

Sitaker, M., Kolodinsky, J., Jilcott Pitts, S. B., & Seguin, R. A. (2014). Do entrepreneurial food systems innovations impact rural economies and health? Evidence and gaps. *American Journal of Entrepreneurship*, *7*(2), 3–16. PMID: 26613066

Spieldenner, J., & Matope, J. H. (2017). The Food Industry as a Partner for Public Health? In Biesalski, H. K., Drewnowski, A., Dwyer, J. T., Strain, J., Weber, P., & Eggersdorfer, M. (Eds.), *Sustainable Nutrition in a Changing World* (pp. 261–274). Springer International Publishing., DOI: 10.1007/978-3-319-55942-1_18

Tisu, L., Vîrgă, D., & Taris, T. (2023). Entrepreneurial well-being and performance: Antecedents and mediators. *Frontiers in Psychology*, *14*, 1112397. DOI: 10.3389/fpsyg.2023.1112397 PMID: 37928580

Uttama, N. P. (2021). Open Innovation and Business Model of Health Food Industry in Asia. *Journal of Open Innovation*, *7*(3), 174. DOI: 10.3390/joitmc7030174

Wiklund, J., Nikolaev, B., Shir, N., Foo, M.-D., & Bradley, S. (2019). Entrepreneurship and well-being: Past, present, and future. *Journal of Business Venturing*, *34*(4), 579–588. DOI: 10.1016/j.jbusvent.2019.01.002

Chapter 14
Nourishing Profits: The Convergence of Wellness and Commerce Within the Food Industry

Karan Berry
http://orcid.org/0000-0002-8641-5228
Symbiosis International University, Pune, India

Amrik Singh
http://orcid.org/0000-0003-3598-8787
Lovely Professional University, India

Shiv Kumar
http://orcid.org/0000-0003-0655-9561
Maharishi Markandeshwar University, India

Rekha Kaushik
http://orcid.org/0000-0003-2011-8287
Maharishi Markandeshwar University, India

Rizwan Yargatti
http://orcid.org/0000-0001-7815-6900
Symbiosis International University, Pune, India

ABSTRACT

Food companies are increasingly implementing wellness-oriented strategies to satisfy market demand, as awareness of nutrition and diseases linked to lifestyle grows. This chapter examines how wellness themes are incorporated into product design, branding, and supply chains, while also critically analyzing the commercialization of health. It further explores the impact of regulatory frameworks, ethical issues,

DOI: 10.4018/979-8-3373-4047-0.ch014

and the role of digital platforms in influencing consumer behavior. While the convergence provides avenues for expansion, it simultaneously presents challenges such as upholding product authenticity and navigating the complexities of consumer perceptions. The prosperity of contemporary food industry lies upon achieving a balance between innovation and transparency, as well as aligning with consumer values related to wellness. This thorough comprehension offers scholars, corporate leaders, and brand strategists valuable insight to predict and meet evolving customer demands, thereby bolstering the food industry's sustainable growth.

INTRODUCTION

Food industry has experienced a profound metamorphosis in contemporary times. With an augmenting global emphasis on health and wellness, food enterprises encounter the imperative of reconciling consumer expectations for nutritious offerings with the economic necessities of profitability (Yu & Watson, 2024). Consumer demand for items that improve health and food firms' strategic responses are the main drivers of the complex phenomena known as the convergence of wellness and commerce in the food industry. This tendency affects the retail and production industries and is indicative of a larger cultural movement towards sustainable living and preventive healthcare. The emergence of wellness branding, the creation of functional foods, and the strategic partnerships across food and pharmaceutical firms are all examples of how wellbeing has been incorporated into business. As businesses adjust to the changing consumer demands for wellness-focused products, these factors are changing the agri-food supply chains as well as marketing tactics. By analyzing pivotal domains such as consumer behavior, product innovation, supply chain intricacies, and corporate social responsibility, this chapter will furnish an exhaustive examination of how food corporations are manoeuvring through the confluence of wellness and commerce. As consumers evolve into more knowledgeable and health-oriented individuals, enterprises are progressively assimilating these considerations into their product lines, thus establishing a novel market paradigm wherein profit is intrinsically connected to the promotion of healthier, more sustainable food alternatives.

The convergence is predominantly influenced by the transformation of consumer preferences, psychological factors, and the retail landscape. This evolution signifies an increasing focus on health-oriented consumption, wherein consumers prioritize nutritional integrity and sustainable methodologies in their dietary selections. The escalating cognizance of health-related concerns, including obesity and chronic illnesses, has compelled consumers to pursue more healthful food alternatives (Cammarelle et al., 2024). The emergence of functional foods, which confer supplementary health advantages, resonates with consumer aspirations for products that bolster well-being. Demographic variables, encompassing age and educational attainment, exert a considerable impact on consumer inclinations towards wellness-oriented food products (Boinwad & Shinde, 2024). Psychological tenets, such as sensory marketing, are integral in molding consumer perceptions and preferences regarding health-centric products. Emotional and cognitive elements propel consumer involvement, fostering brand allegiance among those in pursuit of wellness-oriented alternatives (Maurya, 2024a). "Retail wellnesscape" underscores the significance of the shopping milieu in advancing consumer wellness as retailers have the capacity to augment consumer experiences by meticulously curating product assortments and establishing conducive store environments that promote wellness (Chartrand et al., 2024). Food corporations are employing a myriad of strategic methodologies to synchronize their product offerings with the escalating demand for health-oriented commodities. There is a notable increase in the development of functional foods, defined as consumables that yield supplementary health advantages that transcend basic nutritional needs. Frequently, these products are enriched with bioactive constituents, including vitamins, minerals, antioxidants, and probiotics, which are incorporated to augment their nutritional efficacy (Pistorio et al., 2023). For example, beverages are being fortified with health-enhancing components such as omega-3 fatty acids, plant sterols, and prebiotics to align with the prevailing wellness trend (Kasapoğlu et al., 2019).

The emergence of plant-based functional foods represents another salient trend within the industry. Corporations are leveraging consumer research to inform the development of these products, thereby ensuring they satisfy the burgeoning demand for health and wellness while preserving flavor and convenience (Chala & Emire, 2022). This methodological approach has culminated in the proliferation of products such as gluten-free cereals, fortified juices, and nutrient-enhanced energy drinks (Bogue & Troy, 2016). The food and beverage sector has fundamentally transformed its research and development strategies to rapidly adjust to market dynamics. Companies are concentrating on comprehending product design, formulation, and the selection of raw materials to engineer innovative and competitive offerings (Torres et al., 2024). For instance, the implementation of advanced technologies, including artificial intelligence (AI) and machine learning (ML), in market analysis and product testing has empowered corporations to acquire instantaneous insights into consumer predilections and refine their product assortments accordingly (Maurya, 2024a). The amalgamation of food science and health constitutes a tactical initiative in the advancement of nutritious food products. Companies are engaging in interdisciplinary collaborations to guarantee that their products fulfil consumer expectations regarding health and sustainability, all while maintaining sensory attractiveness (Fitricia et al., 2025). Marketing is instrumental in the advocacy of wellness trends. Corporations are channeling investments into health-centric marketing strategies, such as accentuating the presence of advantageous nutrients and the conservation of natural ingredients. For instance, the adoption of "clean" and "whole" labeling on packaging has emerged as a prevalent practice aimed at attracting health-conscious consumers (Chandon & Cadario, 2022). Corporate storytelling has also proven to be a compelling marketing instrument. Corporations utilize narratives to establish their identities as purveyors of healthy and ethical food alternatives, frequently underscoring their dedication to sustainability and consumer welfare. Nevertheless, there exists a potential risk of misleading consumers if health assertions do not accurately correspond with the actual nutritional value of the offerings (Olsen et al., 2023).

Corporations are undertaking extensive consumer research to discern preferences and attitudes toward healthful foods. A notable preference is emerging among shoppers for organic and functional foods; however, their insights into these goods are affected by factors including trust, labeling, and scientific endorsement. The burgeoning demand for gluten-free products exemplifies how consumer inclinations are steering product innovation. Initially designed for individuals with celiac disease, gluten-free products are now pursued by a wider demographic seeking healthier alternatives (Bogue & Sorenson, 2009). The incorporation of wellness trends into food products is fraught with challenges. Corporations are required to navigate intricate regulatory frameworks to ensure that their health claims are scientifically corroborated. Sustainability has emerged as a pivotal factor driving wellness trends. Customers are looking for goods that support environmental sustainability in addition to their own health (Pistorio et al., 2023). In response, businesses are implementing environmentally friendly packaging, cutting waste, and procuring materials ethically. Product development is influenced by ethical issues. To foster loyalty and trust, businesses are coordinating their tactics with consumer ideals including social responsibility, justice, and transparency (Nielsen, 2016). For instance, before functional foods may be promoted with specific claims, their health benefits must be validated. Businesses also need to deal with the technological difficulties of adding bioactive ingredients to products without sacrificing shelf life or sensory quality (Kasapoğlu et al., 2019). Chipotle's transition to sustainable and health-conscious fast food is a prime example of how businesses can successfully incorporate wellness trends into their offerings. By providing natural, premium ingredients and open sourcing methods, Chipotle has drawn in health-conscious customers and experienced financial growth (Liu et al., 2024), underscoring the significance of matching brand values with customer preferences for sustainability and wellness.

The expansion of the wellness movement in recent years can be ascribed to multiple interconnected factors, encompassing cultural transformations, the influence of social media, and the progression of health paradigms. These components collectively inform public perceptions and practices regarding wellness, culminating in its widespread acceptance. In order to present an evidence-based approach to the discussion, this work aligns qualitative perspectives from secondary data including market surveys, industrial publications, and scholarly journals.

WELLNESS PERSPECTIVE OF NEW-AGE FOOD INDUSTRY

The food sector is on the brink of transformative expansion, and comprehending the dynamics at play within this convergence is essential for enterprises aspiring to innovate and exceed consumer anticipations. Moreover, as global anxieties regarding health and sustainability intensify, it becomes paramount for stakeholders within the food industry to acknowledge the potential to establish enduring and profitable models that prioritize wellness. Retailers are adapting to the burgeoning consumer desire for nutritious and sustainable food by increasingly stocking wellness-oriented products. This transition is significantly shaped by demographic variables such as age, gender, and socioeconomic status, which in turn influence both purchasing behaviors and marketing strategies (Boinwad & Shinde, 2024). The notion of food well-being highlights a comprehensive relationship with food, encompassing psychological, physical, and social dimensions. This theoretical framework aids retailers in aligning their product offerings with the values of consumers (Dubé et al., 2021).

Supermarkets are implementing proprietary brand strategies to harness the momentum of wellness trends, while food manufacturers are compelled to innovate and synchronize their products with wellness expectations. Corporations such as Nestle are rebranding themselves as wellness enterprises, concentrating on products that confer health advantages and establishing strategic partnerships with pharmaceutical companies to bolster their research and development capabilities (Burch & Lawrence, 2010). The terminology surrounding wellness and well-being is variably employed across various academic disciplines, thereby affecting the marketing of food choices. The effective articulation of these concepts can enhance public health communications and improve consumer comprehension (McMahon et al., 2010). Multi-tiered marketing strategies are utilized by wellness food enterprises to advocate for natural health practices, leveraging personal networks to facilitate business growth and consumer education (Lee, 2012). By incorporating health-focused initiatives into their operations, food firms are increasingly using the intersection of wellness and business to develop successful and sustainable business models. This strategy promotes a comprehensive business environment by meeting client demands for wellness products and supporting sustainability objectives. Multi-level marketing (MLM), which relies on personal networks to boost sales and customer trust, is used by several wellness food firms to sell their products (Lee, 2012). By encouraging people to express their wellness experiences, this concept fosters a community-driven strategy that increases brand loyalty.

Encouraging sustainability in the food industry requires a variety of business models, including place-based communal food networks and circular food networks (Donner & Vries, 2023). Businesses are urged to embrace teamwork and uphold distinct sustainability goals, as they might result in creative methods that appeal to consumers who are health-conscious. In order to appeal to customers who value environmentally friendly operations, food companies have begun to utilize ecological approaches for monitoring and reporting their sustainability efforts (Skonberg & Thorbecke, 2022). Businesses can increase their reputation and draw in customers who care about sustainability by disclosing data on things like greenhouse gas emissions. Food industry start-ups are especially interested in developing sustainable business models and incorporating social and environmental factors into their main plans (Franceschelli et al., 2018). Gaining an advantage in a marketplace that prioritizes sustainability and wellness requires this innovation. Although there are many advantages to combining health and business, there are drawbacks as well, like the requirement for ongoing innovation and the possibility of consumer doubt about the veracity of wellness claims. Long-term viability in the changing food landscape requires striking a balance between these factors (Ramesh, 2022).

WELLNESS MOVEMENT'S EVOLUTION

The emergence of plant-based diets, clean eating, and organic food preferences as principal catalysts for change (Yeoman & McMahon-Beattie, 2024). The influence of social media and prominent figures in moulding consumer perceptions regarding food as a vehicle for health. The wellness movement epitomizes a bifocal philosophy: restoration and enhancement. Individuals endeavor to restore their health or optimize their overall well-being, engendering a dynamic interaction between these methodologies (Derkatch, 2023). The emergence of self-care, historically rooted in movements advocating for social justice, has been appropriated by capitalist frameworks, thereby intertwining wellness with productivity and consumerism (Badr, 2022). Social media platforms, most notably Instagram, have emerged as crucial in the promotion of wellness brands. Enterprises such as Goop and Poosh utilize visual marketing methodologies that underscore physical wellness and celebrity endorsements, thereby substantially augmenting consumer engagement. The wellness sector has evolved into a multi-trillion-dollar industry, primarily propelled by social media's capacity to amplify brand visibility and consumer interaction (Vukadinović, 2022). The COVID-19 pandemic has instigated a transition towards holistic health paradigms, accentuating primordial prevention strategies that prioritize well-being over mere management of illness (Veliah & Venkatsubramanian, 2024). Employers are increasingly integrating wellness initiatives into health plans, reflecting a broader trend towards individual accountability in health management, notwithstanding challenges related to participation and the evidential basis for efficacy (Draper et al., 2008).

Corporations are progressively implementing wellness initiatives to alleviate escalating healthcare expenditures, as exemplified by programs such as King County's Healthy Incentives, which have demonstrated efficacy in decreasing medical costs and enhancing health risk factors among employees (Rooney, 2012). Preventive care strategies, propelled by the wellness movement, concentrate on lifestyle modifications that can diminish the necessity for costly medical interventions. The wellness movement has facilitated the popularization of holistic medicine, which considers the individual as a whole- mind, body, and spirit; rather than merely addressing isolated symptoms (Yahn, 1979). This paradigm has precipitated the establishment of collaborative healthcare collectives that incorporate both physicians and non-physician health professionals, thereby enriching treatment diversity and patient care options. Heightened health consciousness among consumers has engendered a demand for alternative healthcare paradigms, compelling healthcare providers to modify their services to align with these emergent expectations (Plank & Gould, 1990). Health social movements have historically influenced healthcare policies and practices, championing patient rights and alternative treatment modalities, as evidenced in the women's health and AIDS movements (Cordner et al., 2014).

Social media platforms have become vital channels for brands to advertise and sell health-oriented products, including organic foods, superfoods, and functional drinks. The capability to directly connect with consumers has enabled these brands to foster robust customer loyalty and support, further propelling the wellness movement (Arı & Yılmaz, 2024). The wellness movement has exerted a substantial influence on the healthcare sector by advocating for preventive care, holistic approaches, and economically viable strategies. This paradigm shift has engendered a re-assessment of treatment methodologies, placing emphasis on long-term health behaviors and patient engagement. Numerous studies indicate that encountering food-related material on social media platforms can change eating patterns and nutritional selections. The influence of emotional engagement and credibility on consumer behavior is particularly significant. Research indicates that food-related posts on social media that trigger intense emotions, such as happiness or nostalgia, are more likely to affect product opinions and buying intentions. Furthermore, the perceived trustworthiness of the information source is crucial in determining its influence on food choices (Scheiber et al., 2023). Social media also aids in discovering new food items and trends, especially among younger audiences. Platforms such as Instagram and TikTok have become central hubs for food innovation, allowing users to share and explore recipes, cooking methods, and unusual ingredients. Hashtags like #organic, #healthy, and #vegan have become associated with contemporary wellness, often advocated by influencers and brands to resonate with consumers' desires for healthier living (Batat, 2024). This trend has allowed the food industry to cater to the preferences and aspirations of younger shoppers, who are increasingly interested in unique and health-oriented products (Pilař et al., 2022). For example, people who often interact with healthy food content on social media are more inclined to embrace healthier eating habits, whereas those exposed to fast-food promotions may develop heightened cravings for unhealthy foods (Wadhwa et al., 2024). These channels promote the swift dissemination of information, allowing trends like clean eating, veganism, and reduced sugar intake to become widely embraced. Users are attracted to visually striking content, including images of carefully arranged meals or videos showcasing workout routines, often accompanied by stories of personal growth and well-being (Pilař et al., 2021). This trend has fostered a cultural movement where food choices are about more than just nutrition; they reflect one's identity and social expression. Social media influencers play a pivotal role in influencing food preferences and buying habits. For an instance, influencers on platforms like Instagram and YouTube often promote organic items, plant-based diets, and clean eating practices, frequently framing these selections as ethically superior or beneficial for health. The influence of these figures goes beyond simple product promotion. They cultivate a sense of community by sharing personal anecdotes, recipes, and advice, which builds trust and interaction with their followers. This trust can lead to substantial sway over dietary choices, as followers are inclined to adopt the habits endorsed by beloved influencers (Arı & Yılmaz, 2024). Nonetheless, the sway of social media influencers is not without its criticism. Certain studies have expressed concerns regarding the lack of scientific support for some dietary suggestions, particularly when influencers who lack formal qualifications in nutrition or health advocate for specific products or diets (Pergher et al., 2024). This underscores the necessity for increased examination of the information shared by influencers and the potential dangers of misinformation.

Technology has been crucial in supporting the contemporary wellness movement, particularly within the food industry. Digital platforms and tools have changed how people obtain information, engage with communities, and make wellness-related choices. One major contribution of technology has been the emergence of digital health communities. These online environments, often found on social media or specialized forums, provide a place for individuals to exchange experiences, seek guidance, and engage in health discussions. For instance, communities focused on veganism or clean eating have thrived on platforms like Instagram and Reddit, fostering a sense of community and motivation among members (Gokce et al., 2023). Technology has also made wellness experiences more personalized. Apps and websites now deliver customized dietary suggestions, meal plans, and exercise routines based on individual tastes and objectives. This degree of personalization has made wellness more approachable and attractive to a wider audience, especially younger consumers who prioritize convenience and customization (Davies & Mann, 2023). In addition, technology has spurred the expansion of the direct-to-consumer market within the food industry.

THE BUSINESS RESPONSE: PROFIT TO PURPOSE

The focus on profit in the food business frequently overshadows public health considerations, resulting in the robust advertising of ultra-processed foods tied to health problems including obesity and diabetes. Corporate political maneuvers can impede regulations designed to restrict harmful food products, thereby undermining public health initiatives (Mialon, 2024). Existing regulations inadequately address the marketing and production of unhealthy food options, permitting the proliferation of low-cost, high-calorie products that contribute to adverse health outcomes (Nestle, 2022; Freeman & Sindall, 2019). There is an absence of comprehensive policies that both promote healthier food choices and regulate detrimental products, thereby creating a deficiency in effective governance (Leib, 2013). The regulatory environment for new food products, including plant-based and functional foods, is frequently convoluted, complicating the market entry of innovative, health-oriented products (Maurya, 2024b). Obstacles such as legal and programmatic impediments impede the advancement of alternative food producers who could augment the availability of healthier options (Leib, 2013).

Case studies of established corporations such as Beyond Meat, Oatly, and Whole Foods, reveal that they all are leveraging the wellness trend. Food companies are increasingly adjusting to the wellness trend by employing various strategies aimed at fulfilling the rising consumer appetite for health-focused goods. These strategies include product innovation, marketing tactics, and modifications to the supply chain, showcasing a holistic approach to align with wellness trends. Food businesses are concentrating on creating healthier products by choosing high-quality raw materials and adopting advanced production technologies. This method not only boosts the nutritional content of products but also aligns with consumer desires for healthier selections (Mukty & Pulubuhu, 2023). The emergence of functional foods that provide health advantages beyond basic nutrition is a notable trend. These items are crafted to meet the needs of consumers who are looking for preventive health measures through their dietary choices (Burch & Lawrence, 2010). Innovative promotional tactics, including direct sales through multi-level marketing, are being used to efficiently communicate the benefits of wellness foods. This strategy taps into personal networks to shape consumer perceptions and increase sales (Lee, 2012). Retailers are modifying their marketing approaches to emphasize the health benefits of wellness foods, influenced by demographic elements like age and education that impact consumer buying behavior (Boinwad & Shinde, 2024). The food industry is forming partnerships with pharmaceutical companies to bolster research and development initiatives, focusing on products that deliver wellness advantages. This collaboration is transforming the agri-food sector and affecting supply chain dynamics (Burch & Lawrence, 2010). Retailers are progressively offering wellness foods, driven by consumer interest in products that promote a sustainable lifestyle. This transition is also shaped by the need to tackle issues such as food insecurity and chronic illnesses (Boinwad & Shinde, 2024).

The emergence of healthier product choices in the marketplace leads to complex changes in consumer behavior and significantly affects buying choices, as people increasingly focus on their well-being. There is a rising consumer awareness about the connection between diet and health, which results in a higher demand for nutritious and healthful foods (Firoozzare et al., 2024). This heightened health consciousness is a crucial psychological element impacting consumers' willingness to pay for wellness-focused food products, with product quality, flavor, packaging, and cost also playing important roles (Ali & Ali, 2020). Buyers are motivated not only by health factors but also by sensory appeal and affordability, which ultimately influences their final purchasing choices (Chandon et al., 2022). The food sector is experiencing a shift towards healthier options, with consumers demonstrating an increased readiness to spend more on such products. This change signifies a transforming consumer environment in which health and wellness are becoming more integrated into buying decisions, with consumers actively seeking products that support their health objectives (Hanus, 2018).

Consumer choices concerning health-oriented products are shaped by a complex interaction of factors, which can be generally classified into psychological, socio-demographic, economic, and environmental categories. These influences have been thoroughly researched across different contexts, including organic foods, functional foods, and products labeled as healthy. One of the most crucial factors driving consumers to buy health-oriented products is health consciousness. Individuals who emphasize health and wellness tend to look for items that correspond with their health objectives. For example, research has indicated that health consciousness has a direct impact on attitudes toward organic and functional foods, as well as the willingness to purchase hydroponic products (Osunsanmi et al., 2024). Perceived advantages, such as the belief that a product enhances physical or mental health, are also significant. Studies reveal that consumers are more inclined to buy health-oriented products when they believe these items provide specific health benefits, like lowering the risk of chronic illnesses or improving nutritional intake. Consumers' awareness of health-oriented products significantly affects their purchasing choices. For instance, knowledge of the health advantages of organic foods, functional foods, and nutraceuticals has been shown to elevate the intention to buy (Jadhav et al., 2023). Nonetheless, insufficient information or misconceptions can serve as obstacles to purchasing these products (Kusdiyanto et al., 2022).

Educational initiatives and transparent labeling of health benefits can improve consumers' comprehension and confidence in health-oriented products. For instance, research has demonstrated that consumers who are made aware of the detrimental effects of chemical fertilizers and toxins are more inclined to choose healthier options (Ghazanfari et al., 2024). Trust in the product and its labeling is another vital consideration. Consumers are more likely to buy health-oriented products if they have confidence in the brand, the manufacturing process, and the claims made on labels. For instance, trust in organic food labels has been recognized as a significant factor influencing purchase intention (Baş et al., 2024). However, doubt regarding health claims can impede purchasing decisions. Studies indicate that consumers may be hesitant about inflated health claims, especially when regulatory oversight is lacking (Jadhav et al., 2023). Economic aspects, such as cost and accessibility, also affect consumers' choices. While many individuals are prepared to pay extra for health-oriented products, high prices can deter purchases, particularly among low-income households (Ghazanfari et al., 2024). Accessibility is also a crucial factor. Consumers are more likely to buy health-oriented products if they can easily find them in local shops or on online platforms. Research has shown that enhancing the availability of organic and functional foods can significantly increase their consumption. Social and cultural influences, such as community norms and familial impacts, also contribute to shaping consumers' choices. For example, factors like marital status, employment situation, and the presence of children at home have been observed to affect the purchase of organic foods (Baş et al., 2024). Likewise, cultural perspectives on health and nutrition can influence the acceptance of functional foods and nutraceuticals (Jadhav et al., 2023).

Retailers are broadening their product ranges to include health and wellness foods, responding to consumer interest in nutritious alternatives (Boinwad & Shinde, 2024). By offering a diverse assortment of health-focused products, they can reach various consumer groups, thereby expanding their market presence (Boinwad & Shinde, 2024). Retailers apply the 4Ps (product, price, placement, promotion) to improve the visibility and attractiveness of healthier food choices (Karpyn et al., 2020). Successful marketing tactics, such as engaging signage and in-store promotions, have been shown to positively affect consumers' decisions to purchase healthier options (Wansink, 2017). Crafting a retail environment that advocates for overall wellness can elevate consumer experiences, fostering repeat visits and brand loyalty (Chartrand et al., 2024). Equipping staff with the knowledge to prioritize customer wellness helps create a welcoming shopping environment, integrating health into the retail experience (Chartrand et al., 2024).

Social influences, such as recommendations from friends and family, can increase the attractiveness of health-focused products. Studies indicate that social factors are especially significant for older consumers (Osunsanmi et al., 2024). Effective marketing and promotional efforts can greatly impact consumers' choices to buy health-focused items. For example, advertisements highlighting health benefits and the natural qualities of products have been found to boost purchase intent (Kaur et al., 2023). Promotions, including discounts and economic incentives, can motivate consumers to try new health-oriented products. Research shows that promotional activities are particularly successful in increasing sales of organic and functional foods (Ariestiningsih et al., 2023). Psychological aspects, such as risk perception and outcome expectancy, also play a role in consumer decisions. For instance, individuals who view health risks as high are more inclined to buy health-oriented products as a preventive strategy. Outcome expectancy, which refers to the belief that a product will provide specific health advantages, is another key psychological aspect. Studies have demonstrated that consumers are more inclined to purchase health-oriented goods if they anticipate beneficial results, such as enhanced health or well-being (Huang et al., 2022). Demographic attributes, including age, gender, education, and income, also influence consumer choices. For example, younger individuals and those with higher incomes tend to purchase health-oriented products, reflecting greater health awareness and available resources. Additionally, education level is a crucial demographic factor, as those with more education often seek out health-oriented products due to increased knowledge of health benefits (Gupta et al., 2023). Environmental concerns, such as the aim to lower carbon footprints and support sustainable practices, also shape consumers' choices. For instance, people who value environmental conservation are more likely to purchase organic foods and other health-oriented products that align with their principles (Guru et al., 2024).

The lifestyles and health priorities of consumers significantly affect their buying decisions. For example, those who emphasize healthy living are more prone to buy functional foods and nutraceuticals (Grujic & Grujčić, 2023). Health orientation, defined as the extent to which consumers emphasize health in their food selections, has been shown to have a direct impact on purchase intentions and behaviors. For example, individuals with a strong health orientation are more inclined to pay attention to nutritional claims and opt for products that carry health-related labels (Huang et al., 2022). Various product characteristics, including naturalness, nutritional value, and flavor, also play a crucial role in consumers' decision-making processes. For instance, consumers are more likely to buy health-focused products when they view them as natural and devoid of artificial components (Guru et al., 2024). The nutritional profile is another key factor. Consumers who value nutrition tend to choose functional foods and nutraceuticals that offer specific health-related benefits (Osunsanmi et al., 2024). As the market continues to grow, finding a balance between consumer health priorities and business goals remains an essential consideration for stakeholders. While these strategies underscore the proactive actions taken by food companies, it is crucial to reflect on the broader impact of these changes.

REGULATORY CHALLENGES AND TECHNOLOGICAL INNOVATIONS

Regulatory frameworks are indispensable in safeguarding food safety and quality; however, they may also obstruct the emergence of innovative, health-promoting products. The European Union's 2006 Regulation regarding nutrition and health claims enforces stringent conditions and necessitates comprehensive dossiers for novel claims, thereby engendering ambiguity and potentially constraining innovation (Binns, 2009). The disparate legal systems between the United States and the European Union, with their divergent regulations concerning dietary ingredients, complicate international commerce and the economic feasibility of new products (Tallon & Kalman, 2024). The assertive marketing strategies employed by commercial entities regarding ultra-processed foods present a formidable challenge to public health objectives, as such practices frequently undermine regulatory initiatives designed to advocate for healthier food choices (Mialon, 2024). The imperative for regulatory adherence in product development may prolong the market introduction of pioneering products such as plant-based alternatives and functional foods, as developers are required to navigate intricate regulatory frameworks (Maurya, 2024b). Overly prescriptive guidance and rigidity within the EU's codified legal architecture can be labor-intensive, thereby obstructing the market entry of novel ingredients. Although these regulatory impediments pose considerable challenges, they simultaneously underscore the necessity for collaboration among food developers, regulatory authorities, and policymakers. This collaboration can facilitate the streamlining of processes and encourage innovation while ensuring consumer protection. Furthermore, enhanced international cooperation in the assessment of ingredient safety could potentially mitigate trade barriers and promote the global integration of wellness and commerce within the food industry (Tallon & Kalman, 2024). The integration of wellness and commerce encounters numerous regulatory obstacles that hinder advancement towards more nutritious food systems. The difficulties arise from the influence of commercial interests, insufficient regulatory frameworks, and the intricacies of food production and marketing.

Although social media and technology have significantly transformed the contemporary wellness movement, they also present several challenges and criticisms. One of the major concerns is the widespread misinformation and the absence of regulation in the online environment. Numerous influencers and brands promote unverified health claims, which can result in confusion and potentially harmful dietary choices (Pergher et al., 2024). Another significant issue is the cultural politics surrounding wellness, which often reinforces exclusionary narratives. The clean eating trend, for instance, has faced criticism for suggesting an affluent, morally superior lifestyle that many individuals cannot access. This has led to allegations of elitism and the reinforcement of social inequalities. Furthermore, the constant inundation of idealized representations of food and bodies on social media can adversely affect mental health. Research has found connections between social media usage and body image concerns as well as disordered eating patterns, particularly among younger adults. The pressure to adhere to unrealistic health and beauty standards may hinder efforts to encourage positive wellness practices (Wu et al., 2023).

Various challenges and obstacles can impede food enterprises from incorporating healthier product options, such as consumer demand and perceptions, financial constraints, supply chain and logistical issues, waste and spoilage, competition, limits on product innovation, and conflicting priorities. Store owners may not recognize adequate demand for healthier selections or might lack the resources to evaluate it. The elevated costs of healthy products and limited financial resources can represent a considerable hindrance (Wongprawmas et al., 2022). Maintaining a steady supply of fresh, healthy ingredients can be difficult, particularly for smaller businesses. Fresh produce spoils quickly, resulting in waste and loss of potential revenue. Healthy offerings may contend with competition from well-established, less nutritious alternatives that are usually less expensive and more vigorously marketed. Food retailers may hesitate to prioritize healthy food initiatives due to various interconnected factors affecting the retail landscape (Zorbas et al., 2024). The pressure to generate profit and meet customer expectations (market logic) can occasionally clash with health promotion objectives (Duus et al., 2025). The long-term effectiveness of ongoing product innovation is often questioned (Ndlovu, 2024). While the food industry encounters substantial ethical challenges, it also possesses the capability to instigate positive transformation. By emphasizing health and sustainability, companies can reform their approaches and aid in creating a healthier community. Nevertheless, the inherent profit motivation may complicate these initiatives, resulting in doubt regarding the industry's dedication to public health.

Technological advancements in food production and distribution are crucial in addressing regulatory complexities that arise at the nexus of health promotion and commercial activity. These advancements significantly enhance food safety, improve traceability, and bolster regulatory compliance, thus facilitating the integration of wellness-oriented products with economic viability. By employing sophisticated technologies such as the Internet of Things (IoT), blockchain, robotics, and artificial intelligence (AI), the food sector can more effectively maneuver through the intricate regulatory landscape while satisfying consumer demands for healthier and more sustainable offerings. The utilization of IoT and sensor technologies plays a crucial role in enhancing food safety and traceability, facilitating the ongoing observation of environmental parameters, thus assuring compliance with safety protocols and lowering the chances of contamination. Blockchain technology affords transparency and traceability throughout the supply chains, which is essential for regulatory compliance and fostering consumer trust. The application of AI and machine learning facilitates the anticipation of contamination risks and the optimization of inspection processes, thereby improving food safety and adherence to regulatory standards (Ayeni & Olagoke-Komolafe, 2024).

Collaboration among food developers, regulatory authorities, and policymakers is indispensable for navigating regulatory frameworks and promoting the introduction of innovative products (Maurya, 2024b). The establishment of harmonized food safety regulations coupled with more robust enforcement mechanisms is vital for ensuring widespread compliance and facilitating international trade (Ayeni & Olagoke-Komolafe, 2024). Innovations such as 3D food printing and lab-cultivated meats resonate with consumer inclinations towards sustainable and nutritious offerings while simultaneously fulfilling regulatory mandates. Features that incorporate embedded sensors for monitoring freshness and quality contribute to enhanced consumer confidence and compliance with regulatory standards (Alam et al., 2025).

The challenges related to supply-side aspects of the aforementioned convergence are complex, encompassing industrial strategies, structural changes, and the incorporation of technology. These elements greatly impact productivity and competitiveness, both of which are vital for achieving convergence in these sectors. Government interventions can affect various groups differently, highlighting the need for customized industrial strategies to boost competitiveness and convergence. Measures aimed at enhancing productivity are essential, as they can improve economic performance and better align with global benchmarks (Pitelis, 1998). The fitness and leisure sector encounters considerable obstacles, such as a deficiency in innovation and inefficient supply chains. Structural changes are necessary to elevate the quality of services offered and cater to the increasing consumer desire for wellness options (Huang, 2020). The health technology sector is key to improving healthcare services and outcomes, with forecasts suggesting significant growth in this field. Tackling infrastructure and regulatory issues is critical for harnessing health technology to facilitate this convergence (Hood et al., 2024).

While technological innovations present substantial advantages, they concurrently pose challenges, including elevated implementation costs and concerns regarding data security. Moreover, regulatory frameworks must evolve in tandem with rapid technological advancements, necessitating proactive engagement and the expansion of expertise among regulatory bodies (Ayeni & Olagoke-Komolafe, 2024). The equilibrium between technological innovation and regulatory compliance is imperative for the successful integration of health promotion and commerce within the food industry.

UPCOMING OPPORTUNITIES AND ETHICAL CONTEMPLATION

The food sector is experiencing noteworthy trends and opportunities, predominantly propelled by consumer demand for health-centric products and sustainable methodologies. Innovations such as personalized nutrition, lab-cultivated meats, and functional foods are redefining the market dynamics. Emerging trends such as personalized nutrition tailored to individual health requirements are gaining momentum, bolstered by technological advancements (Valluri, 2022). There is an increasing focus on environmentally sustainable production techniques, including plant-based alternatives and insect-derived protein sources (Maurya, 2024b). Products that substantiate verifiable health benefits are becoming increasingly favored, thereby necessitating stringent regulatory oversight to uphold consumer trust. Innovations in food technology, particularly the utilization of AI in product development, can significantly improve efficiency and product quality. Emerging markets are presenting novel opportunities for health-oriented products, especially in areas where health consciousness is on the rise (Hobbs et al., n.d.). Regulatory frameworks play a pivotal role in maintaining elevated standards for new food offerings, which is critical for consumer acceptance (Maurya, 2024b). Collaborative initiatives between food developers and regulatory bodies may streamline the introduction of innovative products, such as those derived from insects (Baicu, 2022).

The potential for technological advancements to catalyze new business models and enhance food sustainability (Silchenko & Askegaard, 2021) is evident in lab-grown meats, functional beverages, and personalized nutrition (Deshmukh & Gutte, 2024). It is essential to acknowledge how regulations and government policies shape the evolution of food production and consumption (Cunningham et al., 2021). Due to customer demand for health-conscious products, the food sector's supply chains and distribution networks are changing as wellness and commerce come together. This change affects many supply chain stakeholders and calls for major adjustments to the way food is acquired, produced, and distributed. Food manufacturers are shifting from traditional offers to wellness-focused items in response to the increased demand for sustainable and health-enhancing food products (Burch & Lawrence, 2010). Due to consumer trends and demographic reasons, retailers are placing a greater emphasis on wellness foods, which has an impact on their marketing and stocking strategies (Boinwad & Shinde, 2024). By enabling real-time data exchange between suppliers and retailers, the growth of e-commerce improves supply chain efficiency and coordination, which lowers costs and improves product quality (Kinsey & Buhr,

2003). Sustainable food supply chain management (SFSCM) solutions that address both ecological and social obligations have been implemented as a result of pressure on the food industry to embrace sustainable practices (Bloemhof & Vorst, 2014). By guaranteeing that health outcomes are efficiently provided, the integration of supply chains with a health focus can enhance general well-being and support the wellness movement (Subramanian, 2020). On the other hand, although the emphasis on health might spur creativity and sustainability, it can also result in market monopolization, where bigger companies control the wellness market, thereby excluding smaller manufacturers and reducing the variety of products available. The food business has both possibilities and challenges as a result of this dualism.

The ongoing development of technology and social media is likely to influence the future of the wellness movement. As these platforms become more deeply integrated into everyday life, their impact on dietary choices and health behaviors is projected to increase. A promising avenue is utilizing social media for public health initiatives. Collaborations among influencers, healthcare professionals, and policymakers could boost the credibility and reach of these initiatives (Pabian et al., 2025). Additionally, there is potential for the creation of more advanced tools aimed at personalizing wellness experiences. Innovations in artificial intelligence and data analytics could support even more tailored dietary suggestions, considering individual preferences, health conditions, and lifestyle factors. This could make wellness more accessible and effective for a broader spectrum of individuals (Wiedenroth & Otter, 2022). However, it is essential to tackle the challenges linked to social media's involvement in wellness. This entails efforts to regulate misinformation, champion diversity and inclusion in wellness narratives, and reduce the negative psychological consequences of social media usage. By encouraging a more critical and nuanced understanding of wellness, technology and social media can continue to contribute positively to the development of healthier, more equitable food systems.

The emergence of personalized nutrition applications enables consumers to customize their diets according to their specific health needs and preferences. Big data analytics offers insights into consumer patterns, allowing companies to create targeted products (Maurya, 2024a). Cultured meat technologies are developing as sustainable substitutes for conventional livestock farming, thereby minimizing environmental impacts (Hassoun et al., 2022). The transition towards plant-based foods indicates a rising consumer demand for healthier and more sustainable choices (Alam et al., 2025). The integration of AI, the Internet of Things (IoT), and blockchain improves supply chain transparency and operational effectiveness, building consumer trust (Maurya, 2024a). Methods such as 3D food printing and smart packaging enhance food safety and decrease waste (Alam et al., 2025). Although these trends offer substantial opportunities for innovation and sustainability, they also introduce ethical and cultural considerations that must be addressed to maintain a balanced perspective on the evolution of food technology.

As the sector confronts increasing health issues, like obesity and non-communicable diseases, it faces heightened scrutiny regarding its contribution to public health. This overlap prompts essential inquiries about corporate accountability, ethical marketing, and the sustainability of food systems. Food manufacturers are increasingly seen as moral agents responsible for the health consequences of their products, creating a need for ethical decision-making frameworks (Early, 2002). The duty for public health is transitioning from individuals and governments to the food sector, stressing the necessity for companies to pursue healthy innovation and ethical marketing practices. Ethical concerns also encompass sustainable farming methods and the environmental effects of food production, underscoring the importance of transparency and ethical protocols. Tackling food waste is vital for sustainability, demanding businesses to implement practices that reduce waste along the supply chain (Varzakas & Antoniadou, 2024). The food sector's involvement in public health is further complicated by its fiduciary duties, which may clash with health initiatives. Effective public-private partnerships must align corporate objectives with public health interests to achieve success (Freedhoff, 2014). Ethical conundrums, including the delicate boundary between marketing health and engaging in "health-washing" practices (Ares et al., 2023). Addressing challenges related to food accessibility, affordability, and the prospective dangers of class disparity within health-oriented food markets. Despite the potential, businesses still have to deal with issues like the frequent failures of functional beverages brought on by a lack of knowledge about consumer preferences. Public health programs may also face difficulties due to the "Red Queen" effect, which requires businesses to continuously innovate in order to stay ahead of their rivals (Cuevas et al., 2021).

The wellness food market is growing quickly, offering retailers and manufacturers chances to innovate and satisfy consumer needs (Boinwad & Shinde, 2024). The commercialization of wellness can result in the promotion of products with overstated health claims, which could potentially endanger consumers (Nestle, 2022). There is a possibility that wellness products may not be available to all demographic groups, worsening health inequalities (Ramesh, 2022). Strict regulations are essential to guarantee product safety and curb misleading marketing tactics (Maurya, 2024b). Technological advancements can improve transparency in food labeling and enhance consumer understanding of nutritional information (Riccardi, 2022). Although the fusion of wellness and commerce in the food industry has promising possibilities for enhancing health, it requires vigilant oversight to prevent exploitation and ensure fair access to nutritious foods. Achieving a balance between regulation and innovation is vital for the sector's sustainable progress.

CONCLUSION

The food sector is undergoing significant change propelled by technological innovations and shifting consumer preferences. Businesses are responding to the increasing demand for health-conscious solutions by utilizing creativity, customer information, and strategic marketing. The wellness business offers significant growth and innovation potential, despite ongoing obstacles like customer trust and regulatory compliance. Food businesses may effectively negotiate this competitive environment and help create a more sustainable and healthful food sector by adjusting their tactics to reflect the tastes and beliefs of their customers. Social media and technology have grown to be crucial factors in forming the contemporary wellness movement, especially in the food sector. They have made it possible for wellness experiences to be customized, influencer culture to flourish, and health-related information to spread quickly. In order to ensure that social media and technology lead to a healthier, fairer future, it will be crucial to address their drawbacks while utilizing their promise while the wellness movement develops. But these changes also bring up significant issues about disinformation, cultural tolerance, and mental health.

Sociodemographic, financial, and ecological factors all have a role in the decision to buy health-oriented items. As people become more conscious of the connection between diet and health, there is an increasing desire for healthier food choices. Companies are responding by providing products that emphasize nutritional quality, organic components, and clear labeling. There is a growing emphasis on sustainable methods within the food sector. Shoppers are more likely to support brands that engage in ethical sourcing, eco-friendly production practices, and minimal packaging, which not only aids the environment but also aligns with a health-conscious lifestyle. With advancements in technology and data analysis, brands can now offer tailored dietary suggestions and custom food items. This addresses individual health requirements and tastes, further merging the lines between wellness and mainstream food products. Acknowledging the significance of mental health, numerous brands are including ingredients recognized for enhancing mood and cognitive function, appealing to consumers who desire food that contributes to mental well-being. Trends such as plant-based eating, functional foods, and alternative proteins are gaining popularity. These movements not only attract attention but also resonate with a rising group of consumers who emphasize wellness and ethical aspects in their dietary choices.

Social media platforms like Instagram and TikTok play a significant role in shaping consumer preferences. Healthy meal suggestions, wellness movements, and product reviews are going viral, swaying consumer behavior toward brands that promote healthy living. The effect on consumer habits is significant. Shoppers are increasingly looking for transparency in ingredients and sourcing, and they are prepared to spend more on products they consider healthier, or more sustainable. Furthermore, this change motivates brands to continuously innovate, fostering a competitive market that ultimately provides consumers with more options that meet their wellness requirements.

Notable emerging trends encompass personalized nutrition, lab-grown meat, and the incorporation of Industry 4.0 technologies, which together promise to transform food production, processing, and consumption. These trends enhance efficiency while tackling sustainability issues, thereby shaping the future of the food industry. In response to the changing consumer landscape, retailers and manufacturers are increasingly incorporating health and wellness into their product lines and marketing strategies. This change is fueled by a rising consumer interest in nutrition and preventive health care, which urges businesses to reassess their offerings and engagement strategies. To encourage the use of health-oriented products, marketers, legislators, and public health experts must have a thorough understanding of these elements.

Healthier and environment friendly food choices often come with a higher price tag. This can create accessibility issues for certain consumers, especially within lower-income groups, leading to a gap between those who can afford wellness products and those who cannot. Misleading information regarding nutrition and wellness can contribute to confusion among consumers. Some individuals may not fully grasp the advantages of particular products or may doubt marketing assertions, resulting in hesitance to trust brands that focus on wellness. The food sector is subject to strict regulations, and the intricacies of food safety, labeling standards, and health claims can be overwhelming for businesses. These regulations can hinder innovation and complicate the launch of new wellness products. Acquiring high-quality, organic, or sustainably sourced ingredients can be a daunting task. Variations in availability, pricing, and quality can impede a company's capacity to reliably offer wellness-oriented products. Dietary choices and cultural eating practices differ greatly. Companies might find it challenging to cater to the diverse wellness needs and preferences of all consumer segments, limiting the broader acceptance of wellness-focused products. The increasing interest in wellness has resulted in a surge of options for consumers. In such a saturated market, it can be challenging for businesses to set their products apart, which complicates the establishment of a strong brand identity centered on wellness.

Numerous companies tend to prioritize immediate financial gains over long-term commitments to wellness efforts. This short-sighted approach can discourage companies from wholeheartedly investing in the creation of healthier or more sustainable offerings. Consumer preferences can change quickly, making it hard for businesses to stay current. What qualifies as “wellness” today might not connect with consumers tomorrow, leading to potential financial setbacks for companies that fail to adapt swiftly. Through tackling obstacles like exorbitant costs, ignorance, and restricted accessibility, interested parties can establish a setting that encourages better food selections and sustainable consumption habits. On the other hand, while incorporating health and wellness into retail strategies can be advantageous, some consumers might view these initiatives as marketing ploys instead of authentic health enhancements. This doubt can undermine the effectiveness of health-focused marketing initiatives, indicating a necessity for transparency and genuine communication. After all, the businesses which can successfully convey the health advantages of their goods while preserving customer confidence will be well-positioned to thrive in this competitive market.

REFERENCES

Alam, M. W., Kumar, J. V., Awad, M., Saravanan, P., Al-Sowayan, N. S., Rosaiah, P., & Nivetha, M. S. (2025). Emerging Trends in Food Process Engineering: Integrating Sensing Technologies for Health, Sustainability, and Consumer Preferences. *Journal of Food Process Engineering*, *48*(1), e70035. Advance online publication. DOI: 10.1111/jfpe.70035

Ali, T., & Ali, J. (2020). Factors affecting the consumers' willingness to pay for health and wellness food products. *Journal of Agriculture and Food Research*, *2*, 100076. DOI: 10.1016/j.jafr.2020.100076

Ares, G., Natero, V., Gugliucci, V., Machín, L., Alcaire, F., de León, C., & Otterbring, T. (2023). Health-Washing of Ultraprocessed Products on Instagram: Prevalence and Strategies in an Emerging Market. *Journal of Nutrition Education and Behavior*, *55*(11), 815–822. DOI: 10.1016/j.jneb.2023.09.001 PMID: 37777932

Arı, E., & Yılmaz, V. (2024). *The effects of social media and influencers on consumers' attitudes and purchasing towards organic foods*. Erciyes Üniversitesi İktisadi ve İdari Bilimler Fakültesi Dergisi., DOI: 10.18070/erciyesiibd.1496826

Ariestiningsih, E. S., Syarifah Has, D. F., Suprapti, S., Herawati, A., & Latief, T. S. S. (2023). *Analysis of factors affecting the purchase decision of healthyfood*. Firm Journal of Management Studies., DOI: 10.33021/firm.v8i2.4645

Ayeni, O., & Olagoke-Komolafe, O. E. (2024). *Advancing food safety standards through technology integration and policy development. 2*(1), 035–046. DOI: 10.57219/crrms.2024.2.1.0039

Badr, S. (2022). Re-Imagining Wellness in the Age of Neoliberalism. *New Sociology*, *3*. Advance online publication. DOI: 10.25071/2563-3694.66

Baicu, A. A. (2022). *Regulating emerging food trends.*, DOI: 10.1016/B978-0-12-816011-4.00014-8

Baş, M., Kahriman, M., Çakir Biçer, N., & Seçkiner, S. (2024). Results from Türkiye: Which Factors Drive Consumers to Buy Organic Food? *Foods*, *13*(2), 302. Advance online publication. DOI: 10.3390/foods13020302 PMID: 38254603

Batat, W. (2024). *Identifying the forms of digital food advertising content and their effects on food well-being in the phygital age*. 231–243. DOI: 10.4324/9781003168485-20

Binns, N. (2009). *Session 4: Challenges facing the food industry in innovating for health Regulatory challenges and opportunities for food innovation. 68*(1), 1–10. DOI: 10.1017/S0029665108008860

Bloemhof, J. M., & van der Vorst, J. G. A. J. (2014). *Sustainable Food Supply Chain Networks*. 99–122. https://www.narcis.nl/publication/RecordID/oai%3Alibrary.wur.nl%3Awurpubs%2F452916

Bogue, J., & Sorenson, D. (2009). *Strategic marketing of gluten-free cereal products and beverages* (pp. 149–158). American Association of Cereal Chemists, Inc (AACC). https://doi.org/DOI: 10.1016/B978-1-891127-67-0.50019-4

Bogue, J., & Troy, A. J. (2016). *Functional Beverages: Market Trends and Market-Oriented New Product Designs*. Routledge Handbooks Online., DOI: 10.1201/b19490-3

Boinwad, D. L., & Shinde, P. R.Dr. Dilipkumar L. BoinwadProf. Rajesh S. Shinde. (2024). Health and Wellness Food Products : A Retailers' Perspective. *International Journal of Scientific Research in Science and Technology, 11*(3), 202–216. DOI: 10.32628/IJSRST2411313

Burch, D., & Lawrence, G. (2010). *The "wellness" phenomenon: implications for global agri-food systems*. Earthscan., DOI: 10.4324/9781849774499

Cammarelle, A., Viscecchia, R., De Devitiis, B., Panniello, U., & Gorgoglione, M. (2024). Consumers' Behavior Toward Healthy Foods: A Critical Review. *Food Reviews International*, •••, 1–18. DOI: 10.1080/87559129.2024.2432927

Cardenas, D., & Fuchs-Tarlovsky, V. (2018). Is multi-level marketing of nutrition supplements a legal and an ethical practice? *Clinical Nutrition ESPEN, 25*, 133–138. DOI: 10.1016/j.clnesp.2018.03.118 PMID: 29779808

Chala, D. B., & Emire, S. A. (2022). *Development of plant based functional food products: a review. 46*(1), 169–183. DOI: 10.35219/foodtechnology.2022.1.13

Chandon, P., & Cadario, R. (2022). Healthy in the wrong way: Mismatching of marketers' food claim use and consumers' preferences in the United States but not France. *Journal of the Academy of Marketing Science, 51*(1), 153–173. DOI: 10.1007/s11747-022-00885-4

Chandon, P., Haws, K. L., & Liu, P. J. (2022). Paths to healthier eating: Perceptions and interventions for success. *Journal of the Association for Consumer Research, 7*(4), 383–392. DOI: 10.1086/721842

Chartrand, M.-E., Bélisle, D., Patry-Beaudoin, G., & Cheikhrouhou, S. (2024). The retail wellnesscape: Conceptualizing consumer wellness in a health food retailing context. *Qualitative Market Research, 27*(4), 631–649. Advance online publication. DOI: 10.1108/QMR-09-2023-0127

Cordner, A., Brown, P., & Morello-Frosch, R. (2014). *Health Social Movements*. DOI: 10.1002/9781118410868.wbehibs441

Cuevas, S., Patel, N., Patel, N., Thompson, C., Petticrew, M., Cummins, S., Smith, R. D., & Cornelsen, L. (2021). Escaping the Red Queen: Health as a corporate food marketing strategy. *SSM - Population Health, 16*, 100953. DOI: 10.1016/j.ssmph.2021.100953 PMID: 34815996

Cunningham, M., Azcarate-Peril, M. A., Barnard, A., Benoit, V., Grimaldi, R., Guyonnet, D., & Gibson, G. R. (2021). Shaping the future of probiotics and prebiotics. *Trends in Microbiology, 29*(8), 667–685. DOI: 10.1016/j.tim.2021.01.003 PMID: 33551269

Davies, C., & Mann, A. (2023). Factors influencing women to accept diet and exercise messages on social media during COVID-19 lockdowns: A qualitative application of the health belief model. *Health Marketing Quarterly, 40*(4), 1–19. DOI: 10.1080/07359683.2023.2193076 PMID: 37021625

Derkatch, C. (2023). *Why Wellness Sells: Natural Health in a Pharmaceutical Culture*. DOI: 10.32920/24660234.v1

Desclee, D., Sohinto, D., & Padonou, F. (2021). Sustainability Assessment and Agricultural Supply Chains Evidence-Based Multidimensional Analyses as Tools for Strategic Decision-Making—The Case of the Pineapple Supply Chain in Benin. *Sustainability (Basel), 13*(4), 2060. DOI: 10.3390/su13042060

Deshmukh, V., & Gutte, R. K. (2024). Sustainable Health and Functional Foods. In *The Contribution of Universities Towards Education for Sustainable Development* (pp. 439–451). Springer Nature Switzerland. DOI: 10.1007/978-3-031-49853-4_25

Donner, M., & de Vries, H. (2023). Business models for sustainable food systems: A typology based on a literature review. *Frontiers in Sustainable Food Systems, 7*, 1160097. Advance online publication. DOI: 10.3389/fsufs.2023.1160097

Draper, D. A., Tynan, A., & Christianson, J. B. (2008). Health and wellness: the shift from managing illness to promoting health. *Information and Communication Technologies in Tourism*, 1–4. https://europepmc.org/article/MED/18536150

Dubé, L., Soman, D., & Almeida, F. (2021). *Precision Retailing: Building Upon Design Thinking for Societal-Scale Food Convergence Innovation and Well-Being*. Springer., DOI: 10.1007/978-3-030-54296-2_14

Duus, K. S., Tjørnhøj-Thomsen, T., & Krølner, R. F. (2025). Negotiating healthy food retail initiatives in the research project Healthier Choices in Supermarkets: An ethnographic study of a partnership between health intervention researchers, food retailers, and public health advocates. *BMC Public Health*, *25*(1), 1433. DOI: 10.1186/s12889-025-22633-3 PMID: 40241000

Early, R. (2002). Food ethics: A decision making tool for the food industry? *International Journal of Food Science & Technology*, *37*(4), 339–349. DOI: 10.1046/j.1365-2621.2002.00547.x

Firoozzare, A., Boccia, F., Yousefian, N., Ghazanfari, S., & Pakook, S. (2024). Understanding the role of awareness and trust in consumer purchase decisions for healthy food and products. *Food Quality and Preference*, *121*, 105275. DOI: 10.1016/j.foodqual.2024.105275

Fitricia, G. M., Putri, P. L., Slamet, S., Yuttama, F. R., & Alfizi, A. (2025). Managerial strategies in developing healthy food product: Integrating aspect of health and food science for competitive advantage. *BIO Web of Conferences*, *152*, 01016. DOI: 10.1051/bioconf/202515201016

Franceschelli, M. V., Santoro, G., & Candelo, E. (2018). Business model innovation for sustainability: A food start-up case study. *British Food Journal*, *120*(10), 2483–2494. DOI: 10.1108/BFJ-01-2018-0049

Freedhoff, Y. (2014). The food industry is neither friend, nor foe, nor partner. *Obesity Reviews*, *15*(1), 6–8. DOI: 10.1111/obr.12128 PMID: 24330345

Freeman, B., & Sindall, C. (2019). Countering the commercial determinants of health: Strategic challenges for public health. *Public Health Research & Practice*, *29*(3), e2931917. Advance online publication. DOI: 10.17061/phrp2931917 PMID: 31569200

Ghazanfari, S., Firoozzare, A., Covino, D., Boccia, F., & Palmieri, N. (2024). Exploring Factors Influencing Consumers' Willingness to Pay Healthy-Labeled Foods at a Premium Price. *Sustainability (Basel)*, *16*(16), 6895. DOI: 10.3390/su16166895

Gokce, A., Bazi, S., Safavi, B., Georgiadou, E., & Hajli, N. (2023). The role of social media content on value co-creation in the food sector: A strategic relationship perspective. *British Food Journal*, *125*(10), 3585–3600. Advance online publication. DOI: 10.1108/BFJ-09-2022-0772

Grujic, S., Grujic, R., & Grujčić, M. (2023). Factors affecting consumer preference for healthy diet and functional foods. *Foods and Raw Materials*, 259–271. DOI: 10.21603/2308-4057-2023-2-576

Gupta, A., Sanwal, N., Bareen, M. A., Barua, S., Sharma, N., Olatunji, O. J., & Sahu, J. K. (2023). Trends in functional beverages: Functional ingredients, processing technologies, stability, health benefits, and consumer perspective. *Food Research International*, *170*, 113046. DOI: 10.1016/j.foodres.2023.113046 PMID: 37316029

Gupta, N., Bhattacharjee, M., & Saha, A. R. (2023). Association Between Socio-demographic Factors and the Health Orientation of Urban Consumers Toward the Consumption of High-Value Agricultural Products in India. *Arthshastra Indian Journal of Economics & Research*, *12*(4), 8–24. DOI: 10.17010/aijer/2023/v12i4/172814

Guru, S., Thanki, S. J., & Thakkar, J. J. (2024). *Analysing Factors Driving Purchase and Consumption Behaviour Towards Organic Food*. DOI: 10.1177/09722629231225535

Hanus, G. (2018). Food market innovations as a response to consumer requirements: A review of literature. *Optimum. Economic Studies*, *91*(1), 251–264.

Hassoun, A., Bekhit, A. E.-D. A., Jambrak, A. R., Regenstein, J. M., Chemat, F., Morton, J. D., Gudjónsdóttir, M., Carpena, M., Prieto, M. A., Varela, P., Arshad, R. N., Aadil, R. M., Bhat, Z. F., & Ueland, Ø. (2022). The fourth industrial revolution in the food industry-part II: Emerging food trends. *Critical Reviews in Food Science and Nutrition*, •••, 1–31. DOI: 10.1080/10408398.2022.2106472 PMID: 35930319

Hobbs, J. E., Malla, S., Sogah, E. K., & Yeung, M. T. (n.d.). *Through the Looking Glass*. DOI: 10.4337/9781783474721.00014

Hood, M. M., Kapoor, V., Sawhney, G., & Singh, H. (2024). India's Vision of a Healthy and Developed Nation from the Perspective of the Healthtech Industry. *India's Vision of a Healthy and Developed Nation from the Perspective of the Healthtech Industry.*, *12*(8), 127–132. DOI: 10.35629/3002-1208127132

Huang, B. (2020). *Research on the Optimization Path of Supply side Structural Reform of Fitness and Leisure Industry under the Background of National Fitness*. https://doi.org/DOI: 10.23977/IEESASM.2019.053

Huang, Z., Zhu, Y., Deng, J., & Wang, C. (2022). Marketing Healthy Diets: The Impact of Health Consciousness on Chinese Consumers' Food Choices. *Sustainability (Basel)*, *14*(4), 2059. DOI: 10.3390/su14042059

Inguglia, E. S., Song, Z., Kerry, J. P., O'Sullivan, M. G., & Hamill, R. M. (2023). Addressing Clean Label Trends in Commercial Meat Processing: Strategies, Challenges and Insights from Consumer Perspectives. *Foods*, *12*(10), 2062. DOI: 10.3390/foods12102062 PMID: 37238880

Jadhav, H. B., Sablani, S. S., Gogate, P. R., Annapure, U. S., Casanova, F., Nayik, G. A., Alaskar, K., Sarwar, N., Raina, I., Ramniwas, S., & Mousavi Khaneghah, A. (2023). Factors governing consumers buying behavior concerning nutraceutical product. *Food Science & Nutrition*, *11*(9), 4988–5003. Advance online publication. DOI: 10.1002/fsn3.3518 PMID: 37701202

Karpyn, A., McCallops, K., Wolgast, H., & Glanz, K. (2020). Improving Consumption and Purchases of Healthier Foods in Retail Environments: A Systematic Review. *International Journal of Environmental Research and Public Health*, *17*(20), 7524. DOI: 10.3390/ijerph17207524 PMID: 33081130

Kasapoğlu, K. N., Daskaya-Dikmen, C., Yavuz-Düzgün, M., Karaca, A. C., & Özçelik, B. (2019). *Enrichment of Beverages With Health Beneficial Ingredients*. Academic Press., DOI: 10.1016/B978-0-12-816687-1.00003-5

Kaur, M., Singh, R., Singh, M., & Singh, K. (2023). Can health consciousness drive purchase intention toward packaged immunity boosting food products? *Journal of Foodservice Business Research*, •••, 1–22. DOI: 10.1080/15378020.2023.2298614

Kinsey, J. D., & Buhr, B. L. (2003). E-commerce: a new business model for the food supply/demand chain. *The IUP Journal of Agricultural Economics, 1*(1), 31–47. DOI: 10.22004/AG.ECON.14320

Kusdiyanto, K., Saputro, E. P., Sholahuddin, M., Mabruroh, M., Irawati, Z., Murwanti, S., & Setyaningrum, D. P. (2022). *Identification of intention to buy healthy food*. *5*(1), 32–41. DOI: 10.21744/ijbem.v5n1.1867

Langyan, S., Yadava, P., Khan, F. N., Dar, Z. A., Singh, R., & Kumar, A. (2022). Sustaining Protein Nutrition Through Plant-Based Foods. *Frontiers in Nutrition*, *8*, 772573. Advance online publication. DOI: 10.3389/fnut.2021.772573 PMID: 35118103

Lee, R. C. (2012). A Strategic Thinking on Multi-Level Business Development in Wellness Foods. *American Journal of Industrial and Business Management*, *2*(3), 95–101. DOI: 10.4236/ajibm.2012.23013

Leib, M. E. (2013). The Forgotten Half of Food System Reform: Using Food and Agricultural Law to Foster Healthy Food Production. *Social Science Research Network*. https://doi.org/DOI: 10.2139/SSRN.2343264

Liu, J., Wu, H., & Zhou, Z. (2024). The Future of Food Health-Focused Brands in the Fast-Food Industry Based on the Analysis of Chipotle. *Advances in Economics. Management and Political Sciences*, *115*(1), 52–58. DOI: 10.54254/2754-1169/115/2024BJ0200

Maurya, N. K. (2024a). The Impact of Technology on Food Product Development. *Nutrition and Food Processing, 07*(12), 01–06. DOI: 10.31579/2637-8914/262

Maurya, N. K. (2024b). Regulating Innovation: A Review of Product Development and Regulatory Frameworks in the Food Industry. *Nutrition and Food Processing, 07*(15), 01–08. DOI: 10.31579/2637-8914/276

McMahon, A.-T., Williams, P., & Tapsell, L. C. (2010). Reviewing the meanings of wellness and well-being and their implications for food choice. *Perspectives in Public Health*, *130*(6), 282–286. DOI: 10.1177/1757913910384046 PMID: 21213565

Mialon, M. (2024). The Food industry barrier to achieving the SDGs. *European Journal of Public Health*, *34*(Supplement_3), ckae144.422. Advance online publication. DOI: 10.1093/eurpub/ckae144.422

Mukty, M. I., & Pulubuhu, D. (2023). Strategi Pengembangan Produk Sehat Dalam Bisnis Wirausaha Makanan. *Deleted Journal*, *1*(2), 55–60. DOI: 10.57213/tjghpsr.v1i2.255

Ndlovu, S. G. (2024). Private label brands vs national brands: New battle fronts and future competition. *Cogent Business & Management*, *11*(1), 2321877. DOI: 10.1080/23311975.2024.2321877

Nestle, M. (2022). Regulating the Food Industry: An Aspirational Agenda. *American Journal of Public Health*, *112*(6), 1–e6. DOI: 10.2105/AJPH.2022.306844 PMID: 35446606

Nielsen, K. E. (2016). *Health beneficial consumer products—status and trends.* Woodhead Publishing., DOI: 10.1016/B978-0-08-100329-9.00002-5

Olsen, O., Hari, A. R., & Rival, Y. (2023). Healthy Snacks: Multimodal Critical Discourse Analysis of Traditional Food Brand Corporate Storytelling. *Journal of Pragmatics and Discourse Research*, *3*(1), 19–27. DOI: 10.51817/jpdr.v3i1.322

Osunsanmi, A. S., Ayandibu, A. O., & Heeralal, S. (2024). Assessing the factors that influence consumer's purchase behaviour towards functional foods. *International Journal of Research In Business and Social Science*. DOI: 10.20525/ijrbs.v13i2.3192

Pergher, G., Marçal Vieira Vaz, R. G., & Werner, M. C. (2024). *Content evaluation of instagram posts related to food and health produced by digital influencers.* DOI: 10.56238/sevened2024.037-039

Pilař, L., Kvasničková Stanislavská, L., Kvasnička, R., Hartman, R., & Tichá, I. (2021). Healthy Food on Instagram Social Network: Vegan, Homemade and Clean Eating. *Nutrients*, *13*(6), 1991. DOI: 10.3390/nu13061991 PMID: 34207910

Pistorio, E., Chinnici, G., Zarba, C., Bellia, C., & Pappalardo, G. (2023). *The revolution of functional food: a market analysis (the functional foods market revolution: market analysis of functional food).* DOI: 10.5593/sgem2023V/6.2/s25.53

Pitelis, C. N. (1998). Productivity, Competitiveness and Convergence in the European Economy: Supply-Side Considerations. *Social Science Research Network.* https://papers.ssrn.com/sol3/papers.cfm?abstract_id=811284

Plank, R. E., & Gould, S. J. (1990). Health Consciousness, Scientific Orientation and Wellness. *Health Marketing Quarterly*, *7*(3-4), 65–82. DOI: 10.1300/J026v07n03_06

Ramesh, S. (2022). *The Commerce of Wellness: Integrating Healthcare Treatments into Business Models.* Journal Healthcare Treatment Development., DOI: 10.55529/jhtd.21.7.12

Riccardi, B. (2022). The Added Value of Technology in Food Integration - Holistic Approach. *Nutrition and Food Processing, 5*(4), 01–09. DOI: 10.31579/2637-8914/105

Rooney, P. R. (2012). *Measuring the Impact of a Comprehensive Health and Wellness Initiative.* https://scholarship.claremont.edu/cgi/viewcontent.cgi?article=1426&context=cmc_theses

Roy, B., Hagappa, A., Ramalingam, Y. D., & Mahalingam, N. (2021). A review on lab-grown meat: Advantages and disadvantages. *Quest International Journal of Medical and Health Sciences*, *4*(1), 19–24.

Scheiber, R., Diehl, S., & Karmasin, M. (2023). Analysing the Effects of Social Media Influencers' Food-related Posts on Healthy Eating Intentions, Orthorectic Eating Tendencies, Product Attitudes, and Purchase Intentions. *Medien Journal*, *46*(3), 47–64. DOI: 10.24989/medienjournal.v46i3.2193

Silchenko, K., & Askegaard, S. (2021). Powered by healthism? Marketing discourses of food and health. *European Journal of Marketing*, *55*(1), 133–161. DOI: 10.1108/EJM-04-2018-0296

Skonberg, C., & Thorbecke, M. (2022). *Applying environmental models in the food business context.*, DOI: 10.1016/B978-0-12-822112-9.00009-6

Subramanian, L. (2020). *Enabling health supply chains for improved well-being. 21*(4), 229–236. DOI: 10.1080/16258312.2020.1776091

Tallon, M. J., & Kalman, D. S. (2024). The Regulatory Challenges of Placing Dietary Ingredients on the European and US Market. *Journal of Dietary Supplements*, •••, 1–16. DOI: 10.1080/19390211.2024.2308261 PMID: 38269549

Torres, E. G., Fonseca-Larios, R., & Ramírez-Portilla, A. (2024). *Innovating R&D practices to adapt swiftly to market trends: Insights from the Food and Beverage Industry*. DOI: 10.5772/intechopen.1006672

Valluri, M. (2022). The Future of Food: Trends and Innovations. *International Journal For Multidisciplinary Research*, *4*(2), 6188. Advance online publication. DOI: 10.36948/ijfmr.2022.v04i02.6188

Varzakas, T., & Antoniadou, M. (2024). A Holistic Approach for Ethics and Sustainability in the Food Chain: The Gateway to Oral and Systemic Health. *Foods*, *13*(8), 1224. Advance online publication. DOI: 10.3390/foods13081224 PMID: 38672896

Veliah, G. K., & Venkatsubramanian, P. (2024). Promoting Wellness as a Primordial Prevention Strategy for Achieving Sustainable Public Health in the Post-Covid 19 Era. *American Journal of Lifestyle Medicine*, *18*(4), 608–611. Advance online publication. DOI: 10.1177/15598276241240414 PMID: 39262891

Viroli, G., Kalmpourtzidou, A., & Cena, H. (2023). Exploring Benefits and Barriers of Plant-Based Diets: Health, Environmental Impact, Food Accessibility and Acceptability. *Nutrients*, *15*(22), 4723. DOI: 10.3390/nu15224723 PMID: 38004117

Vukadinović, S. (2022). *Selling Wellness: An Analysis Of Goop And Poosh's Visual Marketing On Instagram*. DOI: 10.32920/19154462.v1

Wadhwa, C. L., Thakker, H., Kaushik, V., Manjunath, H. R., Goyal, S., Thakkar, A., & Grover, M. (2024). Study on Assessing the Evolution of Nutritional Choices through Social Media Influence. *Evolutionary Studies in Imaginative Culture*, •••, 860–869. DOI: 10.70082/esiculture.vi.1084

Wansink, B. (2017). Healthy profits: An Interdisciplinary Retail Framework for Increasing the Sales of Healthy Foods. *The FASEB Journal*, *31*(S1). Advance online publication. DOI: 10.1096/fasebj.31.1_supplement.636.6

Wiedenroth, C. F., & Otter, V. (2022). Can new healthy luxury food products accelerate short food supply chain formation via social media marketing in high-income countries? *Agricultural and Food Economics*, *10*(1), 31. Advance online publication. DOI: 10.1186/s40100-022-00238-3 PMID: 36530963

Wongprawmas, R., Sogari, G., Menozzi, D., & Mora, C. (2022). Strategies to promote healthy eating among university students: A qualitative study using the nominal group technique. *Frontiers in Nutrition*, *9*, 821016. DOI: 10.3389/fnut.2022.821016 PMID: 35187039

Wu, Y. C., Kemps, E., & Prichard, I. (2023). Digging into digital buffets: A systematic review of eating-related social media content and its relationship with body image and eating behaviours. *Body Image*, *48*, 101650. DOI: 10.1016/j.bodyim.2023.101650 PMID: 38039952

Yahn, G. (1979). The Impact of Holistic Medicine, Medical Groups, and Health Concepts. *Journal of the American Medical Association*, *242*(20), 2202–2205. DOI: 10.1001/jama.1979.03300200032018 PMID: 490807

Yeoman, I., & McMahon-Beattie, U. (2024). Signals of change: Eating trends shaping the future of food service. *Research in Hospitality Management*, *14*(2), 104–111. DOI: 10.1080/22243534.2024.2361395

Yu, M., & Watson, S. (2024). Market overview of health and wellness food products. In *Flavor-Associated Applications in Health and Wellness Food Products* (pp. 3–19). Springer International Publishing., DOI: 10.1007/978-3-031-51808-9_1

Zorbas, C., Blake, M. R., Brown, A. D., Peeters, A., Allender, S., Brimblecombe, J., & Boelsen-Robinson, T. (2024). A systems framework for implementing healthy food retail in grocery settings. *BMC Public Health*, *24*(1), 137. DOI: 10.1186/s12889-023-17075-8 PMID: 38195419

ADDITIONAL READING

Gacoska, K. J. (2024). Managing Innovation Through a Business Model in the Food Industry. *International Journal of Research Publication and Reviews*, *5*(5), 4382–4386. DOI: 10.55248/gengpi.5.0524.1245

Kinchla, A. (2023). Increasing Food Safety Preparedness of Small and Emerging Food Businesses with Targeted Food Safety Training. *Food Protection Trends*, •••, 292–303. DOI: 10.4315/FPT-22-031

Omar, I. A., Hasan, H. R., Jayaraman, R., Salah, K., & Omar, M. (2024). Using blockchain technology to achieve sustainability in the hospitality industry by reducing food waste. *Computers & Industrial Engineering*, *197*, 110586. DOI: 10.1016/j.cie.2024.110586

Saha, D., Padhiary, M., & Chandrakar, N. (2025). AI vision and machine learning for enhanced automation in food industry: A systematic review. *Food and Humanity*, *4*, 100587. DOI: 10.1016/j.foohum.2025.100587

Schorung, M. (2024). Quick commerce and the evolving business models of the food retail industry - Investigating the quick commerce supply chain and the urban impacts of dark stores. *Transportation Research Procedia*, *79*, 305–312. DOI: 10.1016/j.trpro.2024.03.041

Spagnoli, P., Vlerick, P., Pareyn, K., Foubert, P., & Jacxsens, L. (2025). Portfolio of interventions to mature human organizational dimensions of food safety culture in food businesses. *Food Control*, *168*, 110937. DOI: 10.1016/j.foodcont.2024.110937

Uttama, N. P. (2021). Open Innovation and Business Model of Health Food Industry in Asia. *Journal of Open Innovation*, *7*(3), 174. DOI: 10.3390/joitmc7030174

Yang, R., Liu, J., Cao, S., Sun, W., & Kong, F. (2024). Impacts of agri-food e-commerce on traditional wholesale industry: Evidence from China. *Journal of Integrative Agriculture*, *23*(4), 1409–1428. DOI: 10.1016/j.jia.2023.10.020

KEY TERMS AND DEFINITIONS

Agri-food supply chains: The procedures that explain how food from a farm makes it to the table are referred to as the agri-food supply chain as well as agri-food system. Production, preparation, transportation, advertising, consumption, and disposal are some of the processes involved in the agri-food supply chain (Desclee et al., 2021).

Clean eating: A modern dietary strategy known as "clean eating" goes beyond simply eating; it is a holistic philosophy focused on choosing whole, least processed foods while deliberately reducing consumption of synthetic additives, processed sugars, and harmful fats. This method promotes switching to simpler, less processed components that replenish the body and enhance general well-being by highlighting the intrinsic nutritional content of foods in their purest form (Inguglia et al., 2023).

Functional beverages: Functional beverages, which frequently contain additives meant to boost particular body functions or enhance general well-being, are drinks that offer health advantages beyond simple nourishment. Additional functional components, such as minerals, vitamins, probiotics, dietary fiber, herbs, or bioactive substances, are added to these beverages to address health concerns or improve specific mental or physical processes (Gupta et al., 2023).

Health washing: The term "health washing" is the practice of portraying a brand, product, or service as healthier than what it actually is, in order to profit on consumers' growing health consciousness. By appealing to the demand for healthier habits with deceptive terminology, labeling, or imagery, this type of marketing or promotion provides the appearance of healthiness without actually offering any health advantages (Ares et al., 2023).

Lab-grown meats: Meat products which are made by growing cells from livestock in a lab environment as opposed to rearing and killing animals are referred to as lab-grown meats, cultured meats, or cell-based meats. In order to create muscle tissue that mimics regular meat, a little sample of animal cells, typically from muscle tissue are taken, grown, and multiplied in a nutrient-rich environment (Roy et al., 2021).

Multi-Level Marketing (MLM): Businesses use a network of autonomous distributors to sell goods and services as part of the multi-level marketing (MLM) strategy. In addition to their own sales, these distributors often profit from sales made by new hires they bring on board. Essentially, the term "multi-level" describes an organizational framework that grows, as distributors add new members to the network, creating several tiers or levels (Cardenas & Fuchs-Tarlovsky, 2018).

Plant-based diets: Fundamentally, plant-based diets are dietary practices that prioritize eating foods that are primarily derived from plants. They include a variety of eating patterns that place an emphasis on fruits, legumes, vegetables, nuts, and whole grains (Langyan et al., 2022). These diets are becoming more popular due to their favorable effects on environmental sustainability as well as possible health benefits, making a strong case for a change in dietary standards (Viroli et al., 2023).

Wellness-oriented products: With an emphasis on preserving mental, physical, and emotional equilibrium, wellness-oriented items are made to improve a person's general health, well-being, and way of life. Generally speaking, these goods support healthy lifestyle choices, encourage improved health outcomes, and complement an all-encompassing approach to wellness (Kapseon et al., 2025).

Chapter 15
Flavoring Social Bonds and HR Practices:
The Influence of Food Culture on Consumer Behavior and Brand Engagement in Marketing Strategies

Amit Kumar Pandey
http://orcid.org/0000-0001-5767-6333
Institute of Management Studies, Ghaziabad, India

Vijit Chaturvedi
http://orcid.org/0000-0001-6757-1340
Amity Business School, Amity University, Noida, India

Jaya Yadav
Amity Business School, Amity University, Noida, India

Prakhar Duggal
Amity School of Engineering and Technology, Amity University, Noida, India

ABSTRACT

This chapter explores the dynamics of food culture, socialisation and human resource (HR) management and how these have influenced consumer and brand relationship and engagement in marketing practices. Food serves as an extremely potent social signifier that helps establishing emotional connections between consumers and brands through culturally based shared experiences. Organizations can reinforce loyalty, inclusivity, and emotional connection, by incorporating culinary

DOI: 10.4018/979-8-3373-4047-0.ch015

traditions into marketing campaigns and HR-led brand storytelling. The paper examines the role that food-focussed events, employee engagement in food rituals, and culturally sensitive branding play in deepening consumer relations and community engagement. It also explores the role of HRM in enhancing the organizational identity and consumer-brand intimacy through food culture. This combination of disciplines provides a tasty trail map for marketers and HR folks wanting to create true, culturally grounded consumer connections.

1. INTRODUCTION

Food as a powerful social and cultural artifact as well as just a biological means of sustenance – is profoundly rooted in the human experience. From culture to culture and generation to generation, food has been at the core of how we gather, connect with one another, and revel in tradition. In today's world dominated by globalization, digital connectivity and multiculturalism in both organizational design and consumer markets, food has become an increasingly popular strategic channel used by brands and HR leaders to create emotional connections and uphold values. The following study takes a "gastro" look behind HRM, focusing on food culture, HR practices and consumer behavior, elaborating on the culinary dimension of things, which has to be acknowledged when it comes to consumer behavior and branding and marketing efforts (madesiya et al., 2024).

Food in culture and society Food is multifaceted. It represents legacy, belongingness, warmth, and acceptance. Breaking bread sharing a meal is associated with trust, comfort, and intimacy with the person across the table all of which brands can mimic with their consumers. In marketing, storytelling with food draws on these associations to create emotional brand stories that span the emotional spectrum, the senses and culture. Now, in corporate ecosystems, HR teams are beginning to understand the benefits of adding food-based rituals and diverse culinary celebrations to their 'bag of tricks.' These undermine the concept of a traditional, authoritative office in favor of a relaxed, fun, and inclusive one. This fusion of cultural sensibility with corporate and marketing strategy is a significant stepping stone from which brands now operate in a competitive landscape where emotional connectivity and experiential value takes supreme precedence (Queiroz et al., 2024).

The world of consumers is changing at a breakneck pace. Consumers today are not the consumers of yesterday--passive, receivers of brands' messages and recipes of their products; they are people who demand authentic experiences, cultural compatibility and emotional relevance with brands. It is in this regard that food becomes a shared tongue connecting generations, geographies and socio-economic strata. Promoting techniques that leverage food culture (via visual storytelling, experiential marketing, influencer partnerships or sensory brand) give special consideration as they are more likely to grab consumers' attention and to build long-term loyalty (Baranidharan et al., 2024).

The HR industry has reportedly started to add culturally-sensitive food related initiatives to employee programs as multi-ethnic potlucks, holiday parties, wellness programs with dietary considerations, etc. These endeavors not only bolster employee engagement, they mirror a brand's internal values to the outside world. As a result of coordinated internal practices and external marketing narratives, consumers can perceive more consistent and authentic brand identity, which in turn strengthens their trust and emotional attachment to the brand. And in this marriage of HR and marketing, food becomes a universal touchpoint, a powerful platform upon which to humanize a company, salute its diversity, and propagate shared values.

Digital platforms have intensified the importance of food culture to marketing. Food has turned itself into a visual and viral experience on social media. With the explosion of food influencers, recipe-sharing platforms and oversized food crazes around the world, what we eat has become incredibly visual and shareable. Brands are flexing their content creation muscles by co-creating with their consumers and employees trading food stories, recipes and rituals that celebrate roots and uphold values, culinary and corporate. Such engagement is not only empowering through participation, but also generates a sense of community and community-focussed consumers. Consumers are more likely to form stronger emotional bonds with and advocate for a brand that resonates with their values, traditions and identity through its food-related content.

There are challenges when it comes to incorporating food culture into brand and HR strategies. Cultural appropriation, exclusion of those with dietary sensitivities, and shallow tokenism can turn consumers off, eroding brand equity. For this reason, efforts which are being initiated by organizations which focus on food must come with cultural intelligence and moral sensitivity, and good faith. This paper seeks to explore the advantages of integrating food culture in HR and marketing practices but also the drawbacks and ethical implications (Chan et al., 2025). Drawing from experiences of sampling, sampling-trials, and mapping-tastescapes in food public relations, the article makes a multidisciplinary lament to the nexus between culture, economy, and community regarding how food-related tactics can culturally season kinship ties, influence consumer purchasing, and deepen brand commitment. In a society obsessed with authenticity and emotional resonance, seasoning brand and HR practice with food culture: is a rich, deep, and inclusive way of creating enduring relationships in the marketplace and in the workplace.

2. FOOD CULTURE AS A SOCIAL CONNECTOR: THE PSYCHOLOGY OF FOOD SHARING AND CULINARY TRADITIONS AS EMOTIONAL ANCHORS

Food culture has long been one of the most deep-seated and powerful social mediators in human society, working on a level far greater than the sustenance it provides, operating on an emotional, psychological, and cultural level. The sharing of food-in family meals, religious feasts, and communal festivals, over the back-yard fence or at the office kitchen-counter-is a foundational social activity, and a social act in which individuals engage on a daily basis (Sharama et al., 2024). On a psychological level, eating together fulfills a basic human need for belonging, for validation. Eating is one of the first commonalities in life, as can be seen when an infant is feeding and is dependent upon another person for food, and we carry into adulthood this connotation of food as a source of emotional support.

Psychology around food sharing has its basis in evolutions, social settings. From an evolutionary standpoint, early human life was frequently dependent on group effort to collect, prepare and distribute food. Those who contributed food were more likely to be granted acceptance and protection by the community, promoting pro-social action and exchange. This evolutionary heritage is reflected in universal customs of hospitality and the sharing of food as one of welcome, good will, and nurturing in present-day societies. Research in social psychology indicates that eating together increases both trust and cooperation, in fact even brief communal eating experiences can lead to greater empathy and understanding amongst people. Indeed, it is this very connection between food and social accord that accounts for the prominence of food in personal and professional relations-establishing situations.

2.1 Festivals, Gatherings, and Community Building

Cultural practices regarding meals further emphasize this aspect of social bonding. Festivals such as Thanksgiving in America, Diwali in India, Eid in the Middle East and Lunar New Year in East Asia include elaborate feasting and help to reaffirm cultural values, the role of family and intergenerational relationships. Every dish that is served is full of stories, meaning and memories that hold people together with their culture and communities. Transmission of culinary knowledge recipes, cooking methods, table manners serves as a form of cultural retention and family cohesion. Shared recipes that are inherited and prepared throughout generations can act as emotional scaffolding and help anchor people in a collective identity. In multicultural societies, this is not the case: people continue to practice and adapt traditional cooking as a way to connect with their heritage and to build connections between cultures (Pugra et al., 2025).

An important aspect of food culture is its emotional dimension, it is the way it enables people to deal with feelings like grief, celebration, love and stress. Comfort foods, similar to comfort blankets, may elicit positive or nostalgic emotion, and contribute to feelings of comfort, irrespective of negative psychological effects. In the same way, festive foods help create a physical memory that we associate with fun and success, injecting good feelings into communal eating. This emotional imprimatur is why food is such a potent driver of memory and feeling. Just a flavor or a scent has the power to trigger strong memories of people, places or moments, thus inextricably linking food and the emotional life. It's no accident that some of life's most meaningful moments births, weddings, reunions, goodbyes are celebrated and mourned with communal eating. This only serves to substantiate the belief that food is not just meant to be eaten; it is felt socially, emotionally, and in terms of cultural perception.

In a contemporary urban context where digital communication replaces physical communication at an accelerating pace food is one of the last remaining tactile experiences that share between different people in one physical space. Whether it's in the form of home-cooked dinners, office lunches, potlucks or food festivals, breaking bread together is a social leveler and community-builder. As video games continue to nudge their way into the digital mainstream, food will follow and bring some of world so uncomfortably close to so many gamers is already a part of the food internet (Sakdiyakorn & Chirakramont, 2024). Matching garments and food are in the same space across platforms too Instagram, TikTok where people invite each other to share food experiences and recipes, to make food for each other in the context of feeding people and caring for people and mourning people and celebrating people, creating digital communities of mutual culinary sharing of interest and emotional resonance.

The business world recognizes the relational power of food. Brands and food marketers salivate over the psychology of sharing when it comes to food, the packaging of social sharing and nostalgia for connecting with consumers emotionally. Ads that feature family dinners, family recipes dishes that are culturally tied – are meant to make you feel good. Foodservice businesses and food brands already develop experiences that act like home or heritage in order to induce emotional comfort or loyalty. In the professional context, HR practices are increasingly incorporating communal eating experiences like cultural food days, food-inclusive celebrations, and nutrition-based dining initiatives to create a greater sense of belonging and inclusiveness among employees (Quang et al., 2025).

Food culture is a universal, all-inclusive language living beyond spoken dialects, political borders and generational separations. Food as a social unifier, then, is shared meaning, emotion memory, cultural persistence. Its distinct power to cultivate emotional and social connections between people has a profound impact on cultural expression, as well as on the health of an organization and the relationships between brands and the consumers they serve. Noticing and leveraging the emotional psychology of food sharing and culinary tradition can therefore yield compelling tactics for strengthening social bonds, forging deeper connections among people, and fostering enduring relationships in personal, professional and consumer settings (Ali & Santos, 2025).

3. HUMAN RESOURCE PRACTICES AND FOOD-BASED ENGAGEMENT

The role of food as a tool to drive engagement, inclusivity and employee wellness is fast gaining rapid acceptance in the evolving context of workplace culture and HR practices. Food-centric engagement tactics go beyond the usual rewards, providing a culturally relevant way to connect and engage and a powerful emotionally loaded way to connect on a human level and convey corporate values (Putra et al., 2023). With inclusive potluck lunches and multicultural food days to wellness-driven nutrition programs and celebratory feasts during festivals, food becomes the glue that brings people together, helping make the workplace a human place and fostering a sense of belonging. This is in line with the psychological evidence that having meals together can increase trust, cooperation and communication key factors of successful team dynamics and a healthy company culture. Utilizing these insights, HR departments at companies across the world are working to build social connections between employees, reduce work stress, and create environments that are inclusive and representative of different cultures (Sulis et al., 2024).

HR party involvement like food-based initiatives makes for a strategic HR move in terms of DEI. By hosting cultural festivals and serving traditional dishes, organizations can recognize the cultural identities of employees from different backgrounds who can then share their culture with their coworkers. This respect for culinary variety is not only a morale booster, but also encourages cross-cultural understanding and education in the workplace. For instance, marking Diwali with Indian sweets, they serve as soft skill trainings in cultural intelligence that help the organization become more agile and more global.

Some HR departments are taking a cue from universities and including nutrition counselling services, healthy café options, or hands-on cooking seminars in their wellness programs. These efforts complement models of overall well-being, emphasizing physical health in the same way as emotional and social well-being. Providing customized dietary options, such as vegan, gluten-free, or halal, sends the message to employees that you care about what matters to them and that everyone is welcome, which helps inspire loyalty and build trust. Food-related HR practices are not simply used as a way to show a friendly gesture of hospitality they're strategic tools for creating a compassionate, engaged and high-performing corporate culture. They demonstrate the company's values, foster real relationships, and continue to inhabit internal branding by sharing in the empathy and community so often extend to our consumer customers. By infusing HR policies with food-based experiences, companies enable a more emotionally intelligent and culturally rich workplace.

4. MARKETING STRATEGIES LEVERAGING FOOD CULTURE

In today's marketing landscape, food culture has become a potent force of consumer influence, experience and self-identity a rich and vibrant canvas for marketers to tell engaging stories, create value and connect emotionally. Place food culture at the heart of marketing strategies, and unlock the power of your brand beyond rational, functional selling propositions to something ventilating social, emotional, and cultural values deeply rooted in the social sharing of food (Khamoushi, 2024). Whether it's about eating on the street or indulgent presentations and global culinary fusions, food is never food for thought but a moving symbolism of a rich, culturally rooted lifestyle, authenticity and belonging. That's why you can not only find food and beverage companies employing food-themed campaigns to reach a wide array of consumers but also other industries such as hospitality, fast fashion, entertainment, and even technology firms. These approaches are often fueled by cultural nostalgia and lore, a dedication to sensorial pleasures and experiential marketing, with food serving as a driver for emotional connection and brand fidelity.

The idea behind these strategies is that food is a common language that triggers memory, emotion and a sense of home. Advertising campaigns that are rooted in regional cuisines, ancestral recipes, and seasonal culinary traditions are generally more successful at creating an immediate emotional connection with consumers. Brands have all famously localized their products to local palates and cultural celebrations serving up spicy paneer burgers in India, for instance, or teriyaki-flavored items in Japan in an effort to appear more relevant and authentic. Such elisions are not only about taste, but rather integrate the branding into the socio-cultural landscape of their communities (Sriram, 2023). Writing and reading about food helps to tell nostalgic stories of a grandmother's dish, a family dinner table, a harvest celebration all of which people can resonate with to build brand trust. This emotional connection now becomes a noteworthy tactical device for adding social context and humanising brands in a highly competitive market-place.

Broadcast and digital platforms have expanded the spread and impact of food culture in advertising. Food has become a content phenomenon, as food porn becomes ever more ubiquitous on social media and home cooks have more reasons than ever to socialize their meals around the conversation, anyway. Brands work with food influencers and chefs to co-create content that elevates the product, and the lifestyle and values it embodies. For instance, plant-based food brands invariably use sustainability, health and ethics as themes in campaigns elements that are appealing to environmentally aware millennials and Gen Z consumers. Marketers can create these communities based on shared experiences, like values or goals, so that customers turn into brand advocates.

Immersive food experiences, where dining and storytelling are combined such as themed dinners, interactive cooking classes, or augmented reality menus leave a lasting mark and a lasting relationship with the brand. These multi-dimensional marketing strategies leverage the emotional and sensory aspects of food culture to bolster brand equity, and carry consumer experiences into lifestyle categories (da Silva & Sehnem, 2025). Seasonal and holiday season marketing is also food culture's stomping grounds, relying on food cultures to stir up excitement among consumers and boost sales. Whether it's the Pumpkin Spice Latte from Starbucks at fall-time, Diwali chocolate boxes from Cadbury's, or the famous Christmas truck from Coca-Cola, delivering seasonal food items becomes a nostalgic prompt or a cultural ritual that consumers eagerly wait for. The stratagems foster a cyclical culture of consumption associated with emotional and cultural rhythms, making a product a symbol of celebration, ritual. And these days, some limited-edition collaborations snacks modeled on fan favorite TV shows or a celebrity-curated menu for once, for now make food a pop cultural currency, a boon in particular among younger consumers seeking out novelty and exclusivity.

Food-based marketing is also becoming more inclusive and representative. With global audiences becoming increasingly culturally diverse, brands are leaning into multicultural food narratives to connect with ethnically varied demographics. By catering to various culinary needs, targeting casual dining, and using bilingual messaging, you show respect for your audience's heritage while broadening your customer base. For instance, featuring African street food, Middle Eastern mezze platters or Latin American fusion dishes in mainstream marketing is an attempt at copying the diverse tapestry of global consumers palates. This is not only a way to strengthen brand relevance, but also brings about cross-cultural appreciation and brotherhood.

Food culture-based marketing draws on the emotion, culture, and sensory aspects of food and has its core purpose to maximize consumer engagement and advertising effectiveness. By incorporating these culinary elements into stories of identity, community, nostalgia, and innovation, marketers can create deeper relationships with consumers that can stand the test of time. As customers look more for meaning, authenticity and experience in their purchase decisions, food-based marketing strategies provide a well-spiced trail to relevance, trust and brand equity whether you're in the real-world or digital marketplace.

5. CONSUMER BEHAVIOR: FOOD, MEMORY, AND DECISION-MAKING

The consumption of food is greatly influenced by complex relationships that exist among food, memory, and decision-making processes, highlighting the role that affective and cognitive processes play in the development of purchase behaviors and brand choices. Food is not only a biological requirement but a symbolic one and a cultural production. It is inextricably associated with memory, identity, and consumption. When people are exposed to such food-related stimuli for example, odors, visual, or taste percepts – a chain of associative memories is triggered that can lead to an emotional response. For instance, the scent of homemade bread will remind us of a family kitchen when we were children; or perhaps, a traditional meal that may remind us of family togetherness or cultural practices. Such emotional memories shape consumer attitudes and selection, which is why food marketing represents one of the most powerful vehicles for behavior change.

Marketers cleverly exploit the memory-food link to influence their purchasing decisions. Sensory branding, which includes colors, packaging, sounds and smells, makes real impressions that affect the way people view a product without their even realizing it. Brands usually seek to implant themselves into consumers' autobiographical memories by associating their products with momentous occasions, cultural icons, or favorite memories (Maspul & Ardhin, 2025). This limited-edition holiday or childhood-flavored retro snack or seasonal flavor activates some sort of happy memory recall and impulse buying. This memory and food connection is especially strong during high-stress or emotional occasions think holidays or life changes when consumers turn to familiar foods for comfort.

The psychology of making choices also extends into our food-related routines and social lifestyles. When we choose food, most of us make heuristic decisions, or mental shortcuts, based on preferred or trusted brands and the learning from past pleasurable experience. Arousal, time pressure, or social circumstances may increase these effects and result in intuitive or habitual decisions rather than rational judgments. For example, a person might buy the same brand of coffee time and again, not only because they like the taste, but because it's a part of their morning routine, associated with feelings of normalcy and comfort.

Social influences and cultural considerations are imposing to consumers' food habits. Communal meals, peer pressure and cultural expectations often determine what and when consumers eat, supporting group identity and brand compliance. Food decision-making, then, is not just self-contained but social. In the era of the digital age with digital influence, user-generated content, influencer recommendation, and peer review influencing memory and perception the memory behavior loop is reinforced by repeated encounter and validation (Ramanayaka, 2025). The nexus of food and memory and food and decision-making reveals the emotional underpinnings of consumer behaviour. When one acknowledges this triad, he or she can create campaigns that are not just about taste but food memory, identity, and emotional fulfillment.

6. CROSS-FUNCTIONAL COLLABORATION: HR-MARKETING SYNERGY

The need for cross-functional collaboration between Human Resources (HR) and Marketing has become a strategic imperative in today's fast changing business world to drive holistic brand identity, internal engagement and organizational culture. Also traditionally thought of as two independent functional silos, HR and Marketing are finally reaching a mutual ground in business operations, by helping in cooperatively aligning employer branding with consumer facing tales, and food culture being the connecting bridge between inner authenticity and outer perceptions. This combination helps organizations design unified experiences for employees as well as customers turning employees into brand champions and customers into committed members of the community (Dharma & Setiawan, 2024). HR is essential to developing a healthy internal culture through inclusivity, care, and engagement; Marketing is the vehicle that takes this culture outward through narrative, campaigns, and consumer contacts. When these departments are aligned, the brand's promise becomes a reality beyond advertising in the daily experiences of employees and in the behavior of customers.

Whether that's through behind-the-scenes team bonding over food, celebrating diversity through food and cuisine, or even company values, such as sustainability, through an eco-friendly approach to food, Marketing get to share the brand's culture in a genuine and emotional way. This draws top talent who believe in the company's mission just as it moves the needle with consumers who value socially conscious, culturally rooted brands. HR-Marketing partnership enables more robust internal communication plans that reflect the tone and language of the brand outside the organization. For when your team knows how to think in your brand's voice maybe through onboarding procedures, local recruitment campaigns, or company retreat-you have effective narrators. That is particularly important in the modern age of social media, where employee advocacy and user-generated content are establishing the way people feel about your brand. HR can leverage Marketing to sharpen EVPs (employee value propositions) by making sure they are emotionally resonant and aligned with consumer brand values, especially in industries such as hospitality, food and beverage, and retail, where service delivery and consumer experience rely on employee engagement (Xavier & Alagappar, 2025).

HR-Marketing co-action creates a purpose-driven, emotionally bonded, and dynamic enterprise. When companies incorporate food culture into the fabric of employee engagement and consumer outreach, they can develop cohesive, culturally rich stories that signify on multiple levels with their multiple stakeholders. It's not only increasing its productivity and retention at work, it is building loyalty to its brand, showcasing its authenticity, and distinguishing itself in a world where personal experiences with companies and brands are becoming more and more important.

7. CHALLENGES AND LIMITATIONS OF THE CHAPTER STUDY

The inclusion of food culture in marketing, consumer engagement and HR practices carries vast potential, however it is not without its obstacles and limitations. As companies look to enhance social connection and brand identity with culinary motifs, there's a lot to consider everything from cultural appropriation to who and how to include, and where to draw the line on the commoditization of symbols that go back thousands of years. These obstacles impede market messages and can even alienate stakeholders or damage reputations. Hence, a mindful and ethical sensibility is essential in negotiating the maze of food, culture, identity and trade.

The more general restriction beside of those mentioned before and that is difficulty to overcome is authenticity in a global market! The larger a brand becomes, and the broader the market it seeks to serve, the more it is forced to universalise food experiences and homogenise culinary identities. This equation of variation with quality threatens to erase some of the things that make food such a powerful connector in the first place, its local distinctiveness and emotional richness. In addition, as consumer awareness grows about social responsibility and cultural sensitivity, any misstep in food-as-a-message marketing or HR action can become a viral issue that impacts brand reputation and employee morale.

While food culture can obviously be a powerful ally in forging social bonds, enlivening a brand and guiding HR programmes, it must be used responsibly, inclusive. The brands that cut through in this area are the ones who don't just see food as a product or well-orchestrated promotion, but as a genuine expression of individuality stories and human connection (Ardiansyah et al., 2024). The manner in which cultural misappropriation, dietary diversity and commercialization are managed with sensitivity and integrity will determine whether food culture will be seen as a force for unity, rather than a source of division in organizational strategies.

7.1 Risks of Cultural Misappropriation

The greatest perils of food-culture marketing is being accused of cultural appropriation when aspects of a culture usually from a historically disadvantaged community are co-opted by brands with no or dubious regard for the people who created them. When businesses exploit monetarily, not culturally ethnic cuisines, ingredients or cooking rituals independent of the communities from whom these traditions come, it can begin to look exploitative and tone-deaf. The appropriation of sacred food customs or traditional dishes for shallow purposes can do the work of robbing such traditions of cultural meaning, turning deep traditions into soulless trends or mere style. The brand not only becomes inauthentic to its core, but runs significant risk of blowing up and being exposed for insensitivity and mere commodification (Luthra et al., 2024). The distinction between cultural appreciation and appropriation is the big issue at stake. This is where brands need to focus on responsible representation by partnering with cultural authorities, recognizing origins and giving credit to communities, and recast advertising as a place for cultural exchange rather than extraction.

7.2 Dietary Restrictions and Inclusivity

Consumer bases are now made up of increasingly mixed religions, health requirements, moral decisions, and cultural differences, and as a result, these groups are extremely sensitive to the complexities of the gastronomic terrain that is modern day dining. Knowledge of religious dietary laws as vegetarianism, veganism, gluten intolerance, allergies and socio-cultural food taboos is crucial as the consequence of ignoring these can lead to people being marginalised or even putting at risk their health. So too evidence of marketing activities portraying one homogenous food culture, excluding consideration of multiple potentially alternate food cultures, may seem alien in multicultural settings. A strategy of inclusivity should be proactive and demands thoughtful planning, gathering of input from a multifaceted stakeholder group and the ability to provide transparent labeling for ingredients and practices. "Those that do inclusivity right communicate that they respect the identities of consumers and employees, which can instill trust and increase loyalty among them (Ford et al., 2025).

7.3 Over-Commercialization of Cultural Symbols

Yet, the vulgarization of cultural symbols of this type, associated with food heritage, is a second issue. To tap into nostalgia or cultural resonance, it's possible some brands will oversimplify or bastardize the authentic meaning of food traditions. For example, the industrialization of cultural holiday meals, alterations to traditional recipes or glamorization of rural culinary practices presented in urban packaging can cause a separation between the authentic and the commodified. The commercialization is apt to be at the expense of cultural authenticity and dignity, with aesthetics and profitability taking precedence. Even if such tactics lead to short-term buzz or sales, they can alienate essential cultural communities and compromise longer term brand credibility. The overreliance on cultural motifs whether ethnic textiles, indigenous tableware or symbolic ingredients without cultural context can turn the meaningful into banal décor (Kunnumpurath et al., 2025). To steer clear of this trap, brands need to find a way to harmonise commercial gain with cultural stewardship, debating with cultural gatekeepers about their designs or working closely with those whose aesthetics they draw on, spending on education and giving back to the communities in which they do business.

8. CONCLUSION

The interconnectedness of food culture, social bonding, human resource management, and marketing strategy evidences a fertile domain for emotional engagement, brand loyalty, and inclusive organizational culture building. "For me, food lets us tell stories, create memories, know who are, be together." When applied thoughtfully, it enhances consumer behavior understanding and employee engagement tactics, enabling brands to create meaningful connections that extend beyond points of purchase. This multi-layering must be conscientiously carried out with cultural sensitivity, ethical accountability, and a focus on inclusion. Confronting issues of cultural appropriation, food diversity, and over-commercialization is key to guaranteeing that food based strategies ultimately do justice to the communities they serve, and are credible to a broad spectrum of participants.

9. FUTURE DIRECTIONS

In terms of next steps in this space, in an ever more changing landscape, these future ways of working will require to be driven through a closer collaboration between HR, Marketing and Cultural experts to truly develop value in a co-created environment. Brands should consider developing food literacy training, inclusive menu ideation and sustainable food sourcing as an inside and outside efforts. Technology will be transformation for sure, AI and data analytics will enable personalized food based marketing and employee wellness programs custom to what individuals like and what their cultural identity is like. Furthermore, upcoming food trends such as Virtual Reality immersive dining experiences, gastronomy tale-telling by social media influencers and hyper-local food tagging how food culture can be utilised for strategic communication. Adopting these new realities, with a balanced focus on authenticity, brands and businesses can elevate food and drink beyond a marketing ploy to a tool of cultural cross-sharing and a universal common ground in humanity navigating the future of consumer and human resource engagement amid a globalized, multicultural society.

REFERENCES

Ali, U. F., & Santos, V. (2025). Glocalization Strategies in the Food Industry: Adapting to Local Needs and Demands. In *Evolving Strategies for Organizational Management and Performance Evaluation* (pp. 237-262). IGI Global Scientific Publishing.

Ardiansyah, N., Aurellia, R. Z., & Anatasya, W., PS, P. C., & Kusumasari, I. R. (. (2024). Transformation of Marketing Strategy in Decision Making in the Era of Globalization: Case Analysis of PT. Indofood Sukses Makmur, Tbk. *Journal of Advances in Accounting, Economics, and Management*, *2*(2), 12–12. DOI: 10.47134/aaem.v2i2.532

Baranidharan, S., Sankarkumar, A. V., Subramani, K., & Madeswaran, A. (2024). Dynamic Strategies and Evolutionary Trajectories: A Comprehensive Review of Experiential Marketing in the Soft Drink Industry. *New Trends in Marketing and Consumer Science*, 159-183.

da Silva, T. H. H., & Sehnem, S. (2025). The utilization of Industry 4.0 technologies to enhance the circular economy through the engagement of stakeholders in Brazilian food technology companies. *Business Strategy and the Environment*, *34*(1), 129–161. DOI: 10.1002/bse.3954

Dharma, B. A., & Setiawan, A. (2024, November). Marketing Management Strategy Alternative for MSMEs. In *BISTIC Business Innovation Sustainability and Technology International Conference (BISTIC 2024)* (pp. 4-11). Atlantis Press.

Ford, H., Dolan, R., Goodman, S., Bastian, S., Pearson, W., & Corsi, A. M. (2025). Exploring consumers' drinking behaviour regarding no-, low-and mid-alcohol wines: A systematic scoping review and guiding framework. *Journal of Marketing Management*, *41*(7-8), 1–31. DOI: 10.1080/0267257X.2025.2499101

Khamoushi, E. (2024). AI in Food Marketing from Personalized Recommendations to Predictive Analytics: Comparing Traditional Advertising Techniques with AI-Driven Strategies. *arXiv preprint arXiv:2410.01815.*

Kunnumpurath, B., Kumar, S., Menon, V. A., Prasad, A., & Ramanath, M. (2025). Behavioural Economics and Korean Food Consumption: Health Environment Sensitivity, Nutrition Application, Cost Saving, and Convenience Practices. In *Behavioral Economics and Neuroeconomics of Health and Healthcare* (pp. 25-52). IGI Global.

Luthra, A., Dixit, S., Singh, A., Garg, S., & Khattar, S. (2024). Sensory Storytelling: Crafting Brand Narratives Through Sight, Sound, Smell, Touch, and Taste. In *Sensible Selling Through Sensory Neuromarketing* (pp. 230-253). IGI Global.

Madesiya, A., & Prachi, D. Rohit, and Neelesh Kumar Maurya, et al. (2024). Exploring the Role of Psychology in the Food Industry: Consumer Behavior, Employee Well-being, and Innovation. *J. Nutrition and Food Processing*, *7*, 15.

Maspul, K., & Ardhin, M. (2025). Kopitiams at Crossroads: Can Malaysia's Cultural Heartbeat Survive Globalization? *Indonesian Journal of Social Development*, *2*(4), 20–20. DOI: 10.47134/jsd.v2i4.3886

Pugra, I. W., Arjana, I. W. B., Suarja, I. K., Sadiyani, N. W., Paramita, R., Sekarti, N. K., & Sunarsa, I. W. (2025). Flavours without borders: A cultural and gastronomic exploration of global cuisines, culinary diversity, and fusion experiences in food courts. *Journal of Education, Social &. Communication Studies*, *2*(2), 101–111.

Putra, F. K. K., Putra, M. K., & Novianti, S. (2023). Taste of asean: Traditional food images from Southeast Asian countries. *Journal of Ethnic Foods*, *10*(1), 20. DOI: 10.1186/s42779-023-00189-0

Quang, T. D., Phan, C. N., Nguyen, H. D., & Bui, T. K. (2025). Culinary dynamics in the digital age: A netnographic exploration of food and beverage trends in Vietnam through user-generated content. *Food, Culture, & Society*, *28*(5), 1–31. DOI: 10.1080/15528014.2025.2485506

Queiroz, L. P., Nogueira, I. B. R., & Ribeiro, A. M. (2024). Flavor engineering: A comprehensive review of biological foundations, AI integration, industrial development, and socio-cultural dynamics. *Food Research International*, *196*, 115100. DOI: 10.1016/j.foodres.2024.115100

Ramanayaka, L. J. (2025). Sensory Neuro-Marketing in Sales: Crafting Irresistible Dining Experiences. In *Impact of Sensory Marketing on Buying Behavior* (pp. 337-366). IGI Global.

Sakdiyakorn, M., & Chirakranont, R. (2024). Brewing social capital: A case study of Thailand's craft beer consumption community. *Journal of Consumer Culture*, *24*(4), 400–419. DOI: 10.1177/14695405241286384

Sriram, H. K. (2023). Harnessing AI Neural Networks and Generative AI for Advanced Customer Engagement: Insights into Loyalty Programs, Marketing Automation, and Real-Time Analytics. *Educational Administration: Theory and Practice*, *29*(4), 4361–4374.

Sulis, Y. D., Anshori, M. I., & Andriani, N. (2024). Analysis of Digital Marketing Strategies in Increasing Sales of Singgasana Cafe and Resto in Tanjung Bumi District Bangkalan Regency. *INVEST: Jurnal Inovasi Bisnis dan Akuntansi*, *5*(1), 114-124.

Xavier, J. A., & Alagappar, P. N. (2025). Harnessing Entrepreneurial Drive, Identifying Market Opportunities, and Leveraging Social Networks: A Malaysian Family Business. In *Strategic Insights and Case Studies on Navigating an Entrepreneurial Landscape* (pp. 207-224). IGI Global Scientific Publishing.

Compilation of References

Abbey, E. L., & Rigg, Q. (2024). A Qualitative Study of the Meaning of Food and Religious Identity. *Journal of Nutrition Education and Behavior*, *56*(6), 380–391. DOI: 10.1016/j.jneb.2024.03.003

Abdullah, A., Mat Isa, N., Azmi, A., Wahab, M. F. A., Tahir, M. S., & Ishak, M. A. (2024). Enhancing Penang Homestay Experience Through Cross-Cultural Benchmarking from Japanese Homestay Hospitality. *Revista de Gestão Social e Ambiental*, *18*(6), e04786. DOI: 10.24857/rgsa.v18n6-001

Access to Nutrition Initiative. (2024). *Global index 2024*. https://accesstonutrition.org

Adan, R. A., Van Der Beek, E. M., Buitelaar, J. K., Cryan, J. F., Hebebrand, J., Higgs, S., Schellekens, H., & Dickson, S. L. (2019). Nutritional psychiatry: Towards improving mental health by what you eat. *European Neuropsychopharmacology*, *29*(12), 1321–1332. DOI: 10.1016/j.euroneuro.2019.10.011 PMID: 31735529

Adkisson, R. V. (2008). Nudge: Improving Decisions About Health, Wealth and Happiness. *The Social Science Journal*, *45*(4), 700–701. DOI: 10.1016/j.soscij.2008.09.003

Ağagündüz, D., Yılmaz, B., Şahin, T. Ö., Güneşliol, B. E., Ayten, Ş., Russo, P., Spano, G., Rocha, J. M., Bartkiene, E., & Özogul, F. (2021). Dairy Lactic Acid Bacteria and Their Potential Function in Dietetics: The Food–Gut-Health Axis. *Foods*, *10*(12), 3099. DOI: 10.3390/foods10123099

Agan, B., & Bayrak, R. (2024). The Future of the Food and Agriculture Sector in Terms of Green Economics and Sustainable Development. *Studies in Systems. Decision and Control*, *576*, 119–146. DOI: 10.1007/978-3-031-77286-3_8

Agurs-Collins, T., Alvidrez, J., ElShourbagy Ferreira, S., Evans, M., Gibbs, K., Kowtha, B., Pratt, C., Reedy, J., Shams-White, M., & Brown, A. G. M. (2024). Perspective: Nutrition Health Disparities Framework: A model to advance health equity. *Advances in Nutrition*, *15*(4), 100194. DOI: 10.1016/j.advnut.2024.100194 PMID: 38616067

Ahmada Kh, A., & Abdo, A.A, A., Khan, S., Aleryani, H., Mi, S., & Wang, X. (2025). Advancing Pickling Techniques to Enhance Bioactive Compounds and Probiotic Content in Pickled Vegetables. *Food Reviews International*, ●●●, 1–27. DOI: 10.1080/87559129.2025.2473009

Ahmad, R., Akter, F., & Haque, M. (2023). Editorial: Diet and nutrition for non-communicable diseases in low and middle-income countries. *Frontiers in Nutrition*, *10*, 1179640. DOI: 10.3389/fnut.2023.1179640 PMID: 37057068

Ahmed, S., Chandra, S., Jain, A., Wongmahesak, K., & Singh, B. (2025). Impact of AI-generated misinformation on electoral integrity and public trust. In *Democracy and democratization in the age of AI* (pp. 57–72). IGI Global Scientific Publishing. DOI: 10.4018/979-8-3693-8749-8.ch004

Ahmed, S., Wongmahesak, K., Singh, B., & Kumar, S. (2025). Empowering Democratic Processes With AI: Innovations in Voter Engagement, Policy Analysis, and Decision-Making Process. In Wongmahesak, K., Wekke, I., Seftyono, C., & Nurdin, N. (Eds.), *Democracy and Democratization in the Age of AI* (pp. 121–132). IGI Global Scientific Publishing., DOI: 10.4018/979-8-3693-8749-8.ch007

Akinsemolu, A. A., & Onyeaka, H. N. (2024). Microorganisms Associated with Food Spoilage and Foodborne Diseases. In Ogwu, M. C., Izah, S. C., & Ntuli, N. R. (Eds.), *Food Safety and Quality in the Global South* (pp. 489–531). Springer Nature Singapore., DOI: 10.1007/978-981-97-2428-4_16

Akinsemolu, A. A., & Onyeaka, H. N. (2025). Mycoproteins as sustainable food sources: Current applications and prospects. *Discover Applied Sciences*, *7*(3), 1–11. DOI: 10.1007/s42452-025-06614-0

Alaimo, L. S., Fiore, M., & Galati, A. (2020). How the Covid-19 Pandemic Is Changing Online Food Shopping Human Behaviour in Italy. *Sustainability (Basel)*, *12*(22), 9594. DOI: 10.3390/su12229594

Alam, M. W., Kumar, J. V., Awad, M., Saravanan, P., Al-Sowayan, N. S., Rosaiah, P., & Nivetha, M. S. (2025). Emerging Trends in Food Process Engineering: Integrating Sensing Technologies for Health, Sustainability, and Consumer Preferences. *Journal of Food Process Engineering*, *48*(1), e70035. DOI: 10.1111/jfpe.70035

Albano-Gaglio, M., Esquerre, C. A., O'Donnell, C. P., Muñoz, I., ElMasry, G., Font-i-Furnols, M., Tejeda, J. F., Brun, A., Lloret, E., & Marcos, B. (2025). Calibration of visible and near-infrared spectral imaging technology to predict the quality evolution of retail fresh pork bellies with different fat content. *Food Research International*, *199*, 115350. DOI: 10.1016/j.foodres.2024.115350 PMID: 39658154

Alegbeleye, O., & Rhee, M. S. (2024). Growth of Listeria monocytogenes> in fresh vegetables and vegetable salad products: An update on influencing intrinsic and extrinsic factors. *Comprehensive Reviews in Food Science and Food Safety*, *23*(5), e13423. DOI: 10.1111/1541-4337.13423 PMID: 39169547

Ali, U. F., & Santos, V. (2025). Glocalization Strategies in the Food Industry: Adapting to Local Needs and Demands. In *Evolving Strategies for Organizational Management and Performance Evaluation* (pp. 237-262). IGI Global Scientific Publishing.

Ali, T., & Ali, J. (2020). Factors affecting the consumers' willingness to pay for health and wellness food products. *Journal of Agriculture and Food Research*, *2*, 100076. DOI: 10.1016/j.jafr.2020.100076

Alonso-Caraballo, Y., Guha, S. K., & Chartoff, E. H. (2020). The neurobiology of abstinence-induced reward-seeking in males and females [Review of The neurobiology of abstinence-induced reward-seeking in males and females]. Pharmacology Biochemistry and Behavior, 200, 173088. Elsevier BV. DOI: 10.1016/j.pbb.2020.173088

Alqatan, S., Maizura, N., Noor, M., Man, M., & Mohemad, R. (2017). Information Technology, in 2000 from University Putra Malaysia. He obtained his degree and Diploma in Computer Sciences. *International Journal of Business Information Systems*, *26*(1), •••.

Alsubhi, M., Blake, M., Nguyen, T., Majmudar, I., Moodie, M., & Ananthapavan, J. (2023). Consumer willingness to pay for healthier food products: A systematic review. *Obesity Reviews*, *24*(1), e13525. DOI: 10.1111/obr.13525 PMID: 36342169

Amirullah, N. A., Samsudin, M. H., Norrrahim, M. N. F., Ilyas, R. A., Nurazzi, N. M., Jenol, M. A., Hawanis, H. S. N., & Gunny, A. A. N. (2024). Regulations for food packaging materials. *Physical Sciences Reviews*, *9*(8), 2711–2735. DOI: 10.1515/psr-2022-0033

Anderson, E. M., Wei, R., Liu, B., Plummer, R., Kelahan, H., Taméz, M., Marrero, A., Bhupathiraju, S. N., & Mattei, J. (2021). Improving healthy food choices in low-income settings in the United States using behavioral economic-based adaptations to choice architecture. *Frontiers in Nutrition*, *8*, 734991. DOI: 10.3389/fnut.2021.734991

Anderson, I. A., & Wood, W. (2020). Habits and the electronic herd: The psychology behind social media's successes and failures. *Consumer Psychology Review*, *4*(1), 83–99. DOI: 10.1002/arcp.1063

Anghelcev, G., Mcgroarty, S. M., Sar, S., Moultrie, J., & Huang, Y. (2020). Marketing Processed Organic Foods: The Impact of Promotional Message Framing (Vice Vs. Virtue Advertising) on Perceptions of Healthfulness. *Journal of Food Products Marketing*, *26*(6), 401–424. DOI: 10.1080/10454446.2020.1792022

Arboix, J. A. (2025). *Sensory Defects in Fermented Sausages* (p. 59) [2025 Update]. Frigomeccanica S.p.A. https://eurocarne.com/daal/a1/informes/a2/Sensory_Defects_in_Fermented_Sausages_2025_LR.pdf

Ardiansyah, N., Aurellia, R. Z., & Anatasya, W., PS, P. C., & Kusumasari, I. R. (. (2024). Transformation of Marketing Strategy in Decision Making in the Era of Globalization: Case Analysis of PT. Indofood Sukses Makmur, Tbk. *Journal of Advances in Accounting, Economics, and Management*, *2*(2), 12–12. DOI: 10.47134/aaem.v2i2.532

Ares, G., Natero, V., Gugliucci, V., Machín, L., Alcaire, F., de León, C., & Otterbring, T. (2023). Health-Washing of Ultraprocessed Products on Instagram: Prevalence and Strategies in an Emerging Market. *Journal of Nutrition Education and Behavior*, *55*(11), 815–822. DOI: 10.1016/j.jneb.2023.09.001 PMID: 37777932

Arı, E., & Yılmaz, V. (2024). *The effects of social media and influencers on consumers' attitudes and purchasing towards organic foods*. Erciyes Üniversitesi İktisadi ve İdari Bilimler Fakültesi Dergisi., DOI: 10.18070/erciyesiibd.1496826

Ariestiningsih, E. S., Syarifah Has, D. F., Suprapti, S., Herawati, A., & Latief, T. S. S. (2023). *Analysis of factors affecting the purchase decision of healthyfood*. Firm Journal of Management Studies., DOI: 10.33021/firm.v8i2.4645

Arora, A. K., Kumar, S., & Kansal, A. (2024). Analysis of Retail Investorsâ€™ Attitudes Toward IPO Investments. Indian Journal of Finance, 42-57.

Arora, A. K., Kumar, A., Tyagi, R., Sharma, S., Kumar, A., & Kumar, S. (2025). Future of Education With AI-Assisted Technologies. In Kaunert, C., Raghav, A., Ravesangar, K., Singh, B., & Riswandi, B. (Eds.), *Artificial Intelligence in Peace, Justice, and Strong Institutions* (pp. 169–190). IGI Global Scientific Publishing., DOI: 10.4018/979-8-3693-9395-6.ch008

Arora, M. K., Lal, S., Singh, B., & Olyaee, M. (2024). Through an Energy Lens: Examining SDGs From a Policy Perspective. In Riswandi, B., Singh, B., Kaunert, C., & Vig, K. (Eds.), *AI Applications for Clean Energy and Sustainability* (pp. 320–343). IGI Global., DOI: 10.4018/979-8-3693-6567-0.ch016

Aşık, İ., Caner, C., Yüceer, M., & Pala, Ç. U. (2025). Ozone Pre-treatment and Equilibrium-Modified Atmosphere Packaging as Elicitors to Enhance Shelf Stability and Nutraceutical Retention in Fresh Aronia (Aronia melanocarpa cv. Nero) Berries. *Food and Bioprocess Technology*, *18*(12), 10636–10654. Advance online publication. DOI: 10.1007/s11947-025-04049-4

Augustin, M. A., Hartley, C. J., Maloney, G., & Tyndall, S. (2024a). Innovation in precision fermentation for food ingredients. *Critical Reviews in Food Science and Nutrition*, *64*(18), 6218–6238. DOI: 10.1080/10408398.2023.2166014

Ayeni, O., & Olagoke-Komolafe, O. E. (2024). *Advancing food safety standards through technology integration and policy development.* *2*(1), 035–046. DOI: 10.57219/crrms.2024.2.1.0039

Azétsop, J., & Joy, T. R. (2013). Access to nutritious food, socioeconomic individualism and public health ethics in the USA: A common good approach. *Philosophy, Ethics, and Humanities in Medicine; PEHM*, *8*(1), 16. DOI: 10.1186/1747-5341-8-16 PMID: 24165577

Azimi, M. N., Rahman, M. M., & Maraseni, T. (2024). The Interplay of Dietary Habits, Economic Factors, and Globalization: Assessing the Role of Institutional Quality. *Nutrients*, *16*(18), 3116. DOI: 10.3390/nu16183116 PMID: 39339718

Backholer, K., Sacks, G., & Cameron, A. J. (2019). Food and Beverage Price Promotions: An Untapped Policy Target for Improving Population Diets and Health. *Current Nutrition Reports*, *8*(3), 250–255. DOI: 10.1007/s13668-019-00287-z PMID: 31300982

Badewa, A. S., & Dinbabo, M. F. (2022). Multisectoral intervention on food security in complex emergencies: A discourse on regional resilience praxis in Northeast Nigeria. *GeoJournal*, *88*(2), 1231–1244. DOI: 10.1007/s10708-022-10679-4

Badr, S. (2022). Re-Imagining Wellness in the Age of Neoliberalism. *New Sociology*, *3*. Advance online publication. DOI: 10.25071/2563-3694.66

Baicu, A. A. (2022). *Regulating emerging food trends.*, DOI: 10.1016/B978-0-12-816011-4.00014-8

Bansal, H. S., & Voyer, P. A. (2000). Word-of-Mouth Processes within a Services Purchase Decision Context. *Journal of Service Research*, *3*(2), 166–177. DOI: 10.1177/109467050032005

Baranidharan, S., Sankarkumar, A. V., Subramani, K., & Madeswaran, A. (2024). Dynamic Strategies and Evolutionary Trajectories: A Comprehensive Review of Experiential Marketing in the Soft Drink Industry. *New Trends in Marketing and Consumer Science*, 159-183.

Barbaro, N., & Pickett, S. M. (2016). Mindfully green: Examining the effect of connectedness to nature on the relationship between mindfulness and engagement in pro-environmental behavior. *Personality and Individual Differences*, *93*, 137–142. DOI: 10.1016/j.paid.2015.05.026

Barbour, L., Lindberg, R., Woods, J., Charlton, K., & Brimblecombe, J. (2021). Local urban government policies to facilitate healthy and environmentally sustainable diet-related practices: A scoping review. *Public Health Nutrition*, *24*(18), 6423–6434. DOI: 10.1017/S1368980021004432

Baş, M., Kahriman, M., Çakir Biçer, N., & Seçkiner, S. (2024). Results from Türkiye: Which Factors Drive Consumers to Buy Organic Food? *Foods*, *13*(2), 302. Advance online publication. DOI: 10.3390/foods13020302 PMID: 38254603

Basso, A., & Serban, S. (2019). Industrial applications of immobilized enzymes—A review. *Molecular Catalysis*, *479*, 110607. DOI: 10.1016/j.mcat.2019.110607

Batat, W. (2024). *Identifying the forms of digital food advertising content and their effects on food well-being in the phygital age*. 231–243. DOI: 10.4324/9781003168485-20

Bateman, I. J., Binner, A., Addicott, E. T., Balmford, B., Cho, F. H. T., Daily, G. C., De-Gol, A., Eisenbarth, S., Faccioli, M., Ferguson-Gow, H., Ferrini, S., Fezzi, C., Gannon, K., Groom, B., Harper, A. B., Harwood, A., Hillier, J., Hulme, M. F., Lee, C. F., & Day, B. H. (2024). How to make land use policy decisions: Integrating science and economics to deliver connected climate, biodiversity, and food objectives. *Proceedings of the National Academy of Sciences of the United States of America*, *121*(49), e2407961121. Advance online publication. DOI: 10.1073/pnas.2407961121 PMID: 39536077

Beal, T., Massiot, E., Arsenault, J., Smith, M. R., & Hijmans, R. J. (2017). Global trends in dietary micronutrient supplies and estimated prevalence of inadequate intakes. *PLOS ONE*, *12*(4), e0175554. DOI: 10.1371/journal.pone.0175554

Beniwal, T., & Mathur, V. K. (2022). Cloud Kitchens and its impact on the restaurant industry. *International Research Journal on Advanced Science Hub*, *4*(12), 324–335. DOI: 10.47392/irjash.2022.076

Berg, G., Lundqvist, E., & Mattsson Sydner, Y. (2024). Useful but overused? The "plate model" as a food educational tool in home economics. *Food, Culture, & Society*, *27*(2), 573–591. DOI: 10.1080/15528014.2024.2319421

Bergstrom, D. M., Wienecke, B., van den Hoff, J., Hughes, L., Lindenmayer, D. B., Ainsworth, T. D., Baker, C. M., Bland, L. M., Bowman, D. M. J. S., Brooks, S. T., Canadell, J. G., Constable, A., Dafforn, K. A., Depledge, M. H., Dickson, C. R., Duke, N. C., Helmstedt, K. J., Holz, A., Johnson, C. R., ... Shaw, J. D. (2021). Combating ecosystem collapse from the tropics to the Antarctic. *Global Change Biology*, *27*(9), 1692–1703. DOI: 10.1111/gcb.15539

Bernardlauwers, B., Islam, R., Muthoifin, M., & Husna Srifyan, J. (2024). Islamic Business Ethics and Political Economy: A Study of Government Policies in Handling the Food Crisis. *Demak Universal Journal of Islam and Sharia*, *2*(02), 91–110. DOI: 10.61455/deujis.v2i02.107

Bertan, S. (2021). Impact of restaurants in the development of gastronomic tourism. *International Journal of Gastronomy and Food Science*, *21*(1), 1–37.

Berthoud, H.-R., Lenard, N. R., & Shin, A. C. (2011). Food reward, hyperphagia, and obesity. *American Journal of Physiology. Regulatory, Integrative and Comparative Physiology*, *300*(6), R1266–R1277. DOI: 10.1152/ajpregu.00028.2011 PMID: 21411768

Bhardwaj, A. K., Chejara, S., Malik, K., Kumar, R., Kumar, A., & Yadav, R. K. (2022). Agronomic biofortification of food crops: An emerging opportunity for global food and nutritional security. *Frontiers in Plant Science*, *13*, 1055278. Advance online publication. DOI: 10.3389/fpls.2022.1055278 PMID: 36570883

Bharti, K., & Agarwal, R. (2026). Consumers adoption of healthy lifestyle: Understanding the influence of upcycling drivers on LOHAS consumer behavior. *Journal of Financial Services Marketing*, *31*(1), 5. DOI: 10.1057/s41264-025-00330-x

Bhatnagar, M., & Rajaram, R. (2024). Correlating investor patterns and ESG performance with neuro marketing insights: Behavioural finance meets sustainability. In *Neuromarketing's Role in Sustainable Finance*. IGI Global., DOI: 10.4018/979-8-3693-9117-4.ch001

Bhutta, Z. A., Ahmed, T., Black, R. E., Cousens, S., Dewey, K. G., Giugliani, E. R. J., Haider, B. A., Kirkwood, B., Morris, S. S., Sachdev, H. S., & Shekar, M. (2008). What works? Interventions for maternal and child undernutrition and survival. *The Lancet*, *371*(9610), 417–440. DOI: 10.1016/S0140-6736(07)61693-6

Bilotta, E., Bertacchini, F., Gabriele, L., Giglio, S., Pantano, P. S., & Romita, T. (2021). Industry 4.0 technologies in tourism education: Nurturing students to think with technology. *Journal of Hospitality, Leisure, Sport and Tourism Education, 29*, 100275. DOI: 10.1016/j.jhlste.2020.100275

Binns, N. (2009). *Session 4: Challenges facing the food industry in innovating for health Regulatory challenges and opportunities for food innovation. 68*(1), 1–10. DOI: 10.1017/S0029665108008860

Blakely, T., Nghiem, N., Genc, M., Mizdrak, A., Cobiac, L., Mhurchu, C. N., Swinburn, B., Scarborough, P., & Cleghorn, C. (2020). Modelling the health impact of food taxes and subsidies with price elasticities: The case for additional scaling of food consumption using the total food expenditure elasticity. *PLoS One, 15*(3), e0230506. Advance online publication. DOI: 10.1371/journal.pone.0230506 PMID: 32214329

Bloemhof, J. M., & van der Vorst, J. G. A. J. (2014). *Sustainable Food Supply Chain Networks.* 99–122. https://www.narcis.nl/publication/RecordID/oai%3Alibrary.wur.nl%3Awurpubs%2F452916

Bogue, J., & Sorenson, D. (2009). *Strategic marketing of gluten-free cereal products and beverages* (pp. 149–158). American Association of Cereal Chemists, Inc (AACC). https://doi.org/DOI: 10.1016/B978-1-891127-67-0.50019-4

Bogue, J., & Troy, A. J. (2016). *Functional Beverages: Market Trends and Market-Oriented New Product Designs.* Routledge Handbooks Online., DOI: 10.1201/b19490-3

Bohm, I., Åbacka, G., Hörnell, A., & Bengs, C. (2025). "Can we add a little sugar?" the contradictory discourses around sweet foods in Swedish home economics. *Pedagogy, Culture & Society, 33*(1), 105–121. DOI: 10.1080/14681366.2023.2190754

Boinwad, D. L., & Shinde, P. R.Dr. Dilipkumar L. BoinwadProf. Rajesh S. Shinde. (2024). Health and Wellness Food Products : A Retailers' Perspective. *International Journal of Scientific Research in Science and Technology, 11*(3), 202–216. DOI: 10.32628/IJSRST2411313

Bolm, S. L., Zwaal, W., & Fernandes, M. B. (2022). Effects of mindfulness on occupational stress and job satisfaction of hospitality and service workers. *Research in Hospitality Management, 12*(1), 61–70. DOI: 10.1080/22243534.2022.2080954

Boobalan, K., Nachimuthu, G. S., & Sivakumaran, B. (2020). Understanding the psychological benefits in organic consumerism: An empirical exploration. *Food Quality and Preference, 87*, 104070. DOI: 10.1016/j.foodqual.2020.104070

Bosco, F. J. (2020). Geographies of Food: Place, Space, and Scale in Food Studies. *Geography Teacher, 17*(3), 73–76. DOI: 10.1080/19338341.2020.1796744

Bouis, H., Foley, J., Lividini, K., Jumrani, J., Reinke, R., Van Der Straeten, D., Zagado, R., Boy, E., Brown, L. R., Mudyahoto, B., Alioma, R., Hussain, M., & Pfeiffer, W. H. (2024). Biofortification: Future challenges for a newly emerging technology to improve nutrition security sustainably. *Current Developments in Nutrition, 8*(12), 104478. DOI: 10.1016/j.cdnut.2024.104478 PMID: 39668944

Bouman, T., van der Werff, E., Perlaviciute, G., & Steg, L. (2021). Environmental values and identities at the personal and group level. *Current Opinion in Behavioral Sciences, 42*, 47–53. DOI: 10.1016/j.cobeha.2021.02.022

Bowman, S. A. (2006). A comparison of the socioeconomic characteristics, dietary practices, and health status of women food shoppers with different food price attitudes. *Nutrition Research (New York, N.Y.), 26*(7), 318–324. DOI: 10.1016/j.nutres.2006.06.012

Brányik, T., Silva, D. P., Baszczyňski, M., Lehnert, R., Almeida, E., & Silva, J. B. (2012). A review of methods of low alcohol and alcohol-free beer production. *Journal of Food Engineering, 108*(4), 493–506. DOI: 10.1016/j.jfoodeng.2011.09.020

Brinkman, H.-J., De Pee, S., Sanogo, I., Subran, L., & Bloem, M. W. (2010). High food prices and the global financial crisis have reduced access to nutritious food and worsened nutritional status and health. *The Journal of Nutrition, 140*(1), 153S–161S. DOI: 10.3945/jn.109.110767 PMID: 19939996

Bronchetti, E. T., Christensen, G., & Hoynes, H. W. (2019). Local food prices, SNAP purchasing power, and child health. *Journal of Health Economics, 68*, 102231. Advance online publication. DOI: 10.1016/j.jhealeco.2019.102231 PMID: 31634764

Brooker, P. G., Hendrie, G. A., Anastasiou, K., Woodhouse, R., Pham, T., & Colgrave, M. L. (2022). Marketing strategies used for alternative protein products sold in Australian supermarkets in 2014, 2017, and 2021. *Frontiers in Nutrition, 9*, 1087194. Advance online publication. DOI: 10.3389/fnut.2022.1087194

Brown, L., Buhalis, D., & Beer, S. (2020). Dining alone: Improving the experience of solo restaurant goers. *International Journal of Contemporary Hospitality Management, 32*(3), 1347–1365. DOI: 10.1108/IJCHM-06-2019-0584

Bruins, M. J., Van Dael, P., & Eggersdorfer, M. (2019). The Role of Nutrients in Reducing the Risk for Noncommunicable Diseases during Aging. *Nutrients, 11*(1), 85. DOI: 10.3390/nu11010085 PMID: 30621135

Brunori, G., Carzedda, M., Iliopoulos, C., D'Haese, M., Lanfranchi, M., Lerro, M., Martino, G., Pettenella, D., van Passel, S., & Troiano, S. (2024). Correction to: Has transformation of food systems reached an impasse? Considerations on the role of agri-food research (Agricultural and Food Economics, (2024), 12, 1, (26),). *Agricultural and Food Economics, 12*(1). https://doi.org/DOI: 10.1186/s40100-024-00308-8

Bui, T.-V. (2014). *Social Media On-A-Stick: A uses and gratification approach toward helping mobile food vendors engage consumers on Instagram.*

Building circular food systems in cities. (2024). World Wildlife Fund. https://foodforwardndcs.panda.org/food-supply-chains/building-circular-food-systems-in-cities/

Burch, D., & Lawrence, G. (2010). *The "wellness" phenomenon: implications for global agri-food systems*. Earthscan., DOI: 10.4324/9781849774499

Burdusel, D., Coman, C., Ancuta, D. L., Hermann, D. M., Doeppner, T. R., Gresita, A., & Popa-Wagner, A. (2024). Translatability of life-extending pharmacological treatments between different species. *Aging Cell, 23*(7), e14208. DOI: 10.1111/acel.14208 PMID: 38797976

Burgaz, C., Gorasso, V., Achten, W. M. J., Batis, C., Castronuovo, L., Diouf, A., Asiki, G., Swinburn, B. A., Unar-Munguía, M., Devleesschauwer, B., Sacks, G., & Vandevijvere, S. (2023). The effectiveness of food system policies to improve nutrition, nutrition-related inequalities and environmental sustainability: A scoping review. *Food Security, 15*(5), 1313–1344. DOI: 10.1007/s12571-023-01385-1

Burkhanov, A. U., Popkova, E. G., Galoyan, D. R., Mkrtchyan, T. M., & Sergi, B. S. (2024). Deep learning, irrigation enhancement, and agricultural economics for ensuring food security in emerging economies. *Global Transitions, 6*, 164–172. DOI: 10.1016/j.glt.2024.06.002

Bustos-Terrones, Y. A., Tariq, R., Rangel-Peraza, J. G., Torróntegui-Chávez, G., & Loaiza, J. G. (2026). Sustaining global food security through digitalization. In *Climate Change Impacts on the Water-Energy-Food Nexus* (pp. 289–302). Elsevier., DOI: 10.1016/B978-0-443-22320-4.00013-X

Çalışkan Koç, G., Özkan Karabacak, A., Süfer, Ö., Adal, S., Çelebi, Y., Delikanlı Kıyak, B., & Öztekin, S. (2025). Thawing frozen foods: A comparative review of traditional and innovative methods. *Comprehensive Reviews in Food Science and Food Safety, 24*(2), e70136. DOI: 10.1111/1541-4337.70136 PMID: 39970035

Calvo-Fernandez, C., Takeuchi-Storm, N., Nauta, M., Sandberg, M., & Lassen, B. (2024). Effect of Post-Chilling Processes and Modified Atmosphere Packing on Campylobacter in Broiler Meat. *Food Control, 111087*. Advance online publication. DOI: 10.1016/j.foodcont.2024.111087

Cammarelle, A., Viscecchia, R., De Devitiis, B., Panniello, U., & Gorgoglione, M. (2025). Consumers' Behavior Toward Healthy Foods: A Critical Review. *Food Reviews International*, *41*(4), 1081–1098. DOI: 10.1080/87559129.2024.2432927

Candau, J., & Axon, S. (2025). Beyond food security: Unleashing the potential of sustainable communities to transform the UK food system. *Land*, *14*(4), 909. DOI: 10.3390/land14040909

Cardenas, D., & Fuchs-Tarlovsky, V. (2018). Is multi-level marketing of nutrition supplements a legal and an ethical practice? *Clinical Nutrition ESPEN*, *25*, 133–138. DOI: 10.1016/j.clnesp.2018.03.118 PMID: 29779808

Carpenter, B. J., Dobbins, T. W., Hernandez, M. S., Barker, S. N., Loomas, K. R., Osburn, W. N., & Legako, J. F. (2024). Comparison of Gas Treatments of High Oxygen, Carbon Monoxide, and Nitric Oxide on Ground Beef Color in Modified Atmosphere Packaging. *Foods*, *13*(6), 902. DOI: 10.3390/foods13060902 PMID: 38540892

Carpentieri, S., Soltanipour, F., Ferrari, G., Pataro, G., & Donsì, F. (2021). Emerging Green Techniques for the Extraction of Antioxidants from Agri-Food By-Products as Promising Ingredients for the Food Industry. *Antioxidants*, *10*(9), 1417. DOI: 10.3390/antiox10091417

Carrión-Antolí, A., Zoffoli, J. P., Serrano, M., Valero, D., & Naranjo, P. (2024). Preharvest Gibberellic Acid Treatment Increases Both Modulus of Elasticity and Resistance in Sweet Cherry Fruit (cv. 'Bing' and 'Lapins') at Harvest and Postharvest During Storage at 0 °C. *Agronomy (Basel)*, *14*(11), 2738. DOI: 10.3390/agronomy14112738

Casas, R., Castro-Barquero, S., Estruch, R., & Sacanella, E. (2018). Nutrition and Cardiovascular Health. *International Journal of Molecular Sciences*, *19*(12), 3988. DOI: 10.3390/ijms19123988 PMID: 30544955

Caso, G., Blasi, E., Cembalo, L., & Vecchio, R. (2023). This cookie will save the planet! The effect of a private sustainability claim on consumers' expectations. *Heliyon*, *9*(3), e14206. Advance online publication. DOI: 10.1016/j.heliyon.2023.e14206

Ćatović, A. (2023). *Dietary Patterns*. IntechOpen., DOI: 10.5772/intechopen.108367

Ceccarini, J., Liu, H., Laere, K. V., Morris, E. D., & Sander, C. Y. (2020). Methods for Quantifying Neurotransmitter Dynamics in the Living Brain With PET Imaging [Review of Methods for Quantifying Neurotransmitter Dynamics in the Living Brain With PET Imaging]. Frontiers in Physiology, 11. Frontiers Media. DOI: 10.3389/fphys.2020.00792

Chala, D. B., & Emire, S. A. (2022). *Development of plant based functional food products: a review. 46*(1), 169–183. DOI: 10.35219/foodtechnology.2022.1.13

Chandon, P., & Cadario, R. (2022). Healthy in the wrong way: Mismatching of marketers' food claim use and consumers' preferences in the United States but not France. *Journal of the Academy of Marketing Science*, *51*(1), 153–173. DOI: 10.1007/s11747-022-00885-4

Chandon, P., Haws, K. L., & Liu, P. J. (2022). Paths to healthier eating: Perceptions and interventions for success. *Journal of the Association for Consumer Research*, *7*(4), 383–392. DOI: 10.1086/721842

Chang, Y. Y. (2020). Lonely or alone? Solitary dining in Japan and Taiwan. *International Journal of Culture, Tourism and Hospitality Research*, *15*(1), 10–25. DOI: 10.1108/IJCTHR-01-2020-0008

Charikleous, M., Voutsas, P., & Stamatis, N. (2024). *Quality Assessment of a new Mullet Mugil cephalus (Linnaeus, 1758) processed product under Active Packaging Systems, at 2-4oC*. HydroMediT 2024, Mytilene, Lesvos, Greece. https://www.researchgate.net/profile/Nikolaos-Stamatis/publication/382888925

Chartrand, M.-E., Bélisle, D., Patry-Beaudoin, G., & Cheikhrouhou, S. (2024). The retail wellnesscape: Conceptualizing consumer wellness in a health food retailing context. *Qualitative Market Research*, *27*(4), 631–649. Advance online publication. DOI: 10.1108/QMR-09-2023-0127

Chaudhary, S., Soni, B., Sindhavad, A., Mamaniya, A., Dalvi, A., & Siddavatam, I. A. (2022). ChefAI.IN: Generating Indian Recipes with AI Algorithm. *International Conference on Trends in Quantum Computing and Emerging Business Technologies (TQCEBT)*, 1-6. DOI: 10.1109/TQCEBT54229.2022.10041463

Chaudhary, S., Vishnoi, V., Chaudhary, S., Tyagi, N., & Consul, P. (2025). Nano-Enhanced and AI-Driven Integration for Food Security and Safety Through Scientific Advances: Systematic Approaches and Societal Implications. In Vaseashta, A., & Stamatin, I. (Eds.), (pp. 339–374). Advances in Computational Intelligence and Robotics. IGI Global Scientific Publishing., DOI: 10.4018/979-8-3373-2883-6.ch010

Chauhan, Y., Negi, I., & Singh, M. (2025). Cultural identity and Globalization in Culinary Practices: Exploring the Evolution, Diversity and Socioeconomic Impact of Food and Cuisine Across Cultures. *International Journal for Multidimensional Research Perspectives, 3*(1), 08–22. DOI: 10.61877/ijmrp.v3i1.225

Chauhan, K., & Rao, A. (2024). Clean-label alternatives for food preservation: An emerging trend. *Heliyon, 10*(16), e35815. DOI: 10.1016/j.heliyon.2024.e35815 PMID: 39247286

Cheewakoset, R., & Sakdapat, N. (2024). Financial skills, Entrepreneurial Qualities, and Leadership Qualities that Influence the Preparatory Behaviours for Business Competition of Undergraduate Students in Thailand. *International Journal of EBusiness and EGovernment Studies, 16*(1), 203–222.

Chen, L., Kuuliala, L., Walgraeve, C., Demeestere, K., & Devlieghere, F. (2024, November 12). *Understanding microbial spoilers in pork: Pseudomonas fragi and its spoilage potential under modified atmospheres.* 38th EFFoST International Conference 2024, Bruges, Belgium. https://biblio.ugent.be/publication/01JCWW4ANG79M5Z7GBEAA9XX62

Cheng, J.-H., Chen, M., & Sun, D.-W. (2024). Ethylene Synergism Control Using Integrated Cold Plasma Technologies to Enhance Fruit and Vegetable Quality. *Food Engineering Reviews.* Advance online publication. DOI: 10.1007/s12393-024-09387-1

Chen, J. C., Wang, R., & Wei, C. C. (2024). Anti-aging effects of dietary phytochemicals: From Caenorhabditis elegans, Drosophila melanogaster, rodents to clinical studies. *Critical Reviews in Food Science and Nutrition, 64*(17), 5958–5983. DOI: 10.1080/10408398.2022.2160961 PMID: 36597655

Chen, J., Li, H., Zhao, T., Chen, K., Chen, M., Sun, Z., Xu, W., Maas, K., Lester, B. M., & Cong, X. (2023). The Impact of Early Life Experiences and Gut Microbiota on Neurobehavioral Development in Preterm Infants: A Longitudinal Cohort Study. *Microorganisms, 11*(3), 814. DOI: 10.3390/microorganisms11030814

Chen, W., Ma, G., & Jia, Z. (2024). Consumer behavior and healthy food consumption: Quasi-natural experimental evidence from Chinese household participation in long-term care insurance. *Frontiers in Sustainable Food Systems, 8*, 1364749. Advance online publication. DOI: 10.3389/fsufs.2024.1364749

Chen, X., Bahramimehr, F., Shahhamzehei, N., Fu, H., Lin, S., Wang, H., Li, C., Efferth, T., & Hong, C. (2024). Anti-aging effects of medicinal plants and their rapid screening using the nematode Caenorhabditis elegans. *Phytomedicine, 129*, 155665. DOI: 10.1016/j.phymed.2024.155665 PMID: 38768535

Chen, X., Mou, Z., Zhao, Y., Su, X., Han, Y., Chen, H., Wei, W., Shan, W., Kuang, J., Lu, W., & Chen, J. (2024). Modified atmosphere packaging maintains stem quality of Chinese flowering cabbage by restraining post-harvest lignification and ROS accumulation. *Food Chemistry: X, 24*, 102006. DOI: 10.1016/j.fochx.2024.102006 PMID: 39655218

Chen, X., Su, L., & Carpenter, D. (2020). Impacts of Situational Factors on Consumers' Adoption of Mobile Payment Services: A Decision-Biases Perspective. *International Journal of Human-Computer Interaction, 36*(11), 1085–1093. DOI: 10.1080/10447318.2020.1722400

Chung, N., Song, H. G., & Lee, H. (2017). Consumers' impulsive buying behavior of restaurant products in social commerce. *International Journal of Contemporary Hospitality Management, 29*(2), 709–731. DOI: 10.1108/IJCHM-10-2015-0608

Conceiving Awareness on Food Habits and Developing Innovative Diet Food Restaurant. (2015, January 1). SciSpace - Paper. https://scispace.com/papers/conceiving-awareness-on-food-habits-and-developing-1em36257i0

Conor, B. (2021). 'How Goopy are you?' Women, Goop and cosmic wellness. *European Journal of Cultural Studies, 24*(6), 1261–1281. DOI: 10.1177/13675494211055735

Cordner, A., Brown, P., & Morello-Frosch, R. (2014). *Health Social Movements.* DOI: 10.1002/9781118410868.wbehibs441

Coro, D. G., Schirmer, K., Van Rhoda, M., McQueen, B., & Morris, C. (2025). An environmental scan of food and drink advertising on public transport around Adelaide schools. *Health Promotion Journal of Australia, 36*(1), e886. DOI: 10.1002/hpja.886 PMID: 38840470

Cronbach, L. J. (1951). Coefficient alpha and the internal structure of tests. *Psychometrika, 16*(3), 297–334. DOI: 10.1007/BF02310555

Cuevas, S., Patel, N., Patel, N., Thompson, C., Petticrew, M., Cummins, S., Smith, R. D., & Cornelsen, L. (2021). Escaping the Red Queen: Health as a corporate food marketing strategy. *SSM - Population Health, 16*, 100953. DOI: 10.1016/j.ssmph.2021.100953 PMID: 34815996

Cuj, M., Grabinsky, L., & Yates-Doerr, E. (2020). Cultures of Nutrition: Classification, Food Policy, and Health. *Medical Anthropology, 40*(1), 79–97. DOI: 10.1080/01459740.2020.1826475

Cunningham, M., Azcarate-Peril, M. A., Barnard, A., Benoit, V., Grimaldi, R., Guyonnet, D., & Gibson, G. R. (2021). Shaping the future of probiotics and prebiotics. *Trends in Microbiology*, *29*(8), 667–685. DOI: 10.1016/j.tim.2021.01.003 PMID: 33551269

Da Costa, J. P., & Corcoran, P. L. (2026). Micro(nano)plastics as soil pollutants. In *Soil Pollution* (pp. 221–240). Elsevier. DOI: 10.1016/B978-0-443-33329-3.00011-8

da Silva, T. H. H., & Sehnem, S. (2025). The utilization of Industry 4.0 technologies to enhance the circular economy through the engagement of stakeholders in Brazilian food technology companies. *Business Strategy and the Environment*, *34*(1), 129–161. DOI: 10.1002/bse.3954

Dallman, M. F., Pecoraro, N. C., & La Fleur, S. E. (2005). Chronic stress and comfort foods: Self-medication and abdominal obesity☆. *Brain, Behavior, and Immunity*, *19*(4), 275–280. DOI: 10.1016/j.bbi.2004.11.004 PMID: 15944067

Davies, C., & Mann, A. (2023). Factors influencing women to accept diet and exercise messages on social media during COVID-19 lockdowns: A qualitative application of the health belief model. *Health Marketing Quarterly*, *40*(4), 1–19. DOI: 10.1080/07359683.2023.2193076 PMID: 37021625

Davis Fred, D. (1989). Perceived Usefulness, Perceived Ease of Use, and User Acceptance of Information Technology. *Management Information Systems Quarterly*, *13*(3), 319–340. DOI: 10.2307/249008

Davis, H. A., Kells, M., Roske, C., Holzman, S., & Wildes, J. E. (2023). A reflexive thematic analysis of #WhatIEatInADay on TikTok. *Eating Behaviors*, *50*, 101759. DOI: 10.1016/j.eatbeh.2023.101759

De Graaf, C., & Kok, F. J. (2010). Slow food, fast food and the control of food intake. *Nature Reviews. Endocrinology*, *6*(5), 290–293. DOI: 10.1038/nrendo.2010.41 PMID: 20351697

de Oliveira Machado, P. M., Kaminsk, R., Perin, G., de Moura, I. F., Januário, E. S., Mendonca, D. B., & de Almeida, A. F. C. (2018). Purchase of products directly from family farms for the National School Feeding Program (PNAE): Cross-sectional study with the universe of Brazilian municipalities. *Ciência e Saúde Coletiva*, *23*(12), 4153–4164. DOI: 10.1590/1413-812320182311.28012016

Derkatch, C. (2023). *Why Wellness Sells: Natural Health in a Pharmaceutical Culture*. DOI: 10.32920/24660234.v1

Desclee, D., Sohinto, D., & Padonou, F. (2021). Sustainability Assessment and Agricultural Supply Chains Evidence-Based Multidimensional Analyses as Tools for Strategic Decision-Making—The Case of the Pineapple Supply Chain in Benin. *Sustainability (Basel)*, *13*(4), 2060. DOI: 10.3390/su13042060

Deshmukh, V., & Gutte, R. K. (2024). Sustainable Health and Functional Foods. In *The Contribution of Universities Towards Education for Sustainable Development* (pp. 439–451). Springer Nature Switzerland. DOI: 10.1007/978-3-031-49853-4_25

Deshpande, S., Mandlik, R., Khadilkar, A. V., Chiplonkar, S. A., & Khadilkar, V. V. (2024). Micronutrient deficiency, dietary diversity, and sociodemographic and lifestyle determinants of dietary diversity among pregnant slum-dwelling women in Pune, India. *BMC Nutrition*, *10*(1), 108. DOI: 10.1186/s40795-024-00915-0 PMID: 39085982

Dewangan, S., Manoharan, G., Sharma, A. K., Kumar, S., & Talukder, M. B. (2024). *Leveraging Blockchain Technology for Enhanced Government Services, Transparency, and Administrative Efficiency*. 202–207.

Dharma, B. A., & Setiawan, A. (2024, November). Marketing Management Strategy Alternative for MSMEs. In *BISTIC Business Innovation Sustainability and Technology International Conference (BISTIC 2024)* (pp. 4-11). Atlantis Press.

Dhir, A., & Tsai, C. C. (2017). Understanding the relationship between intensity and gratifications of Facebook use among adolescents and young adults. *Telematics and Informatics*, *34*(4), 350–364. DOI: 10.1016/j.tele.2016.08.017

Di Rosa, L., De Pasquale, A., Baldassano, S., Marguglio, N., Drid, P., Proia, P., & Vasto, S. (2024). New Regenerative and Anti-Aging Medicine Approach Based on Single-Stranded Alpha-1 Collagen for Neo-Collagenesis Induction: Clinical and Instrumental Experience of a New Injective Polycomponent Formulation for Dermal Regeneration. *Biomedicines*, *12*(4), 916. DOI: 10.3390/biomedicines12040916 PMID: 38672270

Diao, X., Reardon, T., Kennedy, A., DeFries, R., Koo, J., Minten, B., Takeshima, H., & Thornton, P. K. (2023). The future of small farms: Innovations for inclusive transformation. In *Springer eBooks* (pp. 191–212). Springer Nature., DOI: 10.1007/978-3-031-15703-5_10

Ding, X., Ma, X., Meng, P., Yue, J., Li, L., & Xu, L. (2024). Potential Effects of Traditional Chinese Medicine in Anti-Aging and Aging-Related Diseases: Current Evidence and Perspectives. *Clinical Interventions in Aging*, *19*, 681–693. DOI: 10.2147/CIA.S447514 PMID: 38706635

Dolui, M., Sarkar, S., Ghosh, P., & Hossain, M. (2023). Dietary diversity and association with non-communicable diseases (NCDs) among adult men (15-54 years): A cross-sectional study using National Family and Health Survey, India. *PLOS Global Public Health, 3*(4), e0001775. DOI: 10.1371/journal.pgph.0001775 PMID: 37185617

Domingo, A., Yessis, J., Charles, K.-A., Skinner, K., & Hanning, R. M. (2023). Integrating knowledge and action: Learnings from an implementation program for food security and food sovereignty with First Nations communities within Canada. *Implementation Science*, *18*(1), Article 20. DOI: 10.1186/s13012-023-01291-2

Donner, M., & de Vries, H. (2023). Business models for sustainable food systems: A typology based on a literature review. *Frontiers in Sustainable Food Systems, 7*, 1160097. Advance online publication. DOI: 10.3389/fsufs.2023.1160097

Don, S., Lekshmi, M., & Kumar, S. H. (2025). Microbiological quality and safety of processed and packaged fish and fishery products. In *Quality Analysis and Packaging of Seafood Products* (pp. 305–333). Elsevier., DOI: 10.1016/B978-0-443-22082-1.00009-2

Drake, L., Fernandes, M., Aurino, E., Kiamba, J., Giyose, B., Burbano, C., Alderman, H., Lu, M., Mitchell, A., & Gelli, A. (2017). School feeding programs in middle childhood and adolescence. In *Child and adolescent health and development* (pp. 147–164). World Bank., DOI: 10.1596/978-1-4648-0423-6_ch12

Draper, D. A., Tynan, A., & Christianson, J. B. (2008). Health and wellness: the shift from managing illness to promoting health. *Information and Communication Technologies in Tourism*, 1–4. https://europepmc.org/article/MED/18536150

Drewnowski, A. (1995). Energy intake and sensory properties of food. *The American Journal of Clinical Nutrition, 62*(5), 1081S–1085S. DOI: 10.1093/ajcn/62.5.1081S PMID: 7484925

Dsouza, M. P., Shetty, A., Dinesh, T. K., & Damodar, P. (2023). Stimulating employee performance and well-being: A review of mindfulness impact in the hospitality sector. *IIMBG Journal of Sustainable Business and Innovation, 1*(1), 4–17. DOI: 10.1108/IJSBI-06-2023-0037

Dubé, L., Soman, D., & Almeida, F. (2021). *Precision Retailing: Building Upon Design Thinking for Societal-Scale Food Convergence Innovation and Well-Being*. Springer., DOI: 10.1007/978-3-030-54296-2_14

Duffey. (2010). Food price and diet and health outcomes: 20 Years of the CARDIA study (Archives of Internal Medicine (2010) 170, 5 (420-426)). *Archives of Internal Medicine, 170*(12), 1089. DOI: 10.1001/archinternmed.2010.176

Duffey, K. J., Gordon-Larsen, P., Shikany, J. M., Guilkey, D., Jacobs, D. R.Jr, & Popkin, B. M. (2010). Food price and diet and health outcomes: 20 years of the CARDIA study. *Archives of Internal Medicine, 170*(5), 420–426. DOI: 10.1001/archinternmed.2009.545 PMID: 20212177

Duus, K. S., Tjørnhøj-Thomsen, T., & Krølner, R. F. (2025). Negotiating healthy food retail initiatives in the research project Healthier Choices in Supermarkets: An ethnographic study of a partnership between health intervention researchers, food retailers, and public health advocates. *BMC Public Health, 25*(1), 1433. DOI: 10.1186/s12889-025-22633-3 PMID: 40241000

Early, R. (2002). Food ethics: A decision making tool for the food industry? *International Journal of Food Science & Technology, 37*(4), 339–349. DOI: 10.1046/j.1365-2621.2002.00547.x

Edirisinghe, G. S., & Munson, C. L. (2022). Strategic rearrangement of retail shelf space allocations: Using data insights to encourage impulse buying. *Expert Systems with Applications, 216*, 119442. DOI: 10.1016/j.eswa.2022.119442

El Archi, Y., El, Y., & Phd, A. A. (2022). *The role of OTAs in the transformation of tourism: a study on customer satisfaction in the digital era.* https://www.researchgate.net/publication/366014685

Elder, R., & Mohr, G. S. (2020). Guilty displeasures: How imagined guilt dampens consumer enjoyment. *Appetite, 150*, 104641. DOI: 10.1016/j.appet.2020.104641

Errmann, A., Conroy, D., & Young, J. M. (2023). The lab, land, and longing: Discursive constructions of Australian identities in 'future' food consumption. *Journal of Consumer Culture, 24*(1), 193–210. DOI: 10.1177/14695405231207602

Espinosa-Salas, S., & Gonzalez-Arias, M. (2023). Nutrition: Macronutrient intake, imbalances, and interventions. In *StatPearls*. StatPearls Publishing., https://www.ncbi.nlm.nih.gov/books/NBK594226/

Essa, M. M., Bishir, M., Bhat, A., Chidambaram, S. B., Al-Balushi, B., Hamdan, H., Govindarajan, N., Freidland, R. P., & Qoronfleh, M. W. (2021). Functional foods and their impact on health [Review of Functional foods and their impact on health]. Journal of Food Science and Technology, 60(3), 820. Springer Science+Business Media. DOI: 10.1007/s13197-021-05193-3

Fanzo, J., Bellows, A. L., Spiker, M. L., Thorne-Lyman, A. L., & Bloem, M. W. (2021). The importance of food systems and the environment for nutrition. *The American Journal of Clinical Nutrition, 113*(1), 7–16. DOI: 10.1093/ajcn/nqaa313 PMID: 33236086

Fanzo, J., McLaren, R., Bellows, A., & Carducci, B. (2023). Challenges and opportunities for increasing the effectiveness of food reformulation and fortification to improve dietary and nutrition outcomes. *Food Policy, 119*, 102515. DOI: 10.1016/j.foodpol.2023.102515

FAO. (2022). *The state of the world's land and water resources for food and agriculture – Systems at breaking point.* Food and Agriculture Organization of the United Nations.

Farre, G., Gomez-Galera, S., Naqvi, S., Bai, C., Sanahuja, G., Yuan, D., Zorrilla, U., Codony, L. T., Rojas, E., Fibla, M., Twyman, R. M., Capell, T., Christou, P., & Zhu, C. (2012). Biotechnology and nutritional improvement of crops. In Springer eBooks (pp. 1676–1723). DOI: 10.1007/978-1-4419-0851-3_160

Fathiya, K. N.Khansa Nur Fathiya. (2024). Food Security: A Key Component in Promoting Public Health and Nutrition. *International Journal of Health Engineering and Technology, 2*(5). Advance online publication. DOI: 10.55227/ijhet.v2i5.189

Fei, W., Noda, M., Danshiitsoodol, N., & Sugiyama, M. (2024). Skin Anti-Aging Efficacy of a Lactobacillus plantarum GT-17F Fermented Dendrobium officinale Ingredient: A Randomized, Double-Blind, Placebo-Controlled Clinical Study. *Cosmetics, 11*(1), 26. DOI: 10.3390/cosmetics11010026

Feng, Y., Jonathan Ye, H., Yu, Y., Yang, C., & Cui, T. (2018). Gamification artifacts and crowdsourcing participation: Examining the mediating role of intrinsic motivations. *Computers in Human Behavior, 81*, 124–136. DOI: 10.1016/j.chb.2017.12.018

Fernandes, A. C., Morais, C., Franchini, B., Pereira, B., Pinho, O., & Cunha, L. M. (2024). Clean-label products: Factors affecting liking and acceptability by Portuguese older adults. *Appetite, 197*, 107307. DOI: 10.1016/j.appet.2024.107307

Fewtrell, M., Kennedy, K., Singhal, A., Martin, R. M., Ness, A., Hadders-Algra, M., Koletzko, B., & Lucas, A. (2008). How much loss to follow-up is acceptable in long-term randomised trials and prospective studies? *Archives of Disease in Childhood*, *93*(6), 458–461. DOI: 10.1136/adc.2007.127316

Finaret, A. B., & Masters, W. A. (2019). Beyond calories: The new economics of nutrition. *Annual Review of Resource Economics*, *11*(1), 237–259. DOI: 10.1146/annurev-resource-100518-094053

Finaret, A. B., & Masters, W. A. (2025). Food economics: Teaching for the future of agriculture, nutrition, and health. *Applied Economic Perspectives and Policy*, *47*(3), 1232–1247. Advance online publication. DOI: 10.1002/aepp.13517

Find the right cheese product for you | Novonesis. (n.d.). Retrieved October 4, 2025, from https://www.novonesis.com/en/find-right-cheese-product-you

Firoozzare, A., Boccia, F., Yousefian, N., Ghazanfari, S., & Pakook, S. (2024). Understanding the role of awareness and trust in consumer purchase decisions for healthy food and products. *Food Quality and Preference*, *121*, 105275. DOI: 10.1016/j.foodqual.2024.105275

Firth, J., Gangwisch, J. E., Borsini, A., Wootton, R. E., & Mayer, E. A. (2020). Food and mood: How do diet and nutrition affect mental wellbeing? *BMJ (Clinical Research Ed.)*, *m2382*, m2382. DOI: 10.1136/bmj.m2382 PMID: 32601102

Fitricia, G. M., Putri, P. L., Slamet, S., Yuttama, F. R., & Alfizi, A. (2025). Managerial strategies in developing healthy food product: Integrating aspect of health and food science for competitive advantage. *BIO Web of Conferences, 152*, 01016. DOI: 10.1051/bioconf/202515201016

Fitzsimmons, J. A., Kinchla, A. J., & Allingham, C. (2024). Assessing the cost barrier for small and medium food processing businesses to meet Preventive Controls for Human Foods standards. *PLoS One*, *19*(9), e0306618. DOI: 10.1371/journal.pone.0306618 PMID: 39269951

Flanagin, A. J., & Metzger, M. J. (2007). The role of site features, user attributes, and information verification behaviors on the perceived credibility of web-based information. *New Media & Society*, *9*(2), 319–342. DOI: 10.1177/1461444807075015

Flavián, C., Guinalíu, M., & Lu, Y. (2020). Mobile payments adoption – introducing mindfulness to better understand consumer behavior. *International Journal of Bank Marketing*, *38*(7), 1575–1599. DOI: 10.1108/IJBM-01-2020-0039

Floridi, A., Anda-León, M. D., Kozakiewicz, T., Bhattacharyya, M., Thota, A., Burt, P., Tasciotti, L., Selby, J., Premji, Z., & Shisler, S. (2025). Effects of El Niño and the Positive Indian Ocean Dipole (+IOD) on Health, Food Security, Economics, and Conflict in Low- and Middle-Income Countries in the Indo-Pacific: A Systematic Review. *Campbell Systematic Reviews*, *21*(2), e70038. Advance online publication. DOI: 10.1002/cl2.70038 PMID: 40248359

Fogarassy, C., & Finger, D. C. (2020). Theoretical and practical approaches of circular economy for business models and technological solutions. *Resources*, *9*(6), 76. DOI: 10.3390/resources9060076

Food and Drink Federation Scotland. (2023). *Reformulation case study compilation.* https://www.fdf.org.uk/globalassets/resources/case-studies/fdf-scotland/reformulation-case-study-compilation.pdf

Food As Thought Analysis. (2024). https://gradesfixer.com/free-essay-examples/mary-maxfield-food-as-thought-analysis/

Forde, C. G., & Bolhuis, D. P. (2022). Interrelations Between Food Form, Texture, and Matrix Influence Energy Intake and Metabolic Responses [Review of Interrelations Between Food Form, Texture, and Matrix Influence Energy Intake and Metabolic Responses]. Current Nutrition Reports, 11(2), 124. Springer Science+Business Media. DOI: 10.1007/s13668-022-00413-4

Ford, H., Dolan, R., Goodman, S., Bastian, S., Pearson, W., & Corsi, A. M. (2025). Exploring consumers' drinking behaviour regarding no-, low-and mid-alcohol wines: A systematic scoping review and guiding framework. *Journal of Marketing Management, 41*(7-8), 1–31. DOI: 10.1080/0267257X.2025.2499101

Franceschelli, M. V., Santoro, G., & Candelo, E. (2018). Business model innovation for sustainability: A food start-up case study. *British Food Journal, 120*(10), 2483–2494. DOI: 10.1108/BFJ-01-2018-0049

Frascarelli, A., Ciliberti, S., Bartolucci, P. E., & Mastandrea, G. (2025). Correction to: The CAP coherence between redistributive and environmental goals: do the allocation criteria for direct payments play a role? (Agricultural and Food Economics, (2025), 13, 1, (15),). *Agricultural and Food Economics, 13*(1). https://doi.org/DOI: 10.1186/s40100-025-00356-8

Freedhoff, Y. (2014). The food industry is neither friend, nor foe, nor partner. *Obesity Reviews, 15*(1), 6–8. DOI: 10.1111/obr.12128 PMID: 24330345

Freeman, B., & Sindall, C. (2019). Countering the commercial determinants of health: Strategic challenges for public health. *Public Health Research & Practice, 29*(3), e2931917. Advance online publication. DOI: 10.17061/phrp2931917 PMID: 31569200

Freudenberg, N., Willingham, C., & Cohen, N. (2018). The role of metrics in food policy: Lessons from a decade of experience in New York City. *Journal of Agriculture, Food Systems, and Community Development,* *8*(Suppl. 2), 191–204. DOI: 10.5304/jafscd.2018.08B.009

Friel, S., Hattersley, L., Ford, L., & O'Rourke, K. (2015). Addressing inequities in healthy eating. *Health Promotion International, 30*(Suppl_2), ii77–ii88. DOI: 10.1093/heapro/dav073 PMID: 26420812

Gajanan, S. N., & Babu, S. C. (2024). Assessing the economics of fuel for food: Approaches to assessment of time allocations for household chores and roles. In *Handbook on Public Policy and Food Security*. Edward Elgar Publishing Ltd., DOI: 10.4337/9781839105449.00024

Galanakis, C. M., Rizou, M., Aldawoud, T. M. S., Ucak, İ., & Rowan, N. J. (2021). Innovations and technology disruptions in the food sector within the COVID-19 pandemic and post-lockdown era [Review of Innovations and technology disruptions in the food sector within the COVID-19 pandemic and post-lockdown era]. Trends in Food Science & Technology, 110, 193. Elsevier BV. DOI: 10.1016/j.tifs.2021.02.002

García-Castaño, S. G., Pompelli, M. F., Ruiz, A. J. B., & Perneth-Montaño, M. J. (2025). Fruit and Vegetables Harvest and post-harvest. In *Plant Phisiology: Bromeliad Conservation, Stress Signaling, and Post-harvest Innovation* (1st ed., pp. 165–181). Editora Científica Digital. DOI: 10.37885/250619549

García-Salirrosas, E. E., Escobar-Farfán, M., Esponda-Pérez, J. A., Millones-Liza, D. Y., Villar-Guevara, M., Zea, K. L. H., & Gallardo-Canales, R. (2024). The impact of perceived value on brand image and loyalty: A study of healthy food brands in emerging markets. *Frontiers in Nutrition*, *11*, 1482009. Advance online publication. DOI: 10.3389/fnut.2024.1482009

Garg, M., Sharma, N., Sharma, S., Kapoor, P., Kumar, A., Chunduri, V., & Arora, P. (2018). Biofortified Crops Generated by Breeding, Agronomy, and Transgenic Approaches Are Improving Lives of Millions of People around the World. *Frontiers in Nutrition*, *5*, 12. Advance online publication. DOI: 10.3389/fnut.2018.00012 PMID: 29492405

Gems, D., Okholm, S., & Lemoine, M. (2024). Inflated expectations: the strange craze for translational research on aging: Given existing confusion about the basic science of aging, why the high optimism in the private sector about the prospects of developing anti-aging treatments? *EMBO Reports*, *25*(9), 3748–3752. DOI: 10.1038/s44319-024-00226-2 PMID: 39152216

Geny, A., Petitjean, M., Van Wymelbeke-Delannoy, V., & Sulmont-Rossé, C. (2023). Impact of food-based fortification on nutritional outcomes and acceptability in older adults: Systematic literature review. *Frontiers in Nutrition*, *10*, 1232502. DOI: 10.3389/fnut.2023.1232502 PMID: 37964932

George, D. R., Danciu, M., Davenport, P. W., Lakin, M. R., Chappell, J., & Frow, E. K. (2024). A bumpy road ahead for genetic biocontainment. *Nature Communications*, *15*(1), 650. DOI: 10.1038/s41467-023-44531-1

Ghazanfari, S., Firoozzare, A., Covino, D., Boccia, F., & Palmieri, N. (2024). Exploring Factors Influencing Consumers' Willingness to Pay Healthy-Labeled Foods at a Premium Price. *Sustainability (Basel)*, *16*(16), 6895. DOI: 10.3390/su16166895

Gheonea, T. C., Oancea, C.-N., Mititelu, M., Lupu, C. E., Ioni ă-Mîndrican, C.-B., & Rogoveanu, I. (2023). Nutrition and Mental Well-Being: Exploring Connections and Holistic Approaches. *Journal of Clinical Medicine*, *12*(22), 7180. DOI: 10.3390/jcm12227180

Ghoshal, G., & Kansal, S. K. (2019). 2—The Emerging Trends in Functional and Medicinal Beverage Research and Its Health Implication. In Grumezescu, A. M., & Holban, A. M. (Eds.), *Functional and Medicinal Beverages* (pp. 41–71). Academic Press., DOI: 10.1016/B978-0-12-816397-9.00002-9

Gill, R., & Singh, J. (2020). A study of neuromarketing techniques for proposing cost effective information driven framework for decision making. *Materials Today: Proceedings*, *49*, 2969–2981. DOI: 10.1016/j.matpr.2020.08.730

Gittelsohn, J., Trude, A., & Kim, H. (2017). Pricing strategies to encourage availability, purchase, and consumption of healthy foods and beverages: A systematic review. *Preventing Chronic Disease*, *14*, 170213. DOI: 10.5888/pcd14.170213

Global Alliance for Improved Nutrition. (2021). *Food systems and nutrition: Working together for change*. GAIN.

Godfray, H. C. J., Beddington, J. R., Crute, I. R., Haddad, L., Lawrence, D., Muir, J. F., Pretty, J., Robinson, S., Thomas, S. M., & Toulmin, C. (2010). Food Security: The Challenge of Feeding 9 Billion People. *Science*, *327*(5967), 812–818. DOI: 10.1126/science.1185383 PMID: 20110467

Gokce, A., Bazi, S., Safavi, B., Georgiadou, E., & Hajlı, N. (2023). The role of social media content on value co-creation in the food sector: A strategic relationship perspective. *British Food Journal*, *125*(10), 3585–3600. Advance online publication. DOI: 10.1108/BFJ-09-2022-0772

Gómez-Pinilla, F. (2008). Brain foods: The effects of nutrients on brain function. *Nature Reviews. Neuroscience*, *9*(7), 568–578. DOI: 10.1038/nrn2421 PMID: 18568016

Gosliner, W., Brown, D. M., Sun, B. C., Woodward-Lopez, G., & Crawford, P. B. (2019). Corrigendum: Availability, quality and price of produce in low-income neighbourhood food stores in California raise equity issues (Public Health Nutrition (2018) 21:9 (1639-1648) DOI:). *Public Health Nutrition, 22*(1), 184 – 185. https://doi.org/DOI: 10.1017/S1368980018000058

Goukens, C., & Klesse, A. K. (2022). Internal and external forces that prevent (vs. Facilitate) healthy eating: Review and outlook within consumer Psychology [Review of Internal and external forces that prevent (vs. Facilitate) healthy eating: Review and outlook within consumer Psychology]. Current Opinion in Psychology, 46, 101328. Elsevier BV. DOI: 10.1016/j.copsyc.2022.101328

Graham, A. E., & Ledesma-Amaro, R. (2023). The microbial food revolution. *Nature Communications 2023 14:1, 14*(1), 1–10. DOI: 10.1038/s41467-023-37891-1

Grajek, M., Krupa-Kotara, K., Białek-Dratwa, A., Sobczyk, K., Grot, M., Kowalski, O., & Staśkiewicz-Bartecka, W. (2022). Nutrition and mental health: A review of current knowledge about the impact of diet on mental health [Review of Nutrition and mental health: A review of current knowledge about the impact of diet on mental health]. Frontiers in Nutrition, 9. Frontiers Media. DOI: 10.3389/fnut.2022.943998

Green, R., Cornelsen, L., Dangour, A. D., Turner, R. A., Shankar, B., Mazzocchi, M., & Smith, R. (2013). The effect of rising food prices on food consumption: Systematic review with meta-regression. *BMJ*, *346*, f3703. DOI: 10.1136/bmj.f3703

Green, R., Milner, J., Joy, E. J., Agrawal, S., & Dangour, A. D. (2016). Dietary patterns in India: A systematic review. *British Journal of Nutrition, 116*(1), 142–148. DOI: 10.1017/S0007114516001598 PMID: 27146890

Grinin, L., Grinin, A., & Korotayev, A. (2024). Anti-aging as a Key Challenge for the Medicine of the Future. In *Cybernetic Revolution and Global Aging: Humankind on the Way to Cybernetic Society, or the Next Hundred Years* (pp. 459–485). Springer International Publishing. DOI: 10.1007/978-3-031-56764-3_11

Grujic, S., Grujic, R., & Grujčić, M. (2023). Factors affecting consumer preference for healthy diet and functional foods. *Foods and Raw Materials*, 259–271. DOI: 10.21603/2308-4057-2023-2-576

Guarente, L., Sinclair, D. A., & Kroemer, G. (2024). Human trials exploring anti-aging medicines. *Cell Metabolism, 36*(2), 354–376. DOI: 10.1016/j.cmet.2023.12.007 PMID: 38181790

Gunawan, M., Soetjipto, B., & Sudhartio, L. (2023). How to link organizational resilience to transformational entrepreneurship behavior as a theoretical framework gap – A systematic literature review. *F1000 Research, 12*, 1–27. DOI: 10.12688/f1000research.133459.1 PMID: 37441222

Guo, X., Yao, J., Yan, G., & Teng, G. (2025). An intelligent model approach for leakage detection of modified atmosphere pillow bags. *Engineering Applications of Artificial Intelligence, 139*, 109611. DOI: 10.1016/j.engappai.2024.109611

Gupta, A., Sanwal, N., Bareen, M. A., Barua, S., Sharma, N., Olatunji, O. J., Nirmal, N. P., & Sahu, J. K. (2023). Trends in functional beverages: Functional ingredients, processing technologies, stability, health benefits, and consumer perspective [Review of Trends in functional beverages: Functional ingredients, processing technologies, stability, health benefits, and consumer perspective]. Food Research International, 170, 113046. Elsevier BV. DOI: 10.1016/j.foodres.2023.113046

Gupta, B. B., Gaurav, A., Panigrahi, P. K., & Arya, V. (2023). Analysis of artificial intelligence-based technologies and approaches on sustainable entrepreneurship. *Technological Forecasting and Social Change, 186 Part B*(122152), 0040-1625, https://doi.org/https://doi.org/10.1016/j.techfore.2022.122152

Gupta, M., & Sharma, A. (2021). Fear of missing out: A brief overview of origin, theoretical underpinnings and relationship with mental health [Review of Fear of missing out: A brief overview of origin, theoretical underpinnings and relationship with mental health]. World Journal of Clinical Cases, 9(19), 4881. Baishideng Publishing Group. DOI: 10.12998/wjcc.v9.i19.4881

Gupta, N., Bhattacharjee, M., & Saha, A. R. (2023). Association Between Socio-demographic Factors and the Health Orientation of Urban Consumers Toward the Consumption of High-Value Agricultural Products in India. *Arthshastra Indian Journal of Economics & Research, 12*(4), 8–24. DOI: 10.17010/aijer/2023/v12i4/172814

Guru, S., Thanki, S. J., & Thakkar, J. J. (2024). *Analysing Factors Driving Purchase and Consumption Behaviour Towards Organic Food.* DOI: 10.1177/09722629231225535

Hadley, C., Stevenson, E. G. J., Tadesse, Y., & Belachew, T. (2012). Rapidly rising food prices and the experience of food insecurity in urban Ethiopia: Impacts on health and well-being. *Social Science & Medicine, 75*(12), 2412–2419. DOI: 10.1016/j.socscimed.2012.09.018 PMID: 23062966

Ha, M. T., Do Nguyen, G., & Doan, B. S. (2023). Understanding the mediating effect of switching costs on service value, quality, satisfaction, and loyalty. *Humanities & Social Sciences Communications, 10*(1), 288. Advance online publication. DOI: 10.1057/s41599-023-01797-6

Hamburg, I., & Bucksch, S. (2017). Inclusive education and digital social innovation. *Advances in Social Sciences Research Journal, 4*(5). Advance online publication. DOI: 10.14738/assrj.45.2861

Hammami, R., Fliss, I., & Corsetti, A. (2019). Editorial: Application of Protective Cultures and Bacteriocins for Food Biopreservation. *Frontiers in Microbiology, 10*(JULY), 1561. DOI: 10.3389/fmicb.2019.01561

Hammond, S. T., Brown, J. H., Burger, J. R., Flanagan, T., Fristoe, T. S., Mercado-Silva, N., Nekola, J. C., & Okie, J. G. (2015). Food spoilage, storage, and transport: Implications for a sustainable future. *BioScience*, *65*(8), 758–768. DOI: 10.1093/biosci/biv081

Hanus, G. (2018). Food market innovations as a response to consumer requirements: A review of literature. *Optimum. Economic Studies*, *91*(1), 251–264.

Ha, O., & Lim, S.-L. (2023). The role of emotion in eating behavior and decisions. *Frontiers in Psychology*, *14*, 1265074. Advance online publication. DOI: 10.3389/fpsyg.2023.1265074

Hassoun, A. (2025). Food sustainability 4.0: Harnessing fourth industrial revolution technologies for sustainable food systems. *Discover Food*, *5*(1), 171. DOI: 10.1007/s44187-025-00461-z

Hassoun, A., Bekhit, A. E.-D. A., Jambrak, A. R., Regenstein, J. M., Chemat, F., Morton, J. D., Gudjónsdóttir, M., Carpena, M., Prieto, M. A., Varela, P., Arshad, R. N., Aadil, R. M., Bhat, Z. F., & Ueland, Ø. (2022). The fourth industrial revolution in the food industry-part II: Emerging food trends. *Critical Reviews in Food Science and Nutrition*, •••, 1–31. DOI: 10.1080/10408398.2022.2106472 PMID: 35930319

Hayat, U., Li, W., Bie, H., Liu, S., Guo, D., & Cao, K. (2023). An Overview on Post-Harvest Technological Advances and Ripening Techniques for Increasing Peach Fruit Quality and Shelf Life. *Horticulturae*, *10*(1), 4. DOI: 10.3390/horticulturae10010004

Healthy Living Alliance. (2023). *Community monitoring for healthier food environments*. https://heala.org

Heider, F. (1946). Attitudes and Cognitive Organization. *The Journal of Psychology*, *21*(1), 107–112. DOI: 10.1080/00223980.1946.9917275 PMID: 21010780

Herman, C. P., & Polivy, J. (2008). External cues in the control of food intake in humans: The sensory-normative distinction. *Physiology & Behavior*, *94*(5), 722–728. DOI: 10.1016/j.physbeh.2008.04.014 PMID: 18499202

Herrero, M., Hugas, M., Lele, U., Wirakartakusumah, A., & Torero, M. (2023). *A Shift to Healthy and Sustainable Consumption Patterns*., DOI: 10.1007/978-3-031-15703-5_5

Hilgendorf, K., Wang, Y., Miller, M. J., & Jin, Y. S. (2024). Precision fermentation for improving the quality, flavor, safety, and sustainability of foods. *Current Opinion in Biotechnology*, *86*, 103084. DOI: 10.1016/j.copbio.2024.103084

Hiywotu, A. M. (2025). Advancing sustainable agriculture for goal 2: Zero hunger - a comprehensive overview of practices, policies, and technologies. *Agroecology and Sustainable Food Systems*, *49*(7), 1027–1055. DOI: 10.1080/21683565.2025.2451344

Hobbs, J. E., Malla, S., Sogah, E. K., & Yeung, M. T. (n.d.). *Through the Looking Glass*. DOI: 10.4337/9781783474721.00014

Hocquette, J.-F., Chriki, S., Fournier, D., & Ellies-Oury, M.-P. (2025). Review: Will "cultured meat" transform our food system towards more sustainability? *Animal*, *19*, 101145. DOI: 10.1016/j.animal.2024.101145 PMID: 38670917

Hollebeek, L. D., Das, K., & Shukla, Y. (2021). Game On! How Gamified Loyalty Programs Boost Customer Engagement Value. *International Journal of Information Management*, *61*, 102308. https://www.researchgate.net/publication/348565144. DOI: 10.1016/j.ijinfomgt.2021.102308

Hood, M. M., Kapoor, V., Sawhney, G., & Singh, H. (2024). India's Vision of a Healthy and Developed Nation from the Perspective of the Healthtech Industry. *India's Vision of a Healthy and Developed Nation from the Perspective of the Healthtech Industry.*, *12*(8), 127–132. DOI: 10.35629/3002-1208127132

Horgen, K. B., & Brownell, K. D. (2002). Comparison of price change and health message interventions in promoting healthy food choices. *Health Psychology*, *21*(5), 505–512. DOI: 10.1037/0278-6133.21.5.505 PMID: 12211518

Huang, B. (2020). *Research on the Optimization Path of Supply side Structural Reform of Fitness and Leisure Industry under the Background of National Fitness*. https://doi.org/DOI: 10.23977/IEESASM.2019.053

Huang, Z., Du, Y., Xu, F., & Hu, C. (2022). How Does the Horizontal Position of Pictures and Text Affect Product Evaluation? Based on Left and Right Position Effect. *Frontiers in Psychology*, *13*, 841480. Advance online publication. DOI: 10.3389/fpsyg.2022.841480

Huang, Z., Zhu, Y., Deng, J., & Wang, C. (2022). Marketing Healthy Diets: The Impact of Health Consciousness on Chinese Consumers' Food Choices. *Sustainability (Basel)*, *14*(4), 2059. DOI: 10.3390/su14042059

Iacomino, G., Rufián Henares, J. Á., & Lauria, F. (2024). Editorial: Personalized nutrition and gut microbiota: Current and future directions. *Frontiers in Nutrition*, *11*, 1375157. DOI: 10.3389/fnut.2024.1375157 PMID: 38487630

ICMR. (2024). *Dietary guidelines for Indians – 2024*. Indian Council of Medical Research – National Institute of Nutrition. https://www.nin.res.in/dietaryguidelines/pdfjs/locale/DGI07052024P.pdf

Ihssen, N., & Wadsley, M. (2020). A reward and incentive-sensitization perspective on compulsive use of social networking sites – Wanting but not liking predicts checking frequency and problematic use behavior. *Addictive Behaviors*, *116*, 106808. DOI: 10.1016/j.addbeh.2020.106808

Ikram, M. (2022). Transition toward green economy: Technological Innovation's role in the fashion industry.

Inguglia, E. S., Song, Z., Kerry, J. P., O'Sullivan, M. G., & Hamill, R. M. (2023). Addressing Clean Label Trends in Commercial Meat Processing: Strategies, Challenges and Insights from Consumer Perspectives. *Foods*, *12*(10), 2062. DOI: 10.3390/foods12102062 PMID: 37238880

Institute of Medicine (US) Committee on Military Nutrition Research. Carlson-Newberry, S. J., & Costello, R. B. (Eds.). (1997). *Emerging Technologies for Nutrition Research: Potential for Assessing Military Performance Capability*. National Academies Press (US).

Institute of Medicine (US) Food and Nutrition Board. (1989). *Biotechnological developments: Potential for improvements in food formulation, nutrient delivery, and safety*. In *Frontiers in the nutrition sciences: Proceedings of a symposium*. National Academies Press. https://www.ncbi.nlm.nih.gov/books/NBK235299/

Ishak, A. W., & Williams, E. A. (2018). A dynamic model of organizational resilience: Adaptive and anchored approaches. *Corporate Communications*, *23*(2), 180–196. DOI: 10.1108/CCIJ-04-2017-0037

Iwashima, F., & Sato, C. (2022). Revisiting "empowered rural women" in postwar Japan. *Journal of Agrarian Change*, *22*(4), 855–873. DOI: 10.1111/joac.12494

Iweala, E. J., Adurosakin, O. E., Innocent, U., Omonhinmin, C. A., Dania, O. E., & Ugbogu, E. A. (2024). Anti-Aging Potential of Bioactive Phytoconstituents Found in Edible Medicinal Plants: A Review. *Sci*, *6*(2), 36. DOI: 10.3390/sci6020036

Izadi, M., Sadri, N., Abdi, A., Zadeh, M. M. R., Jalaei, D., Ghazimoradi, M. M., Shouri, S., & Tahmasebi, S. (2024). Longevity and anti-aging effects of curcumin supplementation. *GeroScience*, *46*(3), 2933–2950. DOI: 10.1007/s11357-024-01092-5 PMID: 38409646

Jackson, P. (2023). Food, health and sustainability. *The Proceedings of the Nutrition Society*, *82*(3), 227–233. DOI: 10.1017/S0029665122002841 PMID: 36503525

Jadhav, H. B., Sablani, S. S., Gogate, P. R., Annapure, U. S., Casanova, F., Nayik, G. A., Alaskar, K., Sarwar, N., Raina, I., Ramniwas, S., & Mousavi Khaneghah, A. (2023). Factors governing consumers buying behavior concerning nutraceutical product. *Food Science & Nutrition*, *11*(9), 4988–5003. Advance online publication. DOI: 10.1002/fsn3.3518 PMID: 37701202

Jain, P., Sapkal, L. D., Singh, S., & Gaikwad, K. K. (2026). Smart packaging and traceability: Ensuring quality and safety of functional food products. In *Artificial Intelligence in Food Science*. Academic Press, Elsevier. https://www.sciencedirect.com/science/chapter/edited-volume/abs/pii/B9780443264689000266

Jain, V., Crosby, L., Baker, P., & Chalkidou, K. (2020). Distributional equity as a consideration in economic and modelling evaluations of health taxes: A systematic review. *Health Policy*, *124*(9), 919–929. DOI: 10.1016/j.healthpol.2020.05.022

Jaros-Sajda, A., Budzisz, E., & Erkiert-Polguj, A. (2024). Ascorbic acid treatments as effective and safe anti-aging therapies for sensitive skin. *Antioxidants*, *13*(2), 174. DOI: 10.3390/antiox13020174 PMID: 38397772

Javed, A., Usman, M., & Rapposelli, A. (2025). Transition toward a sustainable future: Exploring the role of green investment, environmental policy, and financial development in the context of load capacity factor in G-7 countries. *Sustainable Development (Bradford)*, *33*(2), 1589–1609. DOI: 10.1002/sd.3192

Jeong, S., & Lee, J.-H. (2021). Effects of cultural background on consumer perception and acceptability of foods and drinks: A review of latest cross-cultural studies. *Current Opinion in Food Science*, *42*, 248–256. DOI: 10.1016/j.cofs.2021.07.004

Jeong, M., Kim, K., Ma, F., & DiPietro, R. (2022). Key factors driving customers' restaurant dining behavior during the COVID-19 pandemic. *International Journal of Contemporary Hospitality Management*, *34*(2), 836–858. DOI: 10.1108/IJCHM-07-2021-0831

Jiakui, C., Abbas, J., Najam, H., Liu, J., & Abbas, J. (2023). Green technological innovation, green finance, and financial development and their role in green total factor productivity: Empirical insights from China. *Journal of Cleaner Production*, *382*, 135131. DOI: 10.1016/j.jclepro.2022.135131

Jia, Y., & Clark, K. (2024). The Role of Impulsivity and Addiction in Gambling Behaviors: How Applied Neuroscience Research Can Help in the Monitoring and Management of Mental Health Issues. *Open Journal of Medical Psychology*, *13*(1), 11–24. DOI: 10.4236/ojmp.2024.131002

Jiménez-Trigo, V., Fernández-Ochoa, Á., De La Luz Cádiz-Gurrea, M., Leyva-Jiménez, F. J., Segura-Carretero, A., & Arráez-Román, D. (2025). Current Trends in Reducing Fruit Spoilage from Enzymatic Browning Using Physical Techniques: Avocado Pulp as a Case Study. *Food Reviews International, 41*(9), 1–23. DOI: 10.1080/87559129.2025.2529539

Jones, S., Cain, L., & Deel, G. L. (2024). Virtual Restaurants and Ghost Kitchens: A New Opportunity. *Journal of Hospitality & Tourism Cases, 12(3)*, 108-112. https://doi.org/https://doi.org/10.1177/21649987241241948. (Original work published 2024)

Jönsson, H., Michaud, M., & Neuman, N. (2021). What Is Commensality? A Critical Discussion of an Expanding Research Field [Review of What Is Commensality? A Critical Discussion of an Expanding Research Field]. International Journal of Environmental Research and Public Health, 18(12), 6235. Multidisciplinary Digital Publishing Institute. DOI: 10.3390/ijerph18126235

Kala Kamdjoug, J. R., Djuitchou Chengo, S. M., & Gueyie, J. P. (2021). Factors affecting the adoption of information technologies by small woman-managed enterprises in Cameroon. *Journal of Small Business and Entrepreneurship, 33*(4), 433–451. DOI: 10.1080/08276331.2020.1716134

Kanellos, N., Karountzos, P., Giannakopoulos, N. T., Terzi, M. C., & Sakas, D. P. (2024). Digital Marketing Strategies and Profitability in the Agri-Food Industry: Resource Efficiency and Value Chains. *Sustainability (Basel), 16*(14), 5889. DOI: 10.3390/su16145889

Kang, Y., Kim, S., Sinamo, S., & Christian, P. (2017). Effectiveness of a community-based nutrition programme to improve child growth in rural Ethiopia: a cluster randomized trial. *Maternal & child nutrition, 13*(1), . https://doi.org/DOI: 10.1111/mcn.12349

Kapoor, P. S., Jayasimha, K. R., & Sadh, A. (2013). Brand-related, Consumer to Consumer, Communication via social media. *IIM Kozhikode Society & Management Review, 2*(1), 43–59. DOI: 10.1177/2277975213496514

Kaput, J., Kussmann, M., Mendoza, Y. A., Coutre, R. L., Cooper, K., & Roulin, A. C. (2015). Enabling nutrient security and sustainability through systems research. *Genes & Nutrition*, *10*(3), Article 12. DOI: 10.1007/s12263-015-0462-6

Karlsen, R., & Andersen, A. (2019). Recommendations with a nudge. *Technologies*, *7*(2), 45. DOI: 10.3390/technologies7020045

Karpyn, A., McCallops, K., Wolgast, H., & Glanz, K. (2020). Improving Consumption and Purchases of Healthier Foods in Retail Environments: A Systematic Review. *International Journal of Environmental Research and Public Health, 17*(20), 7524. DOI: 10.3390/ijerph17207524 PMID: 33081130

Kasapoğlu, K. N., Daskaya-Dikmen, C., Yavuz-Düzgün, M., Karaca, A. C., & Özçelik, B. (2019). *Enrichment of Beverages With Health Beneficial Ingredients.* Academic Press., DOI: 10.1016/B978-0-12-816687-1.00003-5

Kathuria, A., & Bakshi, A. (2024). Influence of promotional factors on online impulse buying: Exploring the mediating role of impulse buying tendency. *Current Psychology (New Brunswick, N.J.), 43*(1), 34035–34051. DOI: 10.1007/s12144-024-06911-8

Katre, A., & Raddatz, B. (2023). Low-income families' direct participation in food-systems innovation to promote healthy food behaviors. *Nutrients, 15*(5), 1271. DOI: 10.3390/nu15051271 PMID: 36904271

Katz, E., Blumler, J. G., & Gurevitch, M. (1973). USES AND GRATIFICATIONS RESEARCH. *Public Opinion Quarterly, 37*(4), 509–523. https://poq.oxfordjournals .org/. DOI: 10.1086/268109

Kaur, M., Singh, R., Singh, M., & Singh, K. (2023). Can health consciousness drive purchase intention toward packaged immunity boosting food products? *Journal of Foodservice Business Research*, •••, 1–22. DOI: 10.1080/15378020.2023.2298614

Kearney, J. (2010). Food consumption trends and drivers. *Philosophical Transactions of the Royal Society of London. Series B, Biological Sciences, 365*(1554), 2793–2807. DOI: 10.1098/rstb.2010.0149 PMID: 20713385

Khamoushi, E. (2024). AI in Food Marketing from Personalized Recommendations to Predictive Analytics: Comparing Traditional Advertising Techniques with AI-Driven Strategies. *arXiv preprint arXiv:2410.01815.*

Khan, S. T., Malik, A., Al–Warthan, A., & Shaik, M. R. (2021). The enormity of the zinc deficiency problem and available solutions; an overview. *Arabian Journal of Chemistry*, *15*(3), 103668. DOI: 10.1016/j.arabjc.2021.103668

Khara, T., Riedy, C., & Ruby, M. B. (2021). The Evolution of Urban Australian Meat-Eating Practices. *Frontiers in Sustainable Food Systems, 5*, 624288. Advance online publication. DOI: 10.3389/fsufs.2021.624288

Kinsey, J. D., & Buhr, B. L. (2003). E-commerce: a new business model for the food supply/demand chain. *The IUP Journal of Agricultural Economics, 1*(1), 31–47. DOI: 10.22004/AG.ECON.14320

Kishore, G. M., & Shewmaker, C. (1999). Biotechnology: Enhancing human nutrition in developing and developed worlds. *Proceedings of the National Academy of Sciences of the United States of America, 96*(11), 5968–5972. DOI: 10.1073/pnas.96.11.5968 PMID: 10339525

Klinaki, E., & Ogrodnik, M. (2024). In the land of not-unhappiness: On the state-of-the-art of targeting aging and age-related diseases by biomedical research. *Mechanisms of Ageing and Development, 219*, 111929. DOI: 10.1016/j.mad.2024.111929 PMID: 38561164

Knez, E., Kadac-Czapska, K., & Grembecka, M. (2023). Effect of Fermentation on the Nutritional Quality of the Selected Vegetables and Legumes and Their Health Effects. *Life (Basel, Switzerland), 13*(3), 655. DOI: 10.3390/life13030655

Kohli, A., Omollo, D., & Munyua, H. (2018). Urban gardening cooperatives in Nairobi's informal settlements: Dietary diversity and livelihoods. *Journal of Urban Health*, *95*(3), 456–468. DOI: 10.1007/s11524-018-0266-7

Kolodziejczyk, A. A., Zheng, D., & Elinav, E. (2019). Diet–microbiota interactions and personalized nutrition. *Nature Reviews. Microbiology, 17*(12), 742–753. DOI: 10.1038/s41579-019-0256-8 PMID: 31541197

Korver, O. (1997). 'Healthy' developments in the food industry. *Cancer Letters, 114*(1–2), 19–23. DOI: 10.1016/S0304-3835(97)04617-X PMID: 9103246

Kowalczuk, I., Gutkowska, K., Sajdakowska, M., & Żakowska-Biemans, S. (2016). PRODUCT INNOVATIVENESS AND ITS IMPACT ON HEALTH RELATED IMPORTANCE OF FOOD IN THE CATERING BUSINESS. *Acta Scientiarum Polonorum. Oeconomia, 15*(2), 2.

Kristeller, J. L., & Wolever, R. Q. (2010). Mindfulness-Based Eating Awareness Training for Treating Binge Eating Disorder: The Conceptual Foundation. *Eating Disorders, 19*(1), 49–61. DOI: 10.1080/10640266.2011.533605 PMID: 21181579

Kukla, Q. R. (2024). Healthism, Elite Capture, and the Pitfalls of an Expansive Concept of Health. In *Philosophy and medicine* (p. 275). Springer Nature., DOI: 10.1007/978-3-031-62241-0_21

Kukreti, M., Sehajpal, S., Tiwari, R., & Sood, K. (2024a). Introduction. In *Driving Global Health and Sustainable Development Goals With Smart Technology*. IGI Global. DOI: 10.4018/979-8-3373-0240-9

Kumar, A., Vinod Kumar, K., Sengupta, A., Kundal, K., Sharma, S., Pawar, A., & Kumar, R. (2024). AagingBase: A comprehensive database of anti-aging peptides. *Database : The Journal of Biological Databases and Curation, 2024*, baae016. DOI: 10.1093/database/baae016 PMID: 38470883

Kumar, G. R. (2024). Food tourism research in India – current trends and future scope. *Tourism Review, 79*(3), 640–657. DOI: 10.1108/TR-07-2022-0366

Kumar, S. (2024). The Role of Digital Marketing on Customer Engagement in the Hospitality Industry. In Bansal, R., Ngah, A. H., Chakir, A., & Pruthi, N. (Eds.), (pp. 177–191). Advances in Business Information Systems and Analytics. IGI Global., DOI: 10.4018/979-8-3693-0815-8.ch010

Kumar, S., Dhir, A., Talwar, S., Chakraborty, D., & Kaur, P. (2020). What drives brand love for natural products? The moderating role of household size. *Journal of Retailing and Consumer Services, 58*, 102329. DOI: 10.1016/j.jretconser.2020.102329

Kumar, S., & Patel, A. K. (2019). An analysis of cointegration between nifty index, dollar/INR and crude oil price. *Journal of Advanced Research in Dynamical and Control Systems, 11*(12), 151–159. DOI: 10.5373/JARDCS/V11I12/20193223

Kumar, S., Talukder, M. B., Kabir, F., & Kaiser, F. (2023). Challenges and Sustainability of Green Finance in the Tourism Industry: Evidence From Bangladesh. In Taneja, S., Kumar, P., Grima, S., Ozen, E., & Sood, K. (Eds.), (pp. 97–111). Advances in Finance, Accounting, and Economics. IGI Global., DOI: 10.4018/979-8-3693-1388-6.ch006

Kunnumpurath, B., Kumar, S., Menon, V. A., Prasad, A., & Ramanath, M. (2025). Behavioural Economics and Korean Food Consumption: Health Environment Sensitivity, Nutrition Application, Cost Saving, and Convenience Practices. In *Behavioral Economics and Neuroeconomics of Health and Healthcare* (pp. 25-52). IGI Global.

Kurowska, A., Ziemichód, W., Herbet, M., & Piątkowska-Chmiel, I. (2023). The Role of Diet as a Modulator of the Inflammatory Process in the Neurological Diseases [Review of The Role of Diet as a Modulator of the Inflammatory Process in the Neurological Diseases]. Nutrients, 15(6), 1436. Multidisciplinary Digital Publishing Institute. DOI: 10.3390/nu15061436

Kusdiyanto, K., Saputro, E. P., Sholahuddin, M., Mabruroh, M., Irawati, Z., Murwanti, S., & Setyaningrum, D. P. (2022). *Identification of intention to buy healthy food. 5*(1), 32–41. DOI: 10.21744/ijbem.v5n1.1867

Kuyer, P., & Gordijn, B. (2023). Nudge in perspective: A systematic literature review on the ethical issues with nudging. *Rationality and Society*, *35*(2), 191–222. DOI: 10.1177/10434631231155005

Kvasnička, R., Kvasničková Stanislavská, L., Pilař, L., Kuralová, K., Pilařová, L., & Čejka, M. (2024). Exploring twitter discussions on healthy food: Inspiring, access to healthy food for young, and nutritional economics in focus. *Frontiers in Sustainable Food Systems*, *8*, 1357896. Advance online publication. DOI: 10.3389/fsufs.2024.1357896

La Via Campesina. (2022). *Food sovereignty and nutrition education*. https://viacampesina.org

Laatikainen, T., Pietinen, P., Valsta, L. M., Sundvall, J., Reinivuo, H., & Tuomilehto, J. (2006). Sodium in the Finnish diet: 20-year trends in urinary sodium excretion among the adult population. *European Journal of Clinical Nutrition*, *60*(8), 965–970. DOI: 10.1038/sj.ejcn.1602406

Lacourt, C., Mukherjee, K., Garthoff, J., O'Sullivan, A., Meunier, L., & Fattori, V. (2024). Recent and emerging food packaging alternatives: Chemical safety risks, current regulations, and analytical challenges. *Comprehensive Reviews in Food Science and Food Safety*, *23*(6), e70059. DOI: 10.1111/1541-4337.70059 PMID: 39602345

Lalani, B., Bechoff, A., & Bennett, B. (2019). Which choice of delivery model(s) works best to deliver fortified foods? *Nutrients*, *11*(7), 1594. DOI: 10.3390/nu11071594

Landry, M. J., & Ward, C. (2024). Health Benefits of a Plant-Based Dietary Pattern and Implementation in Healthcare and Clinical Practice [Review of Health Benefits of a Plant-Based Dietary Pattern and Implementation in Healthcare and Clinical Practice]. American Journal of Lifestyle Medicine, 18(5), 657. SAGE Publishing. DOI: 10.1177/15598276241237766

Lang, T., & Heasman, M. (2015). *Food wars: The global battle for mouths, minds and markets* (2nd ed.). Routledge., DOI: 10.4324/9781315754116

Langyan, S., Yadava, P., Khan, F. N., Dar, Z. A., Singh, R., & Kumar, A. (2022). Sustaining Protein Nutrition Through Plant-Based Foods. *Frontiers in Nutrition*, *8*, 772573. Advance online publication. DOI: 10.3389/fnut.2021.772573 PMID: 35118103

Laur, C., McCullough, J., Davidson, B., & Keller, H. (2015). Becoming food aware in hospital: A narrative review to advance the culture of nutrition care in hospitals. *Healthcare*, *3*(2), 393–407. DOI: 10.3390/healthcare3020393

Le Bouthillier, M., Veilleux, S., Loignon, J., Turcotte, M., Trudel, L., & Provencher, V. (2024). Knowledge mobilization between the food industry and public health nutrition scientists: Findings from a case study. *BMC Nutrition, 10*(1), 81. DOI: 10.1186/s40795-024-00889-z PMID: 38845063

Lee, J. Y. (2022). How does psychological safety foster employee performance? A serial multiple mediation of job crafting and thriving. *International Journal of Organization Theory and Behavior, 25*(3/4), 98–112. DOI: 10.1108/IJOTB-12-2021-0239

Lee, M., Angus, D. J., Walsh, H., & Sargeant, S. (2023). "Maybe it's Not Just the Food?" A Food and Mood Focus Group Study. *International Journal of Environmental Research and Public Health, 20*(3), 2011. DOI: 10.3390/ijerph20032011

Lee, M., Bradbury, J., Yoxall, J. S., & Sargeant, S. (2023). "It's about What You've Assigned to the Salad": Focus Group Discussions on the Relationship between Food and Mood. *International Journal of Environmental Research and Public Health, 20*(2), 1476. DOI: 10.3390/ijerph20021476

Lee, R. C. (2012). A Strategic Thinking on Multi-Level Business Development in Wellness Foods. *American Journal of Industrial and Business Management, 2*(3), 95–101. DOI: 10.4236/ajibm.2012.23013

Lee, Y., Kim, G., Jun, J. E., Park, H., Lee, W. J., Hwang, Y., & Kim, J. H. (2023). An Integrated Digital Health Care Platform for Diabetes Management With AI-Based Dietary Management: 48-Week Results From a Randomized Controlled Trial. *Diabetes Care, 46*(5), 959–966. DOI: 10.2337/dc22-1929

Lehmann, U., Mak, T. N., & Bolten, C. J. (2019). Reformulation as a Strategy for Developing Healthier Food Products: Challenges and Recent Developments – An Industry Perspective. Reformulation as a Strategy for Developing Healthier Food Products, 89–110. DOI: 10.1007/978-3-030-23621-2_4

Leib, M. E. (2013). The Forgotten Half of Food System Reform: Using Food and Agricultural Law to Foster Healthy Food Production. *Social Science Research Network*. https://doi.org/DOI: 10.2139/SSRN.2343264

Leni, G., Bonacina, C. E., Principato, L., Galli, R., Negrini, C., Dallolio, G., Bassani, A., & Spigno, G. (2025). Assessment of More Sustainable Packaging Solutions for Sliced Cooked Ham and Mortadella: A Study on Physicochemical Properties and Microbial Quality. *Journal of Food Science, 90*(10), e70574. DOI: 10.1111/1750-3841.70574 PMID: 41017025

Lenoir-Wijnkoop, I., Jones, P. J. H., Uauy, R., Segal, L., & Milner, J. A. (2013). Nutrition economics – food as an ally of public health. *British Journal of Nutrition*, *109*(5), 777–784. DOI: 10.1017/S0007114512005107

Lichtenstein, A. H. (2010). Bring Back Home Economics Education. *Journal of the American Medical Association*, *303*(18), 1857. DOI: 10.1001/jama.2010.592 PMID: 20460625

Lichtenstein, A. H., Appel, L. J., Vadiveloo, M., Hu, F. B., Kris-Etherton, P. M., Rebholz, C. M., Sacks, F. M., Thorndike, A. N., Van Horn, L., & Wylie-Rosett, J. (2021). 2021 dietary guidance to improve cardiovascular health: A scientific statement from the American Heart Association. *Circulation*, *144*(23). Advance online publication. DOI: 10.1161/CIR.0000000000001031 PMID: 34724806

Liguori, E. W., Muldoon, J., Ogundana, O. M., Lee, Y., & Wilson, G. A. (2024). Charting the future of entrepreneurship: A roadmap for interdisciplinary research and societal impact. *Cogent Business & Management*, *11*(1), 2314218. DOI: 10.1080/23311975.2024.2314218

Li, K.-M., Chen, J.-Y., Xiao, Y., Guo, F.-S., Huang, Y.-B., & Lu, Q. (2025). Efficient transformation of starch food wastes into bio-based levulinate products over earth-abundant aluminum salts: Performances and economics. *Biomass and Bioenergy*, *193*, 107570. Advance online publication. DOI: 10.1016/j.biombioe.2024.107570

Li, L., Msaad, H., Sun, H., Tan, M. X., Lu, Y., & Lau, A. K. W. (2020). Green Innovation and Business Sustainability: New Evidence from Energy Intensive Industry in China. *International Journal of Environmental Research and Public Health*, *17*(21), 7826. DOI: 10.3390/ijerph17217826

Lim, X.-J., Cheah, J.-H., Waller, D. S., Ting, H., & Ng, S. I. (2020). What s-commerce implies? Repurchase intention and its antecedents. *Marketing Intelligence & Planning*, *38*(6), 760–776. DOI: 10.1108/MIP-03-2019-0145

Linseisen, J., Renner, B., Gedrich, K., Wirsam, J., Holzapfel, C., Lorkowski, S., Watzl, B., Daniel, H., & Leitzmann, M. (2025). Data in personalized nutrition: Bridging biomedical, psycho-behavioral, and food environment approaches for population-wide impact. *Advances in Nutrition*, *100*(7), 377. DOI: 10.1016/j.advnut.2025.100377 PMID: 39842719

Li, R., Lu, Y., Ma, J., & Wang, W. (2021). Examining gifting behavior on live streaming platforms: An identity-based motivation model. *Information & Management*, *58*(6), 103406. Advance online publication. DOI: 10.1016/j.im.2020.103406

Lisičić-Konaković, M., Mesihović-Dinarević, S., Bajrić, E., Jurišić, S., Musa-Trolić, I., Ćubela, M., Šarac, Z., Prguda-Mujić, J., & Zukanović, A. (2024). Effects of poor eating habits on children's body weight. *Global Pediatrics*, *8*, 100146. DOI: 10.1016/j.gpeds.2024.100146

Liu, Y., Zhao, R., Xiong, X., & Ren, X. (2023). A Bibliometric Analysis of Consumer Neuroscience towards Sustainable Consumption [Review of A Bibliometric Analysis of Consumer Neuroscience towards Sustainable Consumption]. Behavioral Sciences, 13(4), 298. Multidisciplinary Digital Publishing Institute. DOI: 10.3390/bs13040298

Liu, B., Norman, W. C., & Pennington-Gray, L. (2013). A flash of culinary tourism: Understanding the influences of online food photography on people's travel planning process on flickr. *Tourism, Culture & Communication*, *13*(1), 5–18. DOI: 10.3727/109830413X13769180530567

Liu, J., Wu, H., & Zhou, Z. (2024). The Future of Food Health-Focused Brands in the Fast-Food Industry Based on the Analysis of Chipotle. *Advances in Economics. Management and Political Sciences*, *115*(1), 84–90. DOI: 10.54254/2754-1169/115/2024BJ0200

Liu, Y., Ting, H., & Ringle, C. (2023). Appreciation to and Behavior Intention Regarding Upscale Ethnic Restaurants. *Journal of Hospitality & Tourism Research (Washington, D.C.)*, *47*(1), 235–256. DOI: 10.1177/10963480211011544

Li, X., Fu, D., Hu, S., Huang, J., Wang, L., Zhang, Y., Liu, C., Dong, B., & Liu, G. (2026). Non-contact preservation of chilled chicken: Extending shelf life and modulating microbial dynamics using solid spice essential oils and modified atmosphere packaging. *Food Control*, *179*, 111537. DOI: 10.1016/j.foodcont.2025.111537

Li, Y., Wang, Y., Liu, J., Yu, K., Chen, X., Yuan, L., Peng, S., Liu, W., & Zhou, L. (2025). Effect of modified atmosphere packaging on storage quality and lignification process of post-harvest asparagus (Asparagus officinalis L.). *Food Packaging and Shelf Life*, *51*, 101576. DOI: 10.1016/j.fpsl.2025.101576

Ljubičić, M., Sarić, M. M., Klarin, I., Rumbak, I., Barić, I. C., Ranilović, J., Dželalija, B., Sarić, A., Nakić, D., Đjekić, I., Korzeniowska, M., Bartkienė, E., Παπαγεωργίου, M., Tarcea, M., Černelić-Bizjak, M., Kļava, D., Szűcs, V., Vittadini, E., Bolhuis, D. P., & Guiné, R. P. F. (2023). Emotions and Food Consumption: Emotional Eating Behavior in a European Population. *Foods*, *12*(4), 872. DOI: 10.3390/foods12040872

Lock, K., Stuckler, D., Charlesworth, K., & McKee, M. (2009). Potential causes and health effects of rising global food prices. *BMJ (Clinical Research Ed.)*, *339*(7715), 269–272. DOI: 10.1136/bmj.b2403 PMID: 19596718

Lopriore, M. (2025). *Engineering the Shelf Life Predictive Models for Dry Foods Packaged in Bioplastics: An Integrated Approach* [PhD Course in Food and Human Health, University of Udine]. https://air.uniud.it/bitstream/11390/1308526/2/PhD_Thesis_LOPRIORE_MARCO.pdf

Lunetta, E., & Cacciotti, I. (2024). An overview of the packaging industry. In *Nanostructured Materials for Food Packaging Applications* (pp. 1–30). Elsevier., DOI: 10.1016/B978-0-323-99525-2.00006-2

Luthra, A., Dixit, S., Singh, A., Garg, S., & Khattar, S. (2024). Sensory Storytelling: Crafting Brand Narratives Through Sight, Sound, Smell, Touch, and Taste. In *Sensible Selling Through Sensory Neuromarketing* (pp. 230-253). IGI Global.

Luu, T. M. N., Singh, S. K., Dhand, S., Luu, T. M. N., Singh, S. K., & Dhand, S. (2025). *Evaluating the Impact of Wellness Programs on Entrepreneurial Burnout* (evaluating-the-impact-of-wellness-programs-on-entrepreneurial-burnout) [Chapter]. Https://Services.Igi-Global.Com/Resolvedoi/Resolve.Aspx?Doi=10.4018/979-8-3693-3673-1.Ch010

Lv, X., Wu, Y., Gong, M., Deng, J., Gu, Y., Liu, Y., Li, J., Du, G., Ledesma-Amaro, R., Liu, L., & Chen, J. (2021). Synthetic biology for future food: Research progress and future directions. *Future Foods : a Dedicated Journal for Sustainability in Food Science*, *3*, 100025. DOI: 10.1016/j.fufo.2021.100025

M. J. G., Gunny, A. A. N., Devi, M., Hussain, M., & Bibi, A. (2025). Trends and Advances in Quality Management of Horticultural Produce by Lighting Strategies – A Comprehensive Review. *Food and Bioprocess Technology*. Advance online publication. DOI: 10.1007/s11947-025-03948-w

Macdiarmid, J. I. (2013). Is a healthy diet an environmentally sustainable diet? *The Proceedings of the Nutrition Society*, *72*(1), 13–20. DOI: 10.1017/S0029665112002893 PMID: 23186839

Maciel, F. A., & Duarte, D. (2022). The impact of cash transfer participation on unhealthy consumption in Brazil. *Health Policy OPEN*, *4*, 100087. DOI: 10.1016/j.hpopen.2022.100087

Madesiya, A., & Prachi, D. Rohit, and Neelesh Kumar Maurya, et al. (2024). Exploring the Role of Psychology in the Food Industry: Consumer Behavior, Employee Well-being, and Innovation. *J. Nutrition and Food Processing*, *7*, 15.

Madhu, B. (2025). Technological innovations in food grain processing and storage in India: Trends, challenges, and future prospects. *Journal of Stored Products Research*, *114*, 102757. DOI: 10.1016/j.jspr.2025.102757

Madzorera, I., Jaacks, L. M., Paarlberg, R., Herforth, A., Bromage, S., Ghosh, S., Myers, S. S., Masters, W. A., & Fawzi, W. (2021). Food systems as drivers of optimal nutrition and health: Complexities and opportunities for research and implementation. *Current Developments in Nutrition*, *5*(8), nzab062. DOI: 10.1093/cdn/nzab062

Mahecha-Rubiano, Y. R., Garavito, J., & Castellanos, D. A. (2024). Configuration of a combined active packaging system with modified atmospheres and antimicrobial control to preserve fresh strawberry fruits. *Food Packaging and Shelf Life*, *46*, 101390. DOI: 10.1016/j.fpsl.2024.101390

Maicas, S. (2020). The Role of Yeasts in Fermentation Processes. *Microorganisms*, *8*(8), 1142. DOI: 10.3390/microorganisms8081142

Malik, A., Dhir, A., & Nieminen, M. (2016). Uses and Gratifications of digital photo sharing on Facebook. *Telematics and Informatics*, *33*(1), 129–138. DOI: 10.1016/j.tele.2015.06.009

Mandela MarketPlace. (2023). *Community food systems*. https://mandelamarketplace.org

Manfield, R. C., & Newey, L. R. (2018). Resilience as an entrepreneurial capability: Integrating insights from a cross-disciplinary comparison. *International Journal of Entrepreneurial Behaviour & Research*, *24*(7), 1155–1180. DOI: 10.1108/IJEBR-11-2016-0368

Mannar, M. V., Garrett, G. S., & Hurrell, R. F. (2018). Future Trends and Strategies in Food Fortification. In *Elsevier eBooks* (pp. 375–381). DOI: 10.1016/B978-0-12-802861-2.00040-7

Mantzios, M., & Wilson, J. C. (2015). Mindfulness, Eating Behaviours, and Obesity: A Review and Reflection on Current Findings. *Current Obesity Reports*, *4*(1), 141–146. DOI: 10.1007/s13679-014-0131-x PMID: 26627097

Marino, G. (2021). Semiotics of digital cacogastromania. *Digital Age in Semiotics & Communication*, *4*. Advance online publication. DOI: 10.33919/dasc.20-21.3-4.5

Martinez, S., Hand, M. S., Pra, M. D., Pollack, S. L., Ralston, K., Smith, T. A., Vogel, S. J., Clark, S., Lohr, L., Low, S. A., & Newman, C. (2010). *Local food systems: Concepts, impacts, and issues* (Report No. 97). U.S. Department of Agriculture. https://EconPapers.repec.org/RePEc:ags:uersrr:96635

Mason, J. B., Sanders, D., & Musgrove, P. Soekirman, & Galloway, R. (2006). Community health and nutrition programs. In D. T. Jamison, J. G. Breman, A. R. Measham, et al. (Eds.), *Disease control priorities in developing countries* (2nd ed., Chapter 56). The International Bank for Reconstruction and Development / The World Bank. https://www.ncbi.nlm.nih.gov/books/NBK11726/

Maspul, K., & Ardhin, M. (2025). Kopitiams at Crossroads: Can Malaysia's Cultural Heartbeat Survive Globalization? *Indonesian Journal of Social Development, 2*(4), 20–20. DOI: 10.47134/jsd.v2i4.3886

Maurya, N. K. (2024a). The Impact of Technology on Food Product Development. *Nutrition and Food Processing, 07*(12), 01–06. DOI: 10.31579/2637-8914/262

Maurya, N. K. (2024b). Regulating Innovation: A Review of Product Development and Regulatory Frameworks in the Food Industry. *Nutrition and Food Processing, 07*(15), 01–08. DOI: 10.31579/2637-8914/276

Mayorga-Ramos, A., Zúñiga-Miranda, J., Carrera-Pacheco, S. E., Barba-Ostria, C., & Guamán, L. P. (2023). CRISPR-Cas-Based Antimicrobials: Design, Challenges, and Bacterial Mechanisms of Resistance. *ACS Infectious Diseases, 9*(7), 1283–1302. DOI: 10.1021/acsinfecdis.2c00649

McLennon, E., Dari, B., Jha, G., Sihi, D., & Kankarla, V. (2021). Regenerative agriculture and integrative permaculture for sustainable and technology driven global food production and security. *Agronomy Journal, 113*(6), 4541–4559. DOI: 10.1002/agj2.20814

McLeod, A., Pippin, S., & Catania, V. (2009). Using technology acceptance theory to model individual differences in tax software use. *15th Americas Conference on Information Systems 2009, AMCIS 2009, 10*, 6998 – 7008.

McLeroy, K. R., Bibeau, D., Steckler, A., & Glanz, K. (1988). An ecological perspective on health promotion programs. *Health Education Quarterly, 15*(4), 351–377. DOI: 10.1177/109019818801500401 PMID: 3068205

McMahon, A.-T., Williams, P., & Tapsell, L. C. (2010). Reviewing the meanings of wellness and well-being and their implications for food choice. *Perspectives in Public Health, 130*(6), 282–286. DOI: 10.1177/1757913910384046 PMID: 21213565

Mendoza, R. U., & Thelen, N. (2008). Innovations to make markets more inclusive for the poor. *Development Policy Review*, *26*(4), 427–458. DOI: 10.1111/j.1467-7679.2008.00417.x

Meng, Y., Sun, J., Yu, T., & Piao, H. (2024). Plant-derived nanovesicles offer a promising avenue for anti-aging interventions. *Physiologia Plantarum, 176*(2), e14283. DOI: 10.1111/ppl.14283 PMID: 38627963

Messer, K. D., Ganguly, D., & Xie, L. (2025). Mitigating impacts of food production and consumption on climate change: Applications of behavioral economics. *Applied Economic Perspectives and Policy, 47*(4), 1357–1382. Advance online publication. DOI: 10.1002/aepp.13519

Mialon, M. (2024). The Food industry barrier to achieving the SDGs. *European Journal of Public Health, 34*(Supplement_3), ckae144.422. Advance online publication. DOI: 10.1093/eurpub/ckae144.422

Mialon, M., Perez, E., Corvalan, C., Monteiro, C., Jaime, P., & Baeza Scagliusi, F. (2020). Food industry influence on public health policy, research and practice in Latin America. *European Journal of Public Health, 30*(Supplement_5), ckaa165.321. Advance online publication. DOI: 10.1093/eurpub/ckaa165.321

Midjord, N. H., & Bell, C. (2024). To What Extent are Food, Culture, Economics and the Natural Environment Reflected in the Language of the Australian and Brazilian Food-based Dietary Guidelines? *Current Nutrition Reports, 13*(4), 937–949. DOI: 10.1007/s13668-024-00585-1 PMID: 39373940

Miller, K. B., Eckberg, J. O., Decker, E. A., & Marinangeli, C. P. F. (2021). Role of Food Industry in Promoting Healthy and Sustainable Diets. *Nutrients, 13*(8), 2740. DOI: 10.3390/nu13082740 PMID: 34444900

Mingay, E., Hart, M., Yoong, S., & Hure, A. (2021). Why We Eat the Way We Do: A Call to Consider Food Culture in Public Health Initiatives. *International Journal of Environmental Research and Public Health, 18*(22), 11967. DOI: 10.3390/ijerph182211967

Mir Khan, U., & Selamoglu, Z. (2020). Use of Enzymes in Dairy Industry: A Review of Current Progress. *Archives of Razi Institute, 75*(1), 131. DOI: 10.22092/ARI.2019.126286.1341

Mirsch, T., Lehrer, C., & Jung, R. (2017). Digital nudging: Altering user behavior in digital environments. In *Proceedings of the 13th International Conference on Wirtschaftsinformatik* (pp. 634–648). https://aisel.aisnet.org/wi2017/track09/paper/2/

Misopoulos, F., & Bajiraj, P. (2025). Shared Producer Responsibility for Sustainable Packaging in FMCG: The Convergence of SDGs, ESG Reporting, and Stakeholder Engagement. *Sustainability (Basel), 17*(14), 6654. DOI: 10.3390/su17146654

Mohammadian, H. D., & Rezaie, F. (2021). Big data for entrepreneurship towards csr and sustainable development. In *Big Data for Entrepreneurship and Sustainable Development* (pp. 21–48). CRC Press. DOI: 10.1201/9781003090045-2

Mondol, M. S. A., Akbar, U., Mandal, O., Rani, A., Dar, A. H., Chatterjee, A., & Abdi, G. (2025). Advances in agronomic practices, post-harvest technologies, and medicinal potential of dragon fruit (Hylocereus spp.): A comprehensive updated review. *Journal of Agriculture and Food Research*, *22*, 102157. DOI: 10.1016/j.jafr.2025.102157

Monteiro, C. A., Moubarac, J.-C., Cannon, G., Ng, S. W., & Popkin, B. (2013). Ultra-processed products are becoming dominant in the global food system. *Obesity Reviews*, *14*(S2), 21–28. DOI: 10.1111/obr.12107 PMID: 24102801

Monterrosa, E., Frongillo, E. A., Drewnowski, A., de Pee, S., & Vandevijvere, S. (2020). Sociocultural Influences on Food Choices and Implications for Sustainable Healthy Diets. *Food and Nutrition Bulletin*, *41*(2_suppl). Advance online publication. DOI: 10.1177/0379572120975874

Morales, I., & Berridge, K. (2020). 'Liking' and 'wanting' in eating and food reward: Brain mechanisms and clinical implications [Review of 'Liking' and 'wanting' in eating and food reward: Brain mechanisms and clinical implications]. Physiology & Behavior, 227, 113152. Elsevier BV. DOI: 10.1016/j.physbeh.2020.113152

Mora, R. L., Vanare, S. P., & Pegg, R. B. (2025). Mechanisms, Causes, and Solutions: A Comprehensive Review of Lipid Oxidation in Low-Moisture Packaged Snacks. *European Journal of Lipid Science and Technology*, *70044*(9), e70044. Advance online publication. DOI: 10.1002/ejlt.70044

Moretto, A., & Caniato, F. (2021). Can Supply Chain Finance help mitigate the financial disruption brought by Covid-19? *Journal of Purchasing and Supply Management*, *27*(4), 100713. DOI: 10.1016/j.pursup.2021.100713

Morgan, C. (2020). Commensality in Crisis. *Gastronomica*, *20*(3), 46–47. DOI: 10.1525/gfc.2020.20.3.46

Moyeenudin, H. M., Anandan, R., & Shaikjaveedparvez, B. G. (2020). A Research on Cloud Kitchen Prerequisites and Branding Strategies. *International Journal of Innovative Technology and Exploring Engineering*, *9*(3), 983–987. Advance online publication. DOI: 10.35940/ijitee.C8188.019320

Mukherjee, A., Gómez-Sala, B., O'Connor, E. M., Kenny, J., & Cotter, P. D. (2022). Global regulatory frameworks for fermented foods: A review. *Frontiers in Nutrition*, *9*, 902642. DOI: 10.3389/fnut.2022.902642

Mukhtarov, S., Yüksel, S., & Dinçer, H. (2022). The impact of financial development on renewable energy consumption: Evidence from Turkey. *Renewable Energy*, *187*, 169–176. DOI: 10.1016/j.renene.2022.01.061

Mukty, M. I., & Pulubuhu, D. (2023). Strategi Pengembangan Produk Sehat Dalam Bisnis Wirausaha Makanan. *Deleted Journal*, *1*(2), 55–60. DOI: 10.57213/tjghpsr.v1i2.255

Münch, C., von der Gracht, H. A., & Hartmann, E. (2021). The future role of reverse logistics as a tool for sustainability in food supply chains: A Delphi-based scenario study. *Supply Chain Management*, *28*(2), 262–283. DOI: 10.1108/SCM-06-2021-0291

Munialo, C. D., & Mellor, D. (2023). A review of the impact of social disruptions on food security and food choice. *Food Science & Nutrition*, *12*(1), 13–30. DOI: 10.1002/fsn3.3752

Muscaritoli, M. (2021). The Impact of Nutrients on Mental Health and Well-Being: Insights From the Literature. *Frontiers in Nutrition*, *8*, 656290. DOI: 10.3389/fnut.2021.656290 PMID: 33763446

Mu, X., Zhang, H., Shi, J., Hou, J., Ma, J., & Yang, Y. (2024). Fashion intelligence in the Metaverse: Promise and future prospects. *Artificial Intelligence Review*, *57*(3), 67. Advance online publication. DOI: 10.1007/s10462-024-10703-8

Naicker, A., Shrestha, A., Joshi, C., Willett, W. C., & Spiegelman, D. (2021). Workplace cafeteria and other multicomponent interventions to promote healthy eating among adults: A systematic review [Review of Workplace cafeteria and other multicomponent interventions to promote healthy eating among adults: A systematic review]. Preventive Medicine Reports, 22, 101333. Elsevier BV. DOI: 10.1016/j.pmedr.2021.101333

Nasser Eddine, A., Duret, S., Flick, D., & Moureh, J. (2024). Characterising airflow and heat transfer within a multi-package of horticultural produce using a validated CFD model. *International Journal of Refrigeration*, *S014070072400433X*, •••. DOI: 10.1016/j.ijrefrig.2024.12.003

Nawaz, S., & Satterfield, T. (2022). On the nature of naturalness? Theorizing 'nature' for the study of public perceptions of novel genomic technologies in agriculture and conservation. *Environmental Science & Policy*, *136*, 291–303. DOI: 10.1016/j.envsci.2022.06.008

Ndlovu, S. G. (2024). Private label brands vs national brands: New battle fronts and future competition. *Cogent Business & Management*, *11*(1), 2321877. DOI: 10.1080/23311975.2024.2321877

Neff, R. A., Palmer, A. M., Mckenzie, S. E., & Lawrence, R. S. (2009). Food Systems and Public Health Disparities. *Journal of Hunger & Environmental Nutrition, 4*(3–4), 282–314. DOI: 10.1080/19320240903337041 PMID: 23173027

Nelson, J. B. (2017). Mindful Eating: The Art of Presence While You Eat. *Diabetes Spectrum, 30*(3), 171–174. DOI: 10.2337/ds17-0015 PMID: 28848310

Nestlé. (2022). *Creating shared value and sustainability report*. Nestlé Group.

Nestle, M. (2022). Regulating the Food Industry: An Aspirational Agenda. *American Journal of Public Health, 112*(6), 1–e6. DOI: 10.2105/AJPH.2022.306844 PMID: 35446606

Niebel, D., Saha, S., Kunz, W., Evers, B., Löder, M., Ramsperger, A. F. R. M., & Laforsch, C. (2026). Microplastics, Skin Disease, and Dermatology. *Dermatologic Clinics, 44*(1), 125–136. DOI: 10.1016/j.det.2025.08.001 PMID: 41207769

Nielsen, K. E. (2016). *Health beneficial consumer products—status and trends*. Woodhead Publishing., DOI: 10.1016/B978-0-08-100329-9.00002-5

Nisticò, S. P., Greco, M. E., Amato, S., Bennardo, L., Zappia, E., Pignataro, E., & Pellacani, G. (2024). Evaluating the Impact of Oleocanthal and Oleacein on Skin Aging: Results of a Randomized Clinical Study. *Medicina, 60*(6), 947. DOI: 10.3390/medicina60060947 PMID: 38929564

Numa, I. A. N., Wolf, K. E., & Pastore, G. M. (2023). FoodTech startups: Technological solutions to achieve SDGs. *Food and Humanity, 1*, 358–369. DOI: 10.1016/j.foohum.2023.06.011

O'Reilly, G. A., Cook, L., Spruijt-Metz, D., & Black, D. S. (2014). Mindfulness-based interventions for obesity-related eating behaviours: A literature review. *Obesity Reviews, 15*(6), 453–461. DOI: 10.1111/obr.12156 PMID: 24636206

Odoms-Young, A., Brown, A. G. M., Agurs-Collins, T., & Glanz, K. (2024). Food insecurity, neighborhood food environment, and health disparities: State of the science, research gaps and opportunities. *The American Journal of Clinical Nutrition, 119*(3), 850–861. DOI: 10.1016/j.ajcnut.2023.12.019 PMID: 38160801

Oguz, S., Turrisi, V., Kuuliala, L., Somrani, M., & Devlieghere, F. (2025). Listeria monocytogenes growth under well-controlled CO2, pH, and temperature conditions through a novel gas-controlling system. *International Journal of Food Microbiology, 441*, 111343. DOI: 10.1016/j.ijfoodmicro.2025.111343 PMID: 40652695

Ogwu, M. C., & Kosoe, E. A. (2025). Integrating green infrastructure into sustainable agriculture to enhance soil health, biodiversity, and microclimate resilience. *Sustainability*, *17*(9), 3838. DOI: 10.3390/su17093838

Ohanian, R. (1990). Construction and validation of a scale to measure celebrity endorsers' perceived expertise, trustworthiness, and attractiveness. *Journal of Advertising*, *19*(3), 39–52. DOI: 10.1080/00913367.1990.10673191

Okumus, B., Koseoglu, M. A., & Ma, F. (2018). Food and gastronomy research in tourism and hospitality: A bibliometric analysis. *International Journal of Hospitality Management*, *73*, 64–74. DOI: 10.1016/j.ijhm.2018.01.020

Olatunji, O. (2024). A History of Plastics. In O. Olatunji, *Re-envisioning Plastics Role in the Global Society* (pp. 11–26). Springer Nature Switzerland. DOI: 10.1007/978-3-031-48945-7_2

Olsen, O., Hari, A. R., & Rival, Y. (2023). Healthy Snacks: Multimodal Critical Discourse Analysis of Traditional Food Brand Corporate Storytelling. *Journal of Pragmatics and Discourse Research*, *3*(1), 19–27. DOI: 10.51817/jpdr.v3i1.322

Olson, R., Gavin-Smith, B., Ferraboschi, C., & Kraemer, K. (2021). Food Fortification: The Advantages, Disadvantages and Lessons from *Sight and Life* Programs. *Nutrients*, *13*(4), 1118. DOI: 10.3390/nu13041118 PMID: 33805305

Oluwadamilare Usman, F., Louis Eyo-Udo, N., Augustine Etukudoh, E., Odonkor, B., Victoria Ibeh, C., & Adegbola, A. (2024). a Critical Review of Ai-Driven Strategies for Entrepreneurial Success. *International Journal of Management & Entrepreneurship Research*, *6*(1), 200–215. DOI: 10.51594/ijmer.v6i1.748

Onyeaka, H., Nwaiwu, O., Obileke, K., Miri, T., & Al-Sharify, Z. T. (2023). Global nutritional challenges of reformulated food: A review. *Food Science & Nutrition*, *11*(6), 2483–2499. DOI: 10.1002/fsn3.3286 PMID: 37324840

Osunsanmi, A. S., Ayandibu, A. O., & Heeralal, S. (2024). Assessing the factors that influence consumer's purchase behaviour towards functional foods. *International Journal of Research In Business and Social Science*. DOI: 10.20525/ijrbs.v13i2.3192

Ou, C. X., Pavlou, P. A., & Davison, R. M. (2014). Swift guanxi in online marketplaces: The role of computer-mediated communication technologies. *Management Information Systems Quarterly*, *38*(1), 209–230. DOI: 10.25300/MISQ/2014/38.1.10

Owolodun, B., Gmür, D., Felber, S., Ollier, C., Haller, T., & Merten, S. (2025). From diversity to uniformity: Comparing nutritional transition of food consumption in four regions in Senegal. *Food, Culture, & Society*, *28*(3), 503–527. DOI: 10.1080/15528014.2024.2310380

Oyewole, O. S., Raji, M. A., Kazeem, A. A., Ajao, T. O., Ibitoye, O., Abel, O. O., Solomon-Ibuwunwa, O. M., Famakinwa, J. O., & Adewunmi, E. O. (2025). Smart Technological Innovations for Post-harvest Loss Reduction: A Review. *FUDMA Journal of Sciences*, *9*(6), 299–307. DOI: 10.33003/fjs-2025-0906-3605

Öztürk, O. D., Frongillo, E. A., Blake, C. E., McInnes, M. M., & Turner-McGrievy, G. (2020). Before the lunch line: Effectiveness of behavioral economic interventions for pre-commitment on elementary school children's food choices. *Journal of Economic Behavior & Organization*, *176*, 597–618. DOI: 10.1016/j.jebo.2020.03.027

Palo-oja, O.-M., & Nieminen, J. H. (2022). Healthy and Delicious: Responsible Branding of Snacks. *South Asian Journal of Business and Management Cases*, *11*(2), 105–118. DOI: 10.1177/22779779221099749

Pandey, V. K., Shafi, Z., Kumar, A., Rustagi, S., & Singh, S. (2025). Smart Anthocyanin-Fortified Packaging: A Sustainable Approach to Protect Food From Ultraviolet-B Induced Damage. *Journal of Food Process Engineering*, *48*(8), e70196. DOI: 10.1111/jfpe.70196

Parekh, S., Shinghal, K., Agarwal, N., & Raha, S. (2024). Flour power: Women-led millet value chains improve local nutrition. *Millet Revival Project*. https://milletrevivalproject.in/2024/03/29/flour-power-women-led-millet-value-chains-improve-local-nutrition/

Parletta, N., Milte, C. M., & Meyer, B. J. (2013). Nutritional modulation of cognitive function and mental health. *The Journal of Nutritional Biochemistry*, *24*(5), 725–743. DOI: 10.1016/j.jnutbio.2013.01.002 PMID: 23517914

Patwardhan, V., Mallya, J., Kaliappan, S., & Kumar, D. (2024). Influence of social media on young adults' food consumption behavior: Scale development. *Cogent Social Sciences*, *10*(1), 2391016. Advance online publication. DOI: 10.1080/23311886.2024.2391016

Pavlidis, G., & Markantonatou, S. (2020). Gastronomic tourism in Greece and beyond: A thorough review. In *International Journal of Gastronomy and Food Science* (Vol. 21). AZTI-Tecnalia., DOI: 10.1016/j.ijgfs.2020.100229

Pechey, R., & Monsivais, P. (2016). Socioeconomic inequalities in the healthiness of food choices: Exploring the contributions of food expenditures. *Preventive Medicine*, *88*, 203–209. DOI: 10.1016/j.ypmed.2016.04.012 PMID: 27095324

Pell, D., Mytton, O., Penney, T. L., Briggs, A., Cummins, S., Penn-Jones, C., Rayner, M., Rutter, H., Scarborough, P., Sharp, S. J., Smith, R. D., White, M., & Adams, J. (2021). Changes in soft drinks purchased by British households associated with the UK soft drinks industry levy: Controlled interrupted time series analysis. *The Lancet. Public Health, 6*(6), e414–e423. DOI: 10.1016/S2468-2667(21)00058-5 PMID: 33692200

Peres Fabbri, L., Cavallero, A., Vidotto, F., & Gabriele, M. (2024). Bioactive Peptides from Fermented Foods: Production Approaches, Sources, and Potential Health Benefits. *Foods, 13*(21), 3369. DOI: 10.3390/foods13213369

Pérez, J. C. (2021). Fungi of the human gut microbiota: Roles and significance [Review of Fungi of the human gut microbiota: Roles and significance]. International Journal of Medical Microbiology, 311(3), 151490. Elsevier BV. DOI: 10.1016/j.ijmm.2021.151490

Pergher, G., Marçal Vieira Vaz, R. G., & Werner, M. C. (2024). *Content evaluation of instagram posts related to food and health produced by digital influencers.* DOI: 10.56238/sevened2024.037-039

Petty, R. E., & Cacioppo, J. T. (1986). *THE ELABORATION LIKELIHOOD MODEL OF PERSUASION.*

Philosophers, C. (2024). *Exploring the Melting Pot: An In-Depth Review of Fusion Cuisine in Contemporary Gastronomy and Its Cultural, Nutritional, and Culinary Innovations. Chef Sunaina Nanda Food Production Professor.* DOI: 10.13140/RG.2.2.35521.36966

Pietinen, P., Valsta, L. M., Hirvonen, T., & Sinkko, H. (2008). Labelling the salt content in foods: A useful tool in reducing sodium intake in Finland. *Public Health Nutrition*, *11*(4), 335–340. DOI: 10.1017/S1368980007000249

Pilař, L., Kvasničková Stanislavská, L., Kvasnička, R., Hartman, R., & Tichá, I. (2021). Healthy Food on Instagram Social Network: Vegan, Homemade and Clean Eating. *Nutrients, 13*(6), 1991. DOI: 10.3390/nu13061991 PMID: 34207910

Pine, A. (2022). Ambient struggling: Food, chronic disease, and spatial isolation among the urban poor. *Agriculture and Human Values, 40*(3), 1105–1116. DOI: 10.1007/s10460-022-10408-0

Pinho-Gomes, A., Booth, L., & Pettigrew, S. (2023). Public perceptions of responsibility for recommended food policies in seven countries. *European Journal of Public Health*, *33*(2), 299–304. DOI: 10.1093/eurpub/ckad020

Pistorio, E., Chinnici, G., Zarba, C., Bellia, C., & Pappalardo, G. (2023). *The revolution of functional food: a market analysis (the functional foods market revolution: market analysis of functional food).* DOI: 10.5593/sgem2023V/6.2/s25.53

Pitelis, C. N. (1998). Productivity, Competitiveness and Convergence in the European Economy: Supply-Side Considerations. *Social Science Research Network.* https://papers.ssrn.com/sol3/papers.cfm?abstract_id=811284

Plank, R. E., & Gould, S. J. (1990). Health Consciousness, Scientific Orientation and Wellness. *Health Marketing Quarterly, 7*(3-4), 65–82. DOI: 10.1300/J026v07n03_06

Polito, N. D., Stylianakis, A. A., Richardson, R., & Baker, K. (2023). Real-World Intake of Dietary Sugars Is Associated with Reduced Cortisol Reactivity Following an Acute Physiological Stressor. *Nutrients, 15*(1), 209. DOI: 10.3390/nu15010209

Pollari, M., Autio, M., & Elorinne, A.-L. (2024). The transformative potential of textbooks: Food waste knowledge and pedagogical text styles in Finnish Home Economics, Geography, and Biology textbooks. *Nordic Journal of Comparative and International Education, 8*(2). Advance online publication. DOI: 10.7577/njcie.5622

Popkin, B. M. (2006). Global nutrition dynamics: The world is shifting rapidly toward a diet linked with noncommunicable diseases. *The American Journal of Clinical Nutrition, 84*(2), 289–298. DOI: 10.1093/ajcn/84.2.289 PMID: 16895874

Portnoy, A., Jit, M., Helleringer, S., & Verguet, S. (2020). Comparative distributional impact of routine immunization and supplementary immunization activities in delivery of measles vaccine in low- and middle-income countries. *Value in Health,* *23*(7), 891–897. DOI: 10.1016/j.jval.2020.03.012

Pozzi, M., Susini, P., Di Seclì, D., Diluiso, G., Mendes, V. M., Grimaldi, L., & Schettino, M. (2024). The anti-aging role of metformin, clinical applications to pursue the longevity road. *European Journal of Plastic Surgery, 47*(1), 65. DOI: 10.1007/s00238-024-02211-3

Pradhan, M. (2018). *Understanding the demand side of social protection programmes: The case of public distribution of food in India* [Doctoral thesis, University of London]. EThOS. https://ethos.bl.uk/OrderDetails.do?uin=uk.bl.ethos.768446

Prattichizzo, F., Frigé, C., Pellegrini, V., Scisciola, L., Santoro, A., Monti, D., Rippo, M. R., Ivanchenko, M., Olivieri, F., & Franceschi, C. (2024). Organ-specific biological clocks: Ageotyping for personalized anti-aging medicine. *Ageing Research Reviews, 96*, 102253. DOI: 10.1016/j.arr.2024.102253 PMID: 38447609

Premaratna, S. P., Machado, L. J., & Gunawardena, M. N. (2020). Urban consumers' choice of optimal and suboptimal products: Organic and non-organic food choices. *Sri Lanka Journal of Applied Statistics*, *10*(2), 1–16. DOI: 10.4038/sljass.v10i2.7150

Prescott, S. L., Logan, A. C., D'Adamo, C. R., Holton, K. F., Lowry, C. A., Marks, J., Moodie, R., & Poland, B. (2024). Nutritional Criminology: Why the Emerging Research on Ultra-Processed Food Matters to Health and Justice. *International Journal of Environmental Research and Public Health, 21*(2), 120. DOI: 10.3390/ijerph21020120 PMID: 38397611

Pugra, I. W., Arjana, I. W. B., Suarja, I. K., Sadiyani, N. W., Paramita, R., Sekarti, N. K., & Sunarsa, I. W. (2025). Flavours without borders: A cultural and gastronomic exploration of global cuisines, culinary diversity, and fusion experiences in food courts. *Journal of Education, Social &. Communication Studies*, *2*(2), 101–111.

Puri, S., Shaheen, M., & Grover, B. (2023). Nutrition and cognitive health: A life course approach. *Frontiers in Public Health, 11*, 1023907. DOI: 10.3389/fpubh.2023.1023907 PMID: 37050953

Putra, F. K. K., Putra, M. K., & Novianti, S. (2023). Taste of asean: Traditional food images from Southeast Asian countries. *Journal of Ethnic Foods, 10*(1), 20. DOI: 10.1186/s42779-023-00189-0

Qaim, M., & Parlasca, M. C. (2025). Agricultural Economics and the Transformation Toward Sustainable Agri-Food Systems. *Agricultural Economics, 56*(3), 327–335. DOI: 10.1111/agec.70023

Quang, T. D., Phan, C. N., Nguyen, H. D., & Bui, T. K. (2025). Culinary dynamics in the digital age: A netnographic exploration of food and beverage trends in Vietnam through user-generated content. *Food, Culture, & Society, 28*(5), 1–31. DOI: 10.1080/15528014.2025.2485506

Queiroz, L. P., Nogueira, I. B. R., & Ribeiro, A. M. (2024). Flavor engineering: A comprehensive review of biological foundations, AI integration, industrial development, and socio-cultural dynamics. *Food Research International, 196*, 115100. DOI: 10.1016/j.foodres.2024.115100

Que, J. (2023). Treating Mental Illness with Dietary Improvement. *Theoretical and Natural Science, 4*(1), 65–71. DOI: 10.54254/2753-8818/4/20220512

Rabadán, A., Nieto, R., & Bernabéu, R. (2021). Food Innovation as a Means of Developing Healthier and More Sustainable Foods. *Foods, 10*(9), 9. Advance online publication. DOI: 10.3390/foods10092069 PMID: 34574178

Ramadhani, A. M., Nassary, E. K., Rwehumbiza, F. B., Massawe, B. H. J., & Nchimbi-Msolla, S. (2024). Corrigendum: Impact of mulching treatments on growth, yields, and economics of common bean (Phaseolus vulgaris L.) in Eastern Tanzania (Frontiers in Sustainable Food Systems, (2024), 8, (1455206),). *Frontiers in Sustainable Food Systems, 8*. https://doi.org/DOI: 10.3389/fsufs.2024.1455206

Ramanayaka, L. J. (2025). Sensory Neuro-Marketing in Sales: Crafting Irresistible Dining Experiences. In *Impact of Sensory Marketing on Buying Behavior* (pp. 337-366). IGI Global.

Ramenzoni, V. C. (2023). Taboos, food avoidances, and diseases: Local epistemologies of health among Coastal Endenese in Eastern Indonesia. *Frontiers in Sustainable Food Systems*, *7*, 977694. Advance online publication. DOI: 10.3389/fsufs.2023.977694

Ramesh, S. (2022). *The Commerce of Wellness: Integrating Healthcare Treatments into Business Models*. Journal Healthcare Treatment Development., DOI: 10.55529/jhtd.21.7.12

Ranjha, M. M. N., Shafique, B., Khalid, W., Nadeem, H. R., Mueen-Ud-Din, G., & Khalid, M. Z. (2022). Applications of Biotechnology in Food and Agriculture: A Mini-Review. *Proceedings of the National Academy of Sciences. India. Section B, Biological Sciences*, *92*(1), 11–15. DOI: 10.1007/s40011-021-01320-4 PMID: 35035035

Raveendran, S., Parameswaran, B., Ummalyma, S. B., Abraham, A., Mathew, A. K., Madhavan, A., Rebello, S., & Pandey, A. (2018). Applications of Microbial Enzymes in the Food Industry. *Food Technology and Biotechnology*, *56*(1), 16. DOI: 10.17113/ftb.56.01.18.5491

Reardon, T., & Vos, R. (2023). How resilience innovations in food supply chains are revolutionizing logistics, wholesale trade, and farm services in developing countries. *International Food and Agribusiness Management Review*, *26*(3), 455–470. DOI: 10.22434/IFAMR2022.0138

Reddy, G., & van Dam, R. M. (2020). Food, culture, and identity in multicultural societies: Insights from Singapore. *Appetite*, *149*, 104633. DOI: 10.1016/j.appet.2020.104633

Redine, A., Deshpande, S., Jebarajakirthy, C., & Surachartkumtonkun, J. (2022). Impulse buying: A systematic literature review and future research directions. *International Journal of Consumer Studies*, *47*(1), 3–41. DOI: 10.1111/ijcs.12862

Reynolds, A., & Mitri, J. (2024, April 28). Dietary advice for individuals with diabetes. In K. R. Feingold, S. F. Ahmed, B. Anawalt, et al. (Eds.), *Endotext.* MDText.com, Inc. https://www.ncbi.nlm.nih.gov/books/NBK279012/

Rezitis, A. N., & Rokopanos, A. (2019). Asymmetric Price Transmission along the European Food Supply Chain and the CAP Health Check: A Panel Vector Error Correction Approach. *Journal of Agricultural & Food Industrial Organization, 17*(2), 20180002. Advance online publication. DOI: 10.1515/jafio-2018-0002

Riccardi, B. (2022). The Added Value of Technology in Food Integration - Holistic Approach. *Nutrition and Food Processing, 5*(4), 01–09. DOI: 10.31579/2637-8914/105

Richards, M. R., & Sindelar, J. L. (2013). Rewarding healthy food choices in SNAP: Behavioral economic applications. *Milbank Quarterly*, *91*(2), 395–412. DOI: 10.1111/milq.12017

Richter, N., & Hunecke, M. (2022a). Mindfulness, connectedness to nature, personal ecological norm and pro-environmental behavior: A daily diary study. *Current Research in Ecological and Social Psychology, 3*, 100038. DOI: 10.1016/j.cresp.2022.100038

Ridgway, E., Baker, P., Woods, J., & Lawrence, M. (2019). Historical developments and paradigm shifts in public health nutrition science, guidance and policy actions: A narrative review. *Nutrients*, *11*(3), 531. DOI: 10.3390/nu11030531

Rodgers, R. F., Goutama, V., & Sonneville, K. R. (2023). At the Same Table: A Delphi Consensus-Based Model of Health-Promoting Eating Behaviors. *Nutrients, 15*(16), 3601. DOI: 10.3390/nu15163601

Roe, B. E., Bender, K. E., & Qi, D. (2020). The impact of COVID-19 on consumer food waste. *Applied Economic Perspectives and Policy*, *43*(1), 401–411. DOI: 10.1002/aepp.13079

Roe, B. E. (2025). Anti-obesity medication patients' self-reported food savings versus the cost of such medicines: Health Economics. *International Journal of Obesity, 49*(3), 532–535. DOI: 10.1038/s41366-024-01708-y PMID: 39738491

Rojas, C., & Jaenicke, E. (2024). Introduction to Agribusiness special issue: Economics of food reformulation. *Agribusiness, 40*(3), 537–549. DOI: 10.1002/agr.21912

Rokach, A. (2020). Belonging, Togetherness and Food Rituals. *Open Journal of Depression, 9*(4), 77–85. DOI: 10.4236/ojd.2020.94007

Rolle, J., Kisato, J., Rock, P., & Winstanley, J. (2020). Inclusive entrepreneurship: A critical look at the inclusion of persons with disabilities. *International Journal of Business & Economic Development, 08*(02), 20–22. DOI: 10.24052/IJBED/V08N02/ART-01

Roman, S., Campos-Medina, L., & Leal-Mercado, L. (2024). Personalized nutrition: The end of the one-diet-fits-all era. *Frontiers in Nutrition, 11*, 1370595. DOI: 10.3389/fnut.2024.1370595 PMID: 38854164

Rooney, P. R. (2012). *Measuring the Impact of a Comprehensive Health and Wellness Initiative*. https://scholarship.claremont.edu/cgi/viewcontent.cgi?article=1426&context=cmc_theses

Rosenstock, I. M. (1974). Historical origins of the Health Belief Model. *Health Education Monographs, 2*(4), 328–335. DOI: 10.1177/109019817400200403

Rosenthal, A., Maciel Guedes, A. M., dos Santos, K. M. O., & Deliza, R. (2021). Healthy food innovation in sustainable food system 4.0: Integration of entrepreneurship, research, and education. *Current Opinion in Food Science, 42*, 215–223. DOI: 10.1016/j.cofs.2021.07.002

Roy, B., Hagappa, A., Ramalingam, Y. D., & Mahalingam, N. (2021). A review on lab-grown meat: Advantages and disadvantages. *Quest International Journal of Medical and Health Sciences, 4*(1), 19–24.

Rozin, P. (2005). The Meaning of Food in Our Lives: A Cross-Cultural Perspective on Eating and Well-Being. *Journal of Nutrition Education and Behavior, 37*, S107–S112. DOI: 10.1016/S1499-4046(06)60209-1 PMID: 16246277

Rummo, P. E., Meyer, K. A., Green Howard, A., Shikany, J. M., Guilkey, D. K., & Gordon-Larsen, P. (2015). Fast food price, diet behavior, and cardiometabolic health: Differential associations by neighborhood SES and neighborhood fast food restaurant availability in the CARDIA study. *Health & Place, 35*, 128–135. DOI: 10.1016/j.healthplace.2015.06.010 PMID: 26319447

Ruthsatz, M., & Candeias, V. (2020). Non-communicable disease prevention, nutrition and aging. *Acta Biomedica, 91*(2), 379–388. DOI: 10.23750/abm.v91i2.9721 PMID: 32420978

Sacks, F. M., & Campos, H. (2010). Dietary therapy in hypertension. *New England Journal of Medicine*, *362*(22), 2102–2112. DOI: 10.1056/NEJMct0911013

Sahu, P., Bakshi, S., Divya, K. M., Singh, S. V., Keshari, U., Kumar, P., Neelam, K., Singh, P. C., & Singh, V. K. (2024). *Examine the Influence of Social Media in Promoting Regional Cuisine.*, DOI: 10.4018/979-8-3693-7096-4.ch018

Sakdapat, N. (2022). Healthy food consumption behavior of working people in the capital city: A case study in Bangkok, Thailand. *Przestrzeń Społeczna (Social Space), 22*(3), 365–384. https://orcid.org/0000-0002-8689-4046

Sakdapat, N. (2024). Stress Management Behaviour in Working Adults: A Case Study of Operational-Level Private Sector Employees in the Capital City of Thailand. *Przestrzeń Społeczna (Social Space), 24*(2), 469–488. https://orcid.org/0009-0000-0369-1191

Sakdapat, N. (2022). Healthy food consumption behavior of working people in the capital city: A case study in Bangkok, Thailand. [Social Space]. *Przestrzeń Społeczna, 22*(3), 365–384.

Sakdiyakorn, M., & Chirakranont, R. (2024). Brewing social capital: A case study of Thailand's craft beer consumption community. *Journal of Consumer Culture, 24*(4), 400–419. DOI: 10.1177/14695405241286384

Saleem, A., Anwar, S., Nawaz, T., Fahad, S., Saud, S., Ur Rahman, T., Khan, M. N. R., & Nawaz, T. (2025). Securing a sustainable future: The climate change threat to agriculture, food security, and sustainable development goals. *Journal of Umm Al-Qura University for Applied Sciences, 11*(3), 595–611. DOI: 10.1007/s43994-024-00177-3

Salloum, G., & Tekli, J. (2021). Automated and Personalized Nutrition Health Assessment, Recommendation, and Progress Evaluation using Fuzzy Reasoning. *International Journal of Human-Computer Studies, 151*, 102610. DOI: 10.1016/j.ijhcs.2021.102610

Sami, W., Ansari, T., Butt, N. S., & Hamid, M. R. A. (2017). Effect of diet on type 2 diabetes mellitus: A review. *International Journal of Health Sciences, 11*(2), 65–71. PMID: 28539866

Saputro, H., & Wulandari, L. (2023). Gastropreneurship Katupat Kandangan as a Tourism Attraction in the South Hulu Sungai in South Kalimantan. *The Journal Gastronomy Tourism, 10*(1), 82–95. DOI: 10.17509/gastur.v10i1.57919

Sarfraz, M. H., Shahid, A., Asghar, S., Aslam, B., Ashfaq, U. A., Raza, H., Prieto, M. A., Simal-Gandara, J., Barba, F. J., Rajoka, M. S. R., Khurshid, M., & Nashwan, A. J. (2022). Personalized nutrition, microbiota, and metabolism: A triad for eudaimonia. *Frontiers in Molecular Biosciences, 9*, 1038830. DOI: 10.3389/fmolb.2022.1038830 PMID: 36330221

Saurabh Sharma, V. K. G., &, Kumar Rahul, R. S. M. and M. M. (2021). Sustainable Innovations in the Food Industry through Artificial Intelligence and Big Data Analytics. *Logistics, MDPI,* 1–16. https://addepto.com/blog/artificial-intelligence-and-big-data-analytics-in-accounting/

Savarino, G., Corsello, A., & Corsello, G. (2021). Macronutrient balance and micronutrient amounts through growth and development. *Italian Journal of Pediatrics, 47*(1), 109. DOI: 10.1186/s13052-021-01061-0 PMID: 33964956

Scaling Up Nutrition Movement. (2024). *Scaling Up Nutrition Business Network.* https://scalingupnutrition.org

Scheiber, R., Diehl, S., & Karmasin, M. (2023). Analysing the Effects of Social Media Influencers' Food-related Posts on Healthy Eating Intentions, Orthorectic Eating Tendencies, Product Attitudes, and Purchase Intentions. *Medien Journal, 46*(3), 47–64. DOI: 10.24989/medienjournal.v46i3.2193

Schuman-Olivier, Z., Trombka, M., Lovas, D. A., Brewer, J. A., Vago, D. R., Gawande, R., Dunne, J. P., Lazar, S. W., Loucks, E. B., & Fulwiler, C. (2020). Mindfulness and Behavior Change. *Harvard Review of Psychiatry, 28*(6), 371–394. DOI: 10.1097/HRP.0000000000000277 PMID: 33156156

Schüz, B., Meyerhof, H., Hilz, L. K., & Mata, J. (2021). Equity effects of dietary nudging field experiments: Systematic review. *Frontiers in Public Health,* *9*, 668998. DOI: 10.3389/fpubh.2021.668998

Schwartz, H. (2007). *An introduction to behavioral economics: The complicating but sometimes critical considerations* (SSRN Scholarly Paper 960222). Social Science Research Network. DOI: 10.2139/ssrn.960222

Seaton, A., Tran, L., Aitken, R. J., & Donaldson, K. (2009). Nanoparticles, human health hazard and regulation. *Journal of The Royal Society Interface,* *7*(Suppl. 1), S119–S129. DOI: 10.1098/rsif.2009.0252.focus

Seidel, F., Oebel, B., Stein, L., Michalke, A., & Gaugler, T. (2023). The True Price of External Health Effects from Food Consumption. *Nutrients, 15*(15), 3386. Advance online publication. DOI: 10.3390/nu15153386 PMID: 37571323

Serie, K. (2021). *A narrative review of grocery store interventions on improving healthy food purchases* [Master's thesis, South Dakota State University]. Open PRAIRIE. https://openprairie.sdstate.edu/hns_plan-b/6

Setyani, V., Zhu, Y. Q., Hidayanto, A. N., Sandhyaduhita, P. I., & Hsiao, B. (2019). Exploring the psychological mechanisms from personalized advertisements to urge to buy impulsively on social media. *International Journal of Information Management*, *48*, 96–107. DOI: 10.1016/j.ijinfomgt.2019.01.007

Shahbazi, Y. (2024). Effect of modified atmosphere packaging combined with potato starch coating in extending the post-harvest shelf-life of fresh strawberries. *Journal of NutritionFasting and Health*, *12*(3). Advance online publication. DOI: 10.22038/jnfh.2024.81866.1526

Shanaida, M., Lysiuk, R., Mykhailenko, O., Hudz, N., Abdulsalam, A., Gontova, T., Oleshchuk, O., Ivankiv, Y., Shanaida, V., Lytkin, D., & Bjørklund, G. (2025). Alpha-lipoic acid: An antioxidant with anti-aging properties for disease therapy. *Current Medicinal Chemistry*, *32*(1), 23–54. DOI: 10.2174/0109298673300496240416114827 PMID: 38644711

Sharma, P., Malhotra, R. K., Ojha, M. K., & Gupta, S. (2022). Impact of meditation on mental & physical health and thereby on academic performance of students: A study of higher educational institutions of Uttarakhand. *Journal of Medical Pharmaceutical and Allied Sciences*, *11*(2), 4641–4644. DOI: 10.55522/jmpas.V11I2.2309

Shaw, R., & Cassidy, T. (2021). Self-Compassion, Mindful Eating, Eating Attitudes and Wellbeing. *Sumerianz Journal of Social Science*, *42*(42), 73–80. DOI: 10.47752/sjss.42.73.80

Shenoy, K. R., Ranjith, V. K., Nayak, S., & Anirvinna, C. (2024). Conceptualizing organic food consumption: A consumer motive perspective. *Cogent Social Sciences*, *10*(1), 2338864. Advance online publication. DOI: 10.1080/23311886.2024.2338864

Siegel, R., Gordon, K., & Dynan, L. (2021). Behavioral economics: A primer and applications to the UN Sustainable Development Goal of good health and well-being. *Reports*, *4*(2), 16. DOI: 10.3390/reports4020016

Silchenko, K., & Askegaard, S. (2021). Powered by healthism? Marketing discourses of food and health. *European Journal of Marketing*, *55*(1), 133–161. DOI: 10.1108/EJM-04-2018-0296

Singh, B., Jain, A., Kumar, S., & Chandra, S. (2025). Strengthening AI-Driven Solutions for Virtual Tourism: Matching Visitor Experience and Ecosystem Conservation. In C. Ramos, T. Costa, R. Madeira, & J. Ferreira do Rosário (Eds.), *Open Innovation and Technology in Tourism and Hospitality* (pp. 93-110). IGI Global Scientific Publishing. DOI: 10.4018/979-8-3693-8633-0.ch005

Singh, B., & Kumar, S. (2025). Eco-Friendly Practices of Ghost Kitchens Through Smart Technology: Technological Innovations in the Food-Beverage Industry. In Singh, K., Kumar, S., & Talukder, M. B. (Eds.), (pp. 359–378). Advances in Computational Intelligence and Robotics. IGI Global., DOI: 10.4018/979-8-3373-0432-8.ch017

Singh, B., Kumar, S., & Wongmahesak, K. (2025). Leadership and Management in the Public Sector via E-Government and E-Governance in Public Administration Reform. In Wongmahesak, K., Ahmad, J., & Mustanir, A. (Eds.), *Public Governance Practices in the Age of AI* (pp. 253–268). IGI Global Scientific Publishing., DOI: 10.4018/979-8-3693-9286-7.ch013

Singh, P. C., Singh, S. V., Rajauria, S., Singh, V. K., & Sahu, P. (2025). Examine the Role of Short Video Platforms on Tourist's Attitude: A Technology Acceptance Model (TAM) Approach. *PUSA Journal of Hospitality and Applied Sciences*, *11*(1), 12–19. DOI: 10.48165/pjhas.2025.11.1.2

Sitaker, M., Kolodinsky, J., Jilcott Pitts, S. B., & Seguin, R. A. (2014). Do entrepreneurial food systems innovations impact rural economies and health? Evidence and gaps. *American Journal of Entrepreneurship*, *7*(2), 3–16. PMID: 26613066

Skonberg, C., & Thorbecke, M. (2022). *Applying environmental models in the food business context*., DOI: 10.1016/B978-0-12-822112-9.00009-6

Smid, E. J., & Lacroix, C. (2013). Microbe-microbe interactions in mixed culture food fermentations. *Current Opinion in Biotechnology*, *24*(2), 148–154. DOI: 10.1016/j.copbio.2012.11.007

Smith, C., & Fatorachian, H. (2025). Inherently irrational: Exploring the role of behavioural economics and organisational culture in food supply chain disruption management decisions. *Cogent Business & Management*, *12*(1), 2463566. Advance online publication. DOI: 10.1080/23311975.2025.2463566

Sobal, J., & Bisogni, C. A. (2009). Constructing Food Choice Decisions. *Annals of Behavioral Medicine*, *38*(S1), 37–46. DOI: 10.1007/s12160-009-9124-5 PMID: 19787306

Sobarna, A. (2023). Virtual Reality Tourism: Linkage Tourist Intention, Satisfaction, and Quality. [JMI]. *Journal of Marketing Innovation*, *3*(1). Advance online publication. DOI: 10.35313/jmi.v3i1.58

Sokolova, K., & Kefi, H. (2020). Instagram and YouTube bloggers promote it, why should I buy? How credibility and parasocial interaction influence purchase intentions. *Journal of Retailing and Consumer Services, 53*, 101742. Advance online publication. DOI: 10.1016/j.jretconser.2019.01.011

Soldani, J., Tamburri, D. A., & Van Den Heuvel, W. J. (2018). The pains and gains of microservices: A Systematic grey literature review. *Journal of Systems and Software, 146*, 215–232. DOI: 10.1016/j.jss.2018.09.082

Spencer, S. J., Korosi, A., Layé, S., Shukitt-Hale, B., & Barrientos, R. M. (2017). Food for thought: How nutrition impacts cognition and emotion. *NPJ Science of Food, 1*(1), 7. DOI: 10.1038/s41538-017-0008-y PMID: 31304249

Spieldenner, J., & Matope, J. H. (2017). The Food Industry as a Partner for Public Health? In Biesalski, H. K., Drewnowski, A., Dwyer, J. T., Strain, J., Weber, P., & Eggersdorfer, M. (Eds.), *Sustainable Nutrition in a Changing World* (pp. 261–274). Springer International Publishing., DOI: 10.1007/978-3-319-55942-1_18

Sridhar, A., Kapoor, A., Kumar, P. S., Ponnuchamy, M., Sivasamy, B., & Vo, D. V. N. (2021). Lab-on-a-chip technologies for food safety, processing, and packaging applications: A review. *Environmental Chemistry Letters, 20*(1), 901–927. DOI: 10.1007/s10311-021-01342-4

Sriram, H. K. (2023). Harnessing AI Neural Networks and Generative AI for Advanced Customer Engagement: Insights into Loyalty Programs, Marketing Automation, and Real-Time Analytics. *Educational Administration: Theory and Practice, 29*(4), 4361–4374.

Srivastava, S., & Upadhyay, D. P. (2024). Digital Empowerment for Indigenous Communities Using Generative Artificial Intelligence. *GATR Global Journal of Business and Social Science Review (GATR-GJBSSR), Vol.12(2)*(April-June 2024.).

Stephanie, S. (2025). *Impact of Retail Display Case on Shelf-Life, Palatability, and Color-Stability of Fresh Beef Steaks* [Master of Science in Animal Science Thesis]. University of Arkansas.

Stern, A. J. (2021). *Food industry influence on dietary advice in the United States.* Proceedings of the National Conference on Undergraduate Research (NCUR). University of North Carolina at Asheville. https://libjournals.unca.edu/ncur/wp-content/uploads/2021/06/1706-Stern-Aaron-FINAL.pdf

Stevens, G. A., Beal, T., Mbuya, M. N. N., Luo, H., Neufeld, L. M., Addo, O. Y., Adu-Afarwuah, S., Alayón, S., Bhutta, Z. A., Brown, K. H., Jefferds, M. E., Engle-Stone, R., Fawzi, W., Hess, S. Y., Johnston, R., Katz, J., Krasevec, J., McDonald, C. M., Mei, Z., & Young, M. F. (2022). Micronutrient deficiencies among preschool-aged children and women of reproductive age worldwide: A pooled analysis of individual-level data from population-representative surveys. *The Lancet. Global Health, 10*(11), e1590–e1599. DOI: 10.1016/S2214-109X(22)00367-9 PMID: 36240826

Stover, P. J., & Caudill, M. A. (2008). Genetic and epigenetic contributions to human nutrition and health: Managing genome–diet interactions. *Journal of the American Dietetic Association*, *108*(9), 1480–1487. DOI: 10.1016/j.jada.2008.06.430

Subramanian, L. (2020). *Enabling health supply chains for improved well-being. 21*(4), 229–236. DOI: 10.1080/16258312.2020.1776091

Sulis, Y. D., Anshori, M. I., & Andriani, N. (2024). Analysis of Digital Marketing Strategies in Increasing Sales of Singgasana Cafe and Resto in Tanjung Bumi District Bangkalan Regency. *INVEST: Jurnal Inovasi Bisnis dan Akuntansi, 5*(1), 114-124.

Sundaram, D., Vedagiri, H., Subbaraj, G. K., & Kumpati, P. (2024). Repurposing of Drugs in Aging. In *Neuroprotective Effects of Phytochemicals in Brain Ageing* (pp. 333–353). Springer Nature Singapore. DOI: 10.1007/978-981-99-7269-2_15

Suriwong, V., Inrirai, P., Samrit, T., & Swaeng-ngam, S. (2025). Effect of soaking solution and various packaging conditions on shelf life of fresh Bambusa sp. Shoot. *Food Research*, *9*(5), 51. DOI: 10.26656/fr.2017.9(5).047

Swenor, B. K. (2021). Disability inclusion: A missing ingredient for food system equity. *Global Food Security*, *31*, 100584. DOI: 10.1016/j.gfs.2021.100584

Swinburn, B. A., Kraak, V. I., Allender, S., Atkins, V. J., Baker, P. I., Bogard, J. R., Brinsden, H., Calvillo, A., De Schutter, O., Devarajan, R., Ezzati, M., Friel, S., Goenka, S., Hammond, R. A., Hastings, G., Hawkes, C., Herrero, M., Hovmand, P. S., Howden, M., & Dietz, W. H. (2019). The global syndemic of obesity, under-nutrition, and climate change: The Lancet Commission report. *Lancet*, *393*(10173), 791–846. DOI: 10.1016/S0140-6736(18)32822-8 PMID: 30700377

Taheri, B., Pourfakhimi, S., Prayag, G., Gannon, M. J., & Finsterwalder, J. (2021). Towards co-created food well-being: Culinary consumption, braggart word-of-mouth and the role of participative co-design, service provider support and C2C interactions. *European Journal of Marketing*, *55*(9), 2464–2490. DOI: 10.1108/EJM-02-2020-0145

Tallon, M. J., & Kalman, D. S. (2024). The Regulatory Challenges of Placing Dietary Ingredients on the European and US Market. *Journal of Dietary Supplements*, •••, 1–16. DOI: 10.1080/19390211.2024.2308261 PMID: 38269549

Talukder, M. B., & Kumar, S. (2024). Revisiting intention in food service outlet of five-star hotels: A quantitative approach based on food service quality. *Sport i Turystyka. Środkowoeuropejskie Czasopismo Naukowe, 7*(1), 137–156. DOI: 10.16926/sit.2024.01.08

Talukder, M. B., Das, I. R., & Kumar, S. (2025). Future Trends and Prospects of the Food Industry: Perspectives from Hospitality. In Dutta, P. K., Hamad, A., Haghi, A. K., & Prabhakar, P. K. (Eds.), *Food and Industry 5.0: Transforming the Food System for a Sustainable Future* (pp. 289–303). Springer Nature Switzerland., DOI: 10.1007/978-3-031-76758-6_18

Talukder, M. B., & Kumar, S. (2025). Culinary Experiences and Food Tourism in Bangladesh. In Tyagi, P. K., Nadda, V., & Singh, A. K. (Eds.), *Meaningful Tourism* (pp. 201–219). Emerald Publishing Limited., DOI: 10.1108/978-1-83797-837-320251028

Talukder, M. B., Kumar, S., & Das, I. R. (2024). Food Wastage on the Economic Outcome: Evidence From the Hotel industry. In Singh, A., Tyagi, P. K., & Garg, A. (Eds.), (pp. 68–80). Practice, Progress, and Proficiency in Sustainability. IGI Global., DOI: 10.4018/979-8-3693-2181-2.ch005

Tang, J., Abraham, C., Stamp, E., & Greaves, C. (2015). How can weight-loss app designers' best engage and support users? A qualitative investigation. *British Journal of Health Psychology, 20*(1), 151–171. DOI: 10.1111/bjhp.12114 PMID: 25130682

Tapia Granados, J. A. (2002). Fast food nation: The dark side of the all-American meal. *Revista Panamericana de Salud Pública = Pan American Journal of Public Health, 12*(2), 146–147. DOI: 10.1590/S1020-49892002000800019

Tapsell, L. C., Neale, E. P., Satija, A., & Hu, F. B. (2016). Foods, nutrients, and dietary patterns: Interconnections and implications for dietary guidelines. *Advances in Nutrition*, *7*(3), 445–454. DOI: 10.3945/an.115.011718

Tekin, O., Kucuker, E., Aglar, E., Alan, D., & Sumbul, A. (2025). Effects of post-harvest citric, oxalic acid, and modified atmosphere packaging applications on fruit quality and biochemical properties in persimmon. *BMC Plant Biology, 25*(1), 1353. DOI: 10.1186/s12870-025-07368-y PMID: 41068587

Tempels, T., Verweij, M., & Blok, V. (2017). Big Food's Ambivalence: Seeking Profit and Responsibility for Health. *American Journal of Public Health, 107*(3), 402–406. DOI: 10.2105/AJPH.2016.303601 PMID: 28103076

Temple, N. J. (2022). A rational definition for functional foods: A perspective. *Frontiers in Nutrition, 9*, 957516. DOI: 10.3389/fnut.2022.957516 PMID: 36245478

Tenchov, R., Sasso, J. M., Wang, X., & Zhou, Q. A. (2024). Antiaging Strategies and Remedies: A Landscape of Research Progress and Promise. *ACS Chemical Neuroscience, 15*(3), 408–446. DOI: 10.1021/acschemneuro.3c00532 PMID: 38214973

Teng, Y., Jiang, T., & Yan, Y. (2024). The expanded CRISPR toolbox for constructing microbial cell factories. *Trends in Biotechnology, 42*(1), 104–118. DOI: 10.1016/j.tibtech.2023.06.012

Tessier, A. J., Wang, F., Korat, A. A., Eliassen, A. H., Chavarro, J., Grodstein, F., Li, J., Liang, L., Willett, W. C., Sun, Q., Stampfer, M. J., Hu, F. B., & Guasch-Ferré, M. (2025). Optimal dietary patterns for healthy aging. *Nature Medicine, 31*(5), 1644–1652. Advance online publication. DOI: 10.1038/s41591-025-03570-5 PMID: 40128348

Thukral, E., & Ratten, V. (2020). Sport, Health, and Lifestyle Entrepreneurship: Case Studies. In Emerald Publishing Limited eBooks (p. 161). DOI: 10.1108/978-1-83982-836-220201022

Tilman, D., & Clark, M. (2014). Global diets link environmental sustainability and human health. *Nature, 515*(7528), 518–522. DOI: 10.1038/nature13959 PMID: 25383533

Tisu, L., Vîrgă, D., & Taris, T. (2023). Entrepreneurial well-being and performance: Antecedents and mediators. *Frontiers in Psychology, 14*, 1112397. DOI: 10.3389/fpsyg.2023.1112397 PMID: 37928580

Tiusanen, K. (2021). Fulfilling the self through food in wellness blogs: Governing the healthy subject. *European Journal of Cultural Studies, 24*(6), 1382–1400. DOI: 10.1177/13675494211055734

Torres, E. G., Fonseca-Larios, R., & Ramírez-Portilla, A. (2024). *Innovating R&D practices to adapt swiftly to market trends: Insights from the Food and Beverage Industry*. DOI: 10.5772/intechopen.1006672

Tripathi, S., Hakim, L., Gupta, D., Deshmukh, R. K., & Gaikwad, K. K. (2024). Recent Trends in Films and Gases for Modified Atmosphere Packaging of Fresh Produce. In *Novel Packaging Systems for Fruits and Vegetables* (1st ed., p. 27). Apple Academic Press. DOI: 10.1201/9781003415701-3

Tsironi, T. N. (2026). Introduction to food packaging: Historical overview, sustainability, and current trends. In *Safety and Sustainability Aspects of Food Packaging* (pp. 3–28). Elsevier., DOI: 10.1016/B978-0-443-24768-2.00005-3

Tung, A., Takase, L., Fornal, C., & Jacobs, B. (2024). Neuroscience. https://www.sciencedirect.com/journal/neuroscience/vol/134/issue/3

Tuul, S., Banzragch, O., & Saizmaa, T. (2016). E-learning in Mongolian higher education. *International Review of Research in Open and Distance Learning*, *17*(2), 181–197. DOI: 10.19173/irrodl.v17i2.2227

Tyrovola, D., Soulaidopoulos, S., Tsioufis, C., & Lazaros, G. (2023). The Role of Nutrition in Cardiovascular Disease: Current Concepts and Trends. *Nutrients*, *15*(5), 1064. DOI: 10.3390/nu15051064 PMID: 36904064

UNEP. (2021). *Food waste index report 2021*. United Nations Environment Programme.

United Nations. (2015). *Transforming our world: The 2030 agenda for sustainable development*. United Nations General Assembly.

Urfels, A., Mirzabaev, A., Bricx, S., Deb, P., Dewi, K., Evangelista, G., Flor, R. J., Harris, B., Jayasiri, N., Kishore, A., McDonald, A. J., Mondal, M., Quicho, E., Saito, K., Kumar, V., & Laborte, A. (2024). Economics of sustainable irrigation in smallholder agriculture: Implications for food security and climate action. *Environmental Research Letters*, *19*(8), 081008. Advance online publication. DOI: 10.1088/1748-9326/ad6201

Uttama, N. P. (2021). Open Innovation and Business Model of Health Food Industry in Asia. *Journal of Open Innovation*, *7*(3), 174. DOI: 10.3390/joitmc7030174

Valluri, M. (2022). The Future of Food: Trends and Innovations. *International Journal For Multidisciplinary Research*, *4*(2), 6188. Advance online publication. DOI: 10.36948/ijfmr.2022.v04i02.6188

Valpiani, N., Thorne-Lyman, A. L., De Pee, S., Godfrey, S., Gentilini, U., & Bloem, M. W. (2008). Proposed strategies for mitigating the impact of high food prices on nutrition and health in Latin America and the Caribbean. *Perspectives in Agriculture, Veterinary Science, Nutrition and Natural Resources*, *3*, 1–12. Advance online publication. DOI: 10.1079/PAVSNNR20083081

Van Dam, N. T., Van Vugt, M. K., Vago, D. R., Schmalzl, L., Saron, C. D., Olendzki, A., Meissner, T., Lazar, S. W., Kerr, C. E., Gorchov, J., Fox, K. C. R., Field, B. A., Britton, W. B., Brefczynski-Lewis, J. A., & Meyer, D. E. (2018). Mind the Hype: A Critical Evaluation and Prescriptive Agenda for Research on Mindfulness and Meditation. *Perspectives on Psychological Science*, *13*(1), 36–61. DOI: 10.1177/1745691617709589 PMID: 29016274

Varlese, M., Misso, R., Koliouska, C., & Andreopoulou, Z. (2020). Food, internet and neuromarketing in the context of well-being sustainability. *International Journal of Technology Marketing*, *14*(3), 267. DOI: 10.1504/IJTMKT.2020.111500

Varzakas, T., & Smaoui, S. (2024). Global food security and sustainability issues: The road to 2030 from nutrition and sustainable healthy diets to food systems change. *Foods*, *13*(2), 306. DOI: 10.3390/foods13020306

Varzakas, T., & Antoniadou, M. (2024). A Holistic Approach for Ethics and Sustainability in the Food Chain: The Gateway to Oral and Systemic Health. *Foods*, *13*(8), 1224. Advance online publication. DOI: 10.3390/foods13081224 PMID: 38672896

Vecchio, R., & Cavallo, C. (2019). Increasing healthy food choices through nudges: A systematic review. *Food Quality and Preference*, *78*, 103714. DOI: 10.1016/j.foodqual.2019.05.014

Veliah, G. K., & Venkatsubramanian, P. (2024). Promoting Wellness as a Primordial Prevention Strategy for Achieving Sustainable Public Health in the Post-Covid 19 Era. *American Journal of Lifestyle Medicine*, *18*(4), 608–611. Advance online publication. DOI: 10.1177/15598276241240414 PMID: 39262891

Vergères, G., Bochud, M., Jotterand Chaparro, C., Moretti, D., Pestoni, G., Probst-Hensch, N., Rezzi, S., Rohrmann, S., & Brück, W. M. (2024). The future backbone of nutritional science: Integrating public health priorities with system-oriented precision nutrition. *British Journal of Nutrition*, *132*(5), 651–666. DOI: 10.1017/S0007114524001466 PMID: 39320518

Victorson, D., Kentor, M., Maletich, C., Lawton, R. C., Kaufman, V. H., Borrero, M., Languido, L., Lewett, K., Pancoe, H., & Berkowitz, C. (2015). Mindfulness Meditation to Promote Wellness and Manage Chronic Disease: A Systematic Review and Meta-Analysis of Mindfulness-Based Randomized Controlled Trials Relevant to Lifestyle Medicine. *American Journal of Lifestyle Medicine*, *9*(3), 185–211. DOI: 10.1177/1559827614537789

Vilar-Compte, M., Burrola-Méndez, S., Lozano-Marrufo, A., Gaitán-Rossi, P., Teruel, G., & Pérez-Escamilla, R. (2021). Urban poverty and nutrition challenges associated with accessibility to a healthy diet: A global systematic literature review. *International Journal for Equity in Health, 20*(1), 40. DOI: 10.1186/s12939-020-01330-0 PMID: 33472636

Viroli, G., Kalmpourtzidou, A., & Cena, H. (2023). Exploring Benefits and Barriers of Plant-Based Diets: Health, Environmental Impact, Food Accessibility and Acceptability. *Nutrients, 15*(22), 4723. DOI: 10.3390/nu15224723 PMID: 38004117

Vogus, T. J., & Sutcliffe, K. M. (2007). Organizational resilience: Towards a theory and research agenda. *Conference Proceedings - IEEE International Conference on Systems, Man and Cybernetics*, 3418–3422. DOI: 10.1109/ICSMC.2007.4414160

Volpp, K. G., & Lamberton, C. (2024). Behavioral Economics to Enhance Food Is Medicine Programs. *JAMA Health Forum, 5*(7), e241586. DOI: 10.1001/jamahealthforum.2024.1586 PMID: 38995633

von Philipsborn, P., Stratil, J. M., Heise, T. L., Landgraf, R., Hauner, H., & Rehfuess, E. A. (2018). Voluntary industry initiatives to promote healthy diets: A case study on a major European food retailer. *Public Health Nutrition, 21*(18), 3469–3476. DOI: 10.1017/S1368980018002744 PMID: 30334511

Vos, R., & Cattaneo, A. (2021). Poverty reduction through the development of inclusive food value chains. *Journal of Integrative Agriculture*, *20*(4), 964–978. DOI: 10.1016/S2095-3119(20)63398-6

Vukadinović, S. (2022). *Selling Wellness: An Analysis Of Goop And Poosh's Visual Marketing On Instagram*. DOI: 10.32920/19154462.v1

Wadhwa, C. L., Thakker, H., Kaushik, V., Manjunath, H. R., Goyal, S., Thakkar, A., & Grover, M. (2024). Study on Assessing the Evolution of Nutritional Choices through Social Media Influence. *Evolutionary Studies in Imaginative Culture*, •••, 860–869. DOI: 10.70082/esiculture.vi.1084

Waheed, S., & Kumar, S. (2024). Challenges and Future Directions for Promoting Sustainable Gastronomy Tourism. In Jimenez Ruiz, A. E., Bhartiya, S., & Bhatt, V. (Eds.), *Advances in Hospitality, Tourism, and the Services Industry* (pp. 1–16). IGI Global., DOI: 10.4018/979-8-3693-1814-0.ch001

Wang, J., Ding, X., Gao, H., & Fan, S. (2022). Reshaping food policy and governance to incentivize and empower disadvantaged groups for improving nutrition. *Nutrients*, *14*(3), 648. DOI: 10.3390/nu14030648

Wang, X., Ma, L., Jiang, S., Wen, J., Yan, Z., Tian, L., & Zhao, R. C. (2024). Expert Consensus on Prevention and Treatment of Aging-Related Gonadal Dysfunction. *Aging and Disease*, •••, 1–9. PMID: 38739936

Wansink, B. (2017). Healthy profits: An Interdisciplinary Retail Framework for Increasing the Sales of Healthy Foods. *The FASEB Journal*, *31*(S1). Advance online publication. DOI: 10.1096/fasebj.31.1_supplement.636.6

Warren, J. M., Smith, N., & Ashwell, M. (2017). A structured literature review on the role of mindfulness, mindful eating and intuitive eating in changing eating behaviours: Effectiveness and associated potential mechanisms. *Nutrition Research Reviews*, *30*(2), 272–283. DOI: 10.1017/S0954422417000154 PMID: 28718396

Wendt, J., Scheller, D. A., Banik, A., Łuszczyńska, A., Forberger, S., Zeeb, H., Scheidmeir, M., Kubiak, T., Lien, N., Meshkovska, B., Łobczowska, K., Romaniuk, P., Neumann-Podczaska, A., Wieczorowska-Tobis, K., Steinacker, J. M., & Mueller-Stierlin, A. S. (2023). Good practice recommendations on implementation evaluation for policies targeting diet, physical activity, and sedentary behaviour. *BMC Public Health*, *23*(1), Article 1237. DOI: 10.1186/s12889-023-15775-9

Westbury, S., Oyebode, O., Rens, T. van, & Barber, T. M. (2023). Obesity Stigma: Causes, Consequences, and Potential Solutions [Review of Obesity Stigma: Causes, Consequences, and Potential Solutions]. Current Obesity Reports, 12(1), 10. Springer Science+Business Media. DOI: 10.1007/s13679-023-00495-3

White, M. (2021). Urban agriculture in Detroit: Community empowerment through food production. *Journal of Urban Health*, *98*(3), 345–353. DOI: 10.1007/s11524-021-00532-7

Wiedenroth, C. F., & Otter, V. (2022). Can new healthy luxury food products accelerate short food supply chain formation via social media marketing in high-income countries? *Agricultural and Food Economics*, *10*(1), 31. Advance online publication. DOI: 10.1186/s40100-022-00238-3 PMID: 36530963

Wiklund, J., Nikolaev, B., Shir, N., Foo, M.-D., & Bradley, S. (2019). Entrepreneurship and well-being: Past, present, and future. *Journal of Business Venturing*, *34*(4), 579–588. DOI: 10.1016/j.jbusvent.2019.01.002

Willett, W., Rockström, J., Loken, B., Springmann, M., Lang, T., Vermeulen, S., Garnett, T., Tilman, D., DeClerck, F., Wood, A., Jonell, M., Clark, M., Gordon, L. J., Fanzo, J., Hawkes, C., Zurayk, R., Rivera, J. A., De Vries, W., Majele Sibanda, L., & Murray, C. J. L. (2019). Food in the Anthropocene: The EAT-Lancet Commission on healthy diets from sustainable food systems. *Lancet*, *393*(10170), 447–492. DOI: 10.1016/S0140-6736(18)31788-4 PMID: 30660336

Wondirad, A., Kebete, Y., & Li, Y. (2021). Culinary tourism as a driver of regional economic development and socio-cultural revitalization: Evidence from Amhara National Regional State, Ethiopia. *Journal of Destination Marketing & Management, 19*, 100482. Advance online publication. DOI: 10.1016/j.jdmm.2020.100482

Wongprawmas, R., Sogari, G., Menozzi, D., & Mora, C. (2022). Strategies to promote healthy eating among university students: A qualitative study using the nominal group technique. *Frontiers in Nutrition, 9*, 821016. DOI: 10.3389/fnut.2022.821016 PMID: 35187039

Won, Y., Jung, H. J., & Lee, Y. (2024). Online VR store as a sustainable fashion retail space. *International Journal of Retail & Distribution Management, 52*(13), 31–46. DOI: 10.1108/IJRDM-06-2023-0370

World Business Council for Sustainable Development (WBCSD). (2023). *Reducing inequalities for food security and nutrition: A WBCSD business brief.* https://www.wbcsd.org/wp-content/uploads/2023/09/HLPE-FSN-Reducing-inequalities-for-food-security-and-nutrition-Business-Brief.pdf

World Health Organization. (2017). *Biofortification of crops with minerals and vitamins*. e-Library of Evidence for Nutrition Actions (eLENA). https://www.who.int/tools/elena/bbc/biofortification

World Health Organization. (2019). Regional Office for the Eastern Mediterranean. *Healthy diet* (WHO-EM/NUT/282/E). https://applications.emro.who.int/docs/EMROPUB_2019_en_23536.pdf

World Health Organization. (2023). *Noncommunicable diseases: Key facts.* WHO.

World Health Organization. (2024). *Noncommunicable diseases.* https://www.who.int/news-room/fact-sheets/detail/noncommunicable-diseases

Wulandari, K. T., Mukti, M. A., & Kiren, K. (2023). *Operation Efficiency In The F and B Enterprise Through Digitalization and Cloud Kitchen Integration: A Systematic Literature Review*. 1128–1137. DOI: 10.46254/AP04.20230296

Wulandari, W., Rafsanjani, M. A., Dewi, R. M., Zain, R. R., & Irawan, N. (2024). Bibliometric analysis of food waste in economics for Sustainable Development Goals 2030. In S. N., P. B.K., S. M., L. L., A. G. M., & A. S. (Eds.), *E3S Web of Conferences* (Vol. 568). EDP Sciences. DOI: 10.1051/e3sconf/202456801005

Wulandari, A., Marcelino, D., Suryawardani, B., Gusnadi, D., Prabawa, B., & Arumsari, R. Y. (2024). How to Develop Marketing Strategy, Packaging Designs, and Superior Product Processing Education? *Jurnal Penyuluhan, 20*(01), 1–13. DOI: 10.25015/20202448777

Wu, Y. C., Kemps, E., & Prichard, I. (2023). Digging into digital buffets: A systematic review of eating-related social media content and its relationship with body image and eating behaviours. *Body Image, 48*, 101650. DOI: 10.1016/j.bodyim.2023.101650 PMID: 38039952

Xavier, J. A., & Alagappar, P. N. (2025). Harnessing Entrepreneurial Drive, Identifying Market Opportunities, and Leveraging Social Networks: A Malaysian Family Business. In *Strategic Insights and Case Studies on Navigating an Entrepreneurial Landscape* (pp. 207-224). IGI Global Scientific Publishing.

Xin, Y., & Qiao, M. (2025). Towards microbial consortia in fermented foods for metabolic engineering and synthetic biology. *Food Research International, 201*, 115677. Advance online publication. DOI: 10.1016/j.foodres.2025.115677

Xu, X., Meier, F., Blount, B. A., Pretorius, I. S., Ellis, T., Paulsen, I. T., & Williams, T. C. (2023). Trimming the genomic fat: minimising and re-functionalising genomes using synthetic biology. *Nature Communications 2023 14:1, 14*(1), 1–11. DOI: 10.1038/s41467-023-37748-7

Xu, T., Wang, H., Lu, G., Wan, F., Deng, M., Qi, P., Bezerianos, A., Guan, C., & Sun, Y. (2021). E-Key: An EEG-Based Biometric Authentication and Driving Fatigue Detection System. *IEEE Transactions on Affective Computing, 14*(2), 864–877. DOI: 10.1109/TAFFC.2021.3133443

Yadav, K. K., Gaurav, K., Bhalavey, P., Singh, A., Yadav, R. P., & Soni, V. (2025). Post-Harvest Handling and Preservation of Fish. In *Fisheries Science in the 2lst Century Progress and Prospects* (pp. 120–132). Elite Publishing House., https://www.researchgate.net/publication/395946808

Yagishita, S. (2022). Cellular bases for reward-related dopamine actions [Review of Cellular bases for reward-related dopamine actions]. Neuroscience Research, 188, 1. Elsevier BV. DOI: 10.1016/j.neures.2022.12.003

Yahn, G. (1979). The Impact of Holistic Medicine, Medical Groups, and Health Concepts. *Journal of the American Medical Association, 242*(20), 2202–2205. DOI: 10.1001/jama.1979.03300200032018 PMID: 490807

Yang, W., Lu, F., & Liu, Y. (2023). Recent Advances of Enzymes in the Food Industry. *Foods, 12*(24), 4506. DOI: 10.3390/foods12244506

Yeoman, I., & McMahon-Beattie, U. (2024). Signals of change: Eating trends shaping the future of food service. *Research in Hospitality Management, 14*(2), 104–111. DOI: 10.1080/22243534.2024.2361395

Yu, M., & Watson, S. (2024). Market overview of health and wellness food products. In *Flavor-Associated Applications in Health and Wellness Food Products* (pp. 3–19). Springer International Publishing., DOI: 10.1007/978-3-031-51808-9_1

Zamora-Ros, R., & González, C. A. (2020). Diet-disease relationships: Recent advances in nutritional epidemiology. *Mètode Science Studies Journal*, *11*, 115–121. DOI: 10.7203/metode.11.16205

Zanatta, F., Mari, S., Adorni, R., Labra, M., Matacena, R., Zenga, M., & D'Addario, M. (2022). The Role of Selected Psychological Factors in Healthy-Sustainable Food Consumption Behaviors during the COVID-19 Pandemic. *Foods*, *11*(13), 1944. DOI: 10.3390/foods11131944

Zantar, Y., Noutfia, Y., Laglaoui, A., Benicha, M., Baguena, I., Zantar, S., & Hassani, M. (2024). Impact of Enriched CO2 in Modified Atmosphere Packaging on the preservation of "Palmaritas" Strawberries and the extension of their shelf life. *Journal of Microbiology, Biotechnology and Food Sciences*, *14*(2), e10703. Advance online publication. DOI: 10.55251/jmbfs.10703

Zhang, C., Vanschoren, J., van Wissen, A., Lakens, D., de Ruyter, B., & IJsselsteijn, W. A. (2022). Theory-based habit modeling for enhancing behavior prediction in behavior change support systems. *User Modeling and User-Adapted Interaction*, *32*(3), 389–415. DOI: 10.1007/s11257-022-09326-x

Zhang, L., Shao, Z., Li, X., & Feng, Y. (2021). Gamification and online impulse buying: The moderating effect of gender and age. *International Journal of Information Management*, *61*, 102267. Advance online publication. DOI: 10.1016/j.ijinfomgt.2020.102267

Zhang, Z., Yang, R., Zi, Z., & Liu, B. (2024). A new clinical age of aging research. *Trends in Endocrinology and Metabolism*. PMID: 39227191

Zheng, H., Wu, J., Feng, J., & Cheng, H. (2024). Cellular Senescence and Anti-Aging Strategies in Aesthetic Medicine: A Bibliometric Analysis and Brief Review. *Clinical, Cosmetic and Investigational Dermatology*, *17*, 2243–2259. DOI: 10.2147/CCID.S403417 PMID: 39399066

Zheng, L., He, S., Wang, H., Li, J., Liu, Y., & Liu, S. (2024). Targeting cellular senescence in aging and age-related diseases: Challenges, considerations, and the emerging role of senolytic and senomorphic therapies. *Aging and Disease*, *15*(6), 2554. PMID: 38421832

Zhou, Y., Saarniit, K., Jafari, M. S., Rosenvald, S., Laaksonen, O., Tian, Y., & Yang, B. (2025). Storage stability of berry mueslis with special focus on phenolic compounds. *Lebensmittel-Wissenschaft + Technologie*, *228*, 118119. DOI: 10.1016/j.lwt.2025.118119

Zorbas, C., Blake, M. R., Brown, A. D., Peeters, A., Allender, S., Brimblecombe, J., & Boelsen-Robinson, T. (2024). A systems framework for implementing healthy food retail in grocery settings. *BMC Public Health*, *24*(1), 137. DOI: 10.1186/s12889-023-17075-8 PMID: 38195419

Zuroff, T. R., Xiques, S. B., & Curtis, W. R. (2013). Consortia-mediated bioprocessing of cellulose to ethanol with a symbiotic Clostridium phytofermentans/yeast co-culture. *Biotechnology for Biofuels*, *6*(1), 1–12. DOI: 10.1186/1754-6834-6-59

About the Contributors

Kittisak Wongmahesak is a lecturer at the Faculty of Political Science, North Bangkok University, and the Director of the Association of Legal & Political Studies in Thailand. He also holds the position of Research Fellow at Shinawatra University, Thailand, and Universiti Sultan Zainal Abidin, Malaysia. His influence extends to Indonesia, where he is an Adjunct Professor at Sekolah Tinggi Ilmu Administrasi Abdul Haris and an Adjunct Research Professor at several Indonesian universities, including Universitas Muhammadiyah Sinjai, Universitas Muhammadiyah Makassar, and Universitas Muhammadiyah Sidenreng Rappang. With a wealth of academic experience and a robust set of qualifications, Kittisak WONGMAHESAK has held the position of Full Professor of Public Administration at Huanghe Business School, Henan University of Economics and Law in China, and the University of City Island in Cyprus. He has also contributed as an Adjunct Researcher at Ton Duc Thang University and Duy Tan University in Vietnam. His academic qualifications include a Ph.D. in Social Sciences, an M.A., and a B.A. in Political Science, all from Kasetsart University. Additionally, he earned an M.B.A. and an M.P.A. from Ramkhamhaeng University and a B.Pol.Sc. in International Relations and Comparative Government and Politics from Sukhothai Thammathirat Open University. Kittisak WONGMAHESAK's expertise spans Political Science, Public and Private Management, International Political Economy, and Social Research. He is the editor of numerous prestigious journals worldwide, including Sustainability, Frontiers in Psychology, PLOS One, World Food Policy, Asian Academy of Management Journal, International Journal of Public Policy and Administration Research, International Journal of Innovative Research and Scientific Studies, and Recent Advances in Computer Science and Communications. His global recognition as one of the world's top 2% of scientists by Stanford University since 2020 is a testament to his influence. His extensive publication record, with over 450 indexed Scopus/Web of Science documents and an h-index of 56 with more than 10,000 citations, is a wealth of knowledge that informs his significant scholarly contributions.

Roy Marzo currently serves as the Dean of the Faculty of Humanities and Health Sciences and as the Associate Dean of Research and Development at Curtin University, Malaysia. Prior to this, he held the position of Department Chair/Head of Public Health and Head of Research at Management and Science University. His past roles also include Deputy Dean, Chairman of Medical Research and Ethics, and Program Head of the Master in Healthcare Management at Asia Metropolitan University, Malaysia. As an award-winning researcher renowned internationally for his excellence and innovation, Dr. Roy is a member of the editorial board of several international journals. He has published over 100 original research works and books in high-impact journals, covering a wide array of subjects such as epidemiology, health promotion, research methodology, communicable and non-communicable diseases, environmental health, nutrition, aging, quality of life, social and behavioral health, and healthcare management. Dr. Roy also serves as the Vice-President of the International Association on Public Health, which focuses on empowering Public Health professionals worldwide. He is the CEO and Founder of the World Catalysts Research Network (WCRN), a globally recognized center that delivers cutting-edge research solutions. His contributions have significantly advanced rigorous and reproducible research in the fields of data, social, and health sciences. He is an executive board member of Fight Cancer Global (USA) and the International Coordinator for Education Against Tobacco in Southeast Asia. His recent research, encompassing mental health and quality of life during the COVID-19 pandemic, involved studies across 45 countries. Holding a Bachelor of Science in Biology and a Doctor of Medicine from Saint Louis University, Philippines, Dr. Roy completed his Master of Public Health at the same institution, graduating Magna Cum Laude. He also earned a Commonwealth Executive Master in Business Administration in Malaysia, receiving the Outstanding Post-Graduate Thesis Award, and holds Post Graduate Certificates in Teaching Methodology in Malaysia and Distance Education from the University of the Philippines. As a dedicated mentor, he has supervised students from undergraduate to Ph.D. levels and has been repeatedly honored as the Best Research Supervisor. Currently a full scholar at Monash University, Dr. Roy is in the final year of his Ph.D. in Public Health at Monash University, Australia, and is concurrently pursuing a second Ph.D. in Education in Malaysia as a full scholar.

Mohammad Badruddoza Talukder is a distinguished Associate Professor at the College of Tourism and Hospitality Management, International University of Business Agriculture and Technology (IUBAT), Dhaka, Bangladesh. With a Ph.D. in Hotel Management from Lovely Professional University, India, he has been a dedicated educator in tourism and hospitality since 2008. Dr. Talukder is recognized as a leading authority in integrating Artificial Intelligence (AI) and the Internet of Things (IoT) into the global tourism and hospitality landscape. With extensive industry experience, including managerial roles in business-class hotels, he is a visionary force in the hotel industry. Dr. Talukder is also a certified trainer and an honorary facilitator at the Bangladesh Tourism Board, shaping the future of smart tourism and sustainable hospitality practices.

Krisada Chienwattanasook is a Lecturer at the Faculty of Business Administration, Rajamangala University of Technology Thanyaburi, Thailand. He is a former Associate Dean for Research, Development and Academic Service. He earns a DBA. from Burapha University, MBA. from Ramkhamhaeng University and also Eastern Asia University, and BSc. from Srinakharinwirot University. His areas of expertise are Organizational Behavior, Human Resource Development, Organization Development, Management, Strategic Management, CSR, Operation Management, Leadership, Entrepreneurships, Logistics and Supply Chain, and SMEs.

***

Aishwarya Arya Pursuing Ph.D. in Management, Accomplished her Bachelor's and Master's from Institute of Hotel Management and Catering Technology, Lucknow in Hospitality Administration thereafter another Master's in Travel & Tourism Management. She started her academic career in the year 2019 from IHM Lucknow, previously worked with Babu Banarsi Das University, Lucknow as Assistant Professor. She presented and attended many National and International Conferences, seminars and webinars. Her area of specialization includes Room Division, Hospitality Management & Sales and Marketing. She has patents published in Under the office of the controller General of Patents, Designs and Trademarks Department of Industrial Policy and Promotions, Ministry of Commerce and Industry, Government of India.

Chirra Baburao is an esteemed academic and researcher with expertise in public policy, entrepreneurship, start-ups, and the impact of AI on various sectors. Holding Master's degrees in Commerce, Management, and Psychology, he has over a decade of industry experience in IT, operating as a Technopreneur through his MSME-registered firm, Bobbycomputers&Communications. Currently, Research Associate For GNLU ICSSR Project and Doctoral candidate at GITAM School of Business, Visakhapatnam, Baburao excels in qualitative, quantitative, and mixed research methods. He has completed 15 Swayam courses, participated in over 40 webinars, and presented 10 papers at national and international conferences. His research focuses on MSMEs' role in public policy, technological disruptions, and environmental issues. His recent work explores AI's impact on consumer behavior, smart cities, and healthcare, published in reputable journals and conferences, making him a prominent figure in his field

Karan Berry is a dedicated tourism and hospitality academician with experience of over 20 years. Currently employed as Assistant Professor in Symbiosis School of Culinary Arts and Nutritional Sciences, Symbiosis International (Deemed University), Pune-India, he possesses a thorough knowledge of the challenges and prospects of gastronomy tourism. He has authored several book chapters, review articles, and research articles. Dr. Berry also runs a YouTube channel "Research Bay" for all the research scholars, to teach research methodology, and data analysis techniques.

Saurabh Chandra is an accomplished legal scholar and currently serves as an Associate Professor & Assistant Dean at the School of Law, Bennett University, India. With a robust academic foundation, he earned his Bachelor of Arts and Bachelor of Laws (B.A. LL.B.) from the prestigious Aligarh Muslim University (A.M.U.). He further specialized in Business Laws, completing his Master of Laws (LL.M.) at the renowned National Law School of India University (NLSIU), Bangalore. Dr. Chandra's academic journey culminated in a Doctorate in Law (Ph.D.) from the esteemed National Law University (NLU) Delhi. In addition to his impressive legal education from some of India's most prestigious institutions, Dr. Chandra also holds a master's degree in Management with specialization in Human Resources in Management and another in Journalism and Mass Communication. With more than sixteen years of teaching experience, he has numerous publications to his credit. His expertise is complemented by a robust portfolio of scholarly publications. By bridging the gap between theoretical insights and real-world applications, Dr. Chandra's work serves as a valuable resource for academics, legal practitioners, and industry professionals alike. Dr. Chandra brings a wealth of experience in Academic Administration, having successfully held various key administrative positions. His diverse qualifications and extensive experience make him a distinguished figure in the academic and legal communities.

Vijit Chaturvedi is a professor in OB, HR & Psychology with Industry and Academia experience of 19.5 years. She is Doctorate in HR, M.Phil. in Management, MB with specialization in HR and Strategic management. She is an accredited trainer and Industrial Psychologist along with certification in Labour laws. She is currently working as Professor in the area of HR and Psychology and Head of Department-Pratyahara "Department of Spirituality, Research &Consciousness" which conducts

Certificate Programs in Spirituality, consciousness matched in a scientific way. She is also Research Coordinator - Funded Projects of the Institution. Her Research area includes -Strategic, administrative, and behavioural aspects of Human resource/ People management. She has to her credit more than 100 publications in different areas (Including Indexed and Peer Reviewed Journal).Many scholars are perusing PhD under her guidance.

Kiranbhai Ramabhai Dodiya is an experienced Cyber Forensic Expert and Assistant Professor specializing in cyber security and digital forensics. He has taught at prestigious institutions and is currently pursuing a PhD in Biochemistry and Forensic Science. With a strong background in ethical hacking and malware analysis, Kiranbhai is passionate about educating students and contributing to the field of cyber forensics. His expertise includes malware forensic, computer forensics, and data recovery software. Kiranbhai's commitment to professional growth is evident through his participation in workshops, seminars, and research publications. He is dedicated to shaping the next generation of professionals in the field and combatting cybercrimes.

Girdhar Gopal is an experienced academician and researcher with over 19 years in management education, specializing in marketing, business analytics, and operations research. Currently serving as Associate Professor and Head of the School of Business at SHEAT College of Engineering & Management, Varanasi, he holds a Ph.D. in Marketing and has taught a wide range of subjects across several reputed institutions. His academic contributions include multiple publications in Scopus and ABDC-indexed journals, authorship of several management textbooks, and a recently published patent on personalized marketing systems. Dr. Gopal has actively participated in and organized numerous national and international conferences and faculty development programs, and he is known for his dynamic teaching style, strong communication skills, and leadership in academic initiatives.

Gorli Chaitanya Eswara Naidu is Asst Professor in Dept. of Management at Gonna Institute of Information Technology and Sciences. He has more than 4 years of experience in teaching and research in the area of Management. He has been in industry, teaching, research and academic administrator for the past 4 years. His teaching interests include Finance, General Management and Marketing . Dr. Gorli Chaitanya Eswara Naidu has written articles in reputed journals. He has participated and presented various papers in national, international seminars and conferences. He has been Published 8 papers in national and International journals with high Impact factor.

Utkarsh Keshari is currently working on the post of Assistant Professor in SMS college Varanasi and has completed his PhD from FMS, BHU. He has published multiple papers in Scopus, peer reviewed and ABDC listed journals.

Shiv Kumar, working as Associate Professor (Food Science and Technology), Maharishi Markandeshwar Deemed to be University. He has completed M.Sc. in Food Technology, and obtained a Ph.D. in Food Engineering and Technology from SLIET, Longowal, Punjab. Dr. Shiv Kumar was honored with the best PhD thesis award in 2019. He has experience in teaching, with over 8 years, including more than 7 years of post-doctoral and 13 years of research experience in the field of Food Science and Technology. He has filed 7 utility patents, and 2 copyright and 6 of these patents have been published. Dr. Shiv Kumar published around 52 research and review articles, as well as book chapters. He has participated in over 15 National/International conferences, 45 training and faculty development programs. He has been a reviewer for various SCI/Scopus journals. He has working as Editor and co-editor in 01 Wiley and 01 Elsevier book.

Pankaj Kumar is currently working as an Assistant Professor in School of BFSI at Symbiosis University of Applied Sciences, Indore, Madhya Pradesh. He has completed his Ph.D. in Finance from Faculty of Commerce, Banaras Hindu University and published number of research papers in SCOPUS, ABDC and Care listed journals.

Sanjeev Kumar Is a Professor in Lovely Professional University Punjab India. He received Undergraduate in Hotel Management from Osmania University, Postgraduate in Tourism Management from Madurai Kamaraj University. He completed Doctor of Philosophy in Hospitality Management in 2019 from Amity University Jaipur India. His research areas lies in food Service Industry, his research focuses on Alcoholic beverages, Event management and Sustainable Management Practices, Metaverse, AI Machine Learning and Artificial Intelligence. He published more than 80 research papers, articles and chapters in Scopus Indexed, UGC Approved and peer reviewed Journals and books. Dr. Sanjeev Kumar participated and acted as resource person in various National and International conferences, seminars, session chair, research workshops and industry talks and his work has been widely cited. Dr. Sanjeev also edited more than 20 books with various International Publishers such as IGI Global, Cambridge Scholars, Emerald, CABI, Bentham Science, Taylor & Francis. Dr Sanjeev is an active researcher and has published numerous research articles in prestigious National and International journals and books. He has been a reviewer of various national and international journals and also delivers guest lectures at academic conferences and faculty development programs.

Lova Baliji is the Head and Associate Professor of Finance in the Department of MBA at Avanthi Institute of Engineering & Technology. He holds a Ph.D. in Finance, an MBA in Finance & Marketing, and a B.A. from Andhra University. With over six years of teaching experience, he specializes in Risk Management, Security Analysis, Portfolio Management, Marketing Management, Financial Management, and Business Environment. He also has industry experience as a Junior Accountant at Royal Line Ice Cream Pvt. Ltd (Visakha Dairy) from 2012 to 2014. Dr. Baliji has published research in reputed journals such as IJMIE, SJIJIMR, and EPRA International Journal. He actively participates in faculty development programs, workshops, and conferences.

Vijaya Kittu Manda is a multi-dimensional personal. He is a Researcher at PBMEIT, India. He is an Advocate, a Technocrat, an Academician, a Book-writer, Editor, Peer-Reviewer and a stock market enthusiast. He has 12 University Postgraduate Degrees in various disciplines ranging from Arts and Humanities to Sustainability to Regenerative Economy, and from Management to Engineering. He is a Ph.D. in Financial Management. His thesis on Mutual Funds and their Market Competition won the prestigious NSE-IEA Best Thesis Award in 2023. He is currently pursuing his second Ph.D. in Computer Science with focus on Blockchain and Artificial Intelligence. He has nearly 13+ years of experience in capital markets, financial planning, and investing. He writes Research Papers and Case Studies, Case Reports (of Medical Journals) and sits on Editorial Boards of various publishers. He has 141+ Google Scholar publications and 785+ magazine article publications so far. He is the Chief Editor for a Management Book Series and the Editor of several Scopus-indexed books. He is a Peer Reviewer and is a Certified Peer Review Supervisor. He frequently reviews for leading publishers including IEEE, Springer, Emerald, Sage, amongst others. He sits as a Session Chair and an Advisor for various academic and industrial conferences. He is a guest speaker for colleges and universities. He serves as the host for a research talk show called PBMEIT Expert Insights.

Tarun Kumar Patel is a distinguished academician and researcher in the field of biotechnology, currently serving as an Assistant Professor and Head of the Department of Biotechnology at Sant Guru Ghasidas Government P.G. College, Kurud, Dhamtari, Chhattisgarh, India. With a robust academic background and a decade-long teaching career, Dr. Patel has made significant contributions to fungal biology, mass spectrometry, and microbial biotechnology. Educational Background and Qualifications Dr. Patel earned his Postgraduation and subsequently his Ph.D. in Biotechnology with research focused on detecting and analyzing aflatoxin production in Aspergillus flavus strains using advanced mass spectrometry techniques.

His academic excellence is further demonstrated by qualifying the CSIR-NET (Life Sciences) and the GATE examination. Research Contributions Dr. Patel's research encompasses a wide array of topics within biotechnology. His notable works include studies on the biosynthesis of aflatoxin B1 in Aspergillus flavus, identification of genetic relationships in Chlorophytum species, and the exploration of entomopathogenic fungi as biocontrol agents in agriculture. He has contributed to several peer-reviewed journals and book chapters, including publications in Biologia, Biotechnology and Bioprocess Engineering, and contributions to books published by Elsevier and Springer. Professional Experience and Teaching With over ten years of teaching experience at the undergraduate level and seven years at the postgraduate level, Dr. Patel has been instrumental in shaping the academic journey of numerous students. His commitment to education is evident in his active participation in various workshops and training programs, enhancing both his knowledge and teaching methodologies. Professional Affiliations and Recognitions Dr. Patel is an active member of esteemed scientific societies, including the Asian Federation of Biotechnology (AFOB) and the Association of Microbiologists of India (AMI). His research has garnered citations and recognition within the scientific community, reflecting the impact of his work on the field of biotechnology. His dedication to research and education in biotechnology has significantly contributed to advancements in fungal biology and microbial biotechnology. His work continues to inspire students and researchers alike, fostering innovation and excellence in the scientific community.

Rismawati +6281334488341 Universitas Muhammadiyah Palopo Jl. Jenderal Sudirman No. 03 Kota Palopo, Sulawesi Selatan 91922 risma11@umpalopo.ac .id Rismawati is a distinguished academic and consultant with a robust focus on sustainability reporting. She currently holds the position of lecturer and Head of the Quality Assurance Institute at Universitas Muhammadiyah Palopo, where she has been pivotal in ensuring the quality of university processes and outputs since February 2020. Additionally, she serves as an Assurer for Sustainability Reporting at the National Center for Sustainability Reporting in Jakarta, specializing in the evaluation of sustainability reports for mining companies across Indonesia. Her academic qualifications are extensive, comprising a Bachelor's degree in Economics and Accounting, a Master's degree in Accounting Science, and a Doctorate in Accounting from Universitas Brawijaya, Malang. Rismawati is also a certified specialist in sustainability reporting, risk management, and tax planning, holding several prestigious certifications including Certified Sustainability Reporting Specialist (CSRS), Certified Risk Management Practitioner (CRMP), Certified Management Accountant (CMA) and Certified Enterprise Risk Analysis (CERA). In her professional capacity, she has provided consultancy services in financial management and tax compliance for companies such as PT. Reski Barito Timur and PT. Helay Raya. Furthermore, she has authored multiple publications on Social Accounting, Sustainability Accounting, Management Accounting and CSR, contributing significantly to the academic community. Her interests in reading, writing, and travel reflect her commitment to lifelong learning and professional growth in her field

Md. Mehedi Hasan Sawon is a dedicated academic and researcher currently serving as a Senior Lecturer in the Department of Tourism and Hospitality Management at Daffodil International University, Bangladesh. With a strong passion for advancing knowledge in tourism and hospitality, he has made significant contributions through his research and publications. His research interests are diverse and focused on contemporary topics within the tourism and hospitality sectors. Sawon is particularly interested in the intersection of Artificial Intelligence and its applications in tourism, exploring innovative ways to enhance customer experiences and optimize operational efficiency focus on tourism education, seeking to develop new teaching methods and curricula that better align with industry trends. Furthermore, Sawon is interested in social media marketing in the hospitality industry, analyzing how digital platforms shape consumer behavior and business strategies. His work also extends to sustainable tourism, promoting practices that contribute to the long-term preservation of tourism destinations and the environment.

Vinay Seth is currently pursuing his Ph.D. from the Department of Commerce, Mahatma Gandhi Kashi Vidyapith, Varanasi, Uttar Pradesh. He has completed his graduation and post graduation from the Faculty of Commerce, Banaras Hindu University and published a number of research papers in Scopus, ABDC, UGC Care listed journals and in peer reviewed journals.

Liza Shoor is a distinguished scholar who earned her Ph.D. from Punjab Agricultural University (PAU), Ludhiana, India, with her research affiliated to the School of Business Studies at PAU. Her academic pursuits are centered on the evolving landscape of consumer behavior, with a particular focus on impulse buying in the digital era.

Amrik Singh is working as Professor and Head in the School of Hotel Management and Tourism at Lovely Professional University, Punjab, India. He obtained his Ph.D. degree in Hotel Management from Kurukshetra University, Kurukshetra. He started his academic career at Lovely Professional University, Punjab, India in the year 2007. He has published 57 Scopus indexed publications. He has published 12 patents and 01 patent has been granted in the inter-disciplinary domain. Dr. Amrik Singh participated and acted as a resource person in various national and international conferences, seminars, research workshops, and industry talks. He has published 10 books with IGI Global Publication on trending areas such as Food Waste, Solid Waste, Artificial Intelligence in marketing, Mountain Tourism, Virtual tourism, Guest behavior in tourism and hospitality. His area of research interest is accommodation management, ergonomics, green practices, human resource management in hospitality, waste management, AR VR in hospitality, etc. He is currently guiding 8Ph.D. scholars and 5 Ph.D. scholars have been awarded Ph.D. He is PhD thesis external examiner for many national and international universities. He is also editorial team member for Scopus and web of science journals.

Siddharth Singh is currently serving as Deputy Director in the School of Hotel Management at Chhatrapati Shahu Ji Maharaj University, Kanpur (U.P.). He holds a Bachelor's degree in Hotel Management and Catering Technology (BHMCT) and a Master's degree in Hotel Management (MHM). With over 15 years of experience in the hospitality industry and academia, Mr. Singh has developed a deep understanding of food production, culinary operations, and hospitality education. His research interests include integrating hotel management, food technology, and nutrition to create interdisciplinary learning frameworks and promote innovation in food production, packaging, and transport. Chef Siddharth singh siddharthsingh@ csjmu.ac.in

Sujay Vikram Singh is currently serving as Assistant Professor in Amity School of Hospitality, Amity University Uttar Pradesh, Lucknow Campus. Dr. Sujay Vikram Singh is an accomplished academic and researcher with a PhD in Tourism Management from Banaras Hindu University (2024) and extensive expertise in hospitality, tourism marketing, and heritage conservation. He has a strong publication record in ABDC-A, SSCI, and Scopus-indexed journals, along with multiple book chapters in prestigious publications. Awarded UGC-NET/JRF and SRF, he has received several best paper awards and holds patents in tourism-related innovations. With industry experience as a guest relations executive and academic roles including lectures and conference presentations, Dr. Singh specializes in gamification, service quality, and sustainable tourism. His works reflects active participation in workshops, reviewer roles, and a commitment to bridging academia and industry.

Bruno Sousa is an Professor Coordenador of Marketing at Polytechnic University of Cávado and Ave (IPCA), Portugal and holds a PhD in Marketing and Strategy in Universidade do Minho, Portugal. Bruno Sousa is also Head of Masters Program - Tourism Management and Tourism Marketing (IPCA); CiTUR – Center for Tourism

Research, Development and Innovation and UNIAG research member. Bruno Sousa teaching fields include marketing, strategy and tourism. Bruno Sousa research areas include brand management and consumer behavior, strategy implementation, niche marketing, niche tourism and brand attachment. He has published in the Journal of Enterprising Communities, Tourism Management Perspectives, Current Issues in Tourism, Journal of Organizational Change Management, World Review of Entrepreneurship, Management and Sust. Development, among others.

Bikkina Srinivas is a Director at Vingas Industries Private Limited, Visakhapatnam, India. He has over two decades of industrial experience in dealing with industrial gases and related establishments. His areas of speciality involves generating unique ideas and transforming them into practically implementable models. He is a Ph.D. with specialization in Operations Management. He is the author the several journal articles and actively engages in both Industrial and Academic events. He has special interest in Computer Science and Information Technology and has several initiatives that help in the industrial gases industry.

Vanshika Srivastava is a seasoned hospitality professional and educator with a wealth of experience spanning over seven years in both industry and academia. A graduate of IHM Jaipur, she further honed her expertise by earning a Master's degree in Travel & Tourism from IGNOU. She is perusing Ph.D. in hotel management from MMU Mullana, Ambala. Her journey in the hospitality sector began with a dynamic tenure at The Oberoi, New Delhi, where she excelled in the Front Office Department for 2.4 years, gaining hands-on experience in delivering exceptional guest experiences. Driven by her passion for education, she transitioned into academia, serving as Teaching Associate at IHM Panipat for one year. There, she played a pivotal role in shaping future hospitality professionals. She later continued her academic journey as Teaching Associate at IHM Faridabad for three years, further contributing to the development of young minds in the hospitality domain. She has also presented and published various papers in national conferences. She is currently working as Assistant Professor at Chatrapati Sahuji Maharaj University, Kanpur.

Supriadi is a dedicated lecturer in the Informatics Study Program at the Faculty of Computer Engineering, Universitas Cokroaminoto Palopo. He earned his Bachelor's degree in Islamic Studies (S.Ag) from the State Institute of Islamic Studies (IAIN) Ujung Pandang and later pursued a Master's degree in Education (M.Pd) at Universitas Negeri Makassar. His academic expertise lies in the intersection of religious studies and business ethics, which he applies in his teaching of Islamic Studies and Professional & Business Ethics within the Informatics Faculty.

Beyond teaching, Supriadi is actively engaged in research, particularly in the fields of Augmented Reality (AR) and Sharia Tourism. His work focuses on integrating Islamic knowledge with Information Technology, aiming to develop innovative educational tools that enhance the learning experience. By combining religious perspectives with digital advancements, he seeks to bridge the gap between Islamic education and modern technology, making complex subjects more accessible and engaging. Through his research and academic contributions, Supriadi aspires to empower students and professionals with ethical and technological insights that align with Islamic values. His work continues to contribute to the evolving landscape of technology-assisted learning

Theodore Tarnanidis is a professiorial research fellow & marketing scholar, adjunct professor at the International Hellenic University and researcher in Applications of D.Sc. and MCDA. Theodore has six years experience as a marketing and decision making practitioner. He made his post-doc research in the area of sustainable entrepreneurship from the University of Macedonia. He obtained a Ph.D. from the University of London Met., UK. He received his M.B.A from Liverpool University, UK and is a graduate from the University of Macedonia (Business Administration) and Alexander Technological Educational Institute (Marketing). His research focuses on International Marketing, Multi-cultural Marketing, Business Marketing, Consumer science, Marketing Management, Methodology, Advanced Quantitative Methods, Decision Science, Multiple-Criteria Decision Analysis, Management of Education, Sustainable Entrepreneurship. His work has been published in various internationally renowned scientific conferences (Academy of Marketing, European Marketing Academy, PROMETHEE Days, Hellenic Operational Research) and in the Journal of Business Ethics, World Review of Entrepreneurship, Management and Sustainable Development, Journal of Retailing and Consumer Services, Current Issues in Tourism, Marketing Science & Inspirations, European Journal of Educational Management, Management Science Letters, Administrative Sciences and other journals.

Mrigya Tewari, has completed her schooling and higher education from prestigious schools and universities located in Varanasi. She is actively engaged in quality research work in the field of commerce and management. She is currently working as an Assistant Professor in Amity University Madhya Pradesh.

Suraj Yadav is an accomplished professional with a background in Hospitality, holding a bachelor's degree from Pune University and a Master in Hotel Management & Tourism from Madurai Kamaraj University, Madurai. Currently serving as an Assistant Professor and Training & Placement Officer at D Y Patil School of

Hospitality in Kolhapur, Maharashtra, India, he brings extensive expertise to the field. Suraj is also dedicated to furthering his academic pursuits and is actively pursuing a Ph.D. at D Y Patil Agricultural & Technical University in Kolhapur. His commitment to education and training has made a significant impact in the realm of hospitality.

Rizwan Yargatti is currently working as an Assistant Professor in Symbiosis School of Culinary Arts and Nutritional Sciences, Symbiosis International (Deemed University), Pune 412115. He has a vast culinary experience.

Index

A

B

C

D

E

F

G

H

I

K

L

M

N

O

P

R

S

T

W

www.ingramcontent.com/pod-product-compliance
Lightning Source LLC
LaVergne TN
LVHW062336300926
849161LV00007B/1720